Statistics for Psychology Using R

Statistics for Psychology Using R

Vivek M. Belhekar

Faculty Member, Department of Applied Psychology, University of Mumbai

Los Angeles | London | New Delhi
Singapore | Washington DC | Melbourne

First published in 2016 by

SAGE Publications India Pvt Ltd
B1/I-1 Mohan Cooperative Industrial Area
Mathura Road, New Delhi 110 044, India
www.sagepub.in

SAGE Publications Inc
2455 Teller Road
Thousand Oaks, California 91320, USA

SAGE Publications Ltd
1 Oliver's Yard, 55 City Road
London EC1Y 1SP, United Kingdom

SAGE Publications Asia-Pacific Pte Ltd
3 Church Street
#10-04 Samsung Hub
Singapore 049483

Published by Vivek Mehra for SAGE Publications India Pvt Ltd, typeset in ITC Stone Serif Std 9.5/11 pts by Zaza Eunice, Hosur, Tamil Nadu, India.

Library of Congress Cataloging-in-Publication Data

Name: Belhekar, Vivek M., author.
Title: Statistics for psychology using R / Vivek M. Belhekar.
Description: Thousand Oaks, California : SAGE, 2016. | Includes
  bibliographical references and index.
Identifiers: LCCN 2016023057 | ISBN 9789385985003 (pbk. : alk. paper)
Subjects: LCSH: Psychology—Statistical methods. | Psychology—Data
  processing. | R (Computer program language)
Classification: LCC BF39 .B426 2016 | DDC 150.1/5195—dc23 LC record available at https://lccn.loc.gov/2016023057

ISBN: 978-93-859-8500-3 (PB)

SAGE Team: Amit Kumar, Indrani Dutta, Vandana Gupta, Megha Dabral and Ritu Chopra

To

Aai and Dada
(Mom and Dad)
and
Ira and Rutuj
(Daughter and Nephew)

Thank you for choosing a SAGE product!
If you have any comment, observation or feedback,
I would like to personally hear from you.

Please write to me at **contactceo@sagepub.in**

Vivek Mehra, Managing Director and CEO, SAGE India.

Bulk Sales

SAGE India offers special discounts
for bulk institutional purchases.

For queries/orders/inspection copy requests,
write to **textbooksales@sagepub.in**

Publishing

Would you like to publish a textbook with SAGE?
Please send your proposal to **publishtextbook@sagepub.in**

Subscribe to our mailing list

Write to marketing@sagepub.in

Brief Contents

Preface   xi
Acknowledgments   xiii
About the Author   xv

Chapter 1   Probability: Basic Concepts and Random Variables   1
Chapter 2   Statistical Inference   38
Chapter 3   Description of Data: Statistics and Graphical Description   63
Chapter 4   Normal Distribution: Theory, Application, and Testing   78
Chapter 5   Correlation and Association   108
Chapter 6   Regression Analysis   153
Chapter 7   Comparing Means: *t*-test   206
Chapter 8   Analysis of Variance   244
Chapter 9   Non-parametric Methods   298
Chapter 10   Factor Analysis and Structural Equation Modeling   314
Chapter 11   Basic Psychometrics   362

Appendix A: Introduction to R   A-1
Appendix B: Basic Mathematics for Psychologists   A-6
Appendix C: Statistical Tables   A-11
References   R-1
Index   I-1

Detailed Contents

Preface		xi
Acknowledgments		xiii
About the Author		xv

Chapter 1	**Probability: Basic Concepts and Random Variables**	1
	1.1 Sample Space and Event	2
	1.2 Probability	4
	1.3 Random Variable	7
	1.4 Discrete Random Variables	11
	1.5 Continuous Random Variable and Continuous Probability Distribution	20
	1.6 Types of Continuous Random Variables	22
	1.7 Conditional Probability	29
Chapter 2	**Statistical Inference**	38
	2.1 Introduction	38
	2.2 Basic Idea	39
	2.3 The Null Hypothesis	42
	2.4 Point Estimation and Interval Estimation	48
	2.5 Properties of Estimators	49
	2.6 Methods of Estimation	53
	2.7 Important Ideas Underlying Statistical Inference	59
Chapter 3	**Description of Data: Statistics and Graphical Description**	63
	3.1 Introduction	63
	3.2 Descriptive Statistics: Describing Data	63
	3.3 Measures of Central Tendency	64
	3.4 Properties of Measures of Central Tendency	65
	3.5 Measures of Variability	66
	3.6 The Graphical Representation of data	70
Chapter 4	**Normal Distribution: Theory, Application, and Testing**	78
	4.1 Introduction	78
	4.2 Historical Aspects of Normal Distribution	78
	4.3 Normal Distribution: Understanding and Applying Normal Distribution	80
	4.4 Testing Normality	84
	4.5 Problems and Solutions Associated with Non-normal Data	99
	4.6 Multivariate Normal Distribution: Testing multivariate Normality and Outliers	100
Chapter 5	**Correlation and Association**	108
	5.1 Introduction	108
	5.2 Pearson's Correlation	112
	5.3 Special Correlations	123
	5.4 Partial, Part (Semi-partial) and Multiple Correlation	127
	5.5 Testing Difference between Correlation Coefficients	132
	5.6 Methods for Ordinal Data: Spearman's rho and Kendal's tau	135
	5.7 Additional Methods for Ordinal Data: Goodman and Kruskal's Gamma, Kendall's Coefficient of Concordance	139
	5.8 Methods with Categorical/Nominal Data	142

Chapter 6	**Regression Analysis**	153
	6.1 Introduction	153
	6.2 Simple Linear Regression	154
	6.3 Multiple Regression	175
	6.4 Logistic Regression	196
Chapter 7	**Comparing Means: *t*-test**	206
	7.1 Logic of *t*-test	206
	7.2 Single-sample *t*-test	213
	7.3 Independent Samples *t*-test	218
	7.4 Dependent Samples *t*-test	230
	7.5 Power of *t*-test and Estimating Sample Size	235
	7.6 Bootstrapping for *t*-test	241
Chapter 8	**Analysis of Variance**	244
	8.1 Introduction	244
	8.2 Logic of ANOVA	245
	8.3 Independent Samples One-way ANOVA	248
	8.4 Effect-size and Power	253
	8.5 Multiple Comparison Procedures	256
	8.6 Repeated Measures One-way ANOVA	272
	8.7 Factorial Analysis of Variance: Two-way Completely Independent ANOVA	278
	8.8 Multivariate Analysis of Variances (MANOVA)	287
Chapter 9	**Non-parametric Methods**	298
	9.1 Introduction	298
	9.2 The Chi-Square Test of Goodness-of-Fit	298
	9.3 Proportions Tests: Comparing Two Proportions	301
	9.4 Comparing Locations of Independent Samples	304
	9.5 Comparing Locations of Dependent Samples	309
Chapter 10	**Factor Analysis and Structural Equation Modeling**	314
	10.1 Introduction	314
	10.2 Exploratory Factor Analysis	315
	10.3 Confirmatory Factor Analysis (CFA)	333
	10.4 Structural Equations Modeling (SEM)	356
Chapter 11	**Basic Psychometrics**	362
	11.1 Introduction	362
	11.2 The Classical Test Theory	362
	11.3 Item Response Theory	369
Appendix A: Introduction to R		A-1
Appendix B: Basic Mathematics for Psychologists		A-6
Appendix C: Statistical Tables		A-11
References		R-1
Index		I-1

Preface

The first question I had to answer myself before starting to write this book was, "Why one more book when there are plenty others on the same subject?"

Every year I interact with at least 100 students at Department of Applied Psychology, University of Mumbai, in my "Statistics for Psychology" course. Most of them are bright and curious students of undergraduate programs. They start taking the "Statistics for Psychology" course with complex emotions and thoughts—they are eager to learn methods and reasoning of psychological research; however, at the same time, they are also (mostly unnecessarily) scared about the subject (I imagine my early days of being a student in statistics class). When I started teaching random variables, their distributions, jointly distributed random variables, and so on, there was no psychology text that I could refer to and was compelled to make references to books in mathematical statistics and econometrics. I always wondered why economics, a sister social-science discipline, manages to get a plethora of texts that are well grounded in mathematical statistics. On the other hand, psychology, which is also similarly quantitative in its reasoning, sparsely attracts books for publications (and in effect, students and future researchers, and teachers) with such an orientation. I felt that most of the students can, with little training, be better equipped to understand statistical reasoning. This is one of the major reasons why I started writing this book. I have quoted Galib at the very outset keeping this in mind. I am trying to narrate the story differently.

I have tried to keep the order of chapters of this book unlike most of the other textbooks available in the market. I have started with probability and inference and have tried to show that the psychological attribute under investigation is a random variable that needs to be understood in the form of a formal probability distribution. Once this is achieved, the hypothesis regarding the same can be tested with much synchronicity. What is more fascinating is not just the ability of the quantitative techniques to handle the data available from psychological studies, but their ability to design beautifully reasoned abstractions.

This textbook places more weight on the popular methods in psychological research such as *t*-test, ANOVA and MANOVA, correlations and regression, and factor analysis. I have briefly described psychometric methods to show how an R code could be useful for psychometrics. The chapter on psychometrics also introduces a reader to item response theory (IRT). Those who find the first chapter a difficult read may start with Chapter 3 and refer to the first chapter later on. If one has understood Chapter 1, then he/she may give a miss to the descriptive part of Chapter 3. In the process of writing this book, I have started to empathize with authors of textbooks on statistics. They have to perform a job well described by Stephen King while narrating his style of writing, "I try to create sympathy for my characters and then turn the monsters loose."

Software "R" has become one of the most important tools for analyzing statistical data. When I started teaching statistics in 2002, free software packages were not available. It was difficult to give exercises to students. With the availability of R, the situation has improved to a great extent. Students can carry out the assignments on-the-go. R is not just a free software, but it is an environment for statistical computing. The popularity of R is on the rise and most universities and journals have made changes in their curriculum and publications accordingly. This book is full of R codes and exercises. I strongly recommend that students should download R and practice the statistical methods on R. One can start with Appendix A—"Introduction to R." There are many online sources available for free on the same.

The teachers can refer to the presentations and lecture notes available at https://study.sagepub.in/belhekar_SPUR. The presentations are basic outlines and teachers can modify them as per the requirement. I have generally observed that except for computational formula, students skip equations and try to read the text only. It is imperative to understand that equations are not just mathematics but they contain reasoning that needs to be understood and internalized. Students should try to read the equations and say them in terms of the meaning they make. Generally, the reading of a textbook on statistics is not as fast as a textbook on cognitive psychology or evolutionary psychology (and certainly not as fast as a novel). One has to be patient. I have also tried to provide a personal sketch of beings behind the scientists. Stories of Student, Fisher, and Pearson are always fascinating and they open a vista of social-cultural and personal influences on the way science has grown, and perhaps as Max Plank says, "funeral by funeral."

I learned that quantitative reasoning holds the ability to provide smarter tools to unravel mysteries about human mind. Understanding this reasoning is a journey that this book wants to start with. I am trying to initiate a journey for the readers which fascinated me—almost always!

Acknowledgments

There are plenty of people who have contributed to my growth as a student of the discipline of psychology. These influences are largely direct—of the people I have interacted with. But a significant influence is also of the indirect kind—influence of people you have never met or interacted with, that is, influence through the stories narrated by significant others, through the books, through the epics, through the surroundings, and through the institutional cultures. I am thankful to my alma mater—Department of Psychology, University of Pune, which has provided me with the direction for understanding the human mind and the real world. A very open and welcoming environment at the university and always approachable faculty members of most of the departments have certainly created a zeal and zest for knowledge. I am also deeply thankful to the University of Mumbai, particularly the Department of Applied Psychology and Department of Economics who played a major role in my development. I am deeply grateful to Professor P. H. Lodhi who is perhaps the first teacher to infuse enthusiasm and direction for learning statistical methods. I was reasonably unaware of the importance of statistical methods till the time I registered with him for PhD. The UGC Fellowship allowed me to work with him and learn various nuances of statistical methods and psychometrics. The training with him set the way for future learning. His ability to understand data and chose impeccably appropriate methods for its treatment is noteworthy but arduous to emulate. I am genuinely grateful to my dear friend and mentor Neeraj Hatekar (Professor in Econometrics, University of Mumbai). I am fortunate to have shared the treasured friendship with him which opened vistas of thinking about statistical methods. His unimpeachable understanding of statistics and social-sciences theory, ability to transcend the disciplinary boundaries and ever-open attitude to teach, helped me in understanding how to think about statistical methods. I started (whatever little) thinking about psychological attributes in terms of random variables and their distributions and statistical inference in a more mathematical and statistical manner, thanks to Neeraj. If my earlier training helped me learn statistical methods, working with him helped me understand them.

Among the academicians who always inspired me through the sagas are Professor B. N. Mukherjee and Professor Suresh Kanekar, two stalwarts from the universities in Maharashtra (Professor Kanekar was the former head of the Department of Psychology at the University of Mumbai as well; however, I never had the fortune to interact with him). I am thankful to Professor Pethe who has always been a model of an astute academician and lately a mentor in academic administration. I am also grateful to the Vice-Chancellor of University of Mumbai, Professor Sanjay Deshmukh for his support and encouragement, particularly during the last phase of writing.

The UGC-UPE Center for Computational and Experimental Social Sciences and Center for Behavioural Research provided me with an opportunity to use R and conduct training workshops. The national workshops conducted on R and statistical applications, structural equations modeling (SEM), created a much needed urgency to write this textbook. Much of the book has been shaped during the work with the Center for Computational and Experimental Social Sciences. The ICSSR (WRC) has always invited me for training programs on quantitative methods and provided an opportunity to discuss applications of statistical methods. I am thankful to the Directors of ICSSR, Dr Prabhu, Dr Hatekar, and Dr Gawali. I am thankful to my clinical psychology teachers who opened the eye for application of theory, particularly Mr and Mrs Gadkari, and Dr Sanjay Phadke from Pune. Over last 14 years, I have taught statistics at my university as well as many other universities and institutions. It is my good fortune that I had the opportunity to interact with learners of statistical methods from fields of psychology, economics, management, health and medical sciences, education, ecology, and so on. I am thankful to all of them for creating the opportunities for discussing statistical methods. I am thankful to Dr Ramesh Pathare, Dr Anuradha Sovani, Dr Mrunalini Purandare, Dr Nadini Diwan, Dr Aninha Lobo, Dr Kiran Pandya, Dr Vijayendra Pandye, ICSSR-WRC, and AYJ National Institute for Hearing Handicapped for these opportunities. I am also thankful to Professor Shejawal, Dr Wadkar, Professor Sharad Deshpande, and Professor Medha Deshpande, who were always supportive and encouraging. I am grateful to various academic colleagues of the Department of Applied Psychology at University of mumbai, particularly, (late) Dr Sen, Dr Gawali, Dr Satish, Dr Paul, Dr Bankar, Dr Wilbur, and Dr Umesh for support and cooperation. I am thankful to students who helped in proof-reading, particularly Meet Tara Dnyaneshwar, Ketaki Sodhi, Aziz Mukadam, Paras Gala, Snigdha, Trupti, Aditi, Jenai, Pritha, Madhva Galgali, and Buneshte Hakhamaneshy. I am thankful to all my students who made me a better teacher.

I would also like to thank the reviewers of the book for sharing their insightful suggestions: Dr Nasheed Imtiaz and Dr Roomana N. Siddiqui of Aligarh Muslim University; Dr Damanjit Sandhu of Department of Psychology, Punjabi University, Patiala; and Dr Kaveri Chauhan of Galgotias University.

I am fortunately blessed with friends like Abhijeet and Neeraj, who were always ready with the camera for a jungle safari and bird photography. Their company and the DSLR with 200–400 lens were always a fun and relaxing. Pallavi, my loving and caring wife, shared a whole lot of domestic burden during the phase of writing (and otherwise as well). She also was of quick help whenever I needed a proof of a theorem. I cannot find words of appreciation for Harshal and Priya, and my in-laws for understanding the exigencies of situations and permitting me to give a miss to some (important) family functions. I miss three individuals—my maternal uncle Madhavrao Khollam (*mama*), Marutrao Ghodekar (*anna* [maternal uncle]), and Nadkumar Phakatkar (father-in-law) who were always concerned about my academic progress, perhaps since my childhood. The best part in life is to have parents appreciating you while you are enjoying parenting. The highest joy lies in playing with the kids, Rutuj and Ira. They are the most valuable people and their playfulness always brings sheer joy and happiness. I am sincerely thankful to SAGE, particularly Mr Amit Kumar who has been very gentle and professional in getting the work done.

Thank you all.

About the Author

Vivek M. Belhekar is currently Assistant Professor at Department of Applied Psychology, University of Mumbai. He has been teaching at University of Mumbai for the last 13 years. His areas of interest include personality psychology, particularly the five-factor model of personality, personality disorders, evolutionary psychology, cross-cultural psychology, and psychological aspects of economic behavior. He was a part of UGC-UPE Center for Behavioral Research and currently he is also working with Center for Experimental and Computational Social Sciences under UPE-UGC. He has several cross-national collaborations and also adapted quite a few psychological instruments in Marathi. He has published and presented papers in several international and national journals and conferences. At University of Mumbai, he taught courses such as statistics for psychology, advanced applied psychometrics, evolutionary psychology, advanced skills and processes for counseling and psychotherapy. He enjoys travelling, painting, and is also an avid photographer, particularly passionate about wildlife photography.

1 Probability: Basic Concepts and Random Variables

The central problem of statistical application to psychology is to draw general inferences about a population that cannot be directly and completely observed. Observing the entire population is perhaps not realistically possible. So we collect data on a sample representing the population. The population value is estimated using the sample value. For example, a psychologist is interested in knowing the average extraversion score of young adults from Mumbai city. She/he realizes that, given the sheer number of young adults in the city, it is practically not possible to observe extraversion scores of all young adults. So she/he administers a 48-item NEO-PI-3[1] extraversion scale to a sample of young adults from Mumbai. Now, she/he has scores for this sample on the extraversion scale and she/he can compute the average extraversion score for the same. The average score for the sample is not the average for the population. In fact, if she/he draws another sample from the same population, her or his sample average is very likely to change. Now, her or his task is to make a good guess about the average value for all young adults using the value obtained from the sample. This is a typical representation of the central problem of statistics. The central problem of statistics is to "make the best guess" about the population value by using a sample value. This guess is often referred to as "a statistical inference" or "an estimation." This book deals with this problem. In order to make this best guess, we need to understand certain basic aspects of statistics: probability and statistical inference. The first three chapters will introduce you to these concepts. Probability and statistical inference provide the foundations to the understanding of statistics. The discussion in the first two chapters is primarily theoretical. I have included as many examples as possible to make it easy to understand.

This chapter will introduce the concept of probability. Initially, I shall explain the concepts of sample space and events, which are building blocks of probability, and random variable. We shall learn about the probability of events and the process that converts the probability of *n* event into a random variable. A random variable takes some values and we shall learn to compute probabilities associated with those values. The probabilities associated with the values of a random variable are typically represented by probability distribution and, hence, we shall learn about it as well. Random variables are of two types: discrete and continuous. There are different types of each of them. For example, discrete random variables are Bernoulli, binomial, Poisson, and so on, and continuous random variables are exponential, normal, t, F, chi, and so on. We shall cover these types in the upcoming sections since they are very useful in making statistical inference. In addition, there are random variables that are dependent on each other

---

[1] NEO-PI-3 stands for NEO Personality Inventory 3 that is based on the five-factor model of personality. It measures five dimensions, namely neuroticism, extraversion, openness to experience, agreeableness and conscientiousness. It is developed by Paul T. Costa and Robert R. McCrae and published by Psychological Assessment Resources (PAR). Marathi adaptation by Vivek M. Belhekar is available with PAR very soon.

or are jointly distributed. Understanding the probabilities of these random variables also helps us in understanding correlation and regression.

I have provided R codes in each section. You can write them in the R software and also learn to develop skills to use R while learning statistics for psychology. I have also provided examples and exercises wherever needed and you should solve them to understand the concept better. The notes provide additional information about useful concepts; they shall also update you about individuals who contributed to the statistical thinking. Let's begin!

1.1 SAMPLE SPACE AND EVENT

1.1.1 Sample Space

A sample space is defined as a set of all possible outcomes. Let's define a sample space as Ω (omega). Following are examples of a sample space:

Example 1A: Let's define a sample space for tossing a coin. There are two possible outcomes for a coin toss, head (H) and tail (T), and then the sample space can be defined as $\Omega=\{H, T\}$.

Example 1B: The sample space for "a problem-solving task" has two outcomes, either the problem is solved correctly or not solved correctly, which can be defined as $\Omega=\{Success, Failure\}$ or simply $\Omega=\{S, F\}$.

Example 2A: Now, let's define a sample space for tossing two coins together. The first coin will result into two outcomes, head (H) or tail (T), and so will the second one. The possible outcomes will be 2 (H and T for first coin)$\times 2$ (H and T for second coin)=4. If the first coin results in H and so does the second, then the outcome can be represented as HH. Following the same pattern, the sample space for tossing two coins together can be defined as $\Omega=\{HH, HT, TH, TT\}$.

Example 2B: Similarly, if an abstract reasoning experiment involves solving two reasoning problems, then the sample space can be defined as $\Omega=\{SS, SF, FS, FF\}$, where S is success and F is failure.

Example 3A: If we roll a dice and read number on the uppermost surface, then the sample space for rolling a dice can be defined as $\Omega=\{1, 2, 3, 4, 5, 6\}$.

Example 3B: A single item in a psychological survey with a 5-point Likert scale has five options ranging from strongly agree (SA) to strongly disagree (SD), with neutral (N) in between. The sample space for a response to a single-item 5-point Likert scale is $\Omega=\{SA, A, N, D, SD\}$.

Example 4A: Suppose 10 psychology students are presenting research papers in a students' research competition. At the end of the competition, judges will list all students in an order on the basis of their performances. What will be the sample space for the outcome (orders) of the research competition? Since there are 10 students, the possible orders are 10! (ten factorial).[2] Hence, the sample space can be defined as $\Omega=\{10!\}$. All possible outcomes in this case will be 10!=3628800.

Example 4B: In a survey, you have to administer five psychological scales to different participants. You want to administer scales to different participants in different orders and

---

[2] All possible orders or arrangements of n objects are obtained by $n!$ (n factorial). For example, three objects, A, B, and C, can be ordered in the following six ways ABC, ACB, BCA, BAC, CAB, and CBA. In this case, we have three options at the first place (A or B or C), once the first place is filled, we have two options for the second place, and then only one option at third. This is $3\times 2\times 1=6$. So, six orders are possible for three objects. This can be symbolized as 3! (three factorial) which is equal to $3!=3\times 2\times 1=6$. The general form is $n!$ that is defined as $n!$ $=n\times(n-1)\times(n-2)\times\cdots\times 1$. For example, $5!=5\times 4\times 3\times 2\times 1=120$. By convention, $0!=1$ and $1!=1$.

so you need to know all the possible orders in which it can be done. The sample space for all possible orders of administration of five scales is $\Omega=\{5!\}$ which is equal to 120. In R, you can write the following code to get factorial.

```
# R code 1.1. Factorial of 5.
> x <- 5
> factorial (x)
[1] 120
# Manually you can do it as follows.
> 5*4*3*2*1
[1] 120
```

Example 5: Suppose we have to define a sample space for the time taken to solve a problem in an experiment with an assumption that we will not stop the experiment till the problem is solved. The problem can be solved in one second (to be precise, time greater than zero) and it may as well take a long time to solve (generally denoted as less than infinity). Let's define the time taken to solve the problem as x. Then the sample space is $\Omega=\{x: 0<x\leq\infty\}$.

1.1.2 Event

Now, let's define an event. An event is a subset of a sample space. We denote an elementary event by ω and any event (*i*th event) can be denoted as ω_i. The sample space will have events like $\omega_1,\omega_2,\omega_3,\dots,\omega_n$, where sample space Ω has 1 to n events. $\omega_i \in \Omega$ implies that event ω_i is an element of a sample space Ω. For a toss of a single coin, event heads is denoted as $\omega_1=\{\text{Heads}\}$ and event tails is denoted as $\omega_2=\{\text{Tails}\}$. For a reasoning task, event success is denoted as $\omega_1=\{\text{Success}\}$.

All other events in the sample space other than ω_1 are expressed as ω_1^C (omega one complement). In a single-coin toss, event $H^C=T$.

The combination of elementary events also constitutes an event. For example, if we toss two coins, then "heads on the first coin" is a new event, which can be denoted as E={HH, HT}. We can also construct new events by union and intersection[3] of elementary events. An event $E=\omega_1 \cup \omega_2$ (omega1 union omega2). This event is a union of two elementary events ω_1 and ω_2 which occurs when either ω_1 or ω_2 or both are present. For example, if ω_1 is heads on the first coin and ω_2 is heads on the second coin, then event $\omega_1 \cup \omega_2=$E={HH, HT, TH}. Suppose somebody attempts to solve two problems, then the sample space is of four events $\Omega=\{$SS, SF, FS, FF$\}$. Let ω_1 be success on the first task and ω_2 be success on the second task. We can construct a new event G, which is $\omega_1 \cup \omega_2=\{SS, SF, FS\}$, that is, either the first or the second or both are successfully solved.

Furthermore, an event $\omega_1 \cap \omega_2$ (omega1 intersection omega2) can occur when both ω_1 and ω_2 are present. From the same example, $\omega_1 \cap \omega_2=\{HH\}$.

We can further define a null event or an empty set ($\varnothing$). If ω_1 and ω_2 are mutually exclusive events in a sample space, then the event that both occur does not exist. So $\omega_1 \cap \omega_2 = \varnothing$. For example, a toss of a single coin results into two events, H and T. Then an event $H \cap T = \varnothing$ because if H occurs, T will not occur, and vice versa. Similarly, $\Omega^C = \varnothing$, that is, the complement of the sample space is a null event. The events in the sample space follow cumulative, associative, and distributive laws. They are as follows:

$$\text{Cumulative Law: } A \cup B = B \cup A$$
$$\text{Associative Law: } (A \cup B) \cup C = A \cup (B \cup C)$$
$$\text{Distributive Law: } (A \cup B)C = AC \cup BC$$

---

[3] Union and intersection: $A \cup B$ is read as A union B. $A \cup B$ is possible when A exists, or B exists, or both A and B exist. $A \cap B$ is read as A intersection B. $A \cap B$ is possible only when both A and B exist.

1.2 PROBABILITY

1.2.1 Introduction

We generally use the term probability to indicate the chance of occurrence of an event. In behavioral sciences, we need to talk in probabilistic terms because most outcomes in the real world are not certain. For example, whether you will pass a statistics course with A grade, whether a person with a family history of mental illness will have a mental illness, whether a commitment to job leads to a better performance, whether somebody will remember seven words in a working memory experiment, and so on, are those questions that cannot be answered with certainty. Some of the events are highly likely, whereas others are not. The concept of probability helps us to express this uncertainty. Usually, a probability is symbolized as P, and written as P(E) denoting the probability of an event E. Lets answer a simple question: What is the probability of heads if you toss a coin? Some of us instinctively compute this probability as 0.5 (or 50% chances) with the reason that there are two possible outcomes and one desired outcome. So the probability is equal to $1/2 = 0.5$. This is not correct. Let's consider another example that has two outcomes; you are playing a game of badminton against Saina Nehwal which may result in either of two outcomes: you win or Saina wins. Do you think that the probability of you winning = probability of Saina winning = 0.5? Obviously no! The probability of Saina winning is very high, more than 0.99 perhaps. This would also mean that, suppose if you play 1000 games against Saina, she would win more than 990. This results in an **empirical approach** to understand probability.

The term probability has been understood in various ways. The empirical approach, axiomatic approach, and probability, as a measure of belief, are the main approaches to understand probability.

The empirical approach works as follows. If we toss a coin a large number of times (n), then we will get heads for some number of times, denoted as $n(H)$. As we raise n closer to infinity, the ratio of $n(H)/n$ tends to be closer to the probability of H. This can be generally stated as

$$P(E) = \lim_{n \to \infty} \frac{n(E)}{n}$$

where P(E) is the probability of event E, $n(E)$ is the number of times E occurred, and n is the number of times the experiment was conducted. Here, the probability of an event E is equal to n limits[4] to infinity, $n(E)/n$. As n approaches (limits to) infinity, P(E) approaches $n(E)/n$. In other words, the probability of an event E is a limiting proportion of the times E occurs out of n times the experiment was conducted. So to know the probability of the event head, we need to toss a coin for really a large number of times (n times) and take it closer to infinity. While this approach seems intuitively satisfactory, there are two problems with this approach. One, what should be n at which we would stop the experiment? It is not possible to provide a satisfactory answer to this question. Second, if we run the experiment twice for n times to get P(E), then the resulting two P(E) values need not be the same. It also involves a complex assumption that P(E) will be a constant as we increase n to infinity.

1.2.2 Axiomatic Approach

Another approach, the **axiomatic approach** to probability, constructs simpler aspects of probability called axioms. An axiom is a self-evident statement or a statement believed to be

---

[4] Limit: It is used to describe the value that a function "approaches" as the input approaches some value. In formulas, limit is abbreviated as lim, for example, $\lim(x_\infty)$ or by the right arrow ($\to$) as $x \to \infty$ and read as "x limits to infinity." Conventionally, it is written as $\lim_{x \to \infty} f(x) = L$ which means that as x approaches ∞, $f(x)$ will approach L. Theory of limits is essential to perform differentiation and integration in calculus.

true without proof. There are three axioms of probability. We define the sample space as S and any event in S as E_i, such as $E_i \in S$, for $i = 1, 2, \ldots, \infty$; then axioms of probability can be defined as follows.

Axiom 1:

$$0 \le P(E_i) \le 1$$

Axiom 1 implies that the probability of an event (E_i) is from 0 to 1 (both inclusive).

Axiom 2:

$$P(S) = 1$$

Axiom 2 implies that the probability of an entire sample space is 1 or a probability of 1 implies that it is the probability of an entire sample space.

Axiom 3: For any sequence of mutually exclusive events E_1, E_2, E_3, ... (where $E_i \cap E_j = \emptyset$, $i \neq j$ for all i, j),

$$p(_{i=1}^{\infty}E_i) = \sum_{i=1}^{\infty} P(E_i)$$

Axiom 3 implies that if events in a sample space are mutually exclusive, then the probability of their union is the sum of the probability of those events. For example, the sample space for rolling a dice is S={1, 2, 3, 4, 5, 6}. We assume that all six mutually exclusive events are equally likely. Then the probability of each outcome is 1/6. Now, suppose we want to know the probability of odd outcomes (1, 3, and 5) of the dice roll. By using axiom 3, the probability of odd outcomes is:

$$P(\text{odd outcome}) = P(1) \cup P(3) \cup P(5) = P(1) + P(3) + P(5)$$

$$P(\text{odd outcome}) = \frac{1}{6} + \frac{1}{6} + \frac{1}{6} = \frac{3}{6} = \frac{1}{2} = 0.5$$

The axiom also implies that the probability of a null event is zero ($P(\emptyset)=0$).

Now, let's answer the first question: What is the probability of heads in a coin toss? Well, it will depend on the coin, and we have to make an assumption that H and T are equally likely (which is often expressed as the coin is fair or the coin is balanced). Then, P(H)=P(T)=1/2=0.5. If the coin is biased (it is bent) and we believe that the occurrence of H is three times more likely than T, then

$$P(H) = 3/4 = 0.75; \quad P(T) = 1/4 = 0.25$$

1.2.3 Simple Propositions of Probability

By using these axioms, we can show some simple propositions of probability. If events E and E^C are mutually exclusive and $S = E \quad E^C$, then P(S)=1=P (E∪E^C)=P(E)+P(E^C). This leads to Proposition 1.

Proposition 1.

$$P(E^C) = 1 - P(E)$$

For example, in a test cricket match, if the probability of India winning (P(E)) is 0.3, then the probability of all other outcomes is $(P(E^C))=1-0.3=0.7$. These outcomes include India loosing, a draw, a tie, the match abandoned, and so on.

Proposition 2.

$$\text{If } E \subset F, \text{ then } P(E) \le P(F)$$

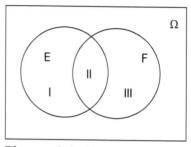

Figure 1.1. *Venn Diagram for Proposition 3*

If an event E is a subset of an event F, then P(E) is smaller than or equal to P(F). When E is a subset of F, then E is a smaller set inside F or set E is equal to set F. For example, even the outcome on a roll of a dice is a subset of all outcomes of the rolls of the dice and will have a probability smaller than the probability of all outcomes.[5] If there are 10 Boys (F) and 10 girls in a class and out of them five boys are day-scholars (E) and you randomly draw one student, then the probability of getting a day-scholar boy (P=5/20=0.2) is smaller than that of getting a male student (P=10/20=0.5).

Proposition 3.

$$P(E \cup F) = P(E) + P(F) - P(E \cap F)$$

If E and F are not mutually exclusive, then P(E∩F) is a part of P(E) and P(F) and is, hence, counted twice while calculating individual probabilities of E and F. Thus, it has to be subtracted once. Look at Figure 1.1.

$$P(E)=P(I)+P(II)$$
$$P(F)=P(III)+P(II)$$
$$P(E)+P(F)=P(I)+P(II)+P(III)+P(II)$$
$$P(E\cap F)=P(II);$$
$$\text{hence, } P(E\cup F)=P(E)+P(F)-P(E\cap F)$$

You will also realize that Proposition 3 can be extended to the union of three events and is expressed as

$$P(E \cup F \cup G) = P(E) + P(F) + P(G) - P(E \cap F) - P(E \cap G) - P(F \cap G) + P(E \cap F \cap G)$$

Proposition 4. This is a general form of Proposition 3 for *n* events. The propositions logically follow the axioms. Rest of the probability can be constructed by using axioms and the propositions. For this reason, the axiomatic approach to probability is preferred over other approaches.

---

[5] Under experimental conditions, Kahneman and Tversky have shown that humans fail to apply this proposition. This is commonly known as conjunction fallacy. They created a Linda example, which is as follows: Linda is 31 years old, single, outspoken, and very bright. She majored in philosophy. As a student, she was deeply concerned with issues of discrimination and social justice, and also participated in anti-nuclear demonstrations. Then which of the following is more probable? (A) Linda is a bank teller. (B) Linda is a bank teller and is active in the feminist movement. Most people judge second as more probable. In reality bank teller who is feminist activist (B) is a subset of bank tellers (A), and hence will have smaller probability than A. Daniel Kahneman was awarded by Nobel Prize in 2002 for his contribution to economic sciences.

1.3 RANDOM VARIABLE

A random variable is a real-valued function defined on the sample space. If S is a sample space with probabilities known for events in that sample space and X is a real-valued function defined over the elements of S, then X is called a random variable. Since the value of a random variable is defined on a sample space, these values can be assigned probabilities. The probabilities associated with random variables can be computed by using probabilities associated with respective events in the sample space. Look at the examples below.

Example 1: Suppose in a learning experiment, you assign one point if a task is correctly solved and zero point if it is incorrectly/not solved. There are two tasks to be solved. Let's assume that the probability of correctly solving (S)=the probability of incorrectly solving (F)=0.5. The elementary events in the sample space are {SS, SF, FS, and FF} with the probability of 1/4 associated with each. The points obtained will be 0 (for event FF), 1 (for events SF and FS each), and 2 (for event SS). Now, let's define a random variable, points obtained (Y), and denote probabilities associated with it. Then

$$P\{Y = 0\} = P\{(FF)\} = \frac{1}{4} = 0.25$$

$$P\{Y = 1\} = P\{(SF),(FS)\} = \frac{2}{4} = 0.50$$

$$P\{Y = 2\} = P\{(SS)\} = \frac{2}{4} = 0.25$$

The sample space consisted of four events with probability measures. One point for success and zero for failure is a real-valued function. The points obtained (Y) are random variables with probability for values of random variables computed from the sample space.

Example 2: Suppose we want to know the average emotional intelligence score of adolescents. We decide to take a sample of 200 adolescents. We will administer an emotional intelligence scale to this sample and compute the average for this sample. Suppose we take another sample, administer the scale, and compute average, then the average will change, and so will be the case with subsequent samples. So the "sample mean" is a random variable.

1.3.1 Probability Distributions

We can write a function for a random variable. Let's think of a game of chance. The game involves rolling two unbiased dice. Each dice results in six outcomes and, hence, the total number of outcomes is $6 \times 6 = 36$. This can be represented as one to six outcomes on the first dice and one to six outcomes on the second dice. For each of the outcome on the first dice, there exist six outcomes on the second dice, that is, total 36 outcomes. Let's now think of a random variable X, where X is equal to the sum of numbers obtained on the two dice. Then X will take values from 2 (1 on first and 1 on second) to 12 (6 on first and 6 on second). To enumerate, $X=7$ is possible in six ways: {(1, 6), (2, 5), (3, 4), (4, 3), (5, 2), (6, 1)}. The probability associated with $X=7$ is equal to 6/36. Table 1.1 shows the probabilities associated with each of the values that X will take. Instead of writing probabilities associated with each of the value of the random variable, it is suitable to write a formula that expresses those probabilities.

This formula can express the probabilities as a function called $f(x)$, where $f(x)=p(X=x)$ for each x within the range of random variable X. That is, a function $f(x)$ is expressing the probability of each of the value (x) of the random variable X. In the above example, $X=$sum of numbers obtained on the two dice, and $x=$the values from 2 to 12 of random variable X.

In the case of the example in Table 1.1, probabilities associated with any value of X (i.e., sum of the outcomes of rolled dice) can be expressed as follows:

Table 1.1 *Sample Space, Random Variable, and Probabilities Associated with the Random Variable*

36 events in the sample space*	Random variable (X)†	p(X=x)
(1, 1)	2	1/36=0.03
(1, 2) (2, 1)	3	2/36=0.06
(1, 3) (2, 2) (3, 1)	4	3/36=0.08
(1, 4) (2, 3) (3, 2) (4, 1)	5	4/36=0.11
(1, 5) (2, 4) (3, 3) (4, 2) (5, 1)	6	5/36=0.14
(1, 6) (2, 5) (3, 4) (4, 3) (5, 2) (6, 1)	7	6/36=0.17
(2, 6) (3, 5) (4, 4) (5, 3) (6, 2)	8	5/36=0.14
(3, 6) (4, 5) (5, 4) (6, 3)	9	4/36=0.11
(4, 6) (5, 5) (6, 4)	10	3/36=0.08
(5, 6) (6, 5)	11	2/36=0.06
(6, 6)	12	1/36=0.03

Notes: * The first number in parenthesis is the outcome on the first dice and the second number is the outcome on the second dice.
† X is the sum of the outcomes on both dice.

$$f(x) = \frac{6 - |x - 7|}{36} \quad \text{for } x = 2, 3, 4, ..., 12.$$

This can be tested by substituting some of the values of the random variable.

$$f(2) = p(X = 2) = \frac{6 - |2 - 7|}{36} = \frac{6 - 5}{36} = \frac{1}{36} = 0.03$$

$$f(5) = p(X = 5) = \frac{6 - |5 - 7|}{36} = \frac{6 - 2}{36} = \frac{4}{36} = 0.11$$

$$f(12) = p(X = 12) = \frac{6 - |12 - 7|}{36} = \frac{6 - 5}{36} = \frac{1}{36} = 0.03$$

The $f(x)$ values will be identical with the $p(X=x)$ values shown in Table 1.1. The function $f(x)=P(X=x)$ for each x within the range of random variable X is called the probability distribution of X in the case of the discrete random variable X. Every probability distribution has a distribution function, which is known as the probability mass function (pmf) in the case of discrete random variables and the probability density function (pdf) in the case of continuous random variables.

Such a probability distribution function $f(x)$ has to satisfy the following conditions:

1. $f(x) \geq 0$ for each value of X
2. $\sum_x f(x) = 1$, where the summation is for all the values of X.

R Code. Distribution of Random Variable
```
pd<-function(x){
  pdx<- (6-(abs(x-7)))/36
  return(pdx)
}
x<-c(2:12)
pd(x)
pdx<-(pd(x))
pdx<-numerical(pdx)
barplot(pdx, main="Dice Distribution", xlab="Value of random
variable", ylab="probability of x")
```

Problem: For Example 1 in the random variable section, find a formula for the probability distribution of total points obtained in the learning experiment. You will recall that this experiment involves solving two problems with equal probability of success and failure where one point is awarded for success.

Solution: We know the probabilities associated with outcomes 0, 1, and 2. They are $p(X = 0) = \dfrac{1}{4}$, $p(X = 1) = \dfrac{2}{4}$, and $p(X = 2) = \dfrac{1}{4}$. You will realize that numerators 1, 2, and 1 are binomial coefficients $\binom{2}{0}$, $\binom{2}{1}$, and $\binom{2}{2}$. So, the formula can be written as

$$f(x) = \frac{\binom{2}{x}}{4} \quad \text{for } x = 0, 1, 2$$

The details of the binomial coefficient are explained in the next section of discrete random variables.

Generally, two types of random variables[6] can be constructed: **discrete random variables** and **continuous random variables**. Discrete random variables take countable, infinite (or finite) values, whereas continuous random variables take uncountable, infinite values.

1.3.2 The Expected Value and Variance

1.3.2.1 Expected Value

An Expected value or expectation of a random variable is one of the very important concepts in probability. Expected value is the average or mean of a random variable. You know that to obtain mean or average you need to do Sum(X)/number of observations or $\bar{X} = \dfrac{\sum x}{n}$. Say, if X=2, 2, 2, 4, 5, then the number of observations (n) is 5. The sum(X)=15 and mean=15/5=3. In this example, you need to know n. In the case of a random variable, you are not aware of n. We need to compute the average without knowing n. What we know is P(x) or f(x). The expected value provides a formulation of the average or mean of a random variable. For the above data, P(2) is 3/5, P(4) is 1/5, and P(5) is 1/5. Now, we compute average as follows:

$$\bar{X} = \frac{2 + 2 + 2 + 4 + 5}{5}$$

The numerator is 3 times 2, plus 1 times 4 and 1 times 5. Let's write it as follows:

$$\bar{X} = \frac{(3)2 + (1)4 + (1)5}{5}$$

Now, we can take each division separately. Then, 3/5 will be the probability of 2, and so on:

$$\bar{X} = \left(\frac{3}{5} \times 2\right) + \left(\frac{1}{5} \times 4\right) + \left(\frac{1}{5} \times 5\right)$$

---

[6] Random variables are broadly classified into two types: discrete and continuous. The third type of random variable is mixed random variable. Part of the random variable is spread like continuous variable and part is concentrated around particular value like a discrete variable. For almost all purposes, understanding of discrete and continuous random variables is sufficient.

Now you will realize that we are multiplying a value of X by its probability and in reality X is only taking three values 2, 4, and 5. This gives us $\bar{X} = 1.2 + 0.8 + 1.0 = 3$. You will understand that if we multiply a value of X by its probability and sum the products, then it is the average. The expectation of random variable is the same concept. The expectation is expressed as:

$$E[X] = \sum_{x:p(x)>0} x \times p(x)$$

where x is value of the random variable, and p(x) is probability of the value. The expression x: p(x)>0 states that the summation is carried out for those x that have p(x) greater than zero. The expected value of X is a weighted average of the possible values that X can take, and the value is weighted by the probability of X. This formalization of expected value is useful for discrete random variables. The expected value for continuous random variables is $f(x)dx \approx P\{x \le X \le x + dx\}$, which is generally stated as

$$E(X) = \int_{-\infty}^{+\infty} x \times p(x)dx$$

This implies that integration (addition of continuous values) from negative infinity to positive infinity of $x \times p(x)$ with respect to x. The details of continuous variable are discussed later.

Example: Suppose a random variable X takes two values 0 and 1 that are equally likely, for example, success (1) and failures (0) on a problem-solving task. Then P(0)=1/2=P(1), which imply that P(X)=½.

The expectation of this random variable is

$$E[X] = \sum_{x:p(x)>0} x \times \frac{1}{2}$$

$$E[X] = 0\left(\frac{1}{2}\right) + 1\left(\frac{1}{2}\right) = 0.5$$

The expectation or average of this random variable is 0.5.

1.3.2.1 Variance

The expectation of random variable provides its average. All the values of random variable are not the expectation of X. Hence, it is necessary to know how far the other values are from expectation. The variance of random variable provides us with this information. If E(X) is denoted as μ, then easy way to do this is to obtain the expectation of the differences between the values and μ, that is E(x−μ). But this sum is zero because the sum of values greater than μ is equal to the sum of values smaller than μ. To get rid of this problem, the difference (x−μ) is squared. The variance of a random variable is obtained as follows:

$$Var(X) = E[(X - \mu)]^2$$

It can be shown that this results into

$$Var(X) = E(X)^2 - (\mu)^2$$

We know that μ=E(X). So it can be expressed as

$$Var(X) = E[X^2] - (E[X])^2$$

for the above example, $(E[X])^2$ is $0.5^2 = 0.25$. The $E[X^2]$ will be $E[X^2] = \sum X^2 \times p(x)$. The X^2 values for 0 and 1 are 0 and 1 only. So $E[X^2] = 0\left(\dfrac{1}{2}\right) + 1\left(\dfrac{1}{2}\right) = 0.5$. Now,

$$\text{Var}(X) = E\left[X^2\right] - \left(E[X]\right)^2$$
$$\text{Var}(X) = 0.5 - 0.25 = 0.25$$

The variance of this random variable is 0.25.

1.4 DISCRETE RANDOM VARIABLES

A discrete random variable is the one that takes a countable infinite or finite number of values. That is, while counting elements belonging to a set, we are using a set of positive integers and counting them as first element, second element,..., and so on, and assigning values such as 0, 1, 2, 3, ..., so on. Friday night turnout for a movie, number of students taking a statistics course, number of patients reporting improvements after therapy, words remembered in a working memory experiment, success or failure on a problem-solving task, number of consumers purchasing a product, and so on, are some examples of discrete random variables.

1.4.1 Types of Discrete Random Variable

We shall look at the Bernoulli distribution, binomial distribution, Poisson distribution, and multinomial distribution as examples of discrete distributions. Nevertheless, there are many more discrete distributions.

1.4.2 The Bernoulli Random Variable and Bernoulli Distribution

Suppose you have provided five problems to a participant in an experiment. The participant can either solve each problem successfully or will fail in solving it. The problems are independent and hence solving one problem will not help or hinder in solving another. So we can assume that the outcome on each of the problem is mutually exclusive. Let's define the probability of success as p and probability of failure as $1-p$, where p is the value between 0 and 1. The probability of failure is also called q which is $1-p$. If we define "success" and "failure" by using numbers and define a new random variable X which takes value 1 for "success" and 0 for "failure." This experiment is called a Bernoulli trial and the random variable is called a Bernoulli random variable after a famous mathematician Jacob Bernoulli[7] (1654–1705) from the Bernoulli family. Now, we can have a pmf of the Bernoulli random variable:

$$P(x) = p^x \times (1-p)^{1-x} \text{ for } x = 0 \text{ or } 1$$
$$P(x) = p^x \times q^{1-x} \text{ for } x = 0 \text{ or } 1$$

If $x=0$, then $P(0)=P\{x=0\}=1-p$. Similarly, if $x=1$, then $P(1)=P\{x=1\}=p$.

---

[7] Jacob Bernoulli is from a famous family of mathematicians, the Bernoulli family. This family has produced seven to eight mathematicians over three generations. He studied mathematics against the wish of parents and travelled Europe to learn recent developments. He joined University of Basel, Switzerland, and soon became Professor. He is known for his work in probability. He is also known for discovery of constant e. He was closely associated with Leibniz and was a proponent of Leibnizian calculus. He is also known for contributions to calculus of variations. He also proved the law of large numbers for binary random variable. He taught mathematics to his younger brother Johann Bernoulli, and Johann went on becoming a competent mathematician and joined Basel. Later, their relations worsened and Johann left Basel and came back only after the death of Jacob. He and his brother carried the Bernoulli trait of mean streak. Johann's son Daniel was also a brilliant mathematician.

Here, we have assumed that the events are independent, that is, the success and failure of the earlier task has no influence on subsequent tasks. For example, if we assume the probability of success as $p=0.4$, then the probability of failure is $q=(1-p)=1-0.4=0.6$. Then the probability of random variable X taking values zero and 1 are: $P(0)=0.4^0 \times (1-0.4)^{1-0}$ which is $P(0)=1 \times 0.6=0.6$ and $P(1)=0.4^1 \times (1-0.4)^0$ which is $P(1)=0.4 \times 1=0.4$. You would quickly realize that the Bernoulli distribution function is stating what is already known, that is, values of p and $1-p$. Hence, the general case of the Bernoulli is useful. It makes use of the same idea. If two events, say M and N, are independent, then the probability of occurrence of both is equal to a multiplication of their respective probabilities $P(M) \times P(N)$. For example, in an experiment, if a participant has to solve five problems out of which s/he fails on first two and successfully solves the next three, the sample space for the same can be expressed as

$$S=(0, 0, 1, 1, 1)$$

So the probability of observing (0, 0, 1, 1, 1) together can be defined as

$$(1-p) \times (1-p) \times (p) \times (p) \times (p) = p^3 \times (1-p)^2 = p^3 \times q^2$$

So, for general case, we can write if $x=1$ and $n-x=0$ in n trials, then we can write the Bernoulli distribution function as $P(x) = p^x \times (1-p)^{n-x}$.

Example: Suppose we assume that the probability of success for solving a problem correctly is 0.40, then we say that $p=0.40$ and then $1-p=0.6$. The probability of occurrence of sequence **S** can be expressed as $p^x \times (1-p)^{n-x} = 0.4^3 \times (1-0.4)^{5-3} = 0.4^3 \times 0.6^2 = 0.02304$. This can be shown as $0.6 \times 0.6 \times 0.4 \times 0.4 \times 0.4 = 0.02304$. Each of the value in this multiplication is obtained via the Bernoulli distribution function $P(x) = p^x \times (1-p)^{1-x}$. R code 1.2 for the same is give below.

```
# R code 1.2. Bernoulli Distribution
library(Rlab)
x=c(0, 0, 1, 1, 1)
dbern (x, .4)
[1] 0.6 0.6 0.4 0.4 0.4
prod (dbern (x, .4)) =0.02304
```

Example: Suppose in a basketball game, a player is trying to shoot a basket from a fixed distance (say, the three-point line) and attempts six throws. Assume that the player is not improving with throws and success/failure on each is independent from other throws. Further, if we know that the probability of success is 0.2, then what is the probability that s/he will make a basket in the following manner: S=(0, 1, 0, 1, 0, 1)?

The $P(0)=1-0.2=0.8$ and $P(1)=0.2$. The Bernoulli distribution function will give the probabilities for each of the event in this sequence in the manner (0.8, 0.2, 0.8, 0.2, 0.8, 0.2). If you multiply them, you will get $P(S)=(0.8 \times 0.2 \times 0.8 \times 0.2 \times 0.8 \times 0.2)=0.004096$. You can also use $p^x \times (1-p)^{n-x}$, where $n=6$ and $x=3$. Then $P(3) = p^3 \times (1-p)^{6-3} = 0.004096$.

Example: The records of clinical psychologists show that 75% of patients improve if treated with particular psychotherapy (i.e., $p=0.75$). If three records are randomly picked up, then what is the probability that the first two are treated successfully and the third is not? The S=(1, 1, 0), $p(0)=1-0.75=0.25$, and $p(1)=0.75$. The Bernoulli distribution function will provide probabilities for each event in this sequence as (0.75, 0.75, 0.25). Their multiplication or $P(2) = p^2 \times (1-p)^{3-2}$ will provide the value 0.140625.

The **expected value**, that is, the average or mean of the Bernoulli distribution is $E(X)=p$ and its **variance** is $Var(X)=p \times (1-p)=p \times q$. The parameter value in the Bernoulli distribution is p, where $0<p<1$. The Bernoulli distribution can be considered as a special case of the binomial distribution.

> **Bernoulli Distribution**
> pmf: $P(x) = p^x \times (1-p)^{1-x}$
> mean: $E(X) = p$
> variance: $Var(X) = p \times (1-p) = p \times q$

1.4.3 Binomial Random Variable and Binomial Distribution

Recall from the earlier section, the example of the problem-solving experiment consisting of five problems. Now, instead of failure on the first two and success on the next three, you are interested in the number of successes out of the five attempts. So the number of "successes" is a random variable (X) which will take any integer number from 0 to 5, where 0 indicates no success and 5 indicates success on all five problems. Suppose you are interested in finding a value $P(X=3)$, that is, the probability that out of five problems a participant correctly solves any three problems, which three are irrelevant. The first task is to define the sample space for this event "success." The participant solving each problem will either succeed (S) or fail (F) on it. Each problem has two possible outcomes. So the total number of outcomes in the sample space S is defined as $2 \times 2 \times 2 \times 2 \times 2 = 2^5 = 32$. The entire sample space can be written as S:

S={(S,S,S,S,S), (S,S,S,S,F), (S,S,S,F,S), (S,S,F,S,S), (S,F,S,S,S), (F,S,S,S,S), (S,S,S,F,F), (S,S,F,S,F),

(S,F,S,S,F), (F,S,S,S,F), (S,S,F,F,S), (S,F,S,F,S), (F,S,S,F,S), (S,F,F,S,S), (F,F,S,S,S),

(S,S,F,F,F), (S,F,S,F,F), (F,S,S,F,F), (S,F,F,S,F), (F,S,F,S,F), (F,F,S,S,F), (S,F,F,F,S), (F,S,F,F,S),

(F,F,S,F,S), (F,F,F,S,S), (S,F,F,F,F), (F,S,F,F,F), (F,F,S,F,F), (F,F,F,S,F), (F,F,F,F,S), (F,F,F,F,F),}.

Since we are interested in finding the value of $P(X=3)$, the elementary events in the sample space S that result into three "success" $(X=3)$ can then be defined as E.

E={(S,S,S,F,F), (S,S,F,S,F), (S,F,S,S,F), (F,S,S,S,F), (S,S,F,F,S), (S,F,S,F,S), (F,S,S,F,S), (S,F,F,S,S),

(F,S,F,S,S), (F,F,S,S,S)}.

If we assume that all elements in S are equally likely (also means that S and F are equally likely), then we can define

$$P(X=3) = \text{number of elements in E/number of elements in S};$$

$$P(X=3) = 10/32 = 0.3125$$

But we have already assumed the probability of success=0.4. Hence, the probability of each of the element in E is already computed as 0.02304 in the Bernoulli distribution. The third axiom of probability tells us that if events are mutually exclusive, then the probability of their union is the sum of the probability of each event. The sum of probabilities associated with each outcome in E equals to 0.2304. So the probability of E, that is, the probability of success on any of the three problems out of five, is 0.2304 and can be expressed as $P(X=3)=0.2304$. It can be obtained simply by multiplying the probability of an element in E by the number of elements in E, which is

$$P(x) = 10 \times p^x \times (1-p)^{n-x}$$
$$P(x) = 10 \times 0.4^3 \times (1-0.4)^{5-3}$$
$$P(x) = 10 \times 0.02304 = 0.2304$$

From the section about combination (Appendix B), we know that the number 10 can be determined by using $\binom{n}{x} = {}^nC_x = \dfrac{n!}{(n-x)! \times x!} = \dfrac{5!}{(5-3)! \times 3!} = \dfrac{120}{12} = 10$. This is also known as binomial coefficient.

Hence, we can rewrite the earlier equation as

$$P(x) = \binom{n}{x} \times p^x \times (1-p)^{n-x}$$

So the probability of solving any three problems successfully out of five problems has the following components: $n=5$, $x=3$, $p=4$ and $1-p=1-0.4=0.6$.

$$P(3) = \binom{5}{3} \times 0.4^3 \times (1-0.4)^{5-3}$$

$$P(3) = 10 \times 0.064 \times 0.36 = 0.2304$$

So the probability of any three successes out of five problems is 0.2304. The pmf for the binomial distribution is

$$f(x) = P(X = x) = \binom{n}{x} \times p^x \times (1-p)^{n-x}$$

$$f(x) = P(X = x) = \binom{n}{x} \times p^x \times q^{n-x}$$

The parameters for this distribution are n and p. The **expectation** (mean) of the binomial distribution is $E(x)=np$ and the **variance** is $var(x)=npq$.

#R code 1.3. Binomial Distribution
```
> dbinom (x, n, p)        # Where (x, n, p) has to be entered.
> dbinom (3, 5, 0.4)         # the solved example
```

Example: You know that the probability of passing an examination is 0.75. If 10 students appear for the examination, what is the probability that randomly chosen four students will pass the examination?

Let's assume that the students are unrelated to each other and the passing or failing of one will not influence any other students' outcome. The random variable is the number of students passing examination, which will take values from 0 to 10; $n=10$, $x=4$, and $p=0.75$. Hence, $q=1-p=1-0.75=0.25$. The probability that four students will pass is

$$P(X = 4) = \binom{10}{4} \times 0.75^4 \times 0.25^{10-4}$$

$$P(X = 4) = \frac{10!}{4! \times (10-4)!} \times 0.75^4 \times 0.25^6 = 0.162$$

So the probability that any four students will pass the examination is 0.0162.

Example: Eye movement desensitization and reprocessing (EMDR) is a psychotherapy discovered by Francine Shapiro that uses eye movements (and other procedures) to reprocess traumatic memories and reduce their negative impact. Research suggests that 80% of posttraumatic stress disorder (PTSD) patients improve if treated with EMDR (i.e., $p=0.80$). If six patients are treated with EMDR, then what's the probability that three of them will show improvement?

If a person shows improvement we call it success (1) and in the case of no improvement we call it failure (0). So the probability of success P(1) is 0.80 and the probability of failure P(0) is $q=1-p=1-0.8=0.2$. Number of persons showing improvement (X) is the random variable that will take values from 0 to 6. We assume that improvement in each person is independent. The

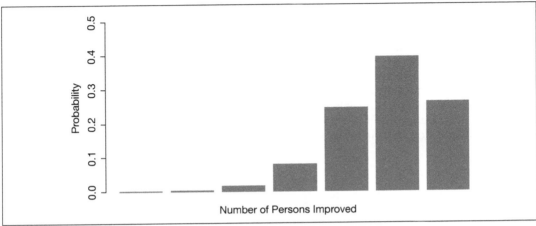

Figure 1.2. *Binomial Distribution for Improvement after EMDR*

probability associated with each value then can thus be computed using the binomial distribution; $n=6$, $p=0.8$ and $q=0.2$. X will take values from zero to 6. Let's compute the probability for each of the outcome:

$$P(X = 0) = \frac{6!}{0! \times (6-0)!} \times 0.80^0 \times 0.20^6 = 0.000064$$

$$P(X = 1) = \frac{6!}{1! \times (6-1)!} \times 0.80^1 \times 0.20^5 = 0.001536$$

$$P(X = 2) = \frac{6!}{2! \times (6-2)!} \times 0.80^2 \times 0.20^4 = 0.01536$$

$$P(X = 3) = \frac{6!}{3! \times (6-3)!} \times 0.80^3 \times 0.20^3 = 0.08192$$

$$P(X = 4) = \frac{6!}{4! \times (6-4)!} \times 0.80^4 \times 0.20^2 = 0.24576$$

$$P(X = 5) = \frac{6!}{5! \times (6-5)!} \times 0.80^5 \times 0.20^1 = 0.393216$$

$$P(X = 6) = \frac{6!}{6! \times (6-6)!} \times 0.80^6 \times 0.20^0 = 0.0262144$$

These are the probabilities associated with each of the values of the binomial random variable, that is, the number of persons improving with EMDR. If you add the probabilities associated with all the outcomes, then $0.00006400+0.001536+0.01536+0.08192+0.24576+0.393216+0.262144=1.00$, which is the probability of the entire sample space.

The probability distribution is shown in Figure 1.2.

Binomial Distribution

pmf: $P(x) = \binom{n}{x} \times p^x \times (1 - p)^{1-x}$

mean: $E(X) = np$

variance: $Var(X) = n \times p \times (1-p) = n \times p \times q$

1.4.4 Poisson Random Variable and Poisson Distribution

Bernoulli trials have led to development of some useful distributions. The Poisson distribution is one of them. Binomial random variable is useful when the number of events is small. If the number of trials increases, that is, they approximate infinity, and p becomes small, that is, almost close to zero, and $\lambda = np$ (a constant), then the Poisson distribution approximates probabilities of the binomial distribution. Under these circumstances, the useful distribution that can be derived from Bernoulli trials and the binomial distribution is the Poisson distribution. The Poisson distribution itself is a very important distribution developed by S. D. Poisson[8] in 1873. The distribution has the following pmf:

$$P(X = x) = e^{-\lambda} \frac{\lambda^x}{x!}$$

where $P(X=x)$ is a probability of any value of $X (x=0, 1, 2,...)$, e is a base of natural logarithm which is a constant 2.718282, λ is a parameter and also mean and variance of the Poisson variable. Note that the mean and variance of the Poisson distribution are identical (λ). Also note that np is a mean of the binomial distribution and $\lambda = np$.

Example: Suppose a footballer practices penalty kick to a goal post each day where only a goalkeeper is present to stop the ball. How many times would a footballer kick the ball outside the goalpost? It's a rare event. The probability (p) is very low. We know that the footballer is practicing 100 kicks a day and we know that once in 5 days he kicks outside the goal post. That is, he fouls once in 500 kicks. Now, every time he sets to kick the ball, there is a 1/500 probability that he would kick outside the post. If the probability of foul is p (success) and the probability of no foul is $1-p$ (failure), then $P(X)$ will follow binomial. In addition, the two fouls are independent from each other, that is, the time between them is random (it won't occur systematically after every 500 kicks but would occur randomly over a number of kicks which will average to 500). Using binomial for this problem is tedious because the n is too large and p is too small. It is easy to think of a binomial distribution that converges to a Poisson distribution.

In the binomial process, where the number of trials or events (n) tends to infinity and the probability of success (p) tends to zero, while np remains constant, let $np=\lambda$, that is, $p = \dfrac{\lambda}{n}$. The limiting form of the binomial distribution obtained is called the Poisson distribution. The binomial distribution is

$$p(x) = \binom{n}{x} \times p^x \times (1-p)^{n-x}$$

Since $p = \dfrac{\lambda}{n}$, we can rewrite the earlier formula as

$$p(x) = \binom{n}{x} \times \left(\frac{\lambda}{n}\right)^x \times \left(1 - \frac{\lambda}{n}\right)^{n-x}$$

The term $\binom{n}{x}$ can be written as $\dfrac{n(n-1)(n-2)\cdots(n-x+1)}{x!}$

---

[8] Siméon Denis Poisson (1781–1840) was a French mathematician who was very close to Pierre-Simon Laplace. He became known for work on correction of Laplace's second-order partial differential equation for potential that is now referred to as the Poisson Equation or potential theory. He worked on definite integrals and Fourier series in pure mathematics. He is also known for Poisson algebra, Poisson regression, Poisson ratio, and so on. In probability theory, his work on the Poisson process and Poisson distribution is well known. In 1837, he wrote a book on probability theory regarding lawsuit, entitled *Recherches sur la prob-abilité des jugements en matière criminelle et en matière civile* (Research on the Probability of Judgments in Criminal and Civil Cases) which contains the first expression of Poisson distribution. Though French revolution happened in his lifetime, he was not a part of it and after the revolution with little difficulty he was back in his academic positions.

$$p(x) = \frac{n(n-1)(n-2)\cdots(n-x+1)}{x!} \times \left(\frac{\lambda}{n}\right)^x \times \left(1-\frac{\lambda}{n}\right)^{n-x}$$

Now, if we divide each of $n(n-1)(n-2)\cdots(n-x+1)$ by n from the denominator of $\left(\frac{\lambda}{n}\right)^x$ and also express $\left(1-\frac{\lambda}{n}\right)^{n-x}$ as $\left[\left(1-\frac{\lambda}{n}\right)^{-n/\lambda}\right]^{-\lambda} \left(1-\frac{\lambda}{n}\right)^{-x}$ then we rewrite the earlier equation as:

$$p(x) = \frac{1\left(1-\frac{1}{n}\right)\left(1-\frac{2}{n}\right)\cdots\left(1-\frac{x+1}{n}\right)}{x!} \times (\lambda)^x \times \left[\left(1-\frac{\lambda}{n}\right)^{-n/\lambda}\right]^{-\lambda} \left(1-\frac{\lambda}{n}\right)^{-x}$$

As we have specified, $n \to \infty$ and λ is constant, then the term $1\left(1-\frac{1}{n}\right)\left(1-\frac{2}{n}\right)\cdots\left(1-\frac{x+1}{n}\right)$ tends to be 1.

The term $\left(1-\frac{\lambda}{n}\right)^{-x}$ also tends to be 1.

And the term $\left(1-\frac{\lambda}{n}\right)^{-n/\lambda}$ tends to e (another constant).

We can rewrite the earlier equation as

$$p(x) = \frac{1}{x!} \times (\lambda)^x \times [e]^{-\lambda} \times 1$$

which is a Poisson distribution commonly written as

$$P(x) = \frac{\lambda^x e^{-\lambda}}{x!} = e^{-\lambda}\frac{\lambda^x}{x!} \quad \text{for } \lambda = 1, 2, 3,\ldots, x > 0$$

Example: Suppose in a game of cricket, the number of "no balls" per game bowled by a bowler is a random variable that follows the Poisson distribution with a mean of 1.5, then what is the probability that five no balls will be bowled in a game?

Assuming that the "number of no balls" bowled in a game (X) follows the Poisson process, then we can use the Poisson distribution to answer this question. The mean is $\lambda=1.5$ and hence the probability of five no balls can be stated as

$$P(5) = e^{-1.5}\frac{1.5^3}{5!}$$

The value of $e=2.718282$ and $e^{-1.5}=0.2231302$.

$$P(5) = 0.2231302 \times \frac{1.5^5}{5!}$$

$$P(5) = 0.2231302 \times \frac{7.59375}{5 \times 4 \times 3 \times 2 \times 1}$$

$$P(5) = 0.01411996$$

The probability of five no balls is approximately 0.014, which can be considered as a low probability.

```
# R code 1.4. Poisson Distribution
> dpois (x, λ) # Where (x, λ) has to be entered.
> dpois (5, 1.5)
[1] 0.01411996
```

Example: From the above example, if we want to know the probability of bowling 2 to 4 no balls, then that can be computed by using the third axiom of probability which states that the union of mutually exclusive events is the summation of their individual probabilities.
Hence, $p(2 \cup 3 \cup 4) = P(2) + P(3) + P(4)$, which is equal to

$$P(2 \cup 3 \cup 4) = e^{-1.5}\frac{1.5^2}{2!} + e^{-1.5}\frac{1.5^3}{3!} + e^{-1.5}\frac{1.5^4}{4!} = 0.251 + 0.1255 + 0.0471 = 0.4236$$

Thus, the probability of bowling 2 to 4 no balls in a given game is 0.4236.

Example: Suppose the probability of having individuals with past suicide attempts in a random sample of adults is 0.002 (estimated value).[9] Then what is the probability that in one of the random samples of size 1000 you will find more than 5 individuals with past suicide attempts? If we assume that x is a random variable (x=number of individuals with history of suicide attempts in a sample) that follows the Poisson distribution with $\lambda = np = 1000 \times 0.02 = 2$, then the probability of $x > 5$ can be determined by applying Proposition 1 of probability. This proposition states that $P(E^C) = 1 - P(E)$. The P(E) in this example is $P(0) + P(1) + P(2) + P(3) + P(4) + P(5)$. Hence, the probability of finding more than five individuals in this group is 1 minus addition of probabilities associated with finding 0, 1, 2, 3, 4, and 5 individuals, respectively:

$$P(x > 5) = 1 - P(E) = 1 - \left[e^{-2}\frac{2^0}{0!} + e^{-2}\frac{2^1}{1!} + e^{-2}\frac{2^2}{2!} + e^{-2}\frac{2^3}{3!} + e^{-2}\frac{2^4}{4!} + e^{-2}\frac{2^5}{5!}\right]$$

$$P(x > 5) = 1 - P(E) = 1 - [0.1353 + 0.2707 + 0.2707 + 0.1805 + 0.0902 + 0.0361$$

$$P(x > 5) = 1 - P(E) = 1 - 0.9835 = 0.0165$$

The probability of obtaining more than five individuals with a history of a suicide attempt is 0.0165.

Example: On an average, 5th graders make two mistakes of spelling or mixing upper and lower case letters on a page. If you obtain a student who made six mistakes on a page, then will you consider these many mistakes as unusually large?
If the number of mistakes on a page (x) follows Poisson, then we can find out the probability associated with six or more mistakes by the following:

$$P(x \geq 6) = \sum_{x=6}^{\infty} e^{-2}\frac{2^x}{x!}$$

This calculation is tedious. We can go by an empirical rule that if $x > (\mu + 2\sigma)$, then it is considered as an extreme value. The mean (μ) of Poisson is 2 and variance (σ^2) is also 2. The standard deviation of this Poisson variable is $\sigma = \sqrt{\lambda} = \sqrt{2} = 1.41$. Hence, we have to calculate the value that is two standard deviations above the mean, which is $2 + (2 \times 1.41) = 2 + 2.828 = 4.828$. This value is smaller than the obtained value of x; hence, we will consider the six errors as an unusual finding.

---

[9] Generally, 11 individuals per 0.1 million commit suicide in India (National Crime Records Bureau, 2011). World Health Organization (WHO) estimated that attempted suicides are 20 times more than committed. With this, 220 individuals per 0.1 million people are attempting suicide. Hence, I am estimating the probability of suicide attempts in India in general population as 220/100000 = 0.0022 or 0.002.

Example: The Poisson distribution should also fulfill axioms of probability like $0 \leq P(x) \leq 1$ and $\sum P(x_i) = 1$. Since $\lambda > 0$ obviously, $P(x) > 0$ for $x = 0, 1, 2, 3, \ldots$ and $P(x) = 0$ otherwise. Now,

$$\sum_{i=0}^{\infty} P(x) = \sum_{i=0}^{\infty} e^{-\lambda} \frac{\lambda^x}{x!} = e^{-\lambda} \sum_{i=0}^{\infty} \frac{\lambda^x}{x!} = e^{-\lambda} e^{\lambda} = 1.$$ We know from Box 1.1 that by following the Taylor

series expansion of the exponential function, the infinite sum $\sum_{i=0}^{\infty} \frac{\lambda^x}{x!}$ results into e^{λ}.

Poisson Distribution

pmf: $P(x) = e^{-\lambda} \dfrac{\lambda^x}{x!}$ for $\lambda = 1, 2, 3, \ldots, x > 0$

mean: $E(X) = \lambda$

variance: $\text{Var}(X) = \lambda$

Example: One of the early applications of the Poisson distribution is shown by Bortkiewicz (1898) to model the number of Persian army soldiers who died due to horse kicks. The probability that a soldier would die due to horse kick (p) is very low and the number of solders (n) is very high. So the Poisson distribution is applicable to this problem.

BOX 1.1. HOW TO KNOW MEAN AND VARIANCE OF RANDOM VARIABLE? AN EXAMPLE OF POISSON DISTRIBUTION

So far, mean and variance of random variable of every random variable was stated. It is interesting to know how we know about the mean or expectation of random variable. If you know the pmf of the random variable, then in case of discrete variables the mean is

$E(X) = \sum_{i=1}^{\infty} X \times P(X)$ and variance is $\text{Var}(X) = E[(X - \mu)^2]$. The pmf of discrete random variable

is known. Then the expectation and variance of random variable can be obtained. Here is an example of Poisson random variable to show its expectation. The expectation of discrete

random variable is $E(X) = \sum_{i=1}^{\infty} X \times P(X)$. Now, if X follows Poisson, then $P(X)$ is replaced with

the pmf of Poisson distribution.

$E(x) = \sum_{i=1}^{\infty} x \times e^{-\lambda} \dfrac{\lambda^x}{x!}$ — replace $P(X)$ with the Poisson distribution pmf and then

$E(x) = \sum_{i=1}^{\infty} x \times e^{-\lambda} \dfrac{\lambda^x}{x(x-1)!}$ — take out $e^{-\lambda}$ since it is a constant and cancel out x.

$E(x) = e^{-\lambda} \sum_{i=1}^{\infty} \dfrac{\lambda^x}{(x-1)!}$ — Now we have to expand summation (assign value of x from 1 onwards)

$E(x) = e^{-\lambda} \times \left[\dfrac{\lambda^1}{(1-1)!} + \dfrac{\lambda^2}{(2-1)!} + \dfrac{\lambda^3}{(3-1)!} + \cdots \right]$ — Now, x is given the values 1, 2, 3,..., onwards.

$E(x) = e^{-\lambda} \times \lambda \left[\dfrac{1^1}{0!} + \dfrac{\lambda}{1!} + \dfrac{\lambda^2}{2!} + \dfrac{\lambda^3}{3!} + \dfrac{\lambda^4}{4!} + \cdots \right]$ — Now, lambda is taken out and the Taylor theorem is applied.

$E(x) = e^{-\lambda} \times \lambda \left[1 + \lambda + \dfrac{\lambda^2}{2!} + \dfrac{\lambda^3}{3!} + \dfrac{\lambda^4}{4!} + \cdots \right]$ — As stated in previous line, here the "Taylor series expansion of exponential function" tells us that $e^{\lambda} = 1 + \lambda + \dfrac{\lambda^2}{2!} + \dfrac{\lambda^3}{3!} + \dfrac{\lambda^4}{4!} + \cdots$; hence, $E(x) = e^{-\lambda} \times \lambda \times e^{\lambda} = \lambda$ now $e^{-\lambda}$ and e^{λ} are cancelled and what remains is λ.

The variance of Poisson distribution can similarly be obtained. $var(X)=E(X^2)-(E(X))^2$. Here we know now that $E(x)=\lambda$ for Poisson and hence $(E(x))^2=\lambda^2$. Now we can show that $E(x^2)=\lambda^2+\lambda$ by following almost similar exercise and Taylor series expansion of exponential function. Hence, $var(X)=\lambda^2+\lambda-\lambda^2=\lambda$. Similarly, other properties like skewness, kurtosis, moment generating function, etc. can be obtained for each distribution.

1.5 CONTINUOUS RANDOM VARIABLE AND CONTINUOUS PROBABILITY DISTRIBUTION

In the earlier section we have learned about discrete random variables that take finite or a countable, infinite set of values. However, there are variables that have a set of uncountable possible values, known as continuous random variables. The examples of continuous random variables are time taken to either solve a problem or complete psychological test or an experimental task; reaction time of the participant; height, weight, or BMI of participant; blood pressure; quantity of food consumed; duration of Internet usage; and so on. These variables will take any (infinite) number of values on any interval. It all depends on how precise measurement is ...! Say, in a typical experiment, the time taken to complete a task is a dependent variable. Now we consider an interval to complete a task, like 20 seconds to 25 seconds. Infinite values of time will exist in this interval. And if you further take a smaller interval, like 21.00 seconds to 21.50 seconds, infinite number of values will exist since we can create infinite fractions of time that is measured as a real number. We stop counting by the process of rounding and due to imprecision of measurement instruments. In this example, since time is a continuous variable, 22.00 seconds is rounding and the "exact" time taken to complete task can be more precisely specified as 21.00010020610710... and so on and, in fact, this process will never have an end, hence infinite. Because of this, it is not possible to specify the probability of a specific value, like the probability that the problem is solved in exact 22.00 seconds and the probability of an exact specific value is going to be zero. That is why, when we specify the probability associated with continuous random variables, we actually specify the probability of an interval and not the probability of a specific value. You will recall that I have specified the probability associated with a specific value of any discrete random variable. It is possible because discrete random variables take countable, finite number of values (e.g., number of problems correctly solved). We generally say that a continuous random variable takes all values between an interval $[a, b]$ such as both a and b are real numbers and $a<b$. There are infinite values possible between a and b. Let's specify the random variable as X; in our example, X is the time taken to complete a task. Since we cannot specify $P(X=x_i)$, that is, probability associated with the specific value of X (e.g., exact x_i time taken to complete a task), we have to specify probability associated with an interval like $P(a\leq x\leq b)$. The expressions $P(a\leq x\leq b)$ and $P(a<x<b)$ are equivalent because probability of both a and b individually is zero. With our example, a could be 20 seconds and b could be 25 seconds and we can specify $P(20\leq x\leq 25)$. That is, what is the probability that a participant will finish the task in 20 to 25 seconds? We also need to define a function $f(x)$. The function $f(x)$ is typically called a distribution function of a continuous random variable for all the values that X will take if it satisfies the following conditions:

Condition 1: $f(x)\geq 0$ for $-\infty<x<\infty$

Condition 2: $\int_{-\infty}^{\infty} f(x)\, dx = 1$.

We can further specify that if $-\infty<a<b<\infty$, then

Condition 3: $\int_{a}^{b} f(x)\, dx = P(a \leq x \leq b)$.

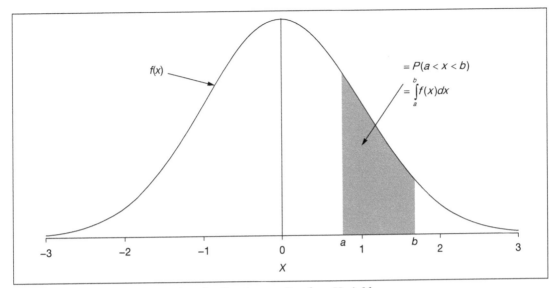

Figure 1.3. *Probability Density of a Continuous Random Variable*

Note: The curve is *f(x)*, also known as pdf, and the probability of area between *a* and *b* is $\int_{a}^{b} f(x)\,dx = P(a \le x \le b)$. Also, note that for a specific value of *x*, for example *a*, there will not be any area under the graph and hence probability will be zero for that value: $\int_{a}^{b} f(x)\,dx = 0$.

The **first condition** states that *f(x)* should be zero or greater than zero for all values of *x*. The **second condition** states that the area under the entire curve is equal to 1. This is similar to the second axiom of probability. These two conditions ensure that probabilities will be between 0 and 1 for any value of *X*. The **third condition** states that for any two values *a* and *b* such as $-\infty < a < b < \infty$, $\int_{a}^{b} f(x)\,dx$ (read: integral of *f*(x) with respect to *x* from *a* to *b*) is equal to the probability of *x* being between values *a* and *b* ($a < x < b$). The *f*(x) *dx* is called as the *probability element* which means the probability associated with an interval of a continuous random variable. Figure 1.3 is a graphical representation.

Most readers who are not familiar with calculus will find these and similar expressions very complex, which they are not. Please refer to Appendix B on "basic mathematics concepts" and read the part on calculus. Nevertheless, I simplify it here as well. Condition 1 is simple. Condition 2 is as follows: $\int_{-\infty}^{\infty} f(x)\,dx = 1$. This is read as "integral of *f*(x) with respect to *x* from negative infinity to positive infinity." $\int$ is an integration sign. Integration is an important aspect of calculus and here it is useful to calculate the area under the curve. $\int_{-\infty}^{\infty}$ means integral from $-\infty$ to $+\infty$. The expression $\int_{-\infty}^{\infty} f(x)\,dx$ means "integral of *f(x)* with respect to *x* from $-\infty$ to $+\infty$." *f(x)* is a function of *x* and read as "*f* of *x*" or simply "*f x*." The function *f(x)* results (generally) in a curve and describes the area under the curve. If you know the value of *x*, which is a continuous random variable, *f(x)* will give you the value of *y* or the height of the curve (Figure 1.3). For each continuous distribution, there are different *f(x)* and we shall know them as we go ahead with distributions. In reality, you need not do the integration to get the probabilities associated with different values of *x*. The table at the end of statistical textbooks will provide you the area under curve, or statistical software like R can do integration for you and compute the area and probability associated with a particular random variable.

Example: Take a simple example: if $f(x) = \dfrac{x^2}{9} = \dfrac{1}{9}x^2$ for *X* taking values between 0 and 3, then, first, *f(x)* will be greater than zero as *x* is greater than zero and otherwise. To know the entire area under the curve, we need to integrate *f(x)* over 0 to 3. That is, $f(x) = \int_0^3 \frac{x^2}{9} dx$ should be equal to 1. This can be tested in R. Write the following code.

We can find out the probability that *x* will take value from 0 to 1. This can be stated as $\int_0^1 \frac{x^2}{9} dx$. That is, integral of *x*-square over 9 with respect to *x* from 0 to 1. This is equal to $\left(\frac{1}{27}x^3\Big|_0^1\right) = \frac{1}{27} = 0.03703704$. The R code provided solves the problem for you.

```
#R code 1.5. Integration
> crv <- function(x)                      #this is a function for defining
                                          f(x)

  {result <- x^2/9
  return(result)
  }
> integrate (crv, 0, 3)                   # this is integration function
                                          in R
1 with absolute error <1.1e-14            # 1 is the total area under
                                          curve
> integrate (crv, 0, 1)                   # integral to find out P(0<x<1)
0.03703704 with absolute error<4.1e-16    # the P(0<x<1)
```

1.5.1 Probability Density Function of a Continuous Random Variable

If the above stated conditions are satisfied, then *f(x)* of the continuous random variable is often referred to as a pdf.

The expectation of continuous random variable is

$$E(X) = \int_{-\infty}^{\infty} x \times f(x)\, dx$$

As specified earlier, expectation is an average of a random variable or population without knowing the size of the population. For continuous random variable, it is an integration of $x \times f(x)$ with respect to *x* for all values of *X*. The variance of a continuous random variable is defined as it is for a discrete random variable. If *X* is a continuous random variable with $E(X)=\mu$, then the variance of *X* is defined as

$$Var(x) = E\left[(x-\mu)^2\right]$$

which is equal to

$$Var(x) = E\left[X^2\right] - \left(E[X]\right)^2$$

As I have specified earlier, variance is also an average or expectation. It is an expectation (or average) of $(x-\mu)^2$.

1.6 TYPES OF CONTINUOUS RANDOM VARIABLES

There are many continuous random variables. The most popular continuous random variable is the normal random variable or normal distribution. Nevertheless, there are many others: they include Beta distribution, Cauchy distribution, chi-squared distribution, exponential distribution, *F*-distribution, gamma distribution, Student's *t*-distribution, uniform distribution,

Weibull distribution, and many more. In this section, we shall refer to uniform, normal, Z, chi-square, F, t, beta, exponential, and gamma distribution. However, we shall give importance to normal, Z, chi-square, F, t, and just illustrate other distributions. In addition, considering its importance, a separate chapter is provided in the book on normal distribution. Hence, the details are avoided here.

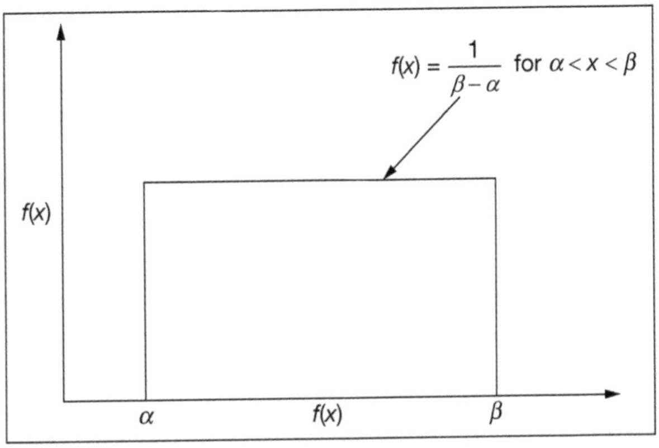

Figure 1.4. *Uniform Distribution*

1.6.1 Uniform Random Variable and Uniform Distribution

The uniform random variable (rectangular distribution) is a symmetric distribution in which any interval of same length will have same probability. The continuous random variable X has uniform distribution if it follows

$$f(x) = \begin{cases} \dfrac{1}{\beta - \alpha} & \text{for } \alpha < x < \beta \\ 0 & \text{elsewhere} \end{cases}$$

Figure 1.4 illustrates uniform distribution. The expectation and variance of uniform distribution is as follows:

$$E(X) = \frac{\alpha + \beta}{2} \quad Var(X) = \frac{1}{12}(\beta - \alpha)^2$$

Even though, uniform distribution can have little application, it can be useful in understanding statistical theory. The real-life examples could be the point on a vehicle tire where next puncture will occur or time for waiting for the next auto or cab on road. However, this distribution assumes that the person waiting for cab will have no information about cab till it comes (hence, at times referred to as no information distribution). In fact, an exponential distribution is a better fit for waiting time than others.

1.6.2 Exponential Distribution

The exponential distribution is most commonly used to model waiting time, particularly, rare events. The utility of the exponential distribution is growing because it can be used to model survival-failure, that is, survival time till an event happens which is also referred to as the waiting time. The exponential distribution has the following distribution function:

$$f(x) = \lambda e^{-\lambda x}$$

If x follows exponential for values of $x > 0$, then $f(x)$ is the distribution function where λ (lambda) is a rate parameter, e is constant ($e \approx 2.71828$). The expectation or mean and variance of the exponential distribution are as follows:

$$E(x) = \lambda^{-1} = \frac{1}{\lambda} \quad Var(x) = \lambda^{-2} = \frac{1}{\lambda^2}$$

A rate parameter is the number of events that occur in a given time interval. One property of this distribution is that it is memory-less. Suppose an event is occurring λ times per hour. Then the average number of times an event will occur in t hours is $t\lambda$. You can recall that a random occurrence of events will follow the Poisson process with mean $t\lambda$. It can be shown that the probability of no event occurs in t hours is $e^{-\lambda t}\dfrac{\lambda t^0}{0!} = e^{-\lambda t}$. If T is the time taken for the first occurrence of event, then $P(T > t) = e^{-\lambda t}$. On the other hand, $P(T > t) = 1 - e^{-\lambda t}$. One of the major applications in psychology is to model the interval between episodes of illness, particularly those that are episodic in nature (e.g., mood disorders). It can also be useful in modeling time of progress of stage-wise progressive illnesses like AIDS or cancer.

Example: If we know that patients of bipolar mood disorder of specific age-gender are in euthymic state (no illness episode or stable mood) for a time interval of eight months on an average, what is the probability that a patient will not have an episode for one year? And if the patient had no episode till eight months, then what is the probability that mood episode will not occur for the next four months? $E(X)=1/\lambda=8$, so the value of $\lambda=1/8$. The probability that episode will not occur for 12 months ($T>12$) is $P(T > 12) = e^{-1/8 \times 12} = 0.223$. If the episode has not occurred for eight months, then the probability that it will not occur for 12 months is $P(T > 12 \mid T > 8) = P(T > 4)e^{-1/8 \times 4} = 0.61$. That is, the probability that episode will not occur for 12 months, given that it has not occurred for eight months, is 0.61.

Example: Suppose you update your status (e.g., upload a picture) on a social networking site. You will expect likes for the update. On an average, there are four likes per hour. What is the probability that you will have to wait up to half an hour for the next like?
    We assume that the waiting time for likes for your upload follows the exponential distribution. The average waiting time per like is $1/\lambda=1/4$ hours (0.25 hours or 15 minutes), which means $\lambda=1/0.25=4$ is the rate parameter. You will realize that the rate parameter is the number of events (e.g., number of likes) that occur in a given time interval (e.g., one hour). If our model (exponential distribution) is correct, the probability that you will have to wait for ½ hour is given by $P(T \geq 1/2) = 1 - e^{-4 \times 0.5} = 0.86467$.
    The R code for both examples follows.

```
#R code 1.6. Exponential Distribution
> 1-pexp(12, 1/8)
[1] 0.2231302
> 1-pexp(4, 1/8)
[1] 0.6065307
> pexp(0.5, 4)
[1] 0.8646647
```

1.6.3 Normal Distribution

Normal random variable and normal distribution is one of the most useful distributions in statistical theory. Most readers with introductory information about statistics have some degree of familiarity with this distribution. A separate chapter is written on normal distribution considering its importance to statistical theory and application, and also considering the fact that most statistical application to psychological data will use normal distribution. Introductory information is provided in this section. If X is a normal random variable, or to say it simply, X is normally distributed, with parameters μ (mu) and σ^2 (sigma square), the density of X is given by

$$f(x) = \frac{1}{\sigma\sqrt{2\pi}} e^{-\left(\frac{(x-\mu)^2}{2\sigma^2}\right)} \quad \text{for } -\infty < x < \infty$$

There are two constants, pi (π) and e, the value of $\pi \approx 3.14159$ and value of $e \approx 2.71828$. The two unknowns μ and σ^2 are also called parameters of normal distribution. The expectation of normal random variable (mean) is μ and variance is σ^2, and obviously standard deviation is σ. $\frac{1}{\sigma\sqrt{2\pi}}$ ensures that $\int_{-\infty}^{\infty} f(x)dx$ will be 1. Some of the important properties of normal distribution are as follows:

- The mean, median and mode are same (μ).
- The bell-shaped curve of normal distribution is symmetric about the mean μ. The normal curve is identical to both sides of its mean.
- Normal distribution has two parameters, μ and σ, and for different values of mean and standard deviation, different normal distributions can be plotted; hence, normal distribution is a family of normal distributions.
- Normal distribution is a continuous distribution that can take values from $-\infty$ to $+\infty$.
- The highest frequency is in the middle and the frequency tapers down at either extremes of normal curve.
- Most of the area under normal curve is within the first three standard deviations at both sides (99.74% area), whereas 68.26% area is within the first standard deviation. To specify:

  o Almost 68.26% (roughly, two-thirds of the area) of the observations fall within 1 standard deviation below and above the mean.
  o Almost 95.44% of the observations fall within 2 standard deviations below and above the mean.
  o Almost 99.73% of the observations fall within 3 standard deviations below and above the mean.

- The skewness and the kurtosis for a normal distribution are both zero. So the normal distribution is known as mesokurtic (if the subtraction of 3 is omitted from the kurtosis formula, then the kurtosis value will be 3 for a normal distribution).

Generally, a normal distribution is denoted as $X \sim N(\mu,\ \sigma^2)$. The examples of a normal distribution are discussed in the separate chapter on normal distribution. However, the example related to statistical theory is given here.

1.6.4 Standard Normal Distribution (Z)

If a variable x is following a normal distribution with mean μ and variance σ^2, then the variable can be converted into standard normal variable (Z) by the following transformation:

$$Z = \frac{x - \mu}{\sigma}$$

The new variable, Z (standard normal distribution) has a mean=0 (zero) and variance=1 (one). The standard normal distribution is a very important distribution in statistical theory as well as it has many psychological applications in psychometric theory. Various variables that follow the normal distribution may have different values of μ and σ^2. The standard normal variable brings normal distributions to identical mean and variance (SD too). Z can also be understood as a normal variable expressed in terms of standard deviations. In routine calculations, the value of μ and σ are not known and, hence, sample values of mean and SD are used. If we set the mean to be zero and standard deviation to be 1 for the pdf of normal, then

$$f(x) = \frac{1}{1\sqrt{2\pi}} e^{-\frac{1}{2}\left(\frac{(x-0)}{1}\right)^2}$$

$$f(x) = \frac{1}{\sqrt{2\pi}} e^{-\frac{1}{2}z^2}$$

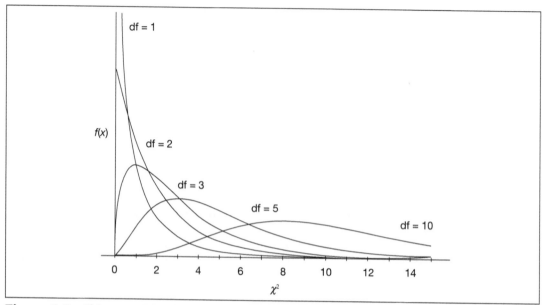

Figure 1.5. *Chi-square Distribution at Different Degrees of Freedom*

Note: The curve is becoming increasing symmetric as df's increase.

This is the pdf of standard normal distribution. The area under normal distribution tables given at the end of statistical books follows Z distribution. And hence, to make use of this table, one has to convert the normal variables into Z.

1.6.5 Chi-Square (χ^2) Distribution

If Z_1, Z_2, ..., Z_k are k *independent* variables that follow standard normal distribution (mean zero and variance 1), then $\chi^2 = \sum_{i=1}^{k} Z_i^2$ with k degrees of freedom (df) where df is the number of independent quantities of Z. The χ^2 is subscripted with k which is df of χ^2 variable (χ_k^2). For example, if Z is one standardized normal variable, the, Z_2 is χ^2 at one df; if Z_1 and Z_2 are two independent standardized normal variables, then $Z_1^2 + Z_2^2$ is χ^2 at two df. The degrees of freedom for a chi-square variable is the number of Z random variables squared and added. Often, young students mistakenly believe that since chi-square test is described in non-parametric statistics, it has nothing to do with normal distribution. The chi-square distribution has the following properties:

1. From Figure 1.5, you will realize that the chi-square distribution is skewed. The degree of skewness depends on its df. The distribution if highly skewed to right with few df's, and as the df's increase, the distribution of chi-square goes closer to the symmetric distribution. In fact, for df above 100 following can be considered as the standardized normal variable (k=df of chi-square):

$$\sqrt{2\chi^2} - \sqrt{(2k-1)}$$

2. The chi-square distribution has a mean k and variance 2k. Remember that k is df of chi-square.
3. If χ_1^2 and χ_2^2 are two independent chi-square variables with k_1 and k_2 df, respectively, then $\chi_1^2 + \chi_2^2$ is also a chi-square variable with df=$k_1 + k_2$.

```
#R code 1.7. chi-square Distribution
> dchisq(x, df)              # x is value of chi-square and df
                             are degrees of freedom
> dchisq(5.99, 2)            # density of chi-square=5.99 at
                             df=2.
[1] 0.02501831
> curve (dchisq (x, 10), 0, 50)  # chi-square density plot at
                             df=10. 0, 50 is limit of x axis
```

1.6.6 *F*-distribution

The *F*-distribution can be obtained in the following manner:

If χ_1^2 and χ_2^2 are two independent chi-square variables with df_1 and df_2 as degrees of freedom of each respectively, then the *F* random variable can be defined as:

$$F = \frac{\chi_1^2 / df_1}{\chi_2^2 / df_2}$$

with df_1 and df_2 as degrees of freedom for the *F*-distribution. The *F*-distribution is shown as $F_{(df1, df2)}$. The *F*-distribution always has two degrees of freedom, one of numerator chi-square and second of denominator chi-square distribution, often called as numerator df and denominator df.

The *F*-distribution is at the heart of analysis of variance (ANOVA) procedures. We shall look at its application in detail in Chapter 8. Some of the characteristics of the *F*-distribution are as follows:

1. The *F*-distribution is skewed to the right. It approaches normal distribution as df_1 and df_2 become large (see Figure 1.6).
2. The expectation (mean) of the *F*-distributed variable is $df_2/(df_2 - 2)$ for $df_2 > 2$ and variance of the *F*-distribution is as follows:

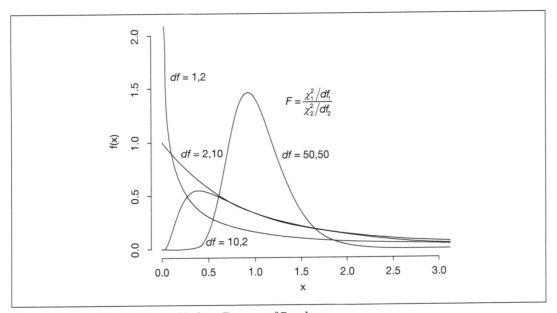

Figure 1.6. *F-distribution at Various Degrees of Freedom*

$$\frac{2df_2^2\left(df_1 + df_2 - 2\right)}{df_1\left(df_2 - 2\right)^2\left(df_2 - 4\right)}$$

3. If the degree of freedom denominator (df_2) of the F-distribution is very large, the relationship between a F-distribution and chi-square distribution is $df_1 \times F \sim \chi^2_{df_1}$, that is, for a very large df_2, the F multiplied by df_1 (i.e., df_1 times F) will approximate the value of chi-square at df_1.
4. If the F-distribution has $df_1 = 1$, the square root of the F-distribution will provide a t-distributed random variable.

1.6.7 Student's *t*-distribution

The Student's t-distribution is a very useful distribution. The Student's t-test utilizes this distribution. t Random variable can be obtained in the following way: If Z is a standardized random variable [$Z \sim N(0, 1)$], and χ^2_k is chi-square distributed random variable at k degrees of freedom, which is independent of Z, then the t-distribution is $t = \dfrac{Z}{\sqrt{\chi^2/k}} = \dfrac{Z/\sqrt{k}}{\sqrt{\chi^2}}$ at k degrees of freedom. Usually, the t-distribution is expressed as t_k, where k is subscript indicating degrees of freedom. While discussing the F-distribution, we learned that if the F-distribution has $df_1 = 1$, the square root of the F-distribution will provide a t-distributed random variable. It can be shown as follows:

$$\sqrt{F_{1,\,df_2}} = \sqrt{\frac{\chi^2_1/1}{\chi^2_2/df_2}} = \sqrt{\frac{Z^2}{\chi^2_2/df_2}} = \frac{Z}{\chi^2_2/df_2} = t_{df_2}$$

The Student's t-distribution has the following properties:

1. The t-distribution is a symmetric distribution.
2. It is similar to the normal distribution but is flatter. As the df increases, it approaches the normal distribution and it is a normal distribution as df equals to infinity. Usually, the t-distribution at df=30 is quite close and similar to normal (try plotting the t-distribution at different df using the following R syntax). And hence, often, $n=30$ is considered as a good number of observations for t-test.
3. The mean of the t-distribution is zero, and its variance is $k/(k-2)$.

```
# R code 1.8. t-distribution
> dt (x, df)          # density of t-value (x) at given degrees of
                      freedom (df)
> dt (1.96, df=Inf)   # density of t-value of 1.96 with df=infinity

#Plotting t-distributions at different df (1, 4, 30 and 120) in different
colors
x <- seq(-3, 3, length=300)  # generate 300 numbers between -3 to 3
hx <- dt(x, 1)               # hx is density of t for x at df=1
gdt <- c(1, 4, 30, 120)      # four degrees of freedom
colors <- c("red", "blue", "darkgreen", "gold")    # colors for graph
plot(x, hx, type ="n", lty=2, lwd=4, xlab="x", ylab=expression(f(x)),
xlim=c(-3,3), ylim=c(0, 0.5), frame.plot=F)  # blank plot is created
for (i in 1:4)               # for loop to plot different graphs
  {
  lines(x, dt(x, df=gdt[i]), lwd=2, col=colors[i])
  }
```

1.6.8 Other Continuous Distributions: Beta, Gamma, and Weibull

This section briefly introduces you to distributions that are comparatively less frequently used in statistics for psychology though they are important in statistical theory. Understanding them will increase the utility as well.

1.6.8.1 Gamma Distribution

The gamma distribution can be considered as the generalization of the exponential distribution. The gamma distribution has two parameters, shape and rate (α, λ), where both are greater than zero (different parameterization is possible in the gamma distribution). The density of the gamma distribution is $f(x) = \dfrac{\lambda e^{-\lambda x}(\lambda x)^{\alpha-1}}{\Gamma(\alpha)}$ where $\Gamma(\alpha)$ is a **gamma function**. The gamma distribution makes use of gamma function in its density function. The gamma function can be obtained by $\Gamma(\alpha) = \int_0^\infty e^{-y} y^{\alpha-1} d_y$. The gamma distribution can be used to answer questions about waiting time like if events are happening randomly, then the amount of time one has to wait till all events occur. The difference between two spikes (inter-spike interval) of given biological function (e.g., heart beats) can be modeled by using the gamma distribution. One such example is hart rate variability (HRV), which is one of the frequently used physiological parameters in psychology.

1.6.8.2 Beta Distribution

The Beta distribution is a very flexible family of distributions. It is one continuous distribution that can take various shapes and at the same time it is bounded between 0 and 1. It can be symmetric or asymmetric and can be U shaped or inverted-U shaped. The pdf of the beta distribution is $f(x) = \dfrac{1}{B(a,b)} x^{a-1}(1-x)^{b-1}$, where x is between 0 and 1. $B(a, b)$ is a beta function.

When $a=b$, the beta distribution is a symmetric distribution. When $a=b=1$, then it is actually a uniform distribution and hence can be considered as a generalization of a uniform distribution. It is useful in studying events occurring on a finite scale. It is often used for probability of probabilities (because probability is between 0 and 1), for example, application as "conjugate prior to binomial" in Bayesian analysis.

1.6.8.3 Weibull Distribution

The Weibull distribution was developed to understand fatigue data. Now it is used to understand various other problems as well. Particularly, it is useful in understanding lifetime of some object which is made up of many parts, and failure of the parts will lead to failure of object. The distribution has two parameters β and α, where α is a scale parameter and β is a shape parameter and both β and α are greater than zero. The pdf is $f(x) = \dfrac{\beta}{\alpha}\left(\dfrac{x}{\alpha}\right)^{\beta-1} e^{-(x/\alpha)^k}$, where $x \geq 0$.

It is useful in modeling reaction time distribution in experimental psychology.

1.7 CONDITIONAL PROBABILITY

In this section, we shall focus on jointly distributed random variables, marginal distribution, conditional probability, conditional expectation, and conditional variance. We shall also look at the useful formulation of conditional probability known as the Bayes rule. We are often interested in problems where more than one variable is measured. For example, think about "intelligence" and "problem-solving ability" measured by their tests. We can ask questions like, what is the average problem-solving ability of individuals with IQ at 110? Or we can also ask, what is the association between IQ and problem-solving? We might be interested in knowing about variance in problem-solving ability for those individuals who have IQ of 110. Is this variance different than the variance of the individuals who have IQ of 145? In order to answer these questions, we need an understanding of joint probability distribution of both the variables. We shall not consider them as individual random variables but we shall look at jointly distributed random variable. The concept of jointly distributed random variable is at the heart of correlations and regression.

In the earlier sections, we have thought of variables that take values on one variable only. For example, number of problems correctly solved take values like 0, 1, 2, 3,..., onwards! In a joint distribution, we think of variables that take two values simultaneously. For example, IQ and problem-solving score. This jointly random variable would appear like (120, 8), (114, 5), (137, 11), (104, 2), and so on. Every parenthesis is one observation where the first number indicates IQ and the second indicates the problem-solving score. Since this is a two-dimensional variable, it will be plotted on a X–Y plane. The pair of values in each parenthesis is a single "value" of a bi-variate random variable. We will call this jointly distributed variable as Z.

1.7.1 Jointly Distributed Random Variable

Suppose you are doing a decision-making experiment and five decision-making tasks are given. Each of them will be either solved correctly or incorrectly. We assume that it is equally likely to succeed and fail on the task. Now, we are interested in the following question: Whether correct solutions on first three tasks are related with correct solutions on all five tasks? Let's denote the number of correct solutions on the first three tasks as X and the number of correct solutions on all tasks as Y. Let's look at the sample space S consisting of 32 events, where C=correct decision and M=mistake:

S={CCCCC, CCCCM, CCCMC, CCMCC, CMCCC, MCCCC, CCCMM, CCMCM, CMCCM,

   MCCCM, CCMMC, CMCMC, MCCMC, CMMCC, MCMCC, MMCCC, CCMMM,

   CMCMM, MCCMM, CMMCM, MCMCM, MMCCM, CMMMC, MCMMC, MMCMC,

   MMMCC, CMMMM, MCMMM, MMCMM, MMMCM, MMMMC, MMMMM}.

The outcome (CCCCM) represents that the first four decisions are correct and the last one is a mistake, that is, $X=3$ and $Y=4$. In the case of (CCMMC), $X=2$ and $Y=3$. In the case of (MMCCC), $X=1$ and $Y=3$. All three can be written as (3, 4), (2, 3), and (1, 3), respectively. Let's look at all values that this random variable $Z=(X, Y)$ will take:

Z={(3, 5), (3, 4), (3, 4), (2, 4), (2, 4), (2, 4), (3, 3), (2, 3), (2, 3), (2, 3), (2, 3), (2, 3),

   (2, 3), (1, 3), (1, 3), (1, 3), (2, 2), (2, 2), (2, 2), (1, 2), (1, 2), (1, 2), (1, 2), (1, 2),

   (1, 2), (0, 2), (1, 1), (1, 1), (1, 1), (0, 1), (0, 1), (0, 0)}.

This has been expressed in Table 1.2.

Table 1.2. *Number of Outcomes of Jointly Distributed Random Variable*

	Y=0	**Y=1**	**Y=2**	**Y=3**	**Y=4**	**Y=5**	**Total X**
X=0	1 (0, 0)	2 (0, 1)	1 (0, 2)	0 (0, 3)	0 (0, 4)	0 (0, 5)	4
X=1	0 (1, 0)	3 (1, 1)	6 (1, 2)	3 (1, 3)	0 (1, 4)	0 (1, 5)	12
X=2	0 (2, 0)	0 (2, 1)	3 (2, 2)	6 (2, 3)	3 (2, 4)	0 (2, 5)	12
X=3	0 (3, 0)	0 (3, 1)	0 (3, 2)	1 (3, 3)	2 (3, 4)	1 (3, 5)	4
Total Y	1	5	10	10	5	1	32

Table 1.3. *Probabilities Associated with the Values of Jointly Distributed Random Variable*

	Y=0	Y=1	Y=2	Y=3	Y=4	Y=5	f(X)
X=0	1/32	2/32	1/32	0	0	0	4/32
X=1	0	3/32	6/32	3/32	0	0	12/32
X=2	0	0	3/32	6/32	3/32	0	12/32
X=3	0	0	0	1/32	2/32	1/32	4/32
f(Y)	1/32	5/32	10/32	10/32	5/32	1/32	1

The entries in Table 1.2 are easy to understand. The table inside heavy lines is for **jointly distributed random variables**. Each intersection of X and Y represents the value of a joint random variable. The number in parenthesis (e.g., 1 and 3) is a value of the variable. It is a combination of the X value from a row and the Y value from a column. The number outside parenthesis represents the number of times a value of bivariate random variable occurred in a sample space. X=1 and Y=3, that is, (1, 3) has occurred three times in our sample space (CMMCC, MCMCC, MMCCC). The last column and bottom row are addition of numbers outside parenthesis. For example, the total of row X=0 is 4, which is an addition of 1+2+1+0+0=4. That is, variable X has taken value 0 four times for all possible values of Y (0, 1, 2, 3, 4, 5). Similarly, you can interpret column totals. The total of column Y=1 is 5 which is 2+3+0+0= 5.

Now let's understand Table 1.3. The X and Y axes are as per the earlier table. The number 3/32 in the intersection of X=1 and Y=3 is a probability of the value (1, 3). There are 32 possible values in the sample space and the value (1, 3) has occurred three times. Hence, the probability of this value is 3/32=0.093. Likewise, the probability of value (2, 3) is 6/32=0.1875. It is usually expressed as P(X=2, Y=3) or P(2, 3), that is, probability of X takes a value 2 and Y takes a value 3. The values in the last column and last row of f(x) and f(y) are called **marginal probabilities**. This is the probability of one variable (either X or Y) taking a specific value.

For example P(X=0)=4/32, P(X=1)=12/32, and so on. It can be shown as:

P(X=0)=P(X=0, Y=0)+P(X=0, Y=1)+P(X=0, Y=2)+P(X=0, Y=3)+P(X=0, Y=4)+P(X=0, Y=5)

P(X=0)=(1/32)+(2/32)+(1/32)=4/32

This can be called **marginal distribution** of X, wherein we have calculated the probability that X takes a value of zero. Similarly, we can think about the probability of other values of X and the probability of values of Y. Marginal distribution is the distribution of individual variable, which is the distribution of X or distribution of Y.

The cumulative density function for a two-dimensional random variable is: $F(x, y)=P(X \leq x, Y \leq y)$, that is, the probability of X takes a value less than a specific value and Y takes a value less than a specific value. For example, F(1, 2) is the probability that there is at the most one correct decision on first three tasks and there are at most two correct decisions on all tasks. It can be obtained by P(X≤1, Y≤2)=1/32+0+2/32+3/32+1/32+6/32=13/32.

1.7.2 Expectation of X and Expectation of Y

With the knowledge of joint and marginal distribution, we can now compute E(X) and E(Y).

We know that E(X)=sum(x×p(x)). This is called **unconditional expectation** of X, because E(X) is independent of any other value of Y. Similarly, we can obtain unconditional expectation of Y.

E(X)=P(X=0) × 0+P(X=1) × 1+P(X=2) × 2+P(X=3) × 3

E(X)=(4/32) × 0+(12/32) × 1+(12/32) × 2+(4/32) × 3

E(X)=0+12/32+24/32+12/32

E(X)=1.5

The variance of X can also be obtained as follows:

$$\sigma_x^2 = E(X^2) - E(X)^2$$

$$= [(4/32) \times 0 + (12/32) \times 1 + (12/32) \times 4 + (4/32) \times 9] - [1.5^2]$$

$$= [0.375 + 1.5 + 1.125] - [2.25]$$

$$= 0.75$$

1.7.3 Obtaining E(X, Y)

When we know that XY are jointly distributed, we can find the E(X, Y). This is the expectation of a jointly distributed random variable:

$$E(X, \ Y) = \sum_i \sum_j x_i \times y_j \times P(X = x_i, Y = y_j)$$

It is to be carried out over the pairs of X, Y. In our example it will be written as

$$E(X,Y) = \sum_i^3 \sum_j^5 x_i \times y_j \times P(X = x_i, Y = y_j)$$

Let's calculate the E(X,Y). First, we do it for i=0 (because i takes values form 0 to 3), which means X=0. Initially, we need to multiply the value of X with the specific value of Y_j and then find a product with value of $P(x_i, y_j)$ in the cell.

For X=0, this entire product is going to be zero because X=0.

Now, let's do it for X=1.

You only look at the row of X=1. In the following expression $[1 \times 2 \times (6/32)]$, 1 is value of X, 2 is the value of Y, and 6/32 is probability of (X=1, Y=2). With this you will be able to understand other expressions:

$$\sum_j^5 x_1 \times y_j \times P(X = 1, \ Y = y_j) = [1 \times 1 \times (3/32)] + [1 \times 2 \times (6/32)] + [1 \times 3 \times (3/32)]$$

$$= [0.09375] + [0.375] + [0.28125] = 0.75$$

Now, Let X=2

$$\sum_j^5 x_2 \times y_j \times P(X = 2, Y = y_j) = [2 \times 2 \times (3/32)] + [2 \times 3 \times (6/32)] + [2 \times 4 \times (3/32)]$$

$$= 0.375 + 1.125 + 0.75 = 2.25$$

Now, let's solve it for X=3

$$\sum_j^5 x_3 \times y_j \times P(X = 3, \ Y = y_j) = [3 \times 3 \times (1/32)] + [3 \times 4 \times (2/32)] + [3 \times 5 \times (1/32)]$$

$$= 0.28 + 0.75 + 0.46875 = 1.5$$

The final sum is E(X, Y)=0.75+2.25+1.5+4.5.

The average or expectation of the random variable (X,Y) is 5.25.

Table 1.4. *Joint Distribution Marginal Distribution of Roll of Dice*

	1	2	3	4	5	6	*f(X)*
Even (1)	0	1/6	0	1/6	0	1/6	3/6
Odd (2)	1/6	0	1/6	0	1/6	0	3/6
f(X)	1/6	1/6	1/6	1/6	1/6	1/6	

1.7.4 Conditional Probability

So far, we have learned about probability of an individual variable. We have also learned about joint and marginal distribution. In the case of a joint distribution, when we know that one event has occurred (e.g., X has taken a particular value), then the probability that a given other event will occur (e.g., Y will take a particular value) is conceptualized in conditional probability. Let's take a simple example. When we roll a fair dice, the probability that any of the six outcomes will occur is 1/6, so the probability of getting 4 is 1/6, that is, $P(4)=1/6=0.167$. The outcome 2, 4, and 6 are even outcomes and 1, 3, and 5 are odd outcomes. Now, if you know that on roll of dice, an "even" outcome has occurred, then what is the probability that 4 has occurred? Now, the probability that 4 will occur is no longer 1/6. There are three equally likely even outcomes possible, 4 is one of the even outcomes; hence, $P(4)=1/3=0.333$. Let's now denote A=event that "4" is rolled and B=event that "even number" is rolled, then the probability of A given that B has occurred is stated as P(A|B), which is read as "the probability of A given B" (Table 1.4).

We can express this as $P(A=4 \mid B=1)$.

Now, take the example of Table 1.3, where joint and marginal probabilities are given. For the ready reference, the table is reproduced here as well.

Now, suppose two decisions are correct out of first 3 ($X=2$), then what is the probability of three correct decisions in all ($Y=3$)?

Table 1.3. *Probabilities Associated with the Values of Jointly Distributed Random Variable*

	Y=0	*Y=1*	*Y=2*	*Y=3*	*Y=4*	*Y=5*	*P(X)*
$X=0$	1/32	2/32	1/32	0	0	0	4/32
$X=1$	0	3/32	6/32	3/32	0	0	12/32
$X=2$	0	0	3/32	6/32	3/32	0	12/32
$X=3$	0	0	0	1/32	2/32	1/32	4/32
$P(Y)$	1/32	5/32	10/32	10/32	5/32	1/32	

$$P(Y = 3 \mid X = 2) = \frac{P(Y = 3, X = 2)}{P(X = 2)}$$

The numerator of this is the probability of joint occurrence of $Y=3$ and $X=2$ (which is 6/32) and denominator is marginal probability of $X=2$ (which is 12/32):

$$P(Y = y_j \mid X = x_i) = \frac{6/32}{12/32} = \frac{0.1875}{0.375} = \frac{1}{2} = 0.5$$

This tells us that the conditional probability that $Y=3$ (i.e., three out of five decisions are correctly made) given that $X=2$ (i.e., two out of first three are correctly made) is 0.5 or 1/2.

The general rule of conditional probability can be written as follows:

$$P(Y = y_j \mid X = x_i) = \frac{P(Y = y_j, X = x_i)}{P(X = x_i)}$$

More generally, for the first example, it's written as

$$P(A \mid B) = \frac{P(A \cap B)}{P(B)}$$

where $P(A \mid B)$ is "probability of A given B," $P(A \cap B)$ probability of "A intersection B" or joint probability that A and B have occurred, and $P(B)$ is the marginal probability of B.

1.7.5 Conditional Expectation

We can ask a question, if we know that four out of five tasks are correctly solved, then what is the average of correctly solved tasks on first three tasks? This will provide us the answer called conditional expectation. This can be expressed as $E(X \mid Y=4)$, that is, expectation of X given $Y=4$. This can be worked out as follows:

$$E(X \mid Y = 4) = \sum_{i=1}^{n} x_i \times P(X = x_i \mid Y = 4)$$

$$E(X \mid Y = 4) = 0 \times P(X = 0 \mid Y = 4) + 1 \times P(X = 1 \mid Y = 4)$$
$$+ 2 \times P(X = 2 \mid Y = 4) + 3 \times P(X = 3 \mid Y = 4)$$
$$E(X \mid Y = 4) = (0 \times 0) + (1 \times 0) + (2 \times 3 / 5) + (3 \times 2 / 5)$$
$$E(X \mid Y = 4) = 0 + 0 + 1.2 + 1.2 = 2.4$$

Similarly, we can calculate the conditional expectation for other values of Y. Let's start from $Y=0$

$$E(X \mid Y = 0) = 0 \times P(X = 0 \mid Y = 0) + 1 \times P(X = 1 \mid Y = 0)$$
$$+ 2 \times P(X = 2 \mid Y = 0) + 3 \times P(X = 3 \mid Y = 0)$$
$$E(X \mid Y = 0) = (0 \times 1 / 1) + (1 \times 0) + (2 \times 0) + (3 \times 0)$$
$$E(X \mid Y = 0) = 0$$

This is obvious; it actually means that when there are zero correct answers on all five tasks, then there will be average zero correct answers on first three tasks as well.

Now, let's do it for $Y=1$

$$E(X \mid Y = 1) = 0 \times P(X = 0 \mid Y = 1) + 1 \times P(X = 1 \mid Y = 1)$$
$$+ 2 \times P(X = 2 \mid Y = 1) + 3 \times P(X = 3 \mid Y = 1)$$
$$E(X \mid Y = 1) = (0 \times 2 / 5) + (1 \times 3 / 5) + (2 \times 0) + (3 \times 0)$$
$$= 0 + (3 / 5) + 0 + 0 = 0.6$$

Similarly, we can do it for $Y=2$.

$$E(X\,|\,Y=2)=0\times P(X=0\,|\,Y=2)+1\times P(X=1\,|\,Y=2)$$
$$+2\times P(X=2\,|\,Y=2)+3\times P(X=3\,|\,Y=2)$$
$$E(X\,|\,Y=2)=(0\times 1/10)+(1\times 6/10)+(2\times 3/10)+(3\times 0)$$
$$=0+(6/10)+(6/10)+0=1.2$$

and for Y=3

$$E(X\,|\,Y=3)=0\times P(X=0\,|\,Y=3)+1\times P(X=1\,|\,Y=3)$$
$$+2\times P(X=2\,|\,Y=3)+3\times P(X=3\,|\,Y=3)$$
$$E(X\,|\,Y=3)=(0\times 0)+(1\times 3/10)+(2\times 6/10)+(3\times 1/10$$
$$=0+0.3+1.2+0.3=1.8$$

For Y=4, the value is calculated and that is 2.4. So let's do it for Y=5

$$E(X\,|\,Y=5)=0\times P(X=0\,|\,Y=5)+1\times P(X=1\,|\,Y=5)$$
$$+2\times P(X=2\,|\,Y=5)+3\times P(X=3\,|\,Y=5)$$
$$E(X\,|\,Y=3)=(0\times 0)+(1\times 0)+(2\times 0)+(3\times 1/1)$$
$$=0+0+0+3=3$$

These values are conditional expectation of X given a specific value of Y. We can actually plot these values against i and that will plot a straight line for us. This line has a slope of 0.60 and the equation of the line can be written as

$$E(X\,|\,Y)=\alpha+\beta Y$$
$$E(X\,|\,Y)=0+0.6\times Y$$

This is not regression analysis. However, what is important to know is that the average X will change with the increase in Y. This will have important implications. For example, as the IQ increases, the average number of problems correctly solved will have a different mean. This can be used later on in psychometrics as well. The idea of correlation and regression depends on this discussion. We shall carry forward this discussion on joint, marginal, conditional distributions, and the associated computation of probabilities in the chapter of correlation and regression.

SUMMARY

Probability is dealing with the chance of occurrence of an event. Defining sample space and event is the basic requirement for working with probability. Axiomatic approach to probability specifies three axioms—probability takes value between 0 and 1, probability of sample space is 1, and union of probabilities of independent events can be the summation of the probability of individual events. The constraints on sample space result into random variable. There are two types of random variables—discrete and continuous. Bernoulli, binomial, Poisson, and so on, are types of random variables. Uniform, exponential, normal, standard normal, chi-square, F-distribution, t-distribution, and so on, are useful continuous random variables. Jointly distributed random variables are a very useful concept. Expectation and variance of jointly distributed random variables are useful. Understanding probability is useful for understanding psychological attributes in terms of random variables.

EXERCISE

1. Define sample space and event. Generate examples of sample space and events.
2. What will be the sample space for tossing of four coins? If the probabilities of H and T are equal, construct a random variable (Y), total number of T and probability associated with (Y).
3. State axioms of probability.
4. Two fair dice are rolled and sum of the outcome is obtained. If E is sum=6, define (E^c). Define P(E) and P(E^c).
5. Two dice are rolled. D is the event that the sum of the dice is even, E is the event that at least one of the dice lands on 2, and F is the event that the sum is 6. Describe the events DE, D$\cup$E, EF, DEF and DE^c.
6. If E and F are mutually exclusive events, with P(E)=0.2 and P(F)=0.6 then, what is the probability that (a) both E and F occur, (b) either E occurs or F occurs, (c) F occurs but E does not occur.
7. Define P(E$\cup$F$\cup$G) if E, F, and G are mutually exclusive.
8. Define P(E$\cup$F$\cup$G) if E, F, and G are not mutually exclusive. Similarly, define P(E$\cup$F$\cup$G$\cup$H). Draw a Venn diagram for both.
9. If 20% people subscribe to a newspaper A, 30% subscribe to newspaper B, 10% subscribe to newspaper C, 15% subscribe to A and B, remaining subscribe to A, B, and C, then (a) probability of a randomly chosen person would subscribe to A and B, (b) probability that a randomly chosen person is not subscribing to C, (c) probability that a randomly chosen person is not subscribing to A and B.
10. Two dice are identically painted and rolled: for each, two sides are red, two are white, and two are green. (a) What is the probability that both will show green? (b) What is the probability that one is red and other is white?
11. Show that P(EF^c)=P(E)−P(EF).
12. If E, F, and G be three events, find expressions for the events so that, out them, (a) only F occurs, (b) G and H occur but E does not occur, (c) all events occur, (d) at least two events occur, (e) at least one event occurs, (f) no event occurs.
13. A student can lend three textbooks from library: there are three cognitive psychology, two statistics, and four personality psychology texts available. S/he can take only one from each category. (a) How many outcomes are there in sample space? (b) If E is an event that one personality book is selected, then how many event will occur in E, (c) if F is event that one statistic book selected, then how many event occur in F, (d) how many events occur in EF.
14. There are 10 chocolate and 15 milk candies in a box. If you randomly take one after another, then what is the probability that all milk candies will be removed before chocolate?
15. In an event, catching a local train on all five days of week follows the Bernoulli distribution. P(1), that is, the probability of catching train is 0.3. What is the probability that you will (a) catch the train on the first and last day of the week, (b) catch the train on the first, third and last days, (c) miss the train on all days, (d) catch the train on all days, (e) catch the train on the last two days, given you have caught the train on the first two days. Test your answers by writing an R code.
16. Five students have applied for a project, where only 20% is chance of success. Write all possible events in the sample space. What is the probability that (a) two students successfully complete the project, (b) all students successfully complete the project, (c) exactly three students successfully complete the project, (d) more than three students successfully complete the project, (e) maximum three students successfully complete the project. Test your answers by writing an R code.
17. State the pmf, mean, and variance of Bernoulli, binomial, and Poisson distribution.

18. The chance of having a subnormal intellectual function in a child (0–16 years) is 1%. Generally, in a town, per year 1000 children are born, and on an average three children have trisomy 21. What is the probability that in a given year (a) five newborns have trisomy 21; (b) in a given year, zero newborn have trisomy 21; (c) in a given year, more than three newborns have trisomy 21; (d) eight newborns had trisomy 21? Is this unusually high $(x > (\mu + 2\sigma))$?

19. If X is a continuous random variable, then why $P(a \leq x \leq b)$ and $P(a < x < b)$ are same statements.

20. State and explain the conditions function $f(x)$ is to follow if it is to be called as a distribution function of a continuous random variable.

21. Suppose that you have to wait for, on an average, 15 minutes to find one participant for your experimental psychology practical. What is the probability that (a) you will have to wait for 20 minutes to find a participant; (b) if you have waited for 10 minutes, what is the probability that you will find the participant in another five minutes; (c) what is the probability that you will not find a participant for 20 minutes.

22. State characteristics of normal distribution.

23. If X follows normal, then define Z which is a standard normal distribution.

24. State relationship between Z, chi-square, F-, and t-distributions.

25. State pdf, mean, and variance of normal, Z, chi-square, F-, and t-distributions.

26. Write an R code for plotting F-distributions at different df (1, 10; 4, 20; 10, 5; 40, 40) in different colors.

27. Write an R code for the density and probability of t-, F-, chi-square, and normal distributions.

28. Explain conditional and marginal distribution with the following example: If four coins are tossed, X=the number of heads on the first two, and Y=the number of tails on all. Find the unconditional expectation of X and unconditional expectation of Y. Find unconditional variance of X. Obtain $E(X,Y)$. Find the conditional expectation of X for all values of Y.

2 Statistical Inference

2.1 INTRODUCTION

The most central problem of statistics, in general, and psychometrics, in particular, is to infer about the population value from the sample value. Suppose, I collect data on 200 individuals on a psychological test that is a measure of power distance. The power distance is defined as "the extent to which the less powerful members of institutions and organizations within a country expect and accept that power is distributed unequally" (Hofstede, 2002). The power distance is a psychological concept which is a part of Hofstede's cultural theory.[1] We have developed a scale to measure power distance.[2] The data is obtained on 200 individuals. The mean of the power distance scale (PDS) is 60 and the standard deviation (SD) is 15. The average of the sample is 60 which does not mean that the population from which this sample is drawn has an average of 60. Perhaps, if we draw another sample of the size 200, we are very likely to get a different mean and SD. We have little interest in the mean value of the sample. The sample values fluctuate with every sample. The population value is stable. We have interest in population values. The population value unfortunately is unknown and not measured. The sample value is known and measured. The task of statistics is to draw a meaningful inference about the population value. This chapter is dealing with this problem. This problem has various aspects to it. What is the logic of such a process of guessing about the unknown population value? Which method should be used to draw an inference about the population value from the sample value? If we pick up a specific sample value, then what are the desirable attributes the sample value should have to be able to guess the population value more accurately? What are the rules or assumptions that are helpful in this process? If the inference is not perfect, can we know the error in making this guess? How to reduce this error in guessing? These and similar other questions are answered in this section.

In this section, we shall discuss the logic of estimation. It involves discussion about sampling distribution, parameter and statistics, and hypothesis testing. The hypothesis testing involves the idea of testing null hypothesis utilizing the distribution of the sample statistics. The chapter shall also discuss properties of estimators. They are desirable attributes the estimators are expected to have. The discussion is also offered on various methods of making this informed

---

[1] The cultural dimension theory by Hofstede is one of the influential theories in industrial organizational psychology and cross-cultural research. The theory is based on the work carried out with IBM employees across cultures. Hofstede's work led to a significant increase in cross-cultural research in business, and psychology utilizing quantitative methods. The dimensions are power–distance index (PDI), individualism-collectivism (IDV), masculinity-femininity (MAS), uncertainty avoidance index (UAI), long-term orientation vs. short-term orientation (LTO), and indulgence vs. restraint (IND).

[2] The scale involves measures of all dimensions of the Hofstede's cultural dimension. The original theory assumed that the dimensions are not the aspects of individual differences. We, on the contrary, believe that the dimensions are aspects of individual differences and can be measured.

guess, or statistical inference. These methods include method of moments (MOM), least square, and maximum likelihood (ML); in addition, Bayesian inference is also discussed. The chapter also offers discussion about some fundamental ideas to inference like central limit theorem (CLT), law of large numbers, Chebyshev's inequality, Cramer–Rao inequality or Cramer–Rao bound (CRB) and Cramer–Rao lower bound (CRLB), and Rao–Blackwell theorem.

2.2 BASIC IDEA

The fundamental problem of inference is that we know the value of sample. The sample is drawn from the population. The population's value is not known because the population is very large. It is virtually impossible to study entire population. It requires more time and energy and perhaps it is not cost-effective. Sample's values are obtained on a (randomly drawn) subset of population called sample. The population value is obtained on all the elements of the population. Sample's value or measurable characteristics of sample are called *statistics* (e.g., sample mean and sample SD) and population value or measurable characteristics of population are called *parameter*, generally population parameter (e.g., population mean or population SD). Generally, Greek alphabets are used to describe a parameter and English alphabets are used to describe sample statistics. For example, μ (pronounce 'mu') is populations mean and $\bar{X}$ is sample mean. Generally sample size is described by n and population size is described as N. Population parameter is unknown whereas sample statistics is known. Since the population parameter is unknown, it is *estimated* by using sample statistics, whereas sample statistics is *calculated* from sampled data. Since the unknown population parameter is estimated from sample statistics, the sample statistics is called *estimator*. The process of estimating a population value from sample statistics is called *estimation* or *inference*. Population parameter is stable and we can consider it as a *constant*, whereas samples statistics is changing as another sample is drawn and hence it is a *variable*. The last property is very useful property.

Let us look at the example above. We know that sample mean is 60 and SD is 15 for a sample of size 200.

The sample mean is 60 and populations mean is unknown. If we obtain another sample from the population, the sample mean will be different, may be 64 or 66 or 57 or 55 also. The sample mean is not a *constant*, it is a *variable*. The sample mean is a statistics. $\bar{X}$ is a statistics, that is, 60 is a statistics. The unknown population mean is a parameter. The process of making a guess about the parameter from the sample value of 60 is called estimation or statistical inference. The sample SD is a useful attribute in this. Let us look at another useful attribute called the sampling distribution.

2.2.1 Sampling Distribution

The sampling distribution is one of the key concepts for understanding statistical inference. Suppose, we take one sample from a population that has mean μ. We calculate a statistics on this sample. Let us assume we calculate sample mean. Let us call this first mean on the first sample as $\bar{X}_1$. Then we return this sample to the population (meaning, we are not going to consider the elements or members of this sample as sample henceforth. Now we shall treat them as members of population itself. This implies that the elements chosen in this sample can also be chosen as members of next sample. This is also called sampling with replacement.). Now we obtain another sample from the population and compute the mean for the second sample. This mean is called $\bar{X}_2$. The second sample is returned to the population. Similarly we keep on drawing the samples from the population, compute the mean of that sample, and return the sample to the population. If we keep on doing this for reasonably large number of times, then we shall have large number of sample means with us. Suppose we have taken 500 such samples, then we shall have 500 sample means. These sample means shall follow a distribution. This distribution is a *distribution of sampling means*. Such a distribution is called the *sampling*

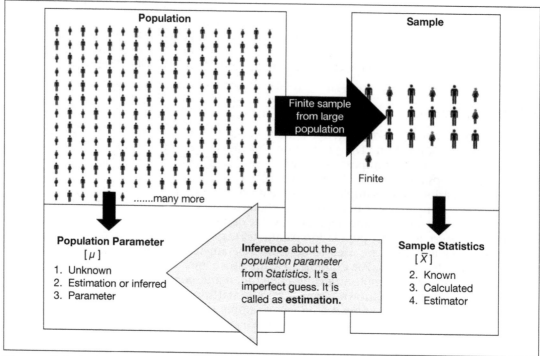

Figure 2.1. *Estimation Process for Mean Estimation*

distribution. The mean of the sampling distribution is the population mean (μ). The SD of the sampling distribution is called *standard error of statistics*, which is a fundamental requirement for testing hypothesis. In the absence of standard error of statistics, no hypothesis can be tested (Figure 2.1). This construction of hypothesis testing is due to seminal efforts of R. A. Fisher, Jerzy Neyman and Egon Pearson. All of them have different views about hypothesis testing; however, what we do today is a combination of both of their ideas. I shall shortly discuss their ideas.

The important idea to be understood is the *sampling distribution of statistics*. In case of the above example of sample mean, suppose, we have 500 sample means available. This distribution of means informs us about the chance of getting a specific value. Every sample mean would be slightly different from each other. This variability of statistics is an important attribute. This variability provides standard error. Let us look R code 2.1 that actually does this process.

R code 2.1. Sampling Distribution of Statistics Mean

```
X<-rnorm(100000, mean=60, sd = 15)    # population of size 100000
mean(X)                               # populations mean
var(X)                                # populations variance
sd(X)                                 # populations sd
nsamp<-500                            # total 500 samples drawn
size <-40                             # each sample of size 40
sam_dist<-numeric(nsamp)              # New variable sam_dist created
for (i in 1:nsamp) sam_dist[i]<- mean(sample(X, size, replace=T))
                                      # repeated samples
mean(sam_dist)                        # mean of sampling distribution
hist(sam_dist, breaks = 32)           # histogram of sampling distribution
qqnorm(sam_dist)                      # normal q-q plot of sam_dist
qqline(sam_dist)
```

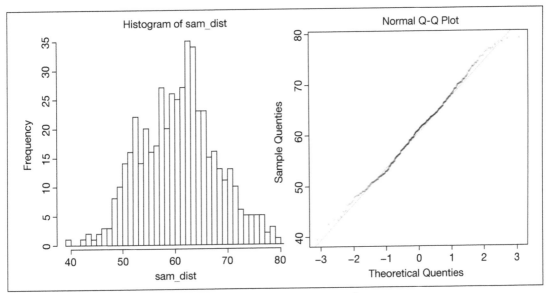

Figure 2.2. *The Result of R Code 2.1. Histogram and the q-q Plot*

The result of the R code is given in Figure 2.2, which shows the histogram and the normal *q-q* plot. For the normal *q-q* plot, if the sample data points are on the diagonal line, then the distribution is normal (details are discussed in Chapter 4).

The distribution of the 500 values of the mean is shown in Figure 2.2. This distribution informs us few interesting things. The distribution has the mean close to 60 which is population mean. The distribution is closely approximating the normal distribution. The normal *q-q* plot informs us that the underlying sampling distribution of the statistics mean is a normal distribution. We also understand that the probability of obtaining a sample mean of 85 or sample mean of 35 is very less likely. Whereas, if the population mean is 60 and SD is 15, then the chance that we shall obtain a sample mean of 55 or 65 is reasonably high. Given this idea, most important thing to note that the sampling distributions are not worked out the way we did. The sampling distributions are worked out mathematically. A statistician developing a specific statistics also works out the sampling distribution for that statistics. For most of the statistics, the sampling distributions take some theoretically known forms of the distribution. Most often, the sampling distributions would take a form of a standard normal distribution. There are statistics that have sampling distribution that take form of *F*-distribution, *t*-distribution, and chi-square distribution. The immediate benefit of using some known statistical distribution is that their probability distribution is well known. This probability distribution can be used as it is. It is almost impossible (very difficult) to work out with hypothesis for which the statistics sampling distribution is not known.

The sampling distribution of the mean is known to us. The sampling distribution of the mean is the normal distribution and the mean of the sampling distribution is population mean and SD of the sampling distribution of the mean is $\sigma_{\bar{x}}$ (standard error of mean).

The $E(\bar{X}) = \mu$, and $\sigma_{\bar{x}} = \sqrt{\dfrac{\sigma_X^2}{n}} = \dfrac{\sigma_X}{\sqrt{n}}$

Figure 2.3 shows the theoretical sampling distribution. This distribution is the standard normal distribution and it can be easily used to test the probability of obtaining the sample value under the null.

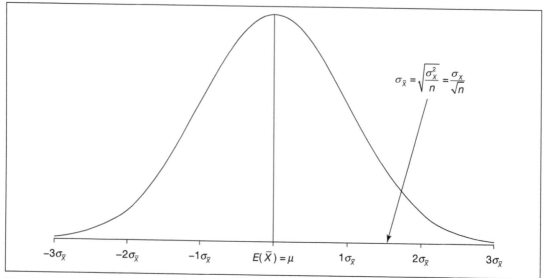

Figure 2.3. *Theoretical Sampling Distribution*

2.3 THE NULL HYPOTHESIS

The null hypothesis is an essential idea for hypothesis testing. The null hypothesis is typically not the researchers' hypothesis. The idea of null hypothesis is by R. A. Fisher. The null hypothesis is a statistical hypothesis (H_0: say H naught or H zero or H null) that is tested for possible rejection under the assumption that it is true. The null usually implies that the observations are result of chance. The hypothesis contrary to null hypothesis is called alternative hypothesis (H_A). The alternative hypothesis is a function real effect.

In case of the power distance scale example, one may have a null hypothesis that the population mean is zero.

$$H_0 : \mu = 0$$
$$H_A : \mu \neq 0$$

The null hypothesis has no sense. Suppose, we have conducted an experiment in which we are recoding the number of errors in experimental task, the null hypothesis is zero time spent in incorrect solutions. The alternative will state that greater than zero time is spent in incorrect solution.

2.3.1 Fisher and Neyman–Pearson on Null Hypothesis

There are two different views about null hypothesis testing. One of them is Fisher's viewpoint about the null hypothesis significance testing. The alternative view is proposed by Jerzy Neyman[3]

---

[3] Jerzy Neyman (1894–1981) was born at Bendery, Bessarabia which was a part of Russian Empire then and now Moldova. The family maintained Polish identity in spite of politically volatile situation. The Russian name of Jerzy was Yuri Czeslawovich. He studied at Kharkov University and developed interests in practical physics and mathematics. He got married with a Russian girl Olga, and in 10 days of marriage he was imprisoned due to Poland–Russia war. In spite of the difficulties, he passed the examination and started teaching at Kharkov. Life was not stable till he received Rockefeller fellowship to work with Karl Pearson. He soon became friends with Egon, Pearson's son. Between 1928 and 1933, they wrote many important papers on hypothesis testing which include *On the problem of the most efficient tests of statistical hypotheses* (1933) and *The testing of statistical hypotheses in relation to probabilities a priori* (1933). In spite of working in the same building and using the theory of R. A. Fisher, he never had good relations with Fisher. In 1938, he left for Berkeley. He worked there for rest of his life.

and Egon Pearson.[4] The basic idea is as follows. The Fisher's idea of null hypothesis is clearly an idea that requires falsification. Fisher would never accept the null hypothesis as it is an indicative of nothingness or random outcomes, the acceptance of which makes no sense in Fisherian logic. The only correct statement for Fisher in null hypothesis is rejected. Fisher's position states that failure to reject null hypothesis means inconclusive results. In Fisherian thinking, there are only two possibilities—reject the null or defer the judgment. The alternative thinking is proposed by Neyman and Pearson. They always contrasted null hypothesis with an alternate hypothesis. Nyman and Pearson would test the null hypothesis and either accept or reject it. The "acceptance of null hypothesis" does not mean that it's proved to be true but for the moment it is accepted as if it is correct.[5] For example, university dean has to make a decision about continuing a community program about "health education." She tests a null hypothesis that participants of the community program have no improvement after attending the program. The null hypothesis is not rejected by the data. If the dean follows Fisher, then she would continue the program looking for more evidence and collect more data; and if she follows Neyman–Pearson she would discontinue the program. This is possibly a simplistic explanation (with great loss of nuances) of the difference. Gigerenzer et al. (1989) and Lehman (1993) have provided a good discussion on the difference between the two approaches. The modern researchers, textbook writers, and statisticians, in general, use the combination of both approaches.

2.3.2 The Null Hypothesis Testing and Sampling Distribution

The null hypothesis is a statement about the population parameter. For example, if a researcher collects the data on intelligence, and she holds a null hypothesis that this sample comes from a population that has a mean 110 with SD=15, then the null in this case is

$$H_0 : \mu = 110$$
$$H_A : \mu \neq 110$$

Once the null and the alternative hypothesis are specified, one needs to work out the sampling distribution of the statistics. The sampling distribution idea has been discussed earlier. The sampling distribution is mathematically obtained for the sample statistics. Here, the sample statistics is mean. The sampling distribution of mean is the normal distribution. The mean of the sampling distribution is μ and the variance is $\frac{\sigma_X^2}{n}$. The SD of sampling distribution is called standard error of statistics. The standard error of statistics mean then can be called standard error of the mean. The standard error of the mean is $\sqrt{\frac{\sigma_X^2}{n}}$ or $\frac{\sigma_X}{\sqrt{n}}$, where σ_x is population value. The population value is never known. Hence the σ_x is estimated by S_X where S_X is SD of the sample. We can now have sample SD and sample size to estimate the SD of the sampling distribution.

---

[4] Egon Pearson (1895–1980) is one of the leading British mathematician and statistician and is a son of Karl Pearson. He succeeded his father as an editor of journal *Biometrika*. He was a recipient of Gay medal and was also a fellow of royal society. He also suffered due to the rivalry between Karl Pearson and R. A. Fisher. Egon started working in University College of London where Fisher and Pearson were already working. In 1933, Pearson retired form Galton Chair. Then the university authorities split the department into two separate departments, Fisher became the Galton Chair successor and Head of department of Eugenics and Egon became reader and Head of Department of Applied Statistics. During the second world war, Egon assisted British Military in statistical analysis of the fragmentation of shells hitting aircraft.

[5] I must make a mention of Popperian idea of epistemology that is philosophically more close to these positions. Popper believed that the scientific knowledge cannot be obtained by proving a hypothesis (or a conjuncture). He argued that a conjuncture or hypothesis is a function of theory and an attempt is made to reject it. If it is not rejected, then we accept it to be true. Some kind of translation of this idea can be viewed in statistical hypothesis testing.

$$\frac{S_X^2}{\sqrt{n}} \to \frac{\sigma_X}{\sqrt{n}}$$

Once the standard error of the statistics is worked out, then it is easy to make judgment about the probability associated with the sample value. Suppose, she obtained a mean of 115 with SD = 15 on a sample of the size 50. She wanted to test the hypothesis that the sample mean of 115 has come from the population that has a mean of 110. The population's mean is unknown for the population represented by the sample. Hence, we test a null hypothesis by specifying that the obtained sample has come from a population that has mean of 110. We know that if we keep on taking random samples from the population that has a mean of 110, there is some chance that we can obtain a mean of 115 and greater than that (Or there is some chance that we obtain mean that differ from population mean by 5 points or more). The null hypothesis significance testing would find the probability of obtaining a value of mean 115 or more when the population mean is 110. This probability can be worked out if we know the standard error of the statistics. The standard error here is

$$\sigma_{\bar{x}} = \sqrt{\frac{S_X^2}{n}} = \frac{S_X}{\sqrt{n}}$$

$$\sigma_{\bar{x}} = \sqrt{\frac{15^2}{50}} = \frac{15}{\sqrt{50}}$$

Since we know that the sampling distribution of the mean is normal around the null, we can convert it into the standard normal distribution by routine transformation. I am assuming the population SD equal to sample SD which may not be true in many cases. These differences are discussed in Chapter 7.

$$Z = \frac{X - \mu}{\sigma} = \frac{\bar{X} - \mu}{\frac{\sigma_X}{\sqrt{n}}} = \frac{115 - 110}{2.12} = \frac{5}{2.12} = 2.357$$

The probability of obtaining the $Z = 2.137$ can be found out from normal tables (Appendix C1) as well as by using R code. This probability is 0.0092 which is considered as a small probability.
    Figure 2.4 shows the basic logic of null hypothesis testing.

2.3.3 How to Use P to Make a Decision?

The probability of 0.0092 has a simple meaning associated with it. It is as follows: if the population mean is 110, then the chance of obtaining 115 is 0.0092 or approximately 0.01.
    I have two options here. First, I have to accept that the sample that I have drawn has come from a population that has a mean of 110. But due to sampling variation the sample I drew resulted in a very unlikely mean of 115. Second, I have to accept that the sample I have drawn has not come from a population that has a mean of 110. If the population's mean is 110, then chance of obtaining the mean of 115 is really very low. So it is unlikely that the present mean has come from a population that has a mean of 110.
    The first option is called "accepting null hypothesis" and second option is called "rejection of null hypothesis."
    Do I know the value of the population mean? NO ... I do not have any idea about what the population mean is. So if I choose any of the two options, I am likely to make a mistake. The other problem is that of choosing a cut-off point for accepting or rejecting the null hypothesis. The probability of obtaining sample mean was 0.01 in this example. What value of probability should be considered as a value that can serve as a cut-off point? General recommendation is probability of 0.05 be taken as a cut-off p-value. Let us understand these two related points in further detail.

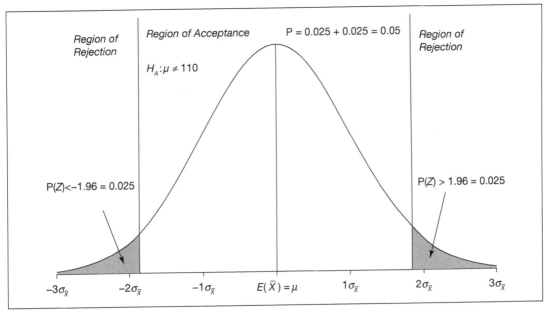

Figure 2.4. *Null Hypothesis and Region of Rejection and Acceptance*

Table 2.1. *Decision Regarding Null Hypothesis and Its Consequences*

	Reality about H_0 in the population	
	H_0 is True	H_0 is False
Decision about null using sample	Do not Reject H_0 Correct Decision $(1-\alpha)$	Type II Error $p=\beta$
	Reject H_0 Type I Error $p=\alpha$	Correct Decision $(1-\beta)$

2.3.4 Types of Errors

The population values are not known. We specify a null hypothesis about the population value. The null is either retained or rejected. In both the cases, there is no guarantee that the decision is in line with the reality of the null hypothesis. Any decision regarding null hypothesis is likely to be erroneous. The acceptance of null hypothesis may be an incorrect acceptance and similarly rejection of the null hypothesis may be an incorrect rejection. The popular tabular presentation is provided in Table 2.1.

Table 2.1 informs us that in reality the decisions are correct when the false null hypothesis is rejected and the true null hypothesis is accepted. The problem occurs when we reject H_0 when we should have accepted it. Incorrect rejection of null is called **Type I error**. The probability of Type I Error is called alpha (α). The probability of correct acceptance of null hypothesis is $1-\alpha$. In general, the α is called level of significance. Lower values of alpha are desirable. The other error occurs when we accept the null hypothesis when we should have rejected it. The incorrect acceptance of null hypothesis is called **Type II Error**. The probability of Type II Error is called β. The ability of the statistics to reject the null hypothesis when it is false is called $1-\beta$ or power of statistics. The statistics should be able to reject the null hypothesis when it is false. The ability of statistics to do so is power. The two errors are intricately associated with each other. As we try to reduce the Type I Error, we increase the chance of Type II Error and vice versa. For example, if we lower the value of α and set it to 0.001, then the chance of Type I Error is greatly reduced. However, we have increased the chance of Type II Error. If the null hypothesis is false, then it would not be rejected unless the probability associated with the statistics is smaller than 0.001. In case of intelligence example, we need a Z value of 3.09 for the null hypothesis to be rejected. The null hypothesis shall not be rejected with the obtained value of 2.357. This increases the chance of accepting a null hypothesis when it is false, that is, Type II Error. One of the problems we face is when the null is rejected, the distribution of H_A is never known to use. What is known is distribution under null.

2.3.5 Level of Significance

The next step is to determine the level of significance or rejection level. This value is called alpha (α) and $\alpha = 0.05$ is most commonly used level of significance. However, it is absolutely not necessary to stick to the value of 0.05. The failure to reject null hypothesis at .05 level implies that null hypothesis is accepted and then there is 5% chance of obtaining finding contrary to the null hypothesis. The exact value of the sampling distribution of the statistics at 5% level is called **critical value**. Most textbooks provide tables for the critical values at the end and hence it is also called tabled value. As we have discussed in Chapter 1, these values are obtained by the cumulative distribution function of the sampling distribution. The critical value for the 5% for Z distribution is 1.96 and at 1% it is 2.58 (two-tailed). This implies that, if the Z statistics values under the null hypothesis are smaller than 1.96, then the null hypothesis is not rejected. If the value of Z statistics is equal to or larger than 1.96, then the null is rejected. What is two-tailed? We shall discuss it. The one-tailed 5% value is 1.64 and one-tailed 1% value is 2.33.

There is no fixed notion of choosing 0.05 at alpha. There are instances when you can also consider the chance up to about 0.10. The choice of significance level of 0.05 is also arbitrary. In fact, Fisher stated, ". . . no scientific worker has a fixed level of significance at which from year to year, and in all circumstances, he rejects hypotheses; he rather gives his mind to each particular case in the light of his evidence and his ideas" (Fisher, 1953).

2.3.6 Directional and Non-directional Hypothesis

We have stated that null is specific value. In the intelligence example, the null was H_0: $\mu = 100$. The alternative hypothesis could be $H_A : \mu \neq 110$. We have already specified this alternative. Once the null is rejected, the alternative states that true population values of the mean could be either above the null value or below the null value. It is not the null value. Suppose, if the researcher knew that the sample consists of brighter participants, then she could have stated an alternative as H_A: $\mu > 110$. In this case, the statistics computed (Z statistics) would be considered significant if it took only positive values (+1.64 and above). The negative Z value leads to acceptance of null hypothesis. The alternative that states that H_A: $\mu > 110$ is also called as directional alternative. The null would be rejected only if the value of statistics is smaller than +1.64 (Figure 2.5).

The chance of rejecting the null hypothesis when the alternative is directional is higher than when the alternative is non-directional. Hence, the power of the statistics is higher when the alternative is directional.

STEPS IN STATISTICAL HYPOTHESIS TESTING

Step 1: Researchers begin with the hypothesis that is driven by psychological theory. Such a hypothesis is called theoretical hypothesis. This hypothesis is expected to predict functional form of relationship between two or more variables. Theoretical hypothesis cannot be null hypothesis. It is against the epistemology of science which always begins with a hypothesis driven from theory. For example, extraversion and risk-taking are correlated; people use availability heuristic in making judgment are theoretical hypothesis. If you don't have theory, then find one. Strictly speaking, no science is possible in the absence of theory.

Step 2: Specify a statistical (probabilistic) form of the psychological theory. The statistical forms are more important than mathematical forms because the relationships between variables are not *exact* or *deterministic*. Next issue is to decide about the population parameter that is responsible for the functional form specified by theory. $y=f(x)$ is the most general functional form. For example, population correlation coefficient between risk-taking and extraversion is some non-zero value or population difference between heuristic manipulated condition and heuristic non-manipulated condition will be non-zero. This leads to what is famously called null and alternative hypothesis. The null hypothesis is a statement that specified that the statistical form of the theory is incorrect, that is, the parameter specified is (most often) not taking any value or takes a value zero. For example, the null states that population correlation between extraversion and risk-taking is zero. The alternative is written in such a way that it covers all remaining conditions than null. The alternative could be non-directional. For example, population correlation is not zero. The directional alternative would (generally) specify what kind of value parameter would take. For example, population correlation between extraversion and risk-taking is greater than zero.

Step 3: Collect the data on sample. Random sampling is technical condition. Most often it is not possible to fulfill the technicality.

Step 4: Specify the alpha level (Type I Error). Most commonly it is set to be 0.05. Compute the statistics. For example, we set alpha=0.05 and compute sample correlation coefficient. For heuristic example, we set the alpha to be 0.05 and compute *t*-statistics.

Step 5: Work out the sampling distribution of the statistics that is the estimator of the parameter. In almost all cases, the sampling distribution of test-statistics follows some theoretically known form. For example, *t*-distribution would be sampling distribution of correlation coefficient (actually it is Z which follows t), and *t*-distribution is also a sampling distribution of differences between means.

Step 6: Test the null hypothesis at level alpha and make decision. Find the probability of obtaining the test-statistics value of the size that we have obtained (p[test statistics > obtained value]). In case, this probability is smaller than alpha, then reject the null and accept the alternative. In case, this probability is larger than the alpha, then retain the null. The acceptance of the null hypothesis implies that the theory specified function form is very likely to be incorrect (given all other explanations are closed).

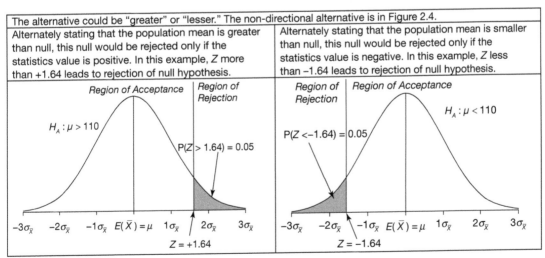

Figure 2.5. *Directional Alternative*

2.4 POINT ESTIMATION AND INTERVAL ESTIMATION

Let us call the **parameter** as theta (θ) and the **estimator** or **statistics** as theta hat ($\hat{\theta}$). Let X be a random variable that follows $f(X, \theta)$, where θ is parameter of the distribution. Given this, we can work out the point estimator and interval estimators.

2.4.1 Point Estimation

Let us assume that we are aware of the functional form of the probability density function (pdf), that is, theoretical pdf. The functional forms are Z distribution, t-distribution, chi-square distribution and so on. However, we do not have knowledge about the θ. We know that θ cannot be known, only the sample statistics can be known. Suppose we have a random sample of the size n, and obtain the function of the sample values as follows:

$$\hat{\theta} = f(X_1, X_2, \dots, X_n)$$

The $\hat{\theta}$ is estimator of the θ. Please recall that the $\hat{\theta}$ changes its value as the sample changes. The $\hat{\theta}$ is a random variable. $\hat{\theta}$ is formula or a rule that is useful in estimating the θ. Suppose we define $f(X) = \frac{1}{n}\Sigma(X_1, X_2, \dots, X_n)$, then the $\hat{\theta} = \frac{1}{n}\Sigma(X_1 + X_2 + \dots + X_n) = \bar{X}$, that is, sample mean is a theta hat, or estimator, or statistics. In this case, the theta, or the parameter is μ or the population mean. In case of power distance scale, 60 is a sample mean ($\hat{\theta}$), that is, estimating a population mean (θ). This estimator is called point estimator. It is called point estimator because it provides a *single point estimate* of the population value. The single value works as a "best guess" or the "best estimate" of the population value. The mean, variance, and regression coefficient are point estimates of the respective parameters. It is generally recommended that point estimator be contrasted with interval estimator.

2.4.2 Interval Estimation

The point estimate obtains a single estimate of the parameter. Instead of obtaining a single estimate of θ, if we obtain two estimates of θ, the results are $\hat{\theta}_1$ and $\hat{\theta}_2$. The $\hat{\theta}_1 = f(X_1, X_2, \dots, X_n)$ and the $\hat{\theta}_2 = f(X_1, X_2, \dots, X_n)$.

The interval estimation is a statement with some confidence (or probability) that the true value of the θ falls between interval of $\hat{\theta}_1$ and $\hat{\theta}_2$. The interval estimation is providing a range of values within which the true value of the parameter may lie. Let us work it out for the power distance example. We need to know the functional form of $f(X, \theta)$. We have learned in the earlier section that as X is normally distributed, the sampling distribution of the $\bar{X}$ is also normally distributed with the mean of $\bar{X}$'s being μ and the SD being $\frac{\sigma_X}{\sqrt{n}}$. We can state this as $\bar{X} \sim N(\mu, \sigma_X^2/n)$. The interval can be constructed as

$$\bar{X} \pm Z_\alpha \left(\frac{\sigma_X}{\sqrt{n}} \right)$$

The $\bar{X}$ is samples mean, and Z_α is value of standard normal deviate at α; generally $\alpha = 0.05$ is taken and the $Z_\alpha = Z_{0.05} = 1.96$. This implies that confidence interval is being created at $1 - 0.05 = 0.95\%$ confidence. σ_X is not known and is replaced with sample estimate. and S_X is used instead and the n is sample size. We can use alpha as 0.01 at 1% confidence interval. The general statement of the confidence interval is

$$P\{(\hat{\theta}_1) \le \theta \le (\hat{\theta}_2)\} = 1 - \alpha$$

where $1-\alpha$ is confidence of this interval. There are two objectives that the confidence interval tries to meet—first, it attempts to keep $1-\alpha$ close to 1 by reducing α; second, it also attempts to keep the interval narrower. Let us work it out with power distance scale example. The $\bar{X}=60$, the $S_x=15$, and $n=200$. The standard error of the mean $\sqrt{\sigma_x^2/n}$ is estimated by $= S_x/\sqrt{n} = 15/\sqrt{200} = 1.06$.

$$P\left\{\bar{X} - Z_\alpha\left(\frac{S_x}{\sqrt{n}}\right) \le \theta \le \bar{X} + Z_\alpha\left(\frac{S_x}{\sqrt{n}}\right)\right\} = 1 - 0.05 = 0.95$$
$$P\{[60 - 1.96(1.06)] \le \theta \le [60 + 1.96(1.06)]\} = 0.95$$
$$P\{(60 - 2.078) \le \theta \le (60 + 2.078)\} = 0.95$$
$$P\{57.92 \le \theta \le 62.08\} = 0.95$$

The true value of the parameter (population mean) is between 57.92 and 62.08 and is possible for 95% of the random samples drawn from the population. Suppose, if we increase the confidence to 99% then the $Z_\alpha=2.58$ and confidence interval will be 57.264 and 62.736. The width of the interval has increased as the confidence is increased. So the only remedy here is to increase the sample size so that the confidence can increase but the width will remain the same or decrease.

2.5 PROPERTIES OF ESTIMATORS

The estimator is a function of sample. The estimator should have certain properties that make an estimator a preferred choice over other estimators. The properties of estimators are broadly categorized into two categories: small sample properties and large sample properties.

2.5.1 Small-sample Properties

There are some useful small-sample properties of estimators. They are unbiasedness, minimum variance, efficiency, linearity, BLUE, and minimum mean-square-error estimator.

2.5.1.1 Unbiased Estimator

The estimator $\hat{\theta}$ is considered as unbiased estimator of the θ, when the expectation of theta hat is theta.

$$E(\hat{\theta}) = \theta$$

It can also be stated that $E(\hat{\theta}) - \theta = 0$. The bias of $\hat{\theta}$ is specified as

$$E(\hat{\theta}) - \theta = Bias(\hat{\theta})$$

Figure 2.6 explains the unbiasedness.

The $\hat{\theta}_1$ is an unbiased estimator because $E(\hat{\theta}_1) = \theta$. However, $E(\hat{\theta}_2) \ne \theta$ and $E(\hat{\theta}_2)$ is a value above the true value of the theta. The bias can be known and the estimator can be adjusted for the bias in estimation.

One of the well-known unbiased estimators is sample mean. For random samples drawn from the population, the sample values would be randomly above and below the true value of the population mean. This leads to expectation of the sample statistics to be equal to parameter. The well-known biased estimator is sample variance. The sample variance is obtained by

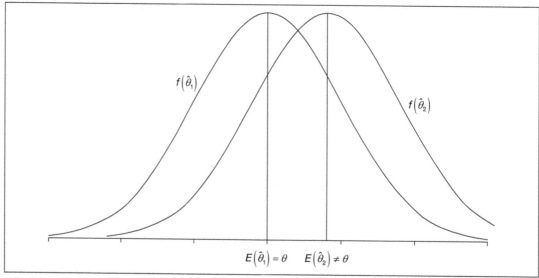

Figure 2.6. *Unbiased and Biased Estimators*

$S_X^2 = \dfrac{\sum\limits_{i=1}^{n}(X - \bar{X})^2}{n}$ and the population variance is $\sigma_X^2 = \dfrac{\sum\limits_{i=1}^{N}(X - \mu)^2}{N}$. The expectation of the sample variance is always an underestimation of population variance as

$$S_{\text{Unbiased}}^2 = \frac{n}{n-1} S_{\text{biased}}^2$$

the quantity $\dfrac{n}{n-1}$ is a correction factor introduced to correct for bias. So generally, the formula of the variance uses $n-1$ as a denominator than n.

$$S_{\text{Unbiased}}^2 = \frac{n}{n-1} \frac{\sum\limits_{i=1}^{n}(X - \bar{X})^2}{n} = \frac{\sum\limits_{i=1}^{n}(X - \bar{X})^2}{n-1}$$

2.5.1.2 Minimum Variance

The minimum variance is another property of the estimator. $\hat{\theta}_1$ is called minimum variance estimator of θ when the variance of $\hat{\theta}_1$ is smaller than the variance of $\hat{\theta}_2$. $\hat{\theta}_2$ is any other estimator of the θ. Figure 2.7 shows the minimum variance estimator. $\hat{\theta}_2$ is a minimum variance estimator among all the estimators of θ.

The point to be noted is that the minimum variance estimator is a biased estimator. It is not necessary that the minimum variance estimator would also be unbiased estimator. $\hat{\theta}_1$ and $\hat{\theta}_3$, both have variance larger than the variance of $\hat{\theta}_2$.

2.5.1.3 Efficient Estimator

The efficient estimator is also called best unbiased estimator. The estimator among the unbiased estimators that has minimum variance is called efficient estimator. The unbiased estimator $\hat{\theta}_1$ is called efficient estimator of θ when it has smaller variance than $\hat{\theta}_2$ which is any other unbiased estimator of θ.

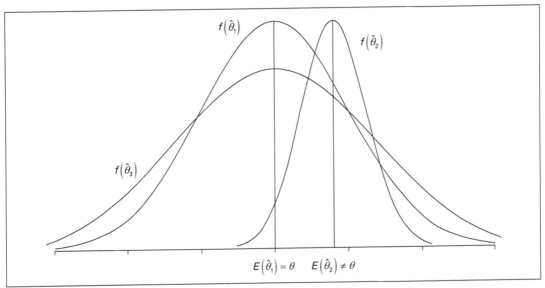

Figure 2.7. *Minimum Variance Estimator*

In Figure 2.7, $\hat{\theta}_1$ is an efficient estimator.

2.5.1.4 Linearity and BLUE

When the estimator is a linear function of sample values, then the estimator is called linear estimator. The sample mean is sum of all sample data point multiplied by a fraction is a linear function. The BLUE estimators are best linear unbiased estimators. If $\hat{\theta}$ is linear and unbiased and has the minimum variance in the category of all linear unbiased estimators, then $\hat{\theta}$ is called BLUE estimator of θ.

2.5.1.5 MSE

The mean square error (MSE) of an estimator $\hat{\theta}$ of a parameter θ is an average squared difference between the estimator and the parameter $\mathrm{MSE}(\hat{\theta}) \equiv E[(\hat{\theta} - \theta)^2]$. The efficiency of the estimator is inversely proportional to the MSE.

$$\mathrm{MSE}(\hat{\theta}) \equiv E[(\hat{\theta} - \theta)^2]$$
$$\mathrm{MSE}(\hat{\theta}) \equiv E\{[\hat{\theta} - E(\hat{\theta}) + E(\hat{\theta}) - \theta]^2\}$$
$$E\{[\hat{\theta} - E(\hat{\theta})]^2\} + [E(\hat{\theta}) - \theta]^2 + 2E[(\hat{\theta}) - E(\hat{\theta})][E(\hat{\theta}) - \theta]$$
$$E\{[\hat{\theta} - E(\hat{\theta})]^2\} + [E(\hat{\theta}) - \theta]^2 + 0$$
$$\mathrm{MSE}(\hat{\theta}) = \mathrm{Var}(\hat{\theta}) + \mathrm{bias}(\hat{\theta})^2$$

The MSE of estimator is variance of estimator plus the bias of the estimator. As the estimator becomes more efficient, its bias and sampling variance decreases.

2.5.2 Large Sample Properties

There are instances when the estimator of the parameter values does not fulfill the properties. However, as the sample size becomes large, they tend to acquire the property more and more.

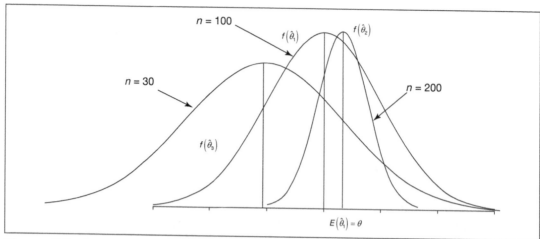

Figure 2.8. *Asymptotically Unbiased Estimators*

As the estimator acquires the property with increasing sample size, it is called asymptotic properties or large sample properties.

2.5.2.1 Asymptotic Unbiasedness

The estimator $\hat{\theta}$ is considered as an asymptotically unbiased estimator of θ when

$$\lim_{x \to \infty} E(\hat{\theta}_n) = \theta$$

The statement is read as "x limits to infinity, expectation of the theta hat is theta." That is, as the sample size increases, the estimator becomes unbiased. When the sample is small, the estimator has a bias and as the sample becomes large, the estimator is less biased. Figure 2.8 explains the asymptotic unbiasedness.

The sample variance with correction of the factor $\dfrac{n}{n-1}$ becomes an asymptotically unbiased estimator. As the sample size increases, the correction factor approaches the value of 1 and the estimator becomes more and more unbiased. The sample variance is an asymptotically unbiased estimator of population variance.

2.5.2.2 Consistency

When $\hat{\theta}$ approaches the true value of θ as the sample increases, it is called consistency. Let δ be a arbitrarily decided small positive quantity, then

$$\lim_{x \to \infty} P(|\hat{\theta} - \theta| < \delta) = 1$$

where $\delta > 0$, and P is probability. This probability approaches 1 as the sample size approaches infinity. The sufficient condition for consistency is that an estimator is asymptotically unbiased and the sampling variance of the estimator approaches zero as n approaches infinity.

2.5.2.3 Asymptotic Efficiency

The estimator $\hat{\theta}$ is called efficient estimator with asymptotic variance and has smaller variance among the consistent estimators than $\hat{\theta}$ and is called asymptotically efficient estimator.

2.5.2.4 Asymptotic Normality

As the sampling distribution of $\hat{\theta}$ approaches the normal distribution with increasing sample size, then $\hat{\theta}$ is called asymptotically normally distributed estimator.

2.5.2.5 Sufficiency

One of the abstract properties of estimator is sufficiency. The statistics $\hat{\theta}$ is called sufficient estimator when $\hat{\theta}$, which is a function of sample observations, uses all the information of the sample about θ. If $(X_1, X_2, \ldots, X_n)$ are sample observations with a probability distribution around parameter θ, and $\hat{\theta} = f(X_1, X_2, \ldots, X_n)$ is function of sample values, then $\hat{\theta}$ is called sufficient estimator for θ if the probability distribution of the observed data is conditional on the value of $\hat{\theta}$.

2.6 METHODS OF ESTIMATION

The estimation of unknown population parameter is the most important issue in statistics. The popular methods of estimation are method of moments (MOM), methods of least squares, and method of maximum likelihood (ML). The Bayesian estimators are gaining popularity. Let us understand them in detail.

2.6.1 Method of Moments

The MOM is perhaps the earliest method of parameter estimation. The MOM is no longer a method in use for parameter estimation. If $X_1, X_2, \ldots, X_n$ are n observations then the MOM estimator for the unknown parameter is based on matching sample moments with the corresponding distribution moments. For example, estimator of the mu is

$$M = \frac{1}{n}\sum_{i=1}^{n} X_i$$

where M is MOM estimator of the population mean. You would recognize that the M is sample average. Let

$$\mu_j(\theta) = E_\theta(X^j)$$

where $\mu_j(\theta)$ is a jth moment of X about 0. Suppose $j=1$, then $\mu_1(\theta) = E_\theta(X^1) = E_\theta(X)$ that is, sample mean is the first moment, which is also the MOM estimator of population mean.

2.6.2 Method of Least Squares

The method of least squares is also called least squares estimation. The method of least squares estimates parameters such that the squared discrepancies between observed data and their expected values are minimized. This method is described in the context of regression analysis in Chapter 6.

If Y is actual values of a variable and Y' is model estimated values of Y from $f(X)$, then the parameters of $f(X)$ estimated such that the squared difference between Y and Y' are minimum. If

$$Y = f(X) + \text{random error}$$

and if we define $f = f_\beta$, then β is estimated by minimizing the quantity

$$\sum_{i=1}^{n}[y_i - f_\beta(X_i)]^2$$

The method of least squares estimator of population mean is $\bar{X} = \dfrac{1}{n}\sum_{i=1}^{n}X_i$, which is also simple average. Please note that if we have a set of X values of observation, then $\sum_{i=1}^{n}(X - \bar{X})^2$ is the smallest value for $\bar{X}$ as an estimator of μ.

2.6.3 Method of Maximum Likelihood

The method of ML is one of the most elegant methods of estimation. It has many desirable properties. Once the ML estimator is derived, the method of ML standard errors, statistical tests and so on can be obtained. I am using an example from Chapter 1 about catching a local train in Mumbai during peak hours. I shall also show how to work out ML in the example. Suppose you are a new visitor to Mumbai and manage to catch the train on 3 occasions out of 10. The sample is (0, 0, 1, 0, 0, 1, 0, 1, 0, 0). The question of the researcher is that what should be a good estimate of the population value of p (probability of success). Generally we express this as

$$P(data \mid parameter) = P(0, 0, 1, 0, 0, 1, 0, 1, 0, 0 \mid p)$$
$$P(data \mid parameter) = (1-p)(1-p)(p)(1-p)(1-p)(p)(1-p)(p)(1-p)(1-p)$$
$$P(data \mid parameter) = P^3(1-P)^{10-3}$$

The P is the parameter in Bernoulli distribution. The value of parameter is fixed, but unknown. The method of estimation is attempting to go closer to this unknown fixed value. The ML is different in its approach. Let the parameter value be between 0 and 1 and consider the probability of observed variable as a function of p. This function is called likelihood function. It is expressed as

$$L(parameter \mid data) = L(p \mid 0, 0, 1, 0, 0, 1, 0, 1, 0, 0)$$

The probability function and the likelihood function are the same. The difference is that the probability function is a function of the data with the value of the parameter fixed whereas the likelihood function is a function of the parameter with the values of data fixed. It is the likelihood of the parameter given data. The role of the parameter and data are reversed in the likelihood function. The probability is probability of data given in the parameter. R. A. Fisher developed the principle of maximum likelihood estimation (MLE). The likelihood function is the principle idea behind the MLE. The ML estimator of the parameter is that value of parameter that maximizes this function.

Let us work out the likelihood function for the above data. The question is to find the likelihood of observing the above data given the value of p (probability of success for binomial). The probability of success will take values form 0 to 1. For each of the value of p, there is some likelihood of observing the present sample data. The value of p, at which the likelihood of observing this data is highest, is called ML. The R code by Charles Geyer (2003) and John White (2010) are useful.

R Code 2.2. Likelihood computation in R (Geyer's code)

```
likelihood.Bernoulli = function(theta, x) {
# theta success probability parameter
# x vector of data
n = length(x)
ans = theta^sum(x) * (1-theta)^(n-sum(x))
return(ans)
```

Table 2.2 *Parameter Values (p values of Binomial Distribution) and Their Likelihood Function*

Parameter of binomial (*p* or probability of success)	*L*(p|data)
0	0
0.1	0.0004782969
0.2	0.001677722
0.3	0.0022236
0.4	0.0017916
0.5	0.0009765625
0.6	0.0003538944
0.7	0.0000750141
0.8	0.0000065536
0.9	0.0000000729
1.0	0

```
}
x<-c(0, 0, 1, 0, 0, 1, 0, 1, 0, 0)
likelihood.Bernoulli(0.4, x)
[1] 0.00179159
```

Table 2.2 shows the various parameter values (*p*-values of binomial distribution) and their likelihood function.

The other useful code is given in R Code 2.3.

R Code 2.3. Likelihood Function for Binomial Data with Plot (by John White)

```
likelihood <- function(sequence, p.parameter)
{
likelihood <- 1
  for (i in 1:length(sequence))
  {if (sequence[i] == 1)
    {likelihood <- likelihood * p.parameter}
    else
    {likelihood <- likelihood * (1 - p.parameter)}}
  return(likelihood)
}
sequence <- c(0, 0, 1, 0, 0, 1, 0, 1, 0, 0)
likelihood(x, .6)
# Plotting likelihood function
possible.p <- seq(0, 1, by = 0.001)
jpeg('Likelihood_Concavity.jpg')
library('ggplot2')
qplot(possible.p,
  sapply(possible.p, function (p) {likelihood(sequence, p)}),
  geom = 'line',
  main = 'Likelihood as a Function of P',
  xlab = 'P',
  ylab = 'Likelihood')
dev.off()
```

Table 2.2 and the R Code 2.2 and R Code 2.3 provide a simple idea about the likelihood function. The full likelihood function is presented in graph in Figure 2.9.

One needs to note that the likelihood function is not the probability density function. The probability density integrates to 1. The likelihood does not integrate to 1. The MLE has some

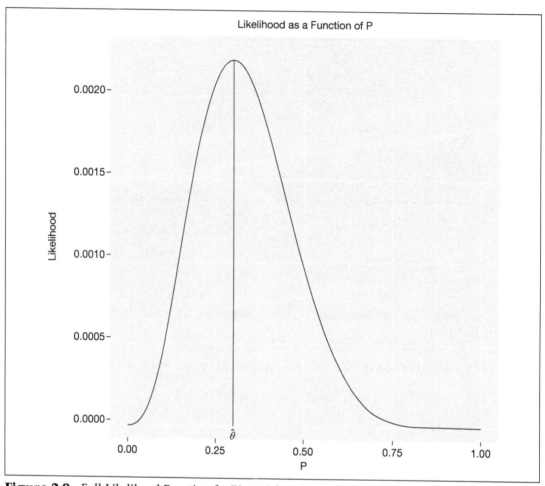

Figure 2.9. *Full Likelihood Function for Binomial Problem*

important properties. The MLEs are consistent. Though there is a bias in small samples, they are asymptotically unbiased. The MLEs are asymptotically efficient. The MLEs are asymptotically normal. If there is sufficient statistics for a parameter, then the MLEs are functions of sufficient statistics for the parameter. The log–likelihood ratio follows the chi-square distribution. It is easy to work out with hypothesis with likelihood ratios.

2.6.3.1 The Wald, Likelihood Ratio and Lagrangian Multiplier Test

The three test statistics—Wald, likelihood ratio (LR), and Lagrangian multiplier test—are very useful while using the ML.

Likelihood Ratio Test

The LR test is formalized as

$$LR = 2\log\frac{L(\hat{\theta})}{L(\theta_0)} = 2\log\frac{\text{Likelihood for theoretical model}}{\text{Likelihood for null model}}$$

$$LR = 2[\log(L(\hat{\theta})) - \log(L(\theta_0))]$$

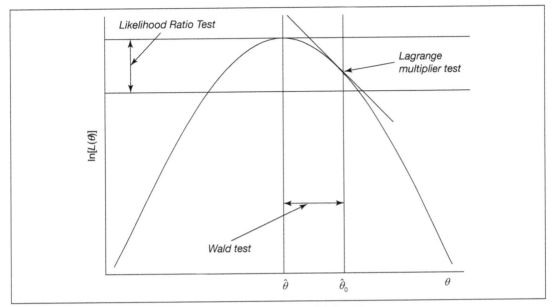

Figure 2.10. *Wald, Likelihood Ratio and Lagrange Multiplier Tests*

The LR follows chi-square distribution under null.

Wald Test

The Wald test approximates LR test. The advantage of the Wald test is that it requires only model parameter estimated. The Wald test evaluates a null hypothesis that parameter is a specific value. The test has following test statistics:

$$W = \frac{(\hat{\theta} - \theta_0)^2}{\text{var}(\hat{\theta})}$$

The W follows the chi-square distribution. The $\hat{\theta} - \theta_0$ is model based ML estimate of θ and θ_0 is value of null model. The variance of $\hat{\theta}$ is asymptotic.

Lagrange Multiplier Test

The Lagrange multiplier test is also called score test.

Only a single model is estimated by the Lagrange multiplier test. The test statistics is

$$S_0 = \frac{S(\theta_0)}{I(\theta_0)}$$

where $S(\theta_0) = \dfrac{\partial \log L(\theta)}{\partial \theta}$ and $I(\theta_0)$ is Fisher's information index. This is distributed asymptotically normally.

Figure 2.10 explains the role of these three tests. The X-axis has various values of theta or parameter. The X-axis is log of the likelihood of the theta. The theta hat zero is under null. The rationale for hypothesis testing using Wald test is as follows: The Wald test divides the distance of $\hat{\theta} - \theta_0$ by $\text{var}(\hat{\theta})$. Large difference between $\hat{\theta}$ and θ_0 leads to rejection of null hypothesis. The likelihood ratio test requires two estimates—model parameter estimate and null model estimate. The log of ratio of the two likelihoods is multiplied by –2. The Lagrange multiplier test is slope of the likelihood function.

2.6.4 Bayes' Rule and Bayesian Inference

Bayesian inference is application of Bayes' theorem to statistical inference. It does not use the typical null hypothesis significance testing (NHST) logic or frequentist logic of statistical estimation. The Bayes Rule is named after Thomas Bayes.[6] The Bayes' theorem is as follows:

$$P(A|B) = \frac{P(B|A)P(A)}{P(B)}$$

A and B are events. $P(A)$ and $P(B)$ are probabilities associated with event A and B. $P(B|A)$ is probability of observing event B given that event A has occurred. $P(A|B)$ is the conditional probability, that is, probability of observing A given that B has occurred. For example, look at the sampled data given below for mental illness (MI) diagnosis by a new test.

		Diagnosis (B)		
		MI	No MI	
Test Result (A)	MI	14	2	16
	No MI	3	81	84
		17	83	100

This implies that out of 100 individuals, 17 had mental illness out of which 14 were having positive test results and 3 were having negative test results. The question is what is the chance that test results would be positive given that one has mental illness? This is the question that Bayes' theorem answers.

$$P(+\text{ve test result}|\text{having MI}) = \frac{P(\text{Having MI}|+\text{ test result})P(+\text{ test result})}{P(+\text{ test result})}$$

The Bayesian inference uses the same idea. The parameter value is considered as a variable. The Bayesian inference begins with prior distribution. The prior is information available beforehand. The uninformative prior can also be used which is "objective information" or not very informative prior. In practice, the uniform distribution is commonly used. Then data is collected to calculate the likelihood of observed distribution and the likelihood function is multiplied by the prior distribution. The obtained probability values are normalized over all possible values. This is referred as the posterior distribution. The mode of this distribution is a parameter estimate. The Bayesian inference is gaining popularity over time and probably would be replacing existing estimation methods in years to come.

2.6.5 The Bootstrap

The bootstrap or resampling methods are alternatives (to non-parametric methods) when the underlying theoretical distribution followed by sample statistics (that is, sampling distribution) is not known. The resampling methods use random sampling with replacement from sample data to make a good judgment about the sampling distribution of statistics. Efron in his *Bootstrap Methods: Another Look at the Jackknife* developed the method in 1979 and it is gaining popularity with resampling being possible with computer. There are many algorithms for bootstrapping. The R provides various dedicated bootstrapping packages. Chapter 7 presents details about application of bootstraps.

---

[6] Thomas Bayes (1701–1761) was an English statistician who is mostly known for his discovery of Bayes rule. Most of the work of Bayes was published after his death. He was also a fellow of royal society.

2.7 IMPORTANT IDEAS UNDERLYING STATISTICAL INFERENCE

Four important ideas underlie the statistical inference: (a) central limit theorem (CLT), (b) law of large numbers, (c) Cremer–Rao inequality, and (d) Rao–Blackwell theorem. Let us have a quick understanding of them before we conclude.

2.7.1 Central Limit Theorem

The central limit theorem (CLT) states that the sum or average of independently distributed random variables is normally distributed irrespective of the underlying distribution. Most of the statistical procedures work because of the CLT as it is one of the most powerful ideas for the statistical inference. Figure 2.11 shows the working of the CLT. The three underlying distributions used to plot this graph are uniform, exponential and normal. The sample size was 5, 20, 50, 100, and 300. The distributions with small sample were not representative of original distribution due to small sample. As the sample is increasing, the distribution is becoming normal. The last column shows the sampling distribution for sample of 300. These distributions are fairly close to normal distribution irrespective of their original distribution.

2.7.2 Law of Large Numbers

The law of large numbers states that as the number of trials of random process increases, the difference between the true value (or expected value) and obtained value approaches to zero (Figure 2.12).

The first graph is showing coin toss experiment which is being repeated 5000 times. The second graph is about a normally distributed variable with mean 60 and SD=15 and the experiments is carried out up to 1000 times. The sample value is approaching the true value represented by horizontal line.The R code for this is law of large number is shown in R code 2.4.

```
R Code 2.4. Law of Large Numbers (for second Figure 2.11)
x<-rnorm(1000,60,15)
size<-c(1:1000)
cs<-cumsum(x)
plot(cs/size, ylim=c(55,65), xlab="Size", type="l")
abline(h = 60, col="red")
# Change the x, size, ylim, and h to obtain figure one.
```

The results of any experiment stabilize as the sample increases. With small sample, the results are more likely to deviate from the true value than the large samples. For example, if the sample mean is defined as $\bar{X} = \frac{1}{n}\sum_{i=1}^{n} X_i$, then as $n \longrightarrow \infty$, the $\bar{X} \longrightarrow \mu$.

2.7.3 Cramer–Rao Inequality

The Cramer–Rao inequality is also referred to as **Cramer–Rao bound** (CRB) or **Cramer–Rao lower bound** (CRLB). The inequality is first derived by Harald Cramer and Calyampudi Radhakrishna Rao.[7] The CRLB is a lower bound on the variance of estimators of a parameter.

---

[7] C. R. Rao (September 10, 1920) is an astute Indian statistician born in Hadagali, Bellary, Karnataka, India. He completed MSc in mathematics from Andhra University and M.A. in statistics from Calcutta University in 1943. Rao worked at Indian Statistical Institute and then completed his PhD from King College, Cambridge University under the supervision of R. A. Fisher. He held several positions of academic importance such as Director ISI, India, Jawaharlal Nehru Professor and National Professor in India, University Professor at the University of Pittsburgh and Eberly Professor and Chair of Statistics and Director of the Center for Multivariate Analysis at

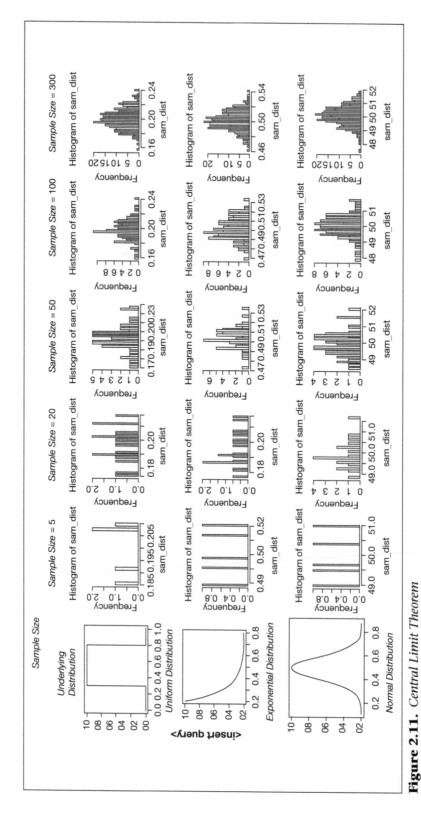

Figure 2.11. *Central Limit Theorem*

Note: Samples of the size 5, 20, 50, 100, and 300 from uniform, exponential and normal distribution. This is obtained by an R code.

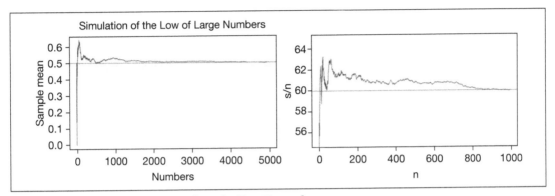

Figure 2.12. *Law of Large Numbers for Two Examples*

The CRLB simply states that the variance of any unbiased estimator is at least as high as Fisher's information.[8] Among all the unbiased estimators, the unbiased estimator that achieves the lowest possible MSE is, therefore, called minimum variance unbiased estimator. Of course, CLRB can also be used with biased estimators. The Fisher's information is the expression that informs about the information that observed variable carries about the unknown parameter.

2.7.4 Rao–Blackwell Theorem

The Rao–Blackwell theorem is at times called **Rao–Blackwell–Kolmogorov theorem**. The theorem is given by C. R. Rao and David Blackwell. According to the theorem, g(X) is any estimator of parameter theta. T(X) is a sufficient statistics, that is, when the statistics which is a function of sample observations uses all the information of the sample about parameter, then the conditional expectation of g(X) given T(X) is a better estimator of theta and is never worse. The Rao–Blackwell theorem is useful in improving a crude estimator by obtaining a conditional expectation of that estimator given another sufficient statistics. This is generally referred to as **Rao–Blackwellization**.

SUMMARY

We have discussed the population parameter and sample statistics. The population parameter is unknown, and statistics is known. The statistics estimates or infers about the population parameter. The null hypothesis is required for testing hypothesis. The alternative covers all possible conditions other than null. The sampling distribution of the statistics under the null hypothesis is required to be worked out. Generally, some known theoretical distributions are followed by the statistics. The decision is either acceptance of the null hypothesis or rejection of the null hypothesis. The alpha of 0.05 is most commonly used to reject the null. In case of the acceptance or rejection of the null, there is always chance of making errors in decision and they are called Type I and Type II Errors. The alternative hypothesis could be directional or

---

the Pennsylvania State University. There are many honors to his credit. He is editor of 32-volume handbook of statistics, importantly the volume 26 is on psychometrics. He is a recipient of Gay medal, Padma Bhushan and Padma Vibhushan (Govt. of India), National Medal of Science (USA), and 38 honorary doctorate degrees of 19 different countries.

[8] Fisher's information refers to the way of measuring the amount of information a random variable contains about a parameter called theta upon which the probability of X depends. It is a variance of a score or expectation of observed value. The Fisher's information matrix is used to calculate variance–covariance matrix associated with maximum-likelihood estimates. It is useful in Wald test.

non-directional. The point estimation and the interval estimation are the ways of estimation. The estimator is required to have certain desirable properties. They are small sample and large sample properties of estimators. The estimation can be achieved by using different methods of estimation. In addition, law of large numbers, CLT, Rao–Blackwell theorem, and Cremer–Rao inequality are important underlying concepts.

EXERCISE

1. Differentiate between parameter and statistics. Identify the three points of difference.
2. Design an R code for sampling distribution.
3. Explain sampling distribution.
4. Work out the relationship between standard error of statistics and sampling distribution.
5. A research hypothesized that the population mean is 20. Specify null and alternative hypothesis.
6. If the obtained mean is 23 and variance is 50, then how to construct null, and alternative, standard error and hypothesis testing.
7. Researchers wanted to test whether an experimental group does better than a control group. Specify null, alternative and decision making logic.
8. The *p*-value of the statistics for the above example is 0.046. What decision you will take? Why?
9. For the above example, specify types of errors.
10. Researcher specifies directional alternative. Other researcher specified non-directional alternative. Rest of the things equal, who has better chance of refuting null. Why?
11. Explain properties of estimators.
12. For a mean 30, var=50, construct a confidence interval for mean for *n*=20. Now do the same for *n*=60. Comment on the difference between both.
13. Explain the role of properties of estimator in hypothesis testing
14. Discuss the MLE in details.
15. Work out the relation between ML associated tests.
16. Explain CLT and law of large numbers (LLN) with R codes.

3 Description of Data: Statistics and Graphical Description

3.1 INTRODUCTION

One of the most essential steps in understanding data is to be able to describe the data. Data can be described by two useful ways. One, the description of data in terms of the statistics or numbers, and second, expression of data in terms of graphs. This chapter introduces descriptive statistical methods and graphical methods of expressing data. Descriptive methods provide the summary of the data. Usually, psychological data are obtained on a large number of individuals on several variables. The data matrix is of $n \times k$ dimensions. The data needs to be expressed in a summarized manner. The purpose of descriptive statistics and graphs is to be able to provide a useful summary of the data. This chapter shall briefly introduce to you descriptive statistics and graphical methods useful for the psychological data. The chapter shall also provide the useful R codes for the same.

3.2 DESCRIPTIVE STATISTICS: DESCRIBING DATA

The data can be described by various measures of central tendency and dispersion. The descriptive statistics provide answers to two useful questions: (a) What is the center of the data? (b) How is the data distributed around the center? To explain and understand the data summarizing techniques, I am using an example data of 50 individuals. The data is shown in R Code 3.1. I refer to the data as Data 3.1.

R Code 3.1: Data and Basic Descriptive
```
x <- c(17, 17, 19, 22, 19, 21, 25, 19, 19, 23, 14, 23, 17, 14, 11, 16,
14, 14, 28, 14, 25, 23, 16, 17, 18, 21, 18, 24, 19, 9, 20, 11, 25, 16,
14, 17, 23, 10, 21, 15, 20, 23, 23, 28, 21, 16, 31, 18, 24, 25)
sum(x)            # sum of the data
> sum(x)
[1] 957
nx <- length(x)   # sample size
sum(x)/nx         # sample mean
[1] 19.14
mean(x)           # sample mean
[1] 19.14
median(x)
[1] 19
```

The first question is answered by measures of central tendency.

3.3 MEASURES OF CENTRAL TENDENCY

The measures of central tendency (also called as measures of location) attempt to locate the center of the data. They reflect the location of the center. The difference between the measures is due to their ability to use the entire data, particularly sensitivity to extreme observations. The three measures of the central tendency are mean, median, and mode.

3.3.1 Mean

Mean ($\bar{X}$) is the most popular measure of a central tendency. It is most commonly described as an average. The mean ($\bar{X}$) is obtained by dividing the sum of the scores (Σ) by number of scores (n):

$$\bar{X} = \frac{\sum_{i=1}^{n} X_i}{n}$$

where $\bar{X}$ is the sample mean, $i = 1, 2, 3, ..., n$ (i.e., any value is referred to as i th value, and i will be from 1 to n), and n is the sample size. The values written below and above the Σ sign indicate the starting and ending points of summation. They imply that the summation starts from $i = 1$ (first value in data) and it will stops as $i = n$. Summation of all the values between $i = 1$ and $i = n$ is carried out. Let's assume that $X = 1, 2, 3, 4, 5$. The sum will be of all the five values and it is 15. The sample size is 5.

$$\bar{X} = \frac{\sum_{i=1}^{n} X_i}{n} = \frac{(1+2+3+4+5)}{5} = \frac{15}{5} = 3$$

The formula at times is also expressed as

$$\bar{X} = \frac{1}{n}\left(\sum_{i=1}^{n} X_i\right) = 0.2 \times (1+2+3+4+5) = 0.2 \times 15 = 3$$

The data in R code 3.1 has the mean of 19.14.

3.3.2 Median

Median (Mdn) is another indicator of centrality. Once the data is arranged in numerical order, the median is the point above which and below which lie 50% data. The median is the 50th percentile of the data. For the data $X = 1,2,3,4,5$, 3 is the score above and below which lie equal number of data points. Formally, median is

$$\text{Median Location} = \frac{n+1}{2}$$

$$\text{Median Location} = \frac{n+1}{2} = \frac{5+1}{2} = \frac{6}{2} = 3$$

When the data is arranged in numerical order, the third score is the median. The third score is 3, and 3 is the median. Suppose the data is $X = 1, 2, 3, 4, 5, 6$, then the median location is $7/2 = 3.5$. That is, median is the average of the third and fourth scores. The median for the data in R code 3.1 is 19.

R Code 3.2: Median Function

```
mdn <- function(x){
nx <- length(x)
modd <- (sort(x))[c((length(x)+1)/2)]       # sort is ranking data
mev <- (sort(x))[c(((length(x)+1)/2)+1)]    # x[i] is ith element in x
meven <- (modd + mev)/2
if((nx %% 2 == 0) ==FALSE)                   # if loop for either odd or even
  {print(modd)}                              # print odd data median
else
  {print(meven)}                             # print even data median
}
mdn(x)                                       # Run the function mdn
```

3.3.3 Mode

Mode is a score in distribution that has highest frequency. Suppose the data is $x=1, 2, 3, 4, 2, 5$. The mode of this data is 2, the value that has highest frequency. If the data is $x=1, 2, 3, 5, 2, 4, 5$, then the data has two modes, 2 and 5. This is bimodal distribution. It is possible to have a multimodal distribution.

3.4 PROPERTIES OF MEASURES OF CENTRAL TENDENCY

All the measures of central tendency reflect a certain definition of center of data. Each of the definitions has some advantages and limitations.

3.4.1 Mean

Being the most popular measure of central tendency, mean has almost become tantamount to central tendency. The mean is a reflection of each score. It also works as a balancing point of distribution; the sum of scores above the mean is the same as that of the scores below the mean. The mean would change if even one of the scores changes. The sum of the scores is translated into mean and mean is preferred when the central tendency has to reflect the sum. The major advantage of mean is that algebraic manipulations are possible with it. In addition, mean, as an estimator of population mean, is the most resistant central tendency to sampling variation. As compared to other measures of central tendency, mean shows less variation in other random samples drawn from the same population. Therefore, it makes mean a natural choice as an estimator of population mean. However, mean suffers a disadvantage. The mean is more sensitive to extreme scores as compared to other measures. For example, if the data is $x=1, 2, 3, 4, 5, 3$, then the mean is 3 and the median is also 3. Suppose the data has one extreme value instead of 5: $x=1, 2, 3, 4, 20, 3$. The addition of one extreme score of 20 (instead of 5) did not make any difference to the median but the mean has now changed to 5.5. The mean quickly responded to change in data. Unfortunately, the mean of the data (5.5) is not a realistic center of this data. This problem can to be taken care of by introducing *trimming*. The trimmed mean is calculated by discarding some percentage of observation in the extreme of the data. The 20% trimming of the present data provides the mean 3. The 10% trimming of the data in R code 3.1 leads to the trimmed mean of 19.125 (instead of 19.14). It is not useful due to the absence of an extreme score. The trimmed mean is considered as a better estimate of the population mean and it also helps in reducing skewness (Wilcox, 2005). Another robust estimator of population mean is Winsorized mean. The trimmed mean does not consider the extreme values. The Winsorized mean are computed by replacing most extreme values by immediate less extreme values. If data of 10 participants are obtained and are arranged in rank order, then the first and tenth observations are replaced by the second and ninth observations, respectively, and then the mean is computed. Rand Wilcox fervently argued in favor of robust estimators like trimmed and Winsorized means (Wilcox, 2005). R Code 3.3 explains trimmed and Winsorized means.

R Code 3.3: Trimmed and Winsorized means

```
mean (x, trim = .1)              # 10% Trimmed mean
library (psych)                  # call library psych
winsor (x, trim = .1)            # winsorizd mean with 10% winsor
sort(winsor(x, trim = .1))       # rank-order of winsor data
```

3.4.2 Median

Median is preferred for the reason that it is less sensitive to extreme scores. It appears that this property makes median a favored choice over mean. We have discussed an example while discussing mean. However, the robust estimators of mean are preferred over median. With large data, the mean turns out to be a better estimate. Another limitation of median is the limitation of the use of median (as compared to mean) in algebraic manipulations. Median is a useful central tendency useful in ordinal or ranked data. Median is favored by researchers who also have problems with scale of measurement in psychological data.

3.4.3 Mode

Mode being the most frequent value, it is a value from data itself. Often mean (and sometimes median) is not a value in data. It is very useful in understanding the most frequent response, for example, whether a particular change is preferred or not in needs assessment research can be ensured by mode. Suppose, 60% respondents strongly agreeing that a counseling psychologist is required in their community is a useful index. In a randomly drawn sample, the chance that a random value is close to the mode is higher than for any other value. Mode is particularly useful when the data is on a nominal scale. For example, among the four screens of a multiplex, screen 2 has maximum attendance. Mode is used to describe sample properties as well, particularly when a homogenous group is used; for example, a researcher reporting the modal age of a sample being 21 years. On the flip side, mode depends on grouping the data and also does not represent the entire data.

3.5 MEASURES OF VARIABILITY

The central tendencies provide measures of average of the data. However, the data points deviate from the average. Some of them are near the average and few are far away from the average. The spread of the data around the average is represented by measures of dispersion or variability. There are quite a few measures of variability. They include range, inter-quartile range, deviation score, and finally variance and standard deviation (SD).

3.5.1 Range

Range is the difference between lowest score and highest score in the data. For $x = 1, 2, 3, 4, 5$, the range is $5 - 1 = 4$. The problem of range is that it heavily depends on extreme scores. For example, if the data is $x = 1, 2, 3, 4, 20$, then the range is 19. Presence of extreme values influences range.

3.5.2 Interquartile Range (IQR)

Interquartile range solves the problem of dependence of range on extreme scores. The interquartile range is usually computed by eliminating upper 25% and lower 25% scores. The point of cut-off for lower 25% scores is called the first quartile (Q1) and the cut-off point for upper 25% scores is called the third quartile (Q3). They are also referred to as 25th and 75th percentile, respectively. The Q2 is the median, that is, the 50th percentile. The difference between the first quartile and the third quartile is called the interquartile range (Q3–Q1). The semi-interquartile range (Q) is obtained by dividing the interquartile range by 2. Though the interquartile range is less sensitive to extreme scores and useful in skewed distributions, it is affected by sampling variation. SD is often better, particularly with distributions that are symmetric. The point to be noted is that the 25% is not a rigid value. Researchers can take 10% cut-offs or 20% cut-offs. They are referred to as Winsorized samples.

3.5.3 Average Deviation

Average deviation calculates deviation around the mean. $(X_i - \bar{X})$ is the deviation of each score from the mean. Since the mean is a balancing point of the distribution, the sum and the average of deviation from the mean is zero, that is, $\sum_{i=1}^{n}(X_i - \bar{X}) = 0$.

3.5.4 Mean Absolute Deviation (m.a.d)

Mean absolute deviation is computed by taking the average of absolute deviations from the mean. For example, $x = 1, 2, 3, 4, 5$ with mean being 3, the absolute deviations are (2, 1, 0, 1, 2) and the average of absolute deviations is 1.2.

3.5.5 Median Absolute Deviations (MAD)

MAD is computed by taking the median of absolute deviations from the median.

$$MAD = \text{Median}(|X_i - \text{median}(X)|)$$

The MAD is considered as a robust measure and is not sensitive to outliers in the data. Since the MAD is actually a median of absolute deviations, it is less sensitive to extreme scores.

3.5.6 Variance

Let us now consider a sample variance. The sample variance is obtained by the following formula:

$$S_X^2 = \frac{\sum_{i=1}^{n}(X_i - \bar{X})^2}{n}$$

$$S_X^2 = \frac{1}{n}\sum_{i=1}^{n}(X_i - \bar{X})^2$$

The sample variance (S^2) is the average of the squared deviation from the mean. Here, S_X^2 is the variance of variable X, $\bar{X}$ is the mean of X, and n is the sample size. When sample variance is used as an estimator of population variance, then the denominator is changed to $n-1$ instead of n. The reason for this is discussed in the next chapter while discussing the unbiased estimators. The reason for this (without much understanding) is that the sample variance with denominator n is a biased estimator and it becomes an unbiased estimator with $n-1$ as the denominator.

For example, if $x=1, 2, 3, 4, 5$, the sample variance is

$$S_X^2 = \frac{\sum_{i=1}^{n}(X_i - \bar{X})^2}{n-1} = \frac{(1-3)^2 + (2-3)^2 + (3-3)^2 + (4-3)^2 + (5-3)^2}{5} = \frac{10}{5} = 2$$

The population estimator of variance is

$$S_X^2 = \frac{\sum_{i=1}^{n}(X_i - \bar{X})^2}{n-1} = \frac{(1-3)^2 + (2-3)^2 + (3-3)^2 + (4-3)^2 + (5-3)^2}{5-1} = \frac{10}{4} = 2.5$$

The variance as the population estimator for the data in R code 3.1 is 23.59. The variance is one of the most popular measures of dispersion.

3.5.7 Standard Deviation (SD)

SD is a positive squareroot of a variance. The symbol representing variance is S. Following is the formula for S:

$$S_X = S_X^2 = \sqrt{\frac{\sum_{i=1}^{n}(X_i - \bar{X})^2}{n-1}}$$

From the above example, the SD is

$$S_X = S_X^2 = \sqrt{2.5} = 1.58$$

In R code 3.1, $S=4.86$. The mean for this data is 19.14. The data can be expressed as $\bar{X} = 19.14$ and $S_X = 4.86$. The score of 24 differs from the mean with 4.86. The score of 24 is one SD above the mean. Similarly, if you want to know the score that is 1.5 SD above the mean, then

$$\bar{X} + (S_X \times 1.5) = 19.14 + (4.86 \times 1.5) = 19.14 + 729 = 26.43$$

The score of 26.43 is 1.5 times above the mean. The variance is the average squared deviation from the mean and the SD squareroot of a variance. R code 3.4 is useful in computing variance and SD.

```
R Code 3.4: Variance and SD and general descriptive
var(x)                                      # variance
[1] 23.59224
sd(x)                                       # SD
[1] 4.857185
varx <- (sum((x-mean(x))^2))/(length(x)-1)  # you can write formula for var
varx
[1] 23.59224
sqrt(varx)                                  # you can compute is using your
function
# Other descriptive statistics
summary(x)                                  # from base packages
```

```
  Min.  1st Qu.  Median  Mean  3rd Qu.  Max.
  9.00   16.00    19.00  19.14  23.00   31.00
```

```
# Descriptive using psych package
library(psych)                          # call library 'psych'
describe(x)                             # most descriptive statistics
```

```
   vars n  mean   sd  median trimmed mad  min max range skew kurtosis se
1   1  50 19.14 4.86 19       19.12  5.93  9   31   22  0.09  -0.46   0.69
```

```
# Descriptive using Hmisc package
library(Hmisc)
describe(x)
x
```

n	missing	unique	Info	Mean	.05	.10	.25	.50	.75	.90	.95
50	0	17	0.99	19.14	11.00	14.00	16.00	19.00	23.00	25.00	26.65

	9	10	11	14	15	16	17	18	19	20	21	22	23	24	25	28	31
Frequency	1	1	2	6	1	4	5	3	5	2	4	1	6	2	4	2	1
%		2	2	4	12	2	8	10	6	10	4	8	2	12	4	8	4	2

The computational alternative for the variance and SD are as follows. The logic of this computational alternative is presented as follows:

$$S_X^2 = \frac{\sum X^2 - \frac{(\sum X)^2}{n}}{n-1}$$

We can derive this formula from the earlier formula. The proof below shows the same:

$$\sum(X - \bar{X})^2 = \sum(X^2 - 2X\bar{X} + \bar{X}^2)$$

$$\sum(X - \bar{X})^2 = \sum X^2 - 2\bar{X}\sum X + n\bar{X}^2$$

$$\sum(X - \bar{X})^2 = \sum X^2 - 2\bar{X}\sum X + n\bar{X}^2$$

$$\sum(X - \bar{X})^2 = \sum X^2 - 2\left(\frac{\sum X}{n}\right)\sum X + n\left(\frac{\sum X}{n}\right)^2$$

$$\sum(X - \bar{X})^2 = \sum X^2 - 2\frac{(\sum X)^2}{n} + \frac{(\sum X)^2}{n}$$

$$\sum(X - \bar{X})^2 = \sum X^2 - \frac{(\sum X)^2}{n}$$

Since the numerator of the variance formula can be expressed as $\sum X^2 - \frac{(\sum X)^2}{n}$, the variance can be written as

$$S_X^2 = \frac{\sum_{i=1}^{n}(X_i - \bar{X})^2}{n-1} = \frac{\sum X^2 - \frac{(\sum X)^2}{n}}{n-1}$$

Often, this expression is referred to as the raw score formula.

One of the properties of SD is that if it is obtained by computing the deviation from the mean, then the SD is the smallest possible value. Let's take a value B such as $B = \bar{X} + d$,

$$\Sigma(X - B)^2 = \Sigma(X - [\bar{X} + d])^2$$

$$\Sigma(X - B)^2 = \Sigma([X - \bar{X}] - d)^2$$

$$\Sigma(X - B)^2 = \Sigma([X - \bar{X}]^2 - 2d[X - \bar{X}] + d^2)^2$$

$$\Sigma(X - B)^2 = \Sigma[X - \bar{X}]^2 - 2d\,\Sigma[X - \bar{X}] + nd^2$$

$$\Sigma(X - B)^2 = \Sigma[X - \bar{X}]^2 - nd^2$$

At step 4, nd^2 is obtained because summation over a constant is that constant multiplied by n. Similarly, summation over $\bar{X}$ is always $n\bar{X}$, that is, the sum of X. Also, note that

$$\Sigma(X - \bar{X}) = \Sigma X - \Sigma \bar{X} = \Sigma X - n\bar{X} = \Sigma X - \not{n}\left(\frac{\Sigma X}{\not{n}}\right) = \Sigma X - \Sigma X = 0$$

and the middle term $2d\,\Sigma[X - \bar{X}]$ will become zero because $\Sigma(X - \bar{X}) = 0$.

The skewness, kurtosis, and z-scores are discussed in Chapter 4. Hence, the discussion on these is avoided here.

3.6 THE GRAPHICAL REPRESENTATION OF DATA

The graphical presentation of data is often very insightful. We shall have a look at some of the useful graphs for psychological data.

3.6.1 Stem-and-Leaf Graph

The steam-and-leaf graph is a useful presentation of the data. It shows the frequency of each value of the data. The steam is the left-hand column and the leaves are the lists on the right-hand rows, showing all the ones digits for each of the tens, twenties, and thirties. Look at a data: 22, 25, 32, 43, 46, 49, 55, 55, 55. The steam-and-leaf graph for this will be as follows:

Stem	Leaves
1	0
2	2 5
3	2
4	3 6 9
5	5 5 5
6	0

The values in the stem represent numbers in the ten space and leaves represent the unit space. Stem 2 has two leaves, 2 and 5, representing 22 and 25. Look at R code 3.5 that shows a stem-and-leaf graph for R code 3.1 data.

R code 3.5: Stem-and-Leaf Graph
```
stem(x)        # plots stem and leaf graph.
The decimal point is at the |

   8 | 0
  10 | 000
  12 |
  14 | 0000000
  16 | 000000000
```

```
18 | 00000000
20 | 000000
22 | 0000000
24 | 000000
26 |
28 | 00
30 | 0
```

```
# This is not a great looking plot since each values is plotted.
# modification in command produces better looking plot
stem(x, scale = .5, width=80)
The decimal point is 1 digit(s) to the right of the |
```

```
 0 | 9
 1 | 011444444
 1 | 566667777788899999
 2 | 001111233333344
 2 | 555588
 3 | 1
```

3.6.2 Box–Whisker Plot (Boxplot)

The boxplot or box–whisker plot is a very useful way of plotting data. The boxplot uses a quartile as its basis. The data is divided into three areas: lower 25%, middle 50%, and upper 25% data. The upper and lower 25% data is represented by whiskers and middle 50% data is represented by a box. The horizontal line in the box represents the 50% cut-off point (or the 50th percentile point) which is also the median. The outliers at either extreme are expressed by separate data points represented by a small dot. R code 3.6 shows the boxplot command in R.

R code 3.6: Box-Whisker Plot
```
boxplot(x, cex.axis = 3, lwd = 2, pch = 16)
# cex.axis increases the axis text size, lwd is line width, and pch is
type of marker.
# the output is shown in figure.
```

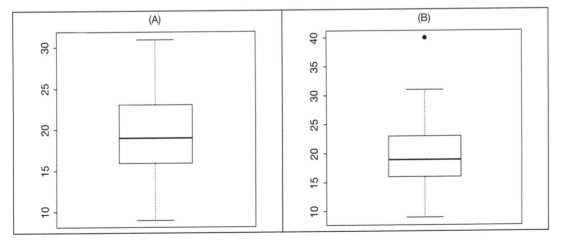

Figure 3.1. *(A) Boxplot of Data; (B) Boxplot with Outlier Value of 40 Added*

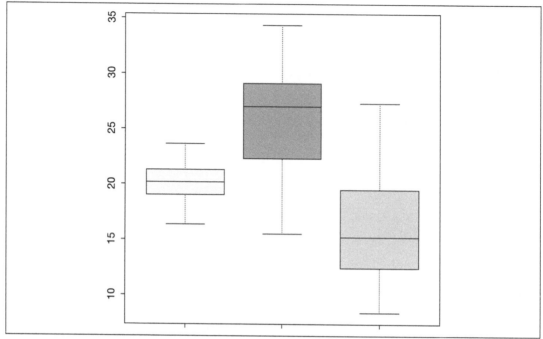

Figure 3.2. *Boxplot for Comparing Groups*

Figure 3.1(A) shows the boxplot for the data. In addition, a value of 40 is added in the data and another boxplot is plotted in Figure 3.1(B).

The box–whisker plot is useful in determining the symmetry, outliers, and distribution across a quartile of the data. The examination of the plot shows that the data is slightly more valued above the median than below. The stem-and-leaf graph also shows the same.

Another useful application of the boxplots is to compare groups in terms of their relative distribution, locations, and outliers. R code 3.7 is generating a random data that is used to demonstrate this utility. The colors can be seen on your screen.

R Code 3.7: Comparing groups with Boxplots
```
set.seed(12345)
x1 <- rnorm(30, 20, 2)
x2 <- rnorm(50, 25, 4)
x3 <- rnorm(40, 15, 5)
col <- c("yellow", "red", "green")
boxplot(x1, x2, x3, col = col, cex = 3, cex.axis = 3, lwd = 2, pch = 16)
```

R code 3.7 generates a boxplot that is shown in Figure 3.2. The comparison is quite telling. Group 1 has smaller variance and a mean around 20. The second and third groups have similar variance; however, group 3 has much lower mean and group 2 has higher mean (centre). The group 3, however, has a very skewed distribution with negatively skewed distribution (or left-skewed distribution). Group 2, however, has a very skewed distribution with negatively skewed distribution (or left skewed distribution).

3.6.3 Histograms

Histogram is one of the most popular ways of plotting data. The histograms represent how frequent the numbers are in the data. The histogram was first introduced by Karl Pearson. Look at the following data: 0, 0, 1, 1, 1, 2, 2, 2, 2, 2, 3, 3, 3, 3, 4, 4, 5, 6.

Table 3.1. *The Values in Data and Their Frequency*

Value	Frequency
0	2
1	3
2	5
3	4
4	2
5	1
6	1

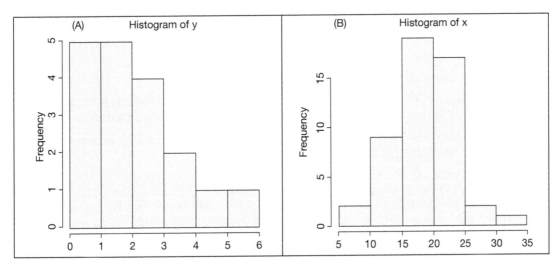

Figure 3.3. *(A) Boxplot of Histogram Data; (B) Data given in the Table of R code 3.1*

Table 3.1 shows the frequency of each value.

The data can be plotted with value on *x*-axis and frequency being on *y*-axis.

Figure 3.3(A) shows the histogram for Table 3.1. Figure 3.3(B) shows the histogram for Data 3.1. The histogram in Figure 3.3(A) is plotting frequency for each value in the data. it is possible since we have fewer data points. When the number of data points increases, this is not a suitable way for representing data. So class intervals were created and frequency in the class interval is plotted in a histogram. The class intervals are 5–10, 10–15, 15–20, etc. This is the most common strategy of plotting a histogram. The histogram in Figure 3.3(A) shows that the frequency distribution is skewed. The histogram in Figure 3.3(B) is reasonably symmetric though slightly heavy on the left side. R code 3.8 is for histograms.

R Code 3.8: Histogram
```
hist(x)    # basic syntax
hist(x, breaks = 6, cex.axis = 2.5, lwd = 2, col = "grey")  # specify details
```

3.6.4 Kernel Density Plots

Kernel density plots are becoming more popular way of presenting data than histograms because of the smoothness in the graph. The kernel density estimator (KDE) is a non-parametric method of estimating the pdf of a continuous random variable. The KDE is at the basis of kernel density plots. The KDE is the solution to data-smoothing problem by drawing an inference about population parameter using finite sample data. The pdf is smooth for a continuous random variable. However, the sample density function is not smooth since it is based on finite data. If $(X_1, X_2, ..., X_n)$ are random sample drawn from a some population distribution with an unknown density function f, the KDE of shape of the function f is

$$\hat{f}_h(X) = \frac{1}{2}\sum_{i=1}^{n} K_h(X - X_i)$$

The KDE is obtained with the following constraints. Every value of pdf has a non-negative $f(x)$, that is, the $f(x)$ results in a positive value of zero; it does not result in less than zero values. The definite integral of the $f(x)$ is set to 1. The idea of KDE is simple. Look at the following data: $x=4$, 5, 6, 10, 12. The value of 4 is one random value taken from population. This value could be 3 or 5. This could be 2 to 6. It is very unlikely that this value could have been 20. Each value has a distribution which is estimated by kernel. They are called "bumps." Each value has a bump, meaning bump_4 is distribution of the first bump. Following steps are taken to obtain the kernel density plot:

Step 1: Choose a kernel, the common one is Gaussian.

Step 2: for each data point, a kernel function is constructed. The function is $h^{-1}K[(X - X_i)/h]$. K is chosen as the kernel function, and the parameter h is called the bandwidth.

Step 3: All the individual scaled kernel functions are added and divided by n; hence, the KDE integrates to 1. The density is plotted.

Figure 3.4 shows the kernel plot computation.

Figure 3.5 shows the final output with each component explained. Figure 3.5(A) shows the individual data points, kernel over individual data points, and kernel density estimate. Figure 3.5(B) shows the R output for the kernel density plot. As an exercise, compare the plot of kernel and histograms. You would obtain a better understanding yourself.

The R code for plotting the kernel density plots is provided in R code 3.9.

R Code 3.9: Kernel Density Plot in R
```
xx <- c(4,5,6,10,12)                        # new data
plot(density(xx), lwd = 4, cex.axis = 3)    # density plot
plot(density(x), lwd = 4, cex.axis = 3)     # density plot for data 3.1
```

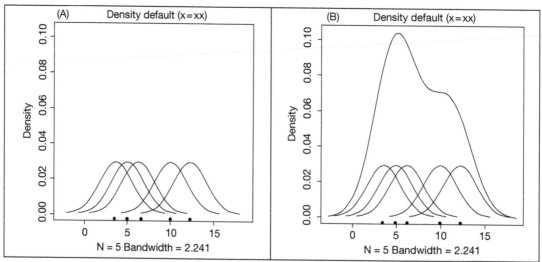

Figure 3.4. *(A) Data Point and Individual Kernels (Steps 1 and 2; bandwidth=2.24); (B) Summation of Kernel to Kernel Density Estimator*

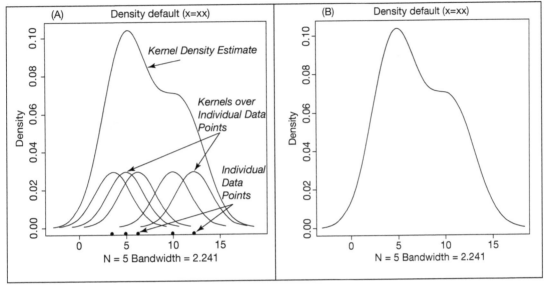

Figure 3.5. *Kernel Density Plot and R Output*

3.6.5 Pie Chart

The pie charts are useful presentation of statistics data over a circle which is divided into slices representing the proportions. Suppose the data is as follows for the sales of five products:

Product	A	B	C	D	E	Total
Sale	10	25	21	44	30	130
%	7.7	19.23	16.15	33.85	23.08	100
Central Angle	27.69	69.23	58.15	121.85	83.08	360

The sales of five products A, B, C, D, and E are given in numbers per day. The percentage is obtained per product and then the central angle is computed by multiplying the percentage by 3.6. These angles are plotted on the circle and the pie chart is obtained. R code 3.10 is useful in plotting the pie chart.

R Code 3.10: Pie Chart
```
sales <- c(10, 25, 21, 45, 30)    # data of sales
product <- c("A", "B", "C", "D", "E")    # lables
pie(sales, labels = product, main="Pie Chart of Sales", cex = 3)   # Pie chart
library(plotrix)    # call library plotrix
pie3D(sales, labels = product, main="Pie Chart of Sales", cex = 3)   # three
dimensional pie-chart
```

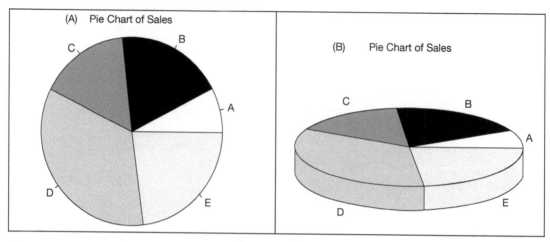

Figure 3.6. *(A) Pie Chart; (B) Three-dimensional Pie Chart*

Figures 3.6(A) and 3.6(B) show the pie chart and the three-dimensional pie chart, respectively.

3.6.6 The ggplot2 and Lattice: Data Visualization with R

The ggplot2 is one of best packages on R to plot graphs. The name is derived from "grammar of graphics." The package is developed by Hadley Wickham (2005).[1] It breaks the visualization of the graph into semantic components of the graph like scales, layers, etc. I strongly recommend that a reader should learn to use ggplot2 (R code 3.11).

R code 3.11: R code for ggplot2
```
install.packages("ggplot2")
library(ggplot2)
# qplot example
qplot(x, geom="histogram", binwidth = 1)
qplot(x, y, data=, color=, shape=, size=, alpha=, geom=, method=,
formula=, facets=, xlim=, ylim= xlab=, ylab=, main=, sub=)
# specify each of the parameter in syntax and obtain fine quality graphs
```

The lattice is another useful graphic package in R, developed by Deepayan Sarkar (2008). The simple plot are shown in R code 3.12.

R Code 3.11: Lattice Plots
```
library(lattice)    # call lattice
densityplot(~x)     # density plot by lattice
xx <- c(x1,x2,x3)   # boxplot data put together
y <- c(rep("A", 30), rep("B", 50), rep("C", 40))  # new variable generated
bwplot(xx~y)        # boxplot
```

SUMMARY

This chapter has provided an introduction to the description of the data as well graphical methods useful for describing the data. The specific graphical methods are avoided since they

---

[1] Please visit http://ggplot2.org to understand more about the ggplot2.

are presented in the respective chapters. For example correlation and regression uses the scatter plot extensively and hence it is not discussed here. The lattice and ggplot2 are very useful R packages to plot high publication quality plots. You should try to play with these packages as much as possible to learn them well.

EXERCISE

1. For the following data, compute measures of central tendency and variability=x (32, 34, 20, 35, 30, 29, 37, 39, 23, 36, 26, 31, 33, 31, 21, 27, 39, 31, 25, 26).
2. Compute the same in R.
3. Write your code for the same in R.
4. Compute 5%, 10%, and 20% trimmed and Winsorized mean.
5. Compute MAD and m.a.d for the above data.
6. Which of them are more sampling resistant? Why?
7. Show that $\Sigma(X - \bar{X})^2 = \Sigma X^2 - \dfrac{(\Sigma X)^2}{n}$.
8. Show that $\Sigma(X - \bar{X}) = 0$.
9. Why deviations taken from mean are smaller than any other value?
10. In a stem–and-leaf graph, a last stem is 6| 2 4 4 4 6 5 7. Tell how many values are above 70. How many values are 67 and 64.
11. For the above data in question 1, plot the stem-and-leaf graph.
12. Plot the box–whisker plot for the same data.
13. For the data (11, 7, 11, 7, 10, 0, 9, 11, 6, 10, 7, 7, 9, 12, 9, 11, 15, 9, 9, 13), plot the boxplot. Any specific finding that you have noted?
14. Plot a histogram for the above data. What measure of central tendency you want to compute? Why?
15. Explain the kernel density plot. Plot the density plot for the above two data sets.

4 Normal Distribution: Theory, Application, and Testing

4.1 INTRODUCTION

The normal distribution and normal random variable are extremely important for developing a good understanding of statistical processes in general and statistical applications for psychology in particular. This chapter provides you with an overview of the history of the normal distribution and its testing. It will also introduce you to the applications and useful transformations of normal distribution that are applied in psychology. A reasonably detailed discussion is provided on testing of normality by various methods. The statistical tests are discussed at length to provide the reader with a good idea of compatible options. At the end, alternatives to normal distribution-based statistics and multivariate normality are discussed briefly.

4.2 HISTORICAL ASPECTS OF NORMAL DISTRIBUTION

The historical aspects associated with statistical modeling with psychological data are generally discussed in notes for each chapter. The history of normal distribution and its testing are interesting and insightful as well. Hence it is maintained here.

4.2.1 Note on History of Normal Distribution

Many historians of statistics would agree that the idea of the normal distribution was first proposed by Abraham de Moivre (1667–1754).[1] He presented a paper "Approximatio ad summam terminorum binomii $\overline{a+b}|^n$ in seriem expansi" on November 12, 1733 to some of his friends. Later on, it was included in the English edition[2] of his book titled *The Doctrine of Chances* (1738). In that paper, he explained the basic form of the normal distribution. He was a friend of Sir Isaac Newton[3] (1642–1727). He dedicated the first edition of this book to Newton and

---

[1] Some do argue that this paper and the book later publish only has the middle term for normal distribution. Stephen Stigler (1986), while studying the history of probability before 1900, argued that de Moivre did not interpret results as approximate rule for binomial coefficient. These views credit Gauss and Laplace for the development of normal distribution.

[2] The first edition of the book was published in Latin in 1711. The English translation was published in 1718. The normal distribution idea was first added in this book in 1738 edition. This is not the first book on probability or statistics. Many historians of science agree that first works on probability were done by Christiaan Huygens (1657), however, "Liber de ludo aleae" (meaning 'Book on Games of Chance'), written by Gerolamo Cardano around 1564 was published in 1663.

[3] Abraham de Moiver was born in France and migrated to England. He read *Principia Mathematica*, one of Newton's valuable contributions and then had discussions with him. It is believed that he spent good deal of time in understanding *Principia* and Newton used to refer individuals saying, "Go to Mr de Moivre. He knows

also discussed his problems with him. The theory of probability was in its infancy at that time, and hence, de Moivre did not use concepts like probability density function. For the next one and half century, no major work was carried out. Carl Friedrich Gauss[4] published a monograph in 1809 titled "Theoria motus corporum coelestium in sectionibus conicis solem ambientium" in Latin [Theory of the Motion of the Heavenly Bodies Moving about the Sun in Conic Sections] in which along with least square he also explained "the normal law of errors" to show that the arithmetic mean is an estimator of location parameter. Marquis de Laplace[5] (1749–1827) proposed a problem of aggregating observation in 1777; then provided normalization constant for normal distribution in 1782, and in 1810, he provided the fundamental central limit theorem. "Laplace's error function" is just another way of describing the normal probability distribution. Because of the contribution of these two mathematicians, normal distribution was at times referred as Laplace–Gaussian curve, or Laplace's second law, or Gaussian law. In 1809, another mathematician, Adrian, provided the derivation of normal probability but it was not known to others for next 60 to 70 years. A single researcher cannot be credited for the name "normal distribution." It was Gauss who coined the term "the normal equation." Later, Pearson popularized the term normal curve. Pearson started using the notation sigma (σ) and Fisher, by specifying location parameter, started writing normal distribution equation the way we write it today. Generally, the normal curve is referred to as "bell-shaped curve."[6] Normal distribution has become popular because of its useful properties. If two variables are normally distributed, then their sum or differences are normally distributed. Statistics based on normal distribution also follow the normal distribution in their test. The only parameters in normal distribution are mean (μ) and variance (σ^2). If they are known, normal distribution can be obtained since other two Pearsonian parameters[7]—skewness and kurtosis—are zero.

4.2.2 Note on History of Testing for Normality

Concern over the normality of observations was expressed in the early days of modern statistics. Fisher's (1930) paper reporting results on the cumulants of the skewness and kurtosis statistics for testing normality, and Bartlett's (1935) work on effect of non-normal distribution on *t*-test, are perhaps the earliest attempts. E. S. Pearson (1931) initially noted the sensitivity to non-normality of "tests comparing two-variances." These findings were confirmed by Geary (1947), who showed that symmetric but non-normal distributions have serious impact on significance levels (*p*-values) for two-sample *z*-test and test of equality of variance. He further showed that the symmetric non-normal distribution has lesser impact than the skewed

---

these things better than I do" (Todhunter, 1865). He became a member of Royal Society in 1697 while Newton was president. He was also a member of commission setup in 1712 to look into claims of Newton and Leibniz as to who discovered calculus.

[4] Carl Friedrich Gauss (1777–1855) was a German Mathematician. He contributed to many areas like number theory, astronomy, algebra, statistics, and geometry. He was a child prodigy. Beside his work on normal distribution, another extremely useful contribution is called as Gauss–Markov Theorem, which is essential in method of least squares. He was sad and depressed through his personal adult life due to the death of his first wife Johanna and it is believed that he never recovered from it. He was hardworking and perfectionist and would not publish until felt that the work is complete in all respects. To honor his contributions, his picture along with normal curve featured on German 10-mark banknote for a long time.

[5] Pierre–Simon Marquis de Laplace (1749–1827) was deeply interested in mathematics and astronomy. His most well-known contribution: Laplace equation and Laplace transformation are significant for many branches of mathematics. He was named Marquis as an honorary title in 1817. One of his well-known students is S. D. Poisson.

[6] "Bell-shaped curve" is not a characteristics description of only normal distribution. Other distributions like logistic, student's *t*-distribution, or Cauchy distribution are also bell-shaped.

[7] Pearson believed that the distribution could be completely described by specifying mean, variance, skewness, and kurtosis. Hence, in the literature, they are at times referred to as Pearsonian parameters.

distribution. Geary concluded that for two-sample *t*-test, its non-normality but similarity of the distributions matter more; the similar distributions in both samples have little impact on probability of rejecting null hypothesis as compared to the dissimilar distributions in both samples. Box (1953) revealed that Bartlett's test of homogeneity of variance was affected by non-normality. Indeed, most statisticians agree that usage of term "robustness" is first documented in this paper. Robustness generally refers to stability of performance of statistical tests in spite of shape of parent population or in spite of deviation from normality. Box wrote "remarkable property of 'robustness' to non-normality which these tests for comparing means possess," was not shared by tests comparing variances (p. 318). However, John Tukey's (1960) paper, "A Survey of Sampling from Contaminated Distributions" and Peter Huber's article, "Robust Estimation of a Location Parameter," are two seminal contributions that provided robustness a status of sub-discipline in statistics. Tukey (1960) employing an unbalanced mixture of two normals with common mean and different variances presented the effects of non-normality on the estimation of location and scale parameters of a distribution. The Pearson and Please's (1975) simulation study confirming lack of robustness of *F*-statistics in homogeneity of variances and Subrahmaniam, Subrahmaniam and Messeri's (1975) study of effect of underlying the location-contaminated normal distribution on various statistics are other noteworthy later works. D'Agostino and Lee (1977) compared the efficiency of several estimates of location parameter, for example, sample mean. They found that with an increase in kurtosis, the efficiency of sample mean was not much affected in student's *t*-distribution but is seriously affected in exponential power distribution. Henry Thode's (2002) book *Testing for Normality* provides a reasonable overview of the developments in the field.

4.3 NORMAL DISTRIBUTION: UNDERSTANDING AND APPLYING NORMAL DISTRIBUTION

If X is a normal random variable, or is normally distributed, with parameters μ (mu) and σ^2 (sigma square), then the density of X is given by

$$f(x) = \frac{1}{\sigma\sqrt{2\pi}} e^{-\left(\frac{(x-\mu)^2}{2\sigma^2}\right)} \quad \text{for } -\infty < x < \infty$$

The equation has two constants, pi (π) and e, the value of $\pi \approx 3.14159$ and value of $e \approx 3.71828$. The two unknowns are μ and σ^2, which are also called the parameters of the normal distribution. The expectation of normal random variable (mean) is μ and variance is σ^2, obviously standard deviation (SD) is σ. $\dfrac{1}{\sigma\sqrt{2\pi}}$ ensures that $\int_{-\infty}^{\infty} f(x)dx$ will be 1.

Given this equation, if you know the values of μ and σ^2, then you can know the probabilities associated with any value of X, that is, $P(a<X<b)$.

4.3.1 Properties of Normal Distribution

Some of the important properties of the normal distribution are as follows:

1. The mean, median, and mode are same: the normal distribution has similar mean, mode and median. Their values are expectation of normal distribution (μ).
2. Normal curve is symmetric: the bell-shaped curve of a normal distribution is symmetric about the mean μ. The normal curve is identical to both sides of its mean. As a result, knowing half of the distribution is enough to understand the probabilities associated with the various values of X. You will realize that the area under the normal distribution tables usually reports values for one side of the distribution.

Table 4.1. *Conversion of Score (X) into Z*

X	$(X - \bar{X})^2$	$Z = (X - \bar{X}) / SD(X)$	$(Z - \bar{Z})^2$
1	4	−1.41	2.00
2	1	−0.71	0.50
3	0	0.00	0.00
4	1	0.71	0.50
5	4	1.41	2.00
$\bar{X} = 3$	$Sum(X - \bar{X}) = 10$	Mean $(Z) = 0.00$	$Sum(X - \bar{X}) = 5.00$
	$Var(X) = 10/5 = 2$		$Var(Z) = 1$
	$SD(X) = 1.4142$		$SD(Z) = 1$

3. Normal is a two-parameter distribution: the normal distribution has two parameters—μ and σ^2. μ (mean) and σ^2 (variance) can take different values. Hence, different normal distributions can be plotted. That is why normal distribution is called a family of normal distributions.
4. The normal distribution is a continuous distribution that can take values from uncountable $-\infty$ to uncountable $+\infty$.
5. The highest frequency is in the middle and the frequency tapers down at either extremes of normal curve. Theoretically, the curve will never have an end, but the frequencies at extreme would be negligibly small.
6. Most of the area under the normal curve is within first three SDs at both sides (99.74% area) whereas 68.26% area is within the first SD. To specify:

   a. Almost 68.26% (roughly, two-thirds of area) of the observations fall within one SD below and above the mean.
   b. Almost 95.44% of the observations fall within two SDs below and above the mean.
   c. Almost 99.73% of the observations fall within three SDs below and above the mean.

7. Zero Skewness and Kurtosis: the skewness value of the normal distribution is zero since normal distribution is symmetric. It is never tilted towards either side. The kurtosis for a normal distribution is also zero (If the subtraction of 3 is omitted from the kurtosis formula, then the kurtosis value will be 3 for a normal distribution). So the normal distribution is known as Mesokurtic. This makes the normal distribution mathematically more tractable distribution.

4.3.2 The Standard Normal Distribution and Standard Score

The standard normal distribution can be obtained by fixing mean to be zero and SD to be 1. This transformation is very useful. We can transform any variable that is normally distributed into Z. This will make computation of probabilities associated with the value of X relatively easy. If X is normally distributed, then Z can be obtained by using following transformation.

$$Z = \frac{x - \mu}{\sigma}$$

Table 4.1 shows that X can be converted into Z by following simple steps. Compute mean and SD for X and compute Z for each X score by applying above formula. If you compute the mean of Z, it will be 0 and if you compute variance and SD of Z, it will be 1.

4.3.3 Finding Area under Normal Distribution: Using Z Score

The Z score is very useful in psychometrics and statistics. Let us learn to use Z for computing probabilities associated with normally distributed variables. Once you compute Z, we can

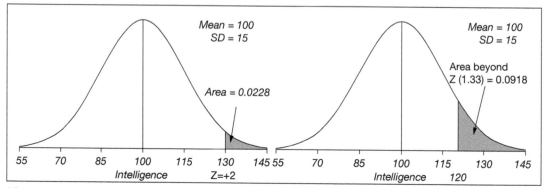

Figure 4.1. *Graphical Illustration of Example 1: Proportion of Cases in a Distribution with μ = 100, and σ = 15*

find out the probabilities associated with *Z* by using the area under normal distribution table (Appendix C1).

Example 1: If intelligence is normally distributed with mean 100 and SD 15, then what is the probability that someone will have a score above 130? What proportion of cases will be above 120?

Let us look at the first problem. We need to compute *Z* associated with 130.

$$Z_{(130)} = \frac{(130-100)}{15} = \frac{+30}{15} = +2.00$$

We want to know the probability of obtaining a score above 130, which actually means that we want to know the probability of getting *Z* greater than +2. Look at *Z* value in the table in Appendix C1. One value is associated with this *Z* value, which is "area between mean and *Z*" and the "area beyond *Z*" is "0.5—area between mean and Z." Since, we are interested in area beyond *Z*, the area beyond *Z* for *Z* = 2 is 0.0228 (0.5 – 0.4772 = 0.0228). The probability of getting IQ above 130 is 0.0228. Figure 4.1 illustrates the same.

Similarly, to find the proportion of cases that will be above 120, we need to find *Z* associated with 120. $Z_{(120)} = \frac{(120-100)}{15} = \frac{20}{15} = +1.33$. Again we shall see the "area beyond *Z*" for *Z* = 1.33. The area beyond *Z* is 0.0918. The probability of "*Z* is greater than 1.33" (which means "equal to and greater than" for continuous variable, since *p* associated with exact value is always zero) can be converted into percentage by multiplying probability by 100. The percentage is 0.0918 × 100 = 9.18%. We can now say that 9.18% cases will be above IQ 120.

Example 2: The neuroticism personality variable is normally distributed with the mean = 85 and SD = 20 for a data of 1000 individuals. Find out the percentage of people who have score less than 75. How many individuals have a score between 70 and 90?

To find percentage of people having score below 75, we need to find *Z* score of 75 for mean of 85 and SD of 20. $Z_{(75)} = \frac{(75-85)}{20} = \frac{-10}{20} = -0.50$. *Z* score is –0.50. Table D1 does not have negative values of *Z*. However, we will make use of useful property of the normal distribution and that is symmetry. The normal distribution is identical on both sides. So knowing one side is enough to know other. Hence, less than 75 actually means an area beyond 75 till negative infinity. So we still need to find the area beyond *Z*. The area beyond *Z* for *Z* score 0.5 (sign of *Z* will not make a difference) is 0.3085. The percentage is 0.3085 × 100 = 30.85% individuals will

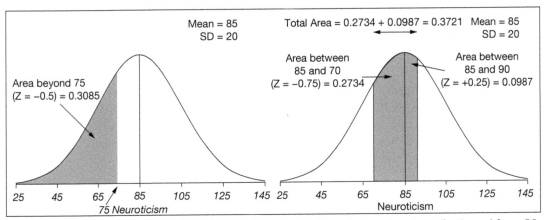

Figure 4.2. *Graphical Illustration of Example 2: Proportion of Cases in a Distribution with μ=80, and σ=25*

have Z score beyond -0.50. That means 30.85% out of 1000 individuals is 308.50 ($\approx$309), and individuals will have a score below 75.

The second part requires finding the individuals having a score between 70 and 90. This can be done in many ways. The mean is 85. One way is to find out the area between mean and 70 and the area between mean and 90. Then we can do addition of these areas. The second way is to find the area beyond 70 and the area beyond 90 and add them up. The entire area is 1. So subtract this from 1 and remaining is area between 70 and 90. Let us do it the first way:

$Z_{(70)}$ is $Z_{(70)} = \dfrac{(70-85)}{20} = \dfrac{-15}{20} = 0.75$. The area between mean and Z for $Z=0.75$ is 0.2734. $Z_{(90)}$

is $Z_{(90)} = \dfrac{(90-85)}{20} = \dfrac{+5}{20} = +0.25$. The area between mean and Z for $Z=0.25$ is 0.0987. The total area between 70 and 90 is $0.2734+0.0987=0.3721$. The percentage is $0.3721 \times 100 = 37.21\%$ and this implies that out of 1000 individuals, 372.1 ($\approx$372) have a score between 70 and 90.

4.3.4 Other Useful Conversions: Percentile, *T*-score, IQ

We have learned to use Z scores for knowing the area under the normal distribution. There are other useful indices in psychology, which can be obtained by converting raw scores into desired scores like IQ, or *T*-score or percentile, and so on.

```
# R code 4.1. Computing area under normal curve
>m<-85              # mean of distribution
>s<-20              # sd of distribution
>z<-(75-m)/s        # compute Z
>z                  # print Z
>1-pnorm(z)         # area beyond Z
>pnorm(z)           # area between mean and Z

# R code 4.2: Converting data into Percentile Rank by using normal
distribution
>x<-c(20, 21, 24, 24, 26, 28, 29, 29, 30, 32, 33, 36, 37, 40) # values of X
>z<-(x-mean(x))/sd(x)                  # z-score of each x
>pnorm(z)*100                          # get the are between mean and Z
>pr<- round(pnorm(z)*100)              # pr for each of value of x
```

The *T*-score is (NOT *t*-distribution or *t*-test statistics) a conversion of normally distributed scores to a distribution with a mean = 50 and SD = 10. The score that is normally distributed can be converted into *T*-score. The conversion is done by the following formula given below.

$$T\text{-score} = 10 \times (Z) + 50$$

From Example 2, the mean for neuroticism was 85 and SD was 20 for a data of 1000 individuals. Let us find out *T*-score for 75. First we need to obtain *Z* for 75, which is −0.5. Now convert it into *T*-score.

$$T\text{-score} = 10 \times (Z) + 50$$

$$T\text{-score} = 10 \times (-0.5) + 50$$

$$T\text{-score} = -5 + 50 = 45$$

T-score for the score 75 is 45. Some of the important psychological tests employ *T*-scores in their scoring scheme. The NEO-PI-3 is a good example to cite.

The distribution of intelligence quotient is generally normal. The IQ generally has a mean of 100 and SD is 15 (or 16). The intelligence test provides you a raw score from a representative population. The score is converted into IQ by using the mean and SD of a normative sample. An individual has a raw score of 37 on IQ test which has mean = 30 and SD = 5. Then IQ can be obtained by

$$IQ = 15 \times (Z) + 100$$

The *Z* for 37 is $(37 - 30)/5 = 7/5 = 1.4$

$$IQ = 15 \times (1.4) + 100 = 121$$

The IQ of an individual on this IQ test is 121. Now, if you look at the area under the normal distribution table, then *Z* can be converted into percentage. The area below *Z* is 0.919, which means approximately 92% scores are below the score of 121. Hence the IQ of 121 can be considered as 92nd percentile.

4.4 TESTING NORMALITY

For many reasons, the normal distribution has been an essential point of discussion in statistics. Normality is a routine assumption made in the development and use of many statistical tests. Knowing whether the collected data comes from a population that is normally distributed seems an important question for researchers. The choice of further statistical procedure is, to some extent, contingent on the results of testing for normality. Normality (or deviation from normality) can have an impact on the inferential procedures and properties of estimators used in the statistical analysis. The magnitude of impact may vary depending on the statistical procedure, parameter estimated, sample size, degree of deviation, kind of deviation, and so on. Statistical applications for psychology are known to make extensive use of procedures based on normal distribution, like *t*-test, ANOVA, tests for regression coefficient, and so on. This section shall introduce some of the commonly used statistical procedures to test normality. However, some researchers have proposed procedures that are not based on the assumption of normality (e.g., Wilcox, 2003, applying contemporary statistical techniques) with an argument that the assumption of normality is difficult to be followed.

Many statistical procedures are available to test normality. In fact, Thode (2002) considered more than 40 procedures to test normality and argued that this list is not exhaustive. The testing of normality is primarily carried out in two ways: first, statistical tests, and second, graphical methods. The statistical tests are procedures that generally test hypothesis that the sample comes from a population that is normally distributed. However, different tests make use of different logics. The graphical methods make use of the properties of the normal distribution to plot the data. The decision rule is subjective judgments about the normality. Neither of the procedures is recommended over another. Researchers need to combine the insights obtained from both procedures and make decisions.

4.4.1 Statistical Tests for Univariate Normality

Many statistical procedures are available to test the null hypothesis that the population represented by the data is normally distributed. For example, quite a few tests utilize sample moment skewness, and kurtosis. The commonly used and reported procedures are discussed here. The tests are presented in three groups: first, the statistical test that make use of moments, second, the tests that are based on goodness-of-fit criterion. In addition, related popular procedures are also described. Some of the tests described in this section are strictly not goodness-of-fit tests. Third, other test procedures that one needs to be aware of. The R codes associated with the tests are also shown.

4.4.1.1 Tests Using Moments

Karl Pearson initiated an idea of using moments for testing normality. Pearson (1930), Fisher (1930), Hsu and Lawley (1939), and Geary and Worlledge (1947) developed a body of knowledge for normally distributed samples for normal moments going up to the seventh moment of the population kurtosis. The moments that are most useful are the estimates of the third and fourth standardized moments in testing for normality.

Population and Sample Moments

The first central moment of a probability density function $f(x)$ is **mean** which is defined as

$$\mu = \mu_1 = \int_{-\infty}^{+\infty} x f(x) dx$$

The second central moment of a probability density function $f(x)$ is **variance** which is defined as

$$\sigma^2 = \mu_2 = \int_{-\infty}^{+\infty} (x - \mu)^2 f(x) dx$$

The square root of second moment is SD. Higher central moment of a probability density function $f(x)$ are defined as

$$\sigma^k = \mu_k = \int_{-\infty}^{+\infty} (x - \mu)^k f(x) dx$$

where, k is a integer greater than 1. The first and second central moments are not too useful to determine normality. However, the central moments are zero for odd values of k for $k > 2$. Hence, standardized moments are useful. The third standardized moment is skewness and fourth standardized moment is kurtosis.

   In the sample, the kth sample moment for a random variable x is defined as

$$m_k = \frac{\sum_{i=1}^{n}(x_i - \bar{x})^k}{n}$$

where, n is number of observation and x_i is ith observation.

Skewness Test

The skewness can be obtained by $g_1 = m_3 / m_2^{3/2}$. When $g_1 > 0$ then the data are skewed to the right and if $g_1 < 0$ then data are skewed to left (at times a notation $\sqrt{b_1}$ is also used for similar expression). It is known that the skewness of the normal distribution is zero. Under the null hypothesis, g_1 is asymptotically normal with mean=0 and variance=6/n. Now it is possible to compute the probability of rejecting this hypothesis. That is a null hypothesis that g_1 is far from zero is tested. Let us use Shapiro (1980) data set of 51 observations, which is given in R code 4.3.

```
#R Code 4.3. Skewness and skewness test
x <- c(3.67, 4.09, 3.73, 1.32, 3.43, 3.01, 2.57, 2.40, 2.29, 3.33, 1.83,
3.55, 1.87, 3.12, 1.84, 1.71, 2.69, 4.83, 2.51, 3.54, 3.93, 2.69, 1.95,
2.94, 1.92, 4.96, 2.37, 2.80, 3.07, 1.62, 2.71, 4.08, 3.20, 2.37, 2.03,
4.75, 4.04, 1.55, 2.44, 2.20, 2.10, 1.77, 2.57, 2.96, 3.77, 3.58, 2.09,
2.28, 2.49, 3.65, 2.63)              # Shapiro (1980) data.
m3<-(sum((x-mean(x))^3))/length(x)   # calculating third moment
m2<-(sum((x-mean(x))^2))/length(x)   # calculating second moment-variance
sk<- m3/(m2^(3/2))                   # calculating skewness
sk                                   # print value of sk (skewness)
library(moments)                     # call package 'moments' from
                                       library

skewness(x)                          # skewness value
agostino.test(x)                     # D'Agostino skewness test
```

The variance can be given as $\text{var}(g_1) = \dfrac{6(n-2)}{(n+1)(n+3)}$. In case of Shapiro (1980), data $\text{var}(g_1) = \dfrac{6(51-2)}{(51+1)(51+3)} = 0.1047$. The exact fourth moment for the distribution of g_1 is $\beta_2(g_1) = 3 + \dfrac{36(n-7)(n^2+2n-5)}{(n-2)(n+5)(n+7)(n+9)}$. D'Agostino (1970) obtains normal transformation of g_1 when sample size is greater than eight, probabilities for which can be evaluated used Z distribution. If

$$Y = g_1 \sqrt{\frac{(n+1)(n+3)}{6(n-2)}} \text{ and } B_2 = \frac{3(n^2+27n-70)(n+1)(n+3)}{(n-2)(n+5)(n+7)(n+9)}$$

then $Z(g_1)$ can be obtained by

$$Z = \delta \log(Y/a + \sqrt{(Y/a)^2 + 1}$$

where, a and d can be defined by

$$W = \sqrt{-1 + \sqrt{2(B_2 - 1)}} \quad \delta = 1/\sqrt{\log(W)} \quad a = \sqrt{2/(W^2-1)}$$

Example: the Shapiro data of 51 observations yields D'Agostino skewness test statistics $Z = 1.069$. The probability associated with this Z value is 0.2847, which indicates that the null hypothesis that skewness=0 cannot be refuted. Other values for same example are as follows: $Y = 1.6122$; $B_2 = 3.447$; $W = 1.101$; $d = 4.889$; $a = 3.68$; and $Z = 1.069$. This indicates that this value of skewness comes from a population that has skewness=0.

The Kurtosis Test

The fourth moment test for testing symmetric departures from normality is calculated by $b_2 = m_4 / m_2^{4/2}$. This is one of the popular tests of normality. Pearson (1935) and Geary

(1947) noted that it is most powerful test of symmetric non-normality. The kurtosis is $b_2 = m_4 / m_2^{4/2} = 1.5667 / 0.781^{4/2} = 2.568$. The table of kurtosis tells us that the upper and lower 2.5 percentiles for normal data with sample size of 51 are 4.34 and 2.08 and the obtained value lies between them. Hence, we fail to reject the hypothesis of normality based on the symmetric departure. The b_2 is asymptotically normal with mean 3 and variance 24/n. The mean of b_2 is $\mu(b_2) = \dfrac{3(n-1)}{(n+1)}$ and variance is $\text{var}(b_2) = \dfrac{24n(n-2)(n-3)}{(n+1)^2(n+3)(n+5)}$. D'Agostino and Pearson (1973) offered a transformation of g_2 to normality. For a sample greater than 20, Anscombe and Glynn (1983) used first three moments of b_2 obtained, adequately approximated by D'Agostino and Pearson (1973) results with simpler transformation to normality. The test statistics for Anscombe–Glynn test of Kurtosis is Z, which is obtained by

$$Z = \frac{\left(\left(1-\dfrac{2}{9A}\right) - \left[\dfrac{1-2A}{1+x\sqrt{\{2/(A-4)\}}}\right]^{1/3}\right)}{\sqrt{2/(9A)}}$$

where, $A = 6 + \dfrac{8}{\sqrt{\beta_1 b_2}}\left(\dfrac{2}{\sqrt{\beta_1 b_2}} + \sqrt{1+4/(\beta_1 b_2)}\right)$ and $x = \dfrac{b_2 - \mu(b_2)}{\sigma(b_2)}$

$\sqrt{\beta_1}(b_2)$ is third moment of b_2 which can be obtained by

$$\sqrt{\beta_1}(b_2) = \frac{E[b_2 - E(b_2)]^3}{[\text{var}(b_2)]^{3/2}} = \frac{6(n^2-5n+2)}{(n+7)(n+9)}\sqrt{\left[\frac{6(n+3)(n+5)}{n(n-2)(n-3)}\right]}$$

#R Code 4.4. Kurtosis and Anscombe–Glynn kurtosis test
```
> m4<-(sum((x-mean(x))^4))/length(x)   # calculating fourth moment
> m2<-(sum((x-mean(x))^2))/length(x)   # calculating second
                                         moment-variance
> kurt <- m4/(m2^(4/2))                # calculating Kurtosis
> kurt                                 # print value of kurtosis
                                         (kurtosis)
> library(moments)                     # call package 'moments' from
                                         library
> kurtosis(x)                          # kurtosis value
> anscombe.test(x)                     # Anscombe-Glynn kurtosis test
```

Example: The Shapiro data of 51 observations yields $Z=-0.4387$. The p-value associated with this Z is 0.6609. Hence, we cannot refute the null hypothesis of Anscombe–Glynn test that kurtosis is from the normal distribution, that is, value of kurtosis is 3. For information, other values are as follows: kurtosis=2.568; mean of b_2=2.885; variance of (b_2)=0.352; the third moment of $b_2 = \sqrt{\beta_1}(b_2) = 1.5745$; $A=20.67$; standardized b_2 statistics=$x=-0.533$; and the test statistics for Anscombe–Glynn test of Kurtosis is $Z=-0.43867$.

ABSOLUTE MOMENT TEST: GEARY'S TEST

Geary (1935) proposed "a test" that could yield small sample properties as an alternative to b_2 test. The test statistics a is ratio of mean deviation to SD.

$$a = \frac{\sum_{i=1}^{n} |x_i - \bar{x}|}{n\sqrt{m_2}}$$

Z transformation for this test has been provided by D'Agostino (1970). The statistics a has an asymptotic mean $= 0.7979$ and $SD = 0.2123 / \sqrt{n}$ which is used for transformation. Z transformation useful for small samples is given below:

$$Z = \frac{\sqrt{n}(a - 0.7979)}{0.2123}$$

```
#R code 4.5. Geary Test for Normality
>library(fmsb)      # call package fmsb. If not available, the install
> geary.test(x)     # Geary test
```

Z is interrelated by using the standard normal distribution. For the Shapiro data, the value of $a = 0.832$ and $Z = 1.147$. The left-tailed p-value $(Z < 1)$ is 0.8743. Hence, we cannot reject the null hypothesis that the data comes from the normal distribution. It is a simple test so you can attempt writing your own R code.

4.4.1.2 Goodness-of-fit Tests

The goodness-of-fit test of normality is one of the most popularly reported tests. They include Kolmogorov–Smirnov test, Shapiro–Wilks test, Jarque–Berra test, Anderson–Darling Test, Cramer–von Mises Test, Kuiper's V test, the χ^2 test, and so on.

Kolmogorov–Smirnov test, Lilliefors test, Anderson–Darling test, Cramer–von Mises tests, and Kuiper's V test are the tests based on empirical distribution function (EDF).

EDF tests are goodness-of-fit tests, which are based on a comparison of the empirical and hypothetical distribution functions. Generally, the hypothesized theoretical distribution (in our case normal distribution) is expressed as $F_0(X)$. The population distribution is represented as $F(X)$ from where the sample is obtained. The **null hypothesis** is H_0: $F(X) = F_0(X)$ which means that the population distribution $F(X)$ from where we have obtained our sample is following a specific theoretical distribution $F_0(X)$. The alternative hypothesis is H_0: $F(X) \neq F_0(X)$ for at least one value of X. The EFD is a simple concept. The EDF for a sample is $F_n(x)$ which is defined in the following manner:

$$F_n(x) = \begin{cases} 0 & x < x_1 \\ i/n & x_i \leq x < x_{(i+1)} \\ 1 & x_n \leq x \end{cases}$$

To state it simply, if no two observations are equal, the EDF is a "step" function that jumps $1/n$ in height at each observation x_k. Take following data: 0, 1, 2, 3, 3, 5, 6, 7, 8, 9. We calculate $F_n(x)$ in the following way: the sample size (n) is 10. $F_n(x) = 0$ for $x < 0$, $F_n(x) = 1/10$ for $0 \leq x < 1$ and $F_n(x) = 1/10$ for $1 \leq x < 2$. Now since there are two values of 3, we need to jump $2/10$ at $x = 3$. Hence, we need to add $F_n(x) = 1/10 + 1/10 = 2/10$ for $3 \leq x < 5$. Similarly, $F_n(x)$ value for the remaining each value of x is going to be $1/10$. The cumulative probabilities are as shown in Table 4.2.

Table 4.2. *Obtaining Cumulative Probabilities for X*

X	0	1	2	3	3	5	6	7	8	9
$P(x<x)$	0.1	0.1	0.1	0.2		0.1	0.1	0.1	0.1	0.1
$F_n(x)$	0.1	0.2	0.3	0.5		0.6	0.7	0.8	0.9	1

Kolmogorov–Smirnov Test

The Kolmogorov–Smirnov test (K–S test) is useful for testing continuous distributions. Normal is one of the continuous distributions that can be tested using K–S test. Kolmogorov (1933) developed one-sample test and Smirnov (1939) independently developed two-sample procedure identical to Kolmogorov's procedure. Hence, the test is popularly called Kolmogorov–Smirnov test. The hypothesis tested is whether the sample of size n is from given theoretical, empirical or probability distribution. Generally, a researcher is interested in retaining the null hypothesis. Though, the K–S test is a non-parametric test, it can be carried out only on **continuous variable**. It makes use of EDF, which is order statistics. **Null hypothesis** for the test is H_0: $F(X) = F_0(X)$ for all values of X and **alternative hypothesis** is H_0:

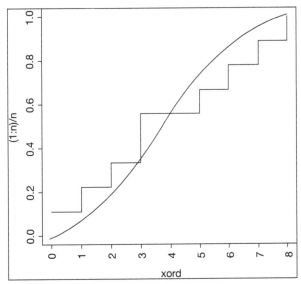

Figure 4.3. *Plot of ECDF for Above Data: The Steps are Data Based whereas Curve Is a Theoretical*

$F(X) \neq F_0(X)$ for at least one value of X. Here, $F(X)$ is the population distribution from where the present sample is obtained and $F_0(X)$ is the hypothesized theoretical or empirical distribution (e.g., normal distribution). In Figure 4.3, you can see that vertical distance between sample cumulative probability distribution and hypothesized cumulative probability distribution can be obtained for each value of X. The test statistics D_n is the largest value for the vertical distance. If the value is larger than the value expected by chance, then the null hypothesis is rejected. This value could be positive or negative depending upon the direction of the difference, and hence it is a two-tailed hypothesis. The test statistics can be obtained by using following formula:

$$D_n = \sup_x [|F_n(X) - F_0(X)|]$$

where D_n is the test statistics, $\sup_x$ is the supremum of x (upper-bound or maximum value of all pairwise differences for $[|F_n(X) - F_0(X)|]$. $F_n(X)$ is EDF based on sample values of X, and $F_0(X)$ as stated earlier, is the hypothesized distribution function (e.g., normal distribution). The mean and SD for the theoretical distribution need to be specified.

Example 1: Let us solve a small sample example with $n=5$. The values of x are 1, 2, 3, 4, 5. (In reality, we should not test normality of such a small sample due to low power, this example is just for illustrative purpose). Since, parameters need to be specified for K–S test, we test the null hypothesis that the population from where this sample is obtained follows normal distribution with $\mu=3$ and $\sigma=1$. The mean and SD of the theoretical distribution need to be specified for K–S test. Following steps also show how to compute test statistics for K–S test.

Step 1: Arrange X score as per order (smallest to largest or largest to smallest) (Column A)

Step 2: Compute $Z=(x-\mu)/\sigma$ for each value of X for a specific mean and SD ($\mu=3$ and $\sigma=1$ in our case), for example, $(1-3)/1=-2$. (Column B)

Step 3: Find $p(\mu$ to $x)$ from the normal distribution table. (Column C)

Step 4: Obtain $F_0(X)$ from p. If Z is negative then subtract p from 0.5 (e.g., $0.5 - 0.4772 = 0.0228$) and if Z is positive then add 0.5 into p (e.g., for $Z = 1$, $F_0(X) = 0.5 + 0.3412 = 0.8413$). (Column D)

Step 5: $S(X_i)$ is obtained by cumulative proportions. (Column E)

Step 6: Obtain absolute (ignoring sign) difference between Column E and Column D. For example, $0.2 - 0.0228 = 0.1772$. The largest value of this difference is labeled as M. So $M = 0.2413$. (Column F)

Step 7: This is an absolute difference between $S(X_i)$ (Column E) and $F_0(X)$ (Column D) but the value for $S(X_i)$ should be from the preceding row for each value of $F_0(X)$. For the first row of $F_0(X)$, there is no preceding row in $S(X_i)$ hence we take the value to be zero for $S(X_i)$. To avoid complication, each computation is shown in the table. The largest value is called as M'. The $M' = 0.2413$. (Column G)

Step 8: Test statistics for K–S test (D_n) is a larger value between M and M'. In this example, since both are identical (though it is less likely to happen in reality), the test statistics value $D_n = 0.2413$.

Step 9: Appendix C-8 provides significance values for $n < 40$. For $n = 5$, two-tailed values are D_n at $p = 0.05$ is 0.563 and D_n at $p = 0.01$ is 0.669. The obtained value of D_n is smaller than D_n at $p = 0.05$, hence we retain the null hypothesis that the population from which the sample is obtained follows the normal distribution with mean = 3 and SD = 1.

It is useful to know that for **large samples** $(n > 40)$ D_n at $p = 0.05$ can be obtained by $1.36 \times \sqrt{n}$ and D_n at $p = 0.01$ can be obtained by $1.63 \times \sqrt{n}$.

```
#R code 4.6. One-sample K-S test in R (Example 1)
x<- c(1,2,3,4,5)                 # enter data of x
ks.test (x, pnorm, 3, 1)   # ks.test function. Mean and SD also specified
```

```
#you can write your own function
n<- length(x)                    # sample size, n, is created as object
p <- pnorm((x-3)/1)              # F₀(X) is obtained
M <- max(seq(1:n)/n-p)           # compute M
Mpr <- max(p-(seq(1:n)-1)/n)     # compute M'
KS <- max(M, Mpr)                # KS is test statistics for K-S test
```

```
# R code 4.7: KS test with output (Example 2)
> ks.test(x, "pnorm", 3, 1)
    One-sample Kolmogorov-Smirnov test
data:  x
D=0.1631, p-value=0.1325
alternative hypothesis: two-sided
```

Example 2: The K–S normality test for the Shapiro data (1980) can be done in R. The null hypothesis tested is as follows: the population represented by a sample follows normal distribution with mean 3 and SD 1.

The K–S statistics value (called D in R output) of 0.1631 has exact probability of 0.1325 (R Code 4.7). This p-value is greater than 0.05 hence we retain the null hypothesis (Table 4.3).

Lilliefors Test: Kolmogorov–Smirnov One-sample Test when μ and σ are Unknown

Now, we know that the location and scale parameters for the normal distribution, mean (μ) and SD (σ) respectively, need to be specified for null hypothesis of Kolmogorov–Smirnov test. In the above example, we have specified it to be $\mu = 3$ and $\sigma = 1$. If the parameters are unknown, then one-sample K–S test cannot be performed. Lilliefors (1967) developed a variation in K–S test, which is known as Lilliefors test. Lilliefors showed that estimates of μ and σ can be used. The estimate of μ is sample mean $(\bar{x})$ and estimate of σ is $SDs_x = \sqrt{\Sigma(x - \bar{x})^2 / n - 1}$. The null

Table 4.3. *Computation of K–S Test Statistics*

A	B	C	D	E	F	G
X	Z	$p(\mu$ to $x)$	$F_0(X)=p\pm0.5$	$S(X_i)$	$S(X_i)-F_0(X_i)$	$S(X_{i-1})-F_0(X_i)$
1	−2	0.4772	0.0228	1/5=0.2	0.1772	0−0.0228=0.0228
2	−1	0.3412	0.1587	2/5=0.4	0.2413	0.2−0.1587=0.0413
3	0	0	0.5	3/5=0.6	0.1	0.4−0.5=0.1
4	1	0.3412	0.8413	4/5=0.8	0.0413	0.6−0.8413=0.2413
5	2	0.4772	0.9772	5/5=1	0.0228	0.8−0.9772=0.1772

and the alternate remain the same. The logic and calculation of D_n for Lilliefors test remains the same. Therefore, detailed example is avoided. The K–S test *p*-values cannot be used for Lilliefors test. The distribution and *p*-values given by Lilliefors are inaccurate and hence Dallal and Wilkinson (1986) modified the *p*-value calculation. However, researchers also suggest the use of Monte–Carlo methods for computing *p*-value.

For Example 1, sample mean is 3 and s_x is 1.58. $D_n=0.1366$. Dallal–Wilkinson *p*-values is 0.9912.

For example 2, the mean is 2.84 and s_x is .893. $D_n=.10692$. Dallal–Wilkinson *p*-values is .1325. In both examples, since *p*-value is greater than 0.05, we accept the null that sample comes from the population that follows the normal distribution. Lilliefors test is known to perform worse than many other EDF tests.

#R code 4.8. Lilliefors Test

```
> library(nortest)    # call package nortest. If not available, then
                        install
> lillie.test (x)     # Lilliefors Test of example 1
> Lillie.test(data)   # Lilliefors test for Shapiro (1980) data
> ks.test(data, "pnorm", mean(data), sd(data)) # Lilliefors test with
ks.test function. the Dn is correct the p-value is incorrect
```

Kuiper's V Test

While discussing K–S test, we have computed *M* and *M'*. The K–S test chooses the maximum form them. Kuiper (1960) suggested an alternative of combining both rather than choosing one of them. His test statistics, *V*, is obtained by

$$V = M + M'$$

The modification of this statistics *V** has a stable distribution across sample sizes (Stephens, 1974).

$$V^* = \left(\sqrt{n} + 0.05 + \frac{0.82}{\sqrt{n}}\right)V$$

M and *M'* values are 0.2413 and 0.2413 for example 1. $V=0.2413+0.2413=0.4826$. *V** is 1.28. The significance can be obtained from Stephens (1967).

Anderson–Darling Test (AD Test)

Anderson and Darling (1952) developed a procedure to test whether a data have a specific continuous distribution function (F_x). The AD test does not require parameter specification (values of μ and σ) and their estimators from sample mean and SD can be used. However, the test can be carried out with parameter specifications as well (either or both values of μ and σ are specified). The test statistics for the AD test is A^2.

$$A^2 = -n - s$$

where

$$s = \sum_{i=1}^{n} \frac{2i-1}{n} [\log(p_i) + \log(1 - p_{(n-i+1)})]$$

$p_i = F_0(X)$ is a value already discussed in the K–S test (Column D of example table), n is a sample size, and log is a natural logarithm with base e. The AD test can be performed if the sample size is above 7. The AD test is useful for a distribution with a heavy tail. Stephens (1986) suggested a correction in AD test since it put more weight on tails. The correction formula is as follows:

$$A^{2}* = \left(1 + \frac{0.75}{n} + \frac{2.25}{n^2}\right) A^2$$

$A^{2}*$ is Stephens corrected AD test statistics and A^2 is AD test statistics. The p-value for $A^{2}*$ can be computed differently for different $A^{2}*$ values and are available in Thode's (2002) and Stephens' (1986) studies. Stephens (1974, 1986) noted that the AD test is one of the most powerful statistical procedures for detecting most departures from the normal distribution. This test can be used to test normal, log-normal, Weibull, exponential, and logistic distributions. The AD test for multiple samples (K-sample AD test) is also available, which tests whether several data sets (K-samples) come from same population.

```
# R code 4.9. Anderson-Darling Test
library(nortest)
ad.test(x)              # this function carries out AD test and reports
                          Stephens correction and p-values.
```

You can write your own function of AD test
```
x<-c(1,2,3,4,5,6, 7, 8)                    # n must be greater than 7
n <- length(x)                             # sample size n
z <- (x-mean(x))/sd(x)                     # standard score or z
p <- pnorm(z)                              # F_0(X) =p+-.5
s <- sum(((((2 * seq(1:n) - 1))/n) * (log(p) + log(1-sort(p, decreasing =
TRUE)))))                                  # calculation of s
A <- -n - s                                #AD test statistics
A
```

AD test on Shapiro Data in R
```
ad.test (x)
Anderson-Darling normality test
data: x
A=0.5566, p-value=0.1434
```

Cramér–von Mises Test

Cramér and von Mises first proposed the Cramér–von Mises criterion in 1928. The generalization was later developed by Anderson (1962). The Cramér–von Mises test statistics is W^2 which is obtained as follows:

$$W^2 = \frac{1}{12n} + \sum_{i=1}^{n} \left(p_i - \frac{2i-1}{2n}\right)^2$$

The critical values (*p*-values) differ as the sample sizes differ. Therefore, the modification suggested in the W^2 is generally used.

$$W^{2*} = \left(1 + \frac{0.5}{n}\right) W^2$$

Watson (1961) proposed a distribution on circle for this test. However, the p-value for W^{2*} can be computed differently for different W^{2*} values and are available in the study of Thode (2002). The significant *p*-values (*p*-value smaller than 0.05) reject the null hypothesis that the sample comes from a population that follows the normal distribution. The R code for Cramér–von Mises test is given below.

```
# R code 4.10. Cramér-von Mises test
> library(nortest)        # call package 'nortest'
> cvm.test(x)             # CvM test in R
```

The following tests are those tests that are generally considered as a goodness-of-fit but they are not distance tests or EDF tests.

Jarque–Bera Test (JB Test)

Jarque and Bera (1987) developed this test for testing normality. This test combines information from skewness and kurtosis. The null hypothesis for the *JB* test is a composite hypothesis that skewness is zero and exact kurtosis is also zero (which is equal to kurtosis being 3 by earlier formula).

$$JB = \frac{n}{6}(S^2 + 0.25(K - 3)^2)$$

where *n* is sample size, *S* is sample skewness, and *K* is sample kurtosis.

The chi-square value obtained from JB test asymptotically follows chi-square distribution. The JB test value is always evaluated at two degrees of freedom. The null hypothesis is rejected when the obtained value of JB is greater than the critical chi-square value at two degree of freedom. Hence, JB$\geq$5.99 is significant at $p = 0.05$ and JB$\geq$9.21 is significant at $p = 0.01$.

Initially, Jarqure and Bera (1980) developed this test for testing the normality of regression residuals. Later on Jarque and Bera (1987) developed test for the normality of observations and the normality of regression residuals. It is a popular measure in economic sciences since regression analysis is most utilized statistics in economics. Robert Hall, David Lilien, et al. (1995) suggested modification in JB formula when applied to multiple regression.

$$JB = \frac{n - k}{6}(S^2 + 0.25(K - 3)^2)$$

where *n* is number of observations, and *k* number of regressors.

```
# R code 4.11: Jarque-Bera Test (JB Test)
> library(tseries)               # call tseries package
> jarque.bera.test(x)            # Jarque-Bera test
# The output for JB Test for Shapiro data looks following:
Jarque Bera Test
data: x
X-squared=2.7094, df=2, p-value=0.258
```

The JB statistics is 2.709 and the *p*-value is greater than 0.05. This clearly indicates that the JB test statistics is not rejecting the null hypothesis.

Hence, we accept the null hypothesis that the data comes from a population that has skewness zero and exact kurtosis also zero, implying that the population represented by sample is normally distributed.

Shapiro–Wilks Test

Shapiro–Wilk test tests whether sampled data comes from a normally distributed population. Shapiro and Wilk (1965) proposed this test. The test statistics is referred to as W. It is obtained by using the following formula:

$$W = \frac{\left(\sum_{i=1}^{n} a_i x_i\right)^2}{\sum_{i=1}^{n} (x - \bar{x})^2}$$

where W is a Shapiro–Wilk statistics, x_i are sampled values from smaller to greater, a_i is a constant generated using mean, variance and covariance of ordered statistics following normal distribution. To compute the values of a (ranging from a_1 to a_n)

$a_1 \ldots a_n = \dfrac{m^T V^{-1}}{(m^T V^{-1} V^{-1} m)^{1/2}}$ is required where, $m = (m_1, \ldots, m_n)^T$ and $m_1, \ldots, m_n$ are expected values

of standard normal order statistics for a sample, and V is the covariance matrix of that order statistics. The null hypothesis is the data that comes from a population that is normally distributed. The larger and closer to 1 (maximum value of W) indicates normality and smaller values indicate non-normality. The smallest possible value of W is $na_1^2 / (n-1)$. If the p-value is smaller than the critical value (that is 0.05) then W is significant and the null hypothesis that data comes from a normally distributed population is rejected. If the p-value is larger than 0.05, then W is insignificant and the null hypothesis that the data comes from a normally distributed population is retained. Following R codes can be used to carry out the Shapiro–Wilk test in R.

One of the noted difficulties with the Shapiro–Wilk test is that V can be exactly computed up to sample size 20 and for sample size 20 to 50, Shapiro–Wilk have given the estimates of a_i values. Hence, Royston (1982) proposed a transformation of W to normality for sample sizes 7 to 2000 and it is commonly used. Razali and Wah (2011) compared the power of four formal tests of normality and concluded that Shapiro-Wilk is most powerful test followed by AD test and KS test.

```
# R code 4.12: Shapiro-Wilk test
> shapiro.test(x)          # Shapiro-Wilk test function
#output for Shapiro data
Shapiro-Wilk normality test
data: x
W=0.9621, p-value=0.102
```

$W = 0.9621$ has a p-value 0.102 which is >0.05 (critical value). Hence, we cannot reject the null hypothesis that the data comes from a population that is normally distributed.

The D'Agostino–Pearson Test (D'Agostino K² test)

D'Agostino and Pearson (1973) developed the D'Agostino–Pearson test of normality. This test is considered as an effective procedure for assessing goodness-of-fit for a normal distribution. It is a particularly better procedure than chi-square test and K–S test.

$$\chi^2 = Z_{g1}^2 + Z_{g2}^2$$

This test value is always evaluated at two degrees of freedom. The computation of Z associated with skewness and kurtosis is provided in an earlier section. The null hypothesis is rejected when the obtained value of JB is greater than the critical chi-square value at two degree of freedom ($\chi^2 = 5.99$, p=0.05; $\chi^2 = 9.21$, p=0.01). At times a notation K^2 is also used and the test is called as D'Agostino K^2 test (D'Agostino, Belanger, & D'Agostino, 1990). $\chi^2 = 2.8282$ for Shapiro (1980) data, which will retain the null hypothesis.

D'Agostino, Belanger and D'Agostino, (1990) argued that popular tests like Kolmogorov–Smirnov or chi-squared goodness-of-fit tests have low power and they should not be seriously considered for testing normality. Thode (2002) suggested that "[i]n general, the performance of moment tests and the Wilk–Shapiro test is so impressive that we recommend their use in everyday practice" (p. 2).

4.4.1.3 Other Tests for Normality

This section will briefly outline the procedures for testing normality that have not been discussed so far. The detailed computation or example is availed. The purpose is to just create awareness about these tests.

Likelihood Ratio Test

Likelihood ratio (LR) tests are the tests that are derived for a specific alternative against a null distribution. The parameters may or may not be specified. The LR test is a ratio of maximum likelihood (ML) function for alternative to ML function for normality (L_1/L_0). L_0 is likelihood for normal whereas L_1 is the likelihood for the alternative distribution. Maximum value of L with respect to unknown parameters is calculated. For computation ease, log of $L = l$ is used. ML estimates are obtained. There will be as many LR tests as there are alternatives.

D'Agostino's D

The D statistic was given by D'Agostino (1971) as an extension of the Wilk–Shapiro test when samples are moderate and large. D'Agostino later on developed a small sample version as well. Locke and Spurrier (1977) argue that when alternatives have considerable asymmetry, the D appears most powerful as a directional test for detecting heavy-tailed alternatives.

```
# R code 4.13: The D'Agostino-Pearson Test
> library(fBasics)
> dagoTest(x)
```

Oja's Test

H. Oja (1981) proposed two statistics for testing normality that are scale and location free. No much information on small samples is available for this test.

Lin and Mudholkar's Test

Lin and Mudholkar (1980) developed a test that is based on interesting aspect of a normal distribution. The mean and variance of normal distribution are independent.

4.4.2 Graphical Methods for Testing Normality

Graphical methods have an important place in statistics. Most statistical methods have a graphical representation. Chambers, Cleveland, Kleiner and Tukey (1983) pertinently pointed out that, "Graphical methods provide powerful diagnostic tools for confirming assumptions, or, when the assumptions are not met, for suggesting corrective actions." John Tukey is a supporter for using graphical displays and specifically argued that graphical methods are a "useful starting point for assessing the normality of data" (Tukey, 1977).

Raw data plotting methods (histogram, stem-and-leaf plot, boxplots or box-and-whisker plots), probability plotting methods (P–P plot, Q–Q plot), detrended probability plots (detrended Q–Q plot), and empirical cumulative distribution function (ECDF) plots are also commonly used for testing normality. This section emphasizes box-and-whisker plot, Q–Q plot, and detrended Q–Q plot as graphical methods of testing normality. Over and above normality testing, it is generally recommended that one should use graphical methods for inspecting data.

4.4.2.1 Plotting Raw Data

Stem-and-leaf plots (Tukey, 1977) provide information that histograms provide; and further provide additional level of details for inspection of data. Like histograms, they display the frequency of observations within bins. In addition, they also show the data values. The median, other percentiles, clustering of values, and ties can be identified. We have learned how to plot the stem-and-leaf plot in Chapter 3. Useful

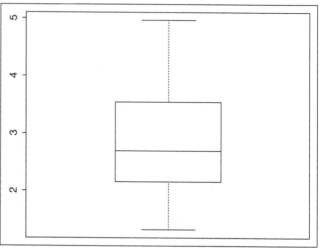

Figure 4.4. *Box-and-whisker Plot of the Shapiro (1980) Data*

indicators for evaluating normality are number of peaks, shape (symmetry–skewness), center, and spread. A symmetric, unimodal (single peak), bell-shaped distribution is an indicator of normality.

Box-and-whisker plot provides less detailed information as compared to histogram or stem-and-leaf plot. Nevertheless, it provides important information about spread and symmetry of the data set and more clearly detect outliers in data (Figure 4.4).

The bottom and top of the box is always first and third quartile which contain 75% of the observations. The horizontal bar inside the box indicates location of the median. The whiskers (lines outside the box) extend to the observation in each tail of the data which is the furthest from the fourths but less than or equal to 1.5 times the fourth spread (This is Tukey's specification which is popularly used. However, there are other specifications as well). The "outliers" are plotted as individual points. Symmetry (or skewness) can be determined by location of the median within box and length of whiskers on both sides. At times, 2, 9, 91, and 98 percentiles are used as additional points (in addition to 50, 25, and 75) to examine symmetry of whiskers.

4.4.2.2 Plotting Probability

Though P–P plot are useful in understanding normality, Q–Q plot are more popularly used. The Q–Q plots are plots of sample order statistics against expected quantiles of the standard normal distribution. The logic of plotting them together is simple: if the observed data is from a normal distribution, then the plot will be linear except for some variations due to sampling variation. If the plot is linear then it is an evidence for normality. To plot the Q–Q plot, observations are plotted from smallest to largest. The common positions for plotting Q–Q plot are $p_i = (i - 0.5)/n$ and $p_i = i/(n + 1)$. Generally, $p_i = i/n$ is not used, because the largest value cannot be used in the plot. A normal Q–Q plot of a normal distribution is typically symmetric and linear in the center of the data. Probability plot is not a formal testing procedure but is primarily a judgmental procedure. Following plots show variations in data and corresponding Q–Q plots. These data are randomly generated in R. Figure 4.5(A) is the Q–Q plot for normally distributed data. You can see that the plot is linear except for a small exception. The straight line drawn inside the plot is the theoretically expected line. The data (empty dots) should be around the line. Small random departures from line are not a problem. You will also realize that a histogram is not a good indicator of normality. Figure 4.5(B) is a Q–Q plot of positively skewed data. The histogram shows the same. The Q–Q plot moves in an upward direction as it moves away from the center. Figure 4.5(C) is negatively skewed data. The Q–Q plot moves in

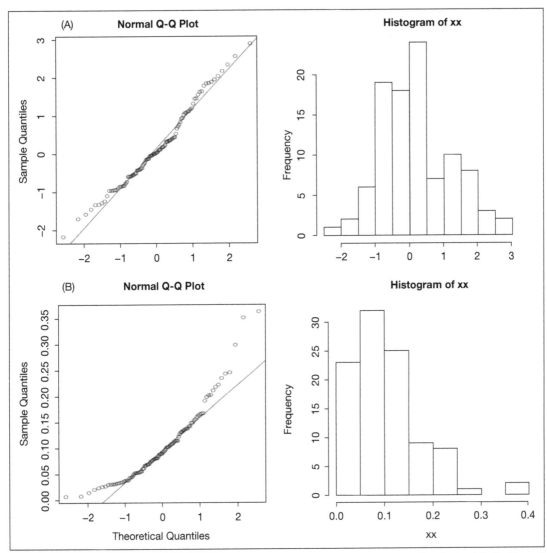

Figure 4.5. *(A) The Q–Q Plot for Normally Distributed Data; (B) The Q–Q Plot for Positively Skewed Data; (C) The Q–Q Plot for Negatively Skewed Data; (D) Normally Distributed Data with a Single Outlier*

a downward direction as it moves away from the center. Figure 4.5(D) is a normally distributed data with a single outlier (extreme score) value. The outlier value is shown as dark black circle for ease of recognition. You will also realize that judgment of outlier is better with Q–Q plot and boxplot. Similarly, judgment of normality is better possible with Q–Q plot, which should be preferred over a histogram. Normality need not be always ascertained by box-and-whisker plot because they may be similar for symmetric distributions (e.g., uniform and normal).

D'Agostino (1986) noted that, though graphical methods are valuable for the identification of distributional characteristics, probability plots "can be sensitive to random occurrences in the data and sole reliance on them can lead to spurious conclusions." Therefore, it is also necessary to have a combination of methods for detecting normality. The objective methods or statistical methods and graphical methods need to be used together to make the judgment to verify distributional assumptions.

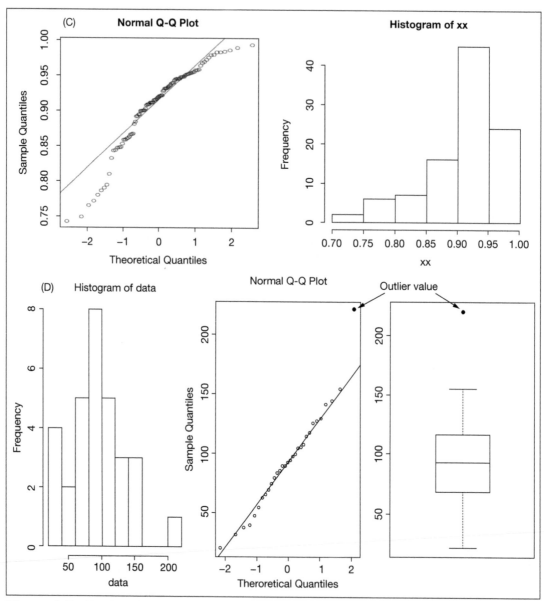

Figure 4.5. *(Continued)*

```
# R code 4.14: Plots to test normality
par(mfrow=c(1,3))   # creates space for three graphs in one, graphical
                      parameter
hist(x, breaks=5)   # plots histogram for x with break of 5
qqnorm(x)           # plot QQ plot for data X
qqline(x)           #plot line in QQ plot
boxplot(x)          # plot box-whisker plot for data x
```

Table 4.4 *Data Transformation: Three Types of Data Transformation*

X	Square Root Transformation	Log Transformation	Inverse Transformation
1	1.00	0.00	1.00
2	1.41	0.30	0.50
3	1.73	0.48	0.33
4	2.00	0.60	0.25
5	2.24	0.70	0.20

4.5 PROBLEMS AND SOLUTIONS ASSOCIATED WITH NON-NORMAL DATA

The distributions normality is an assumption of most parametric statistical procedures. The statistical tests such as t-test, ANOVA, and regression make assumption about normality. Hence, normality is an important issue.

There are specific options that researchers have when they are sure that the distribution is not normal. First alternative is to check for the possibility of transforming the data to a normal distribution. Second alternative is to go for non-parametric statistics that make fewer assumptions and forgo normality. The third alternative is to use computationally intensive procedures like bootstrapping. Chapter 9 and Sections 5.5 and 5.6 of Chapter 5 discuss non-parametric alternatives. The last option is briefly discussed in this section. The bootstrapping procedures are useful but they are beyond the scope of this book.

4.5.1 Data Transformation

The commonly used data transformations methods are square root transformation, log-transformation, and inverse transformation. The square root transformation is to obtain square root of each score. This transformation is useful if the data is slightly skewed. The log transformation is to obtain logarithm of each value. It is useful when the data is moderately skewed. Inverse transformation is to transform data by 1 divided by each score (e.g., 4 is transformed to ¼ = 0.25). Table 4.4 shows each of these transformations.

4.5.2 Non-parametric Statistics

Use of non-parametric statistics or relatively assumption-free tests is another approach of dealing with the non-normal data. The non-parametric statistics usually convert the continuous data into rank–order data. This conversion is obtained by initially arranging data from smallest to largest observations. Then the smallest observation is given rank one, next is given rank two and so on. The ranked data (ordinal data) has a property of order (the consecutive ranks are greater or smaller) but the distance is not equal. The process of ranking leads to the loss of information in the data. However, non-parametric statistics power is reasonably high with moderate to large sample size. The non-parametric procedures are also useful when the sample size is small. Chapter 9 provides a detailed discussion about non-parametric tests.

4.5.3 Computationally Intensive Methods: Bootstrapping

The significant consequence of the non-normal data while using parametric procedures is inferential error. The obtained test statistics is expected to follow some theoretical distribution. Failure to meet assumptions leads to inability of test statistics to follow any theoretical distribution and to judge probability associated with test statistics. For example, while doing t-test, if all assumptions of t-test are followed, then, resulting t-value (test statistics) is following theoretical *t*-distribution at given degrees of freedom (df). As a result, we test the probability of the *t*-value using theoretical *t*-distribution. However, if the distributional assumptions are not followed, then resulting test statistics (*t*-value) will not follow theoretical *t*-distribution. In that case, we cannot know the probability of the obtained *t*-value and cannot test the null hypothesis. Now, is it possible to know the distribution that this *t*-value will follow...? The bootstrapping method empirically creates distribution by using resampling from existing data that the test statistics is likely to follow. The bootstrapping methods will create new statistics (*t** is this example), which will follow the empirically created distribution. The procedures are computationally intensive and require use of computers since resampling are carried out for thousand times. Many good books from Tibshirani and Efron (1998) and Wilcox (2012a) explain use of bootstrapping procedures.

4.5.3.1 Relative Merits and Demerits of these Techniques

The major limitation of data transformation is that the values are changed and difference between true and transformed distribution may lead to inferential error. For example, if time taken to recover from an allergy after consumption of drug follows exponential distribution, which is skewed distribution, the prediction of time taken is possible by using survival model. However, log transformation will make a distribution normal. While predicting the values of transformed distribution, log of each value is required.

4.6 MULTIVARIATE NORMAL DISTRIBUTION: TESTING MULTIVARIATE NORMALITY AND OUTLIERS

Suppose, we have two variables, *X*1 and *X*2 and they are positively associated with each other. We know that each of them is normally distributed. In addition, we can now think of joint distribution of these two variables. This joint distribution is called bivariate normal distribution. For this joint distribution, the mean will be vector of means, and instead of variance, a variance–covariance matrix is used. The bivariate normal distribution will have a rugby-ball like shape. Figures 4.6 and 4.7 show the bivariate normal distribution.

The multivariate normal distribution has certain characteristics that are often used in testing its normality: (a) multivariate normal distribution (MVN) requires that the marginal distributions of each *x* follow univariate normal distribution. This is necessary but not sufficient condition, (b) there is a property called "linearity." It has two implications: first, the correlated variables are strictly linear, and second, any combination of variables is normally distributed, and (c) the last property is the quadratic form of MVN which is used by squared Mahalanobis distance (squared Radii).

There are generally two options available to researchers to test multivariate normality. First approach is to detect multivariate normality by either statistical tests or graphical methods making use of one of the property of MVN. Second, to detect multivariate outliers and dealing with them assures multivariate normality.

In the first approach, there are many tests available. The first line of testing MVN is to test univariate normality. This is also reflected in the first property of MVN. As Gnanadesikan (1977) noted that only in rare cases, multivariate non-normality will not be detected by univariate tests of normality. There are quite a few tests in this approach. The non-normality of univariate marginal distribution is tested by using one of the tests for univariate normality (e.g., Shapiro–Wilk). The limitation of this approach is that the correlation between variables leads to dependency among the test statistics.

4.6.1 Multivariate Outliers and Mahalanobis Distance

The most common approach is to make use of Mahalanobis distance. The squared Mahalanobis distance (squared Radii, Healy, 1968) can be used for determining MVN as well as multivariate outliers.

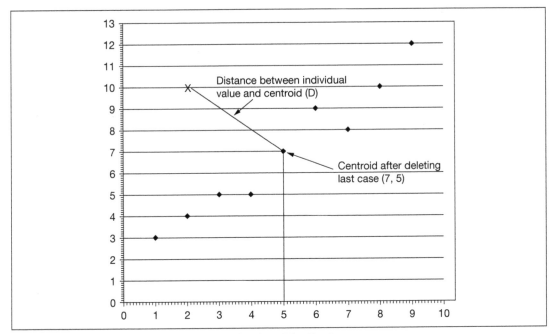

Figure 4.6. *Mahalanobis Distance for Bivariate Distribution*

Table 4.5 *Mahalanobis D^2 Values for Bivariate Distribution*

Age	Motor Skills	Mahalanobis D^2
1	3	2.39
2	4	1.4
3	5	0.69
4	5	0.31
5	7	0.1
6	9	0.64
7	8	0.31
8	10	1.31
9	12	3.04
10	2	7.8
Mean = 5.5	**Mean = 6.5**	

Mahalanobis distance[8] is the distance of an observation from the centroid of remaining observation. Centroid is a point where means of all variables intersect. If MVN is followed, then most observations will be around the centroid. A bivariate scatterplot is the simplest form of multivariate distribution. Each observation is on two variables. Table 4.5 shows two variable

---

[8] Prashant Chandra Malanobis (1893–1972) was a pioneer of statistical research in India. He founded Indian Statistical Institute (ISI) in 1931–1932. The institute was home to many Indian statisticians and students. The Journal *Sankhya* was started which is an important journal in statistics. Now, ISI is premier institute for statistical research in India and since 1959 it is an Institute of National Importance by Act of the Indian Parliament. He also was associated with Jawaharlal Nehru (who later on became first prime minister of Independent India) and obtained initial funding for ISI from him. After independence, he served in Planning Commission of India, and his model, Mahalanobis model was employed in second five-year plan resulting in rapid industrialization and development of infrastructure. He developed life-long friendship with R. A. Fisher and worked together on some committees of planning commission.

data for 10 participants on age and motor skills. The multivariate distribution is shown in Figure 4.6. The centroid is computed after deleting the case for which D is being computed. Then the distance between the case and centroid is squared (D^2). The Mahalanobis distance follows chi-square distribution under MVN. It is usually tested at alpha=0.001 with df being number of variables. The chi-square value at 0.001 for two degrees of freedom is 13.82. Our obtained value for last combination is 7.8 which is still smaller than chi-square value so we shall not declare this as multivariate outlier and treat this distribution as MVN. Please note that for an illustration, I have used only 10 observations, however, in reality MVN will be tested on much larger data.

```
# R Code 4.15. Mahalanobis distance
age <-c(1:10)
ms <-c(3,4,5,5,7,9,8,10,12,2)
x <- data.frame(age, ms)
v <- ncol(x)            # v is number of variables in x. you specify it.
S <- var(x)             # variance-covariance matrix for x
mahal <- mahalanobis (x, colMeans(x), S)     # Malalanobis distance
values for data vector or matrix x
qchisq(.999, v)
plot(density (mahal))  # plot the values of
Mahalanobis (x)        # mahalanobis test for a data vector or matrix x
```

Other statistical measures used for testing MVN are multivariate Q–Q plot, Kowalski's line test (Kowalski, 1970), probability plots using D^2 and Angles, combinations of marginal Wilk–Shapiro W test and extensions of W test, tests for skewness and kurtosis (e.g., Mardia's Tests), which are among the several tests available to assess MVN.

Measures of multivariate outliers are based on leverage, discrepancy and influence. Mahalanobis distance is a leverage-based measure of outliers. The degree to which an observation is in accordance to other observations is referred as discrepancy measures. Influence is a product of leverage and discrepancy. Influence is measured by Cook's distance. The software packages primarily report Mahalanobis distance and Cook's distance. However, research has shown that D^2 or Cook's distance are not very reliable (e.g., Egan and Morgan, 1998; Hadi and Simonoff, 1993) and hence should be used with caution. Once an observation turns out to be multivariate outlier, following steps can be taken. First, you must ensure that the scores are correctly computed and entered in your spreadsheet. Find out the reasons for the case being multivariate outlier. Usually, inconsistent patter of responding to rest of the observation is a major cause of multivariate outliers. Then you can do one of the following: (a) delete the entire case from your sample, or (b) modify the values of observations so the extremity reduces, or (c) keep the case as it is since it is a part of your sample.

Further discussion of multivariate normality and multivariate outliers is beyond the scope of this book. Interested readers may refer to Thode (2002, Chapter 9) and Tabachnick and Fidel (2005).

4.6.2 Statistical Tests for Assessing Multivariate Normality

The MVN is a requirement of many statistical methods. They include multivariate analysis of variance (MANOVA), discriminant function analysis, multiple regression, many generalized linear model (GLM) based procedures, and so on. There are several measures of multivariate normality. Three MVN procedures described here are Mardia's MVN test, Henze–Zirkler's MVN test, and Royston's MVN test.

The multivariate normal distribution function is expressed as:

$$f(x) = \frac{1}{(2\pi)^{m/2} |\Sigma|^{1/2}} \exp\left[-\frac{1}{2}(X - \mu)' \Sigma^{-1}(X - \mu)\right]$$

where X is m-variate observations, μ is a mean vector, and Σ is a covariance matrix. This is expressing multivariate normal distribution of m variables. In sample, Σ is estimated by S the sample variance–covariance matrix, and μ is estimated by vector of sample means.

4.6.2.1 Mardia's MVN Test

The test was proposed by Mardia (1970) to assess the multivariate normality. This is most commonly referred test for multivariate normality. It used sample estimates of multivariate skewness and kurtosis. Let us express squared Mahalanobis distance as $r_{ij} = z_i z_j = (X_i - \bar{X})' S^{-1} (X_j - \bar{X})$ for m variables. I am using r_{ij} because it is often called the squared radii. Marida skewness measures is

$$b_{1,m} = n^{-2} \sum_{i,j=1}^{n} r_{ij}^3$$

and kurtosis measure is

$$b_{2,m} = n^{-1} \sum_{j=1}^{n} r_{ij}^2$$

The test statistics for skewness is

$$(n/6)b_{1,m}$$

with $df = m(m+1)(m+2)/6$. The test statistics for kurtosis is approximately normally distributed with mean $m(m+2)$ and variance $8m(m+2)/n$. Hence,

$$z = \frac{b_{2,m} - (m(m+2))}{\sqrt{8m(m+2)/n}}$$

There are power and type I error issues with sample smaller than 20. However, in psychological research, we shall never apply a multivariate technique for such a small sample.

4.6.2.2 Royston's MVN Test

The Royston's MVN test is useful measure of multivariate normality. Royston's MVN test uses Shapiro–Wilk statistics to assess multivariate normality (it uses Shapiro–Francia statistics for leptokurtic distributions). The Royston test statistics is

$$H = \frac{e \sum_{j=1}^{m} \psi_j}{m}$$

where

$$\psi_j = \{\Phi^{-1}[\Phi(-Z_j)/2]\}$$

and

$$e = m/[1 + (m-1)\bar{c}], \quad \text{and}$$

remaining computational details of $\bar{c}$ and Φ are avoided. They are available in the study of Thode (2002). The test statistics H follows chi-square distribution e degrees of freedom.

4.6.2.3 Henze–Zirkler's MVN Test (HZ Test)

The Henze–Zirkler's MVN test statistics is obtained as follows:

$$HZ = \frac{1}{n}\sum_{i=1}^{n}\sum_{j=1}^{n}\left(\exp\left(-\frac{\beta^2}{2}D_{ij}\right)\right) - 2(1+\beta^2)^{-\frac{m}{2}}\sum_{i=1}^{n}\left(\exp\left(-\frac{\beta^2}{2(1+\beta^2)}D_i\right)\right)n(1+2\beta^2)^{-\frac{p}{2}}$$

where,
  m=number of variable;

$$\beta = \frac{1}{\sqrt{2}}\left(\frac{n(2m+1)}{4}\right)^{\frac{1}{m+4}}$$

$$r_{ij} = z_i z_j = (X_i - \bar{X})' S^{-1}(X_j - \bar{X})$$

$$r_i = z_i z_i = (X_i - \bar{X})' S^{-1}(X_i - \bar{X})$$

HZ measures distance between two distribution functions. The test statistic of HZ follows log-normal distribution if the data is following MVN. The log-normalized mean and SD for HZ statistics are

$$\log(\mu) = \log\left(\sqrt{\frac{\mu^4}{\sigma^2 + \mu^2}}\right)$$

$$\log(\sigma^2) = \log\left(\frac{\sigma^2 + \mu^2}{\sigma^2}\right)$$

The mean and variance of HZ statistics can be used to test the significance of HZ using standard normal distribution as follows:

$$z = \frac{\log(HZ) - \log(\mu)}{\log(\sigma)}$$

The R package MVN is useful to test the multivariate normality. The R Code below provides a test for the three statistics discussed above.

```
R Code. Testing multivariate normality
# Data on three variables x1, x2, and x3
x1 <- c(15, 17, 20, 25, 24, 19, 19, 16, 15, 17, 17, 22, 30, 14, 29, 26,
8, 22, 22, 24, 15, 19, 14, 29, 24, 21, 22, 19, 18, 20)
x2 <- c(2, 4, 3, 5, 3, 4, 1, 4, 4, 3, 4, 4, 7, 2, 5, 6, 1, 4, 7, 5, 2,
4, 4, 5, 5, 4, 5, 3, 2, 4)
x3 <- c(4, 3, 5, 6, 6, 5, 4, 4, 3, 4, 3, 8, 8, 5, 8, 6, 4, 6, 6, 6, 3,
6, 4, 6, 4, 6, 5, 5, 4, 7)

# combining the variables into data matrix
data1 <- cbind(x1,x2,x3)

install.packages("MVN", dependencies = T)  # installing package MVN
library(MVN)                               # call MVN
mardiaTest(data1)                          # Mardia Test
hzTest(data1, qqplot = F)                  # HZ test
roystonTest(data1)                         # Royston test
```

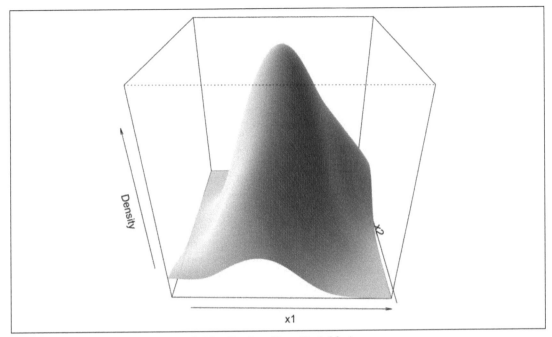

Figure 4.7. *Multivariate Normal Distribution (Two-Variables)*

Note: The figure shows the bivariate normal distribution generated from the R code. This is a distribution for *X*1 and *X*2.

```
# Output showing test statistics, and p-value with decision.
Mardia's Multivariate Normality Test
---------------------------------------
   data              : data1

   g1p               : 0.5647556
   chi.skew          : 2.823778
   p.value.skew      : 0.9852722

   g2p : 13.97667
   z.kurtosis        : -0.511667
   p.value.kurt      : 0.6088841
   chi.small.skew    : 3.264096
   p.value.small     : 0.9745082

   Result : Data are multivariate normal.
---------------------------------------
> hzTest(data1, qqplot = F)
Henze-Zirkler's Multivariate Normality Test
---------------------------------------
data : data1

   HZ : 0.4324797
   p-value : 0.9185043
   Result : Data are multivariate normal.
---------------------------------------
```

```
> roystonTest(data1)
Royston's Multivariate Normality Test
---------------------------------------
   data : data1
   H : 8.604249
   p-value : 0.03376125

   Result : Data are not multivariate normal.
---------------------------------------

################################################################
Plotting bivariate distribution
################################################################
data1 <- cbind(x1, x2)                 # two variables data frame
results <- hzTest(data1)               # HZ test
mvnPlot(results, type =c("persp"))     # plotting MVN
```

The first two tests, Mardia's test and Henze–Zirkler's multivariate normality test are declaring that the data follows multivariate normal distribution. Royston's test is significant at 0.05 level but insignificant at 0.01 level (the actual *p*-value being 0.034). The overall impression is that the data follows MVN for all practical purposes. You can test for Mahalanobis distance and try and find any multivariate outlier.

SUMMARY

This chapter has provided theory application and testing of normality. In most of statistical applications for psychology, normality is a useful concept. Additional reading in this area will provide a good insight into this area. Try solving problems and examples given below. Also practice the R examples that will help you learn the testing part in particular.

EXERCISE

1. State mean, variance and pdf of normal and standard normal distribution. Show that normal pdf converts into standard normal if Z transformation is used.
2. State and explain properties of the normal distribution.
3. If following are the observation on continuous variable X, then obtain Z and mean and variance of Z (2, 3, 5, 6, 7, 4, 8, 1, 4, 10).
4. The conscientiousness dimension of personality is measured for 200 individuals, and found to be normally distributed with mean=35 and SD=4.1. Answer following questions: (a) what is the probability of getting a low score of 20? (b) How many individuals will have score above 40? (c) How many individuals will have score between 37 and 47? (d) How many individuals will have a score between 30 and 40? (e) What is the percentile rank and *T*-score of the individuals having scores like 27, 30, 35, 39, and 45, (f) write R code for all the problems stated above.
5. The mental rotation ability is measured for 300 individuals, and found to be normally distributed with mean=20 and SD=5. Answer following questions: (a) what is the probability of getting a score less than 10? (b) How many individuals will have score above 25? (c) How many individuals will have score between 15 and 25? (d) How many individuals will have a score between 23 and 26? (e) What is the percentile rank and *T*-Score of the individuals having scores like 10, 15, 19, 24, 29 and 35, and (f) write R code for all the problems stated above.

6. Explain first, second, third and fourth central moments. Find kurtosis and skewness for the data in Problem 3.
7. Following is the data on emotional intelligence scale of 25 individuals: (13.29, 10.65, 9.68, 10.52, 7.5, 7.93, 9, 7.19, 9.87, 9.46, 10.8, 8.31, 9.77, 11.37, 12.03, 11.78, 11.7, 15.72, 8.9, 11.35, 9.03, 10.74, 13.95, 10.79, 7.49). Find mean, SD, skewness and kurtosis. Do D'Agostino skewness test, Anscombe–Glynn test of Kurtosis, and Geary's test.
8. For Problem 7, carry out the tests in R.
9. For Problem 7, test the hypothesis that the data comes from a population that has a mean 10 and SD = 2. Solve the same in R. Do Lilliefors test for the same problem.
10. Carry out Shapiro–Wilks, Anderson–Darling, and Jarque–Bera test for Problem 7.
11. Plot box-and-whisker plot, histogram, and Q–Q plots for Problem 7 data.
12. Following is the data of originality scores on creativity scale: (2.04, 9.65, 4.36, 1.44, 2.44, 2.51, 2.95, 8.16, 3.89, 3.62, 5.70, 6.89, 5.23, 2.29, 2.53, 3.12, 6.13, 7.86, 5.52, 4.49, 7.10, 2.61, 6.50, 6.14, 5.23, 6.65, 5.73, 6.36, 2.62, 6.72). Test the data for outlier. After removal of outlier, test whether data comes from population that is normally distributed. Plot box-and-whisker plot, histogram, and Q–Q plots.

5 Correlation and Association

5.1 INTRODUCTION

Being psychologists and behavioral researchers, we measure various psychological attributes along with physical and social attributes of individuals and groups. Often you will realize that change in one of the attributes is associated with the change in another one. To take an example, people who are sensitive towards others' pain (high on empathy) are also more likely to help others than those who are less empathetic. Individuals who are optimistic are more likely to be happy than those who are low on optimism (or pessimistic). This phenomenon can be described as follows: "if one variable is increasing there is higher chance that the other variable will increase." The reverse is also possible, that is, "as one variable is increasing there is higher chance that the other variable will decrease." In statistical terms, this is referred to as correlation. Correlation describes a relationship or association between two (or more) variables. This chapter will introduce you to correlation and associations. A major part of this chapter is primarily concerned with correlation between two variables. We shall understand Pearson's correlation coefficient. This is a useful form of correlation for psychological and social sciences research. We will also understand (about the) special data like dichotomous data on either or both variables. Pearson's correlation makes some assumptions to test the significance. When assumptions are not met or when the data are ordinal or categorical, then use of alternative methods is required. The chapter discusses those methods as well.

5.1.1 Correlation: Meaning and Interpretation

Bivariate correlation is a measure of association between two variables. Typically, one variable is denoted as X and the other variable is denoted as Y. The relationship between these variables is assessed by a statistic called as *correlation coefficient*. Look at the earlier example of optimism and happiness. It states the relationship between one variable, optimism (X) and other variable, happiness (Y). Just have a look at following statements that exemplify correlation:

1. As *conscientiousness* increases, the *academic performance* increases.
2. More the *anxiety* a person experiences, weaker the *adjustment* with stress.
3. As the score on *openness to experience* increases, scores on *divergent thinking tests* also increase.
4. As the *attitude towards a political party* becomes positive (increases), *time spent in reading other party news* decreases.
5. As *savings* increase, a *sense of financial security* increases.
6. On a speed tests, as the *accuracy* increases, the *speed* decreases.
7. Those who are good at *mathematics*, are likely to be good at *science*.
8. As the *age* of the child increases, the *reading speed* increases.
9. As time spent in *practice* increases, the *performance* improves.
10. As *temperature* decreases, the *sales of woolen clothes* increase.

5.1.2 Basic Aspects of Correlation: Direction, Strength, and Linearity

The correlation between two variables can be understood by three aspects: direction, strength, and linearity. Understanding of these concepts provides basic vocabulary for correlation.

5.1.2.1 Direction

Direction indicates whether two correlated variables vary in the same direction (positive correlation) or opposite direction (negative correlation). The relationship between two variables can be described in broadly three directions: positive association, negative association, or no association. Zero correlation (no association) is the absence of any relationship. **Positive correlation** indicates that as the values of one variable increase, the values of other variable also increase (Figure 5.1[A]). Consequently, as the values of one variable decrease, the values of other variable also decrease. This means that both the variables move in a similar direction. From the above examples, "As *conscientiousness* increases, the *academic performance* increases" and "As savings increase, a sense of financial security increases" are indicative of a positive relationship. **Negative correlation** indicates that as the values of one variable increase, the values of other variable decrease. Consequently, as the values of one variable decrease, the values of other variable increase. The two variables move in the opposite (or inverse) directions (Figure 5.1[B]). From the above examples, "On a speed test, as the *accuracy* increases, the *speed* decreases" and "As temperature decreases, the sale of woolen clothes increase" indicate a negative relationship. It is also possible that there is **no relationship** between X and Y. That is, the two variables do not share any relationship. If they do not share any relationship (that is, technically the correlation coefficient is zero), then, obviously the direction of the correlation is neither positive nor negative. It is often called as **zero correlation** or **no correlation**. (Please note that "zero-order correlation" is a different term than "zero correlation," which we will discuss afterwards). For example, guess the relationship between shoe size and intelligence? This sounds an erratic question because there is no reason for any relationship between them. So there is no relationship between these two variables. The data of 100 individuals plotted in Figure 5.1(C) show no relationship.

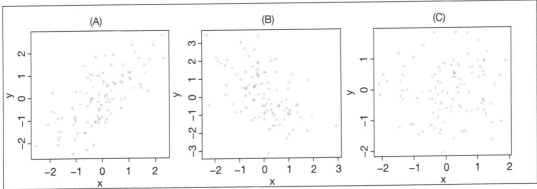

Figure 5.1. *Scatter (A) Positive Correlation, (B) Negative Correlation, (C) No Correlation*

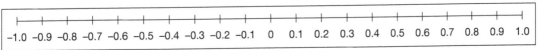

Figure 5.2. *The Range of Correlation Coefficient*

5.1.2.2 Strength

Typically, correlation ranges from –1.00 to +1.00 ($-1.00 \le r \le +1.00$). When correlation is computed by using real data, it is very rarely exactly –1.00 or +1.00 or zero (see Figure 5.2). Hence, the correlation is described in terms of its strength than just direction (for example, high negative, low positive, and so on). As the coefficient is closer to ±1.00, the strength is higher (relationship is strong), and as it approaches zero, the strength is low (relationship is weak). The correlation coefficient of +0.88 (and similarly –0.88) indicates a stronger association, whereas a correlation of +0.12 (and similarly –0.12) indicates lower strength of association.

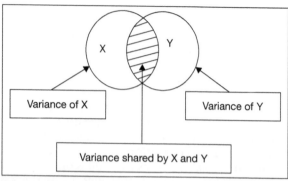

Figure 5.3. *Circles X and Y Represent Variances of X and Y, Respectively*

Note: The shaded part that is common between X and Y is covariance. Covariance indicates the degree to which X shares variance with Y.

However, psychometrics experts differ in opinion about what should be the cutting points about low–moderate–high levels of correlations.

More accurate way to determine strength is to understand the amount of variance that variables explain in each other. The strength of association is common variance between two correlated variables. The correlation coefficient is NOT percentage. So the correlation of 0.25 does NOT mean that 25% variance is common between two variables. The percentage of variance that both variables share can be calculated from correlation. Both variables have variance denoted as S_x^2 (variance of X) and S_y^2 (variance of Y). Out of their variance, X and Y share some variance, which can be called covariance. Figure 5.3 explains this concept. The circle X is the variance of X and, similarly, the circle Y indicates the variance of Y. The overlapping part of X and Y, indicated by shaded lines, shows the shared variance between X and Y.

This is expressed as r^2 (r square). r^2 is the percentage of variance that both the variables share:

$$\text{percentage of variance} = r^2 \times 100$$

For example, if the correlation between X and Y is –0.76, then the percentage of variance is $-0.76^2 \times 100 = 0.577 \times 100 = 57.76\%$. The two variables, X and Y, share 57.76% of variance or 57.76% variance is common to them. Table 5.1 and Figure 5.4 show the correlation and percentage of variance shared.

5.1.2.3 Linearity

Two variables can relate with each other in many ways. A linear relationship is one of the ways they could be related. All other relationships can be called non-linear relationships and techniques called "curve fitting" are useful in handling them. The correlation assumes linear relationship between the variables. *Linear* relationship can be expressed as a relationship between two variables that can be plotted as a *straight* line. The linear relationship can be expressed in the following equation: $Y = a + bX$.

Table 5.1. *Correlation and their Shared % of Variance*

Correlation (r_{xy})	0.1	0.2	0.3	0.4	0.5	0.6	0.7	0.8	0.9	0.99
% of variance	1	4	9	16	25	36	49	64	81	98.01

Here, Y is the dependent variable, "X" is the independent variable, "a" is the constant, and "b" is the slope of the line. Figure 5.5(A) explains linear relationship.

Non-linear relationships can be described as all other forms of relationship between variables other than linear. They can be handled by techniques called as curve fitting. Some of the useful examples of non-linear relationships in psychology are Yerkes–Dodson Law, Steven's Power Law in Psychophysics, and so on. The Yerkes–Dodson Law suggests that performance is poor when stress is too little or too much and it is optimal when stress is moderate. Figure 5.5(B) shows scatter and line for stress–performance relationship.

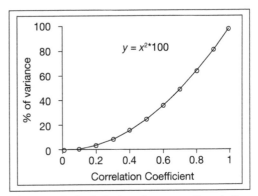

Figure 5.4. *Relation between Correlation and Percentage of Variance*

5.1.3 Types of Correlations and Association

The correlation coefficient and measures of association are of various types. These types depend on the data type as well as computational logic. Generally, I follow distinction clarified by Howell (2008) regarding **correlation and association**. Some sort of order in the data is implied when we speak about correlation so that we can say "as X increases, Y increases." However, such an understanding is not meaningful when order is absent. There we use the term "association." The most popular one is **Pearson's correlation coefficient** (r_{xy}), which is the correlation between two continuous variables. Pearson's correlation is called **point-biserial correlation** (r_{pb}) when the data on one of the variable is dichotomous and other variable is continuous, and non-Pearson correlation for similar data is called **biserial correlation** (r_b). When the data on both the variables are dichotomous, then Pearson's correlation is called **phi coefficient** (ϕ_{xy}) and non-Pearson correlation is called **tetrachoric correlation** (r_{tet}). Pearson's correlation computed on ranked data (ordinal data) is called as **Spearman's rho (r_s)**. The non-Pearson alternative to Spearman's rho is **Kendall's tau (τ_{xy})**. The **Goodman and Kruskal's gamma** is another way to calculate correlations for ordinal data. **Kendall's Coefficient of Concordance** (W) is a similar coefficient for ordinal data generally employed to assess agreement among the ratters. The **contingency coefficient**

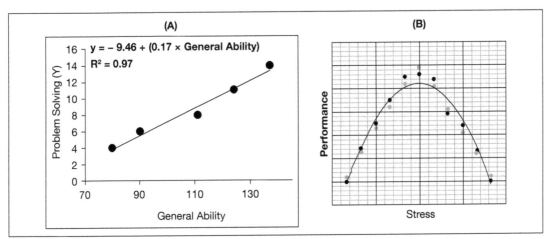

Figure 5.5. *(A) Linear Relationship between Intelligence and Problem Solving with Linear Equation; (B) Non-linear Relationship between Stress and Performance*

test, phi coefficient, Cramér's V coefficient, Yule's Q, odds ratio (odds and RR), Tschuprow's T are other methods for computing correlation for nominal data. In addition, **likelihood ratio, Cochran–Mantel–Haenszel Statistic and Cohen's Kappa** are useful measures of association. These are not Pearson's correlations.

5.1.4 Testing Hypothesis for Correlation

Pearson's product moment correlation describes relationship between variables observed in the sample (r_{xy}). So is the case with other measures of correlation and associations. However, researchers are not interested in sample correlations but they are interested in understanding relationship between X and Y in population represented by a sample. The population correlation (ρ_{xy}), **rho**, is estimated by sample correlation. The null hypothesis significance testing about correlation coefficient generally (but not necessarily) tests the hypothesis that population correlation is zero. The testing of this hypothesis depends on assumptions about the parameter. Null hypothesis testing was a complex and challenging issue in the history of correlation. The work by R. A. Fisher (1915) helped in solving the problem of understanding probability distribution associated with the correlation coefficient.

5.1.5 Correlation and Causality

The relationship between correlation and causality is a complex issue. Generally, given the theory, the causality is implied in correlation. However, correlation is not a statement of causality. In many cases, correlation is not indicative of any direct causal relationship. For example, "as the sales of ice-cream increases, the deaths by drowning increase." In reality, the deaths due to drowning happen particularly in summer when more people go to beaches and rivers and that's precisely the time when the sales of ice-cream increase. This is a spurious correlation between two variables. Quite a few good discussions are available on this issue which include Kenny (1979), Mumford and Anjum (2011), Pearl (2009), Illari and Russo (2014), and so on. Several statistical models make use of non-experimental data to draw causality inferences. They include regression and curve fitting, time series analysis, structural equations modeling, and so on. These techniques basically make use of covariance among the observed variables to draw causal inference. They can be said to be causal only in the presence of causal theory where "exogenous" and "endogenous" variables are clearly specified. If X and Y are correlated, then the following things are possible: (a) X causes Y, (b) Y causes X, (c) a third variable Z causes both X and Y and XY are not causally related, (d) X and Y cause each other cyclically (one after another, generally over time), (e) X causes Z which causes Y, but X may (not) directly cause Y, (f) X and Y are not causally related and the correlation is spurious. All these relations can be modeled by using various statistical methods, and probabilistic inference can be drawn about them.

5.2 PEARSON'S CORRELATION

Pearson's correlation coefficient was developed by Karl Pearson and presented in a monograph published in 1896. However, previous to Pearson, Sir Francis Galton while working on bi-parental inheritance, worked on the idea of correlation intuitively; however, the correlation coefficient was not computed by Galton. In fact, Galton did show a phenomena "regression to mean" that uses some of the ideas later on included in correlation coefficient and regression.

5.2.1 Logic of Pearson's *r*

The computation of correlation is based on covariance (Cov_{xy} or σ_{xy}). Covariance indicates the amount of covariation between two variables. The population covariance is denoted as σ_{xy} and the sample covariance is denoted as S_{xy}:

$$\text{Cov}_{xy} = \sigma_{xy} = \frac{\sum\limits_{i=1}^{N}(X_i - \bar{X})(Y_i - \bar{Y})}{N}$$

Alternatively, the covariance could be written as

$$\text{Cov}_{xy} = \sigma_{xy} = \frac{\sum XY - \dfrac{\sum X \sum Y}{N}}{N}$$

In fact, you would quickly realize that it's an average of the product (multiplication) of the deviation of X from its mean and the deviation of Y from its mean. In the case of random variables (XY), we represent $\sigma_{xy} = E[(X - E(X))(Y - E(Y))]$. If such a number is negative (e.g., –28), then we understand it as follows: Since it's an average (denominator is N), then it will be negative only when the numerator is negative. The numerator will be negative if the sum of $(X_i - \bar{X})(Y_i - \bar{Y})$ is negative. It is possible if one of the deviations is negative. When X is below its mean (X bar), Y is above its mean (Y bar) and vice versa then, on an average as $(X_i - \bar{X})$ is positive, the $(Y_i - \bar{Y})$ is negative and vice versa. This indicates that X and Y move in opposite directions with respect to their means. In such a case, covariance will be negative. On the other hand, it will be positive, if X and Y move in the similar direction with respect to their mean. The covariance value will be zero, if X and Y move independently. That is, for those values of X that are below its mean, some values of Y will be above and some will be below the mean of Y making the product closer to zero. It's important to note that σ_{xy} is an average. Following equations use the same idea to understand its different forms:

$$\sigma_{xy} = E[(X - E(X))(Y - E(Y))]$$
$$\sigma_{xy} = E[XY - XE(Y) - YE(X) + E(X)E(Y)]$$
$$\sigma_{xy} = E(XY) - E(X)E(Y)$$

Three ideas that are relevant here are:

1. If X and Y are independent, then $E(XY) = E(X) \times E(Y)$. If, X and Y are independent, then $\sigma_{xy} = 0$. So we can rewrite the earlier equation as

$$0 = E(XY) - E(X) \times E(Y)$$
$$E(XY) = E(X) \times E(Y)$$

2. If X and Y are two random variables, then $\sigma_{x+y}^2 = \sigma_x^2 + \sigma_y^2 + 2 \times \sigma_{xxy}$.[1]

3. If X and Y are independent random variables, then $\sigma_{x+y}^2 = \sigma_x^2 + \sigma_y^2$. That is, covariance $\sigma_{xxy} = 0$ and hence $2 \times \sigma_{xxy} = 0$ in the second point.

The population covariance (σ_{xy}) is estimated by sample covariance (S_{xy}), which is computed as

$$\text{Cov}_{xy} = S_{xy} = \frac{\sum\limits_{i=1}^{n}(X_i - \bar{X})(Y_i - \bar{Y})}{n-1}$$

---

[1] Proof of $\sigma_{x+y}^2 = \sigma_x^2 + \sigma_y^2 + 2 \times \sigma_{xxy}$

$$\sigma_{x+y}^2 = E(X + Y - E(X + Y))^2$$
$$\sigma_{x+y}^2 = E((X - E(X)) + (Y - E(Y)))^2$$
$$\sigma_{x+y}^2 = E(X - E(X))^2 + E((Y - E(Y))^2 + 2 \times E((X - E(X))(Y - E(Y)))$$
$$\sigma_{x+y}^2 = \sigma_x^2 + \sigma_y^2 + 2 \times \sigma_{xxy}$$

The denominator is not n but $(n-1)$ due to the biased nature of the estimator which has already been discussed in Chapter 2 (please refer to Section 2.2).

5.2.1.1 Correlation Coefficient (r_{xy})

The covariance will change as the scale of measurement changes. If both X and Y are multiplied by a constant C, then $\sigma_{CXCY} = C^2 \sigma_{XY}$. Multiplying the X and Y by a constant will only change the measurement unit and not the relationship between them. However, the value of the covariance will change as the unit of measurement changes in spite of no change in the relationship between X and Y. This makes covariance a difficult statistic to interpret. The correlation coefficient (r_{xy}) is a statistic that is not dependent on the scale of measurement and hence preferred over covariance. Pearson's product moment correlation coefficient removes this drawback of the covariance:

$$r_{XY} = \frac{\sigma_{XY}}{\sigma_X \times \sigma_Y}$$

Correlation coefficient between X and Y is covariance XY divided by the product of standard deviations of X and Y. If variables X and Y are multiplied by a constant C then the correlation is as follows:

$$r_{C_X C_Y} = \frac{\sigma_{C_X C_Y}}{\sigma_{C_X} \times \sigma_{C_Y}}$$

$$r_{C_X C_Y} = \frac{C^2 \sigma_{XY}}{C^2 \times \sigma_X \times \sigma_Y}$$

$$r_{C_X C_Y} = \frac{\sigma_{XY}}{\sigma_X \times \sigma_Y} = r_{XY}$$

This shows that the computation of correlation is unaffected by the unit of measurement. Another point one needs to note is that for correlation, the maximum value the numerator will attain is the value of the denominator. That is, the maximum possible value covariance between X and Y will take is product of the standard deviations of X and Y. Suppose if $X=Y$, then $\sigma_{XY} = \sigma_{XX}$ and the correlation is

$$r_{XY} = \frac{\sigma_{XY}}{\sigma_X \times \sigma_X} = \frac{\sigma_X^2}{\sigma_Y^2} = 1$$

If $X=-Y$, then $r_{XY} = \dfrac{\sigma_{XY}}{\sigma_X \times \sigma_X} = \dfrac{-1 \times \sigma_X^2}{\sigma_X^2} = -1$ In all other cases, the numerator (covariance between X and Y) will be smaller than the denominator (product of standard deviations of X and Y). The covariance can take positive or negative signs and that makes correlation positive or negative. So correlation has an important property, that is, $-1 \leq r_{XY} \leq +1$. Thus, the highest possible correlation is +1 and the lowest possible correlation is –1.

To compute correlation in a sample, the following estimation is used:

$$r = \frac{\text{Cov}_{XY}}{S_X S_Y}$$

where
   Cov_{XY} is the sample covariance between X and Y,
   S_X is the sample standard deviation of X, and

S_Y is the sample standard deviation of Y.
By substituting the covariance equation for covariance, we can rewrite the equation as

$$r = \frac{\frac{\Sigma(X - \bar{X})(Y - \bar{Y})}{n}}{S_X S_Y}$$

By following a simple rule, $a \div b \div c = a \div (b \times c)$, we can rewrite this equation as follows:

$$r = \frac{\Sigma(X - \bar{X})(Y - \bar{Y})}{n S_X S_Y}$$

This formula for computing correlation is often reported in textbooks.

5.2.2 Computation of Pearson's *r*

Suppose, if we have jointly distributed random variables (X,Y), where X is hopelessness and Y is depression, the 10 observations of these random variables are specified as (6,12), (11,15), (5,10), (12,19), (16,16), (10,17), (8,12), (7,11), (14,18), (11,20). The covariance and correlation will be calculated in Table 5.2.

The covariance between depression and hopelessness is 9.55. You would realize that it's a positive number indicating that depression and hopelessness move in the similar direction (as one increases, the other increases, and vice versa). However, due to an absence of a clear unit of measurement of psychological scales, this number is difficult to interpret. The correlation between depression and hopelessness is +0.761, which also indicates that these variables share a good deal of variance with each other. We can actually compute the percentage of variance shared by calculating r^2:

Table 5.2. *Hypothetical Data of 10 Participants on Hopelessness and Depression*

Subject	Hopelessness (X)	Depression (Y)	$(X - \bar{X})$	$(Y - \bar{Y})$	$(X - \bar{X})^2$	$(Y - \bar{Y})^2$	$(X - \bar{X})(Y - \bar{Y})$
1	6	12	-4	-3	16	9	12
2	11	15	1	0	1	0	0
3	5	10	-5	-5	25	25	25
4	12	19	2	4	4	16	8
5	16	16	6	1	36	1	6
6	10	17	0	2	0	4	0
7	8	12	-2	-3	4	9	6
8	7	11	-3	-4	9	16	12
9	14	18	4	3	16	9	12
10	11	20	1	5	1	25	5
n=10	$\Sigma X = 100$	$\Sigma Y = 150$			$\Sigma(X-\bar{X})^2$ = 112	$\Sigma(Y-\bar{Y})^2$ = 114	$\Sigma(X-\bar{X})(Y-\bar{Y})$ = 86
	$\bar{X} = 10$	$\bar{Y} = 15$			$SD_X=3.527$	$SD_Y=3.559$	

$$Cov_{XY} = S_{XY} = \frac{\sum_{i=1}^{n}(X_i - \bar{X})(Y_i - \bar{Y})}{n-1} = \frac{86}{10-1} = \frac{86}{9} = 9.55$$

$$r = \frac{Cov_{XY}}{S_X S_Y} = \frac{9.55}{3.527 \times 3.559} = \frac{9.55}{12.555} = +0.761$$

Percentage of variance shared $= r^2 \times 100 = 0.761^2 \times 100 = 0.5792 \times 100 = 57.92\%$

Now we can say that in this sample, depression and hopelessness share approximately 58% of the variance.

5.2.2.1 Adjusted Correlation Coefficient

The correlation coefficient (r_{xy}) is a biased estimator of population correlation coefficient (ρ_{xy}). The estimator is corrected by the following correction and referred to as the adjusted correlation coefficient (r_{adj}):

$$(r_{adj}) = \sqrt{1 - \frac{(1 - r^2)(n - 1)}{n - 2}}$$

r_{adj} is a relatively unbiased estimator of population coefficient. However, there are other ways of correcting bias as well. As the sample size increases, the sample correlation becomes a less biased estimator. So in large samples, the difference between r and r_{adj} is less. In the case of our example, the adjusted r is

$$(r_{adj}) = \sqrt{1 - \frac{(1 - 761^2)(10 - 1)}{10 - 2}} = \sqrt{1 - \frac{0.4207 \times 9}{8}} = \sqrt{1 - 0.4733} = 0.7257$$

The adjusted correlation is always less than the unadjusted correlation and this difference reduces as the sample size increases. In the case of our example, the sample size is small and, hence, adjustment leads to reasonable reduction in correlation.

5.2.3 Hypothesis Testing about Population Correlation: Significance of Correlation

The correlation coefficient describes relationship between two variables in the sample. To infer about the population correlation coefficient, the correlation coefficient is converted into t-random variable. We know the probability associated with t-distribution. The null and alternatives are as follows:

$$H_0 : \rho = 0$$
$$H_A : \rho \neq 0$$

Rho (ρ_{xy}) is a population correlation and the null hypothesis states that the population correlation is zero. The alternative hypothesis states that the population correlation is not zero. With a large sample, the estimator follows normal distribution, which can be converted into t-distribution by using the following formula:

$$t = \frac{r\sqrt{n - 2}}{\sqrt{1 - r^2}}$$

From the above data,

$$t = \frac{r\sqrt{n - 2}}{\sqrt{1 - r^2}} = \frac{0.7611 \times \sqrt{10 - 2}}{\sqrt{1 - 0.7611^2}} = 3.3188$$

The obtained *t*-value will be tested at df $= n - 2 = 10 - 2 = 8$. The *t*-distribution table shows that $t_{(8)} = 3.555$, $p = 0.01$ and $t_{(8)} = 2.306$, $p = 0.05$.

The value obtained is greater than the critical value at $\alpha = 0.05$ and hence is significant at 0.05 level. The exact probability of obtaining $t_{(08)} = 3.312$ is $p = 0.011$ which is, needless to say, smaller than $p = 0.05$. Hence, we reject the null hypothesis that the population correlation is zero with $\alpha = 0.05$ (probability of type I error). This concludes the hypothesis testing about the correlation coefficient. This does not mean that we only look for significant correlations. Note three points: One, you would realize that as the sample size (*n*) increases, the power of the statistical test increases and the chance that small correlation would turn out to be significant increases. Two, when we compute the correlation as an index for reliability (test–retest), we are not interested in statistical significance (i.e., showing that in population this value is not zero). It is essential to show that it is large value and two administrations share large percentage of variance. Three, we need to understand that significance testing of the correlation coefficient depends on certain assumptions. Hence, they are discussed later. These calculations can be carried out step by step, by writing your function as illustrated in R code 5.1, and R code 5.2 shows the inbuilt function for correlation.

```
#R Code 5.1. Covariance, Correlation, Adjusted r and Significance Testing
hope<-c(6,11,5,12,16,10,8,7,14,11)      # data on x variable
dep<-c(12,15,10,19,16,17,12,11,18,20)   # data on y variable
cov(hope, dep)                          # computes covariance
cor(hope, dep)                          # computes correlation

You can also write you function as well
mycor<-function(x, y)
{
  xd = (x-mean(x))
  yd = (y-mean(y))
  num = sum(xd*yd)
  mcov = num/(length(x)-1)    #covariance between x and y
  print (mcov)                # showing mcov value
  mcor = mcov/(sd(x)*sd(y))   # compute correlation
  print(mcor)                 # showing mcor value on screen
}
mycor(hope,dep)

# Your function to get Adjusted r
radj<-function(r,n)
{
  num = ((1-r^2)*(n-1))/(n-2)   # computes the numerator
  radj = sqrt(1-num)            # computes adjusted r
  print(radj)                   # printing adjusted r
}
radj(.76109, 10) # run the function

# Your Function To Test The Significance of r
rsig <-function(r,n)
{
  t = (r*sqrt(n-2))/(sqrt(1-r^2))   # computes t-value
  pt=pt(t, n-2, lower.tail=F)*2     # computes probability associated with
  t. It is multiplied by 2 to obtained two-tailed probability. One tailed
  can be obtained by removing *2
  print(t)
  print(pt)
```

```
if (pt<=.05) # if loop to print message. Significance level can be
            changed to .01. Change message accordingly.
{
print("The value is significant at .05 level. Reject the null hypothesis
that population correlation is zero.")
}else{
print("The correlation is not significant. Accept the null hypothesis
that population correlation is zero.")
}
}
rsig (.76109, 10)
```

#R Code 5.2. Pearson's Correlation with Function cor.test with Output
```
cor.test (dep, hope, alternative = c("two.sided"), method =
c("pearson"), conf.level = .05)    # cor.test function with specifications
# below is output
Pearson's product-moment correlation
data: dep and hope
t = 3.3188, df = 8, p-value = 0.01056
alternative hypothesis: true correlation is not equal to 0
95 percent confidence interval:
0.2524315 0.9401804
sample estimates:
cor
0.7610917
#alternative could be "less", "greater" meaning alternative states that
rho is #smaller or greater than zero. The method could be "kendall",
"spearman" and #accordingly Spearman's or Kendall's tau correlation will
be computed. To #know more type
help(cor.test) # help for cor.test
```

5.2.3.1 Testing Hypothesis That Population Correlation (ρ_{xy}) Is a Specific Value

We have seen how to test the hypothesis that population correlation is zero. However, researcher may have an interest in testing the hypothesis that population correlation (ρ_{xy}) is of a specific value. Theory or past research may provide specific prediction. The sampling distribution of r becomes more skewed as r approaches ± 1. Further, the estimation of standard error is difficult. This problem affects the test of hypothesis about a specific value of r and testing hypothesis regarding the difference between two values of r. The work by R. A. Fisher (1921) showed that r could be transformed into r' (r prime) which is normally distributed around the value ρ' where ρ' is transformation of ρ similar to that from r to r' (Fisher's original work and most authors refer to it as Z; however, to avoid confusion I have used r'). The standard error of r' is estimated by S_r. r' is the inverse hyperbolic tangent of r (i.e., $\tan h^{-1}(r) = r'$). In R software, you get this value by writing a tan $h(r)$. It is generally referred to as **Fisher's Z transformation of r.**

$$r' = 0.5 \times \log_e \left| \frac{1+r}{1-r} \right| \quad \rho' = 0.5 \times \log_e \left| \frac{1+\rho}{1-\rho} \right|$$

The standard error of r' is denoted by S_r and computed as follows:

$$S_r = \frac{1}{\sqrt{n-3}}$$

With this, r' can be converted into a standard normal variable.

$$z = \frac{\delta_z}{S_{r'}} = \frac{r' - \rho'}{S_{r'}} = \frac{r' - \rho'}{1/\sqrt{n-3}}$$

In the case of our example, if we wish to test a hypothesis that $\rho=0.05$, then we can write the null and alternative as $H_0 = \rho = 0.5$ and $H_A : \rho \neq 0.5$. The computation provides the following results:

$$r = 0.76109 \quad r' = 0.998 \quad \rho = 0.5 \quad \rho' = 0.549$$

$$S' = 0.378 \quad z = \frac{0998 - 0.549}{0.378} = 1.189$$

#R Code 5.3. Function for Testing H₀ about Specific Value of Correlation

```
rdif<-function (r, rho, n)
{
  rt = abs((1+r)/(1-r))
  rp = .5*(log(rt))                          # r' can be computed by "atanh(r)"
  print(rp)
  rhopr = .5*(log(abs((1+rho)/(1-rho)))) #rho prime computation
  print(rhopr)
  srp = (1/(sqrt(n-3)))                      # standard error of r'
  print(srp)
  z = (rp-rhopr)/(srp)                       # Z value computation
  print(z)
}
rdif(.76109, .5, 10) # testing hypothesis rho = .5
```

From Table C1, we know that the probability of obtaining $z \geq |1.96|$ is less than 0.05. So if z is equal to or greater than the absolute value of 1.96, then it is significant at 0.05 level. Hence, the value obtained for our data is not significant. We accept the null hypothesis, and that is, the population correlation is 0.05. If z is significant ($z \geq |1.96|$), then the sign of z can be used to interpret the alternative. Negative z value indicates that the rho is smaller than the null, and positive z indicates that rho is larger than the null.

5.2.3.2 Confidence Interval (CI) on Population Correlation (ρ)

While discussing hypothesis testing, we know that the confidence limit for a parameter can be obtained when we know the standard error of an estimator. We know the standard error of ρ' and not that of ρ. We can still compute the limit for ρ. First, we compute confidence limits for ρ' and then convert those values of ρ' into ρ. We are interested in the following statement: $p\{r_1 \leq \rho \leq r_2\} = 1 - \alpha$ where α is the probability of type I error (which is generally 0.05), and r_1 and r_2 are the estimated values. The statement means that the probability of population value of correlation between r_1 and r_2 is $1-\alpha$. If $\alpha=0.05$, then we are interested in showing $p\{r_1 \leq \rho \leq r_2\} = 1 - 0.05 = 0.95$. So, first we obtain $p\{r_1' \leq \rho \leq r_2'\} = 0.95$ and then convert r_1' and r_2' into r_1 and r_2.

$$\text{CI}(\rho') = r' \pm (z_\alpha \times S_r) = r' \pm \left(z_\alpha \times \sqrt{\frac{1}{n-3}} \right)$$

$r' = 0.998$, $z_{0.05} = 1.96$ and $S_{r'} = 0.378$

$$\text{CI}(\rho') = 0.998 \pm \left(1.96 \times \sqrt{\frac{1}{10-3}}\right) = 0.998 \pm (1.96 \times 0.378) = 0.998 \pm 0.740$$

$$\text{CI}(\rho') = 0.2572 \le \rho' \le 1.7388$$

Now, converting values of ρ' into ρ gives us confidence limits of rho. This conversion is done by

$$r = \frac{e^{2 \times r'} - 1}{e^{2 \times r'} + 1} = \frac{e^{2 \times .2527} - 1}{e^{2 \times .2527} + 1} = 0.253 \quad r = \frac{e^{2 \times 1.7388} - 1}{e^{2 \times 1.7388} + 1} = 0.94$$

$$\text{CI}(\rho) = 0.253 \le \rho \le 0.94$$

which results into $p\{0.253 \le \rho \le 0.94\} = 0.95$, meaning the probability that rho will be between 0.253 and 0.94 is 0.95 or 95% chance that rho will be between these two values. Note that it is not including zero. The confidence is reasonable (0.95) but the interval is too wide. The wide CI is due to small sample size.

```
#R Code 5.4. CI of Correlation
library(psychometric)      #call library psychometric
CIr(.76109, 10, .95)       # function CIr provide CI for correlation. Also
                           use cor.test(x,y)
```

5.2.3.3 Power Calculation of Correlation and Determining the Sample Size

Power is the ability of statistics to reject false a null hypothesis $(1-\beta)$. Let α be the significance level, β be the probability of type II error, and $z_{1-\alpha/k}$ and z_β are $(1-\alpha/k)$th and βth quantiles of the standard normal distribution, respectively. Let $\delta_z = r' - \rho'$, then power (π) can be computed as

$$\pi = \begin{cases} \Phi\left(\dfrac{\delta_z}{S_{r'}} - z_{1-\alpha}\right) & \text{For upper-sided test} \\[3ex] \Phi\left(-\dfrac{\delta_z}{S_{r'}} - z_{1-\alpha}\right) & \text{For lower-sided test} \\[3ex] \Phi\left(\dfrac{\delta_z}{S_{r'}} - z_{1-\alpha/2}\right) + \Phi\left(-\dfrac{\delta_z}{S_{r'}} - z_{1-\alpha/2}\right) & \text{For two-sided test} \end{cases}$$

where $\Phi(\cdot)$ is the cumulative distribution function of standard normal distribution.

Similarly, sample size (n) can also be determined by knowing the power, α, and rho:

$$n = 3 + \left(\frac{z_{1-\alpha} - z_\beta}{\delta_z}\right)^2$$

To obtain power and desired n for a given power, you can use R package "pwr", developed by Champely (2015) which makes use of power calculations elaborated by Cohen (1988).

```
#R Code 5.5. Power and Sample Size for Correlation Coefficient
library(pwr)
pwr.r.test(n, r, sig.level, power, alternative =c("two.sided"))
# to obtain power specify power = NULL. Similarly, specify any of
parameters as NULL that needs to be estimated.
pwr.r.test(10, .76109, .05, power=NULL, alternative =c("two.sided"))
```

```
# to obtain power
# to obtain sample size at power =.9, r = .5, and alpha = .05
pwr.r.test(n = NULL, .5, .05, .9, alternative =c("two.sided"))
```

5.2.4 Assumptions Underling Pearson's *r*

One may recall that the simple descriptive use of the correlation coefficient does not involve any assumption about the distribution of either of the variable. However, using correlation as an inferential statistics requires assumptions about X and Y. These assumptions are as follows:

1. **Independence among pairs of score.**
   This assumption implies that the scores of any two observations (participants in case of most of psychological data) are not influenced by each other. Each pair of observation is independent. This is assured when different subjects provide different pairs of observation.
2. **The population of X and the population of Y follow normal distribution and the population pair of scores of X and Y has a normal bivariate distribution.**
   This assumption states that the population distribution of both the variables (X and Y) is normal. This also means that the pair of scores (X, Y) follows bivariate normal distribution. This assumption can be tested by using statistical tests for normality (refer to Chapter 4).

It should be remembered that the r is a robust statistic. It implies that slight violation of assumption would not influence the distributional properties of t and the probability judgments associated with population correlation.

5.2.5 Factors Influencing Correlation Coefficient

There are some factors that ramify the interpretation of correlation coefficient. These factors are (a) sampling restricted range, (b) combining heterogeneous subgroups, (c) presence of bivariate outliers, and (d) absence of linearity. One should carefully evaluate them before interpreting correlation.

5.2.5.1 Sampling Restricted Range

Selecting the restricted range of X and Y is generally known to attenuate the correlation coefficient. In very unusual circumstances (e.g., if the relation is curvilinear at extreme and the restricting range removes non-linearity) restricted range will improve the correlation. Suppose, you are correlating hours of studies with marks obtained. In reality, time spent in studies will vary from 0 hours to 10–12 hours. However, if you collect data from reputed institutions, then you would realize that they have selected either bright or hard-working students. As a result you will not be able to measure the full range of both variables. The example in Figure 5.6 shows that the correlation for hard-working students (those who study 5 hours or more) is 0.5 and when entire data is considered, the correlation is 0.96. In spite of the fact that this is hypothetical data, the impact of restricted range is visible.

5.2.5.2 Combining Heterogeneous Subgroups

In the study of psychology, often the data on the variable come from specific subgroups, like male–female, urban–rural, etc. In the case of certain variables, these groups may show different patterns of relationship, that is, they may be heterogeneous subgroups, for example, if we are to look at hypothetical data of mental rotation and verbal fluency. Generally, these two variables will show poor relationship. However, if we take the data of a 6th grader and a 10th grader, then the 10th grader will show better performance on both variables as compared to

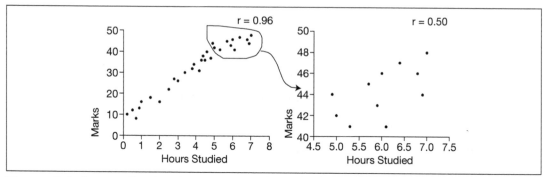

Figure 5.6. *Scatters Showing the Effect of Range on Correlation*

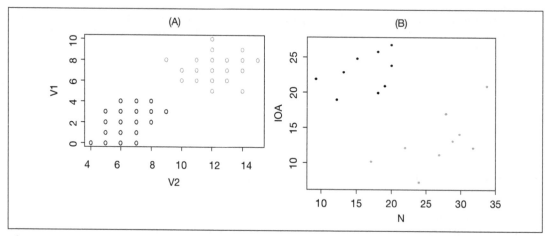

Figure 5.7. *The Correlation of Heterogeneous Subgroups (A) Correlation between V1 and V2 for Separate Groups (r=0.29 for Sixth Graders, and r=0.16 for Tenth Graders. Combined r=0.88) (B) Correlation between IOA and Neuroticism (r=0.40 for Females and 0.65 for Males. Overall Correlation=–0.46)*

the 6th graders. If we combine the data from both grades, then we tend to get high correlation (Figure 5.7[A]). Similarly, the other data (Figure 5.7[B]) shows that two groups (male and female) are heterogeneous because one group, as compared to another, has higher scores on one variable and lower on another. This problem can be controlled to some extent by using partial correlation, which is discussed in Section 5.4.2.

5.2.5.3 Presence of Bivariate Outliers

Outliers are extreme scores on one or both variables. The bivariate outlier is not necessarily an extreme value on each variable individually; however, it is an extreme score on a combination of variables. The presence of a bivariate outlier leads to the reduction of correlation. In Figure 5.8, a score (8, 1) is a bivariate outlier. The correlation computed with the outlier is 0.60, whereas correlation computed after deleting the outlier is 0.84.

5.2.5.4 Absence of Linearity

The linearity of the relationship is a required assumption of the correlation coefficient. In the absence of linearity, Pearson's product moment correlation should not be computed. If the linearity is absent but the monotony in the relation is present, then other non-parametric methods of correlation, like Spearman's rho, can be employed. A monotonous relationship is the one where the pattern remains the same over entire data. For example, if X and Y are increasing, then it is monotonous. This does not mean linear. The linear relations are monotonous but all monotonous relations are not linear.

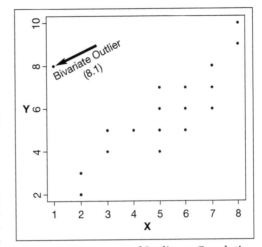

Figure 5.8. *Impact of Outlier on Correlation*

Note: $r=0.84$ without outlier and $r=0.60$ with one outlier.

5.3 SPECIAL CORRELATIONS

Pearson's correlation is computed on continuous data on both variables. However, there are many variables in psychological research that take only two values. For example, responses to ability items on a psychological test (either correct or incorrect), gender (male–female), experimental group and control group, diagnosis (diagnosed–not diagnosed), and many more. Dichotomous variable is the one that can be divided into two sharply distinguished or mutually exclusive categories. Suppose, a researcher is interested in correlating an outcome on a reasoning task (success or failure) with conscientiousness personality, then the reasoning task is a dichotomous variable and conscientiousness is a continuous variable. If reasoning task is correlated with gender, then both variables are dichotomous. The correlations computed under these conditions are referred to as special correlations.

5.3.1 Point-biserial Correlation and Phi Coefficient: Pearson's Correlations

Pearson's correlation computed when there is dichotomous data on one variable and continuous data on another variable is called point-biserial correlation. Pearson's correlation computed when both variables are dichotomous is called phi correlation.

5.3.1.1 Point-biserial Correlation (r_{pb})

The Point-Biserial Correlation (r_{pb}) is Pearson's correlation computed when one variable is dichotomous and another variable is continuous. These are the truly dichotomous variables for which no underlying continuous distribution can be assumed. Now, if we want to correlate these variables, then applying Pearson's formula have problems because of lack of continuity. In this case, the dichotomous variable is usually assigned values zero (0) and one (1) for two levels, respectively. In reality, you can assign any value to one level and any other value to another level (e.g., 14 and 117) and it will not have any relevance. Since r_{pb} is Pearson's correlation, we can calculate it the very same way. Look at hypothetical data in Table 5.3 about outcome on reasoning task (success or failure) with conscientiousness[2] personality. Outcome on task is a dichotomous variable and conscientiousness is a continuous variable.

---

[2] Conscientiousness (C) is the dimension of personality. It's a factor in the five-factor model of personality. People high on C are dutiful, organized, hard-working, orderly, and so on. The other factors are neuroticism, extraversion, openness to experience, and agreeableness.

Table 5.3. *Data on Outcome (Dichotomous) and Conscientiousness (Continuous) Variables*

Participant	1	2	3	4	5	6	7	8	9	10
Outcome	0	1	0	1	1	0	1	0	0	1
Conscientiousness	12	19	13	20	16	15	15	10	09	17

The covariance between outcome and conscientiousness is 1.556, $SD_{Conscientiousness} = 3.63$, $SD_{Outcome} = 0.527$; hence, the correlation is $r_{pb} = \dfrac{Cov_{xy}}{S_x S_y} = \dfrac{1.556}{3.63 \times 0.527} = 0.814$.

The percentage of variance conscientiousness shares with outcome is $r_{pb}^2 = 0.814^2 = 0.66$. This indicates that 66% information in the reasoning task is explained by conscientiousness.

The null hypothesis and alternative hypothesis for testing the significance of r_{pb} are as follows:

$$H_o: \rho = 0$$
$$H_A: \rho \neq 0$$

Since r_{pb} is Pearson's correlation, the significance testing is also similar to it. The *t*-distribution is used for this purpose with $n-2$ as df:

$$t = \frac{r_{pb}\sqrt{n-2}}{\sqrt{1-r_{pb}^2}}$$

The *t*-value for our data is 3.9598. The df$=n-2=10-2=8$. The value is significant at 0.01 level. Hence, we reject the null hypothesis. The R code is identical to R code for Pearson's correlation.

5.3.1.2 Relationship between r_{pb} and t-test and Effect-size

The r_{pb} and independent samples *t*-test are related to each other. The data can be analyzed by independent samples *t*-test (to be discussed in Chapter 7). The outcome in grouping variables creating two groups, and conscientiousness scores can be dependent. The *t*-value is the result of independent samples *t*-test with homogeneity of variance assumed. This requires the calculation of pooled variance (S_p):

$$S_p^2 = \frac{(n_1 - 1)S_1^2 + (n_2 - 1)S_2^2}{n_1 + n_1 - 2}$$

$$t = \frac{\bar{X}_1 - \bar{X}_2}{S_p\sqrt{\dfrac{1}{n_1} + \dfrac{1}{n_2}}}$$

In the case of our data, the t-value is 3.9598 at df$=8$.
The relationship between *t*-value and r_{pb} is expressed as follows:

$$r_{pb}^2 = \frac{t^2}{t^2 + df}$$

$$r_{pb}^2 = \frac{3.9598^2}{3.9598^2 + 8} = 0.66$$

You will also quickly realize that the significance value that we have obtained is also identical to this value (except, at times, for sign).

The point-biserial r can be used as a measure of effect-size. As you know that the effect-size is expressed in terms of Cohen's d. Hedges g and Glass' Δ are alternative ways of expressing effect-size with corrections in d. The relationship between Cohen's d (d) and r_{pb} is as follows:

$$d = \frac{\bar{X}_1 - \bar{X}_2}{S_{pooled}} = \sqrt{\frac{4 \times r_{pb}^2}{1 - r_{pb}^2}}$$

The value of Cohen's d can be similarly converted back into r:

$$r = \frac{d}{\sqrt{d^2 + 4}}$$

In the case of our data, the d value is as follows:

$$d = \sqrt{\frac{4 \times r_{pb}^2}{1 - r_{pb}^2)}} = \sqrt{\frac{4 \times 0.66}{1 - 0.66}} = 2.81$$

The R code for converting r_{pb} to Cohen's d and vice versa and r_{pb} to t is as follows (R code 5.6).

```
# R Code 5.6. Cohen's d from r_pb and Other Useful Conversions
library (psych)        # call package psych
r2d (.814)             # convert r_pb into Cohen's d
d2r (d)                # convert Cohen's d into r_pb
r2t (.814, 10)         # convert r_pb into t-value enter r and sample size
r.con (r, n, p=.95)    # CI for correlation. r=correlation, n=sample size
fisherz (r)            # converting r to Fisher z transformation (r')
fisherz2r (z)          # converting Fisher z into r
```

5.3.1.3 Phi Correlation (ϕ)

The phi correlation (ϕ) is Pearson's correlation computed when both variables are dichotomous, for example, the correlation between the gender of a driver (female–male) and vehicle type (geared–auto transmission). Look at data in Table 5.4.

The value of ϕ is –0.714. The correlation is negative. For gender, the coding is men=0 and female=1, whereas for vehicle type the coding is manual transmission=0 and auto transmission=1. The negative correlation means that as gender takes value from 0 (men) to 1 (female),

Table 5.4. *Data and Calculations of Phi Coefficient*

X: Gender			0=Male					1=Female			
Y: Vehicle Type			0=Manual Transmission					1=Auto Transmission			
X	1	0	1	1	0	1	0	0	1	1	1	0
Y	0	1	0	0	1	1	1	1	0	0	1	1

Calculations

$\bar{X}=0.58$ $S_x=0.51$
$\bar{Y}=0.58$ $S_y=0.51$ $Cov_{XY}=-0.71$

$$r_{XY} = \phi_{XY} = \frac{Cov_{XY}}{S_X S_Y} = \frac{-0.189}{0.51 \times 0.51} = -0.714$$

vehicle type will move from 1 (auto) to 0 (manual). That means as gender becomes women, the vehicle type becomes manual transmission. The variance in vehicle type shared by gender is represented by r^2. The variance explained is $r^2 = \phi^2 = -0.714^2 = 0.509$, whereas 50.9% variance is shared by two variables.

The significance of ϕ can be tested by using the chi-square (χ^2) distribution. The ϕ can be converted into the χ^2 by obtaining a product of n and ϕ^2. The chi-square ($n\phi^2$) will have df=1. The null and alternative are as follows:

$$H_0: \rho=0$$
$$H_A: \rho\neq0$$
$$\chi^2=n\phi^2=12\times0.509=6.10$$

The value of the chi-square at 1 df is 3.84 at .05 level of significance. The obtained value is greater than the tabled value. So we reject the null hypothesis that states that the population correlation is zero. Let's quickly note the relationship between χ^2 and ϕ:

$$\phi = \sqrt{\frac{\chi^2}{n}}$$

So one can compute the chi-square and then calculate the phi coefficient. When χ^2 is obtained, its conversion to ϕ provides an index of practical significance of chi-square.

5.3.2 Biserial (r_b) and Tetrachoric Correlation (r_{tet}): Non-Pearson Correlations

The non-Pearson alternative to r_{pb} and ϕ correlations under conditions of artificial dichotomy are biserial (r_b) and tetrachoric correlations (r_{tet}), respectively. They are presented because traditionally they are discussed, and tradition is heavyweight. Perhaps, if you are referring to research some time back then you will also come across their reporting. The preferred correlations are Pearson's only.

5.3.2.1 Biserial Correlation

The biserial correlation coefficient (r_b) is similar to the point-biserial correlation. Traditionally, r_b is a correlation coefficient between two continuous variables (X and Y), out of which one is measured dichotomously (X). r_b is computed as follows:

$$r_b = \left[\frac{\overline{Y_1} - \overline{Y_0}}{S_Y}\right]\left[\frac{P_0 P_1}{h}\right]$$

where $\overline{Y_0}$ and $\overline{Y_1}$ are the Y score means for data pairs with an X score of 0 and 1, respectively, P_0 and P_1 are the proportions of data pairs with X scores of 0 and 1, respectively, S_y is the standard deviation for the Y data, and h is ordinate or the height of the standard normal distribution at the point which divides the proportions of P_0 and P_1.

The relationship between the point-biserial and the biserial correlation is as follows:

$$r_b = \frac{r_{pb}\sqrt{P_0 P_1}}{h}$$

It is recommended that one should prefer point-biserial correlation to biserial correlation. The distinction of artificially dichotomized and truly dichotomous is not much valuable, given the fact that at the measurement level the variables are dichotomous.

5.3.2.2 Tetrachoric Correlation (r_{tet})

Traditionally, tetrachoric correlation is a correlation between two dichotomous variables that have an underlying continuous distribution. If the two variables are measured in a more refined way, then the continuous distribution will result. For example, attitude to globalization and attitude towards privatization are two variables to be correlated. Now, we simply measure them as having positive or negative attitude. So we have 0 (negative attitude) and 1 (positive attitude) scores available on both the variables. Then the correlation between these two variables can be computed using **Tetrachoric correlation (r_{tet})**. The correlation can be expressed as $\cos(\theta)$.

Here, θ is the angle between vectors X and Y. Using this logic, r_{tet} can also be calculated:

$$r_{tet} = \cos\left[\frac{180^0}{1 + \sqrt{\frac{ad}{bc}}}\right]$$

Look at the hypothetical data in Table 5.5; numbers in the cell indicate frequency of individuals. So the tetrachoric correlation between attitude towards liberalization and attitude towards globalization is a positive one.

5.4 PARTIAL, PART (SEMI-PARTIAL) AND MULTIPLE CORRELATION

So far we have discussed the relationship between two variables. However, the relationship between two variables can get influenced by the presence of third (3rd, 4th, …, Kth) variable(s). Part correlation and partial correlation provide tools to control the influence of other variable or variables on the correlation. Multiple correlations allow us to relate multiple (2 or more) variables with one criterion variable.

5.4.1 Partial Correlation (r_p)

Pearson's correlation (r_{xy}) is the correlation between two variables X and Y. The partial correlation (r_p) is Pearson's correlation between two variables X and Y controlled for third variable Z ($r_{XY.Z}$). Z can be one variable or a set of variables ($Z_1, Z_2, …, Z_k$). The partial correlation controls the influence of Z on X and Y. This correlation is also expressed as correlation between X and Y "partialled out for," "controlled for" or "held constant for" variable Z. The notation $r_{XY.Z}$ is read as correlation between X and Y partialled out for Z. For example, look at the correlation between work locus of control (WLOC) and performance (Pr). So while correlating WLOC with

Table 5.5. *Data on Two Dichotomous Variables*

		Attitude to Globalization	
		Positive	**Negative**
Attitude to Privatization	Positive	70 (a)	20 (b)
	Negative	10 (c)	60 (d)

$$r_{tet} = \cos\left[\frac{180^0}{1 + \sqrt{\frac{ad}{bc}}}\right] = \cos\left[\frac{180^0}{1 + \sqrt{\frac{(70)(60)}{(10)(20)}}}\right] = \cos(32.24^0) = 0.676$$

Pr, we need to control the influence of N. If all variables show linear relations with each other, then it can be achieved by partial correlation ($r_{\text{WLOC Pr. N}}$). It's important to note that the third variable's influence on both (X and Y) is controlled for in partial correlation. The computational formula is as follows:

$$r_p = r_{XY.Z} = \frac{r_{XY} - r_{XZ}r_{YZ}}{\sqrt{(1 - r_{XZ}^2)(1 - r_{YZ}^2)}}$$

where $r_{XY.Z}$ is partial correlation between X and Y controlled for Z, r_{XY} is correlation between X and Y, r_{XZ} is correlation between X and Z, and r_{YZ} is correlation between Y and Z.

The data for $n=50$ is $r_{\text{WOLOC.Pr}} = 0.30$; $r_{\text{WOLOC.N}} = -0.40$ and $r_{\text{Pr.N}} = -0.45$. The correlation between WOLOC and performance ($r_{\text{WOLOC.Pr}} = 0.30$) is significant ($t=2.18$, $p=0.03$). Now, we partial out this correlation for neuroticism:

$$r_p = r_{XY.Z} = \frac{r_{XY} - r_{XZ}r_{YZ}}{\sqrt{(1 - r_{XZ}^2)(1 - r_{YZ}^2)}} = \frac{0.3 - (-0.4 \times -0.45)}{\sqrt{(1 - 0.16)(1 - 0.2025)}} = \frac{0.12}{\sqrt{0.6699}} = \frac{0.12}{0.8185} = 0.147$$

The partial correlation between WOLOC and performance controlled for neuroticism is 0.147, which indicates that the correlation is reducing once it has been controlled for neuroticism. The significance of partial correlation can be tested for the following null hypothesis:

$$H_0 : \rho_p = 0$$

And the alternative hypothesis is

$$H_A : \rho_p \neq 0$$

where ρ_p is the population partial correlation coefficient. The estimator of ρ_p is r_p, which can be converted into t-value that obviously follows t-distribution. The t-value is obtained by

$$t = \frac{r_p \sqrt{n - v}}{\sqrt{1 - r_p^2}}$$

where

r_p = partial correlation computed on the sample, $r_{XY.Z}$
n = sample size,
v = total number of variables employed in the analysis
The significance of the r_p is tested at the df = $n - v$.
In the present example, we can employ significance testing as follows:

$$t = \frac{r_p \sqrt{n - v}}{\sqrt{1 - r_p^2}} = \frac{0.147\sqrt{50 - 3}}{\sqrt{1 - 0.022}} = 1.019$$

The significance of the value is tested at df = $n - v = 50 - 3 = 47$. The two-tailed probability of $t=1.019$ at df=47 is 0.3133. Obviously, the t-value is not significant and we retain the null hypothesis that the population correlation between WOLOC and performance partialled out for neuroticism is zero. Theoretical implication is simple: The apparent correlation between WLOC and performance is due to neuroticism. Once controlled for N, this correlation vanishes.

5.4.2 On Uses of Partial Correlation

There are many uses of partial correlations in psychological research. One, partial correlation is useful when theory makes prediction about the role of the third variable in correlation. The example is already presented. Second, it is useful to statistically control effects of uncontrolled variables, for example, intelligence and personality while correlating cognitive ability and non-cognitive ability with performance. Furnham and Chamorro-Premuzic (2004) found that the correlation of statistics examinations grades (SEG) with intelligence was insignificant (e.g., Wonderlic Test and Alice Heim Test correlated with SEG by 0.17 and 0.18, respectively, $n=91$). After controlling for five-factor model (FFM) personality traits (neuroticism and conscientiousness, more prominently), the correlations changed to 0.32 and 0.33, respectively. They concluded that, "cognitive ability is particularly related to SEG when individual differences in personality are being controlled for" (p. 950). Third, partial correlation is a useful tool to control the impact of developmental changes by partialling out for the age of participants. To take a thoughtless example, the length of index figure and verbal ability will correlate positively if data across early childhood to late adolescence is taken. Both the variables increase in their values as the age increases and hence if we partial this correlation for age, it will be close to zero. Fourth, r_p is useful in controlling for the impact of heterogeneous subgroups in correlational analysis, and fifth, r_p is often used to control for the tendency of social desirability in self-report measures. I shall elaborate the last two.

In Section 5.2.4, the impact of heterogeneous subgroups was considered as one of the factors that affect correlation coefficient. Look at the data in Table 5.6: it's a hypothetical data of nine male and nine female respondents on intolerance of ambiguity (IOA) and neuroticism (N).

The correlation between IOA and N, ignoring the gender for all 18 participants, is –0.46. It is unexpected. However, the correlation for males is 0.648 and that for females is 0.405, which are consistent with the theory. The correlation is influenced by gender. Partial correlation can be employed in order to control the impact of gender. Code gender as male=1 and female=2 and compute partial correlation between IOA and N partialled for gender. The partialled correlation is 0.566, $t=2.56$, df=15, $p=0.0177$. The partial correlation is significant and the null hypothesis that the population partial correlation is zero is rejected. More importantly, the correlation between IOA and N partialled out for gender is +0.567, which is expected when IOA and N are correlated. Notably, partialling out correlation for grouping variable (gender) has controlled the impact of heterogeneous subgroups on correlation.

Self-report instruments are vulnerable to a tendency of faking-good or socially desirable responding (SDR). One common strategy to control SDR is to use SDR scales. Several clinical instruments (e.g., MMPI, MCMI) and personality measures (e.g., EPQ-R) have employed measures of SDR. Researchers often measure SDR by using specialized tools (e.g., BIDR, Marlow–Crowne SD scale, and so on) if parent instrument lack SDR scale. Once the score on the SDR scale is obtained, correlation between content variables is partialled out for response style variables measured by SDR measure. Recently, personality psychologists raised doubts about its utility. McCrae and Costa (1983), Piedmont, McCrae, Riemann, and Angleitner (2000)

Table 5.6. *Data on IOA and Neuroticism (N) for Male and Female Respondents*

Gender	M	M	M	M	M	M	M	M	M
IOA	12	17	7	12	14	11	13	10	21
N	22	28	24	32	30	27	29	17	34

Gender	F	F	F	F	F	F	F	F	F
IOA	27	25	20	19	26	23	24	22	21
N	20	15	18	12	18	13	20	9	19

demonstrated that SDR instruments measure "more substance than style" and, hence, are invalid validity scales.

```
# R Code 5.6. Partial Correlation
library(TripleR)    # call library 'TripleR'
parCor(x, y, z)     # x, y, z are vectors
```

5.4.3 Partial Correlation as Pearson's Correlation between Regression Residuals

Partial correlation can also be understood as a Pearson's correlation between two residuals (errors).

Since, regression is not discussed, this might look unfamiliar. Please revisit this section after having read about regression.

In this, case we can write two linear regression equations and solve them by using ordinary least-squares (OLS). They are as follows:

$$\text{Performance} = a_1 + (b_1 \times N) + e_1$$

where "a_1" is a y intercept of the regression line; "b_1" is the slope of the line; "e_1" is the error in the prediction of performance using N.

$$\text{WLOC} = a_2 + (b_2 \times N) + e_2$$

where "a_2" is a y intercept of the regression line; "b_2" is the slope of the line; "e_2" is the error in the prediction of WLOC using N.

The e_1 and e_2 are residuals of each of the variables after N explains the variation in them. Meaning, e_1 is the remaining variance in performance once the variance accounted for N is removed. Similarly, e_2 is the variance left in the WLOC once the variance accounted for N is removed.

Now, the partial correlation can be defined as Pearson's correlation between e_1 and e_2.

$$r_p = r_{e_1 e_2}$$

This correlation is the correlation of that performance and WLOC, from which a linear influence of N has been removed.

5.4.4 Semipartial Correlation (r_{sp})

Look at the correlation between academic achievement (AA) and intelligence (g). We know that students may do well not only because they are intelligent but also because they are systematic, organized, dutiful, self-motivated, and reflective. These personality traits are referred to as conscientiousness in terms of FFM of personality. So while correlating "AA" with "g," we need to control for the influence of C. If all variables show linear relations with each other, then it can be achieved by partial correlation ($r_{\text{Academic Ach Intelligence. Conscientiousness}}$). However, the theory suggests that C will influence only AA and not "g," correlation between AA and "g" will be computed for controlling the influence of C on AA and not both. This is semipartial correlation (r_{sp}). In semipartial correlations ($r_{sp} = r_{X(Y.Z)}$), the effect of third variable (Z) was partialled out from only one variable (Y) and NOT from both the variables (X and Y). Semipartial correlation is obtained in the following manner:

$$r_{SP} = r_{X(Y.Z)} = \frac{r_{XY} - r_{XZ}r_{YZ}}{\sqrt{1 - r_{YZ}^2}}$$

where

$R_{X(Y.Z)}$ is a semipartial correlation of X with the Y after the linear relationship that Y has with Z is removed,

R_{XY} Pearson's product moment correlation between X and Y,

R_{XZ} Pearson's product moment correlation between X and Z,

R_{YZ} Pearson's product moment correlation between Y and Z.

Suppose, $r_{AA.g} = 0.3$; $r_{AA.C} = 0.4$; and $r_{g.C} = 0.11$ for $n=60$, then correlation between "g" and AA for controlling the influence of C on AA ($r_{sp} = r_{g(AA.C)}$) is obtained by

$$r_{A(B.C)} = \frac{0.3 - (0.4 \times 0.11)}{\sqrt{1 - (0.4^2)}} = \frac{0.256}{0.9165} = 0.279$$

The significance testing of semipartial correlation is similar to partial correlation. The $H_0 : \rho_{sp} = 0$ and $H_A : \rho_{sp} \neq 0$. The null hypothesis is tested using t-distribution.

$$t = \frac{r_{sp}\sqrt{n-v}}{\sqrt{1-r_{sp}^2}} = \frac{0.279\sqrt{60-3}}{\sqrt{1-0.279^2}} = 2.194$$

The calculated t-value 2.19 is greater than the tabled value of 2.002 at df$=57$ for .05 level of significance. Hence, the $H_0 : \rho_{sp} = 0$ is rejected. The theoretical implication is that even of AA is controlled for C, there exists a relationship between intelligence and academic achievement.

5.4.5 Multiple Correlation

The multiple correlation coefficient is a correlation of one variable with multiple other variables. The multiple correlation coefficient is denoted as $R_{A.BCD...k}$ which indicates that A is correlated with B, C, D, up to k variables. For example, we want to compute multiple correlations of A with B and C ($R_{A.BC}$). In this case, a linear combination of B and C is correlated with A. For example, correlation of academic achievement (AA) with two variables, intelligence (g) and conscientiousness (C) is multiple correlations denoted as $R_{(AA).(g C)}$. Often, multiple R is used in the context of regression as the index of total variance explained. In the case when two variables are correlated with one criterion, then multiple R can be calculated as follows:

$$R_{A.BC} = \sqrt{\frac{r_{AB}^2 + r_{AC}^2 - 2r_{AB}r_{AC}r_{BC}}{1 - r_{BC}^2}}$$

from the earlier example, $r_{AA.g} = 0.3$; $r_{AA.C} = 0.4$; and $r_{g.C} = 0.11$ for $n=60$. So the multiple R can be calculated as follows:

$$R_{AA.gC} = \sqrt{\frac{0.3^2 + 0.4^2 - 2 \times 0.3 \times 0.4 \times 0.11}{1 - 0.11^2}} = \sqrt{\frac{0.2236}{0.9879}} = 0.4757$$

Multiple R value 0.4757 is the positive correlation between AA and linear combination of "g" and C. This linear combination explains $R^2 = 0.4757^2 = 0.2263$ (i.e., 22.63%) variance in AA. Similar to correlation coefficient, multiple R square is also not an unbiased estimator of population parameter (P^2). Adjusted multiple R square ($\tilde{R}^2$) is computed to reduce the bias:

$$\tilde{R}^2 = 1 - \frac{(1-R^2)(n-1)}{n-k-1} = 1 - \frac{(1-0.2263)(60-1)}{60-2-1} = 0.1991$$

Here, k is the number of predictor variables (two—"g" and C).

The significance of multiple R is tested for $H_0 : P^2 = 0$ and $H_A : P^2 \neq 0$. The F-distribution is used for calculating the significance of the R^2 as follows:

$$F = \frac{(n-k-1)R^2}{k(1-R^2)} = \frac{(60-2-1) \times 0.2263}{2 \times (1-0.2263)} = \frac{12.89}{1.54} = 8.335$$

The degrees of freedom employed in the significance testing of this F-value are df $_{num}=k$ and df $_{denominator}=n-k-1$. For our example, the degrees of freedom are as follows: df $_{num}=k=2$; and df $_{denominator}=n-k-1=60-2-1=57$. The tabled value of F at df=2, 57 is 3.1588 and the obtained value is greater leading to the rejection of our null hypothesis. The exact probability of $F_{(2,57)} = 8.335$, $p = 0.00067$.

5.5 TESTING DIFFERENCE BETWEEN CORRELATION COEFFICIENTS

Researches might have interest in testing hypothesis about equality of two or more correlations. The correlations can be independent or non-independent. Independent correlations are obtained on two same variables but on different participants, for example, r_{xy} for male and r_{xy} for females. Non-independent correlations are obtained on the same sample. There are two ways of obtaining non-independent correlations. First, one variable (e.g., x) is correlated with two different variables (e.g., y and z) for the same sample leading to two non-independent correlations r_{xy} and r_{xz}; second, two same variables are correlated using the same sample on two different occasions, generally called time 1 (T1) and time 2 (T2). So one has r_{xy} at T1 and r_{xy} at T2. We shall discuss the first case. The generalization of test for independent correlations for more than two variables is also briefly discussed.

5.5.1 Testing Difference in Two Independent Correlations

There are instances when researchers compute correlation between same two variables in different groups or independent samples. The researcher may have an interest in determining whether two population correlations are equal. For example, Borroni, Somma, Andershed, Maffei, & Fossatiand (2014) studied gender differences in correlations between psychopathy and big-five scales. Gender creates independent samples. The correlation between callous-unemotional scale (CUS) and agreeableness (A) is –0.32 for females and –0.35 for males. Now, we can test $H_0 : \rho_{\text{Female}} = \rho_{\text{Male}}$ and the alternative is $H_A : \rho_{\text{Female}} \neq \rho_{\text{Male}}$. However, testing this hypothesis directly has problems that were discussed earlier. Hence, we need to convert them to Fisher's Z-transformation (I am using r' instead of Z to avoid confusion with Z-distribution and Z-score).

$$\text{Fisher's } Z = r' = \tanh^{-1}(r) = 0.5 \times \log \left| \frac{1+r}{1-r} \right|$$

The null is $H_0 : \rho'_{\text{Female}} = \rho'_{\text{Male}}$, where ρ' is Fisher's Z-transformed value of ρ. The r' will be approximately normally distributed with mean ρ' and standard error of $S_{r'} = \frac{1}{\sqrt{n-3}}$.

The null hypothesis now can be tested by

$$z = \frac{r'_1 - r'_2}{\sqrt{\dfrac{1}{n_1 - 3} + \dfrac{1}{n_2 - 3}}}$$

From the above example, the sample sizes were male=429 and female=824. The Z is

$$Z = \frac{r'_1 - r'_2}{\sqrt{\dfrac{1}{n_1 - 3} + \dfrac{1}{n_2 - 3}}} = \frac{-0.3316 - (-0.3644)}{\sqrt{\dfrac{1}{429 - 3} + \dfrac{1}{824 - 3}}} = 0.566$$

The Z-value>1.96 is significant at 0.05 and Z-value>2.58 is significant at 0.01 level. The obtained Z-value is smaller than that and hence is insignificant. This indicates that population correlation of CUS and A are not different for males and females. This suggests that one correlation coefficient should be used for them. This could be by combining data of both male and females. Edwards (1984) suggested the use of weighting procedures for obtaining a single estimate:

$$\bar{r}' = \frac{(n_1 - 3)r'_1 + (n_2 - 3)r'_2}{(n_1 - 3) + (n_2 - 3)}$$

In the case of our example,

$$\bar{r}' = \frac{[(429 - 3) \times -0.3316] + [(824 - 3) \times -0.3644]}{(429 - 3) + (824 - 3)} = -0.3538$$

The $\bar{r}'$ converted to r is –0.3398. Hence, –0.33 can be used as a common estimate of population correlation for males and females.

```
# R Code 5.7. Testing Difference between Two Independent Correlations
library(psych)
r.test(n=429, -.32, -.35, n2=824) # type '?r.test' for alternative tests
```

5.5.2 Testing Difference in More than Two Independent Correlations

There are instances when researchers might have interest in testing the difference between correlation obtained same two variables in more than two (3, 4,..., k) independent groups. Suppose a hypothetical example of correlation between intelligence (g) and creativity (Cr) across three different grades, 5th, 7th, and 9th. The null is $H_0 : \rho_1 = \rho_2 = \cdots = \rho_k$ and the alternative is $H_A : $ NOT H_0. The obtained sample estimates are $r_{g.Cr} = 0.4$ (n=60); $r_{g.Cr} = 0.45$ (n=60); and $r_{g.Cr} = 0.35$ (n=55) for three groups, respectively. For this hypothesis, the chi-square is obtained by

$$\chi^2 = \sum_{j=1}^{k}[(n_j - 3)\, r'^2_j] - \frac{\left[\sum_{j=1}^{k}(n_j - 3)\, r'_j\right]^2}{\sum_{j=1}^{k}(n_j - 3)}$$

where, n_j is the sample size of the jth group, r'_j is Fishers Z transformation of r_j, $j = 1,2,...,k$ are independent groups. In the case of the example, the Fisher transformed values are $r'_{g.Cr} = 0.4236$; $r'_{g.Cr} = 0.4847$; and $r'_{g.Cr} = 0.3654$, respectively, for three groups. The χ^2 is obtained as follows:

$$\chi^2 = [(60 - 3) \times 0.4236^2 + (60 - 3) \times 0.4847^2 + (55 - 3) \times 0.3654^2]$$

$$- \frac{[(60 - 3) \times 0.4236 + (60 - 3) \times 0.4847 + (55 - 3) \times 0.3654]^2}{(60 - 3) + (60 - 3) + (55 - 3)}$$

$$\chi^2 = 1.013$$

The df $= k - 1 = 3 - 1 = 2$. The obtained value of χ^2 is smaller than the tabled χ^2 value of 5.99 at 0.05 level for df$=2$. Hence, we accept the hypothesis that these correlations are homogeneous. If the null hypothesis is retained, then Edwards (1984) suggested that, instead of having separate sample coefficients, a common estimate of correlation be computed for all the groups since all k groups are representing the same population. The weighted estimate is obtained as follows:

$$\bar{z}_r = \frac{\sum_{j=1}^{k}(n_j - 3)r_j'}{\sum_{j=1}^{k}(n_j - 3)} = \frac{(60-3)\times 0.4236 + (60-3)\times 0.4847 + (55-3)\times 0.3654}{(60-3)+(60-3)+(55-3)} = \frac{70.77}{166} = 0.4263$$

The correlation value as a single estimate is now 0.4263 for the entire sample.

5.5.3 Testing Difference in Two Non-independent Correlations

In this section, difference in only one type of non-independent correlations is discussed. The dependence created by same variable in the same sample is correlated with two different variables (r_{xy} and r_{xz}). The non-independence created due to correlating two same variables at different points of time ($T1$ and $T2$) is not discussed.

Let's take an example from Belhekar and Sabnis (2011) data. They reported correlation of borderline personality scale (BPS) with FFI neuroticism (FFIN) and big-five emotional stability (BFES) for $n=246$. Now, one can ask a useful question: Whether two measures of emotional stability, FFIN and BFES, have similar correlation with BPS? The null hypothesis is $H_0 : \rho_{XZ} = \rho_{YZ}$ and the alternative is $H_A : \rho_{XZ} \neq \rho_{YZ}$. In the case of our example, the null is $H_0 : \rho_{\text{FFIN.BPS}} = \rho_{\text{BFES.BPS}}$ and the alternative is $H_A : \rho_{\text{FFIN.BPS}} \neq \rho_{\text{BFES.BPS}}$. $r_{\text{FFIN.BPS}} = 0.43$; $r_{\text{BFES.BPS}} = -0.15$; and $r_{\text{FFIN.BFES}} = -0.44$. For the purpose of this analysis, I shall ignore the signs and only look at magnitude since FFIN and BFES are the opposite ends of same continua. Initial work by Hotelling (1940) paved the way by suggesting T statistics to test this hypothesis. However, it was rejecting null even when it should have been accepted at negligible Type I error. Williams (1959) demonstrated this limitation and proposed a modification in computing T. Steiger (1980) reviewed and remarked that Williams' formula is a better test of hypothesis than Hotelling's. Williams' formula is as follows:

$$T = (r_{xy} - r_{xz})\sqrt{\frac{(n-1)(1+r_{yz})}{2\left(\frac{n-1}{n-3}\right)|R| + \bar{r}^2(1-r_{yz})^3}}$$

where

$$|R| = (1 - r_{xy}^2 - r_{xz}^2 - r_{yz}^2) + (2r_{xy}r_{xz}r_{yz})$$

$$\bar{r} = 0.5\,(r_{xy} + r_{xz})$$

The T statistics follows t-distribution with df$=n-3$. For the present data,

$$|R| = (1 - 0.45^2 - 0.15^2 - 0.44^2) + (r \times 0.45 \times 0.15 \times 0.44) = 0.65576$$
$$\bar{r} = 0.5(r_{xy} + r_{xz}) = 0.5 \times (0.45 + 0.15) = 0.29$$

$$T = (0.43 - 0.15)\sqrt{\frac{(246-1)(1+0.44)}{2\left(\frac{246-1}{246-3}\right)0.65576 + 0.29^2(1-0.44)^3}} = 4.548$$

df=n−3=246−3=243. The tabled value of t=2.596 at 0.01 level for df=250. The obtained value is greater than tabled values and hence is significant. Hence, the $H_0 : \rho_{\text{FFIN.BPS}} = \rho_{\text{BFES.BPS}}$ is rejected. It can be concluded that correlation between FFIN and BPS is different than the correlation between BFES and BPS. This has notable implications to personality theory. The FFIN comes from a theory-driven approach, whereas BFES comes from a psycho-lexical approach. Findings indicate that personality disorder traits are better explained by a theory-driven approach. In addition to Williams' T, Dunn and Clark (1969) introduced a procedure using Fisher's Z-transformation as a useful alternative way to test this hypothesis. Further discussion on advanced topics using ADF estimators is available in Steiger (2004). The R code for Williams' T is given in R code 5.7.

```
# R Code 5.7. Testing Difference in Non-independent Correlations
comcor<-function(rxy, rxz, ryz, n)
{
  rabs<-(1-(rxy^2)-(rxz^2)-(ryz^2))+(2*rxy*rxz*ryz)
  rbar<-.5*(rxy+rxz)
  t<-(rxy-rxz)*(sqrt(((n-1)*(1+ryz))/((2*((n-1)/(n-3)) * rabs) + (rbar^2
  * ((1-ryz)^3))))))
  print(t)
}
comcor(.43, .15, .44, 246) # returns t-value
```

5.6 METHODS FOR ORDINAL DATA: SPEARMAN'S RHO AND KENDAL'S TAU

Pearson's r can be computed on continuous data. Pearson's r is not advisable under two conditions: one, when the data is not continuous, and two, when the assumptions underlying Pearson's r are not satisfied. Alternative correlation procedures are available when the data is ordinal. Some data are ordinal data by nature. For example, a merit list itself is an ordinal data. The ordinal data can also be obtained by rank ordering continuous data. One needs to convert continuous data into ordinal data under circumstances when continous data are not satisfying assumptions of normal-theory-based statistics. These assumptions generally are about normal distribution, equal variances, normal distribution of error terms, homoscedasticity, and so on.

5.6.1 Ranking Data

Ranking data is a relatively simple procedure. Suppose you have the following data to rank: 3, 4, 5, 5, 6, 11, 11, 13, 11, 14.

First, arrange all number from lowest to highest (or the other way round, depending on the purpose and convenience). The lowest rank of 1 is given to the smallest number (3), rank 2 is assigned to value (4). Next two values (5) are identical, called the tied rank. If they were not identical, then they would be given separate ranks of 3 and 4. So we take average of 3 and 4 and give them rank 3.5 each. Next value (6) will get the next rank 5. Three values (11) are tied at the next place; the ranks to be given are 6, 7, and 8. So the average rank is 7=(6+7+8)/3. So the mean rank 7 is assigned to all (11). Last two values (13 and 14) get rank 9 and 10, respectively. The final ranking looks like Table 5.7.

Table 5.7. *Ranking Data*

X	3	4	5	5	6	11	11	11	13	14
Rank X	1	2	3.5	3.5	5	7	7	7	9	10

If the ranking is correct, then the sum of the ranks should be $n \times (n+1)/2$. The sum rank = $(10 \times 11)/2 = 110/2 = 55$. The sum of ranks is also 55, which is indicative that we have ranked correctly.

5.6.2 Spearman's Correlation for Ranked Data (r_s)

A well-known psychologist and intelligence theorist, Charles Spearman (1904), developed a correlation procedure called in his honor as Spearman's rank-order correlation or Spearman's rho (r_s). The null hypothesis states that

H_0: $\rho_s = 0$ and alternative hypothesis states that H_A: $\rho_s \neq 0$. There are specific formulae to compute r_s; however, the simplest way to compute Spearman's r is to compute Pearson's correlation between X and Y, where X and Y are both rank-ordered variables. Pearson's r computed on ranked data is called Spearman's *rho*. There are known issues in significance testing of Spearman's rho since the ranked data cannot be normally distributed. The significance testing for sample smaller than 28 are based on some approximations. Generally, r_s is useful under small sample conditions. Computing the confidence interval does not have much utility. Pearson's r is already well illustrated and the method of ranking is also explained. Given this, there is no need to demonstrate a computational example.

5.6.3 Kendall's *tau* Coefficient (τ)

Kendall's τ coefficient (1938) is an alternative method to Spearman's *rho* to compute correlation with ranked data. The r_s is based on computing similarity mean departures of each group, whereas Kendall's tau is based on *inversions* in the data. Kendall's *tau* is correlation between two sets of ranks, X and Y. The population value of *tau* is symbolized as τ (lower-case Greek letter *tau*) and sample statistics is symbolized as $\tilde{\tau}$. *Tau* ranges from -1.00 to $+1.00$ and is interpreted on basis of sign and magnitude of coefficient. The null hypothesis is $H_0 : \tau = 0$ and the alternative is $H_0 : \tau \neq 0$. Depending on the theory, directional alternatives H_A: $\tau < 0$ or H_A: $\tau > 0$ could be stated. One-tailed test is required for directional alternatives.

5.6.3.1 Logic and Computation of $\tilde{\tau}$

The *tau* is based on concordance and discordance between two sets of ranks. For example, Table 5.8 shows data of four subjects (P, Q, R, and S) on rank of variables X and Y.

Following steps can be taken to obtain concordant and discordant pairs.

Step 1: order one variable (e.g., X) according to ranks (generally, lowest to highest) while keeping pairs intact. After ranking they will look like first two rows in Table 5.9.

Step 2: Take pair of ranks for two subjects Q (1, 1) and P (2, 3) on X and Y. Here pair means two participants (P and Q). The pair of ranks is concordant (i.e., in agreement) when the sign or direction of $R_X - R_X$ for subjects P and Q is similar to the sign or direction of $R_Y - R_Y$ for the same subjects. For subjects P and Q, $R_X - R_X$ is ($1-2 = -1$) and $R_Y - R_Y$ is also ($1-3 = -2$). The sign or direction of the P and Q pair is in agreement. So pair P and Q is called concordant pair (C). Now, considering pair Q and R. $R_X - R_X$ is ($1-3 = -2$) and $R_Y - R_Y$ is also ($1-2 = -1$). The sign or direction of the Q and R pair is in agreement, so it is concordant. Further, considering pair P

Table 5.8. *Small Data Example for tau on Four Subjects*

Subject	P	Q	R	S
R_X	2	1	3	4
R_Y	3	1	2	4

Table 5.9. *Table Showing Computation of Concordant and Discordant Pairs*

Subjects	P	Q	R	S	ΣC	ΣD
Rank of X	1	2	3	4		
Rank of Y	1	3	2	4		
P	1	C	C	C	3	0
Q		3	D	C	1	1
R			2	C	1	0
S				4	0	0
					$\Sigma\Sigma C = 5$	$\Sigma\Sigma D = 1$

$$\tilde{\tau} = \frac{n_C - n_D}{\left[\frac{n(n-1)}{2}\right]} = \frac{5-1}{\left[\frac{4(4-1)}{2}\right]} = \frac{4}{6} = 0.667$$

Table 5.10. *Data of 10 Subjects on X (Rank of NP by Tigers) and Y (Ranks of NP by Visitors)*

	National Parks Being Ranked									
	A	B	C	D	E	F	G	H	I	J
NP by number of tigers (Ranks on X)	1	2	3	4	5	6	7	8	9	10
NP by number of visitors (Ranks on Y)	2	1	5	3	4	6	10	8	7	9

and R. $R_X - R_X$ is $(2-3=-1)$ and $R_Y - R_Y$ is also $(3-2=+1)$. The sign or the direction of pair P and R is not in agreement. This pair is called as *discordant pair* (D). Total number of pairs that need to be evaluated is $n(n-1)/2 = (4 \times 3)/2 = 6$, that is, six pairs. They are: PQ, PR, PS, QR, QS, and RS and the concordance is –C, C, C, D, C, and C, respectively. All the pairs, except the QR pair, are concordant.

$$\tilde{\tau} = \frac{n_C - n_D}{\left[\frac{n(n-1)}{2}\right]}$$

where $\tilde{\tau}$ = value of τ obtained on the sample; n_C = number of concordant pairs; n_D = number of discordant pairs; n = number of subjects. In our case, $n_C = 5$ and $n_D = 1$.

Now, there is a quick illustration to obtain n_C and n_D pairs for this small data in Table 5.9. First, ranks of X are placed in the second row in the ascending order. Accordingly, ranks of Y are arranged in the third row. Then the ranks of Y are entered in the diagonal (see Table 5.9). Start with the first element in the diagonal, which is 1 (row 4). Now move across the row. Compare it (1) with each column element of Y. If it is smaller, then enter C in the intersection. If it is larger, then enter D in the intersection. For example, 1 is smaller than 3 (column 3) so C is entered. In the next row (row 5), 3 is in the diagonal which is greater than 2 (column 4) of Y, so D is entered in the intersection. Then ΣC and ΣD are computed for each row. n_C is obtained from $\Sigma\Sigma C$ (i.e., 5) and n_D is obtained from $\Sigma\Sigma D$ (i.e., 1). Use these values to obtain $\tilde{\tau}$.

5.6.3.2 Computational Alternative for $\tilde{\tau}$

This procedure of computing the *tau* is tedious. There is an easier alternative. Suppose, we want to correlate "rank of national parks by number of visitors" with "their rank in number of tigers." These ranks are available. The data are given in Table 5.10 for 10 national parks. First, we arrange the ranks of the parks by the number of tigers (X) in the ascending order and rank of parks by visitors (Y) be arranged as per the ranks of X. Then draw lines to connect the comparable ranking of X with Y. Please note that lines are not drawn if the subject gets the same rank on both the variables. Now, we calculate the number of inversions. Number of inversions is the number of intersections of the lines. We have five intersections of the lines.

So the following equation can be used to compute $\tilde{\tau}$:

$$\tilde{\tau} = 1 - \frac{2(n_s)}{\frac{n(n-1)}{2}}$$

where $\tilde{\tau}$ = sample value of τ; n_s = number of inversions or $n_s = n_C - n_D$; n = number of subjects.

$$\tilde{\tau} = 1 - \frac{2(n_s)}{\frac{n(n-1)}{2}} = 1 - \frac{2(5)}{\frac{10(10-1)}{2}} = 1 - \frac{10}{45} = 1 - 0.222 = 0.778$$

The value of Kendall's *tau* for this data is 0.78. The relationship between X and Y is positive. This indicates that as the rank on the number of tigers (X) increases, the rank on the number of visitors (Y) increases. Interpretation of *tau* is straightforward. For example, if the $\tilde{\tau}$ is 0.78, then it can be interpreted as follows. If the pairs of NP are sampled at random, then the probability that their order on two variables (X and Y) is similar is 0.778 or higher than the probability that it would be in reverse order. The calculation of *tau* needs to be modified for tied ranks (Hays, 1981).

5.6.3.3 Significance Testing of $\tilde{\tau}$

The statistical significance testing of Kendall's *tau* is carried out by using either Appendix C7 and referring to the critical value provided in it or by using the Z-transformation. Z can be calculated by using the following equation:

$$Z = \frac{\tilde{\tau}}{\sqrt{\frac{2(2n+5)}{9n(n-1)}}}$$

Note that denominator is the standard error of $\tilde{\tau}$. Once the Z is calculated, you can refer to Appendix C1 for finding out the probability.

For our example in Table 5.9, the value of $\tilde{\tau} = 0.664$ for $n = 4$. Appendix C7 provides the critical value of 1.00 at the two-tailed significance level of alpha = 0.05. So $\tilde{\tau}$ is insignificant and, thus, we retain H_0: $\tau = 0$. It implies that the underlying population represented by the sample has no relationship between X and Y.

For the example in Table 5.10, the obtained value of *tau* is 0.778 with $n = 10$.

To test significance, convert $\tilde{\tau}$ into Z. Then use the Z distribution for testing the significance of $\tilde{\tau}$. For this purpose, the following formula can be used:

$$Z = \frac{\tilde{\tau}}{\sqrt{\frac{2(2n+5)}{9n(n-1)}}} = \frac{0.778}{\sqrt{\frac{2(2 \times 10 + 5)}{9 \times 10(10-1)}}} = 3.313$$

The Z table (normal distribution table) in Appendix C1 has a value of $Z = 1.96$ at 0.05 level and 2.58 at 0.01 level. The obtained value of $Z = 3.313$ is greater than these values. So we reject the null hypothesis at 0.01 level of significance.

```
#R Code 5.8. Kendall's Tau
cor.test(x,y, method = c("kendall")) # method may be pearson, or spearman
```

Table 5.11. *Data in Form of Ordered Contingency Table*

			Previous suicide attempt			*r* sum
		No	Thought of self-harm	Attempted self-harm	Suicide attempt	
Depressive episode	No	$n_{11}=42$	$n_{12}=12$	$n_{13}=02$	$n_{14}=04$	57
	Mild	$n_{21}=10$	$n_{22}=33$	$n_{23}=23$	$n_{24}=09$	75
	Severe	$n_{31}=03$	$n_{32}=11$	$n_{33}=20$	$n_{34}=31$	65
c sum		55	56	45	41	197

5.7 ADDITIONAL METHODS FOR ORDINAL DATA: GOODMAN AND KRUSKAL'S GAMMA, KENDALL'S COEFFICIENT OF CONCORDANCE

This section briefly explains two useful alternatives. Kendall's coefficient of concordance (W) is useful in analyzing agreement between multiple raters. Goodman–Kruskal gamma is a bivariate measure of association for data summarized in *ordered contingency tables*.

5.7.1 Goodman and Kruskal's Gamma (γ)

Goodman and Kruskal's gamma (γ) is a measure of correlation between two ordered variables represented in a contingency table (Goodman and Kruskal, 1954, 1972). The gamma takes value between –1 and +1. When the number of ties is very large and the number of values both variables take is small, then data can be converted into an ordered contingency table. An ordered $r \times c$ contingency table is arranged in such a way that both variables are arranged according to their order. Each column or row represents levels of X and Y variables, respectively, and X takes r levels and Y takes c levels. For example, a researcher has two questions, X and Y. Variable X is about self-harm, with responses: "No," "Had thought about it," "Attempted self-harm," and "Attempted Suicide"; and Y is diagnosed with depression: never, depressive episode—mild, depressive episode—severe. The data is ordered on both variables in the same order as described earlier. The ordered contingency table (Table 5.11) is as follows. A sample of 197 respondents answered the two questions, which are represented in the contingency table. Rows relate to depression (Y) and columns relate to self-harm (X). The contingency table is ordered because levels of these variables can be arranged in lower to higher order. A researcher has an interest in correlating ordered categories of depression with ordered categories of self-harm.

The data in Table 5.11 is read in the following manner: $n_{32}=11$ means that sample size (n) of cell specified as row 3 and column 2 is eleven. The statistics computed on the sample for Goodman–Kruskal gamma is $\boldsymbol{G}$ and the parameter estimated is γ (Greek letter gamma). The null hypothesis is $H_0 : \gamma = 0$, meaning that population represented by the sample has a value zero of gamma, and the alternative is $H_A : \gamma \neq 0$. The directional alternatives could be $H_A : \gamma < 0$ or $H_A : \gamma > 0$, depending on theory or previous research. $\boldsymbol{G}$ is computed as follows:

$$G = \frac{n_C - n_D}{n_C + n_D}$$

where n_C are participants who have concordant pair of ordering on X and Y; n_D are participants who have discordant pair of ordering on X and Y. The following procedure is used to obtain n_C and n_D.

Table 5.12 illustrates the computation of concordant and discordant pairs. To get concordant pairs, let's look at cell$_{11}$ which has a frequency 42. The concordant pairs are the product of frequency of that cell and sum of the frequencies of all the cells that fall both below and to

Table 5.12. *Computation of Concordant and Discordant Pairs*

Cell	Concordant pairs		Cell	Discordant pairs	
$Cell_{11}$	42 (33+23+09+11+20+31)	5334	$Cell_{11}$	42 (0)	0
$Cell_{12}$	12 (23+09+20+31)	996	$Cell_{12}$	12 (10+03)	156
$Cell_{13}$	02 (09+31)	80	$Cell_{13}$	02 (10+33+03+11)	114
$Cell_{14}$	31 (0)	0	$Cell_{14}$	01 (10+33+23+03+11+20)	100
$Cell_{21}$	10 (0)	620	$Cell_{21}$	10 (0)	0
$Cell_{22}$	33 (20+31)	1683	$Cell_{22}$	33 (3)	99
$Cell_{23}$	23 (31)	713	$Cell_{23}$	23 (3+11)	322
$Cell_{24}$	09 (3+11+20)	0	$Cell_{24}$	09 (20+11+03)	306
$Cell_{31}$	03 (0)	0	$Cell_{31}$	03 (0)	0
$Cell_{32}$	11 (0)	0	$Cell_{32}$	11 (0)	0
$Cell_{33}$	20 (0)	0	$Cell_{33}$	20 (0)	0
$Cell_{34}$	31 (0)	0	$Cell_{34}$	31 (0)	0
	Sum	**9426**		**Sum**	**1097**

the right of it. It is as follows: $n_{11}(n_{22}+n_{23}+n_{24}+n_{32}+n_{33}+n_{34})$ which is 42(33+23+09+11+2 0+31)=42×127=5334. To get discordant pairs, let's look at $cell_{14}$ which has frequency 01. The discordant pairs are the product of frequency of that cell and the sum of the frequencies of all the cells that fall both below and to the left of it. It is: $n_{14}(n_{21}+n_{22}+n_{23}+n_{31}+n_{32}+n_{33})$ which is 01(10+33+23+03+11+20)=01×100=100.

The n_C=9426 and n_D=751. G is obtained as follows:

$$G = \frac{n_C - n_D}{n_C + n_D} = \frac{9426 - 1097}{9426 + 1097} = 0.7915$$

The significance of G can be tested by using conversion.

$$Z = G\sqrt{\frac{n_C + n_D}{n(1 - G^2)}} = 0.7915\sqrt{\frac{9426 + 1097}{197(1 - 0.7915^2)}} = 9.46$$

The value of Z is significant at 0.01 and, hence, the null hypothesis $H_0 : \gamma = 0$ is rejected.

```
# R Code 5.9. Goodman-Kruskal Gamma
library(vcdExtra)
data <- c(42, 12, 2, 1, 10, 33, 23, 9, 3, 11, 20, 31)
data <- matrix(data, nrow = 3, byrow = TRUE)
GKgamma(data, .95) # .95 is confidence level for a significance test of
                   gamma
```

As is the case with Kendall's *tau*, a positive value of G indicates that concordant pairs are greater than discordant pairs. The negative value indicates that discordant pairs are greater than concordant pairs. The standard error of GK gamma is

$$SE_G = \left[\frac{1}{\sqrt{\frac{n_C + n_D}{n(1 - G^2)}}}\right] \text{ and, hence, } Z = \frac{G}{SE_G}$$

Additionally, Marascuilo and McSweeney (1977) described the procedure to test hypothesis about equality of two gamma values. To test the significance of a specific population value of γ, slight modification can be used to compute Z. Instead of G, use $G - \gamma$ while computing Z,

Table 5.13. *Four Judges Rating 10 Responses on Creativity*

	R1	R2	R3	R4	R5	R6	R7	R8	R9	R10
Judge 1	1	2	3	4	5	6	7	8	9	10
Judge 2	2	1	3	5	4	6	8	9	7	10
Judge 3	3	2	1	5	4	6	8	7	10	9
Judge 4	2	3	1	4	5	7	6	8	9	10
ΣR_j	8	8	8	18	18	25	29	32	35	39
$\Sigma R_j^2 = SS$	18	18	20	82	82	157	213	258	311	381

where γ is the specified value in the null hypothesis. Further, Davis (1967) developed procedures for computing partial correlation with gamma. Alternative procedures of association for an ordered contingency table have been developed by Somers (1962), which is referred to as **delta** (Δ). However, this measure is asymmetrical, and is useful when one of the variables is theoretically pre-specified as more important (or independent) than the other (Siegel and Castellan, 1988). **Yule's Q** is another measure of association that can be considered as a special case of GK gamma. **Yule's Q** is computed only for 2×2 contingency tables that are ordered as well as unordered. Finally, **Kendall's** τ and GK gamma can be computed on the same data sets, but Marascuilo and McSweeney (1977) noted that as the number of ties increase, $|G|$ becomes larger than $|\tilde{\tau}|$.

5.7.2 Kendall's Coefficient of Concordance (*W*)

Researchers at times are interested in correlating more than two sets of ranks. The techniques discussed so far are useful in correlating two sets of ranks (X and Y). Suppose that two judges rank creativity of 10 responses to a item in a test (generally, respondents of creativity test give many responses to an item. Each of the response is scored for creativity), then the inter-judge agreement can easily be computed by using Spearman's rho or Kendall's tau (perhaps, Cohen's Kappa can be the preferred method). Suppose four judges rate creativity of responses, then six different *rho* coefficients will have to be computed. Since these coefficients are different, a single judgment is difficult to frame. Under these circumstances, commonly used estimate of inter-ratter agreement (or Inter-judge agreement) is Kendall's coefficient of concordance (*W*). It was developed independently by Kendall and Babington-Smith (1939) and Wallis (1939). The value of *W* falls between 0 and 1, 0 indicating no agreement and 1 indicating complete agreement. *W* will never be negative. The population value is *W* and sample estimate is $\tilde{W}$. The null hypothesis is H_0: $W=0$ and the alternative is H_A: $W \neq 0$. The alternative will be non-directional. The computational illustration is given in Table 5.13. Four judges have ranked 10 responses (R1 to R10) on creativity.

The Judges are variables (like X and Y in correlation) and things rated (creative responses in our example) are observations. ΣR_j is the sum of columns for each response, whereas ΣR_j^2 is the sum of squares (SS) for each column. Kendall defined the coefficient of concordance as the ratio of variance of the sum of ranks (variance of ΣR_j) and the maximum possible for the sum of ranks. To define $\tilde{W}$,

$$\tilde{W} = \frac{\text{Variance of } \Sigma R_j}{\text{Maximum possible value for } \Sigma R_j}$$

This formulation is computationally slightly lengthy. Little bit of algebra will provide a better alternative.

$$\tilde{W} = \frac{12 \Sigma T_j^2}{k^2 n(n^2 - 1)} - \frac{3(n+1)}{n-1}$$

where T_j is column totals (ΣR_j), n is the number of items (participants or responses) to be ranked, and k is the number of judges.

$$\Sigma T_j^2 = 8^2 + 8^2 + 8^2 + 18^2 + 18^2 + 25^2 + 29^2 + 32^2 + 35^2 + 39^2 = 6076$$

$n=10$ and $k=4$. $\tilde{W}$ is computed as follows:

$$\tilde{W} = \frac{12 \times 6076}{4^2 \times 10 \times (10^2 - 1)} - \frac{3 \times (10+1)}{10-1} = 4.603 - 3.667 = 0.936$$

The value of $\tilde{W}$ is close to 1 and is indicative of a reasonable agreement between the judges. Since, $\tilde{W}$ is not the Pearson correlation, the interpretation of $\tilde{W}$ on the basis of the value is difficult. Hays (1981) suggested that the relationship between $\tilde{W}$ and average of all Spearman's rho ($\bar{r}_s$) can be used for interpretation. The $\tilde{W}$ to $\bar{r}_s$ conversion is simple:

$$\bar{r}_s = \frac{k\tilde{W} - 1}{k - 1}$$

For our data,

$$\bar{r}_s = \frac{k\tilde{W} - 1}{k - 1} = \frac{(4 \times 0.936) - 1}{4 - 1} = 0.915$$

$\bar{r}_s$ is the average of all possible Spearman's rho (r_s) coefficients (six in this data). This value has to be interpreted as Spearman's rho. Generally, $\tilde{W}$ is reported along with $\bar{r}_s$ interpretation.

Chi-square distribution is used to test the null hypothesis that states that there is no agreement between the judges. χ^2 is evaluated at $df=n-1$.

$$\chi^2 = k(n-1)\tilde{W}$$
$$\chi^2 = 4 \times (10-1) \times 0.936 = 33.71$$

χ^2 is significant at 0.01 level since the obtained value is greater than the χ^2 value at 0.01 level at df=9. The chi-square test is not used often, particularly when $\tilde{W}$ is computed as a measure of inter-ratter reliability for the test that has subjective scoring. It must be remembered that a psychometrician has little interest in showing that the population value of $\tilde{W}$ is not zero. The prime interest is to show that $\tilde{W}$ is closer to 1, and hence one should compute $\tilde{W}$ in the form of $\bar{r}_s$. The last point is about relationship between the Friedman test and Kendall's W. Since $\tilde{W}$ can be computed from Friedman's test for within subject design, Kendall's W can be used as a measure of effect-size in Friedman's test.

```
# R Code 5.9. Kendall's W
raw <- c(1, 2, 3, 4, 5, 6, 7, 8, 9, 10, 2, 1, 3, 5, 4, 6, 8, 9, 7, 10, 3,
2, 1, 5, 4, 6, 8, 7, 10, 9, 2, 3, 1, 4, 5, 7, 6, 8, 9, 10) # data input
data <- matrix(raw, ncol = 4, byrow = F) # convert data into matrix
library (irr) # call library irr
kendall (data) # kendall W function
```

5.8 METHODS WITH CATEGORICAL/NOMINAL DATA

The nominal or categorical data does not have any ordering in the categories. For example, gender is a categorical variable wherein order does not exist. Similarly, residential state (e.g.,

Table 5.14. *Contingency Table Showing Frequencies for Two Variables: Preference for Art form (X), and Residential Status (Y)*

		Y: Residential Status			Total
		Metropolitan	**Urban**	**Rural**	
X: Preference for Art Form	Local	20	25	59	104
	Western	60	40	10	110
	Total	80	65	69	$n=214$

Maharashtra and Delhi), color of eyes or hairs, academic discipline (e.g., arts, science, and engineering), and so on are examples of nominal data. The data on nominal categories can be represented in contingency tables. Contingency coefficient test, phi coefficient, Cramér's phi coefficient, Yule's Q, odds ratio are some representative techniques that can be used to understand association among categorical variables. Some of them use Pearson chi-square as a starting point, whereas others do not use it.

5.8.1 Chi-square Test for Independence

Chi-square distribution is discussed in Chapter 1. The detailed discussion about the logic of chi-square statistics is offered in Chapter 9. Readers are requested to read both to develop a better understanding. However, a brief explanation is provided here since the chi-square test for independence can be used to test association between two nominal variables. For example, the researcher has a question about an association between preference for art form (local versus Western) and residential status (metropolitan/urban/rural) and he collects the data as shown in Table 5.14. Number indicates the frequency of the respondent from three residential status registering specific art preference, for example, 20 metropolitan individuals prefer the local art form, and so on. The null hypothesis is that the two variables are independent and the alternative is that they are dependent.

The chi-square test is calculated as follows:

$$\chi^2 = \frac{\Sigma(f_o - f_e)^2}{f_e}$$

where f_o is frequency observed and f_e is frequency expected. The f_o is already provided in the table, whereas f_e needs to be computed. To compute expected frequencies, use the following steps: first, obtain column totals, row totals which are also called marginal totals (since they are in margin). If the E_{ij} is the expected frequency for the ith row and jth column, and R_i and C_j are respective column frequencies, n is the total sample size, then E_{ij} is obtained as follows:

$$E_{ij} = \frac{R_i C_j}{n}$$

In the case of the above example,

$$E_{11} = \frac{80 \times 104}{214} = 38.88; \quad E_{12} = \frac{65 \times 104}{214} = 31.59; \quad E_{13} = \frac{69 \times 104}{214} = 33.53$$

$$E_{21} = \frac{80 \times 110}{214} = 41.12; \quad E_{22} = \frac{65 \times 110}{214} = 33.41; \quad E_{23} = \frac{69 \times 110}{214} = 35.47$$

The chi-square is calculated as follows:

$$\chi^2 = \frac{\Sigma(f_o - f_e)^2}{f_e} = \frac{\Sigma(O_{ij} - E_{ij})^2}{E_{ij}}$$

$$\chi^2 = \frac{(20 - 38.88)^2}{38.88} + \frac{(25 - 31.59)^2}{31.59} + \frac{(59 - 33.53)^2}{33.53} + \frac{(60 - 41.12)^2}{41.12}$$

$$+ \frac{(40 - 33.14)^2}{33.14} + \frac{(10 - 35.47)^2}{35.47}$$

$$\chi^2 = 58.148 \text{ at df} = (R - 1)(C - 1) = (2 - 1) \times (3 - 1) = 2$$

The chi-square value at 0.05 level is 5.99 and at 0.01 level is 9.21. Since the obtained value is greater than the critical value at 0.01 level, the null hypothesis stating that X and Y are independent is rejected. However, the chi-square test cannot be interpreted in terms of the degree of association. It will only make an inference that nominal variables X and Y are dependent or not. Since, these categories are nominal, inference in terms of "as X increases Y increases" or "X and Y share a specific percentage of variance" cannot be made.

```
# R Code 5.10. Independent Chi-square
x<-c(20,25,59,60,40,10)           #data from example
x<-matrix(x, ncol=3, byrow = T)   #converting it to matrix
output<-chisq.test(x, correct=T)  # chi-square test
output                            # view output
output$expected                   # view expected frequencies
```

5.8.2 Chi-Square Based Measures: Phi Coefficient, Contingency Coefficient (C) and Cramer's V

All the three statistics discussed in this section are obtained from Pearson's chi-square. The **phi coefficient** (ϕ) can also be computed for nominal data that are represented in 2×2 contingency tables by using a simple transformation on Pearson's chi-square test.

$$\phi = \sqrt{\frac{\chi^2}{n}}$$

Phi coefficient is Pearson's correlation between two dichotomous variables, discussed earlier (see Section 5.3.1 about phi coefficient).

The Contingency Coefficient (C) is obtained by the following transformation of chi-square:

$$C = \sqrt{\frac{\chi^2}{\chi^2 + n}}$$

The contingency coefficient is generally computed for symmetric contingency tables, that is, when the number of rows and columns are equal; however, it can be computed for data of any dimension. Contingency coefficient suffers from a disadvantage. Since n is always greater than zero, C can *never* be 1. The maximum value C reaches for 2×2 data is 0.707; for 3×3 data is 0.816; and for a 4×4 table, it is 0.866. The maximum value (C_{max}) can be obtained by $C_{max} = \sqrt{(k - 1) \div k}$, where k is smaller between *Row* and *Column* (2 in the earlier example). In the case of 3×3, $C_{max} = \sqrt{(3 - 1) \div 3} = 0.816$. An adjustment in C is suggested by Ott, Larson, Rexroat, and Mendenhall (1992) to take care of this limitation as well as to be able to compare two C values obtained on contingency tables of different dimensions. The adjusted contingency coefficient (C_{adj}) is obtained by $C_{adj}=C/C_{max}$. In the above example, $C_{adj}=0.4622/0.7071=0.654$. However, Sheskin (2007) noted that "it [C_{adj}] still does not allow one to compare such tables with complete accuracy" (p. 417). Cohen (1977, 1988) suggested an effect-size conversion of C to w, where $w = \sqrt{C^2/(1-C^2)}$. The interpretation is small effect-size is between 0.1 and 0.3; medium effect-size is between 0.3 and 0.5; and large effect-size is greater than 0.5 (Cohen, 1988). In the case of the above data, $w = \sqrt{0.4622^2/(1-0.4622^2)} = 0.52$ is a large effect-size.

The Cramér's V (V), also known as **Cramér's *phi*** (ϕ_c), developed by Cramér (1946), is the conversion of a phi coefficient which is applicable to larger than 2×2 tables. Cramér's V can be obtained by

$$V = \sqrt{\frac{\chi^2}{n(k-1)}}$$

where k is smaller among *Row* and *Column* (2 in our example). For 2×2 tables, Cramér's $V=$phi coefficient, that is, $\phi = \sqrt{\chi^2/n} = V = \sqrt{\chi^2/(n\times(2-1))}$. However, in the above example, *phi coefficient* cannot be computed since it's a 2×3 table.

$$V = \sqrt{\frac{58.148}{214(2-1)}} = 0.5212$$

Cramér's V is significant if the chi-square is significant. The alternate hypothesis stating that "population value of V is other than zero" is accepted.

Cohen (1977, 1988) suggested effect-size conversion by $w = V\sqrt{(k-1)}$. Conover (1980, 1999) pointed out that V will increase (and so does chi-square) as the number of rows and columns increase and, hence, it is not possible to compare two or more Cramér's V obtained on contingency tables of different sizes.

```
# R Code 5.13. Phi Coefficient, Contingency Coefficient (C) and Cramer's V
# its continuation form R code 5.10. output is used from R code 5.10
chi <- output$statistic   #saving chi-square value as chi
chi<-output$statistic     # view output
CC<- sqrt(chi/(chi+214))  # CC is Contingency Coefficient
CC                        # View CC
V<-sqrt(chi/(214*(2-1)))  # V is Cramér's V
V                         # View V
```

5.8.3 Measures of Association for Categorical Data not based on χ^2

5.8.3.1 Yule's Q

Yule's Q is a measure of association useful for a 2×2 contingency table developed by G. U. Yule[3] in 1900. It is less popular than *phi coefficient* (ϕ).

---

[3] G. U. Yule was a contemporary of Karl Pearson (KP). He assisted KP and also attended his classes. They had a reasonably good relationship till Yule published a paper about Q. Yule presented a simple criterion that Q will be 0 in the absence of association and ±1 in the case of perfect dependence. KP considered his idea of tetrachoric correlation as better and regarded Q as just approximation. In 1905, Yule criticized KP's assumptions and their relations soured. In addition, it's important to note that Yule was also not associated with eugenics movement. He came to realization due to his work in public health and preventive medicine that the condition of the lower classes is the function of poverty and squalor than genes. He also worked in the War Office during WWI and was honored as Commander of the British Empire. He was a very active member of the Royal Statistical Society and alongside his papers in statistics, his book *An Introduction to Theory of Statistics* (1911) went into multiple

Table 5.15. *Contingency Table Showing Frequencies for Two Variables: Diagnosis of BPD (X), and Past Suicide Attempts (Y)*

		Y: Past Suicide Attempt		Total
		No	Yes	
X: Diagnosis of BPD	Not Diagnosed	95	5	100
	Diagnosed BPD	60	40	100
	Total	155	45	200

$$Q = \frac{ad - bc}{ad + bc}$$

Yule's Q can be tested for statistical significance using Z conversion as suggested by Ott et al. (1992).

$$z = \frac{Q}{\sqrt{\frac{1}{4}\left(1 - Q^2\right)^2 \left[\frac{1}{a} + \frac{1}{b} + \frac{1}{c} + \frac{1}{d}\right]}}$$

The computational example is not provided. However, it needs to be notated that Q can reach a value of ±1 even when there is not a perfect relationship. It takes value ±1 even when one of the cells has zero (Ott et al. 1992).

5.8.3.2 Odds Ratio

The odds ratio (OR) is not based on χ^2. It can be applied to contingency tables of any size. There are two interrelated concepts required for understanding OR: (a) *odds*, and (b) *relative risk* (RR). Odds ratio is the ratio between two *odds*. Let's use the following hypothetical example. The diagnosis of borderline personality disorder (BPD) is also associated with risk of suicide attempt. Let's look at hypothetical data in 2×2 contingency Table 5.15.

Table 5.15 shows that out of 100 non-BPD individuals, only 5 attempted suicide, whereas out of 100 BPD diagnosed individuals, 40 attempted suicide.

Relative risk (RR) is the probability of developing a disorder (or disease, or condition; in this case, attempting suicide) if you are a member of the high-risk group (diagnosed BPD) divided by the probability of developing a disorder (attempting suicide) if you are a member of the low-risk group (not diagnosed as BPD). The probabilities are as follows:

$$P(\text{attempting suicide/Diagnosed BPD}) = 40 / 100 = 0.4$$
$$P(\text{attempting suicide/Not Diagnosed BPD}) = 5 / 100 = 0.05$$
$$RR = \frac{40 / 100}{5 / 100} = \frac{0.4}{0.05} = 8$$

RR=8 means that if an individual is diagnosed as having BPD, then the chance that individual will attempt suicide is eight times greater than when she/he is not diagnosed as having BPD. If we reverse the division, then RR=0.05/0.4=0.125 means that the chance of a suicide attempt is just 0.125 for a non-BPD diagnosed person than a BPD diagnosed individual.

Let's now look at *odds*. **Odds** is the probability that an event (denoted as X) occurs divided by the probability that an event does not occur:

---

editions. The Pearson–Yule controversy was never settled but Yule (1938) commented that in non-intellectual matters, Pearson remained friendly and courteous.

$$\text{Odds}(X) = P(X \text{ will occur}) / P(X \text{ will not occur}).$$

The *odds* for suicide attempt for individuals diagnosed as having BPD can be calculated as *Odds* (Suicide Attempt)=0.4/0.6=0.667. Whereas the *odds* for suicide attempt for individuals not diagnosed as BPD can be calculated as *Odds* (Suicide Attempt)=0.05/0.95=0.052.

The *odds ratio* (OR) is the ratio between these two odds. Generally, the larger number is divided by the smaller number (with an implicit belief that *odds* of the high-risk group is higher). The *odds* of suicide attempt in the high-risk group (diagnosed with BPD), which is 0.6667, is divided by the *odds* of suicide attempts in the low-risk group (not diagnosed with BPD), which is 0.0563. The OR is as follows:

$$OR = \frac{0.4/0.6}{0.05/0.95} = \frac{0.6667}{0.0563} = 12.67$$

If the two *odds* are identical, then the OR will be 1. If the numerator *odds* is smaller than the denominator *odds*, then OR<1. If the numerator *odds* is greater than the denominator *odds*, then OR>1. The OR will take any large value, but it is very rare to get a very large value. The OR of 12.67 is interpreted as "the *odds* of attempting suicide if a person is diagnosed as having BPD is 12.67 times higher than the odds of attempting suicide if a person is not diagnosed as having BPD." To test the significance of OR, the null hypothesis states that the population OR is 1. It means that the two *odds* are equal in population. The null is H_0: OR=1 and the alternative is H_A: OR≠1. Pagano and Gauvreau (1993) showed that this null hypothesis could be tested. It is also known that the sampling distribution of the OR is positively skewed because the OR values below 1 are always bounded between 0 and 1 than the OR values above 1 that are up till infinity. Due to this, logarithmic transformation is used while obtaining a standard normal variable (z).

$$z = \frac{\ln(OR) - 0}{SE_{OR}}$$

where ln(OR) is the natural logarithm of OR, SE_{OR} is standard error of OR that is obtained as

$$SE_{OR} = \sqrt{\frac{1}{a} + \frac{1}{b} + \frac{1}{c} + \frac{1}{d}}$$

In the case of the above example,

$$z = \frac{\ln(12.67) - 0}{0.5022} = \frac{2.539}{0.5022} = 5.056$$

By now, we know that the z value above 1.96 and 2.58 are significant at 0.05 and 0.01 level, respectively. The obtained value is larger than that of 2.58, it is significant at 0.01 level and H_A: OR≠1 is retained. This means that the population value of OR is other than 1. Odds ratio will also be discussed in the context of logistic regression (see Chapter 6).

5.8.4 Additional Measures: Likelihood Ratio Test, Cochran–Mantel– Haenszel Statistic, Cohen's Kappa (κ)

5.8.4.1 Likelihood Ratio Test

The likelihood ratio test (LR test) is an alternative to Pearson chi-square test, though Agresti (1990) pointed out that for a large sample, the LR test and Pearson chi-square are equivalent and for a small sample, exact chi-square is a better alternative than the LR test. The LR test is also useful in analyzing contingency tables that have more dimensions (e.g., $2 \times 2 \times 2$) because of its usefulness in log-linear models. The logic of likelihood is already discussed in details in Chapter 2. In this case, the likelihood of getting the observed data given the null hypothesis is obtained (L_0). If this likelihood is larger than the likelihood of getting the data under alternate hypothesis (L_A), then the null is rejected. Likelihood ratio (ratio of two likelihoods, $L(x)$) is at the basis of this test and uses maximum value of likelihood.

$$L(x) = \frac{\text{likelihood to observe } x \text{ given } H_A}{\text{likelihood to observe } x \text{ given } H_0}$$

The likelihood is a very large number and generally log of likelihood is taken. Given below is a log likelihood statistics often called $-2\log\lambda = \chi^2$, where $\lambda = L_A/L_0$. The chi-square is obtained at df $= (R-1)(C-1)$.

$$\chi^2 = 2\Sigma O_{ij} \log\left(\frac{O_{ij}}{E_{ij}}\right)$$

$$= 2\left[95 \times \log\left(\frac{95}{77.5}\right) + 5 \times \log\left(\frac{5}{22.5}\right) + 60 \times \log\left(\frac{60}{77.5}\right) + 40 \times \log\left(\frac{40}{22.5}\right)\right]$$

$$= 38.96$$

The obtained value of statistics is greater than the tabled value at 0.01 level for df $= 1$. Hence, we reject the null hypothesis. The test has useful application to signal detection theory as well.

```
#R Code 5.11. Likelihood Ratio Test in R
x<-c(95, 5, 60, 40)
x1<-matrix (x, ncol = 2, byrow = TRUE, dimnames=list(PA=c('No', 'Yes'),
BPD = c('No', 'Yes')))
library(MASS)
loglm(~ PA+BPD, data = x1)
```

5.8.4.2 Cochran–Mantel–Haenszel Statistic

The **Cochran–Mantel–Haenszel Statistic (CMH statistics)** is also known as **Mantel–Haenszel Statistic.** William Cochran (1954) Mantel and Haenszel (1959) developed this statistics. It is useful to analyze the relationship between two categorical variables to be controlled for the third variable. The CMH statistics is useful when categorical data is in $2 \times 2 \times k$ format. For example, you have the following data: $X =$ BPD diagnoses (diagnosed as BPD and not-diagnosed as BPD); $Y =$ Past suicide attempt (yes and no); and $Z =$ gender (male and female). The researcher has a question: whether a past suicide attempt is associated with diagnosed BPD if controlled for gender. The contingency table is $2 \times 2 \times 2$ (BPD diagnosis $\times$ past suicide attempt $\times$ gender). The data will have k number of 2×2 tables. In the present data, $k = 2$ (male and female) and hence the data is two 2×2 tables presented in Table 5.16. $H_0 : OR_{111} = OR_{112} = \cdots = OR_{11k} = 1$, that is, the odds ratio is 1 for all k groups. The alternative is it's not 1.

$$CMH = \frac{[\Sigma_k(n_{11k} - \mu_{11k})]^2}{\Sigma_k \text{var}(n_{11k})}$$

where n_{11k} is the left topmost cell in each of k tables, μ_{11k} is the expected frequency of the left topmost cell separately computed for k tables, that is, $\mu_{11k} = n_{1+k} \times n_{+1k} / n_{++k}$ and $\text{var}(n_{11k}) = (n_{1+k} \times n_{2+k} \times n_{+1k} \times n_{+2k}) / n_{++k}^2 \times (n_{++k} - 1)$.

Table 5.16. *Two Contingency Tables for Male and Females Showing Frequencies for Two Variables: Diagnosis of BPD (X), and Past Suicide Attempt (Y)*

		Male			Female		
		Past Suicide Attempt			Past Suicide Attempt		
		No	Yes	Total	No	Yes	Total
Diagnosis of BPD	Not Dig.	30	1	31	60	10	70
	Dig.	5	25	30	30	50	80
	Total	35	26	61	90	60	150

Note: The null hypothesis is specified in the form of *odds ratio* (OR).

Table 5.17. *Two Judges Rating 70 Responses on Creativity*

Judge II	Judge I			Total
	Highly Creative	Slightly Creative	Not Creative	
Highly creative	25	3	2	30
Slightly creative	5	12	3	20
Not creative	1	4	15	20
Total	31	19	20	70

For the part of table for male, $\mu_{11male} = 35 \times 31 / 61 = 17.78$; $\text{var}(n_{11male}) = (35 \times 26 \times 31 \times 30) / (61^2 \times 60) = 3.79$.

For the part of the table for female, $\mu_{11female} = 42$; and $\text{var}(n_{11female}) = 9.02$.

$$\text{CMH} = \frac{[\Sigma_k (n_{11k} - \mu_{11k})]^2}{\Sigma_k \text{var}(n_{11k})} = \frac{[(30 - 17.78) + (60 - 42)]^2}{3.79 + 9.02} = \frac{912.83}{12.81} = 71.26$$

The CMH statistics is evaluated at $df=1$ using the chi-square distribution. The obtained value is significant, hence, we reject the null hypothesis. The alternative "OR are not equal to 1 in population for k tables" is accepted. If the OR in each table is either smaller than or greater than zero, the CMH is a large value. If the ORs are close to 1, then CMH is close to zero. Hence, CMH is interpreted in terms of *OR*. The CMH is not recommended if some ORs are greater than 1 and some ORs are smaller than 1, since they cancel out each other and the CMH is insignificant when ORs are different. Agresti (2007, 2010) provided an excellent discussion about CMH.

```
# R Code 5.12. CMH Test in R
x<-c(30, 1, 5, 25, 60, 10, 30, 50)        # data entered as column vector
dimnames <- list(PSA = c("NO", "YES"), BPD = c("Not_Dig", "Dig"), SEX =
c("male", "female"))                       # names of dimensions
data1<-array(x, dim = c(2,2,2), dimnames)  #creating data in tables
data1                                       # printing data
mantelhaen.test(data1, correct = FALSE)    #CMH test
```

5.8.4.3 Kappa (κ)—Agreement between Ratters

Cohen's Kappa (κ) is a non-chi-square-based statistics. The statistics is generally employed in psychometrics to assess agreement between ratters in reliability analysis. It is a robust measure because it considers agreement occurring by chance. Look at the data in Table 5.17 of two ratters for judging a response to 70 creativity items as "highly creative," "slightly creative," and "non-creative." Note that out of 31 items that were considered as "very creative" by Judge

I, 25 items were also considered as "very creative" by Judge II, but Judge II considered five of them as "slightly creative" and one of them as "not creative." **Simple percentage of agreement** can be calculated as (but not recommended), out of 70 items, judges agreed on 52 items (25+12+15) making it 52/70=0.7429, that is, 74.29% agreement. Some of this agreement can appear by chance as well. The probability of considering an item "highly creative" for Judge I is 31/70=0.4428. The probability of considering an item "highly creative" for Judge II is 30/70=0.4285. If the judges randomly tick-mark items as "highly creative," then the probability that they would classify an item as "highly creative" is $0.4428 \times 0.4285 = 0.1897$, that is, for 70 items, they would agree on $0.1897 \times 70 = 13.279$ items as "highly creative" only by chance. Similarly, they would by chance agree that 5.428 items are "slightly creative" and 5.714 items as "not creative." The measure of agreement should correct for chance agreement. Cohen (1960) proposed a measure, Cohen's Kappa (κ), to assess agreement that corrects for chance agreement.

$$\kappa = \frac{\Sigma f_0 - \Sigma f_e}{n - \Sigma f_e}$$

where f_0 is observed frequencies of agreement (diagonal), f_e is the expected frequencies of agreement by chance, and n is the total number of items rated.
$\Sigma f_0 = 25 + 12 + 15 = 52$ and $\Sigma f_e = 13.279 + 5.428 + 5.714 = 24.421$. The kappa is

$$\kappa = \frac{\Sigma f_0 - \Sigma f_e}{n - \Sigma f_e} = \frac{52 - 24.421}{70 - 24.421} = 0.605$$

One needs to note that kappa (0.61) is smaller than simple percentage of agreement (0.7429) because it is corrected for agreement occurring by chance. Since kappa is employed in psychometrics to assess inter-ratter reliability, it is expected to be close to 1, and the statistical test of significance is often not used. The weighted kappa is also calculated in ordered responses to analyze "disagreements" among ratters separately. The linear weighting or quadratic weighting are used.

```
# R Code 5.13. Cohen's Kappa
x<-c(25, 3, 2, 5, 12, 3, 1, 4, 15)          # data as vector
data <-matrix(x, ncol = 3, byrow = TRUE)    # covert vector into matrix
library (psych)                             # call package 'psych'
cohen.kappa(data)                           # kappa syntax; use unweighted
                                            # kappa estimate
```

SUMMARY

This chapter has provided various methods useful in testing correlation and association between variable. These variables can be of different types, and researchers may also have variety of questions. Depending on that, appropriate methods can be used. One should note that when models in causal form are available, regression and other alternatives should be used rather than correlations. Correlations and associations are useful only when there is absence of causal models or when the underlying theory does not support causality.

EXERCISE

1. Use the following data on X: Attitude to Women Empowerment, and Y: Preference for Egalitarianism. X=2,3,4,3,5,6,5,7,8,6,7,9,7,9,10,11,13,15,13,12. Y=6,5,7,4,5,8,10,11,9,13,15,8,16,18,20,22,14,24,28,27. Gender=M, M, M, M, M, M, M, M, M, M, F, F, F, F, F, F, F, F, F, F. Women Reservation (WR)=Y, N, Y, N, N, Y, Y, N, N, N, N, Y, Y, N, Y, Y, N, Y, Y, Y.

Write the null and alternative hypotheses, and plot scatters. Also compute mean, variance, SD, covariance, and Pearson's r.

2. Test statistical significance for Pearson's r. Interpret results.
3. Use R for computing the above statistics. Also plot your results.
4. Use learning from Chapter 4 and test the normality of the above data for X and Y.
5. Specify the null and alternative, and set the appropriate type I error value. Compute Spearman's rho between X and Y. Also use R for computing *rho*.
6. Compute Pearson and non-Pearson correlation between WR and X; and also between WR and Y. Use an appropriate R code to compute.
7. Compute correlation between gender and WR and use R code. Interpret the findings. Carry out this analysis in R.
8. Use the following data: $X = 6,5,7,8,9,10,11,13,15,12,16,17,18,20$; $Y = 20,18,16,15,13,14,12, 9,10,8,6,21,4,5$. Identify factors that influence this correlation. Take appropriate action and compute correlation. If $r_{xz} = 0.3$ and $r_{yz} = -0.2$, then compute partial correlation.
9. If r_{xy} is to be computed controlling only Y for Z, then compute correlation. Interpret. Use R code.
10. For the above example, compute Kendall's tau. Use R for the same.
11. Three psychologists have ranked four psychotherapy techniques. The rankings are as follows: Ratter 1: 1,2,3,4; Ratter 2: 1,3,2,4; Ratter 3: 1, 2, 4,3; and Ratter 4: 1,2,3,4. Use appropriate statistics to compute inter-ratter agreement.
12. Use the following contingency table. X is grades of students—5th, 7th, and 9th. Y is successful completion of additional activities—completed, partially, completed, and not completed.

		Grades		
		5th	**7th**	**9th**
Activity status	Completed	20	30	25
	Partially	31	19	18
	Not Completed	02	8	10

Test the hypothesis that X and Y are associated. Use R for computing statistics. Interpret results.

13. Use the following contingency table obtained by a school counselor. Test the hypothesis that the choice of discipline depends on gender.

		Gender	
		Male	**Female**
Discipline	Psychology	10	38
	Economics	29	18
	Languages	10	30

Use chi-square and techniques based on chi-square to test this hypothesis.

16. Use the following data. The data is X: Alcoholism in spouse and Y: Conflict in Marital relation. Test the hypothesis that X and Y are associated. Find the chance of conflict.

		Alcoholism in spouse	
		Yes	**No**
Conflict in marital relation	Conflict	31	17
	No Conflict	7	40

15. Use the data below of three organizations A, B, and C on two variables—X: gender (male and female); and Y: office (yes and no). Test the hypothesis that X and Y association is similar across organizations. Use R.

		Org. A Gender		Org. B Gender		Org. C Gender	
		M	F	M	F	M	F
Officer Promotion	Yes	20	4	14	8	9	9
	No	30	20	25	22	40	41

Regression Analysis

6.1 INTRODUCTION

One of the important aims of science is to be able to make predictions. The predictions involve a statement of causality that states that "X" is a cause for "Y" and hence "X" can predict "Y." Here X is called as causal variable or predictor variable. Independent variable (IV) is a generic term used in statistics for causal variables or predictor variables. Y is the effect variable or criterion variable, and dependent variable (DV) is the generic term used for it. The science of psychology considers experimentation as best way to make inferences about causal relationships. The near perfect experiment can always inform us about the causal relationship between X and Y. In an experiment, all other conditions are held constant and only X is changed and then variation in Y is measured. Depending on (a) number and levels of X, (b) measurement level, and (c) distribution of Y, statistical tests like t-test (in case one X takes two levels) or ANOVA (in case X takes more levels and/or there are more than one X) are employed. Experimentation is undoubtedly the most powerful way to demonstrate causality. However, there are many instances when the psychological theory states causality but experimentation is not possible. For example, conducting an experiment is difficult to evaluate hypothesis that "height of parents is cause of height of children." There are two principal reasons because of which experiments cannot be done. The first is that the manipulating IV is beyond the capacity of experimenter, for example, manipulating height of parents, manipulating stress (St) experienced due to life events,[1] natural calamities and disasters, number of dating partners, and so on. Second, the IV cannot be manipulated for ethical and legal reasons. Psychological research works involve human participants and hence need to clear certain ethical standards and must be within the law of the land. For example, variables like maternal separation, brain injuries, deprivation from food, non-treatment conditions for psychiatric patients, atrocious punishment, and private information can be manipulated, however it is unethical and often illegal to do so. And hence, experimentation is not possible for this reason as well. Under such conditions, researchers end up using covariation among the variables as an indicator of causality. Statistical techniques known as "regression" are often useful to analyze the data where X and Y are measured and some causal inference is required. Please note that causality is never a function of statistical technique. Causality requires temporal ordering (temporally X precedes Y), covariation (as X changes Y changes), and absence of alternative explanations. Modeling causality is to be a function of theory than statistics.

The simple linear regression analysis involves predicting one DV (Y) from one IV (X), for example, "predicting performance at work with optimism." Here, work performance is the DV and optimism is the IV. The variables are required to be continuous variables. Multiple

---

[1] Holmes and Rahe (1967) constructed a scale of life events where death of spouse was most stressful life event and other stressful life events included divorce, imprisonment, personal injury, marriage, dismissal from work, etc. The Holmes and Rahe scale has been a popular instrument in stress research.

regression involves predicting one DV (Y) by using more than one IV $(X_1, X_2, X_3, ..., X_k)$, for example, predicting work performance by using optimism (X_1), affective commitment (X_2), normative commitment (X_3), continuance commitment (X_4), and emotional intelligence (X_5). Here we have a model stating that five IVs predict work performance. If the model is significant in predicting work performance, then we shall further evaluate which of the individual IVs are important predictors of Y. The logistic regression is a useful group of techniques when the DV is measured in two categories (Y is dichotomous), for example, passing or failing on test, getting selected after the interview, completing the work assignment in time, getting cured after the treatment, and so on will take only two values. When such a variable is predicted by other IVs the logistic regression analysis is useful technique.

This chapter shall cover the following aspects: (a) introduction to simple linear regression model and examples, (b) hypothesis testing with simple linear regression model, (c) multiple regression model and hypothesis testing, (d) regression assumptions and their evaluations, and (e) logistic regression model and hypothesis testing. The R codes are also provided for most of the analyses. Several exercises are also provided at the end to have hands on practice.

6.2 SIMPLE LINEAR REGRESSION

A simple linear regression model has one IV and one DV. The IV is also known as the "predictor variable" and is denoted by "X." The DV is also known as "criterion variable" and is denoted by "Y." Regression analysis tests whether X can linearly predict Y. In case of simple linear regression, this question resembles to the question asked in Chapter 5 and that is "whether there is linear correlation between two variables." We carried out a Pearson's product moment-correlation to answer this question. The pragmatic distinction between correlation and regression is more with reference to the purpose: when the interest is in *predicting* the values of Y using information about X then the procedure followed is regression. When the interest is in understanding the *covariation* between X and Y without any obvious causal implications then the procedure used is correlation. There are problems with this distinction; nonetheless this serves as a useful specification for practice.

The central question in simple linear regression analysis is "whether X can predict Y." We need data on both X and Y to answer this question. Then we regress Y *on* X and obtain statistics that informs about whether X can predict Y. The linear regression model is explained below.

6.2.1 The Model

The statistical model of the linear regression analysis can be stated as follows:

$$Y = \alpha + \beta X + \varepsilon$$

where
 Y is the DV or criterion variable or effect,
 X is the IV or predictor variable or cause,
 α is the population regression constant and Y intercept of regression line
 β is the population regression coefficient or slope of regression line or per unit change in Y as X changes by one unit.
 ε is the residual or error in the regression equation.

This model is a population level model. The population values of α and β are known as parameters of this model. As you know, parameter values are unknown and need to be estimated from sample values. $Y = \alpha + \beta X$ is expression of linear relationship of Y with X. ε (epsilon) is a random error or noise. In order to estimate variability in Y as a function of linear relation, some assumptions are made about random error term. They are discussed in a later section. The parameters in the model are estimated by using sample estimates or sample statistics. β is estimated by "b" and α is estimated by "a." The sample level regression equation is

$$Y = a + bX + e$$

where
    a is an estimator of α or sample regression constant,
    b is an estimator of β or sample regression coefficient.
    X and Y are sample values of respective variables and e is sample residual.

Example 1: Suppose a researcher is interested in predicting work performance by using conscientiousness personality dimension. I am choosing this example because of direction of causality in this example. It is from personality to behavior and not from behavior to personality. (Similarly, it is fine to have an example of general intelligence predicting performance on a class test). There are a large number of employees in organizations. Getting everyone's data on conscientiousness and performance is practically impossible. All employees are the population. The regression equation for the population is

$$\text{performance} = \alpha + (\beta \times \text{Conscientiousness}) + \varepsilon$$

The performance scores and conscientiousness scores of all employees are not available. Hence we cannot calculate values of α and β. The sample of 120 employees is available to researcher and she can measure their performance scores and conscientiousness scores. The parameters α and β need to be estimated form the sample values of a and b. The sample regression equation is

$$\text{performance} = a + (b \times \text{Conscientiousness}) + e$$

6.2.2 The Scatterplot and Regression

The regression equation is exemplified by using a small data set and a scatterplot. The data of five participants on X and Y values is given in Table 6.1.

The scatter plot of the above data with regression line is shown in Figure 6.1.

Figure 6.1 explains that the five scores of joint distribution of (xy) are not falling on the straight line. The regression line has a slope "b" which is the estimator of population slope β. The regression line also has a Y intercept "a" which is an estimator of α. The ordinary least squares (OLS) logic of plotting the line is explained in the subsequent section. Since this is a sample plot we should have written "a" and "b" instead of α and β.

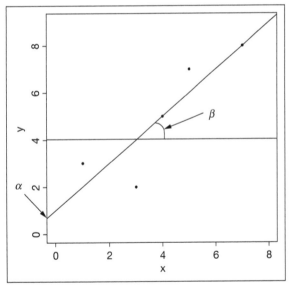

Figure 6.1. *Scatter Plot and Regression Line for Table 6.1 Data*

Table 6.1. *Small Data for X and Y for Example 1*

X	Y
1	3
3	2
5	7
7	8
4	5
Mean = 4	Mean = 5

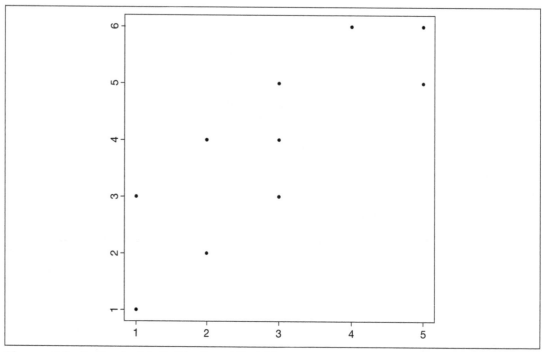

Figure 6.2. *Scatter for Jointly Distributed Variable*

6.2.3 Basics of Regression

The idea of conditional probabilities and jointly distributed random variables has been discussed in Chapter 1. As you know that $E(Y|X)$, expectation of Y given X, is the conditional expectation of Y given value of X. For example, conditional expectation of Y for $X=2$ is $E(Y \mid X = 2) = \sum_{i=1}^{n} Y_i \times P(Y = y_i \mid X = 2)$. Suppose we have a jointly distributed random variable, {(1,1), (1,3), (2,2), (2,4), (3,3), (3,4), (3,5), (4,6), (5,5), (5,6)}. Figure 6.2 shows the scatter for this example.

The scatter diagram shows that $E(Y|X)$ increases as X increases. Some assumptions are required in regression.

Assumption 1: $E(Y|X)$ is assumed to be linear function of X. The linear relationship is expressed as

$$E(Y|X) = a + bX_i$$

Note that relations like $E(Y|X) = a + b(\log X_i)$ or $E(Y \mid X) = a + b\sqrt{X_i}$ or $E(Y|X) = a + bX_i^3$ are also linear relationships. $E(Y|X=2) = 2$. The difference between Y_i and $E(Y|X=2)$ is $Y_i - E(Y|X=2) = Y_i - 2 = e_i$ and e_i can be considered as a random variable and generally, $Y_i - E(Y|X=x) = e_i$. The regression equation is

$$Y_i = a + bX_i + e_i$$

The OLS make the following assumption about e_i:

1. $E(e_i|X_i) = 0$ for $i = 1, 2, \ldots, n$. This implies that conditional expectation of e_i conditioned on X_i is zero.
2. The variance of e_i is constant, that is, variance of e_i remains the same for all values of X. This is generally referred to as homoscedasticity. Absence of constant variance is called as heteroscedasticity.

3. The error is expected to be uncorrelated with previous or future values. When data comes over time, this assumption is important. If the data is obtained two times then $Cov(e_i, e_j) = 0$. This assumption is known as "assumption of no autocorrelation."
4. It is also assumed that e_i is normally distributed.
5. It is assumed that e_i and X_i are independent, where $i = 1, 2, \ldots, n$.
6. All values of X are not same.

6.2.3.1 OLS: The Logic of Estimating α and β

The OLS is the estimation method used to estimate the parameter values α and β. Perhaps estimation of β is of more critical importance than estimation of α. If you look at Figure 6.1, then you can realize that there could be many possible lines one can draw for this data. The central problem of regression is to make a decision about which line to choose from all possible lines. Perhaps the appropriate question is "how to find the value of the slope (that is value of b) that can result in **line of best fit**." The OLS provides a useful logic to do so.

The OLS estimated value of β is such that the sum of square of difference between the actual Y value and predicted Y values is the **smallest**. The difference is denoted as "e" (residual).

The regression equation is

$$Y = a + bX + e$$

The values of Y predicted by the equation are denoted as (Y'). The predicted values are obtained by

$$Y' = a + bX$$

The difference between the actual values of Y and predicted values of Y (that is Y') is called as residual ($Y - Y'$) and denoted as e.

$$e = Y - (a + bX)$$

$$e = Y - Y'$$

Thus, residual is the error of prediction.

The OLS estimation of beta (β) that is OLS estimator "b" is estimated such that the sum of squares of difference between the actual Y value and predicted Y values is the **smallest**.

$$\Sigma e^2 = \min$$

The sum of residuals (Σe) will always be zero since the predicted values of Y can be randomly above and below actual value of Y. So e^2 is taken as a criterion and Σe^2 is set to be minimum. It implies that if we use any other value than the OLS estimated value of β, Σe^2 will be larger for that value than Σe^2 for OLS estimated value of β.

6.2.3.2 The Computation of OLS a and b

The next step is to understand how to compute the OLS estimates of α and β. The covariance between X and Y serves as an important stepping stone for computing a and b.

$$Cov_{xy} = \frac{\Sigma (x - \bar{x})(y - \bar{y})}{n - 1}$$

The OLS estimator "b" is obtained as

$$b = \frac{Cov_{xy}}{S_x^2}$$

where

Cov_{xy} is the covariance between x and y, and
S_x^2 is the variance x

We know that

$$Cov_{xy} = \frac{\sum_{i=1}^{n}(X - \bar{X})(Y - \bar{Y})}{n-1} \qquad S_x^2 = \frac{\sum_{i=1}^{n}(X - \bar{X})^2}{n-1}$$

If we denote $(X - \bar{X}) = x_i$ and $(Y - \bar{Y}) = y_i$, then

$$b_{YX} = \frac{Cov_{xy}}{S_x^2} = \frac{\dfrac{\sum_{i=1}^{n}(X - \bar{X})(Y - \bar{Y})}{n=1}}{\dfrac{\sum_{i=1}^{n}(X - \bar{X})^2}{n-1}} = \frac{\sum_{i=1}^{n}(X - \bar{X})(Y - \bar{Y})}{\sum_{i=1}^{n}(X - \bar{X})^2} = \frac{\sum_{i=1}^{n}x_iy_i}{\sum_{i=1}^{n}x_i^2}$$

a can be obtained by simple transformation of the regression equation.
We know that

$$\bar{Y} = a + b\bar{X}$$

and hence

$$\bar{Y} - b\bar{X} = a$$

In Example 1, using the data, "*a*" and "*b*" can be calculated as follows:
The covariance *xy* can be obtained by

$$Cov_{xy} = \frac{\sum(x - \bar{x})(y - \bar{y})}{n = 1} = \frac{20}{4} = 5$$

b value can be calculated by

$$b = \frac{Cov_{xy}}{S_x^2} = \frac{5}{5} = 1$$

and *a* value can be calculated as

$$a = \bar{Y} - b\bar{X} = 5 - (1 \times 4) = 5 - 4 = 1$$

a and *b* values of Table 6.1 are 1 and 1 respectively. Since it is a simulated data the findings also look artificial. They only serve the purpose of an example (Table 6.2).

Table 6.2. *Some Calculation for Example 1*

x	y	$(x - \bar{x})$	$(y - \bar{y})$	$(x - \bar{x})^2$	$(x - \bar{x})(y - \bar{y})$
1	3	−3	2	9	6
3	2	−1	−3	1	3
5	7	1	2	1	2
7	8	3	3	9	9
4	5	0	0	0	0
Mean=4	Mean=5			20	
$S_x^2 = 20/4 = 5$	$S_x^2 = 26/4 = 6.5$				$\sum(x - \bar{x})(y - \bar{y}) = 20$

6.2.3.3 The Gauss–Markov Theorem

Some desirable properties of estimator have been discussed in Chapter 2. One of the properties is best linear unbiased estimator (BLUE). The essential question is whether the OLS estimators in regression coefficients have those properties?

The population regression coefficient β_{YX} is estimated by b_{YX}. The question essentially is whether b_{YX} is BLUE?

$$b_{YX} = \sum_{i=1}^{n} x_i y_i \bigg/ \sum_{i=1}^{n} x_i^2$$

The **Gauss–Markov Theorem**[2] states that when errors have expectation zero, errors are uncorrelated, and have equal variance then an OLS estimator gives the BLUE of the population regression coefficient.

These assumptions can be stated as

$$E\,(e_i)=0$$

$$\text{Var}\,(e_i)=\text{Constant}$$

$$\text{Cov}(e_i,e_j)=0 \qquad \text{for } i \neq j$$

Then b_{YX} is BLUE.

The OLS estimator b_{YX} is unbiased implying that,

$E(b_{YX}) = \beta_{YX}$ that is, the expectation of b_{YX} is equal to the population value, β_{YX}.

A quick R demonstration can show that b_{YX} is unbiased when x and e are independent. It can also be shown that b_{YX} is biased when x and e are correlated. The R code 6.1 demonstrates the same. A pair of 20 values of x and y is generated 10,000 times and b_{YX} is computed. Then the density of those values is plotted. If the estimator is unbiased, then this plot should have mean equal to the coefficient set (2 in the example). That is if several samples are obtained and b_{YX} values are computed then the mean of those values will be the population value of slope.

R Code 6.1. Distribution of b_{YX}

```
x<- c(147, 136, 114, 130, 141, 161, 114, 123, 148, 122, 156, 149, 100,
138, 101, 104, 125, 131, 127, 153)  # data on X
c <- rep(0,10000) # Column vector of size 10000
i=1
repeat{
    e <- rnorm (20, 0, 1)           # 20 values with mean zero and var =
                                    1 from normal distribution
    y <- 2 + (2 * x) + (e)          # y is specified as linear function
                                    of x where x and e are uncorrelated.
                                    the slope takes value 2
### replace above line by following line to create correlated x and e
### y <- 2 + (2 * x) + (e+(3*x))    ### x and e are related
    cof <- coef(lm(y ~ x))          # in lm the coefficient is stored in cof
    c[i] = cof[2]                   # compute next estimate and store it
                                    in next row of c
```

---

[2] Carl Fredric Gauss (1777–1855) and Andrei Markov (1856–1922) are credited for the theorem. It is interesting to note that Markov is born a year after the death of Gauss. The theorem is popularized by Jerzy Newman. The theorem was a part of Markov's book. However, latest work shows that it is Gauss who has made a primary contribution and Markov did not improve it much. Therefore, some authors call it Gauss theorem only. However, the popularity of the expression Gauss–Markov theorem was so much that it is referred to as Gauss–Markov theorem.

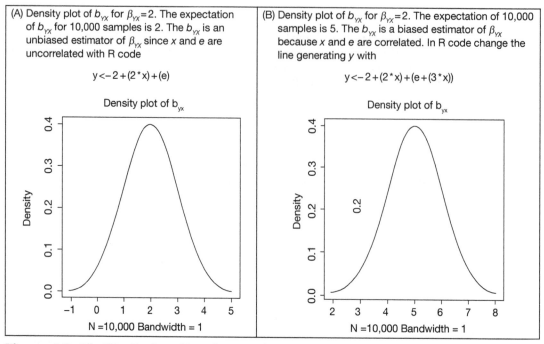

Figure 6.3. *The Distribution of b_{YX} when x and e are (A) Uncorrelated and (B) Correlated*

```
i = i + 1                    # i increases by 1
if (i > 10000)
break
}
plot(density(c, bw = 1), lwd = 5, main = "Density plot of byx", cex.axis
= 2.5) # plotting density
mean(c)                      # mean of b
var(c)                       # var of b
```

The plots resulting from the two R code 6.1 are displayed in Figure 6.3. Their distribution and center need to be examined.

The minimum variance is another property of b_{YX}. This property implies that if OLS b_{YX} is one estimator of β_{YX}, then $Var(b_{YX})$ will be smaller than the variance of $Var(\hat{\theta}_{YX})$ where $\hat{\theta}_{YX}$ is any other estimator of β_{YX}.

b_{YX} is known as an efficient estimator since it has smallest variance in the class of linear unbiased estimators. The OLS estimators are consistent, that is,

$$\lim_{n \to \infty} E(b_{YX}) = \beta_{YX} \quad \text{and} \quad \lim_{n \to \infty} Var(b_{YX}) = 0$$

$\lim_{n \to \infty} E(b_{YX}) = \beta_{YX}$ is already demonstrated. $\lim_{n \to \infty} Var(b_{YX}) = 0$ implies that as the sample size increases, the variance of b_{YX} approaches to zero. The Gauss–Markov Theorem states that OLS estimator has these properties, that is, OLS estimator of regression coefficient is BLUE. This theorem is central to regression analysis. We use OLS estimators of β_{YX} due to this theorem. The proofs of these statements are avoided; they are available in many textbooks on econometrics and mathematical statistics.

Example 2: Predicting Marks from Intelligence

Table 6.3. *Calculation of Example 2*

Test Score (Y)	Intelligence (X)	$(y - \bar{y})$	$(x - \bar{x})$	$(y - \bar{y})^2$	$(x - \bar{x})^2$	$(x - \bar{x})(y - \bar{y})$
3	5	−7	−4	49	16	28
4	7	−6	−2	36	4	12
5	8	−5	−1	25	1	5
6	4	−4	−5	16	25	20
9	6	−1	−3	1	9	3
11	11	1	2	1	4	2
14	9	4	0	16	0	0
16	13	6	4	36	16	24
18	15	8	6	64	36	48
14	12	4	3	16	9	12
Mean = 10	**Mean = 9**			$\Sigma(y - \bar{y})^2$ = 260	$\Sigma(x - \bar{x})^2$ = 120	$\Sigma(x - \bar{x})(y - \bar{y})$ = 154

Example 2 is data of 10 participants for which complete solution is provided. These 10 participants have responded to an intelligence test, which is a measure of general ability (X). These are raw scores. Then, later they took a class test and the test scores (Y) are available. We wish to predict test scores from intelligence. This data is useful from a theoretical perspective as well. We note that: (a) theoretically intelligence scores can cause test scores, and (b) test scores cannot cause intelligence scores (this may sound obvious, but as we see in later examples, it is not so obvious in the psychological data).

Table 6.3 provides data and basic calculations for obtaining *a* and *b*. The mean for test score (TS) and Intelligence (int) are 10 and 9 respectively. The variance for both can be obtained as:

$$S_{int}^2 = 120/9 = 13.33 \quad S_{TS}^2 = 260/9 = 28.89$$

The covariance between intelligence and test score is calculated as:

$$\text{Cov}_{xy} = \frac{\Sigma(x - \bar{x})(y - \bar{y})}{n - 1} = \frac{154}{9} = 17.11$$

The slope (*b*) for this data can be calculated by dividing covariance between intelligence and test score by variance in intelligence.

$$b = \frac{\text{Cov}_{xy}}{S_x^2} = \frac{17.11}{13.33} = 1.28$$

b is the ratio of covariation in X and Y and variation in X. This ratio is closer to zero, which indicates that variation in X does not share any covariation in XY. The Y intercept of the regression line can be obtained as follows:

$$a = \bar{Y} - b\bar{X} = 10 - (1.2833 \times 9) = 10 - 11.5497 = -1.55$$

6.2.3.4 Interpretation of a and b

b is a regression coefficient, indicating *rate of change* in predicted values of Y. It is also considered as a slope of the regression line. *b* can also be interpreted as the amount of change in Y' as X changes by one unit. The regression coefficient or slope of regression line for Example 2 is 1.28, which implies that as raw score on the intelligence test is increasing by one unit, the test score is increasing by 1.28 units. The sign of *b* is also an important attribute. The positive sign of b indicates positive relationship between X and Y and negative sign of b indicates negative relationship between X and Y. A researcher can use regression equation to predict the test score of a new entrant in the class from its intelligence scores. Generally, we are not much interested in using regression equation to make such specific prediction. The primary interest is in general principle of predictability of Y than individual prediction.

The regression constant "a" is the Y intercept of a regression line. It simply implies that "a" is that point on Y-axis where the regression line intercepts the Y-axis. "a" is interpreted as that value of Y when X takes a value zero. This interpretation is meaningful only in some cases. The meaningfulness of this interpretation depends on meaning of $X=0$ and whether there are sufficient values in this range. In case of Example 2, regression constant of −1.55 indicates that value of the test score when score on an intelligence test is zero. However, one would quickly realize that the intelligence test score zero has no real meaning. Most intelligence tests start with the easiest items (very low difficulty) and become progressively difficult. There exists no interpretation of score zero on intelligence test and we shall avoid this interpretation in this context. Suppose we are predicting basketball performance (Y) from height of player (X), then the regression constant has no meaning since zero height is impossibility. The regression constant can be set to the value zero in standardized regression. Most of the research reports prefer to provide standardized regression and the intercept has no meaning in this form. If X is converted into $(x - \bar{x})$ then the mean of $X=0$ and regression analysis is carried out, then intercept is mean of Y.

6.2.3.5 Standardized Regression Coefficients

When a variable is transformed into the standardized form (by subtracting each value form mean and dividing it by SD) the variables are called standardized variables. When X and Y are converted into standardized forms and regression is carried out, the regression coefficients obtained are called **standardized regression coefficients**. The regression coefficients obtained on the unstandardized data (raw data) are called **unstandardized regression coefficients**. The value of 1.28 for Example 2 is the unstandardized regression coefficient. The standardized variables are expressed in terms of standard deviation units. The value of regression coefficient for the standardized regression analysis is 0.8719. It implies that, as intelligence increases by one standard deviation, performance would increase by 0.87 standard deviations. Obviously, the center for both "a" and "b" are zero and hence the intercept will also be zero. The standardized regression coefficient is also a correlation coefficient. The correlation between X and Y is

$$r_{xy} = \frac{Cov_{xy}}{S_x S_y}$$

and the regression coefficient is

$$b = \frac{Cov_{xy}}{S_x S_x}$$

If $S_x = S_y = 1$, r_{xy} will be b. This interpretation of b is very useful in various contexts. A correlation of 0.6 then implies that as X varies by one standard deviation, then Y varies by 0.6 standard deviations. In spite of the similarity between r and b, the causal relation should be carefully inferred.

6.2.4 Accuracy of the Prediction

It is not just the size of the coefficient but accuracy of prediction is also important. The standard error of estimate ($S_{Y.X}$) and r^2 are commonly used as measures of accuracy. The standard error of estimate can be obtained by using the idea of conditional mean. The conditional mean of Y is the value of mean of Y given the values of X. Y' is a conditional mean of Y given X. The variance of Y is obtained by

$$S_Y^2 = \frac{\sum_{i=1}^{n}(Y_i - \bar{Y})^2}{df} = \frac{SS_Y}{df}$$

The residual variance or error variance ($S_{Y\cdot X}^2$) is obtained by replacing $\bar{Y}$ by Y'. Y' is a predicted value of Y by regression equation. The standard error of estimate is

$$S_{Y\cdot X} = \sqrt{\frac{\sum_{i=1}^{n}(Y_i - Y')^2}{df}} = \sqrt{\frac{SS_{residuals}}{n-2}}$$

where
$Y'=a+bX$, that is, Y' is a predicted value of Y by using regression equation

$SS_{residuals}$ is $\sum_{i=1}^{n}(Y_i - Y')^2$, that is, sum of squared deviation of Y from predicted value of Y, or sum of squares residual.
The standard error of estimation is

$$S_{Y\cdot X} = \sqrt{\frac{\sum_{i=1}^{n}(Y_i - Y')^2}{n-2}} = \sqrt{\frac{SS_{Residual}}{n-2}} = \sqrt{\frac{62.37}{10-2}} = \sqrt{7.7958} = 2.792$$

r^2 is computed as

$$r^2 = \frac{SS_{regression}}{SS_{Total}}$$

The SS regression can be obtained by

$$SS_{regression} = \sum_{i=1}^{n}(Y_i' - \bar{Y})^2$$

and SS residual is obtained by

$$SS_{regression} = \sum_{i=1}^{n}(Y - Y_i)^2$$

In case of Example 2,

$$r^2 = \frac{SS_{regression}}{SS_{Total}} = \frac{\sum_{i=1}^{n}(Y_i' - \bar{Y})^2}{\sum_{i=1}^{n}(Y_i - \bar{Y})^2} = \frac{197.6}{260} = 0.76$$

The interpretation of $r^2 \times 100$ is the percentage of variation in Y explained by X. So, $0.76 \times 100 = 76\%$ variation in Y is explained by X. R^2 is also known as **coefficient of determination**. For large samples, r^2 can be used to obtain the standard error of estimate.

$$S_{Y\cdot X} = S_Y \sqrt{(1-r^2)\frac{n-1}{n-2}}$$

$(1 - r^2)$ can be defined as

$$(1 - r^2) = \frac{SS_{\text{residual}}}{SS_{\text{Total}}} = 1 - .7601 = \frac{62.37}{260} = 0.239$$

For large samples, $(n-1)/(n-2)$ is almost 1 and then square root of $(1-r^2)$ scaled by standard deviation of Y is the standard error of estimate. When the samples are small, we need to multiply $(1-r^2)$ by $(n-1)/(n-2)$.

$$S_{Y \cdot X} = \frac{SS_{\text{residual}}}{n-2} = S_Y \sqrt{(1-r^2)\frac{n-1}{n-2}} = 5.37\sqrt{(0.239)\frac{10-1}{10-2}} = 2.792$$

6.2.5 Hypothesis Testing in Regression

The hypothesis testing in regression analysis has two components: (a) testing significance of entire model, and (b) testing significance of each of b. In case of simple linear regression, both are identical. They are separate in multiple regression.

The important part of regression analysis is not just finding the sample estimate of β (that is OLS b), but to be able to make an inference about β. The value of $\beta=0$ implies that Y cannot be predicted by X. That is

$$Y = \alpha + (0 \times X)$$
$$Y = \alpha + \beta \bar{X}$$
$$Y = \alpha + (0 \times X)$$
$$Y = \alpha$$

If b is zero, then predicted values for all X values will be a values, that is, constant. When b is zero, then a become $\bar{Y}$

$$a = \bar{Y} - (b\bar{X})$$
$$a = \bar{Y} - (0 \times \bar{X})$$
$$a = \bar{Y}$$

which implies that regression line will be horizontal line at $\bar{Y}$.

The null hypothesis for regression analysis is

$$H_0: \beta=0$$

The alternative that can be tested for regression analysis is

$$H_A: \beta \neq 0$$

In case of simple linear regression, the significance of β and overall significance of model are not different. In case of multiple regression, the significance of each predictor variable and significance of the model are different. In order to test the significance of a model as per the null hypothesis, one needs to separate variation in Y due to the regression and variation in Y that is not explained by regression. The sum of squares regression is the expression of deviation of each predicted value of Y (that is Y') from the mean of Y (that is $\bar{Y}$). $Y_i' - \bar{Y}$ is the degree to which a regression equation explains deviation of each value of Y from $\bar{Y}$. Since the actual values and predicted values can be below and above the mean of Y, all the deviations are squared before summing them $(Y_i' - \bar{Y})^2$. The sum of squared deviation of predicted values from the mean of Y is called SS regression.

Table 6.4. *Further Computation for Example 2*

Test Score (Y)	Intelligence (X)	$Y' = a + bX$	Residual $Y - Y' =$ $Y - (a + bX)$	SS Residual $(Y - Y')^2$	Regression $Y' - \bar{Y}$	SS Regression $(Y' - \bar{Y})^2$
3	5	4.87	−1.87	3.48	−5.13	26.35
4	7	7.43	−3.43	11.79	−2.57	6.59
5	8	8.72	−3.72	13.81	−1.28	1.65
6	4	3.58	2.42	5.84	−6.42	41.18
9	6	6.15	2.85	8.12	−3.85	14.82
11	11	12.57	−1.57	2.45	2.57	6.59
14	9	10	4	16	0	0
16	13	15.13	0.87	0.75	5.13	26.35
18	15	17.7	0.3	0.09	7.7	59.28
14	12	13.85	0.15	0.02	3.85	14.82
Mean = 10	**Mean = 9**			$\Sigma(Y - Y')^2$ $= 62.367$		$\Sigma(Y' - \bar{Y})^2$ $= 197.623$

SS total is obtained by

$$SS_{Total} = \sum_{i=1}^{n}(Y_i - \bar{Y})^2$$

SS_{Total} is already computed in order to obtain variance and standard deviation of Y. This represents total variation in Y. $SS_{regression}$ is that variation in Y which is explained by regression equation. And $SS_{residual}$ is the deviation in Y that regression equation cannot explain. $SS_{residual}$ is already discussed in the context of standard error of estimate.

Figure 6.4 shows that total distance between $Y_i - \bar{Y}$ can be partitioned in two components. First is regression or explained $(Y'_i - \bar{Y})$: the difference between $\bar{Y}$ and predicted value of Y, this is the distance that is explained by the regression line. Second is residual $(Y - Y'_i)$: the difference between actual value and predicted value, this is the distance that regression equation fails to explain.

Figure 6.1 explains this concept in case of pair of score (13, 16). Let us understand this for $X = 13$, $Y = 16$. The predicted score of Y for $X = 13$ is $Y' = a + bX = -1.55 + (1.2833 \times 13) = 15.13$. This score varies from its mean by $Y_i - \bar{Y} = 16 - 10 = 6$. The difference between $Y'_i - \bar{Y}$, that is, the variance explained by regression equation is $Y' - \bar{Y} = 15.13 - 10 = 5.13$. Out of the total variance of Y value, 5.13 is explained by regression equation. Remaining, that is, $6 - 5.13 = 0.87$ is not explained by the regression equation. This is residual. This is also obtained by difference in actual and predicted value, that is, $Y_i - Y'_i = 16 - 15.13 = 0.87$.

The sum of squares total is expressed as

$$SS_{Total} = SS_{regression} + SS_{residual}$$

$$\sum_{i=1}^{n}(Y_i - \bar{Y})^2 = \sum_{i=1}^{n}(Y'_i - \bar{Y})^2 + \sum_{i=1}^{n}(Y - Y'_i)^2$$

In case of Example 2, Table 6.4 has shown the computation of these components. It can be rewritten as

$$260 = 197.623 + 62.367$$

The degrees of freedom associated with SS_{Total} is $n-1$; degrees of freedom associated with $SS_{regression}$ is k, and degrees of freedom associated with $SS_{residual}$ is $n-k-1$. This is general linear model format that can be tested using ANOVA and F-distribution. The ANOVA table for the above data is given in Table 6.5.

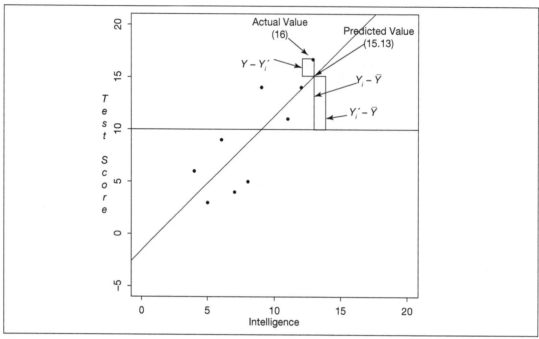

Figure 6.4. *The Scatter with Predicted Values on Regression Line*

Table 6.5. *ANOVA Summary Table for Regression*

Source	SS	df	MSE	F
Regression/ Explained	$\sum_{i=1}^{n}(Y_i' - \bar{Y})^2 = 197.623$	$k=1$	$SS_{regression}/df_{regression} = 197.623$	$F = \dfrac{MSE_{regression}}{MSE_{residual}}$
Residual/ Unexplained	$\sum_{i=1}^{n}(Y - Y_i')^2 = 62.367$	$\begin{aligned}&=n-k-1\\&=10-1-1\\&=8\end{aligned}$	$SS_{residual}/df_{residual} = 197.623$	$F = \dfrac{197.623}{7.796}$
				$F = 25.35$
Total	$\sum_{i=1}^{n}(Y_i - \bar{Y})^2 = 260$	$\begin{aligned}&n-1\\&10-1=9\end{aligned}$		

The critical values of *F* at df 1, 8 can be obtained from Appendix C5 or it can also be obtained by simple R code 6.2.

```
# R Code 6.2. Critical F value
qf(.05, 1, 8, lower = F) # critical F at alpha = .05, df1 = 1,
# and df = 8, lower tail is False. It is [1] 5.317655
```

The critical value of *F* (1, 8) is 5.318 at alpha=0.05. The obtained value of *F* is greater than that and hence, the null stating that H_0: $\beta = 0$ is rejected. The alternative states that H_A: $\beta \neq 0$ is accepted. It is understood that in the population represented by the sample, the regression line has a slope. This implies that intelligence predicts test score in the population represented by sample.

6.2.5.1 Testing Significance of b

I reiterate that testing significance of *b* and significance of entire model are same for simple linear regression. However, for the demonstration purpose, the significance of *b* is discussed. It also has implication to next point, testing significance between independent *bs*.

Let us hypothesize that population value of b is zero. The hypothesis is $\beta_1 = 0$. The standard error of distribution of b is

$$s_b = \frac{S_{Y \cdot X}}{S_X \sqrt{n-1}}$$

In order to test hypothesis that slope of regression line in population is zero, t-statistics can be obtained by

$$t = \frac{b - \beta_1}{s_b} = \frac{b}{\dfrac{S_{Y \cdot X}}{S_X \sqrt{n-1}}} = \frac{b \times (S_X) \times (\sqrt{n-1})}{S_{Y \cdot X}}$$

t is distributed at $n-2$ degrees of freedom. For Example 2, $b = 1.2833$, $S_X = 3.65$, $S_{Y \cdot X} = 2.792$.

$$t = \frac{b \times (S_X) \times (\sqrt{n-1})}{S_{Y \cdot X}} = \frac{1.2833 \times (3.65) \times (\sqrt{10-1})}{2.792} = 5.035$$

The critical value of t at df $= 10 - 2 = 8$ is 2.306. The obtained value is larger than this value and hence null stating $\beta_1 = 0$ is rejected and alternative $\beta_1 \neq 0$ is accepted. The exact two-tailed probability of $t = 5.035$ is 0.001007. This can be obtained by R code.

```
pt(5.035, 8, lower = F)*2
```

6.2.5.2 Confidence Interval for b

The confidence interval (*CI*) for b can be computed as follows:

$$\text{CI}(\beta_1) = b \pm (t_{\alpha/2}) \left[\frac{S_{Y \cdot X}}{S_X \sqrt{n-1}} \right]$$

For Example 2, it is

$$\text{CI}(\beta_1) = b \pm (t_{\alpha/2}) \left[\frac{S_{Y \cdot X}}{S_X \sqrt{n-1}} \right]$$

$$= 1.2833 \pm (2.306) \left[\frac{2.792}{3.65 \times \sqrt{10-1}} \right]$$

$$= 1.2833 \pm 0.588$$

$$\text{CI}(\beta_1) = 1.2833 \pm 0.588 = .6953 \leq \beta_1 \leq 1.781$$

This confidence interval is obtained at $p = 0.95$. It is notable that null hypothesis value (zero) is not in the interval.

6.2.5.3 Test for Significance Difference between Two Independent bs

This section explains test of the significant difference between two independent b values. I modify Example 2 slightly to suit this problem. Suppose, we have 25 students who are provided remedial training and 25 students who did not receive any such training. The question is "whether the slope is steeper for training group than no training group." It is expected that intelligence predicts test score more with training than without training. Simple linear regression analysis is carried out for both groups separately. The summarized regression output is provided in Table 6.6.

Table 6.6. *Data for Testing Difference in Independent bs*

	Remedial Training Group (RTD)	No Remedial Training Group (NRTD)
b	0.338	0.1925
$S_{Y \cdot X}$	4.829	4.583
S_X^2	23.81	23.91
N	25	25

The sample data shows that regression line is steeper for RTD than NRTD. The null hypothesis is H_0: $\beta_1 = \beta_2$. That is, H_0: $\beta_{RTD} = \beta_{NRTD}$. The population slope for both groups are equal. This implies that H_0: $\beta_{RTD} - \beta_{NRTD} = 0$. The sampling distribution of $b_1 - b_2$ has mean zero and standard error $S_{b_1 - b_2} = \sqrt{S_{b1}^2 + S_{b2}^2}$. In previous section, we learned that $s_b = \dfrac{S_{Y \cdot X}}{S_X \sqrt{n-1}}$. The ratio of $b_1 - b_2$ and $S_{b_1 - b_2}$ will follow t-distribution at df$= n_1 + n_2 - 4$.

$$t = \frac{b_1 - b_2}{S_{b_1 - b_2}} = \frac{b_1 - b_2}{\sqrt{S_{b1}^2 + S_{b2}^2}}$$

In case of the example data,

$$S_{b1} = \frac{S_{Y \cdot X_1}}{S_{X_1} \sqrt{n-1}} = \frac{4.829}{4.89 \sqrt{25-1}} = 0.0406$$

$$S_{b2} = \frac{S_{Y \cdot X_2}}{S_{X_2} \sqrt{n-1}} = \frac{4.583}{4.88 \sqrt{25-1}} = 0.0368$$

$$S_{b_1 - b_2} = \sqrt{S_{b1}^2 + S_{b2}^2} = \sqrt{0.0406^2 + 0.0368^2} = \sqrt{0.00165 + 0.00135} = 0.0548$$

$$t = \frac{b_1 - b_2}{S_{b_1 - b_2}} = \frac{b_1 - b_2}{\sqrt{S_{b1}^2 + S_{b2}^2}} = \frac{0.338 - 0.1925}{0.0548} = \frac{0.1455}{0.0548} = 2.655$$

The t-value of 2.665 is evaluated at df$=25+25-4=46$. The critical value of t at 46 degrees of freedom is 2.012. The obtained value is smaller than the critical value and hence the null hypothesis is rejected. There is small improvement possible in these calculations. Since the variances are looking similar, we can use pooled estimate of variances assuming equality. However, the details of such an assumption are better discussed in chapter on t-test. The pooled estimate $(S_{Y \cdot X}^2)$ is obtained by $S_{Y \cdot X}^2 = \dfrac{(n_1 - 2)S_{Y \cdot X_1}^2 + (n_2 - 2)S_{Y \cdot X_2}^2}{n_1 + n_2 - 4}$

Using the pooled estimate, the standard error of $b_1 - b_2$ is calculated by the following formula.

$$S_{b_1 - b_2} = \sqrt{\frac{S_{Y \cdot X_1}^2}{S_{X_1}^2 (n_1 - 1)} + \frac{S_{Y \cdot X_2}^2}{S_{X_2}^2 (n_2 - 1)}}$$

The t-value can be obtained from here.

6.2.6 Simple Linear Regression in R

R code 6.3 explains the regression analysis in R with output. The "lm" is a general purpose linear model command useful in R for carrying out regression, ANOVA and ANCOVA. Though, "aov" is generally preferred for ANOVA. The model is specified by model formula. The argument for "lm" is model formula, which has response variable (DV) on left side of tilde~(read:

is modeled as) and model specification formula on the right. Table 6.7 explains various model formulas that might be useful. For model specification formula, R uses Plus operator (A+B) for combining elementary terms; colon (A:B) as interaction term; and star (A*B) as both main effect and interaction terms (A*B=A + B + A:B).

R Code 6.3. Regression Analysis in R with Output

```
test <- c(3,4,5,6,9,11,14,16,18,14) # Tests Score
int<- c(5,7,8,4,6,11,9,13,15,12) # Intelligence
# lm is linear model command.
fit <- lm (test ~ int)
summary(fit)
Call:
lm(formula = test ~ int)

Residuals:
  Min 1Q Median 3Q Max
-3.717 -1.792 0.225 2.029 4.000

Coefficients:
  Estimate Std. Error t value Pr(>|t|)
(Intercept) -1.5500 2.4580 -0.631 0.54589
int 1.2833 0.2549 5.035 0.00101 **

—

Signif. codes:
0 '***' 0.001 '**' 0.01 '*' 0.05 '.' 0.1 ' ' 1

Residual standard error: 2.792 on 8 degrees of freedom
Multiple R-squared: 0.7601,    Adjusted R-squared: 0.7301
F-statistic: 25.35 on 1 and 8 DF, p-value: 0.001008

# Confidence Interval for b
confint(fit, level = .95)
   2.5 % 97.5 %
(Intercept) -7.2181614 4.118161
int 0.6955724 1.871094

# Useful R functions
fitted(fit) # gives predicted values
residuals(fit) # residuals
anova(fit) # results in anova table
influence(fit) # regression diagnostics
```

The "test" and "int" are two variables specified. (As you know that you can call a .txt or .csv file using read.csv or read.txt command). The output shows the formula use. It also shows the descriptive of the residuals. The coefficients are intercept and regression coefficients, their standard error, t-values, and probabilities. Note the value of intercept being –1.55 and coefficient being 1.2833 with $t=5.035$, $p=0.001$. The regression coefficient is significant and rejects the null that H_0: $\beta=0$. The significance codes below indicate that it is significant at 0.01 level. The standard error is 2.792. R^2 is 0.76 and adjusted R^2 is 0.73. Their interpretation is discussed in previous chapter as well. The F statistics for the entire model is 25.35 which is significant at df$=1$ and 8 (the significance of β and entire model are same in case of simple linear regression). R Code 6.4 shows the plotting of regression line and scatter.

R Code 6.4. Plotting the Regression Line

```
plot(x, y, cex = 3, pch= 20, cex.lab = 3, cex.axis = 2.5, xlim=c(0, 8),
ylim=c(0, 9))
abline(fit, lwd = 3)
```

The R code 6.3 will plot the regression line and scatter. The details of plot command are already discussed in Chapter 3.

6.2.7 Confidence Limits on Y

Once equation is predicting the value of Y, it can be used to predict the value of Y for new score on X. However, we also know that such predictions will be accurate around the mean value of X and when new values are away from mean of X, the confidence interval can be obtained by

$$CI(Y) = Y' \pm (t_{\alpha/2})(S'_{Y \cdot X})$$

where,
  CI(Y) is confidence interval of Y at α,
  Y' is predicted value of Y, and
  $t_{\alpha/2}$ is critical value of t at $p = \alpha/2$.
  $S'_{Y \cdot X}$ can be obtained as follows

$$S'_{Y \cdot X} = S_{Y \cdot X} \sqrt{1 + \frac{1}{n} + \frac{(X_i - \bar{X})^2}{(n-1)S_X^2}}$$

$S'_{Y \cdot X}$ is value that depends on value of $X_i - \bar{X}$. If $X_i - \bar{X}$ is smaller, then $S'_{Y \cdot X}$ will be smaller and if $X_i - \bar{X}$ is larger, then $S'_{Y \cdot X}$ will be larger. Larger the $S'_{Y \cdot X}$, larger the CI, and smaller the $S'_{Y \cdot X}$, narrower the CI.

Suppose, the new value of intelligence is 14, then the CI(Y) can be obtained by first obtaining $S'_{Y \cdot X}$.

$$S'_{Y \cdot X} = 2.792 \sqrt{1 + \frac{1}{10} + \frac{(14 - 9)^2}{(10 - 1)13.33}} = 3.194$$

$$CI(Y) = 16.416 \pm (2.228)(3.194)$$

$$P\{9.3 \leq Y \leq 23.53\} = 0.05$$

The lower side value is 9.3 and upper side value is 23.53. The interval is wide because sample size is small and value of 14 is away from mean of intelligence. Refer to R code 6.5 for computing CI for Y.

```
R Code 6.5. Confidence Interval of Y
newdata = data.frame(int=14)
predict(fit, newdata, interval= "prediction", level = .95)
# Output
  fit lwr upr
1 16.41667 9.052043 23.78129

# Confidence Interval for mean response
predict(fit, newdata, interval="confidence", level = .95)
```

6.2.8 Assumptions Underlying Regression Analysis

The regression analysis has equation $Y = \alpha + \beta X + \varepsilon$. The equation $Y = \alpha + \beta X$ is expression of deterministic linear relationship of Y with X. The ε (epsilon) is a random error or noise. In order to estimate variability in Y as a function of linear relation, some assumptions are made about random error term. These assumptions need to be evaluated before carrying out regression analysis. They are as follows:

1. The random error (ε) is assumed to be **normally distributed**.
2. The error term is assumed to be **homoscedastic**, meaning they all have equal variance
3. The error term is assumed to be **independent** of one another.

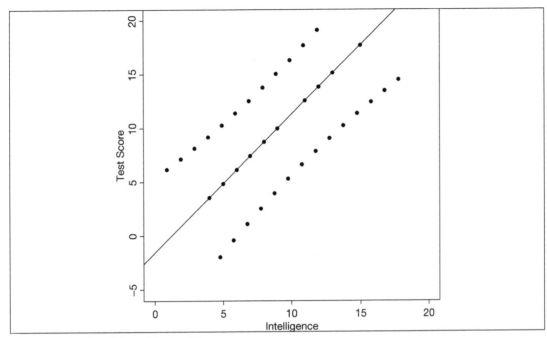

Figure 6.5. *Confidence Limit of Y*

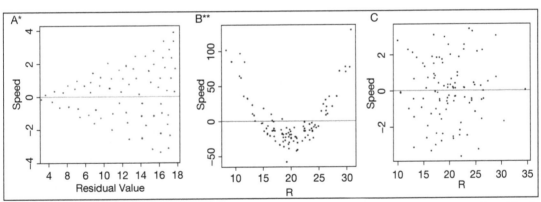

Figure 6.6. *Examples of Violation of Assumption associated with ε (A) Variance of Residuals Increases as X Increases (B) Systematic Curvature of the Residuals (C) Residual Distributed Randomly across the Values of X*
Note: *This violates the assumption of homoscedastic error variance. This is a heteroscedastic error variance. The weighted least squares (WLS) models are better suitable for such data.
**This indicates that the assumption of linear relationship between X and Y is not tenable. This can be dealt with using models that are called as curve fitting.

We know that the residuals sum to zero $\Sigma e=0$. Generally, graphs are used to plot residuals on Y-axis and X is plotted on X-axis and predicted Y values (Y′) are plotted on X-axis. Y values are not plotted since they are related to residuals (e). The Residual versus X plot is expected to provide random scatter below and above the mean residuals (zero line) over all values of X. There should be absence of systematic curvature to this plot.

The normal distribution of error term can be evaluated by using normal Q–Q plot of the residuals. The diagnostic plots also provide such a plot. We have already discussed the issue of evaluating assumption of normal distribution.

R Code 6.6. Diagnostic Plots
```
par (mfrow=c(2,2))
plot (fit, cex = 2, pch=16)
# The residual plots can be obtained by following codes as well
plot (fit$fitted.value, fit$resid, pch = 16, cex = 2)
plot (fit$fitted.value, sqrt(abs(scale(fit$resid))), pch = 16, cex = 2)
qqnorm (fit$resid, cex = 2, pch = 16)
qqline (fit$resid)
```

The regression plots results in Figure 6.7.

The left bottom figure is the square root of standardized residuals versus predicted values, left-top figure plots residuals versus predicted values which is expected to be a flat line. The right top figure is Q–Q plot of residuals which is expected to be scattered tightly around straight line and right bottom figure is residuals versus leverage values in terms of Cook's distance where residuals are not expected to be higher than Cook's distance.

The assumption regarding the error term are discussed so far. Now let us look at other important assumptions.

The assumption of **linearity** is another assumption of regression analysis. This simply implies that if the relationship between X and Y is not linear, then linear regression is not possible.

One of the assumption and implication to psychological research in regression analysis is often ignored by researchers in psychology. This is assumption that X is measured perfectly. This assumption is slightly problematic to psychology researchers given the fact that most of psychological variables are measured with some error (that is the reason we compute reliability of psychological measures). If X is measured with error, then X is

$$X=X_{True}+e$$

The regression equation $Y=a+bX+e$ then can be written as

$$Y=a+b(X_{True}+e_x)+e$$

However, X_{True} is never known and only X is known. As a result, the error term includes measurement error of X as well as random error (e), which also implies that X is not independent of e. This problem is often overlooked by researchers in psychology (with implicitly assuming that measurement is near perfect and reliability is very high). The solution to this problem can be achieved by carrying out structural equations modeling (SEM) which separates measurement error, observed variables and latent variable(s). we shall discuss SEM in Chapter 10.

Example 6.3: Predicting Performance by Conscientiousness Using R

I have a hypothetical data on performance (Y) and conscientiousness (X) of 20 individuals. The data is given below. The prediction looks fine in terms of causality. The performance ratings are average of independent ratings by two supervisors for an employee. The conscientiousness is peer rating for a person. Some useful facts to be noted are that (a) variation in personality dimension can cause variation in performance but other way round is less likely particularly when the personality dimension is measured by peer rating, (b) performance is measured independent of personality, and (c) peer ratings of conscientiousness are not influenced by social desirability.

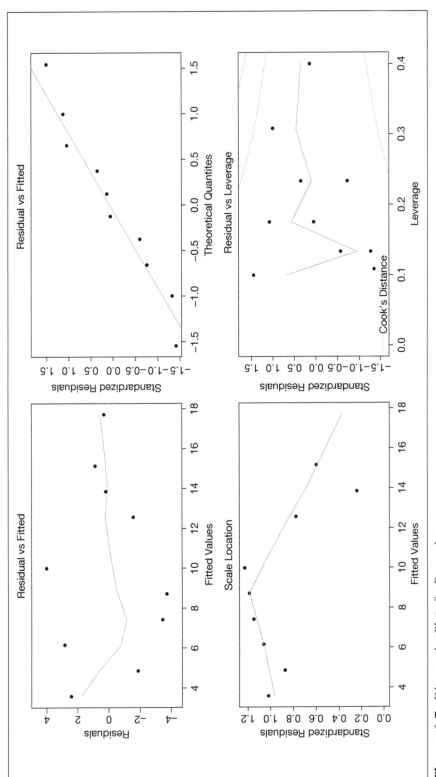

Figure 6.7. *Diagnostics Plots for Regression*

Conscientiousness	147	136	114	130	141	161	114	123	148	122
Performance	110	95	77	95	104	120	79	84	101	80
Conscientiousness	156	149	100	138	101	104	125	131	127	153
Performance	115	102	68	94	79	79	90	83	94	111

The data of 20 subjects is analyzed as follows. The step-by-step analysis is not provided since it has been already discussed. The basic statistics and other details are provided below.

	Performance	**Conscientiousness**
Mean	93.00	131.00
Var	206.84	337.79
SD	14.38	18.37
$Cov_{Perf.Con}$	249.32	

b can be obtained dividing the covariance between performance and conscientiousness by the variance of conscientiousness.

$$b = \frac{Cov_{xy}}{S_x^2} = \frac{249.32}{337.79} = 0.738$$

$$a = \bar{Y} - b\bar{X} = 93 - (0.738 \times 131) = -3.678$$

The R code 6.7 and the output are displayed below.

```
R Code 6.7. Regression for example 6.3
con<- c(147, 136, 114, 130, 141, 161, 114, 123, 148, 122, 156, 149, 100,
138, 101, 104, 125, 131, 127, 153)
perf <- c(110, 95, 77, 95, 104, 120, 79, 84, 101, 80, 115, 102, 68, 94,
79, 79,      90,     83,     94, 111)
fit <- lm(perf ~ con)
summary (fit)

Call:
lm(formula = perf ~ con)

Residuals:
Min                 1Q                  Median              3Q                  Max
-10.0000            -3.6311             -0.0121             3.7025              8.1424

Coefficients:
Estimate Std. Error t value Pr(>|t|)
(Intercept)         -3.68853            8.10139             -0.455              0.654
con                 0.73808             0.06127             12.046              4.75e-10***

---
Signif. codes:
0     `***'    0.001    `**'     0.01     `*'    0.05     `.'    0.1     ` '     1
Residual standard error: 4.909 on 18 degrees of freedom
Multiple R-squared: 0.8896,      Adjusted R-squared: 0.8835
F-statistic: 145.1 on 1 and 18 DF, p-value: 4.746e-10

## Use Following codes for other output.
plot(con, perf, pch = 16, cex = 2)
abline(fit, lwd = 3, cex = 2)
confint(fit, level = .95)
```

6.2.9 Writing Up

The regression is reported depending on the purpose of regression analysis. The example report given below is assuming that performance is predicted using conscientiousness.

In order to predict performance of employees from C, simple linear regression analysis is carried out. The ratings of personality are not affected by social desirability and performance is average of independent ratings. Suitability of regression was evaluated by examining homoscedasticity, normality and independence of errors plots. The OLS estimate of regression coefficient 0.738 is significant ($t=12.05$, df$=18$, $p<0.001$). The multiple $R^2=0.89$ indicating that 89% variation in performance is explained by conscientiousness. The residual standard error is 4.909 and 95% confidence interval is $0.61 < \beta_{YX} < 0.87$ which is not including zero. The conscientiousness is predicting employee performance (EP) well. However, it needs to be noted that it is in the absence of other predictors of EP.

I would not prescribe this example since it suffers due to omitted variable bias.

The problem can be taken care of by using multiple regression analysis that includes more and enough predictors. In general, simple linear regression is not reported in research. The multiple regression analysis is generally reported. The next section deals with multiple linear regression.

6.3 MULTIPLE REGRESSION

The multiple regression analysis is a statistical technique that is useful to predict a DV using multiple predictor variables (IVs). For example, EP can be predicted by conscientiousness, organizational commitment, work locus of control (LOC), agreeableness, job satisfaction, job characteristics and intelligence. The multiple regression analysis is suitable in such a situation. Multiple regression model is a better abstraction of reality since it is able take into account various factors that causes DV. The multiple regression equation is

$$Y = \alpha + \beta_1 X_1 + \beta_2 X_2 + \cdots + \beta_k X_k + \varepsilon$$

where
   Y is a dependent variable,
   α is a population intercept,
   $\beta_1, \beta_2, \ldots, \beta_k$ are population regression coefficients associated respectively with $X_1, X_2, \ldots, X_k$ IVs, and
   ε is error associated with the population regression equation.
   The sample regression equation is

$$Y = a + b_1 X_1 + b_2 X_2 + \cdots + b_k X_k + e$$

where
   a is a sample estimate of population intercept,
   $b_1, b_2, \ldots, b_k$ are sample estimates of population $\beta_1, \beta_2, \ldots, \beta_k$ regression coefficients respectively, and
   e is a sample error term.
   The predicted value of Y (denoted by Y') is expressed as

$$Y' = a + b_1 X_1 + b_2 X_2 + \cdots + b_k X_k$$

As is the case with simple linear regression $e=Y-Y'$, and the OLS estimators of population regression coefficients use the logic of obtaining estimators such that $\sum e^2 = \min$. The primary goal of multiple regression analysis is to make prediction of DV using multiple IVs. In addition, since there are many regression coefficients, one can also ask question about their relative comparisons. The regression techniques involve standard, sequential (hierarchical), and statistical (stepwise) regressions.

Generally, regression analysis require following steps to be taken. First, the researchers identify the set of IVs that are theoretically predictors of DV. This is perhaps the most crucial step in regression analysis. Selecting IV that do not cause each other, and do not show very high association with each other, selecting DV that do not cause any of the IVs, and so on must be taken care of. Generally, these variables are referred to as endogenous and exogenous variables. The endogenous variables (DV) are within the system whereas exogenous variables are outside the system. It is expected that exogenous variables are not affected by changes in the other variables of the model, especially by changes in the endogenous variables. Endogenous variables value is determined by functional relationship with other variables. Problems of exogeneity may occur if uncontrolled confounding variable influences both IV and DV; it may also occur due to loop of causality between IV and DV (for instance, mental health causes physical health and physical health causes mental health). Second, cross-sectional data of IV and DV are obtained. The measurement is assumed to be perfect or near perfect. Time-series data is not discussed here; it is a separate topic for which I do not have any expertise. Third, setting up regression equation and finalizing decision about which variables to retain in equation. Fourth, testing assumption underlying regression analysis and obtaining estimators. Fifth, testing significance of the model and each predictor variable, and writing results.

6.3.1 Purpose of Multiple Regression

The primary purpose of regression analysis is to examine relationship between DV and several IVs. One can also study the effect of some IVs on DV when other IVs are statistically controlled. One can also ask questions about changing in predictability by adding a new IV, for example, whether addition of intelligence as IV brings improvement to predictability of the model in which personality factors are predicting performance. One can also compare several separate set of IVs in predicting DV. For example, set one has job characteristic variables; set two has cognitive variables, set three has components of EI, and so on and each of them separately predicts performance. Interestingly, one can also have IVs that are discrete or categorical. The categorical IV in regression is called as dummy variable. For example, gender (male–female), region, religion, and so on, are categorical variables. Dummy variable coding is quickly discussed at the end.

Tabachnic and Fiddel (2007) have noted several research questions that can be answered by multiple regression analysis: they include understanding degree of relationship between IVs and DV, understanding which IVs are important and which are not, improvement in predictability after addition of new IV, exploring potentially non-linear relationship by converting them to linear form (for example, $Y=bX^2$), comparing set of IVs (having different IVs in each set), predicting DV score for new sample, and parameter estimation are the problems that can be addressed by multiple regression analysis.

Example 4: Let us have a hypothetical example of predicting EP by using EI, C, St, and intelligence (GI). It is well known from the literature that these are theoretically important predictors. We measure performance by averaging ratings by supervisors. The EI, St, and C are measures by averaging anonymous peer-rating, and intelligence is actual performance on intelligence test. The model, the population regression equation, is as follows:

$$EP = \alpha + \beta_1 EI_1 + \beta_2 C_2 + \beta_3 St_3 + \beta_4 GI_4$$

$\beta_1, \beta_2, \ldots, \beta_k$ are estimated by $b_1, b_2, \ldots, b_k$ from the data. The data is as follows. We shall compute $b_1, b_2, \ldots, b_k$ by using matrix algebra. Please refer to Appendix B on basic mathematics for understanding basic matrices. The data is provided in table below.

S. No.	EP	EI	C	St	GI
1	14	33	23	8	18
2	15	37	26	15	24
3	12	19	13	10	32
4	13	30	20	11	18
5	15	35	23	11	24
6	17	34	22	7	30
7	16	32	12	5	31
8	13	31	19	9	23
9	17	28	25	10	26
10	15	29	27	11	19
11	15	31	24	10	26
12	17	30	24	6	27
13	13	24	23	15	21
14	17	37	27	11	25
15	15	29	20	11	25
16	16	28	19	8	36
17	17	33	24	7	34
18	13	23	19	7	26
19	13	36	10	12	29
20	19	28	25	7	32
21	16	42	26	11	25
22	18	43	16	9	30
23	12	25	23	9	22
24	13	32	17	10	26
25	14	31	19	8	26
Mean	15	31.2	21.04	9.52	26.2
SD	1.88	5.28	4.48	2.37	4.56

6.3.2 Matrix Equations

Initially we shall obtain standardized regression coefficient and then transform them into unstandardized regression coefficients.

$$R^2 = \mathbf{R}_{yi}\mathbf{B}_i$$

where
R^2 is percentage of variance explained by regression equation,
$\mathbf{R}_{yi}$ is row matrix of correlations between the k IVs and DV, and
$\mathbf{B}_i$ is column matrix of regression coefficients with same k IVs.
The regression coefficients are obtained by multiplying inverse of $\mathbf{R}_{ii}$ by $\mathbf{R}_{yi}$. $\mathbf{R}_{ii}$ is a correlation matrix among the IVs, and $\mathbf{R}_{yi}$ is column vector of IVs with DV.
The vector of regression coefficients ($\mathbf{B}_i$) can be obtained by

$$\mathbf{B}_i = \mathbf{R}_i^{-1}\mathbf{R}_{iy}$$

where
$\mathbf{B}_i$ is column vector of standardized regression coefficients,
$\mathbf{R}_{ii}^{-1}$ is an inverse of the matrix of correlations among the IVs, and
$\mathbf{R}_{yi}$ is a column matrix of correlations between the DVs and the IVs.

Table 6.7. *Regression Models, R Codes and Description*

Model	R Code Formula	Description
$Y = \alpha + \beta X + \varepsilon$	$Y \sim X$ $Y \sim 1 + X$	Simple linear regression model. Second code explicitly state intercept term.
$Y = \beta X + \varepsilon$	$Y \sim -1 + X$ $Y \sim X - 1$	Regression without intercept term.
$Y = \beta_1 X_1 + \beta_2 X_2 + \varepsilon$	$y \sim x_1 + x_2$	Multiple regression: Y regressed on X_1 and X_2.
$Z_Y = \beta Z_X + \varepsilon$	$scale(Y) \sim scale(X)$	Standardize regression.
$\ln(Y) = \beta_1 X_1 + \beta_2 X_2 + \varepsilon$	$\log(Y) \sim x_1 + x_2$	Transformed variable Y regressed on X_1 and X_2. Multiple regression.

Table 6.8. *The Correlation Matrix for the Data in Example 4*

	EP	EI	C	St	GI
EP	1	0.46	0.38	−0.34	0.46
EI	0.46	1	0.11	0.11	0.01
C	0.38	0.11	1	0.2	−0.37
St	−0.34	0.11	0.2	1	−0.46
GI	0.46	0.01	−0.37	−0.46	1

$$\mathbf{R}_{ii} = \begin{bmatrix} 1 & 0.11 & 0.11 & 0.01 \\ 0.11 & 1 & 0.2 & -0.37 \\ 0.11 & 0.2 & 1 & -0.46 \\ 0.01 & -0.37 & -0.46 & 1 \end{bmatrix} \quad \mathbf{R}_{iy} = \begin{bmatrix} 0.46 \\ 0.38 \\ -0.34 \\ 0.46 \end{bmatrix}$$

$$\mathbf{B}_i = \mathbf{R}_{ii}^{-1} \mathbf{R}_{iy}$$

$$\mathbf{B}_i = \mathbf{R}_{ii}^{-1} \mathbf{R}_{iy} = \begin{bmatrix} 1.03 & -0.13 & -0.15 & -0.12 \\ -0.13 & 1.18 & -0.02 & 0.43 \\ -0.15 & -0.02 & 1.3 & 0.6 \\ -0.12 & 0.43 & 0.6 & 1.44 \end{bmatrix} \begin{bmatrix} 0.46 \\ 0.38 \\ -0.34 \\ 0.46 \end{bmatrix} = \begin{bmatrix} 0.42 \\ 0.59 \\ -0.25 \\ 0.56 \end{bmatrix}$$

The values 0.42, 0.59, −0.25, and 0.56 are standardized regression coefficients associated with EI, C, St, and GI, respectively (Table 6.8). The standardized regression equation that we have obtained is

$$EP = (0.42 \times EI) + (0.59 \times C) + -(0.25 \times St) + (0.56 \times GI) + e$$

R^2 can be obtained by $R^2 = \mathbf{R}_{yi} \mathbf{B}_i$. $\mathbf{B}_i$ is already obtained. $\mathbf{R}_{yi}$ is already computed.

$$R^2 = \mathbf{R}_{yi} \mathbf{B}_i$$

$$R^2 = [0.46 \quad 0.38 \quad -0.34 \quad 0.46] \begin{bmatrix} 0.42 \\ 0.59 \\ -0.25 \\ 0.56 \end{bmatrix} = 0.76$$

$R^2 = 0.76$ implies that the linear combination of IVs explain 76% variance in EP.

In order to convert them into unstandardized coefficients, each standardized regression coefficient is multiplied by ratio of SD of DV and SD of given IV.

$$b_i = B_i \left(\frac{S_Y}{S_i} \right)$$

where
b_i is unstandardized regression coefficient associated with variable i,
B_i is standardized regression coefficient associated with variable i,
S_Y is standard deviation of DV, and
S_i is standard deviation of ith IV.
The unstandardized regression coefficients are computed as follows for each of the variable.

$$b_{EI} = B_{EI} \left(\frac{S_Y}{S_{EI}} \right) = 0.418 \left(\frac{1.96}{5.5} \right) = 0.1489$$

$$b_C = B_C \left(\frac{S_Y}{S_C} \right) = 0.587 \left(\frac{1.96}{4.67} \right) = 0.2461$$

$$b_{St} = B_{St} \left(\frac{S_Y}{S_{St}} \right) = -0.248 \left(\frac{1.96}{2.469} \right) = -0.1968$$

$$b_{GI} = B_{GI} \left(\frac{S_Y}{S_{GI}} \right) = 0.557 \left(\frac{1.96}{4.743} \right) = 0.2301$$

Since the unstandardized coefficients are computed, we can also compute the intercept (a).

$$a = \bar{Y} - \sum_{i=1}^{k}(b_i \bar{X}_i)$$
$$a = \bar{Y} - [(b_{EI}\bar{X}_{EI}) + (b_C\bar{X}_C) + (b_{St}\bar{X}_{St}) + (b_{GI}\bar{X}_{GI})]$$
$$a = 15 - [(0.1488 \times 31.2) + (0.2461 \times 21.04) + (-0.1967 \times 9.52) + (0.2301 \times 26.2)]$$
$$a = 15[(4.643) + (5.1779) + (-1.8735) + (6.026)] = 1.023$$

Once the regression constant (a) and regression coefficients are obtained, the regression equation that will provide the predicted value of EP is as follows:

$$EP' = 1.023 + (0.1488 \times EI) + (0.2461 \times C) + (-0.1967 \times St) + (0.2301 \times GI)$$

6.3.3 Hypothesis Testing

Once the predicted values are obtained from regression analysis, the hypothesis testing can be carried out. There are two steps in hypothesis testing: first, testing hypothesis that entire model predicts DV, and second, once the model predicts DV, the next hypotheses that need to be tested is significance of each predictor variable.

6.3.3.1 Testing Significance of Model

The logic of the significance testing of entire model is identical to the one discussed in simple linear regression. The multiple regression model is

$$Y = a + b_1 X_1 + b_2 X_2 + \cdots + b_k X_k + e$$

Table 6.9. *Calculations of SS of Squares for Multiple Regression*

$(Y_i - \bar{Y})^2$	Y_i	Y_i'	$(Y_i' - \bar{Y})$	$(Y_i' - \bar{Y})^2$	$e = (Y - Y_i')$	$e^2 = (Y - Y_i')^2$
1	14	14.16	−0.84	0.70	−0.16	0.03
0	15	15.50	0.50	0.25	−0.50	0.25
9	12	12.45	−2.55	6.52	−0.45	0.20
4	13	12.39	−2.61	6.82	0.61	0.37
0	15	15.25	0.25	0.06	−0.25	0.06
4	17	17.02	2.02	4.10	−0.02	0.00
1	16	14.89	−0.11	0.01	1.11	1.23
4	13	13.84	−1.16	1.36	−0.84	0.70
4	17	15.36	0.36	0.13	1.64	2.69
0	15	14.19	−0.81	0.65	0.81	0.65
0	15	15.56	0.56	0.31	−0.56	0.31
4	17	16.43	1.43	2.04	0.57	0.33
4	13	12.14	−2.86	8.20	0.86	0.74
4	17	16.76	1.76	3.11	0.24	0.06
0	15	13.85	−1.15	1.32	1.15	1.32
1	16	16.58	1.58	2.49	−0.58	0.33
4	17	18.29	3.29	10.81	−1.29	1.66
4	13	13.73	−1.27	1.62	−0.73	0.53
4	13	13.16	−1.84	3.40	−0.16	0.02
16	19	17.33	2.33	5.43	1.67	2.79
1	16	17.26	2.26	5.12	−1.26	1.59
9	18	16.49	1.49	2.23	1.51	2.27
9	12	13.70	−1.30	1.70	−1.70	2.88
4	13	13.99	−1.01	1.03	−0.99	0.97
1	14	14.72	−0.28	0.08	−0.72	0.52
Sum = 92				Sum = 69.49		Sum = 22.51

We know that

$$SS_{Total} = SS_{regression} + SS_{residual}$$

$$\sum_{i=1}^{n}(Y_i - \bar{Y})^2 = \sum_{i=1}^{n}(Y_i' - \bar{Y})^2 + \sum_{i=1}^{n}(Y - Y_i')^2$$

Table 6.9 provides basic calculation for significance testing for multiple regression. The sum of squares Y is obtained by summing $(Y_i - \bar{Y})^2$, that is the deviation of each Y value form its mean is squared and then added. The degrees of freedom for SS_{total} is $n - 1 = 25 - 1 = 24$.

$$SS_{total} = \sum_{i=1}^{n}(Y_i - \bar{Y})^2 = 92$$

The $SS_{regression}$ is obtained by summing that squared deviations of predicted Y from mean of Y. The degrees of freedom associated with $SS_{regression}$ is $df_{regression} = k = 4$ which is number of predictors.

$$SS_{regression} = \sum_{i=1}^{n}(Y_i' - \bar{Y})^2 = 69.49$$

The $SS_{residual}$ is a squared deviation of predicted value from actual Y value (that is e^2) for all the values. This has degrees of freedom $n - k - 1 = 25 - 4 - 1 = 20$.

$$SS_{residual} = \sum_{i=1}^{n}(Y - Y_i')^2 = 22.51$$

Table 6.10. *ANOVA Summary Table for Multiple Regression*

Source	SS	df	MSE	F
Regression/Explained	$\sum_{i=1}^{n}(Y_i' - \bar{Y})^2 = 69.49$	$k=4$	$SS_{regression}/df_{regression} = 17.37$	$F = \dfrac{MSE_{regression}}{MSE_{residual}}$
Residual/Unexplained	$\sum_{i=1}^{n}(Y - Y_i')^2 = 22.51$	$\begin{aligned}&=n-k-1\\&=25-4-1\\&=20\end{aligned}$	$SS_{residual}/df_{residual} = 1.126117$	$\begin{aligned}F &= \dfrac{17.37}{1.126117}\\ &= 15.42\end{aligned}$
Total	$\sum_{i=1}^{n}(Y_i - \bar{Y})^2 = 92$	$\begin{aligned}&=n-1\\&=25-1\\&=24\end{aligned}$		

The F statistics for the entire model is displayed in Table 6.10.

The obtained F value of 15.43 is significant at 0.01 level given the critical value of $F(4, 20) = 4.43$ at 0.01 level of significance. It can be concluded that in the population represented by sample, the model can predict the EP. The coefficient of determination (R^2) can be computed by

$$R^2 = \frac{SS_{regression}}{SS_{total}} = \frac{69.49}{92} = 0.755$$

6.3.3.2 Testing Significance of Each Predictor Variable

The next question is which of the IVs are important predictors. It can be decided through analysis of each b_i value obtained. The null hypothesis is separately stated for each of the IVs. The general form of the null hypothesis and alternate hypothesis for the purpose is as follows:

$$H_0: \beta_i = 0$$

$$H_A: \beta_i \neq 0$$

In order to obtain significance of each b_i value, the standard error associated with each b_i value needs to obtained. The matrix operation for obtaining the significance for each b_i as follows.

The variance of b_i values can be obtained by $(X'X)^{-1}$ and variance–covariance matrix of b_i is $\hat{\sigma}^2(X'X)^{-1}$. The standard error of b_i is computed by the square root of $C_{jj} = \hat{\sigma}^2[diag((X'X)^{-1})]$
where
$X = X - \bar{X}$ is a $n \times k$ matrix of k IVs and deviation from its mean is obtained for each value.
$\hat{\sigma}^2$ = MSE or error mean square of entire model
For the present data, C_{jj} can be obtained as

$$C_{jj} = \hat{\sigma}^2[diag((X'X)^{-1})] = 1.1255 \times [0.00142 \quad 0.002253 \quad 0.00887 \quad 0.00266]$$
$$C_{jj} = [0.001601 \quad 0.00254 \quad 0.00999 \quad 0.002997]$$

Once the C_{jj} (variance of b_i) is obtained, the standard error is standard deviation of variance term and that is calculated as

$$SE(b_i) = \sqrt{C_{jj}}$$
$$SE(b_i) = [0.04002 \quad 0.05037 \quad 0.09996 \quad 0.05476]$$

Once the standard error associated with each of the b_i is obtained, then significance associated with each predictor variable is calculated by

$$t_i = \frac{b_i}{SE(b_i)}$$

where,

t_i is t value associated with ith predictor variable, b_i is regression coefficient associated with i th predictor variable, and $SE(b_i)$ is standard error associated with b_i. Using this formula, t-values associated with each predictor value can be obtained. The critical t-value at $df_{residual} = n - k - 1 = 20$ is 2.0859.

$$t_{EI} = \frac{0.14885}{0.04002} = 3.72. \quad \text{The obtained value is significant.}$$

$$t_C = \frac{0.2461}{0.05037} = 4.886. \quad \text{The obtained value is significant.}$$

$$t_{St} = \frac{-0.1968}{0.09996} = -1.969. \quad \text{The obtained value is not significant.}$$

$$t_{GI} = \frac{0.23006}{0.05476} = 4.201. \quad \text{The obtained value is significant.}$$

$b_{EI} = 0.149$ which is significant ($t_{EI} = 3.72$, $p < 0.05$). The direction is positive meaning as the EI increases, the EP increases. $b_C = 0.246$ which is significant ($t_{EI} = 4.89$, $p < 0.05$). The direction is positive meaning as the Conscientiousness increases, the EP increases. $b_{St} = -0.197$ which is not significant ($t_{EI} = 1.969$, $p > 0.05$). The St is narrowly missing the significance due to small sample as well as non-directional alternative. Generally, the theory would predict that St is inversely related with performance and the alternative would be H_A: $\beta_{St} < 0$. In case of significant finding, the negative sign of $b_{St} = -0.197$ would mean that in the population, as the St is increasing, the EP is decreasing. $b_{GI} = 0.23$ which is significant ($t_{GI} = 4.2$, $p < 0.05$). The direction is positive meaning as the GI increases, the EP increases.

6.3.4 Types of Multiple Regression

The problem in multiple regression generally arises when IVs are correlated. The correlation among IVs causes shared variance by two or more IVs in the DV. This shared variance cannot be accounted for both explanatory variables. Either we ignore the shared variance or assign it to some specific variable. However, one must remember that high intercorrelation among the IVs is undesirable and leads to a problem of multicollinearity. There are three broad strategies of dealing with the variance in DV shared by more IVs. They are: (a) standard multiple regression, (b) sequential multiple regression (hierarchical multiple regression), and (c) stepwise (statistical) regression.

The **standard multiple regression** considers only unique contribution of the IV to DV. The contribution of the IV shared with other IVs is not considered.

In **sequential multiple regression (hierarchical multiple regression)**, the IVs are entered in the equation one after another in the order specified by the researcher. As a result, the IV that enters first gets all the variation shared with other IVs and so on. In case of earlier example, if the order of entry is C, EI, GI and St, then, all the variance C shares with other predictors goes to C, then EI is entered in the equation, and variance that EI shared with GI and St goes to the credit of EI. Then GI is entered and whatever variance GI shares with St goes to the credit of St, and at the end, St is entered. The actual running of this regression leads to insignificant St. The order of entry is decided on the basis of theory or research question. For example, one may have a question that even after EI explains variance in EP, whether GI can still explain any more variance? This question can be answered by ordering GI after EI.

The **statistical or stepwise regression** is a procedure wherein the order of the entry of the IVs is completely determined by the statistical criterion. The statistical regression uses some statistical criterion to keep the variable in equation. They are "F to enter," "F to remove," "p to enter," and "p to remove" as criterions to keep or remove variables in regression. For example, when we set "p to remove" at 0.05, then we do not keep variables that are not significant at alpha=0.05. The statistical selection can be carried out in three different ways: first, forward selection, second, backward elimination, and third, stepwise regression.

(i) Forward Selection: In forward selection, there are no IVs in the equation to begin with. The IV that meets the statistical criteria for entry is added one at a time. Once the IV is entered in the equation, then it stays in the equation. It is not removed from the equation. This step is repeated until there is no further IV that meet statistical criteria of entry.

(ii) Backward Elimination: In backward elimination process, researcher began equation with all IVs in the equation. Then we run the regression and evaluate various statistical criteria (regression coefficients, partial and semipartial correlation, *t* values of individual IVs, and so on). The insignificant variables that contribute least to the model are then removed from the model. This step is repeated till there are no more variables to be removed from the model. The capitalization on chance is a disadvantage of this process. If variables have suppressor relationship, then it may cause harm to our purpose. The variable that is removed from the earlier step may be a significant predictor, if couple of more variables is removed.

(iii) Stepwise Regression: The stepwise regression tries to combine both the approaches. The stepwise regression starts as forward selection process. It starts with empty equation. We enter the IV that shows highest correlation in step 1. Then all semipartial correlations are carried out for remaining IVs and the IV with highest first-order semipartial correlation is entered. This step is repeated. In addition, before the new variable is added at every step, we test whether variable that was added at the earlier step can be removed on the ground that now it (earlier added variable) is no longer making any significant contribution.

6.3.5 Additional Model Selection Criterion

Which of the explanatory variables in the model should be retained is a critical question to answer. There is no single best way to answer this question. One can think of throwing all possible explanatory variables in the equation and check for significance. This is neither prudent nor practical. One needs to understand that as we keep adding or removing the variables from equation, we are not just changing R^2 but we are also changing the degrees of freedom. The idea is to impose penalty for changing df. The three criteria are presented here:

(i) **R^2 and adjusted R^2**
R^2 for the multiple regression model is defined as

$$R^2 = \frac{ESS}{TSS} = 1 - \frac{RSS}{TSS}$$

Where, ESS is explained sum of squares and RSS is residual sum of squares. R^2 value will be between 0 and 1 and closer to 1 value of R^2 indicates better fit. However, there is an obvious problem with R^2. The problem is that R^2 cannot be reduced if we add irrelevant variable and R^2 may vary with sampling variation. It may be enticing for a researcher to increase the IVs and increase R^2 and obtain better fit. The problem with this strategy is that it does not penalize goodness-of-fit index for increased df. The alternative is adjusted R^2.

$$\bar{R}^2 = 1 - \frac{RSS/(n-k)}{TSS/(n-1)} = 1 - (1 - R^2)\frac{n-k}{n-1}$$

$\bar{R}^2 \le R^2$, that is because adjusted R^2 penalizes R^2 for increasing the regressors.

(ii) **Akaike Information Criterion (AIC):** The AIC is most popular criteria.

$$AIC = e^{\frac{2k}{n}} \frac{\sum_{i=1}^{n} e_i^2}{n} = e^{\frac{2k}{n}} \frac{RSS}{n}$$

where, RSS is residual sum of squares, k is number of regressors (constant included) and n is sample size. The AIC is intuitively easy to understand if the log of two sides is taken.

$$\ln(AIC) = \ln\left(\frac{2k}{n}\right) + \ln\left(\frac{RSS}{n}\right)$$

k is number of predictors. As k increases, the AIC increases if n is not changing (which is what happens). This is a "cost" inflicted for adding new regressor. The RSS is a function of IVs. As the addition regressor is added to the equation, the RSS is expected to decline. This is a "benefit" from adding new regressor. The AIC is evaluation whether reduction in residuals is greater than the penalty for increasing the df. The AIC will be smaller for a model with added IVs (regressors) only if RSS reduces reasonably. So while comparing models, we look for models with smaller AIC.

(iii) **Schwarz Information Criterion (SIC):** The SIC is similar to AIC, the logic of imposing penalty is slightly different.

$$SIC = n^{k/n} \frac{\sum_{i=1}^{n} e_i^2}{n} = n^{k/n} \frac{RSS}{n}$$

For the sake of easier understanding, log of SIC is useful.

$$\ln(SIC) = \left(\frac{k}{n}\ln n\right) + \ln\left(\frac{RSS}{n}\right)$$

The explanation of SIC is similar to AIC and hence avoided. As is the case with AIC, smaller SIC is preferred.

(iv) **Mallows's C_p Criterion:** The C_p criterion is obtained as follows: suppose, we carry out regression with k IVs including intercept and we have $\hat{\sigma}^2$ as an estimator of σ^2. Now we have less than k regressors, p, $p \le k$ and obtain RSS_p that is residual sum of squares for p regressor model. The Mallow's C_p criterion is as follows:

$$C_p = \frac{RSS_p}{\hat{\sigma}^2} - (n - 2p)$$

It is known that $E(\hat{\sigma}^2) = \sigma^2$ that is $\hat{\sigma}^2$ is an unbiased estimator of σ^2. If the model with p regressors fit well, then $E(RSS_p) = (n-p)\sigma^2$. As a result, approximately it is true that

$$E(C_p) \approx \frac{(n-p)\sigma^2}{\sigma^2} - (n - 2p) \approx p$$

It implies that while choosing a model, we choose a model that has smallest C_p values and possibly equal to p.

6.3.6 Importance of IVs

Deciding about the importance of the variable is a concern of researcher. One simple way to make a decision about the importance of variable is the size of regression coefficient. The β_i or β_i^2 is a unique contribution of that variable to the DV. Darlington (1990) made a case against the use of β_i^2 as an important evaluation tool. The sampling variation of β_i^2 values is higher if explanatory variables are correlated. Other than β_i, the useful measure of importance is squared part correlation between i^{th} explanatory variable and DV with remaining explanatory variables are partialled out. Darlington (1990) argued that the semipartial correlation should not be squared; however, the order remains unaffected for absolute values.

6.3.7 Issues in Multiple Regression

There are no free lunches in statistics in general and regression in particular. There are always some concerns and consequences of the decisions made. Some of these specific issues related to multiple regression that researchers need to pay attention to are discussed in this section. They include sample size, multivariate outliers, multicollinearity, heteroscedasticity, and normality. There are problems associated with misspecification of the form, omission of IVs and errors of measurements as well.

6.3.7.1 Sample Size

The sample size for multiple regression is determined by number of predictors, desired power, alpha level, and desired effect-size. Green (1991) provided discussion on sample size for multiple regression in psychological researches. There are some rules of thumb. One such rule is $N \geq 50 + 8k$ for multiple correlation and $N \geq 104 + k$ for each of the individual predictor. In example we have $k=4$ and $N \geq 50 + (8 \times 4) = 50 + 32 = 82$ and $N \geq 104 + 4 = 108$ by using the rules. The larger among the two would be the sample size, that is, $N \geq 108$ would be the sample size. This sample is useful in detecting medium size of beta. Green (1991) describes a complex rule that takes into account the effect-size. The rule is $N \geq (8/f^2) + (k-1)$ where f^2 is effect-size estimate and $f^2 = 0.02$ for small, $f^2 = 0.15$ for medium and $f^2 = 0.35$ for large effect-size. In case of this example, $N \geq (8/0.15) + (4-1) = 56.33$. The sample of size 25 is useful to detect only large effect-size. Kelley and Maxwell (2003) suggested an alternative approach emphasizing *accuracy in parameter estimation* (AIPE). They argued that AIPE approach produces accurate estimates of population parameters by sufficiently narrowing the likely width of CI by providing necessary sample sizes. In case of stepwise regression analysis, more cases are required. It should be noted that too large sample size would lead to very high power that would declare any small value of coefficient to be significant.

6.3.7.2 Multivariate Outliers

The outliers with high leverage values are known to adversely influence regression estimates. The analysis and detection of multivariate outliers is already discussed in Chapter 4. The reader should carry out multivariate and univariate outliers' analysis in order to avoid problems in estimation.

6.3.7.3 Singularity and Multicollinearity

The multicollinearity of correlation matrix implies that two or more predictor variables in correlation matrix are highly correlated. The perfect multicollinearity leads to singularity of matrix. The necessary and sufficient condition to determine singularity is that the determinant of matrix is zero. Such a matrix does not have matrix inverse. If the correlation matrix among IVs is singular, then they will not have an inverse. We know that $B_i = R_{ii}^{-1}R_{iy}$ implies that in order to obtain regression coefficients (**B**$_j$), the inverse of correlation matrix among IVs (R$_{ii}^{-1}$) is required. If such an inverse is impossible, then OLS estimator **B**$_j$ does not exist. In order to avoid these problems, the first step is to detect multicollinearity and take remedial measures if its presence is detected.

Detecting Multicollinearity

Various measures of multicollinearity have been developed. Some of them are discussed here.

(i) Insignificant *t*-values in spite of high *R*²

In case of multicollinearity, the model R^2 will be high and the individual b_i would be small values and *t* values would be insignificant despite of the presence of sound theory. The reason being, one predictor variable shares the common variance and the other highly correlated variables have nothing to explain.

(ii) Correlations among the predictors, Tolerance and Variance Inflation Factor

The pair-wise examination of correlations among the predictor variables is a simple strategy. If any of the correlations are in the range of 0.8 or 0.9, it is a clear indication of multicollinearity. Obtaining tolerance is another way of judging the multicollinearity. Several series of regression are carried out within IVs. Every time, each IV is serving as a DV and remaining IVs are predicting that IV. A very high SMC (squared multiple correlation or R_i^2) or very low tolerances $(1 - SMC$ or $1 - R_i^2)$ indicate multicollinearity. The real limitation of this approach is that even low intercorrelation among IVs may lead to high R^2. One of the solutions to this issue is to obtain variance inflation factor (VIF). The VIF is

$$\text{VIF} = \frac{1}{1 - R_i^2} = \frac{1}{\text{tolerance}}$$

It draws on the idea that closer the R_i^2 to 1, larger is the variance of estimated b_i. In case of multicollinearity, the tolerance will be value closer to zero and VIF will be large value. Some authors suggest that $VIF \geq 10$ be considered as the indicator of multicollinearity.

(iii) Determinant of *X′X*

If *X′X* is obtained on standardized predictor variables, the elements of *X′X* are zero-order correlation coefficients. The determinant of matrix is generalized variance of matrix. The det(*X′X*) closer to zero indicates multicollinearity and det(*X′X*) closer to one indicates independence.

(iv) Theil's Multicollinearity Effect

The Theil multicollinearity effect is a useful tool to detect the structure of multicollinearity. Let R^2 be SMC for DV regressed on all IVs, R_i^2 be the SMC for regression of DV on IVs excluding X_i, then Theil (1971) multicollinearity effect is

$$R^2 - \sum_{i=1}^{k} R^2 - R_i^2$$

In the absence of multicollinearity, this quantity should be zero and in the presence of multicollinearity this quantity should be larger.

(v) Other Methods

Farrar–Glauber test, condition number test, and auxiliary regression are other methods for detecting multicollinearity. Farrar–Glauber test has been criticized for its ineffectiveness. Auxiliary regressions are popular in econometrics data.

Possible Solutions to Multicollinearity Problem

One of the common ways to deal with multicollinearity is to drop the variable that is creating multicollinearity and theoretically less important. Which variable to be deleted is more of theoretical decision than the statistical one. If researchers are not in favor of dropping the IV, then they have few alternatives. Ridge Regression is one procedure that helps to keep the IV in regression by way of stabilizing the estimates of regression coefficients by increasing the variance explained. The procedure once considered valuable is now viewed with considerable doubt (Fox, 1991). If the IVs are showing the pattern of correlations among them, then the principal component analysis of IVs can be carried out and orthogonal (uncorrelated components) can be retained. Transforming variables and adding new data are other methods of dealing with multicollinearity.

6.3.7.4 Heteroscedasticity

The homoscedasticity in multiple regression refers to the distribution of errors across the IVs is uniform and stochastic. Violation of the assumption of homoscedasticity (called as heteroscedasticity) causes problems in the estimation of population regression coefficients. One needs to detect the heteroscedasticity and take steps to remedial measures.

Detecting Heteroscedasticity

There are various ways to identify violation of the assumption of homoscedasticity.

(a) Graphical Methods

The graph of error term against the IV or DV is useful if the sample size is sufficiently large. This plot should have uniform distribution of error term across the values of IV. The absence of which can be considered as a potential violation assumption. Figure 6.3 shows the heteroscedastic pattern in data.

(b) Glejser Test

Glejser (1969) suggested a test for heteroscedasticity that regresses the absolute sample residuals of original regression on IV which is tested for heteroscedasticity. If the absolute error term predicts the independent variable, then it is an indication of the presence of heteroscedasticity. The relationship tested could take various forms. The examples are

$$|e| = a + b_1 X_1 + v$$
$$|e| = a + b_1 \sqrt{X_1} + v$$
$$|e| = a + b_1 \frac{1}{X_1} + v$$

(c) Park Test

The Park (1966) test is an alternative way to test for heteroscedasticity. The Park's test assesses hypothesis that $\hat{\sigma}_i^2$ is a function of IV where $\hat{\sigma}_i^2 = \text{var}(e_i)$. It is expected that $E(e_i \mid X_i) = 0$ for $i = 1, 2, \ldots, n$. Park developed a functional form to be tested as:

$$\sigma_i^2 = \sigma^2 X_i^\beta e^{v_i}$$

The log of both sides is

$$\ln(\sigma_i^2) = \ln(\sigma^2) + \beta \ln(X_i) + v_i$$

if we denote $\ln(\sigma^2) = \alpha$, then

$$\ln(\sigma_i^2) = \alpha + \beta \ln(X_i) + v_i$$

The null hypothesis for Park test is H_0: $\beta = 0$ and alternative is H_A: $\beta \neq 0$.

The steps taken for Park test are as follows:

Step 1: Run the regression $Y_i = a + bX_i + e_i$ and obtain the residual $\hat{e}_i$.
Step 2: Run regression $\ln(\hat{e}_i) = \alpha + \beta \ln(X_i) + v_i$ and test null H_0: $\beta = 0$.

The rejection of null is indication of presence of heteroscedasticity according to Park's criterion.

(d) Goldfeld-Quandt (GQ) Test

Goldfeld and Quandt (1965) suggested a GQ test which assumes that heteroscedastic variance $\hat{\sigma}_i^2$ is positively associated with one of the IVs. As usual we have regression following equation:

$$Y_i = a + bX_i + e_i$$

If the heteroscedastic variance $\hat{\sigma}_i^2$ is positively associated with X_i like

$$\sigma_i^2 = \sigma^2 X_i$$

and σ^2 is a constant, then following steps can be taken to test homoscedasticity.

  (i) Order or rank the observations according to X_i from smallest to largest value of X_i
  (ii) Some predetermined number of observations from center of data (c) are omitted leaving $n-c$ observations. Then divide remaining $n-c$ observations into two groups of $(n-c)/2$ each, having $(n-c)/2$ in first half (containing smaller X values) and $(n-c)/2$ in second half (containing larger X values).
  (iii) Fit two separate regression models for first $(n-c)/2$ and second $(n-c)/2$ data and obtain separate RSS for two observations—RSS_1 for smaller X values and RSS_2 for larger X values. These RSSs will have $df = [(n-c)/2] - k$ where k is number of parameters.
  (iv) Now compute lambda, that is the ratio of

$$\lambda = \frac{RSS_2/df}{RSS_1/df}$$

It is shown that if e_i is normally distributed and null of homoscedasticity is valid, the λ follows F-distribution at $df = [(n-c)/2] - k$. If λ value is greater than critical value of F at $df = [(n-c)/2] - k$, then the null of homoscedasticity is rejected. The decision about c, number of middle values to be deleted, is an important one. Goldfeld–Quandt suggested it to be 8 if $n = 30$ and so on. Later, Harvey and Philips (1974) suggested that maximum one-third observations can be deleted. There are two problems associated with GQ procedure: first, with one explanatory variable, GQ procedure is straightforward; with more explanatory variables, GQ becomes cumbersome procedure since one has to run GQ for each IV separately. Second, the assumption that e_i is normally distributed is critical one and may not be supported by data.

(e) Breusch–Pagan–Godfrey Test

The GQ test needs to be repeated with each X in order to identify heteroscedastic X. The Breusch–Pagan–Godfrey Test (BPG Test) solves this problem. Suppose,

$$Y_i = \alpha + \beta_1 X_1 + \beta_2 X_2 + \cdots + \beta_{kX_{ki}} + e_i$$

is a k variable regression model. Assume that $\sigma_i^2 = f(\varphi_1 + \varphi_2 Z_1 + \cdots + \varphi_k Z_k)$. We further assume that $\sigma_i^2 = f(\varphi_1 + \varphi_2 Z_1 + \cdots + \varphi_k Z_k)$ implies that σ_i^2 is a linear function of Z's. If $\varphi_2 = \varphi_3 = \cdots = \varphi_k = 0$, then $\sigma_i^2 = \varphi_1$ which is a constant. On the basis of this formulation, following test procedures is applied.

  (i) First, run the regression analysis and obtain residuals $e_1, e_2, \ldots, e_n$
  (ii) Obtain $\hat{\sigma}^2 = \sum e_i^2/n$. Note that this is a maximum likelihood (ML) estimator[3] of σ^2.

---

[3] The ML estimator of σ^2 is $\hat{\sigma}^2 = \sum e_i^2/n$. The OLS estimator is $\hat{\sigma}^2 = \sum e_i^2/(n-k)$.

(iii) Define new variable p as residual square divided by $\hat{\sigma}^2$.

$$p_i = e_i^2 / \hat{\sigma}^2$$

(iv) Carry out regression $p_i = \varphi_1 + \varphi_2 Z_1 + \cdots + \varphi_k Z_k + v_i$, where ϕ_1 is constant, and v_i is residual.

(v) Compute ESS for this equation and obtain Θ as

$$\Theta = \frac{1}{2} ESS$$

The $\Theta \underset{asy}{\sim} \chi^2_{k-1}$, that is, Θ follows asymptotically χ^2 distribution at $k-1$ degrees of freedom if e_i is normally distributed. If Θ exceeds the critical value of χ^2_{k-1}, then the homoscedasticity null hypothesis is rejected and if Θ is smaller than critical χ^2_{k-1}, then homoscedasticity null hypothesis is accepted.

(f) White's Test for Heteroscedasticity

The White general test for heteroscedasticity uses the idea of auxiliary regression. An auxiliary regression analysis involves: (a) carrying out regression analysis with original regression model and store squared residuals e_i^2 as variables, and (b) regressing e_i^2 on set of original explanatory variables, their squares and their cross-product. For example, if we have Y predicted by two explanatory variables X_1 and X_2 then $Y = a + b_1 X_1 + b_2 X_2 + e$ is the original model and $e_i^2 = \varphi_1 + \varphi_2 X_1 + \varphi_3 X_2 + \varphi_4 X_1^2 + \varphi_5 X_2^2 + \varphi_6 (X_1 X_2) + v_i$ is referred to as auxiliary regression. White (1980) showed that the n times R^2 for auxiliary regression is Lagrange multiplier[4] (LM) test.

$$LM = n \cdot R^2$$

The LM follows the χ^2 distribution at $df = p - 1$ where $p =$ number of estimated parameters in auxiliary regression. Higher value of LM indicates heteroscedasticity and significant chi-square is rejection of homoscedasticity hypothesis.

(h) Other tests

The Spearman's Rank correlation, Koenker–Bassett (KB) test are other tests to detect heteroscedasticity. KB regresses e_i^2 values on estimated values than explanatory variables. In case of Spearman Rank correlation, the absolute value of residuals is correlated with X and if Spearman's *rho* is significant, then the homoscedasticity null hypothesis is rejected.

R code 6.8 for Heteroscedasticity Tests

```
# The BPG test with EP as DV and EI and C are IVs
# own code
EI1 <- scale(EI)                      # Standardized variable EI
C1<- scale(c)                         # Standardized variable C
fit <- lm((EP)~(EI)+(c))             # original model
usq <- (fit$residuals)^2             # squared residuals
aux <- summary(lm(usq ~ EI + c))     # Regressing residual on IVs
shsq <- sum(usq)/length(c)
pi <- (fit$residuals)^2/shsq          # variable p_i
fit1<-lm(pi~EI1+ C1)                  # regressing p_i on standardized IVs
aov <- anova(fit1)                    # ANOVA table for fit1
(sum(aov$Sum[1:2]))/2 BPG test statistics
```

---

[4] The Lagrange multiplier (LM) test is also known as score test. It is derived from a principle of constrained maximization. The log-likelihood are maximized to the constraints that. The score test was initially proposed by Rao (1948). The test is very useful in evaluating pre-specified model.

```
##############################
### Using lmtest library #########
##############################
library(lmtest)                      # call library lmtest
bptest(fit, studentize= F)           # bptest is function.
gqtest(fit, fraction = 5)            # The Goldfeld-Quandt test; middle 5
                                     cases deleted
hmtest(fit)                          # Harrison-McCabe test
#### whites test ####
aux1 <- lm(usq ~ EI + c + EI^2 + c^2 + (EI*c)) # aux. regression
saul <- summary(aux1)                # summary of aux1
saul$r.sq * length(EP)               # Whites test statistics or LM
bptest(fit, ~ EI*c, + I(EI^2) + I(c^2)) # Whites test with bptest function
```

Dealing with Heteroscedastic Data

The heteroscedasticity in the data is affecting efficiency of the estimators. The estimators in heteroscedastic data are not even asymptotically efficient. The heteroscedasticity is not affecting unbiasedness and consistency properties of the OLS estimator. Since the efficiency cannot be assured, the hypothesis testing in heteroscedastic data is questionable. The possible solutions involve issue of knowledge σ_i^2. When σ_i^2 is known, then the method of WLS can be used to correct the estimators in order to obtain BLUE estimators. The practical hitch is that σ_i^2 are seldom known. White worked through this problem and argued that asymptotically valid parameter estimation is possible. The White's heteroscedasticity-consistent variances and standard errors can be used instead of OLS variance and SE. They are also known as robust standard errors. In addition, researchers can make assumption about the heteroscedasticity pattern. The heteroscedasticity possibly may be minimized or removed by transforming variables. Interaction of IVs with IVs outside regression may also result in heteroscedasticity. Including such a variable may bring homoscedasticity.

6.3.7.5 Independence of Errors

Absence of independent error term is known as "autocorrelation." Most often this problem is associated with time-series data. Durbin–Watson test to detect first order autocorrelation and Durbin's h test, are popular measures of autocorrelation. Most econometrics textbooks provide a neat treatment of autocorrelation problem.

6.3.7.6 Model Specification Errors

Some of the following errors in misspecification of regression model are common in psychological research. They include: (a) omitting a relevant variable, (b) including unnecessary variable, (c) assuming incorrect functional form, and (d) errors in the measurement of X and Y.

(a) Omitting Relevant Variable form Regression Model
This problem would occur if the specified regression model is an under specification. An important predictor variable(s) is not included in the regression model. Suppose, creativity (Cr) is explained by GI and openness to experience, the complete form of regression is

$$Cr = \alpha + \beta_1 GI + \beta_2 O + e_i$$

and we assume that e_i follows all the assumptions specified about stochastic error term. For some reason we do not measure O, and the regression equation is

$$Cr = \alpha^* + \beta_1^* GI + v_i$$

The regression equation is solved for estimating β_1^* by using the estimator $\hat{\beta}^*$. It can be shown that the OLS estimator of the regression coefficient is biased and inconsistent. The omitted variable bias adversely influences two properties of OLS estimator: unbiasedness and consistency. There is no good statistical remedy for such a problem. The only way to get rid of this problem is to resort to a good psychological theory and well-specify the model. The OLS estimator in this case is in trouble. Application of instrumental variable is suggested as a solution in certain cases.

(b) Including Unnecessary Variable(s) in the Model

Inclusion of irrelevant variable in the model is a less serious problem. Suppose, $Y = \alpha + \beta_1 X_1 + e_i$ is a correct functional form. If the specified model is $Y = \alpha * \beta_1^* X_1 + \beta_2^* X_2 + e_i$, where $\beta_2^* = 0$ and there is some correlation between X_1 and X_2, the variance of the OLS estimator would be larger than what it should have been.

One way to take case of this problem is to use model selection criterion: Akaike Information Criterion (AIC) or Schwartz information criterion (SIC) are useful statistical techniques to determine variables that need to be kept in the model.

This problem is encountered for **nested and non-nested models**. The nested regression model is the one where one model can be derived as a special case of another. The non-nested models are separate models and neither can be considered as a special case of each other.

Nested Model: let us have a model $EP = \alpha + \beta_1 EI + \beta_2 C + \beta_3 GI + \beta_4 St + \varepsilon_i$. Let us call this model as unrestricted model (UR). Let us have another model $EP = \alpha + \beta_1 EI + \beta_2 C + \beta_3 GI + \varepsilon_i$ which is a restricted model (R). The restricted model is special case of UR model with restriction that $\beta_4 = 0$.

Non-Nested Model: let us have Model 1 as $EP = \alpha_1 + \beta_1 EI + \beta_2 C + \varepsilon_i$ and Model 2 as $EP = \alpha_2 + \beta_3 St + \beta_4 GI + \upsilon_i$. These models are called non-nested models.

Non-Nested Model F test: the non-nested model F test is explained for a simplified form of models. Suppose, the two non-nested models are:

Model 1: $Y = \alpha_1 + \beta_1 X_i + e_i$

Model 2: $Y = \alpha_2 + \beta_2 Z_i + \upsilon_i$

to solve the problem of comparison, create restriction in Model 2 as follows:

Specify a new artificially UR model $Y = \alpha_3 + \beta_3 X_i + \beta_4 Z_i + \eta_i$ which is an artificial nesting model for Model 2 and has no psychological theory backing up, and if we impose a restriction $\beta_3 = 0$, then the model reduces to Model 2 which is a restricted model. Then the F test can be carried out using the RSS under the null hypothesis that $\beta_3 = 0$.

$$F = \frac{\dfrac{RSS_R - RSS_{UR}}{1}}{\dfrac{RSS_{UR}}{n-3}}$$

The F statistical is evaluated for df$=1$, and $n-3$.

The J test: this test is useful for testing non-nested models. It starts with artificial nesting model.

$$Y_i = \lambda(\alpha_1 + \beta_1 X_i) + (1-\lambda)(\alpha_2 + \beta_2 Z_i) + e_i$$

If $\lambda = 1$, then $Y_i = 1(\alpha_1 + \beta_1 X_i) + (1-1)(\alpha_2 + \beta_2 Z_i) + e_i = (\alpha_1 + \beta_1 X_1) + e_i$ is Model 1 and If $\lambda = 0$, then $Y_i = 0(\alpha_1 + \beta_1 X_i) + (1-0)(\alpha_2 + \beta_2 Z_i) + e_i = (\alpha_2 + \beta_2 Z_i) + e_i$ is Model 2. Davison and MacKinnon suggested following steps:

Step 1: replace α_1 and β_1 in artificial nested model by their estimates of Model 1 by OLS procedure. $Y_{i1}' = (\alpha_1 + \beta_1 X_i)$ and the model is $Y_i = \lambda Y_{i1}' + (1-\lambda)(\alpha_2 + \beta_2 Z_i) + e_i$.

Step 2: now $\hat{\lambda} = 0$ is tested and Model 2 is supported and is it is not rejected.

(c) Incorrect Functional Form

Specifying an incorrect functional form might be another error. Suppose, St is explanatory of EP and the functional form is non-linear. If the regression is carried out with a linear form it is referred to as an incorrect specification of the functional form. Transforming variables suitably is the most useful remedy. One can test the specification error. Regression specification error test (RESET), which is also popularly known as Ramsay reset specification test, is a useful method to detect the incorrect specification functional form. It estimates the RSS of restricted and unrestricted models specifying the different functional forms, and tests the difference by using F test. The Rainbow test is another test for testing the misspecification of functional form.

(d) Errors in Measurement

The measurement error is common problem that psychologists face. The entire theory of reliability (true score model) in psychometrics is due to the problem of measurement error. This section is particularly useful to psychological measures such as self-report inventories, questionnaires, and so on. There could be three possibilities: first, DV is incorrectly measured, second, IV is incorrectly measured, and third, both IV and DV are incorrectly measured. Let us look at them. The OLS estimator is in trouble when measurement is with error.

(i) DV is Measured with Error and IV is Measured Accurately

Suppose, we have a DV Y, which is measured inaccurately, the measured value is Y and true value is Y^*. The true value is not observable. Then

$$Y_i = Y_i^* + e_i$$

Most would recognize this is a fundamental equation of reliability theory. We assume that e_i is uncorrelated with Y_i^*. The regression model to be estimated is

$$Y_i^* = \alpha + \beta X_i + v_i$$

But we do not know Y_i^* and only have Y_i. Hence we actually estimate

$$Y_i = \alpha + \beta X_i + v_i - e_i$$

if we define $\eta_i = v_i - e_i$ then

$$Y_i = \alpha + \beta X_i + \eta_i$$

This has a direct impact on the estimation of variance associated with OLS estimator. The numerator of the variance of estimator will be $\sigma_\eta^2 = (\sigma_{v_i}^2 + \sigma_{e_i}^2) \geq \sigma_{v_i}^2$

When Y is incorrectly measured, the estimator remains a BLUE estimator. However, the variance of the estimator increases leading to small t-values. As a result the OLS estimator is more inaccurate.

(ii) Explanatory Variable is measured with Error and DV is Measured Accurately

Suppose, the true value of explanatory variable is given by X_i^* but the measured variable X_i is having error $X_i = X_i^* + e_i$. Then e_i is a stochastically disturbance term that follows all assumption about e_i. The regression equation to be estimated is

$$Y_i = \alpha + \beta X_i^* + v_i$$

Suppose, v_i is also satisfying classical assumption about stochastic error term, and is uncorrelated with e_i then the regression that we actual carry out is

$$Y_i = \alpha + \beta(X_i - e_i) + v_i$$
$$Y_i = \alpha + \beta X_i - \beta e_i + v_i$$

and if we specify $\phi_i = v_i - \beta e_i$ then $Y_i = \alpha + \beta X_i + \phi_i$

Now we can evaluate covariance between ϕ_i and X_i

$$\text{Cov}(X_i, \phi_i) = E[(X - E(X))(\phi - E(\phi))]$$
$$\text{Cov}(X_i, \phi_i) = E[e_i(v_i - \beta e_i)]$$
$$\text{Cov}(X_i, \phi_i) = E(e_i v_i - e_i \beta e_i) = E(e_i v_i) - \beta E(e_i^2)$$
$$\text{Cov}(X_i, \phi_i) = -\beta \sigma_e^2$$

This implies that OLS estimator is not consistent and it is also not unbiased. X and ϕ are correlated. Given this, there is a serious problem in estimating regression equation with OLS estimator. The better strategy under these circumstances is to be able to specify model in term of latent variables where the sources of the error are part of the model. Thanks to this problem, the SEM has immerged as an important approach to deal with psychological data in recent past.

6.3.8 Mediated and Moderated Variable Regression

Baron and Kenny's (1986) paper on the JPSP website is one of the popular papers that distinguishes between moderation and mediational analysis. Both, mediation and moderation analysis used third variable that influences regression model.

6.3.8.1 Simple Mediation Model

The simple mediation model has one causal variable (X), one consequent variable (Y) and one mediator variable (M). Suppose, we have optimism (X) causing happiness (Y) and this relationship is mediated through self-esteem (M). The graphical presentation of this model is as follows:

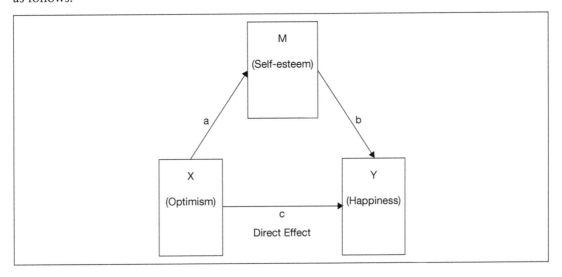

There three effects conceptualized and computed for mediational analysis are: direct effect, indirect effect, and total effect.

Direct Effect is the effect of causal variable (X) on consequence variable (Y) without any other variable in-between.

Indirect Effect is the effect of causal variable on consequence variable through mediating variable.

The two linear models are then evaluated. Basic equations for mediational analysis are as follows:

$$M = i_1 + aX + e_M$$
$$Y = i_2 + cX + bM + e_Y$$

where, i_1 and i_2 are regression intercepts, e_M and e_Y are errors associated with M and Y respectively, a, b, and c are regression coefficients, ab is indirect effect and c is direct effect. The mediation analysis can be carried out with the R package called lavaan. I am using read-ymade example of lavaan in R code 6.9. I shall also show how to obtain a, b, c as well as ab.

R Code 6.9. Mediational Analysis Using R

```
library(lavaan) # call package lavaan
set.seed(1234) # set.seed so that random generated data is idetical.
X <- rnorm(100)
M <- 0.5*X + rnorm(100)
Y <- 0.7*M + rnorm(100)
Data <- data.frame(X = X, Y = Y, M = M)
# lavaan requires model specification. Details are discussed in factor
# analysis chapter
model <- ' # direct effect
  Y ~ c*X
  # mediator
  M ~ a*X
  Y ~ b*M
# indirect effect (a*b)
  ab := a*b
# total effect
total := c + (a*b)
'
fit <- sem(model, data = Data) # running path model
summary(fit) # viewing results
```

 # Complete Outcome:
```
lavaan (0.5-18) converged normally after 12 iterations

Number of observations                 100

Estimator                              ML
Minimum Function Test Statistic        0.000
Degrees of freedom                     0
Minimum Function Value                 0.0000000000000

Parameter estimates:

Information                            Expected
Standard Errors                        Standard
```

```
      Estimate Std.err Z-value P(>|z|)

Regressions:
Y ~
X (c) 0.036 0.104 0.348 0.728
M ~
X (a) 0.474 0.103 4.613 0.000
Y ~
M (b) 0.788 0.092 8.539 0.000

Variances:
Y 0.898 0.127
M 1.054 0.149

Defined parameters:

ab      0.374  0.092  4.059  0.000
total   0.410  0.125  3.287  0.001

#############################
##same can be achieved by using OLS regressions
# Regress Y on X. The result is total effect of mediation.
fit1<-lm(Y~X)
summary(fit1)
# Selected output
# X 0.4100 0.1260 3.254 0.00156 **
# Regress Y on X and M. This shall provide c and b effects.
fit2 <- lm(Y ~ X + M)
summary (fit2)
# Selected output

# X   0.03635  0.10605  0.343  0.7325
# M   0.78832  0.09373  8.410  3.58e-13 ***

# Regress M on X to obtain effect a, that is, M ~ X
fit3 <- lm(M ~ X)
summary (fit3)
# Selected output

# X   0.47392  0.10378  4.567  1.44e-05 ***

In order to obtain ab we need b
fit4<- lm(Y~M)
summary(fit4)
# Selected output

# M   0.80178  0.08473  9.463  1.78e-15 ***

# In order to compute effect ab multiply a and b
0.47392* 0.80178 # should provide ab
# To obtain standard error of ab
sqrt((0.47392^2* 0.08473^2)+(0.80178^2* 0.10378^2)-(0.08473^2*
0.10378^2))
```

The above R code has worked out an example. The total effect of X on Y is significant ($b=0.410$, $z=3.287$, $p<0.01$), out of which, the direct effect of X on Y is not significant ($b=0.036$, $z=0.348$, $p=$ns), and indirect effect (ab) of X on Y is significant ($b=0.374$, $z=4.059$, $p<0.001$). This is an example from random data, but, if we have to interpret this in terms of our example, then, effect of optimism on happiness is insignificant. It implies that though happiness is predicted by optimism it is not because of optimism itself but because of the indirect route, by way of influencing self-esteem. Mediational analysis can be more complex involving more mediating variables. You can refer to Hayes (2013) for further details.

6.3.8.2 Moderated Variable Regression

The moderated variable regression has been suggested as a strategy to evaluate the significance of the moderating variable (Saunders, 1956). Moderated regression has been usually recommended due to its strengths and superiority over other techniques like median-split (Borkenau & Ostendorf, 1992; Piedmont, McCrae, Riemann, & Angleitner, 2000). A criterion (*Y*), a predictor (*X*), and a moderator (*M*) variable are modeled in hierarchical regression equation in moderated regression. The moderated variable regression poses a question that whether the effect of *X* on *Y* is different for different values of *M*. That is, as *M* changes its values, the relationship between *X* and *Y* changes. In terms of regression, the regression coefficients for *Y* regressed on *X* change as *M* changes its values. The basic equations are

$$Y = a + b_1 X_i + b_2 M_i + e_i$$
$$Y = a + b_1 X_i + b_2 M_i + a + b_3 X_i M_i + e_i$$

X and *M* are first entered in the regression equation and then the product term (*XM*) is entered in the equation. If *M* is moderating the relationship between *X* and *Y*, then b_3 is significant. b_3 is an estimator of β_3 with null hypothesis being $H_0 : \beta_3 = 0$. The rejection of this null hypothesis results into establishing the moderated relationship. The moderated variable strategy has become popular in testing the validity of lie scale correction (Piedmont et al., 2000, Belhekar, in press). For further details, reference can be made to Hayes (2013).

6.4 LOGISTIC REGRESSION

Over last decade or so, the logistic regression has become a popular method in psychological research. It is very useful in medical and health researches. The logistic regression is useful to make predictions when the DV is dichotomous and IVs are continuous. The most common situation in medical research is whether or not client has recovered: 0 for not-cured and 1 for cured. One can quickly think of psychotherapy (e.g., CBT [cognitive behaviour therapy], EMDR [eye movement desensitization therapy], STDT [Short Term Dynamic Therapy], and so on) to specific client groups (individuals diagnosed as having major depression). The other technique useful for such a problem is discriminant function analysis (DFA), which is mathematically identical to MANOVA, and can be used with DV that are at more than two levels. It is also useful in obtaining more dimensions of discrimination that cannot be achieved logistic regression. However, DFA requires many assumption (please refer to Chapter 8) and most of them are relaxed with logistics regression. For example, predicting examination outcome by using hours spent in study. The examination outcome is either pass or fail. The DV examination Outcome is dichotomous, and predictor is continuous. This prediction can be carried out by using logistic regression. Look at the following data in R code 6.10.

```
R code 6.10. Data for Logistic and Plot
iv<- c(22, 28, 41, 29, 24, 30, 32, 37, 38, 31, 38, 25, 14, 27, 36, 24,
44, 35, 38, 29, 44, 53, 34, 39, 54, 47, 53, 40, 39, 36)
y<- c(0, 0, 0, 0, 0, 0, 0, 0, 0, 0, 0, 0, 0, 0, 0, 1, 1, 1, 1, 1, 1, 1,
1, 1, 1, 1, 1, 1, 1, 1)
plot (iv, y, cex = 2, pch = 16, cex.axis = 2)
range <- c(15,20,25,30,35,40,45,50,55) # range of iv values
prob <- c(0,0, .25, .2, .5, .56, .67, 1, 1) # probability of y
associated with range
plot(range, prob, cex = 2, pch = 16, cex.axis = 2, cex.lab = 2.5)
```

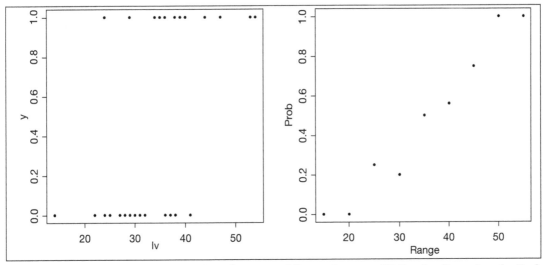

Figure 6.8. *(A) Scatterplot of Number of Hours and Exam Outcome (B) Passing Percentage by Each Hours of Study Level*

The following plots are insightful (Figure 6.8). Plot A shows the scatterplot of number of hours and exam outcome. Plot B shows the passing percentage by each hours of study level.
The frequency table for examination outcome is as follows:

Range	n	Examination Outcomes		P (Proportion Passing)
		0=Fail	1=Pass	
10–15	1	1	0	0
16–20	0			
20–25	4	3	1	0.25
26–3	5	4	1	0.2
31–35	4	2	2	0.5
36–40	9	4	5	0.56
40–45	3	1	2	0.67
46–50	1	0	1	1
51–55	3	0	3	1
Total	30	15	15	0.52

The table shows that though the DV is dichotomous, the probability of Y taking value 1 changes as the study hours change. The scatterplot is not much interpretable, but $P(Y=1)$ by study hours is more interpretable. It can be seen that the probability of $Y=1$ is gradually increasing with increasing value of X. In general we can say that X (time spent in studies) and Y (exam outcome) are positively related. The logistic regression models this relationship.

6.4.1 Fundamentals of Logistic Regression

The basic regression equation we have learned is

$$Y_i = a + b_1 X_i + e_i$$

a and b are OLS estimators of their population parameters. The logistic regression models the probability of Y. the basic model is

$$Y_i = \frac{e^u}{1+e^u}$$

where $u = a + b_1X_i + e_i$; e is constant; and Y_i is the estimated probability that observed case is in either of the category. u is general regression equation, in which, a is estimated regression constant, b is regression coefficient, and e_i is error of prediction. The linear regression creates log of the odds or logit:

$$\ln\left(\frac{Y}{1-Y}\right) = a + \sum b_1X_i$$

The ML estimation is used to estimate regression coefficients. The idea of ML is different than OLS. The ML tries to estimate best linear combination of predictors that maximize the likelihood of obtaining observed data. In order to accomplish ML estimation, some initial estimates of coefficients are arbitrarily taken. Then ML estimates are derived. The basic process is as follows: the ML methods require construction of *likelihood function*. The probability of the actual data as function of parameters is expressed by this function. ML estimators are obtained such that they maximize this function. Y is coded as 0 or 1. Let us specify

$$\pi(x) = \frac{e^{a+b_1X_i}}{1+e^{a+b_1X_i}}$$

$\pi(x)$ provides conditional probability that Y is 1 given X, that is, $P(Y=1|X)$. $1-\pi(x)$ provides the $P(Y=0|X)$. Hence, for the pairs X_i, Y_i where $Y=0$, contribution to likelihood function is $1-\pi(x)$ and when $Y=1$, contribution to likelihood function is $\pi(x)$. It is expressed as

$$\pi(x_i)^{y_i}[1-\pi(x_i)]^{1-y_i}$$

The likelihood function for vector of coefficients (β) is expressed as a product of terms

$$l(\beta) = \prod_{i=1}^{n} \pi(x_i)^{y_i}\,[1-\pi(x_i)]^{1-y_i}$$

Generally log of ML function is useful which is expressed as *log-likelihood* (LL).

$$L(\beta) = \ln[l(\beta)] = \sum_{i=1}^{n}\{y_i \ln[\pi(x_i)] + (1-Y_i)\ln[1-\pi(x_i)]\}$$

In order to obtain β that maximizes value of LL of beta $[L(\beta)]$, $L(\beta)$ is required to be differentiated with respect to a and b. Typically, a closed solution of estimating parameter values does not work for these estimates. The estimation of parameters of logistic regression equation hereafter is an iterative process. The details for this process are beyond the scope of this book. I have used an R code to obtain the estimates. For the data provided, R code 6.10 can be analyzed. R code 6.11 for the same is given below.

R Code 6.11. Logistic Regression

```
fit <- (glm(y~iv, family= binomial()))
summary(fit)

Call:
glm(formula = y ~ iv, family = binomial())
```

```
Deviance Residuals:
   Min        1Q      Median       3Q        Max
-1.63898  -0.79826   0.02501   0.88865   2.06869
```

Coefficients:

	Estimate Std.	Error	z value	Pr(>|z|)	
(Intercept)	-6.32772	2.51067	-2.520	0.0117	*
iv	0.17972	0.07045	2.551	0.0107	*

—

```
Signif. codes:
0 `***' 0.001 `**' 0.01 `*' 0.05 `.' 0.1 ` ' 1

(Dispersion parameter for binomial family taken to be 1)

Null deviance: 41.589 on 29 degrees of freedom
Residual deviance: 30.268 on 28 degrees of freedom
AIC: 34.268
Number of Fisher Scoring iterations: 5
```

The R code above is used for estimating the beta values. The intercept value is -6.33 and regression coefficient is 0.18. These two values are estimated by ML estimates.

$$\pi(x) = \frac{e^{-6.33+(0.18 \times X_i)}}{1 + e^{-6.33+(0.18 \times X_i)}}$$

To understand in linear manner, let us use following expression as an estimated *logit transformation* $g(\hat{x})$

$$g(\hat{x}) = \ln\left(\frac{Y}{1-Y}\right) = -6.33 + 0.18 \times \text{Hours}$$

The R code also has been computed which is summarized in the table below.

	Estimate	Std. Error	z value	Pr(>|z|)
Intercept	-6.33	2.51	-2.52	0.01
IV	0.18	0.07	2.55	0.01

In addition to estimates, this table displays standard errors. The Z values column is given by ratio of estimate and standard error.

$$Z_a = \frac{-6.33}{2.51} = -2.52 \qquad Z_b = \frac{0.1797}{0.0705} = 2.551$$

The last column is probabilities associated with each of the Z values.
   Once the estimates are obtained, the model evaluating the adequacy of the model.

6.4.2 Significance Testing of the Coefficients

The process of significance testing in reality is more complex than the description provided below. However, this section provides explanation of all elementary components in this process. Once the coefficients are estimated, the statistical significance testing of the null hypothesis is carried out. This would tell us which of the predictor variables are "significant." The significance testing asks a basic question: whether the model that has explanatory variables is better than the model that does not have any explanatory variable (constant only model)? The question is answered by using two models: one, a constant only model, second, a model with the explanatory variable(s). The values predicted by model that has variables in it are better fitting than when there are no variables, then the model is considered as significant. Unlike the OLS regression model, where the difference between actual and predicted values is in the absolute sense, the logistic model is evaluated on difference between constant only model and theoretical model. This is generally called as goodness-of-fit. We shall look at LL statistics, Wald Statistics, Pseudo R^2, and information criteria in this section.

6.4.2.1 Log-Likelihood Statistics

The LL is expressed as

$$L(\beta) = \ln[l(\beta)] = \sum_{i=1}^{n} \{y_i \ln[\pi(x_i)] + (1 - y_i)\ln[1 - \pi(x_i)]\}$$

An essential building block is *deviance*. The deviance is $-2 \times log\text{-}likelihood(-2LL)$. The deviance is used instead of LL for the easy of interpretation since $-2LL$ follows chi-square distribution. The deviance is analogous to RSS in linear regression. The $-2LL$ can be calculated for different models. Generally, $-2LL$ for constant only model and $-2LL$ for model with variables are compared. This ratio is expressed as G or χ^2

$$G = \chi^2 = -2\ln\left[\frac{\text{likelihood constant only}}{\text{likelihood with Variables}}\right]$$

$$G = \chi^2 = [-2LL(\text{constant only})] - [-2LL(\text{with Variables})]$$

$$G = \chi^2 = 2LL(\text{with Variables}) - 2LL(\text{constant only})$$

$$df = k_{\text{with Variables}} - k_{\text{constant only}}$$

The chi-square is obtained as

$$G = \chi^2 = 41.58883 - 30.26812 = 11.32071$$
$$df = 29 - 28 = 1$$

The probability of obtaining chi-square 11.32 at df=1 is 0.0007665. These results can be obtained by R code 6.12.

```
R Code 6.12. Chi-square Test in Logistic Regression
model_chi <- fit$null.deviance-fit$deviance
model_chi # returns model chi-square
df_chi <- fit$df.null - fit$df.resid
df_chi  returns model df
pchisq(model_chi, df_chi, lower = F) # probability of chi-square
# Easier way to obtain al this is to write
anova(fit, test = "Chisq") # model chi-square test
Analysis of Deviance Table
Model: binomial, link: logit
Response: y
Terms added sequentially (first to last)
Df Deviance Resid. Df Resid. Dev Pr(>Chi)

NULL                29    41.589
iv     1   11.321   28    30.268   0.0007665 ***
```

—

```
Signif. codes:
0 `***' 0.001 `**' 0.01 `*' 0.05 `.' 0.1 ` ' 1
```

In R the constant only model can be specified by writing the following R code 6.13.

R Code 6.13: Constant Only Model
```
fit0 <- (glm(y~1, family= binomial("logit")))
```

The obtained chi-square is significant. It implies that when "model with variables" is better than "constant only model", then the chi-square has actually taken the difference between the two deviances (some sort of residuals) and the deviance of "constant only model" is 41.58 and deviance of "model with variables" is 30.268. The difference is chi-square distributed. The test has verified whether deviance has significantly reduced because of inclusion of variables in the model. If we had more predictor variables, we would have carried out significance testing of each of the predictor variable since the "model" is better than "no model." It is usually accomplished by Wald statistics.

6.4.2.2 Wald Statistics

The Wald test is a ratio of ML estimate of β (slope parameter estimated by b) and its standard error. The Wald statistics developed by Abraham Wald[5] is called z statistics.

$$Z_b = \frac{b_1}{SE_{b1}} = \frac{0.1797}{0.0705} = 2.551$$

z is standard normal distributed variable. The probability of obtaining value of 2.551 and more is 0.0107. Since the probability is low, we reject the hypothesis that population value of b is zero. Menard (2001) argued that one should be carefully use this statistics since the standard errors inflate as estimated β increases. The R code described in the box has already displayed Wald statistics.

6.4.2.3 R and R²

The model can be evaluated by using R and R^2. The most popular options are Cox and Snell R^2, McFadden R^2, and Nagelkerke R^2. These R^2 are often referred to as pseudo R^2. Since there are different ways to calculate R^2, there is no consensus about which one is best. Menard (2000) and Mittlbock and Schemper (1996) reviewed various measures of R^2 and made different recommendations.

Let L_0 be the likelihood function of the model that has no predictors (constant only model) and let L_M be the likelihood function for model that has predictors.

Then the McFadden R^2 is defined as

$$R^2_{McF} = 1 - \frac{\ln(L_M)}{\ln(L_0)}$$

$\ln(L_M) = -15.1340627$ and $\ln(L_0) = -20.7944154$. The McFadden R^2 is

$$R^2_{McF} = 1 - \frac{\ln(L_M)}{\ln(L_0)} = 1 - \frac{-15.1340621}{-20.7944154} = 0.2722055$$

The R code 6.14 given below is useful for obtaining the LL of model and null.

---

[5] Abraham Wald was a Hungarian mathematician and statistician. He contributed to the solution of many statistical problems. He contributed to statistical decision theory and sequential analysis.

R Code 6.14 for Likelihood of Model and Likelihood of Baseline
```
library(pscl)
pR2(fit)
     llh        llhNull         G2       McFadden       r2ML        r2CU
-15.1340621   -20.7944154   11.3207066   0.2722055   0.3143287   0.4191049
```

The McFadden R^2 is similar to R^2 of linear regression where $\ln(L_M)$ is similar to sum-of-squares error and $\ln(L_0)$ is similar to sum of squares total (SST). R^2 is a ratio of likelihood of constant only model and likelihood of null model (constant only model) and hence is an indicator of improvement due to adding variables in the model. The likelihood is always between 0 and 1. The log of likelihood is always zero or smaller than zero. When the model has low likelihood (closer to zero), the log is larger and when the model has high likelihood (closer to 1), the log has smaller magnitude. When improvement in likelihood due to adding variable is large, then the ratio would be smaller number. As a result 1, ratio of likelihoods will be a larger number.

The Cox and Snell R^2 is another popular measure of R^2. It is a ratio of likelihoods that account for the improvement due to addition of predictors, obviously, smaller the ratio, greater the improvement. R_{CN}^2 is obtained as

$$R_{CN}^2 = 1 - \left[\frac{(L_0)}{(L_M)}\right]^{2/n} = 1 - \left[\frac{(0.00000000093132)}{(0.0000002675225)}\right]^{2/30} = 0.3143287$$

The Cox and Snell Pseudo R^2 can be also expressed as

$$R_{CN}^2 = 1 - \exp\left[\frac{(-2LL_M) - (-2LL_0)}{n}\right] = 1 - \exp\left[\frac{30.26812 - 41.58883}{30}\right] = 0.3143287$$

It should be noted that Cox and Snell R^2 cannot have maximum value of 1. Assuming that the full model is perfect fit and has likelihood equal to 1, $R_{CN}^2 = 1 - \left[\frac{(L_0)}{1}\right]^{2/n} = 1 - [L_0]^{2/n}$ which is less than 1. This is a useful expression to understand Nagelkerke modification.

Noticing the problem that R_{CN}^2 does not reach its maximum value, Nagelkerke (1991) suggested a modification in R_{CN}^2. This is expressed as

$$R_{Ng}^2 = \frac{R_{CN}^2}{1 - [L_0]^{2/n}} = \frac{0.3143287}{1 - \left[(0.00000000093132)\right]^{2/30}} = 0.4191049$$

It can also be expressed as

$$R_{Ng}^2 = \frac{R_{CN}^2}{1 - \exp\left(-\frac{2LL_0}{n}\right)} = \frac{0.3143287}{1 - \exp\left(-\frac{41.58883}{30}\right)} = \frac{0.3143287}{1 - 0.25} = 0.4191049$$

Among other measures, McKelvey and Zavoina R^2, Efron's R^2, and so on, are popular approaches. Generally, R^2 can be interpreted not exactly like OLS R^2. R^2 is logistic regression are pseudo-R^2. They appear like R^2, that is they are from 0 to 1 scale (some do not reach 1), and large values indicate better fit of the model, they cannot be interpreted in terms of percentage of variance. You can refer to Kvålseth (1985) for discussion about properties of R^2.

6.4.2.4 Information Criterion

Two most popularly used information criteria to interpret the model fit are AIC and Bayes information criterion (BIC).

As we have discussed in multiple regression, the information criteria penalizes R^2 for having more predictors.

$$AIC = -2LL_M + 2k = 30.26812 + (2 \times 2) = 34.268$$

The AIC for the constant only model is 41.589. Generally AIC is evaluated on the basis of reduction in value for a better fitting model.

The BIC changes the penalty by slightly modifying the AIC formula

$$BIC = -2LL_M + 2k \times \ln(n) = 30.26812 + (2 \times 2)\ln(30) = 43.87291$$

6.4.3 The Odds Ratio

The odds ratio is very useful indicator in logistic regression, since it is very useful in health and clinical research. It captures a change in the odds of occurrence of an event from the unit change in predictor. The odd ratio is already discussed in the correlation chapter and its computation and details are avoided here. The R can compute the odds ratio by following simple command.

R code 6.15 for Odd's Ratio
```
exp(coef(fit)) # exp of coefficients provides odds
# Output
(Intercept) iv
0.001786108 1.196877134
```

The coefficients of logistics regression are log odds. The odds ratio can be obtained by exponentiation of the coefficients. The exponent of coefficient 0.17972 is the odds ratio for this predictor. The odds ratio for the predictor is 1.197. The odds ratio is as the name indicates—a ratio between two odds. The odds ratio of 1 indicates that the odds of passing do not change if hours spent in study change by a unit. The odds ratio above 1 (e.g., OR=1.197) indicates the odds of passing (occurrence of event) is 1.197 as time spent in studies increases by a unit. There is a small increase in the chance of passing as one studies for a minute more per session of the day.

6.4.4 Classification

One way to determine whether the logistic model is useful in predicting the outcome variable is to do the classification. This involves predicting the outcome variable by using the logistic model that we have developed. Then we check how many of those values are correctly predicting the outcome. R code 6.16 below carries out this task for you.

R code 6.16 for Classification in logistic regression
```
fit<- (glm(y~iv, family= binomial("logit")))
mystep <- (step(fit, fity~iv, family= binomial("logit")))
fitted(mystep)
classDF <- data.frame(response = y, predicted = round(fitted(mystep),0))
xtabs(~ predicted + response, data = classDF)
         response
predicted   0   1
        0  10   4
        1   5  11
```

The classification table is given below.

		Actual		Total
		Pass	**Fail**	
Predicted	**Pass**	10 (66.67%)	4	14
	Fail	5	11 (73%)	16
Total		15	15	30

This table indicates that out of 15 students who passed the exam, 5 are incorrectly classified as "fail" and out of 15 failed students, 4 are incorrectly classified as "pass." The accuracy of classification is 70%. The accuracy is reasonably satisfactory. There is a limitation of this approach. The data on which model is built is also used for validating the model. This creates a classification bias. A process called Jackknifed classification is used to adjust this bias. This process is as follows: (a) first case is removed from the data, (b) logistic model is developed and this case is classified. It is noted whether it is a correct classification or not, (c) this process is repeated for second case, and third case, till all cases are kept out of the model and predicted and (d) the classification table is prepared. The logic of this process is simple. Every time a classified case is not included in model building. So, classification is independently done.

6.4.5 Writing the Results

The results of logistic regression are written the same way you write the results of the multiple regression. Here is an example:

The logistic regression analysis is performed on the exam outcome as DV and time spent in studies per session as predictor. There are three sessions a day and average of the time spent is taken. Data on 30 participants were obtained. The full model as compared to constant only model turned out to be statistically significantly better ($\chi^2=11.32$, df=1, $p=0.0008$). The 95% confidence interval ranged from 0.06 to 0.35 that is not including zero. The predictor time spent in studies has turned out to significant ($z=2.55$, $p<0.01$). The classification is showing 70% accuracy that is satisfactory. The odds ratio indicates that as individuals study a minute more per session per day then the odds of passing increase by 1.19.

SUMMARY

This chapter has three main aspects associated with prediction: first, simple linear regression, second, multiple linear regression, and third, logistic regression. The R codes were also provided. It is recommended that you carry out more analysis on the simulated data and data provided in exercises. The practice with data analysis would help you understanding this topic better. I reiterate that understand statistics cannot be replaced by learning R or any other statistical analysis software for that matter.

EXERCISE

1. For following data: $x=1, 3, 5, 4, 6, 7, 5, 8, 9, 11$; $y=13, 8, 9, 7, 6, 8, 5, 4, 3, 5, 2$, plot scatter.
2. Estimate regression parameters for above data.
3. Specify Gauss–Markov theorem.
4. Compute standardized regression coefficients for the above data.
5. Use following data: EI=12, 13, 14, 16, 18, 22, 9, 8, 10, 17, 18, 20; empathy: 2, 3, 4, 6, 8, 13, 11, 1, 3, 2, 4, 6. Compute the regression coefficients, and test whether population regression coefficient is zero. Specify the null, alternative and critical values. Interpret the data.

6. Test the null hypothesis that population regression coefficient is 0.8.
7. Evaluate accuracy of prediction for Q1 and Q5 data.
8. Plot Q1 and Q5 data and regression line.
9. Carry out this analysis in R.
10. Write a report for Q5.
11. Specify assumption underlying regression analysis.
12. Use following data: Positive schizotypy=1, 2, 3, 4, 3, 4, 5, 6, 4, 5, 7, 6, 7, 8, 9, 8, 7, 10, 13, 12, 14, 15, 17, 19, 22. Intelligence=3, 4, 5, 6, 7, 8, 6, 8, 9, 10, 12, 13, 15, 16, 13, 10, 12, 11, 10, 14, 12, 10, 9, 11, 16. Remote association=2, 3, 4, 3, 5, 4, 3, 6, 7, 6, 5, 6, 7, 8, 7, 8, 9, 10, 14, 15, 18, 17, 15, 16, 17, 18, 14, 19. Estimate coefficients for predicting remote association using positive schizotypy and intelligence.
13. Test significance of the entire model and individual variable for Q12.
14. Test multicollinearity in the Q12
15. Test heteroscedasticity for Q12.
16. Carry out Q12, Q13, Q14, and Q15 in R.
17. X=5, 9, 8, 7, 9, 10, 8, 9, 6, 9, 9, 7, 10, 7, 11, 9, 7, 6, 6, 9, 6, 6, 9, 7, 7, 10, 9, 6, 8, 9; X_1=5, 6, 5, 5, 5, 4, 7, 5, 5, 6, 5, 4, 5, 5, 3, 5, 5, 5, 3, 7, 4, 5, 8, 4, 3, 5, 5, 4, 5, 6; Y=34, 20, 30, 33, 29, 31, 34, 29, 38, 32, 22, 29, 33, 31, 23, 21, 30, 33, 26, 32, 33, 35, 33, 31, 22, 27, 34, 32, 26, 32. Conduct multiple regression analysis with Y as dependent and X and X_1 as independent.
18. For Q18, conduct mediational analysis with Y and $X1$ as M.
19. X=16, 14, 22, 17, 16, 25, 20, 18, 23, 25, 24, 16, 18, 21, 15, 18, 20, 20, 21, 21, 24, 20, 17, 20, 19, 20, 26, 22, 27, 24; Y=0, 0, 1, 1, 0, 1, 1, 1, 1, 1, 1, 1, 1, 1, 1, 1, 0, 0, 0, 0, 1, 1, 1, 1, 0. Carry out logistic regression for this data.
20. Write results for Q1, Q5, Q12, Q17, and Q19.

7

Comparing Means: *t*-test

Comparing groups is one of the most popular research questions that psychologists ask. Many times researchers are interested in testing hypotheses regarding two means. The data from laboratory experiments (control group and experimental group) or treatment effectiveness studies (pre-test and post-test) are good examples. In addition, there are instances when researchers want to compare naturally occurring (or human-made) groups, such as gender-based, cultural, linguistic, and so on. There are instances when we have only one group assessed only once and we want to know whether the mean of this sample is similar to some hypothetical population value. This chapter is dealing with many problems of this nature. The *t*-test is one popular option to answer these types of questions. It is also known as Student's *t*-test because Gosset (alias "Student") developed its necessary statistical foundations. Student's *t*-test asks a question about population mean when we do not have full information about population. The *t*-test is of various types—one-sample *t*-test, independent samples *t*-test, and dependent samples *t*-test are three general types of *t*-tests. One-sample *t*-test is carried out when we want to know whether the obtained sample comes from a specific population. For example, a researcher obtained a mean of 7.8 on a visual-pattern span for 23 participants of age 5 and wants to know whether this sample comes from a population that has 8 as the mean visual-pattern span. The independent samples is carried out when the difference between the means of two independent samples is used to test whether the population mean difference has a specific value (generally, zero). For example, a researcher has obtained means of 18.8 and 19.4 for 8-year-old male and female samples, respectively. Independent samples' *t*-test is useful in testing the question of whether the respective male–female population have the same mean or not. The dependent samples' *t*-test asks similar question, but the samples are either repeated or matched (samples are some way dependent), for example, whether an intervention carried out to improve a specific memory mechanism leads to difference in pre-intervention mean and post-intervention mean in the population. Though two means are compared, they are obtained from the same group leading to dependence.

This chapter shall explain *t*-tests and their variations, which result due to varying positions about assumptions underlying the *t*-test. The chapter discusses issues associated with the power of the *t*-test. It shall also introduce basic bootstrap alternatives in *t*-test. Necessary R codes are also provided, some with outputs as well. It is expected that you will not only run them but also try and understand the syntax and logic. I am assuming that you have read Chapters 1 and 2, which is required to understand the logic of *t*-test as well as the inference associated with it.

7.1 LOGIC OF *t*-TEST

In this section, we shall look at mathematical notes about *t*-distribution and *t*-test statistics. We shall also look at the sampling distribution of mean and the sampling distribution of variance. These ideas are central to further discussion about *t*-test. The statistical foundations were worked out by William Sealy Gosset (1876–1937), nicknamed Student,[1] in his most famous paper "The Probable Error of a Mean" published in *Biometrika* in 1908. R. A. Fisher further refined certain aspects related to it.

7.1.1 The *t*-distribution and *t*-test—Basic Principles

You are familiar with the *t*-distribution through Chapter 1. The *t*-distribution is a continuous distribution. The *t* random variable is obtained by using chi-square and standard normal random variables. If Z is a standard normal random variable $[Z \sim N(0, 1)]$, and χ_k^2 is the chi-square distributed random variable at k degrees of freedom, which is independent of Z, then $t = \dfrac{Z}{\sqrt{\chi^2/k}}$ at k degrees of freedom. The distribution of t is given by the following distribution function:

$$f(t) = \frac{\Gamma\left(\dfrac{v+1}{2}\right)}{\sqrt{\pi v}\,\Gamma\left(\dfrac{v}{2}\right)} \times \left(1 + \frac{t^2}{v}\right)^{-\frac{v+1}{2}} \qquad \text{for } -\infty < t < +\infty$$

where Γ is the gamma function (you are familiar with it through Chapter 1), v is degrees of freedom (pronounce v as "nu"), π is constant (pi = 3.1416), and t is the random variable. Note that t random variable will take values between $-\infty$ and $+\infty$, whereas the probabilities associated with these values are obtained by $f(t)$, the distribution function of t random variable. Since t is a continuous random variable, probability is not of a specific value of t but it is of a specific range, that is, $P(a < t < b)$ implying the probability that t will take a value between a and b.

Now, in this chapter we are discussing *t*-test for testing hypotheses about population mean/s. let's understand the use of a t random variable in doing so.

Suppose if we obtain random samples from a normally distributed population that has a mean μ and variance σ^2, and compute $\bar{X}$ for each sample, then we will have a large number

---

[1] Student was a nickname taken by William Sealy Gosset to avoid problems at work. He completed his education from New College, Oxford, and joined Arthur Guinness, Son & Co. as a statistician-brewer. Guinness banned publishing by its employees in scientific journals due to bad-past experience in maintaining trade secrets. Gosset met Karl Pearson in 1905 and remained friends throughout. Pearson encouraged Gosset to write in *Biometrika* during his work at Pearson's statistical laboratory during 1906–1907. Gosset wrote his first paper in 1907 in *Biometrika* with the nickname Student to get rid of problems at Guinness. In 1908, he published his most celebrated paper "The probable error of mean" where he argued that the test assuming normality is useful only for large samples and developed an alternative which he called the z-test till 1922. R. A. Fisher and Gosset replaced z with $t = \sqrt{n-1}z$. R. A. Fisher wrote to Gosset in 1912 supplying rigorous proof of the frequency distribution of the z-statistic (now *t*-statistic) and argued that $n-1$ should be used instead of n in computing the SD (Fisher was student at Cambridge at that time). Gosset did not understand Fisher's idea fully. Fisher noted, "One immense advantage which Student possessed was his concern with, and responsibility for, the practical interpretation of experimental data." Gosset also tried to work on the problem of distribution of r (correlation coefficient) for samples of 4 to 8 and concluded, "I hope they [three distributions of r] may serve as illustrations for the successful solver of the problem." The successful solver was no one else but R. A. Fisher. Gosset had difference of opinion with R. A. Fisher over the use of randomized blocked designs and preferred balancing over randomization within blocks. Gosset was a humble and down-to-earth man and did not strive to take credit of Students work to his original identity. When Gosset was praised for discovering *t*-statistic and *t*-distribution in 1937, he humbly replied "Oh, that's nothing—Fisher would have discovered it all anyway" (Boland, 1984). He had many interests like gardening and carpentering, and he developed hybrid species and boat-designs that were acknowledged by experts of those fields. Fisher in his obituary to Gosset wrote, "His life was one full of fruitful scientific ideas and his versatility extended beyond his interests in research. In spite of his many activities it is the student of Student's test of significance who has won, and deserved to win, a unique place in the history of scientific method."

of $\bar{X}$. As you know, this is known as a sampling distribution of the mean. The sampling distribution of $\bar{X}$ will be normally distributed with mean μ and variance σ^2/n. This can be stated as $\dfrac{X-\mu}{S/\sqrt{n}}$, which follows z (standard normal distribution). However, in most of the cases, the population value of σ^2 is not known and hence we substitute it with its estimator, $\hat{\sigma}^2 = S^2$. Obviously, $\dfrac{X-\mu}{S/\sqrt{n}}$ will not result in z but it will result in a t random variable. If $\bar{X}$ is obtained only once from the population (one sample is drawn from population) and specifies a hypothetical value of μ, then it is a t–statistic. Now, let's understand why $\dfrac{X-\mu}{S/\sqrt{n}}$ will be a t random variable and will follow t-distribution.

We know that $t = \dfrac{z}{\sqrt{\chi^2/k}}$ at df$=k$ that follows t-distribution. If we show that $t = \dfrac{z}{\sqrt{\chi^2/k}} = \dfrac{\bar{X}-\mu}{S/\sqrt{n}}$, then it will imply that the sample statistics that we shall obtain by $\dfrac{\bar{X}-\mu}{S/\sqrt{n}}$ will be the t-random variable and will also follow t-distribution at $n-1$ degrees of freedom.

Let's start with $t = \dfrac{z}{\sqrt{\chi^2/k}}$.

In this equation, z and χ^2 are independent. It is known that

$$\chi^2_{n-1} = \frac{(n-1)S^2}{\sigma^2} \quad \text{and} \quad z = \frac{\bar{X}-\mu}{\sigma/\sqrt{n}}$$

Then, we substitute them and obtain

$$t = \frac{z}{\sqrt{\chi^2/k}} = \frac{\dfrac{\bar{X}-\mu}{\sigma/\sqrt{n}}}{\sqrt{\dfrac{(n-1)S^2}{\sigma^2}\Big/ n-1}} = \frac{\dfrac{\bar{X}-\mu}{\sigma/\sqrt{n}}}{\sqrt{\dfrac{(n-1)S^2}{\sigma^2}\Big/ n-1}} = \frac{\dfrac{\bar{X}-\mu}{\sigma/\sqrt{n}}}{\sqrt{\dfrac{S^2}{\sigma^2}}} = \frac{\bar{X}-\mu}{\left(\dfrac{\sigma}{\sqrt{n}}\right)\left(\dfrac{S}{\sigma}\right)} = \frac{\bar{X}-\mu}{S/\sqrt{n}}$$

This shows that sample statistics obtained through $\dfrac{\bar{X}-\mu}{S/\sqrt{n}}$ will be a t random variable and, obviously, it will follow t-distribution.

In the above exercise, we assumed that $\chi^2_{n-1} = \dfrac{(n-1)S^2}{\sigma^2}$; however, we can show this—If we take a random sample of size n from a population with mean μ and variance σ^2, and obtain sample mean as $\bar{X}$ and sample variance as S^2, and if we further assume that $\bar{X}$ and S^2 are independent (proving independence is beyond the scope of this book), then we use the following term:

$$\sum_{i=1}^{n}(X_i-\mu)^2 = \sum_{i=1}^{n}(X_i-\bar{X})^2 + n(\bar{X}-\mu)^2$$

We can substitute $(n-1)S^2$ for $\sum_{i-1}^{n}(X_i-\bar{X})^2$ because sample variance $S^2 = \dfrac{\sum_{i=1}^{n}(X_i-\bar{X})^2}{(n-1)}$ can be written as $S^2(n-1) = \sum_{i=1}^{n}(X_i-\bar{X})^2$.

If both sides are divided by σ^2, then

$$\sum_{i=1}^{n}\left(\frac{X_i - \mu}{\sigma}\right)^2 = \frac{S^2(n-1)}{\sigma^2} + \frac{(\bar{X} - \mu)^2}{\sigma^2(1/n)}$$

$$\sum_{i=1}^{n}\left(\frac{X_i - \mu}{\sigma}\right)^2 = \frac{S^2(n-1)}{\sigma^2} + \left(\frac{(\bar{X} - \mu)}{\sigma^2/\sqrt{n}}\right)^2$$

The left-hand side term is Z^2 (standard normal) and the second term on the right-hand side is also Z^2, so we rewrite the above statement as

$$\sum_{i=1}^{n} Z^2 = \frac{S^2(n-1)}{\sigma^2} + Z^2$$

We know from Chapter 1 that $\chi^2 = \sum_{i=1}^{k} Z_i^2$ at df=k. Hence, the left-hand side term is χ^2 at df=n, and the second term on the right-hand side is also χ^2 at df=1. We use the property that "If χ_1^2 and χ_2^2 are two independent chi-square variables with k_1 and k_2 df, respectively, then k is also chi-square variable at df k_1+k_2." We can rewrite as $\chi_n^2 = \frac{S^2(n-1)}{\sigma^2} + \chi_1^2$ and this is equivalent to $\chi_{n-1}^2 = \frac{S^2(n-1)}{\sigma^2}$, that is, $\frac{S^2(n-1)}{\sigma^2}$ will follow χ^2 distribution at df=$n-1$.

7.1.2 Sampling Distribution of Mean

Sampling distribution of the mean is a simple idea. If a population has mean=μ and variance=σ^2 and random samples of the mean are obtained from this population, then their distribution will be referred to as a sampling distribution of the mean. We, behavioral scientists, generally tend to believe that a sample consists of individuals. It is not correct. If we obtain a random sample of individuals of size n (say, n=50) and measure their extraversion score, then, in reality, we have sampled 50 extraversion scores from a population of extraversion scores and not sampled 50 individuals. The mean of these 50 extraversion scores is $\bar{X}_1$ of extraversion scores. We return the first sample to the population and members of this and any sample can be a member of the next sample as well—called sampling with replacement. Now, if we again sample 50 extraversion scores, the next mean is $\bar{X}_2$ and the next means are $\bar{X}_3, \bar{X}_4,..., \bar{X}_n$ for n samples. The means are likely to be different from each other and, hence, the sample mean is a random variable (... and, for that matter, any sample statistics is a random variable). We can find probability associated with values of random variable if we know its distribution. The mean of sampling distribution of $\bar{X}_i$ is μ, that is, $E(\bar{X})=\mu$. Hence, $\bar{X}$ is an unbiased estimator of μ. It can be stated as

$$E(\bar{X}) = \sum_{i=1}^{n} \frac{1}{n}\mu = n\left(\frac{1}{n}\mu\right) = \mu$$

The variance of $\bar{X}$ is $\frac{\sigma^2}{n}$, and the SD of $\bar{X}$ is $S_{\bar{X}}$. The expression $S_{\bar{X}}$ is also usually called **standard error of the mean**. The standard error of mean is obtained by $SD(\bar{X}) = S_{\bar{X}} = \sqrt{\frac{\sigma^2}{n}} = \frac{\sigma}{\sqrt{n}}$

You would also realize that as the sample size (n) increases, standard error of the mean reduces. As the sample size increases, $\bar{X}$ is closer to the value μ, and hence, the variance of $\bar{X}$ is reduced. Table 7.1 is a worked out example of the same. The hypothetical population is created of size 3 (N=3), and all the possible random samples of size 2 (n=2) are taken from this population.

Table 7.1. *Sampling Distribution of Mean, Variance, and SD for Small Population of N=3, and Sample Size=n=2 for 9 Samples*

Population	3	5	7	Mean=5	Variance=2.667		SD=1.633		
	P1	P2	$\bar{X}$	$s^2 = \dfrac{\Sigma(x-\mu)^2}{n}$	$s^2 = \dfrac{\Sigma(X-\bar{X})^2}{n-1}$	$S^2 = \dfrac{\Sigma(X-\bar{X})^2}{n}$	$S = \sqrt{\dfrac{\Sigma(X-\bar{X})^2}{n-1}}$	$S = \sqrt{\dfrac{\Sigma(X-\bar{X})^2}{n}}$	$S_X = \dfrac{\sqrt{\dfrac{\Sigma(X-\bar{X})^2}{n-1}}}{\sqrt{n}}$
Sample 1	3	3	3	4	0	0	0.00	0	1.41
Sample 2	3	5	4	2	2	1	1.41	1	1.00
Sample 3	3	7	5	4	8	4	2.83	2	1.41
Sample 4	5	3	4	2	2	1	1.41	1	1.00
Sample 5	5	5	5	0	0	0	0.00	0	0.00
Sample 6	5	7	6	2	2	1	1.41	1	1.00
Sample 7	7	3	5	4	8	4	2.83	2	1.41
Sample 8	7	5	6	2	2	1	1.41	1	1.00
Sample 9	7	7	7	4	0	0	0.00	0	1.41
			$E(\bar{X})=5$	$E(S^2)=2.667$	$E(S^2)=2.667$	**1.333**	$E(S)=1.517$	0.889	$E(S_X)=1.517$

Note: $\mu=5$; $\sigma^2=2.667$; and $\sigma=1.633$.

Mean, variance with population mean known, variance with sample mean and $n-1$ as denominator, SD for both, and the standard error of the mean are computed. The population mean $(\mu)=5$; population variance $(\sigma^2)=2.667$, and Population SD$(\sigma)=1.633$. The mean of sample means is also 5 since the sample mean is an unbiased estimator. The mean of sample variances with $n-1$ as denominator is 2.667 since sample variance is an unbiased estimator. However, sample SD is not an unbiased estimator of population SD since the square root transformation of a variance is non-linear.

7.1.3 Sampling Distribution of Variance

The sample variance as an estimator of population variance is computed by

$$S^2 = \frac{\Sigma(X - \bar{X})^2}{n-1}$$

The denominator is df$=n-1$. The purpose of taking $n-1$ as df can be explained as follows. If the sample variance is computed with n as the denominator, then it is an underestimation of population variance and, hence, it is a biased estimator of population variance. If we take expectation of a sample variance, then

$$E(S^2) = E\left(\frac{\Sigma(X - \bar{X})^2}{n}\right) = \frac{(n-1)\sigma^2}{n}$$

The bias is of $(n-1)/n$ proportion. If the denominator is $(n-1)$, then this bias can be corrected. The $(n-1)$ in numerator and denominator will cancel out and what remains is σ^2 and sample variance becomes an unbiased estimator of population variance:

$$E(S^2) = E\left(\frac{\Sigma(X - \bar{X})^2}{n-1}\right) = \sigma^2$$

Table 7.1 shows that $E(S)^2=\sigma^2$ with $(n-1)$ as denominator. When the denominator is n, then $E(S^2)<\sigma^2$. For this example, $(n-1)/n=1/2=0.5$ is bias in estimation. Now, if we multiply 2.667 by 0.5, then we obtain $[(n-1)/n] \times S^2=0.5 \times 2.667=1.33$ which is equivalent to the biased estimator of σ^2. Also, note that S^2 is computed even when the population mean is estimated by $\bar{X}$. Henceforth, when I refer to sample variance, I am referring to an unbiased estimator of population variance. However, sampling distribution of variance is unbiased in just one point. The distribution is not symmetric, it is positively skewed. The skewness is more when sample size is small. Figure 7.1 demonstrates this for mean and variance. I have specified a population with $\mu=5$ and $\sigma^2=50$ of the size 100,000. I have obtained two sets of random samples (5,000 samples each) from this population, one with $n=5$ in each sample and other with $n=40$ in each sample. I have calculated the mean and variance of each of these 5,000 samples. So we have 5,000 means and variances for each set. The distribution of these means and variances is shown in Figure 7.1. The mean for Figures 7.1(A) and (B) were 5.016 and 5.006 for sample sizes 5 and 40, respectively; both of them are very close to the population mean of 5. The normal Q–Q plots for both show that sampling distribution is normally distributed. The findings are different in the case of distribution of sample variance. The mean variance is 50.61 and 50.012 for sample sizes 5 and 40 respectively; both of them are very close to population variance of 50. However, the distribution is positively skewed for both sample sizes (5 and 40) and more of so for small samples ($n=5$). The normal Q–Q plot clearly indicates the same. This implies that though S^2 is an unbiased estimator of σ^2, probability is always higher to get an individual value that is an underestimation of σ^2. It is stated as $P[(S^2)<\sigma^2]>p[(S^2)\geq\sigma^2]$ and as n approaches infinity, $P[(S^2)<\sigma^2]>\lim_{n\to\infty} p[(S^2)\geq\sigma^2]$. Note that σ is used while computing z, and S is used while

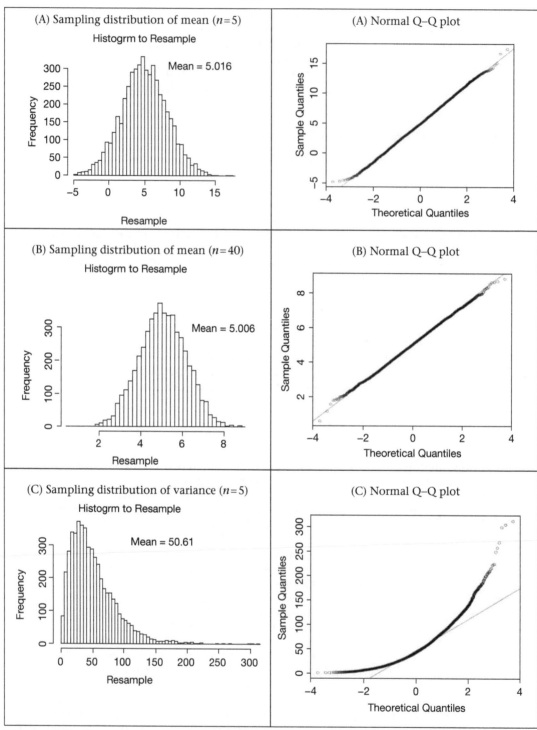

Figure 7.1. *Histograms and their Associated Normal Q–Q Plots for Sampling Distribution of Mean and Variance for Sample Size (n) being 5 or 40 (Total Samples are 5,000)*

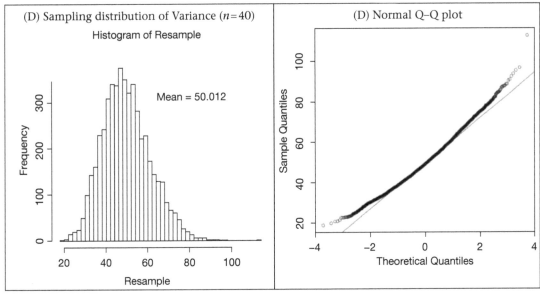

Figure 7.1. *(Continued)*

computing *t*-statistics. Since the probability of obtaining $S < \sigma$ is higher, the resulting *t*-value is larger than the value of *z*. R code 7.1 is useful for this exercise.

R Code 7.1. Sampling Distribution of Mean and Variance.

```
mu <- 5                        # population mean is 5
varp <- 50                     # population variance is 50
sdp<- sqrt(varp)               # population standard deviation is square
                                 root of varp
x <- rnorm(100000, mu, sdp)    # normally distributed population with mean
                                 5 and var 50 is created.
nsample<-5000                  # sample size 5000
size <- 40                     # size is 40. You can change to 5 or any
                                 other number.
resample <- numeric(nsample)   # numeric variables of size 5000
for(i in 1:nsample) resample[i] <- var(sample(x, size, replace = T))
                               # for loop
#replace var with mean to get sampling distribution of mean
mean(resample)                 # mean of 5000 samples
hist(resample, breaks = 50)    # histogram of 5000 samples
qqnorm(resample)               # normal q-q plot of 5000 samples
qqline(resample)
```

7.2 SINGLE-SAMPLE *t*-TEST

When we have only one sample obtained from the population with a hypothesis about the population mean, then a single sample test can be carried out. Suppose, we have a sample of 30 participants measuring their spatial ability and assume that they come from the population that has a mean of 25, then we can test the hypothesis that this sample comes from a population that has a spatial ability score of 25. This hypothesis can be tested by a single sample test. When the *population variance is known*, then the suitable test is **one-sample Z-test** and when the *population variance is not known*, the suitable test is **one-sample *t*-test**.

7.2.1 Single Mean Test—σ Known

The z-test is useful when we have one sample taken from population, and null hypothesis states that population mean is a specific value. The condition is that the *population variance is known* (or if unknown, the sample is very large).

Example 1: Suppose there is common aptitude test for all schools in a town. The data for all schools state that mean=40 and SD is 5. Now, a teacher from one of the school has a curious question: whether the students from her school, on an average, perform as well as other schools? Now she has mean of her school know. It is 38.9 for 60 students of her school. She can carry out a z-test.

z-test formula and computation:

The $z = \dfrac{x - \mu}{\sigma}$ will be $z = \dfrac{\bar{X} - \mu}{\dfrac{\sigma}{\sqrt{n}}}$, since $\sigma_{\bar{x}} = \dfrac{\sigma}{\sqrt{n}}$; z can be stated as $z = \dfrac{\bar{X} - \mu}{\dfrac{\sigma}{\sqrt{n}}}$.

For the present data: $\mu=40$; $\sigma^2=25$; $\sigma=5$; $n=60$, and $\bar{X}=38.9$.

$$H_0 : \mu = 40$$
$$H_A : \mu \neq 40$$

The computation is

$$z = \frac{\bar{X} - \mu}{\dfrac{\sigma}{\sqrt{n}}} = \frac{38.9 - 40}{\dfrac{5}{\sqrt{60}}} = \frac{-1.1}{\dfrac{5}{7.746}} = \frac{-1.1}{0.645} = -1.704$$

The two-tailed probability of getting a z-value of ±1.704 is 0.088 from Appendix C1. The probability of obtaining a value of ±1.704 or greater is 0.088. Generally, we use $\alpha=0.05$ as a critical p-value. Hence, we retain the null since we do not have sufficient evidence to reject the null. As far as the teachers question is considered, on an average, the performance of her students is at par with other schools' students. R code 7.2 is for a one-sample test.

R Code 7.2. One-sample z-test

```
ztest = function(x, mu, var, n){
  z = (mean(x) - mu)/(sqrt(var/n))
  p<-pnorm(z)*2    # for two-tailed test.
  print(z)
  print(p)
}
ztest(38.9, 40, 25, 60)
```

7.2.2 Single-sample *t*-test: Testing One-sample Mean with σ Unknown

When the sample mean is obtained from a single sample and population variance is unknown (which is usually the case), a single-sample *t*-test can be carried out. In general, a researcher does not know the population variance (σ^2) and it is estimated using sample variance (s^2).

When sample mean and SDs are used to estimate the population mean, then the sampling distribution of s^2 is useful since s^2 is an estimator of σ^2.

The formula developed for z requires modification:

$$z = \frac{\bar{X} - \mu}{\sigma/\sqrt{n}}$$

Table 7.2. *Data of IQ for 10 Participants*

Participant	A	B	C	D	F	G	H	I	J	K
IQ	119	96	130	109	103	111	129	91	124	105

Since σ^2 is unknown, s^2 is used as an estimator. The resulting value is not going to follow normal distribution. This value will change with sample size (n) and s^2. The resulting value will follow t-distribution:

$$t = \frac{\bar{X} - \mu}{S/\sqrt{n}} = \frac{\bar{X} - \mu}{\sqrt{S^2/n}} = \frac{\bar{X} - \mu}{S_x}$$

You would also realize that as n increases, $S \Rightarrow \sigma$, and as $n=\infty$, $t_\infty = z$. The t-distribution is a standard normal distribution as sample size approaches infinity.

Degrees of freedom: The degrees of freedom for a one-sample t-test is $(n-1)$. We know that the t-distribution is a sampling distribution obtained at some df (1 to infinity). The $n-1$ is because we use sample mean to estimate variance and a df is lost in this. The df, as you know, is the number of elements that can be set free to vary.

Example 2: A school psychologist sampled a small data of 10 students on an IQ test. The data is given in Table 7.2. The psychologist has the question of whether the sample comes from population that has IQ=110. If we assume that the population variance is not known, then the z-test is not possible. Hence, we will have to do the one-sample t-test for this problem. The null and alternative are

$$H_0 : \mu = 110$$
$$H_A : \mu \neq 110$$

For these data, $\bar{X} = 111.7$; $S = 13.51$; and $n=10$. Following convention, the probability of type I error (α) can be set to 0.05 value. The t-value is

$$t = \frac{\bar{X} - \mu}{S_{\bar{x}}} = \frac{\bar{X} - \mu}{\dfrac{S}{\sqrt{n}}} = \frac{111.7 - 110}{\dfrac{13.51}{\sqrt{10}}} = \frac{1.7}{4.27} = 0.3979$$

The obtained t-value is evaluated at df=$n-1$=10$-$1=9. From Appendix C4, the t-value at df=9 at α=0.05 is 2.262. The obtained t-value of 0.398 is smaller than two-tailed t-value of 2.262 at df=9. This indicates that the probability that the obtained sample came from a distribution that has a mean other than 110 is reasonably low to refute null hypothesis. Hence, null hypothesis stating that the sample mean comes from a population that has a mean 110 is retained.

7.2.2.1 One-tailed and Two-tailed Tests

The alternate hypothesis could be directional or non-directional. When the alternate hypothesis is non-directional, a two-tailed test is carried out. For example, if the null is H_0: μ=0 and the alternate is H_A: $\mu \neq 0$, the null could be refuted in the case of μ<0 or μ>0. The sampling distribution of t will have to be tested on both sides of the null because according to the alternate, we do not know on which side the population mean will be, and hence, a two-tailed test. Figure 7.2(A) shows this. The critical value is at α/2=0.05/2=0.025 for each side (0.025+0.025=0.05). However, in the case of a directional alternate hypothesis, a one-tailed test is carried out. For the

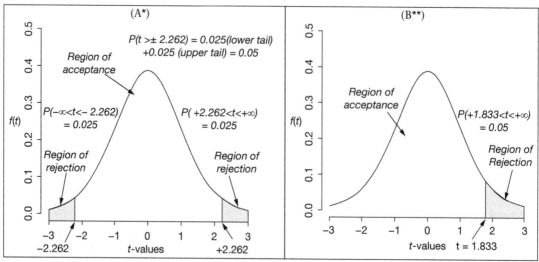

Figure 7.2. *(A) t-distribution at df=9 Two-tailed Test (B) t-distribution at df=9 One-tailed Test*
Notes:*The null can be rejected only if the calculated *t*-value is greater than ±2.262.
    **The null can be rejected only if the calculated *t*-value is greater than +1.833.

H_0: $\mu=0$, if the alternative is H_A: $\mu>0$, then the area of sampling distribution of t that we should examine is only above the mean. If the mean is below the *mu*, then we accept the null. We can refute the null only if the *t*-value is in the upper area (positive value). In the case of the earlier example, if the alternate is H_A: $\mu \neq 110$, then $t_9=+2.262$ has $p=0.025$, and $t_9=-2.262$ has $p=0.025$. Addition of these p-values leads to $p(t_9 > \pm 2.62) = 0.025 + 0.025 = 0.05$. If we had the alternate as H_A: $\mu>110$, then $t_9=+1.833$ has $p=0.05$ (see Figure 7.2(B)). Needless to say that one-tailed values at given α and df will be smaller than the respective two-tailed values. Hence, the chance that the null with directional alternate gets rejected is always higher than that of the null with a non-directional alternate. This opens issue of power, which we shall discuss in Section 7.5.

7.2.2.2 Confidence Interval on μ

The confidence interval (CI) computation is intuitively very simple to understand; $CI_{1-\alpha} = \bar{X} \pm (t_{\alpha/2} \times S_X)$. $CI_{1-\alpha}$ is the confidence interval at $1-\alpha$ that is the level of significance, $\bar{X}$ is the sample mean (111.7), $t_{\alpha/2}$ is the critical two-tailed value in the t-distribution (±2.262) at df$=n-1=9$, and S_X is the standard error of mean (4.2715). The logic and computation is simple:

$$t_{\alpha/2} = \frac{\bar{X} - \mu}{S_x} \quad \pm 2.262 = \frac{111.7 - \mu}{4.2715} = (\pm 2.262 \times 4.275) + 111.7 = \pm 9.67 + 111.7$$

Using 9.67 to add and subtract from the sample mean, we can obtain confidence limits at 95% confidence:

$$CI_{Upper} = 111.7 + 9.67 = 121.37$$
$$CI_{Lower} = 111.7 - 9.67 = 102.03$$

This CI is obtained at 0.05 level of significance. This leads to $P(102.03 \leq \mu \leq 121.37) = 1 - 0.05 = 0.95$, that is, the probability that the population mean will lie between 102.03 and 121.37 is 0.95 or 95% confidence that the population value will be between these two numbers.

The general expression of CI is

$$CI_{1-\alpha} = \bar{X} \pm (t_{\alpha/2} \times S_X) = \bar{X} \pm \left(t_{\alpha/2} \times \frac{S}{\sqrt{n}} \right)$$

If we need to compute 99% confidence interval, then we shall use the critical value of $t_{\alpha/2} = t_{0.01/2} = t_{0.005/2} = \pm 3.25$. Taking this value, the

$$CI_{99} = \bar{X} \pm (t_{\alpha/2} \times S_{\bar{X}}) = 111.7 \pm (3.25 \times 4.275) = 97.818 < \mu < 125.581$$

One needs to understand that the value of *mu* is unknown but a fixed value, whereas the value of the sample mean is known but changes with every sample. The population mean cannot be known, but CI is an interval estimate of the population mean. The sample mean is a random variable, however, *mu* and *specific interval* are not random variables. Useful point to note is that if the result is obtained from an experiment, the confidence is not about the interval but it is about the method (Good, 1999). In the above example, you have also noted that as the confidence increased from 0.95 to 0.99, the interval widened. Two lessons that we have learned in Chapter 2 are relevant here: One, the width of interval is disproportionate to confidence. As confidence increases, interval widens. Two, CI can be reduced by increasing the sample size. As *n* increases, the standard error of mean reduces, leading to narrowing of the interval.

```
#R Code 7.3. One-sample t-test with Output
x<-c(119, 96, 130, 109, 103, 111, 129, 91, 124, 105)
t.test(x, mu = 110, alternative = c("two.sided"), conf.level = .95)

One Sample t-test

data: x
t = 0.398, df = 9, p-value = 0.6999
alternative hypothesis: true mean is not equal to 110
95 percent confidence interval:
102.0372      121.3628
sample estimates:
mean of x
  111.7
```

For R code 7.3, x=variable, mu=hypothesized population mean, alternative=directionality of the alternative ("two.sided" for two-tailed test, "less" and "greater" for one-sided test), and conf.level is $1-\alpha$. For the output, t=obtained *t*-value, df=n−1, *p*-value is the exact probability associated with the *t*-value at df. The "95 % confidence interval" matches with our calculation except for rounding errors. Rest of the output is self-explanatory.

7.2.2.3 Alternate Use

The one-sample *t*-test can be used to identify cases that have an extreme score, particularly when *n* is small. It is useful in tests/scale that have norms based on small samples. Crawford and Howell (1998) suggested the use of *t*-distribution instead of Z. Suppose we have small normative data on suicide ideation scale of individuals having depressive disorder and had suicide ideation but did not attempt. The mean=30 and SD=4 for normative data of 20 patients. Now, we have a new case that has a score 35. The question is whether this patient deviates from this normative data. We can use *t*-distribution instead of Z:

$$t = \frac{X - \bar{X}}{S\sqrt{\frac{n+1}{n}}} = \frac{35 - 30}{4\sqrt{\frac{20+1}{20}}} = \frac{5}{4\sqrt{1.05}} = \frac{5}{4 \times 1.025} = \frac{5}{4.098} = 1.22$$

The one-tailed critical t-value at df$=n-1=20-1=19$ is 1.729. Since the obtained value is smaller than the critical value, it is insignificant and we accept that the value of 35 comes from the normative sample. In fact, simple interpolation states that the score of 39 and above (exactly, 38.32 and above, but such values do not exist on psychological scales) will be a significant departure from a normative sample.

7.3 INDEPENDENT SAMPLES *t*-TEST

The t-test is perhaps most frequently used to test the difference between two independent samples on the same dependent variable. The most common example is independent groups experimental designs. Suppose you have an experiment with participants randomly assigned to control group (no training, for example) and experimental group (training), and measured on some dependent variable (e.g., time taken to solve the problem). We can apply the independent samples t-test to analyze the data of such experiments. Therefore, comparing two treatment groups (experimental conditions) or comparing two naturally occurring groups (e.g., men–women, class comparison, language-based groups, and so on) on some variable is the most general use of t-test for independent groups. Comparing two experimental conditions usually have random assignments of participants, but in the case of natural groups (gender differences) random assignments are not possible. Therefore, we shall look at this issue while discussing assumptions underlying the t-test.

Suppose you carry out an experiment with randomly assigned 60 participants to experimental and control groups and obtain $\bar{X}_{\text{expt}} = 20$ and $\bar{X}_{\text{control}} = 15$. Now, you can find the difference in the sample means $(20-15=5)$. But none of us have any interest in showing that the difference is observed in sample means. If the same experiment is carried out again and again, we shall keep on getting different values of difference. The "difference in sample mean" $(\bar{X}_1 - \bar{X}_2)$ is a random variable. Since we are interested in generalizing our finding, the question of interest is—can we make a logical guess about the difference in population means $(\mu_1 - \mu_2)$ by using the difference in sample means $(\bar{X}_1 - \bar{X}_2)$? That is, is it possible to state with reasonable confidence that the population means of the experimental group and control group differ from each other? The independent samples t-test is a useful test for this purpose. Initially, we shall look at logic of independent samples t-test, solve an example using t-statistic, and examine theoretical and practical issues.

7.3.1 Distribution of Difference between Means

Sampling distribution of difference between means is an important idea to independent samples t-test. Let's specify the null and alternative hypotheses for independent samples t-test. The null is H_0: $\mu_1 - \mu_2 = 0$, thus implying that H_0: $\mu_1 = \mu_2$. The alternative hypothesis is H_A: $\mu_1 - \mu_2 \neq 0$ implying that H_A: $\mu_1 \neq \mu_2$. The null implies that the first population mean and the second population mean are identical. To test this null hypothesis using sample means, we need information about the sampling distribution of $\bar{X}_1 - \bar{X}_2$ under the null. We do not know μ_1 and μ_2. We have only sample means $\bar{X}_1$ and $\bar{X}_2$ for both populations. The difference between sample means is $\bar{X}_1 - \bar{X}_2$. Now, let μ_1 and μ_2 be population means, σ_1^2 and σ_2^2 be the variance of each population, $\bar{X}_1$ and $\bar{X}_2$ be sample means from respective population, and n_1 and n_2 be the sample sizes of samples taken from the population. Now, if we take a random sample of size n_1 and n_2 from those populations and obtain the mean for each, we will have $\bar{X}_1$ and $\bar{X}_2$. Both samples means, drawn simultaneously from their respective populations, are independent. Now we obtain the sample mean difference, $\bar{X}_1 - \bar{X}_2$. Now, further imagine that we keep on doing this exercise for an infinite number of times; we will have large number of values of $(\bar{X}_1 - \bar{X}_2)$. The distribution of these values has been worked out.

Before we move further, let's understand the concept of *variance sum law*. Suppose we have two variables, X and Y, then the variance of sum or difference (addition and subtraction) of two variables is obtained as

$$\sigma^2_{X\pm Y} = \sigma^2_X + \sigma^2_Y \pm 2\rho\sigma_X\sigma_Y$$

When X and Y are added, then $\sigma^2_{X+Y} = \sigma^2_X + \sigma^2_Y + 2\rho\sigma_X\sigma_Y$

When X and Y are subtracted, $\sigma^2_{X-Y} = \sigma^2_X + \sigma^2_Y - 2\rho\sigma_X\sigma_Y$

Here, $\sigma^2_{X\pm Y}$ is the variance of the sum or difference of X and Y, σ^2_X and σ^2_Y are the variance of X and Y, respectively, ρ is the population correlation between X and Y.

When X and Y are independent, $\rho = 0$ and variance of the sum or difference is

$$\sigma^2_{X\pm Y} = \sigma^2_X + \sigma^2_Y \pm (2 \times 0 \times \sigma_X \times \sigma_Y)$$

$$\sigma^2_{X\pm Y} = \sigma^2_X + \sigma^2_Y$$

This implies that "when variables are independent, the variance of sum or difference between (addition and subtraction) two variables is the addition of their variances." Knowing this, we can move ahead with the sampling distribution of the difference between means.

We also know that the variance of $\bar{X}_1$ is σ^2_1/n_1 and the variance of $\bar{X}_2$ is σ^2_2/n_2.

$$\sigma^2_{\bar{X}_1 - \bar{X}_2} = \sigma^2_{\bar{X}_1} + \sigma^2_{\bar{X}_2}$$

$$\sigma^2_{\bar{X}_1 - \bar{X}_2} = \frac{\sigma^2_1}{n_1} + \frac{\sigma^2_2}{n_2}$$

Then, the SD of $\bar{X}_1 - \bar{X}_2$ can be stated as

$$\sigma_{\bar{X}_1 - \bar{X}_2} = \sqrt{\sigma^2_{\bar{X}_1 - \bar{X}_2}} = \sqrt{\sigma^2_{\bar{x}_1} + \sigma^2_{\bar{x}_2}} = \sqrt{\frac{\sigma^2_1}{n_1} + \frac{\sigma^2_2}{n_2}}$$

We also know that the SD of the sampling distribution of $\bar{X}_1 - \bar{X}_2$ is the standard error of $\bar{X}_1 - \bar{X}_2$.

We have already specified that $z = \dfrac{\bar{X} - \mu}{\sqrt{\sigma^2/n}}$. If we apply it to the present problem, then we obtain:

$$z = \frac{(\bar{X}_1 - \bar{X}_2) - (\mu_1 - \mu_2)}{\sqrt{\dfrac{\sigma^2_1}{n_1} + \dfrac{\sigma^2_2}{n_2}}}$$

$$z = \frac{(\bar{X}_1 - \bar{X}_2) - (\mu_1 - \mu_2)}{\sigma_{\bar{X}_1 - \bar{X}_2}}$$

In reality, σ^2_1 and σ^2_2 are not known. Hence, we estimate them using S^2_1 and S^2_2 which are the sample variances. As we have seen in the single-sample t-test, if we substitute S^2 for σ^2, then the resulting value is not z-statistics but it is t-statistics.

$$t = \frac{(\bar{X}_1 - \bar{X}_2) - (\mu_1 - \mu_2)}{S_{\bar{X}_1 - \bar{X}_2}}$$

$$t = \frac{(\bar{X}_1 - \bar{X}_2) - (\mu_1 - \mu_2)}{\sqrt{\dfrac{S^2_1}{n_1} + \dfrac{S^2_2}{n_2}}}$$

where $\bar{x}_1$ and $\bar{x}_2$ are sample means; s^2_1 and s^2_2 are variances; n_1 and n_2 are the sample sizes of groups 1 and 2, respectively; and $(\mu_1 - \mu_2)_{\text{hypo}}$ is the statement of the null hypothesis. Often the statement of the null hypothesis is $\mu_1 - \mu_2 = 0$. Hence, in such a case, the formula of the t-test is written as

$$t = \frac{(\bar{x}_1 - \bar{x}_2)}{\sqrt{\dfrac{s_1^2}{n_1} + \dfrac{s_2^2}{n_2}}}$$

Learners often consider this as the formula of t-test. However, when $\mu_1 - \mu_2$ is not zero, then one needs to use $(\bar{x}_1 - \bar{x}_2) - (\mu_1 - \mu_2)_{\text{hypo}}$ as a numerator.

7.3.2 Assumptions Underlying Independent Samples *t*-test

Independent samples t-test has the following assumption which needs to be verified before its application:

1. **Normal distribution:** Samples are obtained from populations that are normally distributed.
2. **Equality of variances:** The population variances are equal, that is, $\sigma_1^2 = \sigma_2^2$.
3. Samples are independent.
4. Samples are drawn from the population at random.

Let's look at the assumptions in details.

The populations are normally distributed is the first assumption. We can test the normality assumption by using certain statistical tests (Jarque–Bera test; Shapiro–Wilks test, A-D test, and so on) as well as by using plots like boxplots and normal Q–Q plots. The detailed discussion is provided in Chapter 4 about each of the methods. If both populations are normally distributed, then it implies that the difference between them is also normally distributed.

Now let's look at the third assumption (yes, I shall discuss the second one at last). **The samples being independent** implies that the selection of elements in one sample has no consequence in the selection of elements in the second sample. Suppose, you obtain a sample of males and females from a university campus (say, to study gender difference in dyadic trust) and select male and female samples irrespective of who is in other group, then the selection is independent. But, if we select girls and boys who are in a relationship with each other, meaning if we select a female participant and her boyfriend is also selected, then the dependence is brought in the sample. As a consequence, the term ρ (population correlation) will not be zero. The scores X_1 and X_2 will be correlated and the variance of the mean difference will take into account its full form, that is,

$$\sigma_{X-Y}^2 = \sigma_X^2 + \sigma_Y^2 - 2\rho\sigma_X\sigma_Y$$

Generally, dependent samples most commonly occur in psychological research under repeated measures experiments as well as matched group experiments.

The fourth assumption is of random sampling. This assumption is generally not followed. Random assignment and not random sampling is done while performing experiments. This assumption is of little significance if samples are large.

The second assumption stated that the sample comes from populations that have equal variance $(\sigma_1^2 = \sigma_2^2)$. Let's first understand the reason for this assumption. We have learned that if a constant is added or subtracted from all scores, the variance remains unchanged. In the context of experiments, this constant is the treatment for the experimental group. That is, $X_{\text{control}} + \text{treatment(Constant)} = X_{\text{experimental}}$, which lead to $\sigma_{\text{control}}^2 = \sigma_{\text{experimental}}^2$ because all scores change by constant.[2]

---

[2] The change by constant is not directly observed in sample data. It's a part of the mathematical model underlying experimental designs. We shall discuss it while discussing ANOVA. The sample results are affected by secondary variance that remain out of control in behavioral experiments.

Testing $\sigma_1^2 = \sigma_2^2$: the most popular test to evaluate the assumption of equality of variances is Leven's test. The Leven's test statistics evaluates that the null hypothesis is $H_0 : \sigma_1^2 = \sigma_2^2$ and the alternate is $H_A : \sigma_1^2 \neq \sigma_2^2$; however, this test is sensitive to the sample size and, hence, rejection of H_0 by Leven's test should only be considered as an indication of the potential violation of assumption (see Section 7.3.6). As of now, we stick to the assumption of homogeneity of variances. We shall inspect this assumption later on. One of the consequences of the homogeneity assumption is pooling variance.

Pooling variance: The assumption of homogeneity of variances leads to change in the denominator of *t*-test statistic. The denominator is a standard error of sampling distribution of $\bar{X}_1 - \bar{X}_2$.

$$S_{\bar{X}_1 - \bar{X}_2} = \sqrt{\frac{S_1^2}{n_1} + \frac{S_2^2}{n_2}}$$

If $\sigma_1^2 = \sigma_2^2 = \sigma^2$, then the legitimate question is—why do we need two estimators (S_1^2 and S_2^2) to estimate one parameter (σ^2). So it is appropriate to have some kind of average of these two estimators in order to have a better estimate of σ^2. Since the sample size (n_1 and n_2) may be different, the average is calculated by

$$S_P^2 = \frac{(n_1 - 1)S_1^2 + (n_2 - 1)S_2^2}{n_1 + n_2 - 2}$$

The numerator is the weighted sum of variances (weighted by their respective df=$n-1$) and the denominator is df of S_P^2. In the case of $n_1 = n_2$, $S_P^2 = \frac{S_1^2 + S_2^2}{2}$. Now, with S_P^2 being the single estimator of σ^2, we can re-write the standard error of sampling distribution of $(\bar{X}_1 - \bar{X}_2)$.

$$S_{\bar{X}_1 - \bar{X}_2} = \sqrt{\frac{S_P^2}{n_1} + \frac{S_P^2}{n_2}} = \sqrt{S_P^2\left(\frac{1}{n_1} + \frac{1}{n_2}\right)} = S_P\sqrt{\frac{1}{n_1} + \frac{1}{n_2}}$$

The *t*-test formula with homogeneity of variances assumed can be expressed as

$$t = \frac{(\bar{X}_1 - \bar{X}_2) - (\mu_1 - \mu_2)_{\text{hypo}}}{S_P\sqrt{\frac{1}{n_1} + \frac{1}{n_2}}}$$

Example 3: Mood congruent recall hypothesis[3] argues that a material is more likely to be recalled if material's emotional tone is similar to individuals' emotional state at the time of retrieval. It implies that if you are in a happy mood then you will recall more happy instances and if you are sad then you will recall more sad instances than happy. However, Bower (1981) and Isen (1984) showed that mood-congruent memory is asymmetrical. Happy mood facilitates recall of happy memories and inhibits recall of sad memories; sad mood only inhibits recall of happy memories but generally does not increase recall of sad memories. Suppose we design a hypothetical experiment, where happy and sad are two experimentally manipulated conditions, by randomly assigning participants to two groups. Mood is manipulated

---

[3] The mood congruent memory is known to be asymmetrical. In addition, it is also influenced by meta-memory—participants who were asked to feel happy/sad showed similar results. Nature of task and aspects of learning also influence it. The results of mood congruent memory are more stable than state-dependent memory.

Table 7.3. *Mood Congruent Recall Data for Independent Samples t-test*

Happy manipulation	4, 5, 6, 7, 5, 6, 4, 8, 7, 6, 8, 7, 8, 9, 7	$\bar{X}_1 = 6.47$	$S_1 = 1.51$	$n_1 = 15$
Sad manipulation	3, 3, 6, 4, 6, 5, 4, 5, 4, 7, 8, 4, 4, 8, 5	$\bar{X}_2 = 5.07$	$S_2 = 1.62$	$n_2 = 15$

by showing comedy and sad films to respective groups[4] (Forgas, 2002). As a baseline, we have recall of sad (for the sad group) and happy (for the happy group) memories without manipulation. Again we take recall of sad memories for the sad group after the manipulation and do the same for happy memories for the happy group. Then we subtract the baseline of each participant from their respective experimental condition to obtain change in mood congruent memories. Now, we have two sets of scores for the change in mood congruent memory scores. If there is no asymmetry, then both groups will have a similar population mean. This is our null hypothesis—population means of both groups are equal. $H_0: \mu_{\text{Happy}} = \mu_{\text{Sad}}$. The alternative is $H_A: \mu_{\text{Happy}} \neq \mu_{\text{Sad}}$. The data of mood congruent recall for 15 happy condition participants and 15 sad condition participants are given in Table 7.3 with a comma as a separator. The calculation of *t*-statistics is as follows:

$$t = \frac{(\bar{X}_1 - \bar{X}_2) - (\mu_1 - \mu_2)_{\text{hypo}}}{S_P\sqrt{\dfrac{1}{n_1} + \dfrac{1}{n_2}}}$$

The estimate of a pooled variance is $S_P^2 = \dfrac{(15-1)2.27 + (15-1)2.64}{15+15-2} = \dfrac{31.73 + 36.93}{28} = 2.452$

However, you know that when $n_1 = n_2$ we can use simpler formula $S_P^2 = \dfrac{S_1^2 + S_2^2}{2} = \dfrac{2.27 + 2.64}{2} = 2.452$

$$S_P = \sqrt{2.452} = 1.566$$

Now *t*-statistics can be computed as follows:

$$t = \frac{(6.47 - 5.07) - (0)_{\text{hypo}}}{1.566\sqrt{\dfrac{1}{15} + \dfrac{1}{15}}} = \frac{1.4}{1.566 \times 0.36515} = \frac{1.4}{0.5718} = 2.448$$

The degrees of freedom for an independent samples *t*-test is

$$df = (n_1 - 1) + (n_2 - 1) = (15 - 1) + (15 - 1) = 14 + 14 = 28$$

Appendix C4 for Student's *t*-distribution shows that two-tailed values are $t_{28} = 2.048$ at 0.05 level and $t_{28} = 2.763$ at 0.01 level. The obtained value is 2.448, which is greater than the value at the 0.05 level and obviously will have lower probability. So we can say that $t_{28} = 2.448$ is significant at the 0.05 level. The decision is to reject the null hypothesis. We conclude that mood congruent recall is higher under a happy condition than under a sad condition. The mean recall of happy memories increased significantly more under a happy condition than the mean of increase in recall of sad memories under a sad condition. This indicates that mood congruent memory is not working similarly for both mood states; it is biased towards happy mood. This is generally explained as a motivational function in literature of emotions.

---

[4] There are several ways to induce mood. Listening to music, showing comedy, neutral, and sad types of videotapes (or pictures), Velten's reading of emotionally charged sentences task, self-referential mood induction by asking participants to describe their own life event where they experience a specific emotion, telling (reading) a story that is having a specific emotional valence, or combinations of these strategies are used for the manipulation of human mood in laboratory conditions. Usually a manipulation check is used after manipulation. Care need to be taken to maintain minimal risk while choosing material.

7.3.2.1 Confidence Interval for $\mu_1 - \mu_2$

Confidence interval is one useful tool to demonstrate effectiveness of experimental treatment. We have learnt the logic of CI while discussing a one-sample t-test. The CI is set on $(\mu_1 - \mu_2)$. The CI for the independent samples t-test at $\alpha = 0.95$ can be computed as follows:

$$CI_{0.95} = (\bar{X}_1 - \bar{X}_2) \pm t_{0.025} S_{\bar{X}_1 - \bar{X}_2}$$

From Example 3, the CI can be computed as

$$CI_{0.95} = (6.47 - 5.07) \pm \left(2.048 \times 1.566\sqrt{\frac{1}{15} + \frac{1}{15}}\right) = 1.4 \pm 1.172 = (0.228, \ 2.572)$$

$$CI_{0.95} = 0.228 \le (\mu_1 - \mu_2) \le 2.572$$

In terms of probability, $P\{0.228 \le (\mu_1 - \mu_2) \le 2.572\} = 1 - \alpha = 0.95$. The CI is not including zero and it is reasonably narrow. The CI supports the argument about asymmetry in mood congruent recall.

7.3.3 Effect-size

Generally, when H_0 is rejected, the accepted hypothesis is that there is non-zero difference. How large is the difference can be answered by effect-size. Cohen (1960) provided procedure for calculating effect-size. There are many measures of effect-size. Cohen's d is most popular amongst all. Cohen's d value is easy to interpret as well. To calculate Cohen's d,

$$d = \frac{\bar{X}_1 - \bar{X}_2}{S_p}$$

The d value between 0.2 and 0.5 is considered as the small effect-size, d value between 0.5 and 0.8 is considered as the medium effect-size, and value of 0.8 and above is considered as the large effect-size. The d is an expression of mean difference in SD terms. For example, if $d = 0.5$ for an experiment, then the experimental group is 0.5 SD units above the control group.

In case of Example 3, Cohen's d can be computed.

$$d = \frac{6.47 - 5.07}{1.566} = 0.894$$

This effect-size is large, suggestive of a large difference between population means. The happy condition group recalled 0.89 SD units more mood congruent memories than the sad condition group.

The d can be obtained by

$$d = t\sqrt{\frac{1}{n_1} + \frac{1}{n_1}}$$

For small samples, Hedges (1981) and Hedges and Olkin (1985) suggested a correction referred to as Hedge's g:

$$\text{Hedge's } g = \text{Cohen's } d \times \left(1 - \frac{3}{(4 \times df) - 1}\right)$$

This is unbiased Cohen's d. There is little difference between them for $n > 20$ and usually Cohen's d is reported (Cumming, 2012). From Example 3, Hedge's g can obtained as

$$\text{Hedge's } g = 0.894 \times \left(1 - \frac{3}{(4 \times 28) - 1}\right) = 0.8698$$

Cohen's d can be converted into point-biserial correlation (r_{pb}): $r_{pb} = \dfrac{d}{\sqrt{d^2 + 4}} = \dfrac{0.894}{\sqrt{0.894^2 + 4}} = \dfrac{0.894}{2.1907} = 0.4081$.

7.3.3.1 Magnitude of Treatment Effect: ω^2 and η^2

The significance of t-statistics is a function of sample size. Very small difference in population means can be detected if very large samples are employed. On the other hand, small samples will not be able to detect large differences in populations. In experimental research and applied research, investigators are interested in estimating the magnitude of difference and not just significance. The most common estimate of magnitude is ω^2 (omega square):

$$\omega^2 = \frac{t^2 - 1}{t^2 + n_1 + n_2 - 1}$$

Often, ω^2 will be between zero and 1.[5] Keppel (1991) pointed out that it is unusual for ω^2 to exceed the value of 0.25 in the experimental literature in psychology. Needless to say, it is difficult to control experimental error in behavioral and social sciences research. The eta square $\eta^2 = t^2/(t^2 + df)$ is a comparatively less used method. Cohen (1988) provided guidelines to interpret ω^2 as small effect-size when $0.0099 < \omega^2 < 0.0588$, medium effect size when $0.0588 < \omega^2 < 0.1379$ and large effect size when $0.1379 < \omega^2$. The ω^2 for Example 3 is

$$\omega^2 = \frac{2.45^2 - 1}{2.45^2 + 15 + 15 - 1} = 0.14$$

The ω^2 is also indicative of large effect-size.

R Code 7.4. Independent Samples t-test with Homogeneity Assumption

```
happy <- c(4, 5, 6, 7, 5, 6, 4, 8, 7, 6, 8, 7, 8, 9,7)
sad <- c(3, 3, 6, 4, 6, 5, 4, 5, 4, 7, 8, 4, 4, 8, 5)
t.test (happy, sad, alternative = c("two.sided"), mu = 0, paired = F,
var.equal = T, conf.level = .95)

Two Sample t-test

data: happy and sad

t = 2.4483, df = 28, p-value = 0.02088
alternative hypothesis: true difference in means is not equal to 0
95 percent confidence interval:
0.2286691 2.5713309
sample estimates:
mean of x mean of y
6.466667 5.066667
```

7.3.4 Reporting Results

The t-test results can be reported in the form of table or text. Young students should note that details of calculations are not reported. Brevity is virtuous. The example report could be as follows.

The assumptions underlying independent samples t-test were carefully evaluated. The normal Q–Q plot as well as statistical test ($JB = 1.67$, $p = 0.43$) ensured normality. The mood congruent recall of a happy condition ($\bar{X}_1 = 6.47$; $SD = 1.51$, $n = 15$) is significantly higher than that of a sad condition ($\bar{X}_1 = 5.07$; $SD = 1.62$, $n = 15$) with $t_{28} = 2.45$, $P = 0.021$. The 95% confidence interval of $0.228 \le (\mu_1 - \mu_2) \le 2.572$ is not including zero. The large effect-size (Cohen's

---

[5] The ω^2 can be negative when the absolute value of $t > 1$.

Table 7.4. *Data for Independent Samples t-test*

Male	25, 26, 19, 27, 24, 24, 28, 29, 21, 28, 22, 25, 26, 25, 20, 23, 29, 25, 22, 22	$\bar{X}_{men} = 24.5$	$S_{men} = 2.91$	$n = 20$
Female	30, 27, 24, 26, 28, 32, 24, 25, 29, 25, 31, 30, 21, 28, 22, 22, 27, 27, 26, 30	$\bar{X}_{women} = 26.7$	$S_{women} = 3.13$	$n = 20$

$d = 0.894$) indicates that mood congruent recall of a happy Condition is 0.89 SD units higher than that of a sad Condition.

7.3.5 Evaluating Null Stating Non-zero Value of $\mu_1 - \mu_2$

As a researcher, one may have a hypothesis stating specific difference in population means. The *t*-test for independent samples can be used in such a case. Let's look at Example 4.

Example 4: In meta-analysis of object location memory (OLM)[6], Voyer, Postma, Brake, and Imperato-Mcginley (2007) concluded that OLM is higher in women than men by $d = 0.27$, particularly for the age above 13. Now, assume that we have a test of OLM with a mean 24 and SD = 4 for men. We can argue that women's population mean will be approximately $(0.27 \times 4 = 1.08 \approx 1.1)$ 1.1 above the mean of men. Imagine that we have the data for 20 male and 20 female young-adult participants as shown in Table 7.4.

The null and alternative hypotheses are as follows:

$$H_0 : \mu_{Women} - \mu_{Men} = 1.1$$
$$H_0 : \mu_{Women} - \mu_{Men} \neq 1.1$$

The null is not zero difference between population means. It is specifying some value (1.1) on the basis of prior research. This value can come from theory as well. However, in behavioral sciences there are very few theories that will have such an exact predictability about location parameter.

7.3.5.1 Calculations

We also know that independent samples *t*-statistics can be done with the following formula. Here, we are using separate variances if we do not explicitly wish to make homogeneity assumption. I shall discuss consequences of separately using variances in the next section. The null is $H_0: \mu_{Women} - \mu_{Men} = 1.1$ and, hence, $(\mu_1 - \mu_2)_{hypo} = 1.1$ for calculating *t*-statistic:

$$t = \frac{(\bar{X}_1 - \bar{X}_2) - (\mu_1 - \mu_2)_{hypo}}{\sqrt{\dfrac{S_1^2}{n_1} + \dfrac{S_2^2}{n_2}}}$$

The formula is using separate variances, since equal variances are not assumed. The H_0: $\mu_{Women} - \mu_{Men} = 1.1$ can be tested by using the equal-variance formula as well. The unequal variances create some problems, which are discussed in the next section.

---

[6] OLM is a kind of visual memory. Eals & Silverman (1992) developed various tasks to test OLM. They argued that hunter-gatherer theory explains advantage females have in recall of object arrays. This hypothesis claim that in history of 1.7 million years of human evolution, females were primarily gatherers and males were primarily hunters. Hence, selection favored ability to remember location for females and selection favors ability to manipulate object in their spatial context form males. Stable gender differences were observed in spatial ability in favor of males. The idea of using principles of theoretical evolutionary biology to understand psychological processes has become mainstream approach known as evolutionary psychology.

$$t = \frac{(26.7 - 24.5) - (1.1)_{\text{hypo}}}{\sqrt{\dfrac{9.8}{20} + \dfrac{8.47}{20}}} = \frac{2.2 - 1.1}{\sqrt{0.49 + 0.424}} = \frac{1.1}{0.9559} = 1.1507$$

The degrees of freedom for this example are

$$\text{df} = (n_1 - 1) + (n_2 - 1) = (20 - 1) + (20 - 1) = 19 + 19 = 38$$

The *t*-value that we shall use needs to be a two-tailed value since the alternative is non-directional. The null can be rejected if the population mean difference is greater or smaller than 1.1. The *t*=2.024, at 0.05 (two-tailed) level of significance. The obtained *t*-value of 1.1507 is smaller than the critical *t*-value at the 0.05 level. As a result, we retain the null hypothesis and that states that the population mean difference is 1.1 in favor of women. This exercise has explained how to evaluate the null that states the non-zero difference between two populations. As a practice, you can carry out the *t*-test on this data with the null being $\mu_{\text{female}} - \mu_{\text{male}} = 0$ and alternative being $\mu_{\text{female}} > \mu_{\text{male}}$, and try to interpret findings. R code 7.5 exemplifies the same.

R Code 7.5. Testing Hypothesis That $\mu_1 - \mu_2$ Is Specific Value
```
female<-c(30, 27, 24, 26, 28, 32, 24, 25, 29, 25, 31, 30, 21, 28, 22,
22, 27, 27, 26, 30)
male<-c(25, 26, 19, 27, 24, 24, 28, 29, 21, 28, 22, 25, 26, 25, 20, 23,
29, 25, 22, 22)
t.test(female, male, mu = 1.1, var.equal = F)
```

There is one problem that I overlooked in this section. This is associated with using separate S^2 while estimating the standard error of the mean difference. This is usually done when homogeneity assumption is violated. The resulting statistics necessarily may not follow *t*-distribution. The next section addresses the issue of heterogeneous variances.

7.3.6 Heterogeneous Variances: Possible Solutions

The variances were not pooled in Example 4. Let's call this test statistics that is obtained without pooling variance as *t'* instead of *t*.

$$t' = \frac{(\bar{X}_1 - \bar{X}_2) - (\mu_1 - \mu_2)_{\text{hypo}}}{\sqrt{\dfrac{S_1^2}{n_1} + \dfrac{S_2^2}{n_2}}}$$

where S_1^2 and S_2^2 are separate estimators of heterogeneous[7] variance. Strictly speaking, *t'* is not following the assumptions of *t*-statistics, then sampling distribution of *t'* will not be *t*-distribution (since, *t'* is not *t* random variable) and we cannot use probabilities associated with the *t* random variable from the *t*-distribution to evaluate the null hypothesis. It seems that we are in trouble, but there are many solutions to this problem, though there is no single best solution.

7.3.6.1 Behrens–Fisher Problem

Initial work on the problem of unequal population variances was done by Behrens (1929) that was further extended by Fisher (1930, 1935). The Behrens–Fisher's solution to the unequal

---

[7] Some textbooks (e.g., Wilcox, 2012b) refer to this as heteroscedasticity instead of heterogeneous and homoscedasticity instead of homogeneity.

variance problem is to work out the distribution of t' so that one can find the probability of t' at the given df. We know from the one-sample t-test that $\mu = X + t\sqrt{S^2/n}$ which can be extended to a two-sample t-test:

$$(\mu_1 - \mu_2) = (\bar{X}_1 - \bar{X}_2) + t_2\sqrt{S_2^2/n_2} - t_1\sqrt{S_1^2/n_1}$$

Fisher argued that the fiducial distribution of $(\mu_1 - \mu_2)$ could be used to draw fiducial inference about $(\mu_1 - \mu_2)$ and to create fiducial confidence intervals. The fiducial confidence intervals are based on fiducial statistical theory that views an unknown parameter as a random variable. To state simply, the fiducial confidence interval of $100(X)$ implies that probability that the parameter will fall in that interval is X. The t' then,

$$t' = \frac{(\mu_2 - \mu_1) - (\bar{X}_2 - \bar{X}_1)}{\sqrt{\dfrac{S_1^2}{n_1} + \dfrac{S_2^2}{n_2}}} = t_2\cos\theta - t_1\sin\theta$$

and $\tan\theta = \dfrac{S_1\sqrt{n_1}}{S_2\sqrt{n_2}}$

if θ is in the first quadrant (both value positive in graph), then

$$t' = \frac{(\mu_2 - \mu_1) - (\bar{X}_2 - \bar{X}_1)}{\sqrt{\dfrac{S_1^2}{n_1} + \dfrac{S_2^2}{n_2}}} = \frac{(\mu_2 - \bar{X}_2)}{\sqrt{\dfrac{S_1^2}{n_1} + \dfrac{S_2^2}{n_2}}} - \frac{(\mu_1 - \bar{X}_1)}{\sqrt{\dfrac{S_1^2}{n_1} + \dfrac{S_2^2}{n_2}}} = \frac{(\mu_2 - \bar{X}_2)}{S_2\sqrt{n_2}}\left(\frac{S_2\sqrt{n_2}}{\sqrt{\dfrac{S_1^2}{n_1} + \dfrac{S_2^2}{n_2}}}\right) - \frac{(\mu_1 - \bar{X}_1)}{S_1\sqrt{n_1}}\left(\frac{S_1\sqrt{n_1}}{\sqrt{\dfrac{S_1^2}{n_1} + \dfrac{S_2^2}{n_2}}}\right)$$

$$= t_2\cos\theta - t_1\sin\theta$$

Then the distribution of t' is the Behrens–Fisher distribution defined by $(n-1, n-2, \theta)$. If $P[t' > t_{\alpha/2}(n_1 - 1, n_2 - 1, \theta)] = \alpha/2$, then $100(1-\alpha)\%$ fiducial interval is

$$(\bar{X}_2 - \bar{X}_1) \pm t'_{\alpha/2}(n_1 - 1, n_2 - 1, \theta)\sqrt{S_1^2/n_1 + \sqrt{S_2^2/n_2}}$$

The computation of CDF of θ is provided by some texts. Various books and papers also provide tables for the Behrens–Fisher distribution. They include Sukhatme (1938), Sukhatme et al. (1957), Fisher and Yates (1957), Kim and Cohen (1998), and so on. However, they are complicated computations and evaluation. Cochran and Cox (1957) presented a method to calculate the critical value of t' at any value of n_1 and n_2:

$$\hat{t} = \frac{t_1[S_1^2/n_1] + t_2[S_2^2/n_2]}{S_1^2/n_1 + S_2^2/n_2}$$

where t_1 is the tabled critical value of t at $\alpha/2$ significance level for df=n_1-1.

The $\hat{t}$ will generally be larger than nominal value and will result in a conservative test. R code 7.6 is useful to carry out these computations.

R Code 7.6. Function for Behrens–Fisher Critical Value by Cochran and Cox (1957)

```
BFCrt <- function (x, y, alpha){
   sbn1 <- var(x)/length(x)                    # variance by sample size
   sbn2 <- var(y)/length(y)
   t1 <- qt(alpha/2, length(x)-1, lower.tail=F) # critical value of t
```

```
t2 <- qt(alpha/2, length(y)-1, lower.tail=F)
t_hat <- ((t1*sbn1)+(t2*sbn2))/(sbn1+sbn2)    # BF Critical value
round (t_hat, 2)
}
BFCrt(x,y,.05)                                # run BFCrt function.
                                              Input x, y and alpha
                                              (two-tailed)
```

7.3.6.2 Welch–Satterthwaite Solution

Unlike Behrens–Fisher, who tried to find the distribution of t', Welch (1938) and Satterthwaite (1946) attempted to solve this problem by considering t' as a value that follows t-distribution but not at df=n_1+n_2-2. They argued that if variances are unequal, then for t', we should compute df'. The formula[8] is give below:

$$df' = \frac{\left(\dfrac{S_1^2}{n_1} + \dfrac{S_2^2}{n_2}\right)^2}{\left(\dfrac{S_1^2}{n_1}\right)^2 \bigg/ (n_1 - 1) + \left(\dfrac{S_2^2}{n_2}\right)^2 \bigg/ (n_2 - 1)}$$

Since S^2 are not integers, the resulting df' is a fraction. It is generally suggested that df' be rounded to the nearest integer. The p-value changes negligibly (usually at the third decimal) by rounding. The df' will always remain between min (n_1-1, n_2-1) and n_1+n_2-2. R code 7.7 for the Welch–Satterthwaite t-test is given below for Example 3.

R Code 7.7. Welch–Satterthwaite t-Test
```
happy <- c(4, 5, 6, 7, 5, 6, 4, 8, 7, 6, 8, 7, 8, 9,7)
sad <- c(3, 3, 6, 4, 6, 5, 4, 5, 4, 7, 8, 4, 4, 8, 5)
t.test (happy, sad, alternative = c("two.sided"), mu = 0, paired = F,
var.equal = F, conf.level = .95)
# OUTPUT
Welch Two Sample t-test
data: happy and sad
t=2.4483, df = 27.84, p-value = 0.02092
alternative hypothesis: true difference in means is not equal to 0
95 percent confidence interval:
  0.2283664 2.5716336
sample estimates:
mean of x mean of y
  6.466667   5.066667
```

---

[8] Welch (1947) suggested that while computing modified df, 2 should be subtracted. The formula becomes

$$df' = \left[\frac{\left(\dfrac{S_1^2}{n_1} + \dfrac{S_2^2}{n_2}\right)^2}{\dfrac{\left(\dfrac{S_1^2}{n_1}\right)^2}{n_1 - 1} + \dfrac{\left(\dfrac{S_2^2}{n_1}\right)^2}{n_2 - 1}}\right] - 2$$

However, the result changes by negligibly small amount.

The Behrens–Fisher distribution is not so much used; however, the Welch–Satterthwaite solution is generally a preferred choice.

7.3.6.3 Tests for Homogeneity of Variances

We have seen alternatives for the problem of inequality of variances. The next problem is the detection of heterogeneous variance. There are many tests for detecting homogeneity. The most popular among them is the Levene's test for equality of variance. The Bartlett's test and the F_{max} test are other examples of a homogeneity test.

Levene (1960) developed a test that is intuitively very easy to understand. It can be used with more than two groups and so it will be useful in ANOVA as well. The null is $H_0 : \sigma_1^2 = \sigma_2^2$ and $H_A : \sigma_1^2 \neq \sigma_2^2$. The steps are as follows: (a) compute $Z_{ij} = | X_{ij} - \bar{X}_j |$, that is, obtain absolute difference between every score and mean of its group. We will have two sets of Z_{ij} scores since we have two groups. (b) Run the t-test on two scores (run ANOVA in case of multiple groups). If the p-value of the t calculated is smaller than α, then reject H_0. R code 7.8 is provided for homogeneity tests.

R code 7.8. Homogeneity of Variance Tests

```
library(car)
gp <- factor(gp)
levene.test (daat~gp, center = mean)      # Leven's test
levene.test (daat~gp, center = median)    # Brown-Forsythe test
fligner.test (daat, gp, daat~gp)          # Fligner-Killeen test
bartlett.test (daat~gp)                    # Bartlett test
var.test (daat~gp)                         # F test
#you can easily write your own code for Levene's test
z1 <- abs(x-mean(x))
z2 <- abs(y-mean(y))
levene <- t.test(z1, z2, equal.var=F)
(levene$statistic)^2                        # Levene's test statistic
(levene$p.value)                            # p-value for test statistic
```

For the Levene's test, the deviation of X_i is taken from the mean of that group. If the deviations are taken from the median of X_i, then the test is sometimes referred to as the Brown–Forsythe test. Brown and Forsythe (1974) argued that it is a robust test since it is relatively insensitive to non-normality, skewness of distribution and heavy-tailed distribution. Fligner and Killeen (1976) proposed a test based on the sum of absolute deviations from a combined sample. Among traditional tests, the Fmax test is a simple test that takes a ratio of large and small variances, $F_{max} = S_l^2 / S_s^2$, where S_l^2 is larger variance and S_s^2 is smaller variance between two variances. The details are provided in Sheskin (2007). It is not recommended due to problems with non-normal data. Bartlett's test of homogeneity is another test that can be used with more than two samples as well. The Bartlett's test statistics follows chi-square distribution at df$=k-1$. The Bartlett's test is computed by following the formula: If n is the sample size, $k=$number of groups, n_i is the sample size of a specific group, S_i^2 is the sample variance of each group, and S_p^2 is the pooled variance, then

$$\chi^2 = \frac{(n-k)\ln(S_P^2) - \sum_{i=1}^{k}(n_i - 1)\ln(S_i^2)}{1 + \left(\dfrac{1}{3(k-1)}\right)\left(\sum_{i=1}^{k}\left(\dfrac{1}{n_i - 1}\right) - \left(\dfrac{1}{n-k}\right)\right)}$$

It should be noted that most tests of homogeneity provide acceptable results if two or more of the following conditions are obeyed: normal distribution, equal means (or location parameter), reasonably equal sample size, and sufficiently large n to have an asymptotic approximation to test statistics distribution. The R code 7.8 provides various homogeneity tests. In a useful and interesting investigation, Hayes and Cai (2007) questioned the utility of homogeneity tests and evaluated the effect of three conditions—keeping variances pooled, keeping variance separate, and making decision on the basis of homogeneity tests. Their analyses resulted in a recommendation that keeping variances separate is always a better strategy. So in spite of all the discussion about homogeneity, you will gain much at little cost by keeping variances separate.

7.3.6.4 Robustness of t-Statistic

A statistics is called robust when it is not affected or minimally affected by some violation of assumptions. It implies that test statistics more or less follow a theoretical distribution in spite of moderate departure from assumptions and p-values from theoretical distribution and can be used with little difficulty. The assumption of homogeneity and assumption of normality are two critical assumptions in the case of a t-test. If the sample size is equal and distributions are symmetric, the t-test remains a robust procedure. If distributions are very skewed, in particular, in opposite directions, then the use of the theoretical distribution is problematic. Problems worsen when samples are very unequal and skewness is high. Wilcox (2012a, 2012b) cogently argued in favor of using trimmed means to test mean differences; he further argued for the use of bootstrap methods (resampling methods) to deal with problems associated with the violation of assumptions. I have discussed the bootstrap alternatives in the last section.

7.4 DEPENDENT SAMPLES t-TEST

The t-test requires modification when samples are matched or repeated. Let's understand the conditions that create dependence. One, if the same group of individuals is assessed twice in an experiment, then it is a repeated measures experimental design. One group pre-test/post-test experimental design creates repeated measures. It is commonly used in studying effectiveness of interventions where participants are measured before and after an intervention. Two, dependence also occurs when matched-group designs are employed. For example, if a researcher is interested in studying the effect of two types of training methods on absenteeism at work and assign a participant to two training-programs (A and B) by matching on organizational commitment scores (OC), it will result in a matched-group design. The researcher will initially assess OC and arrange participants in descending (or ascending) order on the basis of organizational commitment score (OCS) and take pairs of individuals in successive positions (1 and 2, 3 and 4, and so on). She will then randomly assign participants from each pair to one of the training programs. In this case, as one participant moves to Training A (albeit, randomly), the other participant in the pair has to move to Training B, and hence leading to dependence. Three, dependence will occur if selection of a participant in one group is determined by the selection of participants in another group by some design mechanism. For example, for some reason, if a researcher is studying difference in attitudes of siblings and selecting participants who are siblings, then this created dependent groups. Here, as one member is selected (say, the elder sibling group), then who will be in the other group is determined (obviously, the younger sibling). In all these cases, the two groups are dependent. The t-test computation has to take into account the dependence. The dependent samples t-test (also known as repeated measures t-test, matched groups t-test, t-test for correlated means)[9] is a useful solution.

---

[9] There are various names to dependent samples t-test: repeated measures t-test, matched groups t-test, t-test for correlated means, and dependent samples t-test. I prefer dependent samples simply because the rest of the names are exclusive for specific condition. The common aspect of this t-test is the lack of independence in selection

7.4.1 Basic Principles and Computation

The null hypothesis and alternative hypothesis are same. The null is H_0: $\mu_1 = \mu_2$ and the alternative is H_A: $\mu_1 \neq \mu_2$. The independent t-test formula is

$$t = \frac{(\bar{X}_1 - \bar{X}_2) - (\mu_1 - \mu_2)_{\text{hypo}}}{\sqrt{\dfrac{S_1^2}{n_1} + \dfrac{S_2^2}{n_2}}}$$

The numerator is fine for dependent samples. However, we cannot use the same denominator. It is the standard error of distribution of mean differences. We used the variance sum law to obtain it. The *variance sum law* states that suppose we have two variables, X and Y, the variance of sum or difference between of two variables is obtained as $\sigma_{X \pm Y}^2 = \sigma_X^2 + \sigma_Y^2 \pm 2\rho\sigma_X\sigma_Y$. Here, $\sigma_{X \pm Y}^2$ is the variance of the sum or difference of X and Y, σ_X^2 and σ_Y^2 are the variances of X and Y, respectively, and ρ is the population correlation between X and Y. Since we are subtracting X and Y, $\sigma_{X-Y}^2 = \sigma_X^2 + \sigma_Y^2 - 2\rho\sigma_X\sigma_Y$.

The $p=0$ (zero) in the case of the independent samples t-test. However, there is dependence, $\rho \neq 0$ (zero) and hence the estimation of standard error needs to take into account the correlation between X and Y. Further, in the case of the t-test, we are not dealing with $X - Y$, but with the distribution of $\bar{X}_1 - \bar{X}_2$. So, the variance of $\bar{X}_1$ is $\sigma_1^2 / n_1 = \sigma_{\bar{X}_1}^2$ and the variance of $\bar{X}_2$ is $\sigma_2^2 / n_2 = \sigma_{\bar{X}_2}^2$. Hence, $\sigma_{\bar{X}_1 - \bar{X}_2}^2$ could be expressed as $\sigma_{\bar{X}_1 - \bar{X}_2}^2 = \sigma_{\bar{X}_1}^2 + \sigma_{\bar{X}_2}^2 - (2\rho\sigma_{\bar{X}_1}\sigma_{\bar{X}_2})$. This is the variance of distribution of $\bar{X}_1 - \bar{X}_2$ when $\rho \neq 0$ (zero) and the SD of this distribution is $\sqrt{\sigma_{\bar{X}_1 - \bar{X}_2}^2} = \sqrt{\sigma_{\bar{X}_1}^2 + \sigma_{\bar{X}_2}^2 - (2\rho\sigma_{\bar{X}_1}\sigma_{\bar{X}_2})}$. While using it with a sample, the values of population correlation (ρ) and population variances (σ^2) are unknown and are estimated by their sample values. This results in $\sqrt{S_{\bar{X}_1}^2 + S_{\bar{X}_2}^2 - (2rS_{\bar{X}_1}S_{\bar{X}_2})}$ and *the t-test formula for dependent samples* is as follows:

$$t = \frac{(\bar{X}_1 - \bar{X}_2) - (\mu_1 - \mu_2)}{\sqrt{S_{\bar{X}_1}^2 + S_{\bar{X}_2}^2 - (2rS_{\bar{X}_1}S_{\bar{X}_2})}}$$

where $\bar{X}_1$ and $\bar{X}_2$ are means and $S_{\bar{X}_1}^2$ and $S_{\bar{X}_2}^2$ are squared standard errors of the mean of the first and second set of scores, respectively. The $S_{\bar{X}_1}$ is obtained by $S_{\bar{X}_1} = \dfrac{S_{X_1}}{\sqrt{n_1}}$ and similarly $S_{\bar{X}_2} = \dfrac{S_{X_2}}{\sqrt{n_2}}$; r is Pearson's correlation between the two sets of scores.

Let's make one more useful point: If the variances are homogeneous, then $\sigma_1^2 = \sigma_2^2 = \sigma^2$. In this case, we can write $\sigma_{\bar{X}_1}^2 + \sigma_{\bar{X}_2}^2 - (2\rho\sigma_{\bar{X}_1}\sigma_{\bar{X}_2})$ as $\sigma_{\bar{X}_1 - \bar{X}_2}^2 = 2\sigma^2 - 2\rho\sigma^2 = 2\sigma^2(1-\rho)$ and SD is $\sigma_{\bar{X}_1 - \bar{X}_2} = \sigma\sqrt{2 \times (1-\rho)}$.

In case of homogeneity assumption, the formula of the dependent samples t-test can be written as

$$t = \frac{(\bar{X}_1 - \bar{X}_2) - (\mu_1 - \mu_2)}{\sigma\sqrt{2 \times (1-\rho)}}$$

Now we have formula of t with and without homogeneity assumption. But, we can make life much simpler by making use of difference scores in the case of the dependent samples t-test. Let's follow this process: Let $D = X_1 - X_2$, that is, D is one set of score, that is, the difference between X_1 and X_2. It is also known as **gain score** or **difference score**. We can use

---

of elements. The name, *t*-test for correlated means, is also indicative of the same. It indicates that population correlation is not zero for the sampling distribution of means.

Table 7.5. *Pre-test and Post-test Data for 17 Participants**

X_1: Pre-therapy	12, 14, 15, 10, 20, 29, 11, 25, 19, 15, 25, 25, 21, 14, 15, 9, 33	$\bar{X}_{pre} = 18.35$	$S_{pre} = 7.04$	$n = 17$
X_2: Post-therapy	16, 3, 6, 9, 7, 6, 4, 18, 5, 13, 6, 10, 8, 2, 10, 0, 21	$\bar{X}_{post} = 8.47$	$S_{pre} = 5.74$	$n = 17$
Difference $D = (X_1 - X_2)$	−4, 11, 9, 1, 13, 23, 7, 7, 14, 2, 19, 15, 13, 12, 5, 9, 12	$\bar{D} = 9.88$	$S_D = 6.63$	$n = 17$

Note: * Scores are ordered according to participants (e.g., participant 1 has pre-test=12 and post-test=16; and so on).

D as one-sample scores with n=number of pairs. If X_1 and X_2 are from normally distributed populations with the same variance, then we can use D as a normally distributed population. If the null is H_0: $\mu_1 = \mu_2$, then $\mu_1 - \mu_2 = 0$, that is, $\mu_D = 0$. We can use the logic implemented in the one-sample t-test and get the formula for difference scores:

$$t = \frac{\bar{D} - \mu_D}{S_{\bar{D}}} = \frac{\bar{D} - \mu_D}{S_D / \sqrt{n}}$$

This is a simpler formulation of dependent samples t-test. The degrees of freedom for dependent samples t-test is df=$n-1$, where n=number of pairs, so, df=number of pairs−1.

Example 5: The example is based on Rachman's (1997) idea of cognitive theory of obsessive-compulsive disorder (OCD) but the data is simulated.[10] Rachman proposed within the cognitive theory framework that OCD is a function of erroneous cognitive mechanisms—catastrophic misinterpretation and responsibility bias. He also proposed treatment procedure (1998). Let's assume that data of 17 patients for eight session of cognitive therapy using Rachman's framework are available. All patients were assessed using Y-BOCS II,[11] a measure of OCD before and after therapy. The data are given in Table 7.5.

The null for this example is H_0: $\mu_{pre} = \mu_{post}$ and the alternative is H_A: $\mu_{pre} > \mu_{post}$. Lower scores on Y-BOCS II indicate lover levels of OCD symptoms. The alternative translates into H_A: $\mu_D > 0$ if $\mu_D = \mu_{pre} - \mu_{post}$. The t-statistics can be computed as follows:

$$t = \frac{\bar{D} - \mu_D}{S_D / \sqrt{n}} = \frac{9.88 - 0}{6.63 / \sqrt{17}} = \frac{9.88}{1.609} = 6.144$$

df=number of pairs −1=17−1=16.

The critical value for t-statistic at df=16 is 1.746 at p=0.05 (one-tailed) and t=2.58 at p=0.01 (one-tailed). The one-tailed test was carried out considering that the alternative is directional, and upper-tailed probability is used since the alternative states that the mean difference will be positive. The obtained value is greater than the critical value. The t-value is significant and the null is rejected. We accept the alternative stating that the post-test mean will be smaller than the pre-test mean. We can conclude that the CBT has significantly reduced Y-BOCS II scores. R code 7.9 is useful to do it in R.

---

[10] I have used this procedure with few clients and observed 60–70% improvement in my clinical practice.
[11] Yale–Brown Obsessive Compulsive Scale (Y-BOCS) was developed by Goodman et al. (1989) and revised 2006 as Y-BOCS II. It is one of the most popular and quick measures of OCD. Yale and Brown are names of Universities where these researchers are/were based during the development of Y-BOCS I.

7.4.2 Confidence Limits for Dependent Samples *t*-Test

The confidence interval for the *t*-test can be computed as follows. If *t*-statistics is defined as $t = \dfrac{\bar{D} - \mu_D}{S_{\bar{D}}}$, then the confidence interval (CI) is computed as

$$CI_{0.95} = \bar{D} \pm t_{0.05/2} S_{\bar{D}} = \bar{D} \pm t_{0.05/2} \frac{S_D}{\sqrt{n}}$$

$$CI_{0.95} = 9.88 \pm 1.746 \times \frac{6.63}{\sqrt{17}} = 9.88 \pm 1.746 \times 1.609 = 9.88 \pm 2.8083 = 7.071,\ 12.688$$

There is a small correction required. The formula is good for two-tailed. For one-tailed alternative, lower side CI is enough computation. The range will be from lower side CI to positive infinity. The confidence is reasonably away from zero.

7.4.3 Effect-size Calculation

The idea of Cohen's *d* has been explained. Cohen's *d* is

$$d = \frac{\mu_1 - \mu_2}{\sigma}$$

For dependent samples, the *d* value can be computed as

$$d = \frac{\bar{D} - \mu_D}{\sigma_D} = \frac{9.88 - 0}{6.632} = 1.49$$

Cohen's *d* is indicating large effect-size. It implies that CBT resulted in large change in the means. The mean difference is approximately 1.5 SD units large.

7.4.4 Reporting Results

The difference between pre-test (mean = 18.35, SD = 7.04) and post-test (mean = 8.47, SD = 5.74) was evaluated using dependent samples *t*-test. The results ($t_{16} = 6.14$, $p < 0.05$, one-tailed; Cohen's $d = 1.49$) indicated that the Y-BOCS scores have significantly reduced after eight sessions of CBT with large effect-size. The 95% confidence interval did not include zero and resulted in a lower side value of 7.071 for H_A: $\mu_D > 0$.

R Code 7.9. Dependent Samples *t*-test

```
pre <- c(12, 14, 15, 10, 20, 29, 11, 25, 19, 15, 25, 25, 21, 14, 15, 9,
33)
post <- c(16, 3, 6, 9, 7, 6, 4, 18, 5, 13, 6, 10, 8, 2, 10, 0, 21)
t.test (pre, post, paired = T, var.equal = T)

Paired t-test
data: pre and post
t = 6.1437, df = 16, p-value = 1.414e-05
alternative hypothesis: true difference in means is not equal to 0
95 percent confidence interval:
  6.472421 13.292285
sample estimates:
mean of the differences
          9.882353

diff <- pre-post     # Difference Score
t.test(diff)         # One sample t-test on difference score. Output of is
                       identical to paired t-test
```

Example 6: The self-report studies of attitude and prejudice always had a deficit: people can fake attitude. Greenwald and Banaji (1995) developed measures of attitude that offered a solution of this problem. This is called an implicit attitude test (IAT) that uses reaction time for classification of "stereotype congruent trial" and "stereotype non-congruent trials" to assess prejudice. The detailed procedure is described by Nosek, Greenwald, and Banaji (2007); however, I am illustrating only by using three steps just to explain the idea. Suppose we take the hypothetical example of study of prejudice towards the Dalit community in the contest of caste-based prejudice in India. The typical experiment is as follows:

Step 1: Show Dalit and non-Dalit symbols on screen and ask participants to classify them as Dalit (key m) or non-Dalit (key z) by pressing a key.

Step 2: Similar task to classify some attribute (e.g., words) as good (or pleasant) or bad (or unpleasant). For example, display the word JOY and participants classify them as "pleasant" or "unpleasant."

Step 3: Participant classifies using a combined set of terms. For example, a Dalit and non-Dalit symbols and pleasant and unpleasant words are classified into "Dalit or unpleasant" or "non-Dalit or pleasant" category (stereotype congruent classification).

Later, the Dalit and non-Dalit symbols and pleasant and unpleasant words are classified as "Dalit or pleasant" or "non-Salit or unpleasant" (stereotype non-congruent classification). The idea is simple—the stereotype congruent condition (SCC) will take less time for pressing key than the stereotype non-congruent condition (SNCC). Please note that the complete experiment will have more conditions and balancing.[12] Now, we conduct an experiment to test the attitude of general population and obtain data on the average reaction time for SSC and SNCC. Since we have to do both conditions on the same participants, we have repeated measures designs. Let's simulate hypothetical data.[13]

Condition	Mean	SD	Correlation (r)	Sample size	Standard Error of Mean
SCC	0.996 ms	0.232	0.3	30	$0.232/\sqrt{30} = 0.0423$
SNCC	1.12 ms	0.254			$0.254/\sqrt{30} = 0.0464$

The *t*-test for dependent samples can be carried out on this data by using an alternate formula.

$$t = \frac{(\bar{X}_1 - \bar{X}_2) - (\mu_1 - \mu_2)}{\sqrt{S_{\bar{X}_1}^2 + S_{\bar{X}_2}^2 - (2rS_{\bar{X}_1}S_{\bar{X}_2})}} = \frac{(1.12 - 0.996) - (0)}{\sqrt{0.0423^2 + 0.0464^2 - (2 \times 0.3 \times 0.0423 \times 0.0464)}}$$

$$= \frac{0.124}{0.00395 - 0.00118} = 2.358$$

The df=n_{pairs}−1=30−1=29 and critical value of t at df=29 is 2.045. The obtained value is greater than the critical value and, hence, we reject the null hypothesis stating that the mean population reaction time for SCC and SNCC are the same. This indicates that the IAT is measuring prejudice towards the Dalit community.

---

[12] The Typical IAT experiment for this data will have the following steps. There are seven Blocks. All Blocks shall have 20 trials and Block 4 and 7 shall have 40 trails each. Block 1 to 3 and 5 and 6 are practice trials. Block 1 has Dalit and non-Dalit symbols; Block two has pleasant and unpleasant words, Block three and four has Pleasant + Dalit and unpleasant + non-Dalit symbols. Block five has Dalit and non-Dalit symbols reverse keyed. Block six and seven has Pleasant + Non-Dalit and unpleasant and Dalit symbols. The complete designed experiment on OpenSesame experiment builder is available with me. R has a package "IAT" which uses the *D*-scoring algorithm.

[13] The *t*-test on raw reaction time means is not the best way to analyze IAT or reaction time data. Nosek et al. (2007) explained the analysis algorithm for IAT data. Analysis of reaction time is a complex issue. Refer to Van Zandt (2002) for the analysis of response time distributions.

7.5 POWER OF *t*-TEST AND ESTIMATING SAMPLE SIZE

The issue of power is already discussed in Chapter 2. Power of statistical test is referred to the probability of rejecting a null hypothesis when it is false. We actually never know about the falsity of null. We know that the decision to reject the null could be correct or incorrect. The probability to make a correct rejection of null is power, and so Power=$1-\beta$, where β is the probability of a type II error. The power calculations related to the *t*-test are partly illustrated here. The useful R-code is also provided to calculate the power. The power of the *t*-test is a function of (a) the probability of type I error, (b) sample size, (c) alternative hypothesis, (d) whether one-tailed versus two-tailed tests is used.

As α (**probability of type I error**) increases, the power increases. That is, power is higher for $\alpha=0.05$ than for $\alpha=0.01$. Generally, we take $\alpha=0.05$ for a one-tailed test and $\alpha=0.05/2=0.025$ for a two-tailed test. As the **sample size** increases, the power of statistical test increases. This is because the standard error reduces as n increases. For example, in the case of a one-sample *t*-test, $t=(X-\mu)/(S_x/\sqrt{n})$, where denominator $S_x/\sqrt{n}$ will become small as n becomes large. Consequently, *t*-statistic will be a large value even if $(X-\mu)$ is a small value.

The **true alternate hypothesis** produces greater $(\mu_0-\mu_1)$ if μ_1 is away from μ_0. As the difference $\mu_0-\mu_1$ increases, the power increases. The power of a **one-sided test** is higher than two-sided test, because we know that the chance that the null with directional alternate gets rejected is always higher than that of the null with non-directional alternate. I have demonstrated this issue while discussing one-tailed and two-tailed alternative hypotheses (Figure 7.2).

To calculate power associated with independent samples *t*-test, we need to know effect-size (Cohen's *d*), significance level, non-centrality parameter, and degree of freedom. We know everything else but the non-centrality parameter.

The **non-centrality parameter** is a family of distributions that is associated with a relevant central distribution. The central distribution describes how test statistics will be distributed when the null is true. The non-central distribution is the distribution of test statistics when the null is false. Student's *t*-distribution, *F*-distribution, and chi-square distribution will have the corresponding non-central distributions. The non-central parameter helps in describing how much the mean of distribution of test statistic is away from its mean when the null is true. For example, for a one-sample *t*-test, when the null (H_0: $\mu=0$) is false, then $t=(X-\mu)/(S_x/\sqrt{n})$ will not be distributed around zero, but some other value. The reason is simple, while computing $(X-\mu)$ we should not be using $\mu=0$ but some other value. The distribution would not be centered around null, but it will be centered around $\delta=\dfrac{\mu_1-\mu_0}{\sigma/\sqrt{n}}$. Here, δ is called the *non-centrality parameter*. The non-centrality parameter is expressing how far the center of alternative is from the center of distribution under null hypothesis (or how wrong the null is!). We use non-central *t*-distribution for this purpose. The non-central *t* random variable is defined as $t''=\dfrac{Z+\delta}{\sqrt{\chi^2/df}}$ where t'' is the non-central *t* random variable. It's useful to note that the non-central *t*-distribution is asymmetric, right tail is heavier when $\delta>0$, and left tail will be heavier when $\delta<0$.

The issue now is to calculate the non-centrality parameter. The effect-size calculation comes handy for this. The non-centrality parameter is a function of Cohen's *d*. Non-central parameter is Cohen's *d* scaled by the function (squareroot) of the sample size. Once the non-centrality parameter is computed, it is easy to compute the power associated with the test statistic. We can also use understanding of power to estimate the required sample size before starting research instead of post-hoc computation of power. If you know desired Cohen's *d* value and non-centrality parameter (or desired power), then you can also compute the required sample size before you start your research.

7.5.1 Power and Sample Size Computation for One-sample *t*-test

Let's calculate the power of a one-sample *t*-test. We start with calculating Cohen's *d*. Once we calculate *d*, we compute the non-centrality parameter (δ) as $\delta = d\sqrt{n}$. The δ can be used to calculate power by using power tables. I shall illustrate the logic of computation from δ to power (though explicit computations cannot be shown here).

For one-sample t-test (Example 2) that we discussed, the H_0: $\mu = 110$. Cohen's *d* is calculated as follows:

$$\text{Cohen's } d = \frac{\bar{X} - \mu}{S_{\bar{X}}} = \frac{1.7}{13.51} = 0.1253$$

The $\delta = d\sqrt{n} = 0.1253\sqrt{10} = 0.3962$.

The power table has no value for this *delta*. However, R code 7.10 can compute it for you. Power=0.065. Obviously, it's a negligible power given, that is, the null and alternative distribution overlap to a great extent and *t* is insignificant.

Now, let's twist this example a bit. Suppose that the null in population mean is 105. Then,

$$\text{Cohen's } d = \frac{\bar{X} - \mu}{S_{\bar{X}}} = \frac{6.7}{13.51} = 0.4959$$

$$\delta = d\sqrt{n} = 0.4959\sqrt{10} = 1.568$$

The power tables for δ to power can be used. You can, however, use R code 7.10 provided.

R Code 7.10. Power Calculation for One-sample *t*-test
```
# from default stats package
power.t.test(n = 10, delta = 6.7, sd = 13.51, sig.level = .05, power =
NULL, type = c("one.sample"))

# by using pwr package.
library(pwr)
pwr.t.test(n = 10, d = .4959, sig.level = .05, power = NULL, type =
c("one.sample"), alternative = c("two.sided"))
# NULL shall be calculated

#Output
One-sample t test power calculation
              n = 10
          delta = 6.7
             sd = 13.51
      sig.level = 0.05
          power = 0.2889036
    alternative = two.sided

# The output of the default stats package is shown. The value of power
is .289. The probability of rejecting false null hypothesis is .29. It's
a low probability. That is probability of Type II error is 1 - .29=.71.
This is because power is a function of sample size. The sample size is
too small and hence power is low.
```

Let's understand the computational logic in the case of a one-sample *t*-test. It requires computing quantile and CDF. Quantile is an inverse of CDF, that is, the cumulative distribution function finds out probability for a given value and above (or below), whereas a quantile function provides the value for a given probability. R code 7.11 shows the relation.

The quantile for the probability of 0.025 is –1.962 in *t*-distribution at df=1000, that is, the *t*-value –1.962 (to negative infinity) will have the probability of 0.025.

And if we do the reverse of this process, then (in R, "pt") we will get the probability of 0.025 for the *t*-value of –1.962 (to negative infinity).

R Code 7.11. Relation between Quantile and CDF for t-distribution
```
alpha = .05
qtl<-qt(alpha/2, 1000)    # quantile for probability of .025 at df = 1000
pt(qtl, 1000)
[1] 0.025    # output, CDF of qtl. It is exactly equal to .025
```

To compute power, we need a **quantile function** at $\alpha/2$ for df=n–1 that will provide $t_{\alpha/2,df}$ for a two-sided alternative (for one-sided alternative, one should compute quantile at α). Now, we can compute the **CDF** for this *t*-value at df = n–1, and non-centrality parameter=*delta*. This CDF will be the power of the *t*-test statistic. For the two-tailed alternative, we compute it for both sides and then add them. In this example, the power of *t* statistics is the probability of obtaining *t* greater than |2.262157| with the non-centrality parameter being 1.568. Simple R code 7.12 is given below. The power can be actually calculated by using R, since CDF with the non-centrality parameter can also be computed using R. Figure 7.3 describes the concept of power clearly.

R Code 7.12. Power Calculations
```
Qtl <- qt(.05/2, 9, lower = F)   # quantile value is 2.262157
p1 <- pt(qtl, 9, ncp = 1.568, lower = F)           # CDF upper
p2 <- pt(-qtl, 9, ncp = 1.568, lower = T)          # CDF lower
p1 + p2                          # Upper + Lower to obtain power
```

7.5.1.1 Determining Sample-size before Data Collection

We can use the logic of power to determine the sample size before we start data collection. We need to know the expected value of power (1 minus probability of type II error), level of significance (probability of type I error), and the expected effect-size. We can obtain an expected value of *delta* from power. Once we know *delta*, computation of the expected sample size is easy.

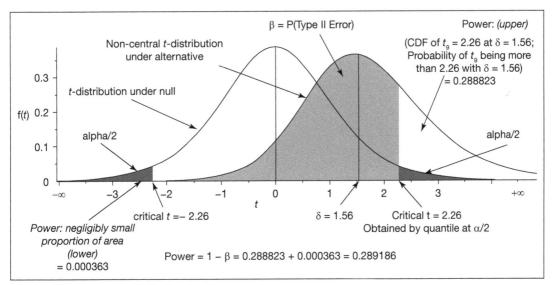

Figure 7.3. *Power Calculation for One-sample t-test*

$$\delta = d \times \sqrt{n}$$

$$\sqrt{n} = \frac{\delta}{d}$$

$$n = \left(\frac{\delta}{d}\right)^2$$

Example: Suppose you want to determine the sample size for obtaining power = 0.8, effect-size = 0.5, and $\alpha=0.05$. Then, *delta* value is 2.8. Now, the sample size is

$$n = \left(\frac{2.8}{0.5}\right)^2 = 31.36 \approx 32$$

The exact computation can be done by using R code 7.13. The estimated sample size is 33.367, which indicates that a sample of size 34 is required to have the approximate power of 0.8 and effect-size of 0.5. As we have noted earlier, we will need a larger sample to detect a small difference, that is, if we reduce the value of Cohen's *d* (we believe that the difference in population means is small), then we need a large sample.

R Code 7.13. Estimating Sample Size for One-sample *t*-test
```
library(pwr)
pwr.t.test(n = NULL, d = .5, sig.level = .05, power = .8, type = c("one.
sample"), alternative = c("two.sided"))
```

7.5.2 Power and Sample-size Computation for Independent Samples *t*-test

The null hypothesis for independent samples *t*-test is $\mu_1 - \mu_1 = 0$ which is the center of distribution under null. The effect-size in terms of Cohen's *d* is calculated as

$$d = \frac{(\mu_1 - \mu_2) - (\mu_1 - \mu_2)_{\text{hypo}}}{\sigma}$$

Since the null hypothesis value is zero and *mu* is estimated from the sample mean, we compute Cohen's *d* by

$$d = \frac{\bar{X}_1 - \bar{X}_2}{S_p}$$

The non-centrality parameter, *delta*, for a two-sample *t*-test is obtained by

$$\delta = d\sqrt{\frac{n}{2}}$$

where *n* refers to *n* of one group only (assuming equal *n* and the total sample size is 2n). As you know that once we have the value of *delta*, we can use power tables and obtain power. I would prefer to use an R code to obtain the exact value.

For Example 3 (mood-congruent memory) of independent samples *t*-test, the *d* and *delta* (δ) are computed as follows.

Cohen's *d* was 0.894. The non-centrality parameter *delta* (δ) can be obtained as

$$\delta = d\sqrt{\frac{n}{2}} = 0.894 \times \sqrt{\frac{15}{2}} = 0.894 \times 2.7386 = 2.448$$

The non-centrality parameter $\delta=2.448$ is a *t*-value around which alternative hypothesis distribution is centered. We can also say that the center of the alternative is 2.448 above null. Now, you can refer to the power table that converts δ into power values. I would prefer to use R code 7.14 to obtain the exact value.

R Code 7.14. Power for Independent Samples *t*-test

```
library(pwr)
pwr.t.test(n = 15, d = .894, sig.level = .05, power = NULL, type =
c("two.sample"), alternative = c("two.sided"))
#OUTPUT
Two-sample t test power calculation
              n = 15
              d = 0.894
      sig.level = 0.05
          power = 0.6568111          # This is power of t-test
    alternative = two.sided
NOTE: n is number in *each* group     # note that n is of each group
```

At times, sample size may not be the same in each group. In case of **unequal sample size**, we compute **harmonic mean ($\tilde{n}_k$)** of the sample size instead of *n*. It is computed as

$$\tilde{n}_k = \frac{k}{\dfrac{1}{n_1} + \dfrac{1}{n_2} + \cdots + \dfrac{1}{n_k}}$$

where $\tilde{n}_k$ is the harmonic mean for *k* groups, *k* is the number of groups (in this case its 2), and $n_1, n_2, \ldots, n_k$ are sample sizes of each group. Use $\tilde{n}_k$ instead of *n*. If one group has 13 and other group has 17 participants, then $\tilde{n}_k = \frac{2}{(1/13) + (1/17)} = \frac{2}{0.1357} = 14.733$.

7.5.2.1 Determining Sample Size for Independent Samples t-test

The power we have obtained is 0.66, but this is a post-hoc calculation of power. The better practice is to determine the sample size before data-collection for reasonable power. The sample size estimation for the independent samples *t*-test is similar to that of the one-sample *t*-test, with a little difference.

$$\delta = d\sqrt{\frac{n}{2}}$$

$$\left(\frac{\delta}{d}\right)^2 = \frac{n}{2}$$

$$\left(\frac{\delta}{d}\right)^2 \times 2 = n$$

The *n* obtained by this process is a one-group sample size. We need to multiply it by 2 to get the entire sample. R code 7.15 can be used for this. Suppose, we want to know the sample size for power=0.8 and the effect-size of 0.5, then the result is $n=63.77$, that is, the sample of 64 in each group is required. The total sample required is $64 \times 2 = 128$. You would quickly realize that our sample size was almost 100 shorter than required. Then, how did we obtain power of 0.66? Simple, Cohen's *d* estimate of effect-size was large ($d=0.894$) resulting in less overlap between central and non-central distributions.

R Code 7.15. Sample Size for Independent Samples *t*-test
```
library(pwr)
pwr.t.test(n = NULL, d = .5, sig.level = .05, power = .8, type = c("two.
sample"), alternative = c("two.sided"))
```

7.5.3 Power and Sample-size Computation for Dependent Samples *t*-test

We have already discussed the computation of Cohen's d for dependent samples *t*-test. The mean of difference score is $\bar{D} = \sum D / n_D$ and $t = \dfrac{\bar{D} - \mu}{S_{\bar{D}}}$. The effect size is $d = \dfrac{\bar{D} - \mu_D}{S_D}$. The non-centrality parameter (δ) can be obtained by

$$\delta = d \times \sqrt{\frac{n}{2}}$$

From Example 5, Cohen's *d* value is 1.49 and sample size is 17. The *delta* can be computed as

$$\delta = d \times \sqrt{\frac{n}{2}} = 1.49 \times \sqrt{\frac{17}{2}} = 4.344$$

The value of the non-centrality parameter indicates how wrong the null was. As you know, we can use power tables to obtain approximate power or use R to get the exact value. R code 7.16 for obtaining power for dependent samples *t*-test is given later.

R Code 7.16. Power for Dependent Samples *t*-test
```
library(pwr)
pwr.t.test (n = 17, d = 1.49, sig.level = .05, power = NULL, type =
c("paired"), alternative = c("two.sided"))
```

The resulting value of power is 0.99. The power is very high; it's almost certain that if the null is wrong, then it will be rejected. It is high given the mean difference and large effect-size.

Another point to be noted is the role of *rho* (population correlation in dependent samples) in understanding power. The SD of the difference between means for dependent samples was known as

$$\sigma_{\bar{X}_1 - \bar{X}_2} = \sigma\sqrt{2(1 - \rho)}$$

where ρ is the population correlation between two groups. Let's look at the effect of ρ on power. The quantity $1 - \rho$ will be smaller as ρ is larger and viceversa. The $\sigma_{\bar{X}_1 - \bar{X}_2}$ will be a smaller value for large ρ. While computing Cohen's *d*, $\sigma_{\bar{X}_1 - \bar{X}_2}$ is a denominator. This implies that if ρ is large, then Cohen's *d* will be large and the power will also be large. The ρ is zero in the case of independent samples. This is a revealing point: The power of dependent samples *t*-test is likely to be larger than the power of independent samples *t*-test. The methodological implications to experimentation is that repeated measured experimental designs are likely to have more power than that of independent groups experimental designs for statistical reasons if *t*-statistics is used.

The estimation of the required sample-size is not different. R code 7.17 is provided below for determining *n* for *d*=0.5, power=0.8 at alpha=0.05.

R Code 7.17. Sample Size for dependents Sample *t*-test
```
library(pwr)
pwr.t.test(n = NULL, d = .5, sig.level = .05, power = .8, type =
c("paired"), alternative = c("two.sided"))
```

7.6 BOOTSTRAPPING FOR *t*-TEST

Bootstrapping is a resampling method (Efron and Tibshirani, 1993). The *t*-test procedures for violation assumptions, heavy tailed and skewed distributions, and heterogeneous variances are discussed in earlier sections. Bootstrapping is a resampling solution to all such problems. It is an attempt to approximate distribution from which the sample is taken. There is no fixed procedure that can be called the bootstrapped *t*-test. The basic principle of bootstrapping is simple: lager numbers of samples are taken with replacement from the sample itself. The statistic of interest is computed on each of it. The distribution of statistic from those many samples can be used as the approximation of sampling distribution. Wilcox (2005) has made fervent arguments in favor of utility of bootstrapping methods over theoretical distributions. I am illustrating a methods described by Wilcox (2005).

7.6.1 One-sample Bootstrap-*t* Method

Wilcox (2005) described a simple bootstrap example in the case of a one-sample *t*-test. He explained the percentile Bootstrap method and the Bootstrap-*t* method as bootstrap methods for hypothesis testing. I am only illustrating the Bootstrap-*t* method. Suppose you have taken a sample of size n and want to do a one-sample *t*-test, then

$$t = \frac{\bar{X} - \mu}{S/\sqrt{n}}$$

Your sample is $x_1, x_2, x_3, \ldots, x_n$. One needs to take the following steps to do simple bootstrap.

1. Generate a bootstrap sample of size n, that is, $x_1^*, x_2^*, x_3^*, \ldots, x_n^*$.
2. Calculate mean ($\bar{X}^*$), SD (S^*) for the bootstrap sample.
3. Calculate *t*-statistic for the bootstrap sample: $t^* = \frac{\bar{X}^* - \bar{X}}{S^*/\sqrt{n}}$.
4. Repeat this process B times. Here B is a very large number. It represents the number of samples with replacements that you wish to take to estimate sampling distribution. Let's set $B = 5000$.
5. As a result of step 4, we will have $t_1^*, t_2^*, t_3^*, \ldots, t_B^*$ *t*-values. That is, now we have 5,000 values of t^*.

The distribution of t_b^* values is used to determine the probability associated with calculated t on one sample. The t_b^* is not distribution of t. It is an approximation of distribution from which the sampled *t*-value has come. It is quite useful in estimating confidence interval (CI) at $p = \alpha/2$. Now, the next step is to order t^* values from smallest to largest. We will have $t_1^* < t_2^* < \cdots < t_B^*$. Then we define $l = \alpha B/2$ and $u = B - l$. The null hypothesis is rejected if $t < t_l^*$ or $t > t_u^*$. The $1 - \alpha$ confidence interval can be obtained by

$$\left(\bar{X} - t_u^* \frac{S}{\sqrt{n}}, \bar{X} - t_l^* \frac{S}{\sqrt{n}} \right)$$

This will provide confidence interval. This is the bootstrap-*t* method for a one-sample *t*-test. Basic R code 7.18 for the data in Example 2 is provided.

R Code 7.18. Bootstrap-*t* for One-sample
```
x<-c(119, 96, 130, 109, 103, 111, 129, 91, 124, 105)
one_t_boot <- function(x){ # function for resampling
n1 <- length(x)
xstar <- sample(x, length(x), replace = T) # sample of size n1
tstar <- (mean(xstar)-mean(x))/(sd(xstar)/sqrt(n1)) # t on resample
return(tstar)
}
```

```
B <- 5000                          # You can specify B as other value
t_rest<-replicate(B, one_t_boot(x))  # repeating this process B times
ordert<-sort(t_rest)               # sorting and ordering
```

7.6.2 Bootstrap for Independent Samples

Let me extend the same method to independent samples t-test. The independent samples t is

$$t = \frac{(\bar{X}_1 - \bar{X}_2) - (\mu_1 - \mu_2)_{\text{hypo}}}{\sqrt{\dfrac{S_1^2}{n_1} + \dfrac{S_2^2}{n_2}}}$$

Your sample is $x_{11}, x_{12}, x_{13}, \ldots, x_{1n}$ and $x_{21}, x_{22}, x_{23}, \ldots, x_{2n}$ for groups 1 and 2, respectively. Now, take the following steps to do bootstrap.

1. Generate bootstrap samples of sizes n_1 and n_2, that is, $x_{11}^*, x_{12}^*, x_{13}^*, \ldots, x_{1n}^*$ and $x_{21}^*, x_{22}^*, x_{23}^*, \ldots, x_{2n}^*$ from both groups.
2. Calculate mean ($\bar{X}_1^*$ and $\bar{X}_2^*$), SD (S_1^*, S_2^*) for both groups.
3. Calculate t-statistic for this sample: $t^* = \dfrac{(\bar{X}_1^* - \bar{X}_2^*) - (\bar{X}_1 - \bar{X}_2)}{\sqrt{\dfrac{S_1^{2*}}{n_1} + \dfrac{S_2^{2*}}{n_2}}}$.
4. Repeat this process B times. Here, B is a very large number. It represent the number of samples with replacements that you wish to take to estimate the sampling distribution. Let's set $B=5{,}000$.
5. As a result of step 4, we will have $t_1^*, t_2^*, t_3^*, \ldots, t_B^*$ t-values. That is, now we have 5,000 values of t^*.

The distribution of t_b^* values are useful in estimating the confidence interval (CI) at $p = \alpha/2$. Now, the next step is to order t^* values from smallest to largest. We will have $t_1^* < t_2^* < \cdots < t_B^*$. Then, we define $l = \alpha B/2$ and $u = B - l$ rounded to the nearest integer. The null hypothesis is rejected if $t < t_l^*$ or $t > t_u^*$. The $1 - \alpha$ confidence interval can be obtained by

$$\left((\bar{X}_1 - \bar{X}_2) + t_u^* S_{\bar{X}_1} S_{\bar{X}_2}, (\bar{X}_1 - \bar{X}_2) + t_l^* S_{\bar{X}_1} S_{\bar{X}_2} \right)$$

The null hypothesis is rejected if CI does not contain zero. This is bootstrap-t method for the independent samples t-test. This method is just an illustration and bootstrap can be achieved by multiple other ways. R code 7.19 shows how to do resampling. You can complete rest of the computation. Note that the confidence interval will change if you repeat the procedure. I am not giving any solution because when you will repeat the process you may not obtain the same solution. Nevertheless, almost always your decision about the null will be identical to mine.

R Code 7.19. Basic Resampling Function for Independent Samples t-test

```
x <- c(4, 5, 6, 7, 5, 6, 4, 8, 7, 6, 8, 7, 8, 9, 7)
y <- c(3, 3, 6, 4, 6, 5, 4, 5, 4, 7, 8, 4, 4, 8, 5)
f <- function() {
      Xs <- (sample(x, length(x), replace = T))
      Ys <- (sample(y, length(y), replace = T))
      T <- ((mean(Xs)-mean(Ys))-(mean(x)-mean(y)))/(sqrt((var(Xs)/
length(Xs))+(var(Ys)/length(Ys))))
}
B<-5000                           # number of resamples
res_t<-replicate(B, f())          # repeating f() for 5000 times
ord1<-(sort(res_t))       # ordering from small to large
```

Wilcox (2005) recommended Yuen–Welch modification for the two-sample *t*-test that uses trimmed means. Yuen procedure without trimming is Welch *t*-test. Wilcox further illustrated Bootstrap-*t* methods for comparing trimmed means. He provided R codes for the same. You can download the file Rallfun-v27.txt (or recent version), then use R command source("Rall-fun-v27.txt") which contains more than 1100 R codes written by Wilcox. The URL is "http://dornsife.usc.edu/assets/sites/239/docs/Rallfun-v27.txt". R code 7.20 is given below. You can also read Wilcox (2012b, 2016) for further details.

R Code 7.20. R Code from Rallfun-v27.txt for Yuen–Welch and Bootstrap
```
yuen(x,y, tr = .2, alpha = .05) Yuen-Welch modification
yuenbt(x,y, tr = .2, alpha = .05, nboot = 5000, side = F) # Bootstrap
```

SUMMARY

This chapter was aimed at understanding *t*-distribution and *t*-test statistics. We have discussed types of *t*-test, specific issues associated with *t*-test, and R codes for most part of it. The discipline of statistics is ever-changing and new procedures are emerging to analyze data. Analysis of data from two groups is no exception. Bootstrapping is one of them and we have discussed it as well. I recommend that you solve the problems using R and play with the data sets. I have not used plots extensively, but I recommend that you use them since it is a useful learning tool. Once, you learn these aspects, you can also read the references mentioned in the chapter to improve understanding.

EXERCISE

1. Show that $t = \dfrac{z}{\sqrt{\chi^2/k}} = \dfrac{\bar{X} - \mu}{S/\sqrt{n}}$.

2. Show that $\chi^2_{n-1} = \dfrac{(n-1)S^2}{\sigma^2}$.

3. Work out the sampling distribution of the mean with R.

4. For a population values of 1,2,3,4 work out sampling distribution for sample of size 3 and obtain population and sample values of mean, variance and sd.

5. The sample mean is 10 and the population SD is 2. Test the hypothesis that the population mean is 12.

6. For the above example, population SD is not known. Sample SD=3. Test the null.

7. Carry out problems 5 and 6 in R.

8. Work out the sampling distribution of mean difference for $H_0: \mu_1 - \mu_2 = 0$.

9. State assumptions of independent *t*-test and their verification.

10. X = (44 53 47 44 41 46 44 44 58 44 55 53 46 47 48 51 48 54 49 39) and Y = (48 40 52 45 43 45 51 39 49 44 48 51 51 55 49 45 58 47 52 52). Test the null that mean X=mean Y. They are independent groups.

11. Create confidence interval, effect-size for the precious problem.

12. Explain the ways to deal with the homogeneity problem.

13. Imagine that problem 10 is dependent groups. Test the null that means are equal.

8 Analysis of Variance

8.1 INTRODUCTION

The analysis of variance (ANOVA) is one of the very popular procedures in psychological data analyses. Under many experimental and non-experimental conditions, the ANOVA comes in handy. While the previous chapter focused on t-test, which is useful for evaluating hypothesis about population mean difference for two groups, this chapter will focus on ANOVA. When there are more than two groups and the differences between their population means need to be evaluated, the t-test is not a suitable statistic. The reasons for this have been discussed further. The useful statistic under such a condition is ANOVA and it was Sir Ronald Aylmer Fisher[1] who first developed this technique. The ANOVA is an omnibus test that evaluates the null hypothesis that the population means of all k-groups are equal. For example, if there are three treatments of depression (CBT, BT [behaviour therapy], and SPT [supportive psychotherapy]) applied to three separate groups of patients and their depression is measured by Beck Depression Inventory-II (BDI-II) after the treatments. The effectiveness of the treatment can be tested using ANOVA in single analysis. However, which treatment is most effective cannot be concluded with F-statistics in ANOVA and further multiple comparison procedures (MCP) are required to be carried out. We have looked at the possibility of having more levels of the independent variable (IV). The ANOVA can also be useful when there are multiple IVs. ANOVA with two or more IVs is called factorial ANOVA. For example, if we extend the above example and have the presence of borderline personality as another IV then we have IV1: treatment (CBT, BT, and SPT) and IV2: BPD (present and absent), and DV is the depression score after the treatment for individuals diagnosed with depression. This is the factorial ANOVA problem. This provides us with additional information of joint effect of both IVs on DV. This joint effect is also called interaction effect. The multivariate extension of ANOVA is referred to as MANOVA. The MANOVA is carried out when there are more DVs. Table 8.1 explains the general schematic representation of these techniques.

---

[1] R. A. Fisher is a British statistician and is called the father of modern statistical methods. He introduced the concept of likelihood (1921). The maximum likelihood is single maximum value of a function of likelihood, and likelihood of a parameter is proportional to the probability of data. Fisher wrote many texts; however, Statistical Methods for Research Workers (1925) was the first of its kind of book that was written for non-statistician and ran into many editions. He contributed extensively to experimental designs and wrote "The design of experiments" (1935) and contributed extensively through crop-field experiments. He made numerous contributions to statistics. He had an impaired vision in childhood and started solving problems in algebra by imagining them in geometry, a habit that helped him to solve many of his problems as statistician. The feud between Karl Pearson and R. A. Fisher is well-known in the history of statistics, both being sever critiques of one another (professionally). Pearson also used his position as editor of Biometrika to criticize Fisher. The irony is that, Fisher was appointed at Galton Chair of Eugenics in University College London in 1933 which was previously held by his rival Karl Pearson.

Table 8.1. *Schematic Representation of Group Difference Techniques*

Statistical Technique	IV (Factor)	Levels of IV	DV	Example
Independent Samples *t*-test	One	Two	One	Experimental and control group comparison
Dependent samples *t*-test	One	Two	One	Pre-test post-test design
Independent samples One_Way ANOVA	One	More than two	One	Comparisons of three treatments (BT, CBT, SPT) for depression
Dependent samples One-way ANOVA	One	More than two	One	Comparison of same participants under three experimental conditions
Factorial ANOVA	Two or More	Two or more for each IV	One	3×2 factorial design; IV1: Treatment (CBT, BT, and SPT) and IV2: BPD (present and absent) and DV is depression
MANOVA	One or More	Two or more for each IV	More than one	Gender differences on four measures of neuroticism

8.2 LOGIC OF ANOVA

ANOVA is the preferred choice when the number of groups (conditions) is more than 2. Suppose we want to compare population means of four groups by using the *t*-test, then the number of comparisons (r) that we need to carry out is $(k \times k - 1)/2 = (4 \times 3)/2 = 12/2 = 6$. When so many comparisons are carried out, the probability of type I error for at least one of the comparisons is inflated. This probability is $P = (1 - (1 - \alpha)^r) = 1 - (1 - 0.05)^3 = 1 - 0.95^3 = 1 - 0.857 = 0.1426$. The real problem is not that we need to do more *t*-tests, the real problem is that the P (type I error) for one comparison inflates. This implies that when three comparisons are performed, the chance that we reject the null when we should have accepted it is 0.1426 for at least one comparison which is much higher than the expected value of 0.05 for all comparisons. The main advantage of ANOVA is that it manages this error during *F*-statistics computation. When the *F*-statistics is significant, the issue of multiple comparisons appears again. Traditionally, the significance of F is required for multiple comparisons. Once F is significant, it indicates that multiple comparisons are required to test which population means differ from each other. While performing these, we once again need to guard further statistical procedures from committing type I error.

8.2.1 Foundations of ANOVA

You know the *F*-distribution from Chapter 1. The *F*-distribution is named after Sir Ronald A. Fisher, one of the founding fathers of modern statistical methods. We have discussed *F*-distribution as a ratio of two independent random variables following chi-square distribution. To represent an *F* random variable:

$$F = \frac{\chi_1^2 / v_1}{\chi_2^2 / v_2}$$

where χ_1^2 and χ_2^2 are chi-square distributed random variables with v_1 and v_2 degrees of freedom, respectively. The probability density is given by

$$f(x) = \frac{\Gamma\left(\frac{v_1 + v_2}{2}\right)}{\Gamma\left(\frac{v_1}{2}\right)\Gamma\left(\frac{v_2}{2}\right)} \left(\frac{v_1}{v_2}\right)^{\frac{v_1}{2}} \cdot x^{\frac{v_1}{2} - 1} \left(1 + \frac{v_1}{v_2} x\right)^{\frac{1}{2}(v_1 + v_2)}$$

For $x > 0$, $f(x) = 0$ elsewhere. The pdf is generally not directly required.

The F-distribution is very useful in dealing with variances and is useful in answering questions about the equality of variance. We know that a chi-square variable is used in computing F random variables. We also know from Chapter 7 that the first chi-square variable is $\chi_1^2 = \frac{(n_1 - 1)S_1^2}{\sigma_1^2}$ and the second chi-square variable is $\chi_2^2 = \frac{(n_2 - 1)S_2^2}{\sigma_2^2}$ at $(n_1 - 1)$ and $(n_2 - 1)$ degrees of freedom. The F variable can be stated as

$$F = \frac{\chi_1^2 / df_1}{\chi_2^2 / df_2}$$

If we substitute the above chi-square expressions then

$$F_{n_1 - 1, n_2 - 1} = \frac{\dfrac{(n_1 - 1)S_1^2}{\sigma_1^2}}{\dfrac{(n_1 - 1)}{(n_2 - 1)S_2^2}} = \frac{\dfrac{(n_1 - 1)S_1^2}{\sigma_1^2}}{\dfrac{(n_1 - 1)}{(n_2 - 1)S_2^2}} = \frac{S_1^2 / \sigma_1^2}{S_2^2 / \sigma_2^2}$$

Now, we may wish to test the hypothesis that $\sigma_1^2 = \sigma_2^2$. Suppose we have a sample from a normally distributed population that has variance σ_1^2 and obtain sample variance S_1^2, and similarly have another sample from a normally distributed population that has variance σ_2^2 and obtain sample variance S_2^2, then we can find F as

$$F_{n_1 - 1, n_2 - 1} = \frac{S_1^2 / \sigma_1^2}{S_2^2 / \sigma_2^2} = \frac{S_1^2}{S_2^2}$$

The null and alternative hypotheses are stated as $H_0 : \sigma_1^2 = \sigma_2^2$ and $H_A : \sigma_1^2 \neq \sigma_2^2$.

Example 8.1: Suppose sample 1 is $X_1 = 30, 28, 21, 22, 23, 26, 23, 29, 24, 14$ and sample 2 is $X_2 = 27, 18, 32, 23, 21, 24, 30, 17, 28, 22$. The sample variances are $S_1^2 = 24.84$ and $S_2^2 = 21.78$. The F-test can be carried out as follows:

$$F = \frac{S_1^2 / \sigma_1^2}{S_2^2 / \sigma_2^2} = \frac{S_1^2}{S_2^2} = \frac{24.84}{21.78} = 1.141$$

The $df_1 = n_1 - 1 = 10 - 1 = 9$, and $df_2 = n_2 - 1 = 10 - 1 = 9$. Appendix C5 describes F-values from theoretical F-distribution at df_1 and df_2. The critical values of F are 3.178 and 5.351 at 0.05 and 0.01 levels of significance, respectively. The obtained value is smaller than the critical value at 0.05 level and, hence, we accept the null hypothesis that two variances are equal. R code 8.1 is useful in this case.

R Code 8.1. *F* test for Testing Variances
```
x1<- c (30, 28, 21, 22, 23, 26, 23, 29, 24, 14)
x2 <- c (27, 18, 32, 23, 21, 24, 30, 17, 28, 22)
var.test(x1, x2, ratio = 1, alternative = c("two.sided"), conf.level = .95)
```

Let's now work out the fundamentals of ANOVA. They include obtaining the total sum of squares, between sum of squares, and within sum of squares, and showing that between and within variances or a mean square ratio follows F-distribution. Imagine that we have independent random samples from k populations of size n. We denote χ_{ij} as the ith value in the jth population. For example, if we sample 10 individuals from 3 populations each, then $j=1, 2, 3$ (j^{th} population), $i=1,2,\ldots,10$ (i^{th} sample), $n=30$ ($10\times3=30$; total sample), $n_j=10$ (sample in the jth group), and $k=3$ (number of populations). If the random variable χ_{ij} is normally distributed with mean μ_j and variance σ^2, then we can state that

$$x_{ij} = \mu_j + e_{ij}$$

Here, x_{ij} have a common variance and mean=0. It can be written as

$$x_{ij} = \mu + \tau_j + e_{ij}$$

where $j=1,\ldots,k$, $i=1,2,\ldots,n$, $\mu=$grand mean, and τ_j is a treatment effect of the jth group. The treatment effect is stated as $\sum_{j=1}^{k} \tau_j = 0$. This implies that the mean of a specific population $\mu_j = \mu + \tau_j$ and since $\sum_{j=1}^{k} \tau_j = 0$, the $\mu_j=0$. This also implies that $\tau_j = \mu_j = \mu$ and $e_{ij} = x_{ij} - \mu_j$. Now, we specify the null as $H_0 : \mu_1 = \mu_2 = \cdots = \mu_k$ which can be stated as H_0: $\tau_j=0$ for $j=1,\ldots,k$; and H_A: $\tau_j \neq 0$ for at least one j. To state it differently, $\mu_j=\mu+\tau_j$ and if $\tau_j=0$, then it implies that the null is $\mu_j=\mu$. The alternative can be stated as $\mu_j \neq \mu$ for at least one j.

The ANOVA is statistics that tests this null hypothesis. The test is based on total variability.

$$\sum_{j=1}^{k}\sum_{i=1}^{n}(X_{ij} - \bar{X})^2 = n\sum_{j=1}^{k}(\bar{X}_j - \bar{X})^2 + \sum_{j=1}^{k}\sum_{i=1}^{n}(X_{ij} - \bar{X}_j)^2$$

$\sum_{j=1}^{k}\sum_{i=1}^{n}(X_{ij} - \bar{X})^2$ is called the total sum of squares (SS_T), $n\sum_{j=1}^{k}(\bar{X}_j - \bar{X})^2$ is called **treatment sum of squares** or **sum of squares between** (SS_{bet}) and $\sum_{j=1}^{k}\sum_{i=1}^{n}(X_{ij} - \bar{X}_j)^2 SS_T \sum_{j=1}^{k}\sum_{i=1}^{n}(X_{ij} - \bar{X}_j)^2$ is called the **error sum of squares** or **sum of squares within** (SS_{within}). We can write it as

$$SS_T = SS_{bet} + SS_{within}$$

SS_T is the total variation, SS_{within} is the variation by chance, and SS_{bet} is also the variation by chance if null is true but it will contain variation in population mean when H_0 is false.

These are three sets of random variables. In order to use F-distribution with them, we need to show that SS_{bet} and SS_{within} follow *chi-square* distribution. Let's first look at SS_{within}.

The $SS_{within} = \sum_{i=1}^{n}(X_{ij} - \bar{X}_j)^2$ for one population (j^{th} population). Let's use the idea discussed in Chapter 7 that $\frac{(n-1)S^2}{\sigma^2}$ is a chi-square random variable at df=$(n-1)$. This will imply that $(n-1)S^2 = \sum_{i=1}^{n}(X_{ij} - \bar{X}_j)^2$ and $\frac{(n-1)S^2}{\sigma^2}$ is a chi-square random variable at df=$(n-1)$. This will further imply that $\dfrac{\sum_{j=1}^{k}\sum_{i=1}^{n}(X_{ij} - \bar{X}_j)^2}{\sigma^2}$ will be a chi-square random variable at df=$k(n-1)$. Additionally, we know that df of chi-square is also the mean of the chi-square distribution. Hence, $\frac{SS_{within}}{\sigma^2}$ has a mean of $k(n-1)$ and so $\frac{SS_{within}}{k(n-1)}$ can be used as an estimator of σ^2. We can refer to $\frac{SS_{within}}{k(n-1)}$ as the **mean square error (MSE)** or **mean square within** (MSW). Now, let's look at SS_{bet}. $\bar{X}_j$ are the means of a normally distributed random variable with mean μ and variance $\sigma^2/\sqrt{n}$.

We can apply the similar logic as earlier. $\dfrac{\sum\limits_{j=1}^{k}(\bar{X}_j - \bar{X})^2}{\sigma^2/\sqrt{n}} = \dfrac{SS_{bet}}{\sigma^2/\sqrt{n}}$ is a chi-square random variable

at df=$k-1$. The mean of the chi-square is $k-1$ and, hence, we can use $\dfrac{SS_{bet}}{k-1}$ as an estimate of

the second variance. Now, we call $\dfrac{SS_{bet}}{k-1}$ as the **mean square treatment** or **mean square**

between (MSTr or **MSBet)**. If the null hypothesis is false, then MSBet contains variance due to difference in treatments, that is, difference in population means. Otherwise there is no reason to have a large difference between MSBet and MSW. The null can be rejected if the MSBet is reasonably larger than MSW. The ratio of MSBet/MSW follows the F-distribution. We can state that

$$F = \frac{SS_{bet}/k-1}{SS_{within}/k(n-1)} = \frac{MSBet}{MSW}$$

Just to reiterate, the basic model of ANOVA is

$$x_{ij} = \mu + \tau_j + e_{ij}$$
$$x_{ij} = \mu + (\mu_j - \mu) + (x_{ij} - \mu_j)$$

It is also referred to as the structural model of one-way ANOVA. Under certain assumptions, we realized that model estimation could be useful to test the null hypothesis that all populations have the same mean. The MSBet and MSW are chi-square random variables divided by their respective degrees of freedom and, hence, the ratio of MSBet/MSW follows F-distribution.

8.3 INDEPENDENT SAMPLES ONE-WAY ANOVA

One-way ANOVA for independent samples evaluates an omnibus null hypothesis regarding equality of population means for all k-groups. Independent samples are often acquired through random assignment of participants to separate treatment conditions in order to control individual differences. The independent samples are also obtained through selecting individuals from different groups (e.g., organizations, linguistic groups, cultural groups, and so on) that ensure independence. Discussion regarding the assumptions and their ramifications, specification of hypothesis, computation of test statistics and interpretation is offered in this section. In addition, effect-size and power-related issues as well as MCP are discussed in sections to follow.

8.3.1 Assumptions of ANOVA

8.3.1.1 Normality

One of the assumptions of ANOVA is that the samples are drawn from populations that are normally distributed. There are various ways to test this assumption that have already been discussed in Chapter 4. We have tested similar assumptions for t-test as well. In the case of our example of three groups, we assume that each of them is drawn from populations that are normally distributed.

8.3.1.2 Homogeneity of Variances

The assumption of homogeneity states that population variances of all groups are equal. It is stated as

$$\sigma_1^2 = \sigma_2^2 = \sigma_3^2 = \cdots = \sigma_k^2 = \sigma^2$$

As you know, at times homoscedasticity is another term used for homogeneity of variances. There are tests of homogeneity of variances such as Bartlett's test and Levene's test that were discussed in Chapter 7. We can extend them to multiple groups readily. In later sections we shall further discuss that the ANOVA can be carried out even if there is a minor departure from the assumption of homogeneity. R code 8.2 explains the test of homogeneity.

Bartlett's K-squared $= 1.1441$, df$= 2$, p-value$= 0.56$, and Levene's Test for homogeneity of variance $F(2, 27) = 1.0126$, $p = 0.3767$ testing null hypothesis of homogeneity of variances are insignificant for the data and have failed to reject the null. We can safely assume homogeneity of variance. However, even if the test had rejected the null hypothesis of homogeneity, we would have only taken it as a potential case of violation of assumption.

R Code 8.2. Homogeneity Test for ANOVA
```
gp<-c(rep("G1", 10), rep("G2", 10), rep("G3", 10)) # groups
data<-c(26, 24, 27, 22, 23, 17, 27, 23, 25, 20, 32, 26, 25, 25, 28, 22,
26, 27, 20, 26, 18, 26, 23, 13, 24, 21, 18, 19, 15, 22)  #data
library(car)                    # call package 'car'
leveneTest(data~gp, center = mean)      # Levene's test
bartlett.test(data~gp)                  # Bartlett's test
```

8.3.1.3 Independence

The assumption of independence states that observations are independent from each other. In model form, this assumption actually means that e_{ij} are independent. A simple way of obtaining independence is to randomly assign participants to groups.

8.3.2 The Null and Alternative Hypothesis

The null hypothesis states that all k populations have identical means.

$$H_0 : \mu_1 - \mu_2 = \cdots = \mu_k$$

The null is stating equality of all population means and, hence, it is called omnibus null hypothesis. The null can be refuted in multiple ways. Even if one pair of means is not equal, the null is rejected. So the alternative can be simply stated as "NOT null." However, the null can be written as $H_0: \mu_j \neq \mu$ for $j = 1, 2, \ldots, k$. The alternative can be written as $H_A: \mu_j \neq \mu$ for at least one j.

8.3.3 ANOVA Computations

Example 8.2: The data of the following experiment is from three groups. Each group has 10 participants and the total sample size is 30. Table 8.2 shows the data for the experiment. Group 1, Group 2, and Group 3 are three groups and scores of the participants are shown.

Now, we need to compute (a) sum of squares total (SS$_T$), sum of squares between (SS$_{beta}$), and sum of squares within (SS$_{within}$); (b) degrees of freedom total df$_{tot}$, degrees of freedom between df$_{bet}$, and degrees of freedom within df$_{within}$; (c) **mean square within** (MSE or MSW) and **mean square between** (**MSTr** or **MSBet**), and (d) the F-ratio.

Table 8.2. *Data for One-way ANOVA*

Group 1	26	24	27	22	23	17	27	23	25	20
Group 2	32	26	25	25	28	22	26	27	20	26
Group 3	18	26	23	13	24	21	18	19	15	22

Let's start with sum of squares.

The sum of squares total (SS_T) is defined as $\sum\limits_{j=1}^{k} \sum\limits_{i=1}^{n}(X_{ij} - \bar{X})^2$.

Let's denote the grand mean as $\bar{\bar{X}}$ instead of $\bar{X}$ for the ease of understanding. The sum of squares total is computing difference between each value of X_{ij} and grand mean $(X_{ij} - \bar{X})^2$. The SS_T is equal to $\sum\limits_{i=1}^{n_{total}}(X_{ij} - \bar{\bar{X}})^2$. The grand mean ($\bar{\bar{X}}$) is 23.

$$\sum_{i=1}^{n_{total}}(X_{ij} - \bar{\bar{X}})^2 = (26-23)^2 + (24-23)^2 + (27-23)^2 + (22-23)^2 + (23-23)^2$$

$$+ (17-23)^2 + (25-23)^2 + (25-23)^2 + (28+23)^2 + (22-23)^2 + (32-23)^2$$

$$+ (26-23)^2 + (25-23)^2 + (25-23)^2 + (28-23)^2 + (22-23)^2 + (26-23)^2$$

$$+ (27-23)^2 + (20-23)^2 + (26-23)^2 + (18-23)^2 + (26-23)^2 + (23-23)^2$$

$$+ (13-23)^2 + (24-23)^2 + (21-23)^2 + (18-23)^2 + (19-23)^2 + (15-23)^2$$

$$+ (22-23)^2$$

$$= 9 + 1 + 16 + 1 + 0 + 4 + 9 + 81 + 9 + 4 + 4 + 25 + 1 + 9 + 16 + 9 + 9$$

$$+ 25 + 9 + 0 + 100 + 1 + 4 + 25 + 16 + 64 + 1$$

$$= 504$$

The sum of square between (SS_{bet}) is defined as $n\sum\limits_{j=1}^{k}(\bar{X}_j - \bar{X})^2$. Since we denote the grand mean as $\bar{\bar{X}}$, the sum of squares between is the difference between $\bar{X}_j$ and grand mean $(\bar{X}_j - \bar{\bar{X}})^2$. SS_{bet} is equal to $n\sum\limits_{j=1}^{k}(\bar{X}_j - \bar{\bar{X}})^2$. The mean of Group 1=23.4, mean of Group 2=25.7, and mean of Group 3=19.9.

$$SS_{beta} = n\sum_{j=1}^{k}\left(\bar{X}_j - \bar{\bar{X}}\right)^2 = 10(23.4+23)^2 + 10(25.7-23)^2 + 10(19.9-23)^2$$

$$SS_{beta} = n\sum_{j=1}^{k}\left(\bar{X}_j - \bar{\bar{X}}\right)^2 = 96.1 + 72.9 + 1.6 = 170.6$$

The sum of squares within (SS_{within}) is $\sum\limits_{j=1}^{k} \sum\limits_{i=1}^{n}(X_{ij} - \bar{X}_j)^2$. The sum of squares within is the difference between score (X_{ij}) and mean of the group of that score ($\bar{X}_j$). That is, every score of Group 1 (X_{j1}) minus the mean of Group 1 ($\bar{X}_1$), then every score of Group 2 (X_{j2}) minus the mean of Group 2 ($\bar{X}_2$) and then every score of Group 3 (X_{j3}) minus the mean of Group 3 ($\bar{X}_3$). These differences are squared and then summation is carried out.

$$SS_{within} = \sum_{j=1}^{k} \sum_{i=1}^{n}(X_{ij} - \bar{X}_j)^2$$

$$= \sum_{i=1}^{n}(X_{j1} - \bar{X}_1)^2 \qquad + \qquad \sum_{i=1}^{n}(X_{j2} - \bar{X}_2)^2 \qquad + \qquad \sum_{i=1}^{n}(X_{j3} - \bar{X}_3)^2$$

$$= \begin{bmatrix} (26-23.4)^2 + (24-23.4)^2 + \\ (27-23.4)^2 + (22-23.4)^2 + \\ (23-23.4)^2 + (17-23.4)^2 + \\ (27-23.4)^2 + (23-23.4)^2 + \\ (25-23.4)^2 + (20-23.4)^2 \end{bmatrix} + \begin{bmatrix} (32-25.7)^2 + (26-25.7)^2 + \\ (25-25.7)^2 + (25-25.7)^2 + \\ (28-25.7)^2 + (22-25.7)^2 + \\ (26-25.7)^2 + (27-25.7)^2 + \\ (20-25.7)^2 + (26-25.7)^2 \end{bmatrix} + \begin{bmatrix} (18-19.9)^2 + (26-19.9)^2 + \\ (23-19.9)^2 + (13-19.9)^2 + \\ (24-19.9)^2 + (21-19.9)^2 + \\ (18-19.9)^2 + (19-19.9)^2 + \\ (15-19.9)^2 + (22-19.9)^2 \end{bmatrix}$$

$$= \begin{bmatrix} 6.76+0.36 \\ +12.96+1.96 \\ +0.16+40.96 \\ +12.96+0.16 \\ +2.56+11.56 \end{bmatrix} + \begin{bmatrix} 39.69+0.09 \\ +0.49+0.49 \\ +5.29+13.69 \\ +0.09+1.69 \\ +32.49+0.09 \end{bmatrix} + \begin{bmatrix} 3.61+37.21 \\ +9.61+47.61 \\ +16.81+1.21 \\ +3.61+0.81 \\ +24.01+4.41 \end{bmatrix}$$

$$= \quad 90.4 \quad + \quad 94.1 \quad + \quad 148.9$$

$$= 333.4$$

The SS total is equal to the sum of SS between and SS within.

$$SS_T = SS_{bet} + SS_{within}$$
$$504 = 170.6 + 333.4$$

The degrees of freedom are computed as follows:

$$df_{Total} = (n_{total} - 1) = 30 - 1 = 29$$
$$df_{Between} = k - 1 = 3 - 1 = 2$$
$$df_{within} = (n_1 - 1) + (n_2 - 1) + \cdots + (n_k - 1)$$
$$df_{within} = (10 - 1) + (10 - 1) + (10 - 1) = 9 + 9 + 9 = 27$$

We know that $df_{Total} = df_{Between} + df_{within}$ and for our data its $29 = 2 + 27$. The **MSBet** can be computed as

$$MSBet = SS_{between} / df_{Between}$$
$$MSBet = 170.6/2 = 85.3$$

The **MSW** can be obtained by

$$MSW = SS_{Within} / df_{Within}$$
$$MSW = 333.4/27 = 12.348$$

The *F*-statistics can now be computed.

$$F = \frac{SS_{bet}/(k-1)}{SS_{within}/[k(n-1)]} = \frac{MSBet}{MSW} = \frac{85.3}{12.348} = 6.908$$

The *F*-statistics is obtained at $df = (2, 27)$. Now we refer to Appendix C5 for values of *F*-distribution. The critical *F*-value at 0.05 level is 3.354 and at 0.01 level is 5.488.

R Code 8.3. Probability of *F*-value
```
qf(.01, 2, 27, lower.tail = F)   # F value at .01 level for df = 2, 27
pf(6.908, 2, 27, lower.tail = F) # probability of F value 6.908 df = 2,27
```

The obtained value is greater than the critical value. Hence, we decide to reject the null. The omnibus null hypothesis which stated that population means of all three groups are identical is rejected. The alternative states that the population means of at least one comparison is not identical. The *F*-statistics does not give information regarding which of the population means differ from each other. The post-hoc comparisons and planned comparisons are used for that. The findings of ANOVA are traditionally reported in a summary table. Table 8.3 is the summary table for our example. Please note that journal editors discourage reporting the entire table.

Table 8.3. *Summary Table of One-way ANOVA*

Source	SS	df	MS	F
Between	170.6	3−2=2	85.30	6.908
Within	333.4	9+9+9=27	12.35	
Total	504	30−1=29		

R Code 8.4. One-way ANOVA
```
gp<-c(rep("G1", 10), rep("G2", 10), rep("G3", 10)) # groups
data<-c(26, 24, 27, 22, 23, 17, 27, 23, 25, 20, 32, 26, 25, 25, 28, 22,
26, 27, 20, 26, 18, 26, 23, 13, 24, 21, 18, 19, 15, 22)  #data
gp<-factor<-(gp)   # gp is defined as factor
fit<-aov(data~gp)   # aov is function; data~gp is formula
summary(fit)
          Df  Sum Sq  Mean  Sq    F value     Pr(>F)
gp         2   170.6  85.30  6.908  0.00378 **
Residuals  27  333.4  12.35

---

Signif. codes:
0 `***' 0.001 `**' 0.01 `*' 0.05 `.' 0.1 ` ' 1
```

The One-way ANOVA can be carried out in R by using the following R code 8.4.

R code 8.4 for ANOVA is simple. It requires IV that is a factor. Hence, we did [factor(gp)]. It's not required since gp is a character vector. If you are using numeric vector as a grouping variable, then you must convert it into a factor. The formula is DV ~ IV for ANOVA. Generally, store the output of ANOVA in some object (e.g., fit) and use summary function on that object. The output is in the form of a summary table that is familiar to you by now. To plot your results use R code 8.5.

R code 8.5. Boxplot for ANOVA and Plotting F-distribution
```
boxplot(data~gp, main = "BoxPlot for ANOVA", xlab = "Groups", ylab =
"Scores")    # Boxplot for ANOVA
curve(df(x, 2, 27), from = 0, to = 8, main = "F distribution at df = 2,
27 ", xlab = "F value", ylab = "Density")    # Plot F-distribution
```

Figure 8.1(A) shows the boxplot using R code 8.5. The boxplot also indicates that there are two potential outliers in Group 2 which we did not pay attention to. Figure 8.1(B) shows the F-distribution at df=2, 27.

8.3.4 Assumptions of ANOVA and their Ramifications

The assumptions of normality and homogeneity are the most critical. The real data sometimes do not follow these assumptions. The ANOVA is a robust statistical procedure. It is more so in the case of the normality assumption. Initial work by Box (1953, 1954) led to the foundation of robustness as a sub-discipline of statistics. Most of the reviews indicate that the non-normality is not a major problem of ANOVA, particularly when distributions are skewed in a similar manner. Minor variations from the homogeneity of variances is not a serious problem. The formal tests of homogeneity (Levene's test and Bartlett's test) are known to be more sensitive and reject the null in the case of a minor departure, and are considered as more conservative tests.

Box (1954) procedure is one approach if violations are more than tolerable. However, the procedure is a conservative estimate. Hence, we can use the Welch (1951) procedure for dealing with data that violates assumptions. The F'' is computed which is distributed with df=$k-1$, df'. The F'' is obtained by

$$F'' = \frac{\dfrac{\sum w_k (\bar{X}_k - \bar{X}')^2}{k-1}}{1 + \dfrac{2(k-2)}{k^2-1} \sum \left(\dfrac{1}{n_k-1}\right)\left(1 - \dfrac{w_k}{\sum w_k}\right)^2}$$

where

$$w_k = \frac{n_k}{S^2_k} \quad \text{and} \quad \bar{X}' = \frac{\sum w_k \bar{X}_k}{\sum w_k}$$

$$\text{df}' = \frac{k^2-1}{3\sum \left(\dfrac{1}{n_k-1}\right)\left(1 - \dfrac{w_k}{\sum w_k}\right)^2}$$

The computational function for R is available with me.

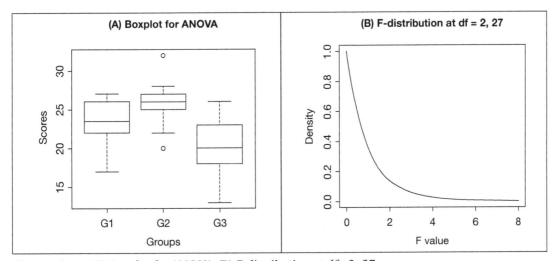

Figure 8.1. *(A) Boxplot for ANOVA (B) F-distribution at df=2, 27*

8.4 EFFECT-SIZE AND POWER

Some techniques developed to evaluate effect-size for ANOVA are discussed below. In addition, evaluation of statistical power of ANOVA and its use in estimating sample size are also discussed.

8.4.1 Effect-size: Estimating Magnitude of Treatment Effect

The treatment effect can be estimated by effect-size measures that belong to Cohen's *d-family* as well as those that belong to the *r-family*. The *d*-family measures are based on difference between the means, whereas the *r*-family estimates are based on the correlation between IV and DV. The eta-squared (η^2) and omega-squared (ω^2) are useful in ANOVA as estimators of magnitude of treatment effect. We have discussed them in the case of *t*-test (Section 7.3.3).

8.4.1.1 Eta-squared ($\hat{\eta}^2$)

The eta-squared ($\hat{\eta}^2$) calculated after ANOVA is an estimator of the population parameter eta-squared (η^2). The η^2 can be obtained by

$$\eta^2 = \frac{SS_{bet}}{SS_{Total}}$$

Eta-squared is the proportion of SS treatment effect in the SS total. This formula is similar to the r^2 expression in regression that states that $r^2 = \frac{SS_{regression}}{SS_{Total}}$ and obviously eta-squared is the r-family measure. For Example 8.2, the eta-squared is

$$\eta^2 = \frac{SS_{bet}}{SS_{Total}} = \frac{170.6}{504} = 0.338$$

The SS_{bet} and SS_{Total} are biased estimators and hence η^2 is a biased estimator. Darlington and Carlson (1987) suggested modification in eta-square computation to make it an unbiased estimator.

$$\text{Adjusted } \eta^2 = 1 - \frac{MSW}{MST}$$

where MST = $SS_{Total}/n_{total} - 1$. In the case of Example 8.2, MST = 504/30 – 1 = 504/29 = 17.3793.

$$\text{Adjusted } \eta^2 = 1 - \frac{12.35}{17.3793} = 1 - 0.7106 = 0.2894$$

The eta-squared is interpreted directly as a squared correlation coefficient. We can state that 33.8% of information in the dependent variable is explained by the IV. Judd and McClelland (1989) argued that eta-squared is percent reduction in error (PRE). Since, SS_{bet} can be viewed as the amount by which SS_{Within} reduces, the ratio of SS_{bet} and SS_{Total} (that is η^2) can be considered as the percent reduction in error.

8.4.1.2 Omega-squared (ω^2)

Omega-squared is one useful estimator of the proportion of treatment effect. It is obtained by dividing treatment variance by the addition of treatment and error variance. Omega-squared as a sample statistic is computed as follows:

$$\omega^2 = \frac{SS_{bet} - (k-1) \times MSW}{SS_{Total} + MSW}$$

In the case of Example 8.2, omega-squared is calculated as follows:

$$\omega^2 = \frac{170.6 - (3-1) \times 12.35}{504 + 12.35} = \frac{145.9}{516.35} = 0.283$$

The omega-squared, being an r-family effect-size estimator, can directly be interpreted in terms of the percentage of variance treatment explained. In the above example, 28.3% of variation in the dependent variable is explained by the IV. Cohen (1977) provided useful guidelines to interpret omega-squared as (a) $0.0099 < \omega^2 < 0.0588$ as a small effect-size; (b)

$0.0588 < \omega^2 < 0.1379$ as medium effect-size; and (c) $\omega^2 > 0.1379$ as large effect-size. The obtained value is indicating large effect-size. The ω^2 will be between 0 and 1 when $F > 1$. When $F < 1$, ω^2 can be a negative value. ω^2 and η^2 are computed in the case of significant F and practically the value will range between 0 and 1.

8.4.1.3 Cohen's f

Cohen (1977, 1988) suggested Cohen's f as a generalization of the d index. Though a separate formula is available, I shall use the one that makes use of omega-squared.

$$f = \sqrt{\frac{\omega^2}{1-\omega^2}}$$

In the case of Example 8.2, Cohen's f is obtained by

$$f = \sqrt{\frac{0.283}{1-0.283}} = \sqrt{0.3938} = 0.6275$$

Cohen (1977) provided useful criteria for interpretation of f values. A small effect-size is $0.1 < f < 0.25$; medium effect-size is $0.25 < f < 0.4$; and $f > 0.4$ suggests large effect-size.

8.4.2 Power Calculations for One-way ANOVA

We know that F-distribution (let's call this as central F-distribution) is about $F = \frac{\chi_1^2/df_1}{\chi_2^2/df_2}$ random variable with mean of $E(F) = df_2/(df_2-2)$. When null is true, the F-distribution is centered around $df_2/(df_2-2)$ mean. In F-calculation, $df_2 = df_{Within}$. However, if χ_1^2 is a non-central chi-square variable[2] with a non-central parameter λ (lambda), then F is called non-central F-distribution (ncF). The ncF is distributed around mean $\frac{df_2(df_1+\lambda)}{df_1(df_2-2)}$. When the null hypothesis is false, the F-distribution under H_A is not centered around mean $df_2/(df_2-2)$ but it is centered around mean $\frac{df_2(df_1+\lambda)}{df_1(df_2-2)}$.

The value of λ is called a non-centrality parameter in the case of the F-distribution.
    In order to calculate power, we shall make use of Cohen's f:

$$f = \sqrt{\frac{\omega^2}{1-\omega^2}} = 0.6275$$

Often, in power literature, f is described by the symbol ϕ' which is an effect-size estimator. The non-centrality parameter can be obtained first obtaining ϕ.

$$\phi = f\sqrt{n}$$

where n is size of one group. If the groups are unequal, the harmonic mean of n is computed.

---

[2] The non-central chi-square distribution is the generalization of the chi-square distribution. The central chi-square is the sum of squared standard normal variables (Z^2). The $Z \sim N(0,1)$, that is, Z follows normal with mean 0 and variance 1. If the chi-square is obtained by squaring X (instead of Z), which is normally distributed with mean μ and unit variance, then the chi-square is called non-central chi-square. This chi-square has two parameters: (a) df; (b) λ, where $\lambda = \sum_{i=1}^{k}\mu_i$ is called the non-centrality parameter.

$$\phi = 0.6275\sqrt{10} = 1.9843$$

We know that $\phi = \sqrt{\lambda/k}$ so, $\phi^2 = \lambda/k$ and then lambda is $\phi^2 k = \lambda$

$$\lambda = \phi^2 k = 1.984329^2 \times 3 = 11.81268$$

The λ can be called a non-centrality parameter.

Once we have lambda, the power can be computed by using R code 8.6.

R Code 8.6. Power of One-way ANOVA
```
n = 10                                   # sample-size per group
omega<-(170.6-(2*12.35))/(504+12.35)     # computing omega
f<-sqrt(omega/(1-omega))                 # computing f(effect size)
phi<-f*sqrt(n)                           # computing f
ncF<-phi^2*3                             # non-centrality parameter
crit<-qf(.05, 2, 27, lower = FALSE)      # computing critical F value
pf(crit, 2, 27, ncF, lower = FALSE)      # computing power
```

Once the non-central parameter is computed, the power is the probability of obtaining $F(df_1, df_2)$ greater than the critical value of F for a given non-central parameter. As you know from power discussion in the context of t-test, the idea of power is useful in determining the sample size.

Since we know that $\phi = f\sqrt{n}$, we can state that

$$\phi/f = \sqrt{n}$$
$$\phi^2/f^2 = n$$

Now, suppose we want to carry out an experiment which has four experimental conditions, the effect-size (f) is 0.4, level of significance is 0.05, and the expected power is 0.8. Then the required sample size can be computed as follows using R.

R Code 8.7. Power and Sample Size Computation for ANOVA
```
library(pwr)                    # call package pwr
pwr.anova.test(k = 4, n = NULL, f = .4, sig.level = .05, power = .8)
# Sample size estimation
pwr.anova.test(k = 3, n = 10, f = .6275, sig.level = .05, power = NULL)
# Power for example 8.2 data with output.
Balanced one-way analysis of variance power calculation
          k       = 3
          n       = 10
          f       = 0.6275
sig.level         = 0.05
      power = 0.8366323
NOTE: n is number in each group
```

The computation is very easy with R. Hence, I am omitting the tables for converting lambda into power values.

8.5 MULTIPLE COMPARISON PROCEDURES

The significance testing for ANOVA evaluates an omnibus null hypothesis which states that all population means are the same. Rejecting this hypothesis only mean that at least one of the comparisons is non-zero. The *F*-statistics does not provide information regarding anything specific about these comparisons. The further investigation regarding comparisons of each population means is generally referred to as "multiple comparisons."

8.5.1 Basic Ideas in Multiple Comparisons

There are some important concepts that we need to understand before going ahead with multiple comparisons.

8.5.1.1 Error Rate

Error rates are of two types.

1. **Per comparison type I error rate:** The type I error (α) for single comparison is set by researchers. Generally, we set it to be $\alpha_{pc} = 0.05$, that is, the probability that one comparison results in type I error is α_{pc}.
2. **Family-wise type I error rate:** When many comparisons are carried out (*c* comparisons), then the probability that one of the *c* comparison results in type I error is the family-wise error rate (FWER), α_{fw}. $P = (1 - (1 - \alpha_{pc})^C) = 1 - (1 - 0.05)^3 = 0.1426$.

As the comparisons increase, the probability of type I error increases. Often researchers carry out comparisons that they are interested in and not all comparisons. In those cases, the α_{fw} will be applicable only for the comparisons carried out. Two separate strategies are used to adjust the family-wise type I error. They are called (a) planned comparisons (or a priori comparison) and (b) post-hoc comparisons (or unplanned comparisons, or posteriori comparisons).

8.5.1.2 Post-hoc and Planned Comparisons

The *F*-test has provided information about the omnibus null in one shot. This is saving us from making type I error. We know that carrying out multiple *t*-tests (3 in this case) will inflate the probability of family-wise type I error. The significance of *F* has actually brought us at the point where we again face the problem of type I error. Since *F* is significant, we need to compare individual groups to know the specific alternative. Traditionally, two strategies are employed: (a) planned comparisons; (b) post-hoc comparisons.

(a) **Planned comparisons:** They are also called as **a priory comparisons**. Planned comparisons are planned prior to the data collection. A researcher has specific comparisons that she wishes to carry out. Those comparisons are carried out once data is available. Attempt is made to keep α_{fw} under control. The planned comparisons are simple or complex. Simple comparisons are comparing two groups (e.g., evaluating difference between mean 1 and mean 3 with H_0: $\mu_1 = \mu_3$). Complex comparisons involve comparing more groups. For example, a comparison can be set to test whether the average of mean 1 and mean 2 is equal to mean 3. That is, H_0: $(\mu_1 + \mu_2)/2 = \mu_3$ which can be written as $H_0 : (0.5 \times \mu_1) + (0.5 \times \mu_2) = \mu_3$, this implies that $H_0 : [(0.5 \times \mu_1) + (0.5 \times \mu_2)] - \mu_3 = 0$.

(b) **Post-hoc comparisons:** They are also known as **unplanned comparisons** or **posteriori comparisons**. Post-hoc comparisons are those that researchers decide to carry out after data collection. Specifying a value of α_{fw} is a tricky issue in post-hoc comparisons. For example, $\alpha_{fw} = 0.2$ is liberal when the number of comparisons (*c*) is 3, whereas the same value looks stringent when the number of comparisons (*c*) is 10. There is some degree of disagreement among researchers regarding this issue.

8.5.1.3 Significance of F

Traditionally, it is believed that the significance of *F*-statistics is necessary for MCP. The traditional wisdom was based on the idea that *F*-tests omnibus null hypothesis $H_0 : \mu_1 = \mu_2 = \cdots = \mu_k$

and the rejection of it implies that at least one comparisons is significant. The acceptance of omnibus null imply that there is not a single comparison that is significant and, hence, no point in looking for it. Most traditional textbooks carry this advice.

Modern insights (actually, not so modern) inform that this general recommendation is not correct. Many have shown that, theoretically, it possible that the overall F is significant but none of the simple comparisons are significant (e.g., Grissom & Kim, 2005; Kirk, 1995; Maxwell & Delaney, 2000) particularly when we employ stringent procedures for multiple comparisons (like Scheffé's test). Most of the MCP logically do not require significance of the overall F-test. The null tested by the overall F and the null tested by comparison procedures have different probabilities to reject the null hypothesis. Hence, there could be instances when the overall F is insignificant but some of the comparisons are significant because F may have less power than some of the comparisons. Wilcox (1987) recommends that there is no reason to carry out the overall F-tests, and researchers should start with multiple comparisons (p. 39). If the issue is so clear that multiple comparisons are not contingent on the significance of the overall F, then why psychologists have been practicing it so many years? I agree with Howell's conclusion that "The only reason I think of is 'tradition,' and that is a powerful force" (p. 373). Please note that some of comparison procedures may require MSW, which does not mean that they require significance of F.

8.5.2 Planned Comparisons

One important idea in planned comparisons is **contrasts**. The comparisons that are planned earlier are called contrasts or planned contrasts. Linear contrasts are a part of planned comparisons that attempt to evaluate the null hypothesis that the difference between two means or linear combination of more than two means is zero. So simple contrast is H_0: $\mu_1 = \mu_2$. However, more complex contrasts can be setup. For example, a contrast H_0:$(\mu_1 + \mu_2)/2 = \mu_3$ is more a complex one. Let's understand linear combinations of means first. The linear combination of means takes the following general form:

$$\sum_{j=1}^{k} a_j \bar{X}_j = a_1 \bar{X}_1 + a_2 \bar{X}_2 + \cdots + a_k \bar{X}_k = \psi$$

where $a_1, a_2, \ldots, a_k$ are weights or are called coefficients (c_j), $\bar{X}_1, \bar{X}_2, \ldots, \bar{X}_k$ are sample means, and $\sum_{j=1}^{k} a_j \bar{X}_j$ is a sum of means weighted by a coefficient which is referred to as Ψ (Greek letter "*psi*"). A linear combination is a weighted sum of means. This expression can be written as $\sum_{j=1}^{k} c_j \bar{X}_j$. When a condition $\sum_{j=1}^{k} = 0$ is set, the linear combination is called **linear contrast**. The linear combination is a statement of null hypothesis.

Example: We can set a contrast for $\bar{X}_1 - \bar{X}_3$ when we have three means $\bar{X}_1, \bar{X}_2, \bar{X}_3$.

This can be done by setting coefficients as $a_1 = 1, a_2 = 0, a_3 = -1$. The sum of the coefficients $\sum_{j=1}^{k} c_j = 1 + 0 + (-1) = 0$ is zero and the contrast is

$$\Psi = (1)\bar{X}_1 + (0)\bar{X}_2 + (-1)\bar{X}_3 = \bar{X}_1 - \bar{X}_3$$

Example: If we are interested in setting a contrast with the mean of the first group minus the average of means of the last two groups, then the contrast can be set as follows.

The coefficients are $a_1 = 1, a_2 = -1/2, a_3 = -1/2$. The sum of the coefficients is $\sum_{j=1}^{k} c_j = 1 + (-1/2) + (-1/2) = 0$ and the contrast is $\Psi = (1)\bar{X}_1 + (-1/2)\bar{X}_2 + (-1/2)\bar{X}_3 = \bar{X}_1 - \dfrac{\bar{X}_2 + \bar{X}_3}{2} = \bar{X}_1 - \dfrac{1}{2}(\bar{X}_2 + \bar{X}_3)$.

8.5.2.1 Planned Comparisons with Contrasts

Let's assume that we want to test a null hypothesis using linear contrasts. The null hypothesis is H_0: $\mu_1 = \mu_3$. The null can be stated as $\psi = (1)\mu_1 + (0)\mu_2 + (-1)\mu_3 = \mu_1 - \mu_3$. Let's now see the data from Example 8.2. Three means are 23.4, 25.7, and 19.9. The coefficients (c_j) are 1, 0, and −1 (the sum of c_j is zero). While computing Ψ, estimates of population mean (sample mean) are used. $\psi = (1)23.4 + (0)25.7 + (-1)19.9 = 23.4 - 19.9 = 3.5$. Note that $\psi = \sum_{j=1}^{k} c_j \bar{X}_j$. The sum of the square of coefficients is $\sum c_j^2 = 1^2 + 0^2 + (-1)^2 = 2$. The test statistics for the comparison is F_{comp}. To obtain F_{comp} we need to compute SS_{comp} and MS_{comp}. The MSW is taken from the main ANOVA computation (12.348).

$$SS_{comp} = \frac{n\psi^2}{\sum c_j^2} = \frac{10(3.5)^2}{2} = \frac{122.5}{2} = 61.25$$

$df_{comp} = k_{comp} - 1 = 2 - 1 = 1$ where k is the number of comparisons.

$$MS_{comp} = SS_{comp}/df_{comp} = 61.25/1 = 61.25$$
$$F_{comp} = MS_{comp}/MSW = 61.25/12.348 = 4.96$$

The tabled F-value at df=1, 27 is 4.21. The obtained F-ratio is significant at 0.05 level. Since the F-ratio is significant for the contrast, we can conclude that Group 1 has a larger population mean than Group 3. This also implies that population coefficients are not summing to zero. In reality, there is no reason to believe that the coefficients do not sum to zero, but it means that when multiplied by coefficients, they do not turn out to be equal.

Example: Complex Contrasts
Suppose we have a hypothesis that states that Group 1 is equal to the average of Groups 2 and 3. If the null hypothesis is stated as $H_0 : \mu_1 = (\mu_2 + \mu_3)/2$ and the alternate as $H_A : \mu_1 \neq (\mu_2 + \mu_3)/2$, then planned comparisons can be carried out. The coefficients (c_j) are 1, −1/2, and −1/2 (the sum of c_j is zero). ψ is obtained by $\psi = (1)23.4 + (-1/2)25.7 + (-1/2)19.9 = 23.4 - 22.8 = 0.6$. The sum of squares of the coefficients is $\sum c_j^2 = 1^2 + (-0.5^2) + (-0.5)^2 = 1.5$. The test statistic for the comparison is F_{comp}. To obtain F_{comp}, we need to compute SS_{comp} and MS_{comp}. The MSW is taken from the main ANOVA computation (12.348).

$$SS_{comp} = \frac{n\psi^2}{\sum c_j^2} = \frac{10(.6)^2}{1.5} = \frac{3.6}{1.5} = 2.4$$

$df_{comp} = k_{comp} - 1 = 2 - 1 = 1$ where k is the number of comparisons.

$$MS_{comp} = SS_{comp}/df_{comp} = 2.4/1 = 2.4.$$
$$F_{comp} = MS_{comp}/MSW = 2.4/12.348 = 0.194$$

Since the obtained F_{comp} value is insignificant (critical F-value is 4.21 at df=1, 27, P=0.05), the null hypothesis stating that $\mu_1 = (\mu_2 + \mu_3)/2$ is accepted.

8.5.2.2 Orthogonal Comparisons

Generally researchers are not interested in carrying out as many comparisons as possible. They are interested in few comparisons driven by theory. Too many planned comparisons may inflate α_{fw}, but the general recommendation is that if the number of planned comparisons is kept equal or below df_{bet} for full model (i.e., omnibus F-test), then researchers need not worry about α_{fw}. In the case of Example 8.2, $df_{bet} = 2$, implying that we can carry out two comparisons. Orthogonal comparison is a way of determining how many such comparisons can be carried out. Orthogonal (literally mean uncorrelated) comparisons are comparisons that are independent of one another. The information provided by orthogonal comparisons is independent. The two comparisons are called orthogonal when

$$\sum_{j=1}^{k} c_{j1}c_{j2} = 0$$

where c_{j1} and c_{j2} are comparisons 1 and 2 for the jth group.

Let's test whether the two comparisons above are orthogonal.

The coefficient for comparison are (1, 0, –1) and (1, –1/2, –1/2) for, c_{j1} and c_{j2}, respectively.

$$\sum_{j=1}^{k} c_{j1}c_{j2} = (1)(1) + (0)(-1/2) + (-1)(-1/2) = 1 + 0 + (1/2) = 1.5$$

Since the sum is not zero, the two comparisons that we have carried out are not orthogonal. They are providing overlapping information.

Suppose that the set of coefficients are (0, 1, –1) and (1, –1/2, –1/2), then

$$\sum_{j=1}^{k} c_{j1}c_{j2} = (0)(1) + (1)(-1/2) + (-1)(-1/2) = 0 + (-1/2) + (1/2) = 0$$

This is summing to zero and, hence, the two comparisons with coefficients (0, 1, –1) and (1, –1/2, –1/2) are independent or orthogonal.

Suppose, there are four groups to be compared, the comparisons can be arranged in the following manner for comparison for sets 1, 2 and 3, 4. Table 8.4 shows the comparisons, coefficients and their sum.

$$\sum_{j=1}^{k} c_{j1}c_{j2} = (0.5)(0.5) + (0.5)(0.5) + (-0.5)(-1) + (-0.5)(0) = 0.25 + 0.25 + 0.5 + 0 = 1$$

$$\sum_{j=1}^{k} c_{j1}c_{j3} = (0.5)(1) + (0.5)(-1) + (-0.5)(0) + (-0.5)(0) = 0.5(-0.5) + 0 + 0 = 0$$

$$\sum_{j=1}^{k} c_{j2}c_{j3} = (0.5)(1) + (0.5)(-1)(0) + (0)(0) = 0.5 + (-0.5) + 0 + 0 = 0$$

For k groups, there are $k-1$ orthogonal comparisons possible within each complete orthogonal set. The orthogonal comparisons are important because they provide independent (non-redundant) pieces of information. The F-test can be calculated for each of the orthogonal comparison. To test whether you have created all orthogonal contrasts, you should add all SS_{comp} which should be equal to SS_{bet}. The last point to note is that it is not necessary to test orthogonal contrasts. One can test non-orthogonal contrasts if there is underlying theory that supports such a test.

Table 8.4. *Contrasts and Coefficients*

Contrast	Group	vs	Group	Coefficients Group 1	Coefficients Group 2	$\sum_{j=1}^{k} c_j$	$\sum_{j=1}^{k} c_j^2$
1	1, 2	vs	3, 4	½, ½,	–½, –½	0	1
2	1 vs 2			1, –1	0, 0	0	2
3			3 vs 4	0, 0	1, –1	0	2

8.5.2.3 Multiple t-test

Multiple *t*-test is one of the oldest ways of dealing with the problem of multiple comparisons. The *t*-test has pooled estimate of variance, which is replaced by MSW of the overall *F*-test for multiple *t*-test.

$$t = \frac{\bar{X}_i - \bar{X}_j}{\sqrt{\frac{MSW}{n} + \frac{MSW}{n}}} = \frac{\bar{X}_i - \bar{X}_j}{\sqrt{\frac{2MSW}{n}}}$$

Suppose you wish to compare Group 1 with 2 and Group 2 with 3, then for the first comparison (Group 1 with Group 2):

$$t = \frac{23.4 - 25.7}{\sqrt{\frac{12.348}{10} + \frac{12.348}{10}}} = \frac{23.4 - 25.7}{\sqrt{\frac{2 \times 12.348}{10}}} = \frac{-2.3}{\sqrt{2.4696}} = 1.46$$

For the second comparison (Group 2 with Group 3)

$$t = \frac{25.7 - 19.9}{\sqrt{\frac{12.348}{10} + \frac{12.348}{10}}} = \frac{25.7 - 19.9}{\sqrt{\frac{2 \times 12.348}{10}}} = \frac{5.8}{\sqrt{2.4696}} = 3.69$$

(The *t*=2.227 for the comparison of Group 1 and Group 3.)

The multiple *t*-test is not the recommended approach for its inability to control α_{fw}. Multiple *t*-test is particularly worse when there are many comparisons. It might be useful if there are few (two or three) planned comparisons to be carried out.

Instead of multiple *t*-tests, **Fisher's LSD test** (or **Fisher's protected *t***) is a better alternative. One can carry out **Fisher's LSD test** for the comparisons that a researcher is interested in. This test is also useful in post-hoc comparisons. The LSD is discussed in the next section.

8.5.2.4 The Bonferroni–Dunn Test

The Bonferroni–Dunn (BD) test uses Bonferroni inequality. The **Bonferroni inequality** (also known as **Boole's inequality**)[3] states that the probability of occurrence of union of events cannot be more than the sum of probabilities of individual events.

If the P(E_i) is the probability of E_i, and $P\left(\bigcup\limits_{i=1}^{n} E_i\right)$ is the probability that either of $E_1, E_2, ..., E_n$

occurs, the Bonferroni inequality is stated as

$$P\left(\bigcup_{i=1} E_i\right) \leq \sum_{i=1} P(E_i)$$

---

[3] Carlo Emilio Bonferroni (1892–1960) is an Italian mathematician who was an excellent pianist and composer and deeply interested in music. He also served as an officer in WWI and came back to teaching after the war. Bonferroni wrote two articles (1935, 1936) which include what are referred to as the "Bonferroni inequalities" today. George Boole (1815–1864) discovered the basic idea much before Bonferroni and it is believed that Bonferroni based his ideas on them. George Boole was an English mathematician and logician. Boolean Algebra is work developed in his famous book *The Laws of Thought* (1854). Boolean logic is considered as the foundation of the information age and is applied in computer construction, switching circuits, and so on.

It implies that the probability of occurrence of one or more events can be smaller or equal to the sum of their individual probabilities. Suppose, we are doing three comparisons, then $c=3$, and if we set $\alpha_{pc}=0.05$, the probability of type I error for one of the comparisons cannot be more than $0.05 + 0.05 + 0.05 = 0.15$. So the maximum value of α_{fw} will be less than or equal to $\alpha_{pc}c$.

R Code 8.8. Critical *t*-value at $\alpha_{pc}=0.0167$
```
qt(.0167/2, 27, lower=F)
```

If we want α_{fw} as the required type 1 error for any one comparison, then $\alpha_{fw}/c = \alpha_{pc}$. $\alpha_{fw} \le c\alpha_{pc} = c(\alpha_{fw}/c)$. For example, if $c=3$, then $\alpha_{fw} \le (3 \times 0.01667) = 3 \times (0.05/3) = 0.05$. This inequality becomes equality when union is of disjoint sets. However, we know that if $\alpha_{pc}=0.05$, then $\alpha_{fw}=0.1426$ and hence $\alpha_{fw} \le c\alpha_{pc}$. Dunn (1961) used this inequality to develop extensive tables to evaluate t at these α levels. To carry out the BD t-test, we need to take the following steps: (a) compute multiple t, (b) compute $\alpha_{pc} = \alpha_{fw}/c = 0.0167$, (c) evaluate the calculated t at α_{pc}. An easy R code can be used to compute the critical t-value at $\alpha_{pc}=0.0167$ which provides critical t-value$=2.552$ for BD.

In order to calculate t:

$$t = \frac{\bar{X}_i - \bar{X}_j}{\sqrt{\frac{2MSW}{n}}} \quad \text{or} \quad F = \frac{\psi^2}{\sum a_j^2 \frac{MSW}{n}}$$

The Bonferroni t can be carried out on linear contrasts by using $t = \frac{\psi}{\sqrt{\sum \alpha_j^2 \frac{MSW}{n}}}$.

Hence, the Bonferroni test is contrasts or multiple t-test with modified α_{pc}. The limitation of the BD procedure is obvious. It will become increasingly conservative with the increasing number of comparisons. A general caution is to not use BD as a post-hoc procedure since it will use all possible comparisons (unlike a select few in a priori comparison) leading to a large value of c and very small value of α_{pc}. For example, for IV having five levels, $c=10$ and $\alpha_{pc} = 0.05/10 = 0.005$, which is a very conservative value. As a post-hoc procedure, BD has lower power (ability to reject false null$=1-\beta$) since it has the smallest possible α_{pc}. Šidák (1967) proposed modification in the Bonferroni procedure. Šidák used multiplicative inequality $P(\alpha_{fw}) \le 1-(1-\alpha_{pc})^c$ and modified α_{pc} by $\alpha_{pc} = 1-(1-\alpha_{fw})^{1/c}$. For example, if we desire $\alpha_{fw}=0.05$, for $c=3$, then

$$\alpha_{pc} = 1-(1-0.05)^{1/3} = 1-0.95^{1/3} = 1-0.9833 = 0.0169$$

You would quickly realize that Dunn–Šidák (DŠ) does not differ much from BD (0.0169 and 0.0167, respectively). The t-value at df$=27$, $\alpha=0.0169/2$ is 2.546 (can be obtained by the R code shown above). If any of the comparisons results in a t-value greater than this, then we reject the null for DŠ. The t-values are already computed in the section on multiple t. The comparisons are as follows:

Group 1 with 2: $t=1.46$. Not greater than the critical BD and not greater than the critical DŠ.
Group 1 with 3: $t=2.227$. Not greater than the critical BD and not greater than the critical DŠ.
Group 2 with 3: $t=3.69$. Greater than the critical BD and greater than the critical DŠ.

The only comparison that turned out to be significant is that between Group 2 and Group 3 for BD as well as DŠ.

To add a note, BD can be used with critical difference (CD) idea. The CD is the difference that is required in means for it to turn out to be significant. Many MCP use this idea. If the difference between two means is larger than the CD, then the mean difference is considered as significant at α for that comparison procedure. The critical difference for BD (CD_{BD}) can be obtained by first finding Z at $\alpha/2$. The Z at alpha=0.0167/2 is 2.394. Then CD_{BD} is obtained by first computing t_{BD} and then computing CD_{BD}.

$$t_{BD} = Z + \frac{Z^3 + Z}{4(df_w - 2)} = 2.394 + \frac{2.394^3 + 2.494}{4(27 - 2)} = 2.55$$

$$CD_{BD} = t_{BD}\sqrt{\frac{2MSW}{n}} = 2.55\sqrt{\frac{2 \times 12.35}{10}} = 4.014$$

$\bar{X}_1 - \bar{X}_2 = 2.3$; $\bar{X}_1 - \bar{X}_3 = 3.5$; and $\bar{X}_2 - \bar{X}_3 = 5.8$. The difference of $\bar{X}_2 - \bar{X}_3 = 5.8$ is larger than $CD_{BD}=4.014$ hence is significant.

8.5.2.5 Holms and Larzelere and Mulaik Test

Holm (1979) and Larzelere and Mulaik (1977) have argued in favor of a multistage test. I am not elaborating the Larzelere and Mulaik test that makes use of correlation coefficients. I am elaborating Holm's procedure. Their method focuses on changing the value of c in the formula $\alpha_{fw}/c = \alpha_{pc}$ as the number of comparisons tested change. If the t-values for all comparisons are ordered and then the first null hypothesis for the largest t is rejected, the next largest t needs to be evaluated at $c-1$ instead of c. The simple logic states that the number of null likely to be falsely rejected are now only $c-1$ and not c. Similarly, for the next largest, it will be $c-2$, and so on. The steps are as follows: (a) compute the t-values as is discussed in BD; (b) disregarding the sign, arrange all t-values as per the ascending order, like, $|t_1| \leq |t_2| \leq \cdots \leq |t_c|$, and c is the number of contrasts tested or comparisons carried out; (c) the $|t_c|$ is tested for significance using Dunn's critical value at c contrasts. Then $|t_{c-1}|$ is tested for significance using Dunn's critical value at $c-1$ contrasts, and so on. This implies that $|t_{c-1}|$ is tested at $\alpha_{pc} = \alpha_{fw}/(c-1)$; (e) the process continues for $|t_{c-2}|$, $|t_{c-3}|$ to $|t_1|$ at denominator being $c-2, c-3, \ldots, 1$. The Holm's test obviously will have higher power than the Bonferroni test since the α_{pc} is the changing value. This test can be used as a post-hoc test as well.

8.5.3 Post-hoc Tests

Post-hoc tests are those types of tests that do not necessarily require beforehand specification of comparison. A priory comparisons idea is to know comparisons in advance and set up contrasts. A scientific theory is expected to make such specific prediction. A priori comparisons are ideal in this situation, particularly when the number of comparisons is limited. At times, researcher may not have the luxury of a priori theoretical knowledge and may also have many comparisons that create serious problems in the application of contrasts. The alternatives are plenty—they all are referred to as post-hoc tests.

8.5.3.1 Least Significant Difference (LSD)

The LSD is obtained by

$$LSD = t_{\alpha/2, dfw}\sqrt{MSW\left(\frac{1}{n_1} + \frac{1}{n_2} + \cdots + \frac{1}{n_k}\right)}$$

where dfw is degrees of freedom within (27 for our data), and MSW is the mean square within (MSW=12.35). In the case of our example, $t_{0.05/2,27} = 2.052$ and

$$LSD = 2.052\sqrt{12.35\left(\frac{2}{10}\right)} = 3.225$$

The null is rejected if $|\bar{X}_1 - \bar{X}_2|$. For the three comparisons:

$|\bar{X}_1 - \bar{X}_2| = 2.3 < 3.225$ null $\mu_1 - \mu_2 = 0$ is accepted. The difference is insignificant.
$|\bar{X}_1 - \bar{X}_3| = 3.5 > 3.225$ null $\mu_1 - \mu_3 = 0$ is rejected. The difference is significant.
$|\bar{X}_2 - \bar{X}_3| = 5.8 > 3.225$ null $\mu_2 - \mu_3 = 0$ is rejected. The difference is significant.

The point to be noted is simple. The LSD is a very liberal test and, hence, $\mu_1 - \mu_3 = 0$ is rejected which was not rejected by other methods of comparisons. Fisher–Hayter test is a modification in Fisher's LSD suggested by Hayter (1986) that attempts reduce the liberal nature of LSD.

```
# R Code 8.9. LSD and Other Tests
library(agricolae)                          # call package agricolae
LSDout<-LSD.test(fit, "gp", p.adj = c("none"))  # LSD test
LSDout                                       # LSD value is 3.22446
# p.adj can be "none" "holm", "hochberg", "bonferroni", "BH", "BY",
"fdr"
# Holm (1979) ("holm"), Hochberg (1988) ("hochberg"), Hommel (1988)
#("hommel"), Benjamini & Hochberg (1995) ("BH" or its alias "fdr"), and
#Benjamini & Yekutieli (2001) ("BY")
```

8.5.3.2 Dunnett's Procedure

Psychologists often conduct experiments that have one control group and some experimental groups. When one control group has to be compared with some treatments then most appropriate procedure is Dunnett's procedure. The critical value of Dunnett's procedure t_D is obtained from tables at $df = k - 1, n - k$. Once it is obtained from the tables, the Dunnett's critical difference can be calculated by

$$CD_D = t_D\sqrt{\frac{2MSW}{n}}$$

Now, for the sake of example, we assume that Group 3 is a control group, then $df = 3 - 1, 30 - 3 = 2, 27$ and t_D is the critical value from the table at $df = n - k, k$. It is 2.33.

$$CD_D = 2.33\sqrt{\frac{2 \times 12.35}{10}} = 3.66$$

The comparisons are as follows since Group 3 is a control group.
$|\bar{X}_1 - \bar{X}_3| = 3.5 < 3.66$ null $\mu_1 - \mu_3 = 0$ is accepted. The difference is insignificant.
$|\bar{X}_2 - \bar{X}_3| = 5.8 > 3.66$ null $\mu_2 - \mu_3 = 0$ is rejected. The difference is significant.

The first comparison is insignificant since we have used a two-sided value of t_D. However, we actually expect the difference to be positive and, hence, the alternative is $\mu_2 > \mu_1$ and $\mu_3 > \mu_1$. The one-tailed value of t_D is 2.00. The CD is

$$CD_D = 2.00\sqrt{\frac{2 \times 12.35}{10}} = 3.14$$

Now, both differences are significant. I am not providing the Dunnett's table for one-tailed and two-tailed values. Instead, I encourage you to use R code. This R code requires control group values to come first in ANOVA. So change the R syntax accordingly so that the control group values are entered first, and then run the 'aov' syntax. You shall have to run the ANOVA syntax with grouping variable specified as numerical vector.

```
R Code 8.10. Dunnett's Procedure
library(multcomp)
fit2<- glht(fit, linfct = mcp(gp = "Dunnett"), alternative = "greater")
# write "greater". Fit is output of 'aov'
summary(fit2)
```

8.5.3.3 Studentized Range Statistics (q)

Many statistical procedures, particularly MCP, utilize studentized range statistics (q). The studentized range statistics is

$$q_r = \frac{\bar{X}_L - \bar{X}_S}{\sqrt{MSW/n}}$$

where $\bar{X}_L$ and $\bar{X}_S$ are the largest and smallest mean in the set of comparisons, r is the number of treatments (groups) in a set, and MSW is mean square within of ANOVA. The q can be converted into t by $t = q/\sqrt{2}$ or $q = t\sqrt{2}$.

The table of studentized range statistics is provided in Appendix C6.

Let's carry out the computation.

$$\bar{X}_1 = 23.4, \bar{X}_2 = 25.7, \quad \text{and} \quad \bar{X}_3 = 19.9. \quad \text{The } q \text{ is}$$

$$q_r = \frac{\bar{X}_L - \bar{X}_S}{\sqrt{MSW/n}} = \frac{25.7 - 19.9}{\sqrt{12.35/10}} = \frac{5.8}{1.11} = 5.21$$

The transformation of q to t gives us $t = 5.21/\sqrt{2} = 3.690$. Obviously, the only difference in t and q formula is that 2MSW is used in the denominator for t and only MSW is used for q. The table provided $q_{0.05}$ for $df=27$, $r=3$ which is 3.51. You can obtain it by using an R code. The obtained value $5.21 > 3.51$ and is significant at 0.05 level implying that there is a significant difference between the largest and smallest mean.

R Code 8.11. Studentized Range Statistics
```
qtukey(p, r, df, lower = F)     # compute studentized range value
qtukey(.05, 3, 27, lower = F)   # for the data
```

8.5.3.4 Tukey's HSD or WSD Test

John Tukey[4] is one of the early workers in the area of MCP. Tukey's honestly significant difference (HSD) or wholly significant difference (WSD) is MCP that used studentized range statistics. The critical difference is HSD:

$$HSD = q\sqrt{\frac{MSW}{n}}$$

where q is the studentized range statistics obtained from table ($q=3.506$) and MSW is the mean square within. The HSD for the above example is

$$HSD = q\sqrt{\frac{MSW}{n}} = 3.506\sqrt{\frac{12.35}{10}} = 3.506 \times 1.11 = 3.897$$

---

[4] John Tukey (1915–2000) is an American mathematician who is famous for his contribution to the fast Fourier transform algorithm (Cooley–Tukey FFT algorithm), estimation of spectra of time series, and so on. He also contributed to the distinction between exploratory analysis and confirmatory analysis. Tukey introduced the term "bit" for binary digits. He introduced boxplots in his work *Exploratory Data Analysis* (1977). Tukey Lambda distribution, Tukey's test of additivity, Tukey's lemma, Jackknife estimation (Quenouille–Tukey jackknife) are some of his other notable contributions to statistics. He is credited for creating a robust estimation as a sub-discipline of statistics.

The null is rejected if $|\bar{X}_1 - \bar{X}_2| > \text{HSD}$. For the three comparisons,
$|\bar{X}_1 - \bar{X}_2| = 2.3 < 3.90$ null $\mu_1 - \mu_2 = 0$ is accepted. The difference is insignificant.
$|\bar{X}_1 - \bar{X}_3| = 3.5 < 3.90$ null $\mu_1 - \mu_3 = 0$ is accepted. The difference is insignificant.
$|\bar{X}_2 - \bar{X}_3| = 5.8 > 3.90$ null $\mu_2 - \mu_3 = 0$ is rejected. The difference is significant.
This implies that the mean difference of 3.90 and greater is significant at 0.05 level of significance. The $\bar{X}_2 - \bar{X}_3$ is the only difference that is larger than 3.90 and is significant at 0.05 level. We conclude that $\mu_2 > \mu_3$. The R code for HSD is as follows:

R Code 8.12. Tukey HSD Statistics and Plot
```
fit <- aov(data~gp)                                     # aov is function
TukeyHSD(fit)                                           # Output of HSD
library(multcomp)                                       # load multcomp
fit.mc<-glht(fit, linfct = mcp(gp = "Tukey"))          # HSD by multcomp
summary(fit.mc)                                         # output of HSD
plot(cld(fit.mc))                                       # groupwise boxplot
library("HH")                                           # call HH library
fit.mmc <- mmc(fit, linfct = mcp(gp = "Tukey"), focus = "gp") # HSD
plot(fit.mmc)                                           # 95% confidence interval
HSD plot
```

8.5.3.5 Tukey–Kramer Procedure: HSD for Unequal Sample

The Tukey HSD is devised for equal sample sizes. For unequal sample sizes, a variant of Tukey's HSD has been proposed by Tukey and Kramer. $\sqrt{\text{MSW}/n}$ is replaced by $\sqrt{\dfrac{\dfrac{\text{MSE}}{n_1} + \dfrac{\text{MSE}}{n_2}}{2}}$

The remaining calculations are similar to the Tukey HSD. The problem of unequal n doesn't occur in case of our example, and even of you solve it using Tukey-Kramer, the solution is identical to HSD for equal sample-size.

8.5.3.6 Games–Howell Procedure: Unequal n and Unequal Variances

The Games–Howell procedure is more popular than the Tukey–Kramer procedure since it adjusts for the inequality of variances as well as the inequality of sample size. The Games–Howell procedure used Tukey's idea to compute the critical difference, but it employs separate estimates of variances, and also computes df adjusted for difference in sample size and variances. The Games–Howell procedure makes use of the Behrens–Fisher problem. The critical difference for Games–Howell is

$$\text{CD}_{\text{GH}} = q_{0.05(r,\text{df}')}\sqrt{\dfrac{\dfrac{S_1^2}{n_1} + \dfrac{S_2^2}{n_2}}{2}}$$

The CD_{GH} is the critical difference for a given comparison, q is a studentized range statistics, df' is obtained by the following formula per comparison and rounded to the nearest integer.

$$\text{df}' = \left(\dfrac{S_1^2}{n_1} + \dfrac{S_2^2}{n_2}\right) \Bigg/ \dfrac{\left(\dfrac{S_1^2}{n_1}\right)^2}{n_1 - 1} + \dfrac{\left(\dfrac{S_2^2}{n_1}\right)^2}{n_2 - 1}$$

It's obvious that the CD_{GH} will be a different value for different comparison. The df' for $|\bar{X}_1 - \bar{X}_2|$ is 17.992; df' for $\bar{X}_1 - \bar{X}_3$ is 16.98; and df' for $\bar{X}_2 - \bar{X}_3$ is 17.129. The CD_{GH} for $\bar{X}_1 - \bar{X}_2$

Table 8.5. *Summary of Games–Howell Procedure*

Mean Diff	$|\bar{X}_i - \bar{X}_j|$	df'	CD$_{GH}$	Significance
$\bar{X}_1 - \bar{X}_2$	$23.4 - 25.7 = 2.3$	$17.99 \approx 18$	3.65	*ns*
$\bar{X}_1 - \bar{X}_3$	$23.4 - 19.9 = 3.5$	$16.98 \approx 17$	4.18	*ns*
$\bar{X}_2 - \bar{X}_3$	$25.7 - 19.9 = 5.8$	$17.13 \approx 17$	4.22	P<0.05

is 3.65; CD$_{GH}$ for $\bar{X}_2 - \bar{X}_3, \bar{X}_1 - \bar{X}_3$ is 4.18; CD$_{GH}$ for $X_2 - X_3$ is 4.21. $\bar{X}_2 - \bar{X}_3 \bar{\chi}_2 - \bar{\chi}_3$ is larger than the CD$_{GH}$ (5.8>4.21) and, hence, the Games–Howell procedure concluded that for $\bar{X}_2 - \bar{X}_3$ the population mean difference is non-zero (see Table 8.5). Generally, the power of Tukey's test is better than that of BD when all possible comparisons are carried out. The BD may have advantage when a smaller subset of comparisons is used.

8.5.3.7 Scheffé Test

The Scheffé[5] test is historically the most popular procedure for multiple comparisons. Scheffé test, like Tukey's HSD, uses constant critical values for all comparisons. The Scheffé test is useful for unplanned comparisons. It is considered as one of the most conservative procedures. The Scheffé test can be computed as follows:

$$CD_S = \sqrt{(k-1)(F_{\text{dfb,dfw}})}\sqrt{\frac{2MSW}{n}}$$

In the case of our example, the Scheffé test critical difference is as follows:
For $F_{2,27} = 3.35$ at alpha$=0.05$, $k=3$, MSW$=12.35$, the

$$CD_S = \sqrt{(3-1)(3.35)}\sqrt{\frac{2 \times 12.35}{10}} = 2.588 \times 1.57 = 4.068$$

The only mean difference that is larger than 4.068 is $\bar{X}_2 - \bar{X}_3$ which is $25.7 - 19.9 = 5.8$.
The other way to compute is $F_S = F_{\text{dfb,dfw}}(k-1)$ which will provide critical *F*-value for the Scheffé. Then compute *F* for all possible comparisons and if the critical value is smaller than computed, then it is significant. Due to the conservative nature of the Scheffé test, some have suggested to use $\alpha_{fw} = 0.10$ instead of 0.05. This test is useful if the same α_{fw} is to be maintained across comparisons. Generally BD will have more power than Scheffé for smaller number of comparisons. However, as Bonferroni inequality suggests, Scheffé will have more power for a smaller subset.

8.5.3.8 Newman–Keuls Procedure

Newman (1939) and Keuls (1952) developed this procedure that uses studentized range statistics and at times is referred to as the Student–Newman–Keuls test. The procedure is as follows. First, the means are arranged in order (from lowest to highest).

$$\bar{X}_3 = 19.9 \quad \bar{X}_1 = 23.4 \quad \bar{X}_2 = 27.7$$

---

[5] Henry Scheffé (1907–1977) was an American statistician who worked in different areas of statistics. He started his career in pure mathematics and later worked with Jerzy Neyman, Samuel Wilks, John Tukey, and others on statistical problems, primarily at Princeton. His comprehensive review of nonparametric methods (1943) and work on the analysis of variance (1959) are his important contributions.

This procedure uses steps (*s*) in computing critical *q* value. The number of steps in comparison of two adjacent means (e.g., 19.9 and 23.4) is 2. The step is counting the number of means from a lower mean to a higher mean (both included). So a comparison between $\bar{X}_3$ and $\bar{X}_2$ requires three steps. The critical value of *q* (studentized range statistics) is computed on the basis of number of steps as the number of group. The *q* value differs as the steps differ and, hence, this is called stepwise or layered procedure. The Newman–Keuls (NK) procedure is carried out in following manner. First, the maximum difference is tested for significance, then the second bigger difference, and so on. This shall stop once any of the differences turns out to be insignificant. Then further smaller differences are not evaluated. The critical difference for the NK procedure is

$$\mathrm{CD}_{\mathrm{NK}} = q_{(\mathrm{steps,dfw})}\sqrt{\frac{\mathrm{MSW}}{n}}$$

where $\mathrm{CD}_{\mathrm{NK}}$ is the critical difference required, $q_{(\mathrm{steps,dfw})}$ is the tabled value of *q* at df=steps, dfw. The alternative way to compute the significance of comparison is to compute $q = \dfrac{\bar{X}_l - \bar{X}_s}{\sqrt{\dfrac{\mathrm{MSW}}{n}}}$ and

test it against $q_{(\mathrm{steps,dfw})}$ which is the tabled value for the comparison. The problem with NK is that the family-wise error rate is larger than 0.05 when comparisons are performed with 0.05. Because of this limitation, NK is becoming less recommended a procedure.

8.5.3.9 Ryan–Einot–Gabriel–Welsch Q (REGWQ) Procedure

The **Ryan–Einot–Gabriel–Welsch Q (REGWQ)** procedure is a modification of Ryan's work (1960). It was subsequently modified by others and is now known as REGWQ. Ryan (1960) used the Bonferroni approach to adjust the error rate, however, with a modification. Bonferroni kept $\alpha_{\mathrm{fw}}/c = \alpha_{\mathrm{pc}}$ constant across comparisons. Ryan suggested α_{pc} be modified per step. Similar suggestion was given by Newman–Keuls; however, unlike Newman–Keuls, Ryan's modification keeps family-wise error rate at α_{fw}. If means are *k*, and step size is *r*, then, according to Ryan (1960), the critical value of q_{steps} can be computed at the $\alpha_r = \dfrac{\alpha_{\mathrm{fw}}}{k/r} = \dfrac{r\alpha_{\mathrm{fw}}}{k}$ level of significance. That is, if steps are 2 and *k*=3, then α_r=0.033. The critical value of *q* is to be computed at α_r=0.033. Einot and Gabriel (1975) introduced a modification in computing α_r at

$$\alpha_r = 1 - (1 - \alpha_{\mathrm{fw}})^{1/(k/r)}$$
$$\alpha_r = 1 - (1 - \alpha_{\mathrm{fw}})^{r/k}$$

level of significance leading to a slight increase in the α_r value resulting in a slightly smaller critical *q* value. You would quickly realize that Einot and Gabriel (1975) are using Šidák's idea rather than Bonferroni's idea as used by Ryan. Welch (1977) suggested that Ryan–Einot–Gabriel computation for critical *q* should use α_{fw} instead of α_r when *r*=*k* and *r*=k–1. α_{fw} now remains at α with these modifications. The name REGWQ reflects the contributions of all. Various R codes are available for these computations; however, I suggest using your own function that is a quick solution. Use [qtukey] to obtain critical value.

8.5.3.10 Hochberg GT2

The Hochberg GT2 (Hochberg, 1974) is a test that is a modification which uses the Tukey–Kramer *t*-test, modifies Šidák inequality and evaluates that by using studentized maximum modulus

(SMM) distribution. This test is known to be more conservative (meaning less powerful) than Tukey–Kramer with unequal n and more conservative than Tukey with equal n. Stoline and Ury (1979) provided tables for SMM values. Gabriel (1978) proposed another method that is more liberal than Hochberg GT2, which uses the SMM distribution.

8.5.3.11 Hochberg H2, Tamhane T2, and Dunnett T3

Hochberg proposed a procedure (H2) that used Bonferroni inequality and Welch approximation. Tamhane (1979)[6] modified this procedure by using Šidák multiplicative inequality. Dunnett (1980) modified T2 by using Kimball inequality and referred to it as the T3 procedure. The details are avoided since better procedures are available and present description is provided to keep the reader informed.

8.5.3.12 Benjamini–Hochberg Test

The Benjamini–Hochberg test uses false discovery rate (FDR) as a central concept. Other tests aim to maintain the FWER (α_{fw}) at a certain value for all comparisons and some of them focus on changing α_{pc} in a sequential manner. Benjamini and Hochberg (1995, 2000) have developed an alternative thinking focusing on FDR that is becoming increasingly popular. The FDR is an interesting idea. The traditional idea focuses on type I error (as if it is the only error in statistical inference) and tries to control α_{pc}, and if one of the comparisons is wrong, then the entire set of comparison is considered as erroneous. Benjamini–Hochberg looks at the percentage of significant results or discoveries that are false significant results or false discoveries. The FDR is conceptualized as

$$\text{FDR} = \frac{\text{False Significant Results}}{\text{Total Significant Results}} = \frac{\text{No. of False Rejection of } H_0}{\text{No. of } H_0 \text{ Rejected}}$$

Suppose we test 20 null hypotheses and reject 10 of them. If two of the rejections are false, then the FDR is $2/10 = 0.20$. If you straightway interpret 0.20 as the FWER, then it looks outrageously high, but Benjamini and Hochberg (1995, 2000) showed that over many trials it will settle to 0.05. They have proposed many tests that do this job. I shall explain Benjamini and Hochberg's linear step up (BH-LSU) procedure that is useful for pairwise contrasts. For our example, we have three pairwise contrasts; hence, $k = 3$. The t-statistic and probability associated with t-statistics can be computed for these contrasts. You have to rank the contrast by p-values. Table 8.6 shows the illustration. The rank of p column ranks p-values from lowest to highest, and contrasts in the table are arranged accordingly. The $p_{crit} = \alpha \left(\dfrac{i}{k} \right)$ is obtained by setting the desired FDR $= \alpha = 0.05$. We move from the highest value of i to lower values. The decision rule is as follows: if $p > p_{crit}$, the null is accepted and the next comparison is evaluated; if $p < p_{crit}$, then the null is rejected for this and further comparisons.

Table 8.6. *Summary of Benjamini–Hochberg Procedure*

Pair for contrast	t-value	p-value	I (rank of p)	p_{crit}	Significance
$\bar{X}_1 - \bar{X}_2$	1.463	0.1549	3	0.05	No
$\bar{X}_1 - \bar{X}_3$	2.227	0.0345	2	0.0333	No
$\bar{X}_2 - \bar{X}_3$	3.691	0.00099	1	0.01667	Yes

---

[6] Ajit Tamhane is working at Northwestern University and his primary contributions are in data-analytics, experimental designs, and multiple comparison procedures. He worked with Yosef Hochberg on MCP and developed variations of few.

The Benjamini–Hochberg procedure is popular since it is slightly more liberal without compromising on FDR. There are few more procedures elaborated by Benjamini and Hochberg which are not explained here.

8.5.3.13 Waller–Duncan Bayesian Test

The Waller–Duncan (WD) test uses the Bayesian approach[7] and it does not typically aim at controlling type I error. The WD test attempts to minimize the Bayes risk for the additive loss function. The additive loss function is a sum of loss functions for each comparison. You have to specify the value of K. The value of $K = 50$, $K = 100$, $K = 500$ are approximately corresponding to alpha = 0.10, 0.05, and 0.001, respectively. $K = k_1/k_0$. The k_0 is a constant with which mean difference is multiplied when null is incorrectly accepted and k_1 is a constant with which mean difference is multiplied when the null is incorrectly rejected. K implies that k_1 is K-times higher than k_0. The critical difference required for WD is

$$CD_{WD} = t_B \sqrt{\frac{2MSW}{n}}$$

The null is rejected by Waller–Duncan if the difference between means is larger than the critical difference required for WD.

$$\bar{X}_i - \bar{X}_j \geq t_B \sqrt{\frac{2MSW}{n}}$$

where t_B is the Bayesian *t*-value which is a decreasing function of *F*-value. The R code for Waller–Duncan is given below.

```
# R Code 8.13. Waller-Duncan Bayesian Test
library(agricolae)   # Call package 'agricolae'
fit<-aov(data~gp)
wdout<-waller.test(fit, "gp", K = 100, console=F)   # WD test
wdout$parameters     # Waller is t_B
wdout$statistics     # CriticalDifference is CD_WD
wdout$means
```

8.5.4 Comparison of MCP and Choosing MCP

Choosing an appropriate MCP is not an easy task, not just because of the multiplicity of a test but also because researchers' need (research question) determines the appropriateness of a test. A general caution I suggest is that if you are planning a priori tests, then do the comparisons that you have planned and don't plan the comparisons after doing them (though one may feel tempted). For few planned comparisons I would recommend orthogonal contrasts. For small number of planned comparisons, Holm or DŠ is a useful option. In the case of a large number of (not necessarily all) comparisons, REGWQ is a good option. The Tukey HSD is also a good option though slightly more conservative. In the case of unequal sample sizes and unequal variances, the Games–Howell procedure is recommended. The use of the NK procedure is not recommended for the reasons discussed. Dunnett's procedure is useful in the case of experiments with control-group. The Benjamini–Hochberg and Waller–Duncan

---

[7] The Bayesian approach uses Bayes theorem to infer posterior probability by using a prior probability and a likelihood function obtained from a statistical model for observed data. Generally, non-informative prior is used to obtain objective Bayesian estimates.

Table 8.7. *Comparison of MCP*

Test	Error rate	Comparison	Power*	Type (a priori/ Post-hoc)	Conditions for use	Limitation
Usual t	PC	Pairwise	Highest	A priori		Large p
Bonferonni DŠ	FW	Any Contrast	Reasonably high with small c	A priori	Small c	Not recommended for large c
Linear Contrasts	PC	Any Contrast	Reasonably high	A priori	Few pre-specified contrasts	Not useful for unspecified comparisons
Holm	FW	Any Contrast	>Bonferroni	A priori or Post-hoc	As above+better control FWER	Not for large c
LSD	FW	Pairwise	Too Liberal	Post-hoc	Not recommended	Liberal
Dunnett's	FW	Control group	Reasonably high	Post-hoc	Compare with Control group	Useful only for control group
HSD	FW	Pairwise	> Bonferroni for all comparisons	Post-hoc	Tighter control over type I	Conservative
Scheffé	FW	Any contrast	Very conservative	Post-hoc	As above	Very Conservative
NK	FW	Pairwise	Problems	Post-hoc	Not recommended	Higher than specified alpha
REGWQ	FW	Pairwise	Reasonable	Post-hoc	Stepwise, all pairwise comparisons	Low power for less than all pc
Benjamini–Hochberg	FDR	Any Contrast	High	Post-hoc	Control on FDR	
Waller–Duncan	Bayesian Loss Function	Pairwise	High	Post-hoc	Controlling K	

Note: * A direct comparison of power is generally not recommended since tests have different form of comparisons. This column is indicative and not absolute.

procedures do not control for FWER like traditional ones. The Benjamini–Hochberg controls for FDR, whereas Waller–Duncan uses the Bayesian loss function logic. As Howell (2008) noted, Benjamini–Hochberg is the preferred option because it is not invalidating family of comparisons for one false rejection. I would also prefer Waller–Duncan because of inherent properties of the Bayesian logic. Table 8.7 provides a summary of comparisons of the multiple comparison procedures.

8.6 REPEATED MEASURES ONE-WAY ANOVA

8.6.1 Basic Ideas

The preceding section has discussed the one-way ANOVA procedure for independent groups. This section introduces repeated measures one-way ANOVA. The repeated measures ANOVA is also known as ANOVA for dependent samples and correlated means ANOVA. The dependence is created because the participants are matched on some variable (matched group designs) or the same set of participants is exposed to all conditions. The following section discusses the structural model of repeated measures ANOVA, logic of split of variance, computational formulas, and R codes. The major advantage of the repeated measures design is that participants act as their own control. In psychological experiments, individual differences has been a troublesome source of contamination in randomized experiments and repeated measures experiments have been considered as experimental designs with higher power. Another advantage of repeated measures design is drastic reduction in the number of participants required. The experiment with three conditions and 10 participants per condition (total 30 participants for independent groups) requires only 10 participants for the entire experiment. However, **practice effect** is one limitation of repeated measures experiments. The performance of participants may improve with practice as they are exposed to experimental conditions or may deteriorate when tasks are demanding and lead to fatigue. This is generically referred to as practice effect. Practice Effect can be controlled by many ways; two most prominently used methods are (a) counterbalancing and (b) randomization of orders.

Counterbalancing: It provides crossover designs and Latin square designs. For the **crossover designs**, all possible orders need to be obtained. For example, in the case of three conditions (A, B, C), the possible orders are $3! = 3 \times 2 \times 1 = 6$. They are *ABC, ACB, BAC, BCA, CAB*, and *CBA*. Equal number of participants are allotted to each order. Even if we allot five participants, we shall need $5 \times 6 = 30$ participants. The counter-ordering is also a control available (BAC and CAB). The **Latin squares design** is another option. Latin square designs can be diagrammatically represented in Table 8.8. Latin square[8] is a repeated measures design in which each condition in each row (order) and column (position in the order) occurs only once. Suppose, we have four levels of IV, then total orders are $4! = 4 \times 3 \times 2 \times 1 = 24$. So many orders cannot be

Table 8.8. *Latin Square for Single Factor Four-Level Repeated Measures Design: The Levels Are A, B, C, D and Position in the Order is Are P1, P2, P3, P4.*

Order	Position in Order			
	P1	**P2**	**P3**	**P4**
1	A	C	B	D
2	B	A	D	C
3	C	D	A	B
4	D	B	C	A

[8] The term Latin is originally used because Euler used Latin characters in the squares.

manipulated. Hence, only those orders in which each condition is once at each position (in order) are used[9].

Randomization of orders: The statistical theory underneath repeated measures designs assume that the order of experimental conditions is randomly created. Since all orders are equally likely, there is no systematic bias created by orders. The error term contains the variance that is due to orders experienced by participants.

8.6.2 Structural Model of Repeated Measures ANOVA

The structural model for one-way repeated measures ANOVA is as follows:

$$X_{ij} = \mu + \pi_i + \tau_j + e_{ij}$$

where

X_{ij} is a score of the ith participants in the jth treatment

μ is a grand mean

π_i is a constant of the ith person

τ_j is a constant associated with the jth treatment

e_{ij} is the error associated with the ith participants in the jth treatment

π_i represents the extent to which each person's/subject's score departs from the mean of the person/subject. It is assumed to be distributed with mean zero. τ_j is representative of the difference between treatment mean and average treatment mean.

e_{ij} is distributed around the mean zero. It is further assumed that e_{ij} and π_i are independently distributed and they have identical variance across treatments.

The treatment effect is stated as $\sum_{j=1}^{k} \tau_j = 0$. This implies that the mean of a specific population

is $\mu_j = \mu + \tau_j$, and since $\sum_{j=1}^{k} \tau_j = 0$, the $\mu_j = 0$. The null is $H_0 : \mu_1 = \mu_2 = \cdots = \mu_k$ which can be stated

as $H_0 : \tau_j = 0$ for $j = 1, \ldots, k$; and $H_A : \tau_j \neq 0$ for at least one j.

The complete model is stated as

$$X_{ij} = \mu + \pi_i + \tau_j + (\pi\tau)_{ij} + e_{ij}$$

The notation $(\pi\tau)_{ij}$ represents an interaction between the ith subject and the jth experimental condition. The estimate of $(\pi\tau)_{ij}$ is not possible, since there is only one score per participant per condition. And for the same reason, the model reduces to

$$X_{ij} = \mu + \pi_i + \tau_j + [(\pi\tau)_{ij} + e_{ij}]$$

It is generally expressed as

$$X_{ij} = \mu + \pi_i + \tau_j + e_{ij}$$

The partition of the sum of squares is as follows:

$$SS_T = SS_{treat} + SS_{sub} + SS_{error}$$

---

[9] The Latin square with odd number of conditions requires such two tables. For odd number of conditions randomly permuted, Latin square can be used.

8.6.3 Computation for Repeated Measures One-way ANOVA

The computation of repeated measures one-way ANOVA requires computation of the respective sum of squares. The sum-of-squares total is

$$SS_T = \sum_{i=1}^{n_{total}} \left(X_{ij} - \overline{\overline{X}} \right)^2$$

where $\overline{\overline{X}}$ is the grand mean which is an estimator of μ, X_{ij} is a value of ith individual in the jth group, and SS_T is the sum-of-squares total. The sum-of-squares treatment (SS_{treat}, between or IV) is

$$SS_{treat} = \sum_{j=1}^{k} n \left(\overline{X}_j - \overline{\overline{X}} \right)^2$$

where $\overline{X}_j$ is the mean of the jth condition, k is the total number of conditions of levels of IV, and n is the sample size. The sum-of-square subject (SS_{Sub}) is

$$SS_{sub} = \sum_{i=1}^{n_{sub}} k \left(\overline{X}_{sub} - \overline{\overline{X}} \right)^2$$

where $\overline{X}_{sub}$ is the mean of the ith subject. The sum-of-squares error is obtained by

$$SS_{error} = SS_T - \left(SS_{treat} + SS_{sub} \right)$$

The degrees of freedom are as follows:

$$df_T = n_{total} - 1; df_{treat} = k - 1; df_{sub} = n_{sub} - 1; \quad \text{and} \quad df_{error} = df_{treat} \times df_{sub}$$

The mean square is computed as follows:

$$MS_{treat} = SS_{treat} / df_{treat}$$
$$MS_{error} = SS_{error} / df_{error}$$

The *F*-ratio is obtained as $F = \dfrac{MS_{treat}}{MS_{error}}$.

Example: Denis Dutton (2009) argued in favor of evolutionary foundations of art and aesthetic taste. Dutton argued that certain artistic values are universal and shaped by natural selection. One of the well-cited examples is preference for landscapes (Balling & Falk, 1982; Orians & Heerwagen, 1992)—the visual landscapes having characteristics resembling the habitat of savanna (low-relief, sparsely wooded tropical grassland, presence of vegetation, animal, or bird life, presence of water in the view, road extending to distance, mountains in far). I tried to test this hypothesis by presenting three types of landscape drawings (rain forests, deciduous forest, and savanna) to children for rating the most desirable place to live.[10] The participants were shown drawings of three landscapes randomly and they rated them on a 10-point scale. A subset of data of average rating is shown in Table 8.9.

---

[10] This is part of one of the experiments conducted to evaluate human landscape preferences at Center for Experimental and Computational Social Sciences (CECSS) at University of Mumbai. The center has conducted research in the field of experimental and behavioral economics, evolutionary determinant of human preferences, and decision-making.

Table 8.9. *Data for Landscape Preferences Experiment*

Participants	Rain forest	Deciduous forest	Savanna	$\bar{X}_{sub}$	$\hat{\pi}_i = \bar{X}_{sub} - \bar{\bar{X}}$
P1	1	2	4	2.33	−2.17
P2	4	4	7	5.00	0.50
P3	2	3	7	4.00	−0.50
P4	5	4	6	5.00	0.50
P5	5	6	7	6.00	1.50
P6	5	6	7	6.00	1.50
P7	3	3	5	3.67	−0.83
P8	4	3	8	5.00	0.50
P9	5	4	4	4.33	−0.17
P10	1	5	5	3.67	−0.83
Mean	**3.5**	**4**	**6**	**4.50**	

Estimate of τ_j is $\hat{\tau}_j = \bar{X}_j - \bar{\bar{X}}$. They are as follows:

$$\hat{\tau}_{RF} = \bar{X}_{RF} - \bar{\bar{X}} = 3.5 - 4.5 = -1$$

$$\hat{\tau}_{DF} = \bar{X}_{DF} - \bar{\bar{X}} = 4 - 4.5 = -0.5$$

$$\hat{\tau}_{SAV} = \bar{X}_{SAV} - \bar{\bar{X}} = 6 - 4.5 = 1.5$$

$$\sum_{j=1}^{k} \hat{\tau}_j = (-1) + (-0.5) + (1.5) = 0$$

8.6.3.1 Calculations

$$SS_T = \sum_{i=1}^{n_{total}} \left(X_{ij} - \bar{\bar{X}} \right)^2 = (1 - 4.5)^2 + (4 - 4.5)^2 + \cdots + (4 - 4.5)^2 = (5 - 4.5)^2 = 93.5$$

$$SS_{treat} = \sum_{j=1}^{k} n \left(\bar{X}_j - \bar{\bar{X}} \right)^2 = 10(3.5 - 4.5)^2 + 10(4 - 4.5)^2 + 10(6 - 4.5)^2 = 35$$

$$SS_{sub} = \sum_{i=1}^{n_{sub}} k \left(\bar{X}_{sub} - \bar{\bar{X}} \right)^2 = 3(2.33 - 4.5)^2 + 3(5 - 4.5)^2 + \cdots + 3(3.67 - 4.5)^2 = 34.83$$

$$SS_{error} = SS_T - (SS_{treat} + SS_{sub}) = 93.5 - (35 + 34.83) = 23.67$$

The R code for one-way repeated measures ANOVA is as follows.

```
# R Code 8.14. One-way Repeated Measures ANOVA
rating <- c(1, 4, 2, 5, 5, 5, 3, 4, 5, 1, 2, 4, 3, 4, 6, 6, 3, 3, 4, 5,
4, 7, 7, 6, 7, 7, 5, 8, 4, 5)          #
subject <- c("A", "B", "C", "D", "E", "F", "G", "H", "I", "J","A", "B",
"C", "D", "E", "F", "G", "H", "I", "J","A", "B", "C", "D", "E", "F",
"G", "H", "I", "J")      # A to J are 10 participants
```

Table 8.10. *Summary Table for Repeated Measures ANOVA*

Source	SS	df	MS = SS/df	F	P
SS_{sub}	34.83	$df_{sub} = n_{sub} - 1 = 10 - 1 = 9$	3.87	$F = \dfrac{MS_{treat}}{MS_{error}}$	<0.01
SS_{treat}	35.00	$df_{treat} = k - 1 = 3 - 1 = 2$	17.50		
SS_{error}	23.67	$df_{error} = df_{treat} \times df_{sub} = 2 \times 9 = 18$	1.315	$= \dfrac{17.5}{1.315} = 13.31$	
SS_T	93.50	$df_T = n_{total} - 1 = 30 - 1 = 29$			

```
land <- c("RF", "RF", "RF", "RF", "RF", "RF", "RF", "RF", "RF", "RF",
"DF", "DF", "DF", "DF", "DF", "DF", "DF", "DF", "DF", "DF", "SAV",
"SAV", "SAV", "SAV", "SAV", "SAV", "SAV", "SAV", "SAV", "SAV") # RF =
# Rain forest; DF = Deciduous forest; SAV = savanna
land <- factor (land)
data <- data.frame (rating, subject, land)   # Type data to know data
                                                       entry
attach (data)
fit <- aov (rating ~ land + Error(subject/land), data)
summary (fit)         # generates summary table
# Error(subject/land) is specification of SS subject.
#Output
Error: subject
              Df   Sum Sq   Mean  Sq F value   Pr(>F)
Residuals   9    34.83    3.87

Error: subject:land
              Df   Sum Sq   Mean     Sq F value   Pr(>F)
land        2    35.00    17.500   13.31          0.000283 ***
Residuals   18   23.67    1.315

---

Signif. codes:
0 '***' 0.001 '**' 0.01 '*' 0.05 '.' 0.1 ' ' 1
```

The null hypothesis stating that the population means of all conditions (RF, DF, SAV) are identical is rejected. The alternative stating that at least one pair of means is significantly different is accepted. The summary of ANOVA is provided in Table 8.10.

8.6.4 Contrasts for Repeated Measures Design

As we have tested contrasts for independent samples designs, we can also test for contrasts for repeated measures designs. Suppose we want to compare SAV with RF and with DF, we specify two contrasts: 1, 0, −1 and 0, 1, −1.

For the first contrast, the t-value is 4.87, at df=18, P<0.05 (tabled value of t=2.10 at df=18).

Similarly, if you test the second contrast (0, −1, 1), the t-value is 3.90, at df=18, P<0.05. Both the t-values indicate that the population mean of DV (ratings desirability of a place to live) for savanna landscapes is higher than the population mean for rain forest and deciduous forests respectively, thus providing support to the evolutionary argument about landscape preferences. You can also test contrast −0.5, −0.5, 1, implying that the average of RF and DF is equal to SAV (t will be 5.07). Table 8.11 is a schematic representation of the contrast computation.

Table 8.11. *Contrast Computation for Repeated Measures ANOVA*

	RF	DF	SAV	
Mean	3.5	4	6	
Coefficient	−1	0	1	$\sum a_i^2 = 2$
$a_j \bar{x}_j$	−3.5	0	6	$\psi = \sum a_j \bar{X}_j = 2.5$

$$\sqrt{\frac{(\sum a_j^2)MS_{error}}{n}} = 0.513 \qquad t = \frac{\psi}{\sqrt{\frac{(\sum a_j^2)MS_{error}}{n}}} = 4.87$$

8.6.5 Post-hoc Test: Example with Tukey's HSD

The Tukey's HSD is exemplified here; however, one should wisely choose options.

$$\text{HSD} = q\sqrt{\frac{\text{MS}_{\text{error}}}{n}}$$

q is obtained at $\text{df}_{\text{residual}}$, that is $q_{(3,18)} = 3.61$ at $p=0.05$. The HSD is 1.309. The mean differences are as follows:

$|\overline{X}_{\text{RF}} - \overline{X}_{\text{SAV}}| = |3.5 - 6| = 2.5$ is greater than 1.309 and is significant.
$|\overline{X}_{\text{DF}} - \overline{X}_{\text{SAV}}| = |4 - 6| = 2$ is greater than 1.309 and is significant.
$|\overline{X}_{\text{RF}} - \overline{X}_{\text{DF}}| = |3.5 - 4| = 0.5$ is smaller than 1.309 and is insignificant.

This leads to the conclusion that the population mean of savanna is greater than the other two conditions but population means of RF and DF do not differ.

8.6.6 Assumption of Sphericity

The assumption of sphericity refers to the constant variance and constant covariance of the population variance–covariance matrix (Σ), which is estimated by the sample variance–covariance matrix ($\hat{\Sigma}$) which is shown in Table 8.12 for our data.

Mauchly's sphericity test is commonly used for testing this assumption. It is a stringent test and options like Greenhouse and Geisser (1959), Huynh and Feldt (1976) are also available. They are not recommended due to issues associated with them.

```
# R Code 8.15. Mauchly's Test and Repeated Measures ANOVA
library(car)        # call package "car"
mat <- with(data, cbind(rating[land=="RF"], rating[land=="DF"],
rating[land=="SAV"]))      # binding the columns
lmmodel <- lm(mat ~ 1)     # creating multivariate linear model
fact <- factor(c("RF", "DF", "SAV"))   # list IV
# Now carry out ANOVA and Mauchly Tests for Sphericity
aov <- Anova(lmmodel, idata=data.frame(fact), idesign=~fact, type="III")
summary(aov, multivariate=F)

# Alternative way to do Mauchly test
library(ez)         # call package 'ez'
ezANOVA(data=data, dv=. (rating), wid=. (subject), within=. (land),
type=3)
This code will provide similar results.
```

The Mauchly test statistics value is 0.978 and the *p*-value is 0.916, indicating that the null hypothesis of sphericity is accepted. Hence, we need not look for more options.

Table 8.12. *Variance–Covariance Matrix for Data*

	RF	**DF**	**SAV**
RF	2.72	1.11	0.89
DF	1.11	1.78	0.56
SAV	0.89	0.56	2.00

8.7 FACTORIAL ANALYSIS OF VARIANCE: TWO-WAY COMPLETELY INDEPENDENT ANOVA

8.7.1 Basic Ideas

So far the two ANOVA examples that we have discussed are concerned with one IV (or factor) that was manipulated at more than two levels. The two sub-types were independent groups and repeated measures ANOVA. However, when there is more than one IV (or factors) then the designs are called as factorial designs. The statistical analysis is referred to as factorial ANOVA. Two-way ANOVA refers to two factors (as one-way refers to one factor). The two factors can take two or more levels each. Interesting options for designing experiments and studies open up with factorial designs. There could be three sub-types of two-way factorial ANOVA that one can quickly imagine. (a) When the first and second factors are independently manipulated, this is referred to as two-way completely randomized ANOVA, (b) when one factor is randomly manipulated and repeated-measures are obtained on the other factor, it is referred to as two-way mixed ANOVA, and (c) when repeated-measures were obtained on both factors, the designs are referred to as two-way ANOVA with completely repeated-measures. I shall explain only the first design in detail. The other two designs are very briefly explained with R codes and one example.

8.7.2 Main Effect and Interaction Effect

The factorial designs are the preferred type of analysis when there is more than one factor. Suppose if there are two factors in a given data, then two separate one-way ANOVA can be carried out for each factor (which is called **main effect**). However, factorial ANOVA provides additional information about interaction between two IVs. This is called **Interaction effect**, which is an advantage of factorial ANOVA. Let's understand this with an example.

Example: Creativity is an important area of psychological research. Creativity is defined as the ability to produce a novel, original, and useful solution to the problem. Mark Runco is one of the major advocates of use of experimentation in creativity research. Personality theories like Eysenck's PEN model (1995) and the FFM (McCrae, 1987) attempted to explain creativity.[11] I am using an example from Runco and Pezdek's (1984) paper and adding personality ideas to it. Runco and Pezdek (1984) tested the effect of the mode of presentation (audio versus video) on creativity. They exposed participants to an African folklore story of a magical old woman using an audiotape or a videotape and, after the story was completely presented, asked participants for "alternatives for a possible end." Suppose, if we take the personality process into account and create one more IV—openness to experience (O)—which can be manipulated through selection, and take participants who are either high-O or low-O (by using upper 73 and lower 27 percentile participants) and randomly assign them to either conditions of the first IV—media conditions, then we obtain a 2×2 factorial design. Here, IV 1 is media conditions (2 levels: audiotape or videotape) and IV 2 is openness to experience (2 levels: low-openness and high-openness), and the dependent variable is the score of participants on creativity in the alternative possible end by using the Torrance (1974) process. Suppose we have 60 high-openness and 60 low-openness participants (they are independent anyways) who are randomly assigned to either audiotape or videotape condition (30 each), then the resulting layout will be as shown in Table 8.13.

---

[11] Eysenck argued that creativity is a function of moderately high psychoticism scores which lead to lowering of cognitive inhibition and over-inclusive thinking. He also argued that mental illness is associated with creativity through the same channel. The FFM argued that high O is a more suitable condition for creativity. Openness leads to primary process thinking that creates remote associations and creative responses.

Table 8.13. *The 2×2 Layout with Sample Size for Two-way ANOVA*

		IV 1: Media Condition		
		L1: Audiotape	**L2: Videotape**	
IV2: Openness	L1: Low-Openness	Low-O & Audiotape $n=30$	Low-O Videotape $n=30$	Low-O $n=60$
	L2: High-Openness	High-O & Audiotape $n=30$	High-O & Videotape $n=30$	High-O $n=60$
		n Audiotape$=60$	n Videotape$=60$	Total $n=120$

Note: O=Openness to Experience; IV=Independent variable; L1=level 1; L2=level 2; n=sample size.

8.7.2.1 Main Effect

The main effect in factorial ANOVA is referred to as the impact of an individual factor or IV on the dependent variable. The presence of other factor/s (IVs) is ignored while obtaining main effect. For example, we shall have two main effects in the above example (number of main effect is always equal to the number of IVs or factors). First main effect is of IV1: media condition. This main effect is tested for the following null and alternative hypotheses:

$$H_0 : \mu_{\text{Audiotape}} = \mu_{\text{Videotape}}$$
$$H_A : \mu_{\text{Audiotape}} \neq \mu_{\text{Videotape}}$$

This is tested by computing the *F*-ratio for this factor. The sample size is 60 for audiotape and 60 for videotape condition.

Second main effect is of IV2: openness to experience (O). This main effect is tested for the following null and alternative hypotheses:

$$H_0 : \mu_{\text{Low-O}} = \mu_{\text{High-O}}$$
$$H_A : \mu_{\text{Low-O}} \neq \mu_{\text{High-O}}$$

This is tested by computing the *F*-ratio for factor O. The sample size is 60 for low-O condition and 60 for high-O condition.

The significance of the two main effects is independent of each other. The null is rejected and the alternative is accepted if the *F*-ratio is significant. In the case of only two levels of IV, no further analysis is required since comparison of means can be informative for conclusion regarding which the mean is higher in population. However, if the factor has more than two levels, then MCP (planned or post-hoc) need to be carried out. They are already discussed in the preceding section. Figure 8.2 presents some prototypes of significant main effect. Figure 8.2(A) shows main effect of media condition (videotape better than audiotape) and no main effect of openness condition. Figure 8.2(B) shows no main effect of media condition and main effect of openness condition (high-openness better than low-openness). Figure 8.2(C) shows main effect of media condition (videotape better than audiotape) and main effect of openness condition (high-openness better than low-openness).

8.7.2.2 Interaction Effect

The interaction effect is the joint effect of IVs that are independent of main effect. The interaction effect is present when the impact of one of the factors on DV changes as levels of the other factor changes. The question that a researcher is concerned about is whether the effect of one factor on DV is constant for all levels of another factor? The interactions effect is absent when

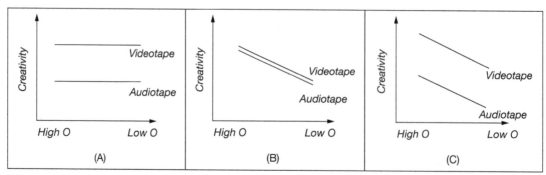

Figure 8.2. *Prototypical Graphical Presentation of Significant Main Effect and Absence of Interaction Effect (A) Presence of Main Effect for Media Condition (B) Presence of Main Effect for Openness to Experience (C) Presence of Main Effect for Both Factors*

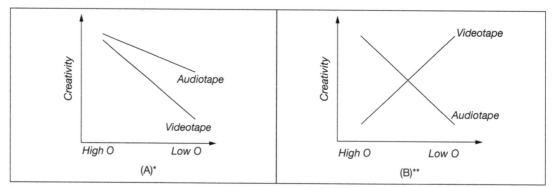

Figure 8.3. *Graphical Presentation of Significant Interaction Effect (A) Significant Main Effect of O and Interaction Effect (B) Insignificant Main Effect and Significant Interaction Effect*

Notes: * Audiotapes improve performance for low O; however, high-O individuals do well irrespective of media condition.
** Audiotapes benefiting high O and videotapes benefiting low O.

the effect of one factor on DV is constant for all levels of another factor. The interaction effect is present when the effect of one factor on the DV is different for different levels of another factor. The third *F*-ratio is obtained for interaction effect in two-way factorial designs. Figure 8.3 presents prototypes of significant interaction effects. Figure 8.3(A) is showing that the low-O individuals are benefited by audiotape conditions than videotape condition, whereas high-O individuals are doing well irrespective of media condition. Figure 8.3(B) is theoretically a very unlikely outcome for this example, though it implies that high-O are doing well under videotape and low-O are doing well under audiotape condition.

8.7.3 The Structural Model and Partitioning Sum of Squares

The structural model for one-way ANOVA is $X_{ij} = \mu + \tau_j + e_{ij}$ in which τ_j is $(\mu_j - \mu)$ treatment effect. In the case of one-way ANOVA, there is only one treatment that is represented by τ_j. In the case of two-way ANOVA, there are three treatment effects—two for the two factors and one for the interaction. The treatment effects can be represented as A and B and interaction effect can be represented as A*B. The structural model for two-way ANOVA is

$$X_{ijk} = \mu + \alpha_j + \beta_k + (\alpha\beta)_{jk} + e_{ijk}$$

where

X_{ijk} is any the ith observation for a combination of $(jk)^{th}$ cell

μ is the constant population mean

α_j is the effect of the first factor (A) which is $\mu_j - \mu$

β_k is the effect of the second factor (B) which is $\mu_k - \mu$

$(\alpha\beta)_{jk}$ is the interaction effect between the first and second factor (A*B)

e_{ijk} is the error associated with observation X_{ijk}. The error follows normal distribution with mean zero and variance σ^2.

The split of the sum of squares for two-way ANOVA is expressed as

$$SS_T = SS_{IV1} + SS_{IV2} + SS_{IV1 \times IV2} + SS_{error}$$

where SS_T is the sum of squares total, SS_{IV1} is the sum of squares due to IV 1 or main effect 1, SS_{IV2} is the sum of squares due to IV2 or main effect 2, $SS_{IV1 \times IV2}$ is the sum of squares due to interaction of IV1 and IV2 or interaction SS, and SS_{error} is the error sum of squares (also called within-cell sum of squares).

8.7.4 Computational Formula

The two-way ANOVA requires computation of SS_T, SS_{IV1}, SS_{IV2}, $SS_{IV1 \times IV2}$, and SS_{error}, their associated degrees of freedom, MS errors, and three F-ratios.

SS_T is the same SS that we have been computing for ANOVA.

$SS_T = \sum_{i=1}^{n} \left(X_{ijk} - \bar{\bar{X}} \right)^2$, that is, the sum of squared deviation of each value from the grand mean is obtained.

$SS_{error} = SS_{WC}$ is similar to one-way within SS. In the case of two-way designs, each value is subtracted from the mean of the cell. In Example 8, there are four cells and we shall have four cell means. $SS_{error} = SS_{WC} = \sum_{i=1}^{n} (X_{ijk} - \bar{X}_{jk})^2 = \sum_{i=1}^{n} (X_i - \bar{X}_{cell})^2$.

For SS of IV1 and SS of IV2, the computations are reasonably easy.

$SS_{IV1} = \sum n_j \left(\bar{X}_j - \bar{\bar{X}} \right)^2$ $\bar{X}_j$ are the mean of audiotape and videotape conditions.

$SS_{IV2} = \sum n_k \left(\bar{X}_k - \bar{\bar{X}} \right)^2$ $\bar{X}_k$ are the mean of low-O and high-O conditions.

The interaction sum of squares can be estimated separately, but they are the easiest of computations.

$$SS_{IV1 \times IV2} = SS_T - (SS_{IV1} + SS_{IV2} + SS_{error})$$

The computation of the interaction SS can be obtained through the computation of

$$SS_{cell} = \sum n_{jk} \left(\bar{X}_{jk} - \bar{\bar{X}} \right)^2$$
$$SS_{IV1 \times IV2} = SS_{cell} - (SS_{IV1} + SS_{IV2})$$

Similarly, $SS_{WC} = SS_{Total} - SS_{cell}$ can also be obtained through SS_{cell}

8.7.4.1 Data and Calculation

For example, I am using a small hypothetical data set. The data are given in Table 8.13 ad the descriptive data are provided in Table 8.14.

Let's now compute sum of squares.

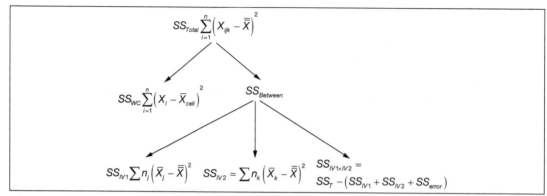

Figure 8.4. *Sum of Squares for Two-way ANOVA*

Table 8.14. *Data and Computations for Two-way ANOVA*

	High O		**Low O**	
	Audiotape	**Videotape**	**Audiotape**	**Videotape**
	3	3	3	2
	5	4	3	0
	4	2	3	1
	3	3	2	1
	4	5	3	2
	5	4	4	1
	4	3	3	0
	3	4	1	1
	4	5	1	2
	5	4	2	0
Σ or Sum	**40**	**37**	**25**	**10**
$\bar{X}_{jk}$	**4**	**3.7**	**2.5**	**1**

$$SS_{Total} = \sum_{i=1}^{n}\left(X_{ijk} - \bar{\bar{X}}\right)^2 = (3-2.8)^2 + (5-2.8)^2 + \cdots + (2-2.28)^2 + (0-2.8)^2 = 84.4$$

$$SS_{IV1} = \sum n_j\left(\bar{X}_j - \bar{\bar{X}}\right)^2 = 20(3.25-2.8)^2 + 20(2.35-2.8)^2 = 8.1$$

$$SS_{IV2} = \sum n_k\left(\bar{X}_k - \bar{\bar{X}}\right)^2 = 20(1.75-2.8)^2 + 20(3.85-2.8)^2 = 44.1$$

$$SS_{cell} = \sum n_{jk}\left(\bar{X}_{jk} - \bar{\bar{X}}\right)^2 = 10(4-2.8)^2 + 10(3.7-2.8)^2 + 10(2.5-2.8)^2 + 10(1-2.8)^2 = 55.8$$

$$SS_{WC} = SS_{Total} - SS_{cell} = 84.4 - 55.8 = 28.6$$
$$SS_{IV1\times IV2} = SS_{cell} - (SS_{IV1} + SS_{IV2}) = 55.8 - (44.1 + 8.1) = 3.6$$

The degrees of freedom computation is as follows:

$$df_{Total} = n_{total} - 1 = 40 - 1 = 39$$
$$df_{IV1} = J - 1 = 2 - 1 = 1$$
$$df_{IV2} = K - 1 = 2 - 1 = 1$$

Table 8.15. *Mean and SD for All Cells and IV's and Entire Data*

		IV 1: Media Condition		
		L1: Audiotape	**L2: Videotape**	
IV2: Openness	**L1: Low-Openness**	$\bar{X}=2.5$ $S=0.97$	$\bar{X}=1.0$ $S=0.82$	$\bar{X}_{\text{low-O}}=1.75$ $S=1.16$
	L2: High-Openness	$\bar{X}=4.0$ $S=0.82$	$\bar{X}=3.7$ $S=0.95$	$\bar{X}_{\text{high-O}}=3.85$ $S=0.88$
		$\bar{X}_{\text{Audiotape}}=3.25$ $S=1.16$	$\bar{X}_{\text{Videotape}}=2.35$ $S=1.63$	$\bar{\bar{X}}=2.8$ $S=1.47$

Table 8.16. *Summary Table for Two-way ANOVA*

	Sum Sq	df	Mean Sq	F-value	Pr(>F)
Media	8.1	1	8.1	10.196	0.00292
Opn	44.1	1	44.1	55.51	<0.0001
Opn × Media	3.6	1	3.6	4.531	0.04019
Residuals	28.6	36	0.79		
Total	84.4				

where J and K are levels if IV1 and IV2, respectively.

$$df_{IV1 \times IV2} = (J-1) \times (K-1) = 1 \times 1 = 1$$
$$df_{WC} = \Sigma(n_{jk}-1) = (10-1)+(10-1)+(10-1)+(10-1) = 36$$

The mean square (MS) is obtained by dividing SS by the respective df.

$$MS_{IV1} = SS_{IV1}/df_{IV1} = 8.1/1 = 8.1$$
$$MS_{IV2} = SS_{IV2}/df_{IV2} = 44.1/1 = 44.1$$
$$MS_{IV1 \times IV2} = SS_{IV1 \times IV2}/df_{IV1 \times IV2} = 3.6/1 = 3.6$$
$$MS_{WC} = SS_{WC}/df_{WC} = 28.6/36 = 0.79$$

The *F*-ratio for IV1, IV2 and interaction are obtained as follows:

$$F_{IV1} = MS_{IV1}/MS_{WC} = 8.1/0.794 = 10.20$$
$$F_{IV2} = MS_{IV2}/MS_{WC} = 44.1/0.794 = 55.51$$
$$F_{IV1 \times IV2} = MS_{IV1 \times IV2}/MS_{WC} = 3.6/0.794 = 4.53$$

The tabled *F*-value for df (1, 36) is 4.11 at 0.05 level of significance and 7.40 at 0.01 level of significance. The *F* for IV1 and IV2 are greater than the tabled value at 0.01 level of significance and the null is rejected for IV1 and IV2 at 0.01 level of significance. The *F* of the interaction effect is larger than 4.11 and, hence, we can state that there exists an interaction in this data. The summary table for the ANOVA is presented in Table 8.16.

There are no more than two levels for any of the IV and, hence, we shall not carry out the post-hoc of planned comparison. R code 8.16 explains how to do a two-way ANOVA in R. Please note that you can have entire data in .csv format and call it directly in R by using (`read. csv`) command.

```
# R Code 8.16. Two-way ANOVA
dv <- c(3, 5, 4, 3, 4, 5, 4, 3, 4, 5, 3, 4, 2, 3, 5, 4, 3, 4, 5, 4, 3,
    3, 3, 2, 3, 4, 3, 1, 1, 2, 2, 0, 1, 1, 2, 1, 0, 1, 2, 0) # data
opn <- c("hi", "hi", "hi", "hi", "hi", "hi", "hi", "hi", "hi", "hi",
    "hi", "hi", "hi", "hi", "hi", "hi", "hi", "hi", "hi", "low",
    "low", "low", "low", "low", "low", "low", "low", "low", "low", "low",
    "low", "low", "low", "low", "low", "low", "low", "low", "low", "low") #
    factor openness
media <- c ("au", "au", "au", "au", "au", "au", "au", "au", "au", "au",
    "vid", "vid", "vid", "vid", "vid", "vid", "vid", "vid", "vid", "vid",
    "au", "au", "au", "au", "au", "au", "au", "au", "au", "au", "vid",
    "vid", "vid", "vid", "vid", "vid", "vid", "vid", "vid", "vid") #
    factor media condition
data <- data.frame (dv, opn, media) # creating data.frame
fit <- aov(dv ~ opn + media + opn*media, data = data) # running #two-way
    NAOVA
summary (fit)        # this is summary table.
interaction.plot (opn, media, dv, fun = mean, type=c("c"), lwd=6, cex.
    lab=2, cex.axis=2) # plotting interaction
# Use print (model.tables) to obtain means across conditions
print (model.tables (fit, "mean"), digits = 3)
```

The interaction plot is easy to draw. The *Y*-axis is the dependent variable, the *X*-axis has one of the factors, and lines of different kinds are another factor. The R-generated interaction plot is given n Figure 8.5.

The two-way ANOVA findings are interpreted as main effects of each IV and interaction effect. The main effect is the impact of individual IVs on the DV. In the above case, the impact of media condition is significant ($F (1, 36) = 10.20$, $p < 0.001$). The examination of sample mean

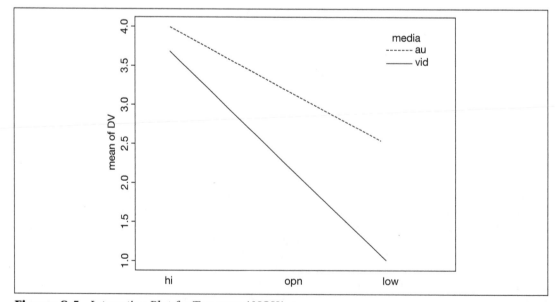

Figure 8.5. *Interaction Plot for Two-way ANOVA*

Note: It implies that low O participants are benefited by audiotape condition, whereas high-O participants were less sensitive to media conditions.

indicates that mean creativity is greater under auditory conditions (3.5) as compared to videotape condition (2.5). The impact of openness is significant ($F(1, 36)=55.51$, $p<0.001$). The sample means lead to the conclusion that high-openness individuals have better creativity than low-openness individuals. The interaction effect is significant ($F(1, 36)=4.53$, $p<0.05$) and the examination of the interaction plot suggests that high-openness participants are insensitive to media conditions and low-openness participants are better under auditory condition than videotape condition.

8.7.5 The Alternative Factorial ANOVA Designs

Two other types of factorial ANOVA designs are briefly explained here: (a) Mixed-factorial design; (b) Completely repeated factorial design. I shall explain the basic logic and R codes; the explicit computation formulation is avoided.

8.7.5.1 Mixed-factorial ANOVA

Let's start with the 2×2 mixed factorial design for the purpose of illustration. Here, one factor randomized (or independent) and another factor is repeated measures. The SS is divided as follows

$$SS_{Total} = SS_{IV1} + SS_{within} + SS_{IV2} + SS_{IV1 \times IV2} + SS_{IV2 \times within}$$

where IV1 is the independently (randomly) manipulated factor and IV2 is the repeatedly measured factor.

Example: It is known that subvocal rehearsal mechanism of phonological loop of working memory naturally develops around the age of 7 but with training it can be activated at age of 5.[12] We take age as IV1 (4 years and 5 years as two levels), training as IV2 (pre and post as two levels), and word-length effect (WLE) as DV. The WLE, which is poorer memory for long words than for short words, is used as an indicator of the presence of rehearsal mechanism. We have two age Groups, 4 year old and 5 year old, that are independent. These groups are assessed on WLE before (pre-test) and after the training (post-test). The effect of training is repeatedly measured IV. So we have one factor (IV1: age) that is independent and second factor (IV2: training) that is repeated. The DV is WLE measured as proportional correct responses for longer words. Such a design is called a mixed-ANOVA design. The R code provides data and analysis.

R Code 8.17. Mixed Two-way ANOVA

```
age <- c("four", "four", "four", "four", "four", "four", "four",
    "four", "four", "four", "five", "five", "five", "five", "five", "five",
    "five","five","five","five") # Age IV 1
train <- c("pre", "pre", "pre", "pre", "pre", "post", "post", "post",
    "post", "post", "pre", "pre", "pre", "pre", "post", "post",
    "post", "post", "post") # Age IV2

sub <- c("A", "B", "C", "D", "E", "A", "B", "C", "D", "E", "F", "G",
    "H", "I", "J", "F", "G", "H", "I", "J") # Subjects

wle <- c(0.85, 0.9, 1.1, 1.2, 1.1, 0.9, 0.85, 0.95, 1.05, 0.99, 0.95,
    1.1, 1.08, 1.1, 0.9, 0.6, 0.4, 0.56, 0.43, 0.76) # DV scores
```

---

[12] The work in the area of working memory is also showing growing evidence for variation in the development of working memory. Alan Baddely developed the initial framework to which Logie, Gathercole, etc., have contributed.

```
data <- data.frame(age, train, sub, wle)    # data frame of variables
attach(data)         # attaching data

# ANOVA command where train is specified as within
fit <- aov(wle ~ (age*train) + Error(sub/train), data = data)
summary(fit) # summary table
model.tables(fit, c("mean")) # Tables for mean
```

 # The R Output is as follows
```
Error: sub
           Df  Sum Sq   Mean Sq  F value  Pr(>F)
age        1   0.2020   0.20201  15.01    0.00472 **
Residuals  8   0.1077   0.01346

---

Signif. codes:
0 `***' 0.001 `**' 0.01 `*' 0.05 `.' 0.1 ` ' 1

Error: sub:train
            Df  Sum Sq   Mean Sq  F value  Pr(>F)
train       1   0.3892   0.3892   25.21    0.00103 **
age:train   1   0.1940   0.1940   12.57    0.00756 **
Residuals   8   0.1235   0.0154

---

Signif. codes:
0 `***' 0.001 `**' 0.01 `*' 0.05 `.' 0.1 ` ' 1
```

Table 8.17 provides summary of the mixed-two way ANOVA. The main effect of age (IV1) is significant with WLE for "5 year old" being slightly prominent. The main effect of training (IV2) is also significant $[F(1,8),=25.21, p<0.001]$ with post-test showing lowering of proportional correct responses for longer words (pre=1.028; post=0.749). This suggests that a subvocal rehearsal mechanism can be activated with training. Figure 8.6 shows the interaction effect. The interaction effect states that as the age becomes 5, the WLE appears with training. No such effect is seen for both age groups without training. The interaction effect is significant $[F(1,8)=12.57, p<0.001]$. The mixed-two way ANOVA is a very useful technique for the simple reason that it saves upon the participants and allows researchers the luxury of factorial designs.

8.7.5.2 Completely Repeated Measures Factorial ANOVA

With the illustration of the 2 × 2 factorial design, if the same set of participants are exposed to all conditions (four conditions in this case), then the resulting ANOVA design is called completely repeated measures or two-way within subject ANOVA. I am using a completely

Table 8.17. *The Summary Table for Mixed Two-way ANOVA*

Source	SS	df	MSE	F
Factor 1 (IV1): Age	0.2020	1	0.2020	15.01**
Within	0.1077	8	0.01346	
Factor 2 (IV2): Training	0.3892	1	0.3892	25.21**
Interaction (IV1 × IV2):Age × Training	0.1940	1	0.1940	12.57**
Factor 2 × Within (IV2 × within): Training × Within	0.1235	8	0.0145	
Total	1.0164	19		

Note: *p <.05; **p <.01.

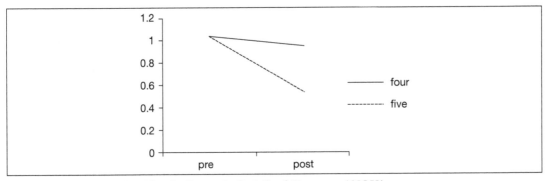

Figure 8.6. *Interaction Plot for Example for Mixed Two-way ANOVA*

hypothetical example for R code so that interested readers can at least be able to run it in R.

```
R Code 8.18. Completely Repeated Measures Two-way ANOVA
# The first iv take two levels A and B
iv1 <-c("A", "A", "A", "A", "A", "A", "A", "A", "A", "A", "B", "B", "B",
  "B", "B", "B", "B", "B", "B", "B")
# The second IV takes two leves a and b
iv2 <- c("a", "a", "a", "a", "a", "b", "b", "b", "b", "b", "a", "a",
  "a", "a", "a", "b", "b", "b", "b", "b")
# Five Subjects (V, W, X, Y, and Z) are repeated four times
sub <- c("V", "W", "X", "Y", "Z", "V", "W", "X", "Y", "Z", "V", "W",
  "X", "Y", "Z", "V", "W", "X", "Y", "Z")
# Scores on DV
dv <- c(5, 2, 1, 4, 3, 3, 6, 5, 7, 6, 10, 11, 13, 12, 14, 1, 3, 2, 4, 5)
# ANOVA command syntax and Summary table
fit <- aov(dv ~ (iv1*iv2) + Error (sub/(iv1*iv2)))
# ANOVA command syntax
summary(fit)
```

The residual is associated with each of the three effects and in addition, variation due to subject is separated. The three *F*-values are significant for the above data, but nothing much to read from it since it's a simulated example.

The factorial ANOVA in general is a very useful technique that allows us not only to examine the main effect of each individual factor but also the joint effect of the factors on the dependent variables. The factorial ANOVA is a more powerful test from a methodological perspective since the within-cells variance is reduced. Now we shall move to a more general or multivariate form of ANOVA design generally referred to as the MANOVA.

8.8 MULTIVARIATE ANALYSIS OF VARIANCES (MANOVA)

The MANOVA is a general form of ANOVA when there are more dependent variables and DVs are intercorrelated, for example, if the researcher who is interested in studying gender difference (or cultural differences) in neuroticism employs anxiety (A), impulsiveness (Im), vulnerability (Vu), and hostility (Ho) subscales of NEO-PI-3 as measures of neuroticism. Now s/he has IV (or factor) that takes two levels (male–female) and scores on four DV measures (scores on A, Im, Vu, and Ho scales). You can think of four *t*-tests for four DVs separately. (One can also think of four separate ANOVAs if the IV has more levels, for example, in the case of cultural differences, the IV may take Indian, Sub-Saharan, and American as three levels.) One problem is the intercorrelation among the DVs, resulting in an increased chance of type I error. The other limitation is that such an analysis results in four separate pieces of information regarding gender difference in neuroticism. The alternative statistical technique is MANOVA.[13] ANOVA evaluates the significance of mean difference among groups on one DV. MANOVA evaluates the significance of mean difference among groups on a linear combination of several DVs. A new linear combination of DVs is created in the MANOVA that maximizes the difference in a set of DVs. A statistical test similar to ANOVA is carried out and the null hypothesis is evaluated. The factorial MANOVA is also possible when more DVs are employed in a factorial design. Overall, MANOVA provides better understanding because it provides information about changes in the DVs due to treatment. In addition, MANOVA guards against type I error when DVs are intercorrelated. Under specific conditions it may also be able to detect group differences that cannot be detected by univariate ANOVAs. Tabachnick and Fidell (2007) listed various research questions that can be answered by MANOVA. However, the most popular use of MANOVA is to study the main-effect of IV (or IVs). In the case of the neuroticism example, the main effect is the effect of gender on a linear combination of DVs measuring neuroticism. The significant main effect of MANOVA indicates that maximally differing linear combination of four DVs is different in population for males and females. Once the main effect turned out to be significant, the next important question for a researcher is, "Which of individual DVs are significantly different across levels of IVs and which are not?" For example, one may conclude that male–female differ on anxiety and hostility; however, no gender difference is observed on the remaining two DVs. Interaction among IVs, parameter estimation, specific comparison and trend analysis, effect-size, and effect of covariates are other important researcher questions answered by MANOVA (Tabachnick & Fidell, 2007).

8.8.1 Assumptions and Other Important Aspects of MANOVA

MANOVA makes certain assumptions and a researcher should evaluate them before the application of MANOVA. Since MANOVA is a multivariate technique, other considerations such as sample size, outliers and power need to be paid attention to.

8.8.1.1 Multivariate Normal Distribution (MVN) and Outliers

As ANOVA requires an assumption of univariate normal distribution of sampling distribution of means across groups, MANOVA requires similar assumption of MVN of means of DVs across groups. It can also be verified by using tests like Mardia's MVN test, Henze–Zirkler's MVN test, and Royston's MVN test. These test are available in the MVN package of R. They are also described in the chapter on normal distribution (Chapter 4). Mardia (1970) argued that the sample size of 20 and more in the smallest cell would ensure robustness to MVN. The multivariate normality can be assured by deleting multivariate outliers. The presence of multivariate outliers has a detrimental impact on multivariate test and, hence, the general recommendation is to do outliers analysis before MANOVA. Finally, one should note that univariate normality does not ascertain multivariate normality, but generally it is useful.

---

[13] Discriminant function analysis is another technique used to predict group membership (logistic regression is also an alternative to do the same), which is mathematically MANOVA. The MANOVA focuses on mean differences among groups, whereas discriminant function analysis predicts group membership and dimensions of differences. Though this is not a rule, generally MANOVA is used under experimental conditions where the manipulation of IV (either experimentally or by selection) and random assignment (with equal number in each group) of participants is carried out and discriminant function analysis is carried out in non-experimental contexts.

8.8.1.2 Homogeneity of Variance–Covariance Matrices

Homogeneity of variance assumptions of ANOVA is extended to homogeneity of variance–covariance matrices for MANOVA. The population variance–covariance matrix (generally called the covariance matrix) is exemplified in the form of null hypothesis. Note that the upper diagonal is omitted since it's a mirror image of the lower diagonal.

$$
\begin{bmatrix}
\sigma_A^2 & & & \\
\text{Cov}_{A.Im} & \sigma_{Im}^2 & & \\
\text{Cov}_{A.Vu} & \text{Cov}_{Im.Vu} & \sigma_{Vu}^2 & \\
\text{Cov}_{A.Ho} & \text{Cov}_{Im.Ho} & \text{Cov}_{Vu.Ho} & \sigma_{Ho}^2
\end{bmatrix}_{Female}
=
\begin{bmatrix}
\sigma_A^2 & & & \\
\text{Cov}_{A.Im} & \sigma_{Im}^2 & & \\
\text{Cov}_{A.Vu} & \text{Cov}_{Im.Vu} & \sigma_{Vu}^2 & \\
\text{Cov}_{A.Ho} & \text{Cov}_{Im.Ho} & \text{Cov}_{Vu.Ho} & \sigma_{Ho}^2
\end{bmatrix}_{Male}
$$

The diagonal values are population variances for four DVs and non-diagonal elements are population covariances among DVs. The assumption is that the two matrices are equal. The sample variance–covariance matrices are used as estimators for the purpose of a statistical test. Box's M test is the most popular test of homogeneity of variance–covariance matrices. If the homogeneity assumption is retained, then a single estimate of the variance–covariance matrix needs to be used. This single estimate is the pooled variance–covariance matrix (S_p). Box's M test is known for its sensitivity and often rejects the null hypothesis.

8.8.1.3 Mutlicollinearity and Singularity

When a DV is completely linearly dependent on other DVs, then that leads to errors in statistical inferences. Absence of such complete linear dependence is assumed in MANOVA. Tabachnick and Fidell (2007) recommended that if such a DV has to be kept in the MANOVA, then component scores of principal components analysis (PCA) of pooled within-cells correlation matrix should be entered as an alternate set of DVs. The presence of singularity or multicollinearity can be suspected, as the determinant of the within-cell correlation matrix is closer to zero. Any correlation above 0.7 is suspicious and that above 0.8 is an indication of multicollinearity. A complete absence of correlation among the DVs is also not suitable for MANOVA, and, in such a case, separate univariate ANOVAs may be used.

8.8.1.4 Linearity

Linearity assumption expects that all DV pairs be linearly related with each other (and so are covariates, if employed). The absence of linearity leads to failure in maximizing the differences across groups.

8.8.1.5 Homogeneity of Regressions

This assumption states that the regressions are same in all groups for Roy–Bargmann stepdown analysis of covariates as well as for the stepdown analysis of DVs.

8.8.1.6 Reliability of Covariates

A reliable covariate in the case of MANCOVA leads to higher power of test statistics.

8.8.1.7 Sample Size

Minimally, each of the cells should have more cases than the number of DVs (more than 4 in each cell in our example); otherwise, the cell becomes singular and the related assumptions cannot be tested. The sample size is expected to be 6–10 times the number of DVs per group. Generally, the sample size is associated with power.

8.8.2 The Null and Alternative Hypothesis for MANOVA

The null hypothesis of ANOVA is that all groups have the same population mean. The null of MANOVA is a more general statement. It states that all groups have the same vector of population means. For the example of gender difference in four measures of neuroticism, the null and alternate hypotheses are as follows:

$$H_0: \begin{array}{c}\text{Male}\\ \begin{bmatrix} \mu_A \\ \mu_{\text{Im}} \\ \mu_{\text{Vu}} \\ \mu_{\text{Ho}} \end{bmatrix}\end{array} = \begin{array}{c}\text{Female}\\ \begin{bmatrix} \mu_A \\ \mu_{\text{Im}} \\ \mu_{\text{Vu}} \\ \mu_{\text{Ho}} \end{bmatrix}\end{array} \qquad H_A: \begin{array}{c}\text{Male}\\ \begin{bmatrix} \mu_A \\ \mu_{\text{Im}} \\ \mu_{\text{Vu}} \\ \mu_{\text{Ho}} \end{bmatrix}\end{array} \neq \begin{array}{c}\text{Female}\\ \begin{bmatrix} \mu_A \\ \mu_{\text{Im}} \\ \mu_{\text{Vu}} \\ \mu_{\text{Ho}} \end{bmatrix}\end{array}$$

8.8.3 Statistical Test

The most popular statistical test for MANOVA is Wilks's Lambda (Λ)[14]

$$\Lambda = \frac{|S_{\text{error}}|}{|S_{\text{effect}} + S_{\text{error}}|}$$

where S is the sum of squares and cross products (SSCP) matrix, the S_{error} is the SSCP of within, and S_{effect} is the SSCP of effect (or between). The $|S_{\text{error}}|$ is a determinant of S_{error} and $|S_{\text{effect}} + S_{\text{error}}|$ is a determinant of the addition of $S_{\text{error}} + S_{\text{error}}$ matrices. The Λ will be close to 0 if S_{error} is small, and close to 1, if S_{error} is large. If IV has a significant impact on the linear combination of DVs, then S_{effect} will be large and Wilks Λ will be close to zero. The SSCP is a multivariate analogue of sum of squares in ANOVA. The mutivariate sum of squares will involve multiple DVs and their interaction. An example of SSCP for example data is

$$\begin{bmatrix} SS_A & & & \\ CP_{A.\text{Im}} & SS_{\text{Im}} & & \\ CP_{A.\text{Vu}} & CP_{\text{Im.Vu}} & SS_{\text{Vu}} & \\ CP_{A.\text{Ho}} & CP_{\text{Im.Ho}} & CP_{\text{Vu.Ho}} & SS_{\text{Ho}} \end{bmatrix}$$

where SS is the sum of squares and CP is the cross-products. The upper diagonal is omitted since it's a mirror image of the lower diagonal.

Table 8.18. *Small Data for Anxiety and Vulnerability for Both Genders*

Variables	Male		Female	
	Anxiety	**Vulnerability**	**Anxiety**	**Vulnerability**
	6	5	9	5
	5	4	8	6
	8	6	7	7
	7	7	6	6
	4	6	8	5
Mean	6	5	8	6

---

[14] Samuel Stanley Wilks (1906–1964) worked at Princeton and contributed to fields like unit-weighted regression, and is known for the Wilks theorem. His paper "Certain Generalizations in the Analysis of Variance" (Wilks, 1932) contains ideas regarding MANOVA, particularly Wilks's lambda distribution.

8.8.4 Small Sample Worked Out Example

Let's do MANOVA for a small sample example with anxiety and vulnerability as DVs and gender as IV to have some understanding of the computational component. The data is shown in Table 8.18.

Grand Mean for anxiety = 7, and grand mean for vulnerability = 5.5

Let's first compute the SSCP error and SSCP between, the addition of which will give us the SSCP total. Then we shall compute their determinants followed by lambda.

8.8.4.1 SSCP within, Between, and Total

$$\text{Within SS anxiety} = (6-6)^2 + (5-6)^2 + (8-6)^2 + (7-6)^2 + (4-6)^2 + (9-8)^2$$
$$+(8-8)^2 + (7-8)^2 + (6-8)^2 + (9-8)^2 + (8-8)^2 = 20$$
$$\text{Within SS Vulnerability} = (5-5)^2 + (4-5)^2 + (6-5)^2 + (7-5)^2 + (6-5)^2 + (5-6)^2$$
$$+(6-6)^2 + (7-6)^2 + (6-6)^2 + (5-6)^2 = 8$$
$$\text{Within CP}_{\text{anxiety.Vulnerability}} = [(6-6) \times (5-5)] + [(5-6) \times (4-5)] + [(8-6) \times (6-5)]$$
$$+[(7-6) \times (7-5)] + [(4-6) \times (6-5)] + [(9-8) \times (5-6)]$$
$$+[(8-8) \times (6-6)] + [(7-8) \times (7-6)]$$
$$+[(6-8) \times (6-6)] + [(8-8) \times (5-6)]$$
$$= 2$$

The sum of squares cross-products matrix for within is

$$\text{SSCP}_{\text{Within}} = \begin{bmatrix} \text{SS}_{\text{An}} & \text{CP}_{\text{An.Vu}} \\ \text{CP}_{\text{An.Vu}} & \text{SS}_{\text{Vu}} \end{bmatrix} = \begin{bmatrix} 20 & 2 \\ 2 & 8 \end{bmatrix}$$

Similarly, SSCP between can be computed. You have to use the deviations of groups mean from grand mean. The sum of squares cross-products matrix for between is

$$\text{SSCP}_{\text{Between}} = \begin{bmatrix} 10 & 5 \\ 5 & 2.5 \end{bmatrix}$$

$$\text{SSCP}_{\text{Between+Within}} = \text{SSCP}_{\text{Between}} + \text{SSCP}_{\text{Within}}, \quad \text{that is,}$$

$$\begin{bmatrix} 10 & 5 \\ 5 & 2.5 \end{bmatrix} + \begin{bmatrix} 20 & 2 \\ 2 & 8 \end{bmatrix} = \begin{bmatrix} 10+20 & 5+2 \\ 5+2 & 2.5+8 \end{bmatrix} = \begin{bmatrix} 30 & 7 \\ 7 & 10.5 \end{bmatrix}$$

The determinant of $\text{SSCP}_{\text{Within}}$ is

$$\det \begin{bmatrix} 20 & 2 \\ 2 & 8 \end{bmatrix} = 156$$

The determinant of $\text{SSCP}_{\text{Between+Within}}$ is

$$\det \begin{bmatrix} 30 & 7 \\ 7 & 10.5 \end{bmatrix} = 266$$

$$\Lambda = \frac{156}{266} = 0.586$$

The significance of the Wilks lambda is tested by using approximate *F*-transformation.

$$\text{Approximate } F(df_1, df_2) = \left(\frac{1-y}{y}\right)\left(\frac{df_2}{df_1}\right)$$

where approximate F is the F-ratio, $y = \Lambda^{1/s}$, and $s = \min(p, df_{effect})$, p is the number of DVs,

$$df_1 = p(df_{effect})$$

$$df_2 = \left[(df_{error}) - \frac{p - df_{effect} + 1}{2}\right] - \left[\frac{p(df_{effect}) - 2}{2}\right]$$

In the same example, $y = 0.586^{1/1} = 0.586$

$$df_1 = p(df_{effect}) = 2(1) = 2$$

$$df_2 = \left[(8) - \frac{2 - 1 + 1}{2}\right] - \left[\frac{2(1) - 2}{2}\right] = 7$$

$$\text{Approximate } F(2,7) = \left(\frac{1 - 0.586}{0.586}\right)\left(\frac{7}{2}\right) = 2.472$$

The tabled F at df (2, 7) is 4.73 at 0.05 level of significance. The obtained F of 2.47 is smaller than and, hence, the null is accepted. χ^2 test is also possible at df=$p(k-1)$.

$$\chi^2 = -[(N - 1) - 0.5(p + k)]\ln \Lambda$$

$$\chi^2 = -[(10 - 1) - 0.5(2 + 2)]\ln 0.586 = 3.741$$

X^2 is at df = $p(k - 1) = 2(2 - 1) = 2$ is 5.99 at $p=0.05$. we accept the null and do not carry out further univariate comparisons.

The effect-size for MANOVA can be obtained by transformation of lambda.

$$\eta^2 = 1 - \Lambda$$

where η^2 is effect-size of MANOVA. It represents variance explained in linear combination of DVs by IVs. The $|S_{error}|$ is error variance and $|S_{effect} + S_{error}|$ is total variance since determinant is generalized variance. The lambda is the proportion of variance in DVs, which is not accounted by IVs out of total variance. So, $1 - \Lambda$ is proportion accented in the DVs by IV. In the case of the above data,

$$\eta^2 = 1 - 0.586 = 0.414$$

This implies that 41.4% information in linear combination of anxiety and vulnerability is explained by gender. When $s>1$, partial η^2 is used as an effect-size estimate which is Partial $\eta^2 = 1 - \Lambda^{1/s}$. In the case of our example, $s=1$ and hence there is no difference between η^2 and partial η^2.

The R code for MANOVA is as follows:

```
# R Code 8.19. MANOVA Example
an <- c(6, 5, 8, 7, 4, 9, 8, 7, 6, 10) # Data on dv1
vu <- c(5, 4, 6, 4, 6, 5, 6, 7, 5, 7) # data on dv2
sex <- c("m", "m", "m", "m", "m", "f", "f", "f", "f", "f") # iv
sex <- factor(sex) # specifying IV as factor
data <- data.frame(sex, an, vu) # creating data.frame
fit <- manova(cbind(an, vu) ~sex, data) # running MANOVA
```

```
summary (fit, test= "W") # Summary of MANOVA gives Wilks lambda
# Use R for Roy, P for Pillai lambda

# The MANOVA Output is as follows
> summary(fit, test= "W")
           Df  Wilks approx  F num  Df den  Df  Pr(>F)
sex        1    0.58647         2.468  2        7   0.1545
Residuals  8

# Note that Wilks lambda is .586

# Individual ANOVA table for Univariate analysis
summary.aov (fit) # individual ANOVA summary tables
# The ANOVA Output for each DV is as follows
Response an:
           Df  Sum Sq Mean  Sq F value  Pr(>F)
sex        1   10   10.0     4            0.08052.
Residuals  8   20   2.5

---
Signif. codes:
0 `***' 0.001 `**' 0.01 `*' 0.05 `.' 0.1 ` ' 1

Response vu:
           Df  Sum Sq  Mean Sq  F value  Pr(>F)
sex        1   2.5     2.5      2.5      0.1525
Residuals  8   8.0     1.0
```

8.8.5 Testing Homogeneity of Variances

The homogeneity assumption can be tested by the log-likelihood ratio test or Box's M test.

8.8.5.1 Log-likelihood Ratio Test

Log-likelihood ratio test is multivariate generalization of Bartlett's test of homogeneity of variances in the form of the log-likelihood ratio test. The test statistics is

$$-2\log \lambda = n\log|\mathbf{S}| - \sum_{i=1}^{k} n_i \log|\mathbf{S}_i| = \sum_{i=1}^{k} n_i \log|\mathbf{S}_i^{-1} - \mathbf{S}|$$

where $\mathbf{S}_i$ is sample-biased covariance matrix, and $\mathbf{S}$ is maximum likelihood estimated common covariance for all the groups under the null hypothesis. The statistic follows asymptotic chi-square distribution at df $= 0.5(p+1)(k-1)$.

8.8.5.2 Box's M Test

Box (1949) proposed an alternative called the Box's M test. Box's M also follows asymptotic chi-square distribution at df $= 0.5(p+1)(k-1)$. Box's M is defined as

$$M = \gamma \sum_{i=1}^{k} (n_i - 1)\log|\mathbf{S}_i^{-1} - \mathbf{S}_p|$$

where

$$\gamma = 1 - \frac{2p^2 + 3p - 1}{6(p+1)(k-1)} \left(\sum_{i=1}^{k} \frac{1}{n_i - 1} - \frac{1}{n - k} \right)$$

The $\mathbf{S}_i$ is the unbiased covariance matrix per group, and $\mathbf{S}_p$ is the pooled covariance matrix. $\mathbf{S}_p$ is

$$\mathbf{S}_p = \frac{\sum_{i=1}^{k} (n_i - 1)\mathbf{S}_i}{n - k}$$

The Box's M test is known for its sensitivity, particularly when n is large. The significance of the test is only indicative and should not be considered as violation of assumption. Generally, when sample sizes are equal, then significant Box's M can be ignored. This robustness has problems with unequal sample sizes and significant Box's M. In such a case, the examination of log-determinants of variance–covariance matrices for groups as well as pooled is used. If the log-determinants of variance–covariance matrices for each group ($\mathbf{S}_i$) and pooled covariance matrix ($\mathbf{S}_p$) are not widely very different, then homogeneity is usually assumed. Please note that the determinant of variance–covariance matrix is known as generalized variance of a matrix. Understandably, this is a not an objective judgment.

 # R Code 8.20. The Boxes M Test for Homogeneity of Variance–Covariance Matrices

```
library (biotools) # call package biotools
dv <- data.frame(an, vu)  # cbind DVs
boxM(dv, sex)             # Box M test
```

8.8.6 MANOVA Example with R

The hypothetical data is given in R code 8.21 component for three cultural groups, Indian, American, and Sub-Saharan. The data is on the same four DVs discussed earlier. The data is in the form of R code instead of table. Since there are four DVs ($p=4$) and three groups ($k=3$) and DVs are likely to be moderately correlated, MANOVA is a suitable option. The data and MANOVA is run in R code 8.21 and the output is also presented.

 # R Code 8.21. MANOVA Full Example

```
# Data on 60 participants (20 each) on four variables
Ax <- c(4, 5, 4, 6, 7, 5, 6, 5, 4, 5, 6, 7, 4, 5, 6, 7, 6, 4, 7, 5, 8,
    7, 9, 8, 7, 6, 7, 8, 9, 6, 5, 4, 6, 5, 6, 5, 4, 6, 5, 7, 5, 6, 7, 6,
    8, 7, 6, 5, 4, 5, 3, 4, 5, 6, 3, 4, 3, 5, 6, 4)
Vu <- c(2, 3, 2, 4, 3, 5, 6, 5, 4, 5, 3, 4, 3, 2, 6, 7, 5, 6, 8, 5, 6,
    5, 6, 5, 4, 5, 3, 4, 2, 3, 2, 3, 2, 4, 2, 4, 3, 2, 3, 2, 2, 1, 3, 4,
    3, 2, 1, 2, 1, 0, 2, 1, 0, 2, 1, 3, 4, 3, 2, 1)
Ho <- c(12, 11, 13, 14, 12, 9, 15, 13, 8, 10, 15, 13, 10, 8, 7, 15, 14,
    13, 12, 11, 14, 13, 12, 13, 14, 15, 14, 13, 16, 15, 14, 13, 12, 13,
    11, 12, 13, 11, 11, 12, 18, 19, 17, 18, 16, 15, 16, 17, 18, 19, 18,
    17, 16, 15, 14, 13, 16, 17, 16, 17)
Im <- c(1, 2, 3, 3, 2, 1, 3, 4, 3, 4, 5, 4, 3, 2, 3, 4, 3, 2, 2, 1, 2,
    1, 3, 4, 3, 2, 1, 2, 3, 3, 2, 1, 2, 3, 4, 5, 3, 2, 1, 2, 5, 6, 5, 4,
    7, 5, 6, 7, 5, 4, 3, 4, 2, 3, 4, 6, 4, 3, 2, 1)

# Grouping variable gp
gp <- c(rep("Ind", 20), rep("SS", 20), rep("AM", 20))
DV <- cbind(Ax, Vu, Ho, Im)    # cbind the DVs
```

```
fit <- manova(DV ~ gp)          # MANOVA syntax
summary(fit)                    # MANOVA Results
summary.aov(fit)                # Indiavidual ANOVA results

# MANOVA output
> summary(fit, test = "W")
            Df  Wilks approx  F num   Df den   Df   Pr(>F)
gp          2   0.23067       14.608  8         108  2.733e-14
Residuals   57

gp       ***
Residuals
---
Signif. codes:
0 `***' 0.001 `**' 0.01 `*' 0.05 `.' 0.1 ` ' 1

# Indiavidual ANOVA output for each DV
> summary.aov(fit)
Response Ax:
            Df  Sum Sq   Mean Sq  F value  Pr(>F)
gp          2   18.533   9.2667   5.1083   0.009106 **
Residuals   57  103.400  1.8140

---
Signif. codes:
0 `***' 0.001 `**' 0.01 `*' 0.05 `.' 0.1 ` ' 1
Response Vu:
            Df  Sum Sq   Mean Sq  F value  Pr(>F)
gp          2   64.133   32.067   15.811   3.447e-06 ***
Residuals   57  115.600  2.028

---
Signif. codes:
0 `***' 0.001 `**' 0.01 `*' 0.05 `.' 0.1 ` ' 1

Response Ho:
            Df      Sum Sq   Mean Sq  F value      Pr(>F)
gp          2 252.1  126.050  36.379   6.578e-11 ***
Residuals   57       197.5    3.465

---
Signif. codes:
0 `***' 0.001 `**' 0.01 `*' 0.05 `.' 0.1 ` ' 1

Response Im:
            Df  Sum Sq   Mean Sq  F value  Pr(>F)
gp          2   39.433   19.7167  11.364   7.026e-05 ***
Residuals   57  98.900   1.7351

---
Signif. codes:
0 `***' 0.001 `**' 0.01 `*' 0.05 `.' 0.1 ` ' 1
```

The cultural differences among three cultures, Indian, Sub-Saharan, and American, on four dependent variables (anxiety, vulnerability, hostility, and impulsivity) are evaluated using MANOVA. Testing the underlying assumptions ensured the suitability of MANOVA. The multivariate normality is assumed by the Mardia test and the deletion of multivariate outliers using Mahalanobis distance. The Box's $M = 20.56$ (df=20, $p=0.4234$), indicating homogeneity of variance covariance matrices. The MANOVA yielded Wilk's Lambda = 0.2306, Approx. $F (8, 108) = 14.61$, $p < 0.0001$. Since the Wilks lambda is significant, the multivariate null hypothesis of equal mean vectors of neuroticism variables across cultures is rejected. Univariate F-test were carried out for each of the DVs. The three cultural groups showed significant difference on anxiety $(F_{(2,57)} = 5.1083; p=0.009)$, vulnerability $(F_{(2,57)} = 15.811, p<0.0001)$, hostility $(F_{(2,57)} = 36.379, p<0.001)$, and impulsivity $(F_{(2,57)} = 11.364, p<0.001)$. The mean differences in cultures were further evaluated by using Tukey's HSD multiple comparison method. The results are as follows.

8.8.7 Writing up MANOVA Results

Generally, the MANOVA results can be reported without tables in the text format. An example report is described in the box above.

I would briefly describe HSD or other suitable MCP results after describing the results. I am avoiding reporting MCP results since they are already discussed earlier in this chapter. Readers interested in MANOVA further are requested to refer to Tabachnick and Fidell (2007), Huberty and Petoskey (2000), and Huberty and Olejnik (2006).

SUMMARY

This chapter attempted to provide introduction to ANOVA and its variation, MCP and multivariate ANOVA. The R codes supplied will be useful for analyzing the data and playing around the example data. Generally, it is advisable to carry out all computations manually, at least once.

EXERCISE

1. A researcher is comparing five independent groups for mean comparisons with alpha=0.05. define the probability of type I error.
2. Show that the F random variable leads to the ratio of two variances.
3. A researcher has two groups with variances being 30.22 and 39.21. Test the hypothesis for equal population variances using F-ratio.
4. A researcher has data on two groups, X and Y. X=2,3,4,3,5,6,7,6,5,4,7,8,7; Y=1,2,3,2,1,5,6, 4,5,3,9,8,10,14. Test the hypothesis that the population variance of X and Y are equal with F-test.
5. Show that F random variable is useful in testing the structural model of ANOVA.
6. Explain various assumptions of independent samples ANOVA and their evaluation.
7. A researcher conducted an experiment having four levels of IV (training) used with randomly assigned participants to four groups. The post-training data is given below.

Group 1	9	8	7	8	9	6	11	12	10	10
Group 2	11	13	12	16	14	18	12	10	11	9
Group 3	10	11	9	8	12	13	14	9	10	5
Group 4	14	15	16	14	13	17	14	15	17	18

State the null and alternative hypotheses, state the assumptions, and test them for one-way ANOVA. Compute descriptive statistics, ANOVA, write the summary table, and evaluate the null hypothesis. Plot bar graphs of means.

8. For exercise 7, (a) carry out planned comparisons for orthogonal contrasts; (b) test contrasts that $G1 < G2 = G3 < G4$; (c) do BD and Bonferroni–Šidak tests (d) do HSD, REGWQ, LSD, and Waller–Duncan tests.

9. For the following data across three linguistic groups, evaluate assumptions of ANOVA. Take corrective steps.

Group 1	4	5	3	6	7	6	5	3	6	8	6	7
Group 2	4	5	1	0	3	4	5	4	2	3	4	6
Group 3	5	8	11	15	16	5	4	2	7	9	10	

10. Report results for (a) Exercises 7 and 8; (b) Example 9.
11. Write R code for exercises 7, 8, and 9.
12. Consider the null hypothesis that all population means are equal. Work out the application of F-distribution to this problem.
13. For the following data, carry out ANOVA for independent samples X = (32 36 29 24 28 28 31 26 33 25 38 37 28 31 28 25 18 30 30 37); Y = (16 22 29 27 26 22 26 24 26 22 30 30 31 23 24 23 31 24 25 27); Z = (32 28 40 25 23 29 37 29 29 33 29 29 34 29 26 31 24 22 28 24).
14. Write the null alternative hypothesis for the above problem.
15. State assumptions of independent ANOVA and verify them for the above data.
16. Carry out planned comparisons for the above data.
17. Carry out post-hoc comparisons for the above data.
18. Do exercises 3, 4, 5, 6, in R.
19. Compute effect-size and power of ANOVA for the above data.
20. Carry out MANOVA for the data Dv1 <- c(5, 7, 3, 5, 4, 5, 8, 7, 1, 6) # Data on dv1. Dv2 <- c(8, 4, 5, 9, 8, 4, 6, 7, 8, 9) # data on dv2 sex <- c("m", "m", "m", "m", "m", "f", "f", "f", "f", "f") # iv

9 Non-parametric Methods

9.1 INTRODUCTION

Non-parametric methods are a set of procedures that are useful to deal with data that is not measured using a scale below the interval scale. For example, you have a data of a number of symptoms of anxiety disorder. The difference between symptom numbers 1 and 2 is not similar to the difference between symptoms 4 and 5. And hence, the data cannot (should not) be analyzed by using earlier discussed procedures such as dependent samples t-test. Procedures such as t-test and ANOVA are useful in cases when the data is on at least an interval scale. However, they further require some critical assumptions to be satisfied by the data. The most important assumptions include assumption of normality and assumption of homogeneity of variances. At times the data does not follow these assumptions to the extent that even robustness of these methods cannot salvage the analysis. Under these circumstances, if one has to analyze the pre-test, post-test data of symptoms, then the only alternatives they are left with are non-parametric tests. The bootstrapping option discussed in t-test section may not save the analysis due to the measurement scale issues. This chapter introduces non-parametric methods of data analysis for psychological data. The techniques covered in this chapter are chi-square test statistics, binomial test, proportions test, median test, Wilcoxon-signed rank test, Wilcoxon rank-sum test (and U test), Kruskal–Wallis test, and Friedman's rank test for k correlated samples. The chi-square test, binomial test, and proportions test are useful in analyzing *nominal or categorical* data. They include the number of individuals preferring the particular football team in European league, proportion of individuals re-visited the clinic after initial assessment for psychiatric disorders, and so on. Other statistical methods are useful in analyzing the *ordinal or ranked* data. Example of these data types are ranks in school or college examinations, and so on. Suitable R codes are also provided to carry out the analysis of the data. Given the rise in the bootstrapping theory, the bootstrapping alternative should be preffered over non-parametric analysis, particularly when measurement level is preserved and assumptions underlying the statistical methods are violated.

9.2 THE CHI-SQUARE TEST OF GOODNESS-OF-FIT

The chi-square test for assessing association between nominal categories (which is also known as chi-square test for independence) is discussed in Chapter 5 of correlation and association. Given this, chi-square test for goodness-of-fit is discussed here. The chi-square test for goodness-of-fit is used when questions about the proportions of the categorical data is asked. For example, in a sample survey, 200 individuals reported their support to one of the five top T20 team participating in the World Cup. These teams are Australia, India, South Africa, Pakistan, and England. You want to know whether the teams are equally supported in the population represented by the sample. If the teams were equally supported, then the ideal sample values are 200/5=40 per team. We also know that samples generally show random noise and the sample data usually fluctuate from the population values. It is also expected that there is high chance of these fluctuations being small than these fluctuations being large. And hence large fluctuation should create a doubt about the hypothesis. Suppose the data states that the teams are supported in following manner: Australia=51; India, 53; South Africa=41, Pakistan=29; and England=26. The general appearance of the data casts doubt about the hypothesis. Nevertheless, a statistical test is required to be done to confirm the same. The chi-square test is suitable option.

$$\chi^2 = \frac{\Sigma(f_o - f_e)^2}{f_e}$$

Where χ^2 is chi-square test statistics, f_o is frequency observed, and f_e is frequency expected. The observed frequencies are given for the data. The expected frequencies are 40 for all the teams. Then χ^2 is

$$\chi^2 = \frac{\Sigma(f_o - f_e)^2}{f_e}$$

$$\chi^2 = \frac{(51-40)^2}{40} + \frac{(53-40)^2}{40} + \frac{(41-40)^2}{40} + \frac{(29-40)^2}{40} + \frac{(26-40)^2}{40}$$

$$\chi^2 = \frac{121}{40} + \frac{169}{40} + \frac{1}{40} + \frac{121}{40} + \frac{196}{40} = \frac{608}{40} = 15.2$$

The degrees of freedom for chi-square test is df=c−1, where c is number of categories. The chi-square value in the Appendix C9 at df=5−1=4 at 0.05 level is 9.49. The obtained value of 15.2 is larger than the 0.05 level critical value of 9.49. Hence the null that all teams are equally supported is rejected. The alternative is that all teams are not equally supported. The specific form of inequality is not revealed by the chi-square test. The R code to test the hypothesis is given in R Code 9.1.

R code 9.1. Chi-square test for goodness-of-fit
```
x <- c(51, 53, 41, 29, 26)      # data
chisq.test(x)                    # chi-square test
        Chi-squared test for given probabilities
data: x
X-squared = 15.2, df = 4, p-value = 0.004304
```

R code 9.1 shows the similar output. The null hypothesis is rejected since the probability of the obtaining chi-square value greater than 15.2 is equal to .0043.

I am sure that no T20 experts will agree with the kind of hypothesis tested in earlier example. The real hypothesis will actually state the probabilities of winning the T20-WC differently for different teams. Suppose, intelligent specification of the hypothesis is as follows: 0.25, 0.3, 0.2, 0.1, 0.15. The probabilities can be converted into expected frequencies by multiplying them by 200. The expected frequencies are 50, 60, 40, 20, 30. The chi-square is as follows:

$$\chi^2 = \frac{\Sigma(f_o - f_e)^2}{f_e}$$

$$\chi^2 = \frac{(51-50)^2}{50} + \frac{(53-60)^2}{60} + \frac{(41-40)^2}{40} + \frac{(29-20)^2}{20} + \frac{(26-30)^2}{30}$$

$$\chi^2 = \frac{1}{50} + \frac{49}{60} + \frac{1}{40} + \frac{81}{20} + \frac{16}{30} = 0.02 + 0.8167 + 0.025 + 4.05 + 0.533 = 5.45$$

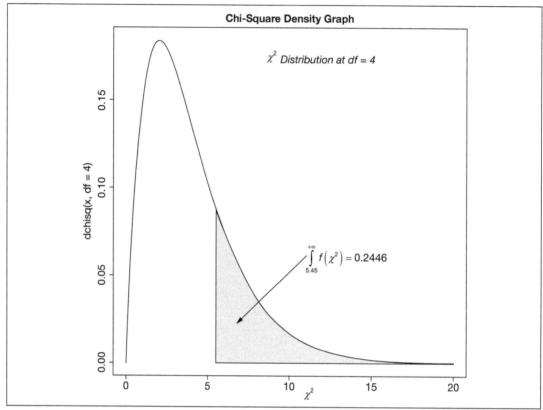

Figure 9.1. *Chi-square Redistribution at df=4 and Area beyond 5.45*

The calculated chi-square value of 5.45 is smaller than the critical chi-square value of 9.49 at 0.05 level of significance. It implies that the null hypothesis specifying the proportions as 0.25, 0.3, 0.2, 0.1, 0.15, respectively, is retained.

Let us look at the chi-square statistics in details. The numerator is the difference between the observed data (f_o) and theory based expectations (f_e). If the data is in line with the theoretical expectations, then the difference between observed and expected $(f_o - f_e)$ would be smaller and closer to zero. It is unlikely to always be zero because the sampled data is an imperfect representation of the population and contains sampling error. The difference is squared because the differences in $f_o - f_e$ can be positive and negative and then they will cancel each other. The chi-square is not a function of how big this difference is in absolute value; chi-square is a function of the ratio of this difference to f_e. The small f_e, as compared to the difference between f_o and f_e, leads to large chi-squares. The chi-square is a very popular goodness-of-fit test used to test the data-model fit. Figure 9.1 shows the chi-square distribution at df=4. It also shows the area beyond the value 5.45 and integrates (addition of continuous data) to a probability of getting a value more than 5.45.

9.2.1 Assumptions of Chi-square Test Statistics

No non-parametric statistics are assumption-free statistics. They forgo assumptions like normality, and homogeneity to make a researcher's life better. The chi-square makes certain assumptions:

1. It is assumed that data is obtained randomly from the population.

2. It is assumed that the observations are independent. It is expected that one participant's response should not influence other participants' response.
3. In repeated experiments, the observed frequencies are normally distributed around the expected frequencies.

There are certain attributes of chi-square that one needs to remember. The chi-square is always a positive value or zero. It will be zero only if observed frequencies are exactly equal to expected frequencies. The chi-square depends on number of differences (c) used to compute chi-square, and hence df=$c-1$.

9.3 PROPORTIONS TESTS: COMPARING TWO PROPORTIONS

The proportions test is useful in testing whether the two proportions observed in the sample are in line with the hypothesis about the population proportions. Most often the hypothesis states that the population proportions are identical. The test is possible for dependent proportions as well as independent proportions.

9.3.1 Proportions Test for Dependent Proportions: McNemar's Chi-squared Test

Let us start with an example: I am providing an example from Cosmides' (1989) work on cognitive adaptations for social exchanges. She argued that our ability to reason is highly domain-specific and not much useful across domains. She exemplified this with a series of experiments using Wason selection task.[1] The task is as follows: there is a rule. The task of the participant is to identify potential violators of the rule. Let us call this ability "cheater detection module." If this ability is an evolved ability and highly domain specific, then the participants should identify violations of rule only in "social contract (SC) situations," which is a adaptive problem that human species has been solving for last 1.7 million years of evolution. The same ability should not be useful to us to solve problems that are "abstract" and do not involve any SC. Let us understand the abstract problem first. There are four cards. They have a color (red or brown) on one side and a number (odd or even) on the other side. The Rule is "If the card has an *even number* on one side, then it has *red* on other side." The simple formulation of this problem is "if p then q," where p=even number and q=red. Now you are presented with four cards, two showing up numbers—one is 4 and other is 7, and two showing up colors—one is red and other is brown (Figure 9.2A). The question is: which of these cards you would flip to test whether the rule is violated or not? This represents an abstract condition. Similarly, the problem representing SC condition is expressed in Figure 9.2B (do not rush to the answer if you have never done this problem; solve it and then look at the answer).

The logically correct answer for all Wason selection problems is "p, and not-q", that is, 4 and brown in abstract problem and drinking beer and 16 in the second problem. I am sharing a small data from a classroom experiment: 65 students were given two problems. 12 students solved abstract problem correctly and 55 students have solved SC problem correctly. The two proportions 12/65 and 55/65 are obtained on the same sample. The split of the cases across condition is provided in Table 9.1. So they are dependent proportions. The question that I wanted to ask is that does the population represented by the sample has same proportions? The data is shown in Table 9.1.

The data shown in four cells are named as a, b, c, and d. The McNemar test statistics is

$$\chi^2 = \frac{(b-c)^2}{(b+c)}$$

---

[1] Wason selection task is designed to test reasoning ability. The experiments by Cosmides and Tooby made it very popular. However Fodor criticized it for having deontic logic.

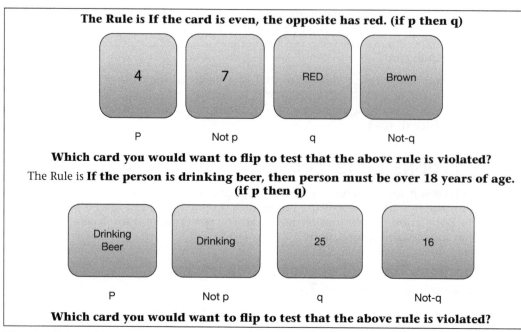

Figure 9.2. *(A) Wason Selection Task Problem: Abstract Condition, (B) Wason Selection Task Problem: Social Contact Condition*

Table 9.1. *The Data for Modularity of Reasoning Experiment*

		Social Contract		Total
		Correct	**False**	
Abstract	**Correct**	10 (a)	2 (b)	**12**
	False	45 (c)	8 (d)	**53**
Total		**55**	**10**	**65**

The null and alternative hypotheses are

$$H_0 : P_b = P_c \quad \text{and} \quad H_A : P_b \neq P_c$$

The null hypothesis is evaluated at df=1.

$$\chi^2 = \frac{(2-45)^2}{(2+45)} = 39.34$$

The critical chi-square value is 3.841 for df=1 at 0.05 level of significance. The value is smaller than the obtained value and hence the null hypothesis is rejected. The alternative state that the correct answers differ under abstract and SC conditions is accepted. The examination of the data tells us that the number of correct answers is much higher in SC condition than abstract, thus supporting Consmides' prediction that the ability to reason is domain specific ability. The R code for the proportions test is R code 9.2.

R Code 9.2. McNemar Test in R
```
data <- matrix(c(10, 2, 45, 8), nrow = 2, byrow = T, dimnames = list("ab-
stract" = c("true", "false"), "SC" = c("true", "false")))
data   # Print data matrix
```

```
mcnemar.test(data, correct= F)  # McNemar test and output
```

```
        McNemar's Chi-squared test
data: data
McNemar's chi-squared = 39.34, df = 1, p-value = 3.56e-10
```

Among other tests that are useful for similar purpose are Westlake–Schuirmann test for equivalence for two-dependent proportions, Bowker test for internal symmetry, Stuart–Maxwell test for marginal homogeneity, and so on.

9.3.2 Proportions Test for Independent Proportions

Let us continue with the same example. One of the rival hypothesis for the above finding may be that the correct answers in SC situation are a function of formal education, and urban social conditions. Hence I repeated this experiment in the rural areas of Maharashtra. The small subset of data is presented here—the success on SC problem for rural and urban samples. Out of 60 rural participants, 49 solved it correctly and out of 65 urban participants, 55 solved it correctly. I want to test the hypothesis that whether the proportion of success is same for both groups in population. The data is as shown in Table 9.2.

The null and alternative are as follows:

$$H_0 : P_U = P_R \quad \text{and} \quad H_A : P_U \neq P_R$$

The population parameter P_1-P_2 is estimated by sample proportions $\hat{P}_1 - \hat{P}_2$. The sample estimate $\hat{P}_1 - \hat{P}_2$ is normally distributed around the mean P_1-P_2 with the variance being $\dfrac{\hat{P}_1(1-\hat{P}_1)}{\hat{n}_1} + \dfrac{\hat{P}_2(1-\hat{P}_2)}{\hat{n}_2}$. The common estimate of p can also be computed. z can be obtained as

$$z = \frac{\hat{P}_1 - \hat{P}_2}{\sqrt{\dfrac{\hat{P}_1(1-\hat{P}_1)}{n_1} + \dfrac{\hat{P}_2(1-\hat{P}_2)}{n_2}}}$$

z is directly convertible into χ^2 with simple know transformation $\chi^2 = Z^2$.

The common estimate of p is $\hat{p} = \dfrac{55+49}{65+60} = \dfrac{104}{125} = 0.832$

$$z = \frac{\hat{P}_1 - \hat{P}_2}{\sqrt{\hat{p}(1-\hat{p})\left(\dfrac{1}{n_1} + \dfrac{1}{n_2}\right)}} = \frac{0.8461538 - 0.8166667}{\sqrt{0.832(1-0.832)\left(\dfrac{1}{65} + \dfrac{1}{60}\right)}} = 0.441$$

The chi-square is obtained by square transformation. $\chi^2 = Z^2 = 0.441^2 = 0.194$. The chi-square of 3.841 at df=1 is the 0.05 level value. The obtained value of 0.194 is smaller than the critical value of 3.841 and hence we retain the null hypothesis that proportion one is equal to proportion two in population. This implies that the population proportion of rural and population

Table 9.2. *Data Showing the Urban Rural Proportions in SC–WS Tasks*

	Urban	Rural
Correct answer	55	49
Incorrect	10	11
Total	65	60
Proportion of success	0.846	0.82

proportion of urban in solving SC Wason selection task is same. This also refutes the hypothesis that performance on SC Wason selection task is determined by social milieu. The R code for the proportions test is 9.3.

```
R Code 9.3. Independent Samples Proportions Test
x <- c(55,49)
y <- c(65, 60)
prop.test(x, y, correct=F)
        2-sample test for equality of proportions without
        continuity correction

data: x out of y
X-squared = 0.19408, df = 1, p-value = 0.6595
alternative hypothesis: two.sided

95 percent   confidence interval:
-0.1019635   0.1609378

sample estimates:
prop 1       prop 2
0.8461538    0.8166667
```

9.4 COMPARING LOCATIONS OF INDEPENDENT SAMPLES

Comparing a hypothesis about the population locations of independent samples is a common problem that the applied researchers have to tackle. The parametric methods provide tools like t-test for independent samples, ANOVA for independent samples, and factorial ANOVA. With some violation of assumptions, the bootstrapping can be used with these methods. The non-parametric alternatives include the median test, Wilcoxon rank-sum test, Kruskal–Wallis test, Mann–Whitney U test, and so on. The present section discusses these tests.

9.4.1 The Median Test

The median test is a procedure to evaluate a hypothesis that two independent samples are drawn from a population that have same median. The samples can be of different sizes since they are drawn independently. The null hypothesis is that two groups have same median and alternate hypothesis is that they do not have same median. The test is useful when the data is on the ordinal scale. Following steps are involved in computing the test statistics for median test:

Step 1: Combine data from both samples and rank the data.
Step 2: Compute a median on combined sample
Step 3: For each group, find individuals that are above the median and below the median.
Step 4: Carry out chi-square for the 2×2 data of groups $\times$ above–below median and test the significance.

Example: Daniel Kahneman, a noble laureate in Economic sciences in 2002 for the work carried out with Amos Tversky, made an incredible argument that fundamental assumption of economic sciences about human rationality is seriously questionable. Kahneman and Tversky conducted series of experiments to test whether individuals act rationally. They argued that humans use heuristics, mental shortcuts or rules of thumb that are much faster than algorithmic thinking. Heuristics may not necessarily give correct answers. They argue for the presence of three heuristics: availability, representativeness, and anchoring-and-adjustment. Availability refers to the ease with which related instances come to mind. They developed problems in which the participants were given a rule for the construction of instances and the participants were to estimate their frequency. According to them, if availability hypothesis is correct, that

Table 9.3. *Data for Extrapolation Experiment for Availability Heuristics*

Descending Presentation	1,250	2,334	2,260	1,004	800	880	710	1,300	2,001
Ascending Presentation	456	800	768	510	240	512	900	1,280	2,080
Descending Presentation	1,300	2,100	1,200	980	890				
Ascending Presentation	310	740	800						

Table 9.4. *Individuals Above and Below in Both Presentations*

	Presentation Method		Total
	Descending	**Ascending**	
Above Median	**10**	**3**	13
Below Median	**4**	**9**	13
Total	14	12	26

is, judgments are based on the assessment of the ease with which instances could be brought to mind. They created problems of two kinds: first, classes whose instances are easy to construct or imagine, and second, classes whose instances are not constructed or are difficult to construct or imagine. They expected that first kind of instances would be judged to be more frequent than the second. In the extrapolation experiment, the subjects were to estimate the numerical expression that was written on the blackboard in 5 seconds. One group of participants estimated a product $8\times7\times6\times5\times4\times3\times2\times1$ and another group of participants estimated a product $1\times2\times3\times4\times5\times6\times7\times8$. Suppose, we rerun the experiment and obtain data as shown in Table 9.3.

The combined median of the data is 895. Group-wise numbers of scores above the median and below the median are given in Table 9.4.

The 2×2 contingency table can be analyzed with chi-square statistics. Instead of computing expected frequencies for each cell, there is a simpler way to compute chi-square for 2×2 contingency table.

$$\chi^2 = \frac{n(ad-bc)^2}{(a+c)(b+d)(a+b)(c+d)}$$

$$\chi^2 = \frac{26(90-12)^2}{(10+4)(3+9)(10+3)(4+9)} = 5.572$$

The chi-square is evaluated at 1 df. The 0.05 level value of chi-square at one degree of freedom is 3.841. The obtained value is larger than the critical value which means that the null hypothesis of equal population median is rejected. The type of presentation leads to difference in the median answers in the populations represented by samples. We can conclude that the participants used availability heuristics to make a judgment about the product. Those who have seen large numbers to begin with estimated product to be larger than those who have seen small number to begin with. The decision rule for median test is as follows: if the chi-square is significant, then the null hypothesis is rejected. If the chi-square is insignificant, then the null hypothesis is retained. The median test has the same power that of sign test when interval level measure is used (Mood, 1954). The test has better power for heavy-tailed distribution. Considering the lower power of median test even in the instances where it was expected to have better power (double exponential distribution, for example), Freidlin and Gastwirth (2000) questioned whether median test should be retired from general use. The Wilcoxon test has far better power as compared to the median test. The users should keep these issues in mind while applying median test. The R Code 9.4 demonstrates median test in R.

R Code 9.4. Median Test
```
data <- matrix(c(10, 3, 4, 9), nrow = 2, byrow = T, dimnames = list(median
= c("above", "below"), method = c("dec", "asc")))
```

9.4.2 Wilcoxon Rank-sum Test

Wilcoxon rank-sum test is one of the powerful non-parametric options to compare independent groups. This is a popular non-parametric alternative to independent samples *t*-test. The Wilcoxon rank-sum test is slightly different from *t*-test, which exclusively tests a null about a location parameter, which is the mean. The Wilcoxon rank-sum test evaluates a null that the two population distributions represented by two samples are similar. The refutation of the null is influenced by the population differences in location parameters. Most often, rejection of the null is interpreted as difference in the two population locations. However, it should be noted that the rejection of null may result also due to other attributes of the distribution.

The Wilcoxon rank-sum test has relatively simple underlying logic. Suppose, two random samples are drawn from a population and the two random samples are combined and ranked. The ranks of the first samples and ranks of the second sample are added. Let us call them ΣR_x and ΣR_y, respectively. Since the two samples are drawn from the same population, they are overlapping. As a result, ΣR_x and ΣR_y values would not differ much from each other. On the other hand, if two samples are obtained from separate distributions that show less overlap and the combined ranking is done, the distribution that is at left side will take most of lower ranks and distribution on the right side will take most of the higher ranks. As a result, ΣR_x and ΣR_y will be different values. Figure 9.3 demonstrates the same.

Let us look at the example.

Behavioral economics has emerged as an interdisciplinary science that integrates insights from psychology and economics. It translates the economic equilibrium into experiments. The ultimatum game is one of the extensively reported games in which participants are divided into two groups: one is proposers and other is responders. The proposers are given some real money. Say, for example, ₹100. The proposer has to offer some fraction of this money (0 to 100) to the responder. If the responder agrees to split, the split happens and the money is divided. If the responder disagrees to split, then the split does not happen and the money goes back to the experimenter. The proposers and responders do not have any information about each other. I have carried out an experiment where all proposers

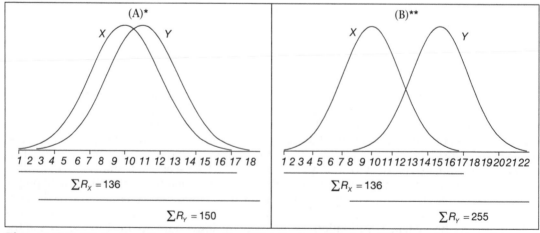

Figure 9.3 *(A) Sum of Ranks when Two Distributions Overlap (B) Sum of Ranks when Two Distributions Do Not show much Overlap*

Notes: * The sum of the ranks is reasonably nearby.
** The sum of the ranks is reasonably far.

Table 9.5. *Data for Wilcoxon Test*

Female Responders		Male Responders	
Amount Proposed	**Rank**	**Amount Proposed**	**Rank**
46	14	45	12.5
44	10.5	50	20.5
33	1	51	22
42	7.5	47	15.5
34	2.5	53	24
34	2.5	47	15.5
43	9	48	17
41	5.5	49	18.5
42	7.5	52	23
45	12.5	49	18.5
41	5.5	55	26.5
37	4	54	25
		44	10.5
		55	26.5
		50	20.5
sum	$\Sigma R_X = 82$		$\Sigma R_Y = 296$

were male and proposers were told about the gender of responder (Either Male or Female). The idea is very simple: It is a test of the hypothesis that the gender plays an important role in economic behavior in sample. If the decision is not influenced by gender, then male proposer shall offer identical amount to responders irrespective of their gender. The data is shown in Table 9.5.

The sum of the ranks of the smaller group is the test statistics. The test statistic is denoted as W_s. In case of the example, the test statistics is 82.

For sample of 25 and above, W_s is normally distributed. The mean is

$$\bar{W}_S = \frac{n_1(n_1 + n_2 + 1)}{2}$$

The variance is

$$\sigma^2_{Ws} = \sqrt{\frac{n_1 n_2 (n_1 + n_2 + 1)}{12}}$$

W_s value can be converted into Z, and probability of Z can be found. If $Z \geq |1.96|$, then we reject the null.

$$W_s = \sum (\text{Rank in Fem res}) = 82$$
$$\sum (\text{Rank in Male res}) = 296$$

$$z = \frac{W_s - \dfrac{n_1(n_1 + n_2 + 1)}{2}}{\sqrt{\dfrac{n_1 n_2 (n_1 + n_2 + 1)}{12}}}$$

$$z = \frac{82 - \dfrac{12(12 + 15 + 1)}{2}}{\sqrt{\dfrac{12 \times 15(12 + 15 + 1)}{12}}} = \frac{-86}{20.4939} = -4.19$$

The two-tailed probability associated with $z=4.19$ is 0.000027. The probability is much smaller than the alpha of 0.05 and hence the null is rejected. This implies that there is enough evidence to say that male proposers send smaller proposals to females than that of males.
Wilcoxon W_s can be converted into Mann–Whitney U.

$$U = \frac{n_1(n_1 + 2n_2 + 1)}{2} - W_s$$

U and W are linearly related. And hence U is not discussed here separately.

R Code. Wilcoxon Rank-sum Test
```
female<- c(46, 44, 33, 42, 34, 34, 43, 41, 42, 45, 41, 37)
male <- c(45, 50, 51, 47, 53, 47, 48, 49, 52, 49, 55, 54, 44, 55, 50)
wilcox.test (female, male, correct = F)
```

9.4.3 The Kruskal–Wallis H Test

The Kruskal–Wallis H test is a useful alternative to independent samples ANOVA. The test uses similar logic that is discussed in Wilcoxon rank-sum test. The sum ranks of each group are used. The test can be used when the measurement scale is not interval level and when ANOVA cannot be used. It is also used when the assumptions underlying ANOVA are also severally violated.

Once combined ranking is obtained for the entire data, and if the samples are from the same population, then ΣR_1, that is, sum rank for group one, divided by n_1, will not be different from other groups' rank-sum. The sum of rank-sum of each group is large when sum ranks are different from each other. These differences determine the H statistics.

The test statistics for Kruskal–Wallis is

$$H = -3(n_{total} + 1) + \frac{12}{n_{total}(n_{total} + 1)}\left[\frac{(\Sigma R_1^2)}{n_1} + \frac{(\Sigma R_2)^2}{n_2} + \cdots\right]$$

where ΣR_1 is the sum of the rank for group one and so on, n_1 is sample-size group 1, n_{total} is total sample in study. The H follows chi-square distribution at df$=k-1=3-1=2$.

Look at the data in Table 9.6. The table shows the data of scores obtained by three different training groups.

The H can be calculated as follows:

$$H = -3(n_{total} + 1) + \frac{12}{n_{total}(n_{total} + 1)}\left[\frac{(\Sigma R_1)^2}{n_1} + \frac{(\Sigma R_2)^2}{n_2} + \cdots\right]$$

$$H = -3(17 + 1) + \frac{12}{17(17+1)}\left[\frac{(42)^2}{6} + \frac{(83.5)^2}{6} + \frac{(27.5)^2}{5}\right]$$

$$H = -54 + 0.03922[1607.2917]$$

$$H = -54 + 63.031 = 9.031$$

Table 9.6. *Data for Scores Obtained by Three Groups under Three Training Conditions*

	Training A	Rank	Training B	Rank	Training C	Rank
	3	3.5	7	11.5	5	7.5
	4	5.5	10	16	2	1.5
	2	1.5	8	13	6	9.5
	5	7.5	9	14.5	4	5.5
	9	14.5	11	17	3	3.5
	6	9.5	7	11.5		
Rank-sum		42		83.5		27.5

The H, Kruskal–Wallis statistics, follows χ^2 distribution. $df = k-1 = 3-1 = 2$, where k is number of groups. The critical chi-square value at 0.05 level of significance for $df = 2$ is 5.99. The obtained value of 9.031 is greater than the critical value and as a result, the null hypothesis is refuted. The null states that all groups have similar distribution. That is there is no difference in distribution of any two groups. The alternative implies that there are at least two groups for which the distribution is not similar. Dunn (1964) suggested that if the null hypothesis is rejected, then for all pairs of comparisons (A with B, A with C, and B with C) should be carried out by employing Mann–Whitney U test with revised alpha value. The correction is similar to Dunn multiple comparison procedure using Bonferroni inequality. The correction is $\alpha_p = \alpha/c = 0.05/3 = 0.017$, where c is number of comparisons. One should be using Wilcoxon rank-sum test as well with the same correction. The effect-size for Kruskal–Wallis test can be obtained by epsilon-squared (E_R^2).

$$E_R^2 = \frac{H}{\left(n_{total}^2 - 1\right)/\left(n_{total} + 1\right)} = \frac{9.031}{\left(17^2 - 1\right)/\left(17 + 1\right)} = 0.564$$

The effect-size falls between 0 and 1 and hence can be interpreted in terms of association between independent and dependent variable.

R Code 9.6. Kruskal–Wallis Test
```
score <- c(3, 4, 2, 5, 9, 6, 7, 10, 8, 9, 11, 7, 5, 2, 6, 4, 3)
gp <- c(1, 1, 1, 1, 1, 1, 2, 2, 2, 2, 2, 2, 3, 3, 3, 3, 3)
kw <- kruskal.test (score, gp)   # Kruskal-Wallis test
kw                                #output of KW test
n <- length(score)               # n is ntotal
(kw$stat/((n^2-1)/(n+1)))         # computes epsilon-square
```

9.5 COMPARING LOCATIONS OF DEPENDENT SAMPLES

The above section presented non-parametric procedures for statistically analyzing the data of independent samples. This section shall discuss the non-parametric statistical tools useful for inference with dependent or correlated samples. The techniques discussed here are sign test, Wilcoxon signed-rank test, and Friedman's rank test.

9.5.1 The Sign Test

The sign test is perhaps the simplest of tests in terms of understanding and computing ease. It is an easy alternative to dependent samples *t*-test. However, sign test is not a preferred alternative. The Wilcoxon signed-rank test is preferred alternative. The sign test can be performed on ordinal data or on the interval data that does not follow the assumptions of *t*-test.

The university is running a 20-session course on science and society that is aiming at increasing the scientific temper in the society. The participants of this course are tested before and after the course on scientific temperament scale. The scores of the participants are dependent (due to repeated measures). The data is not analyzed using *t*-test since the scale of measurement is not assumed to be interval. The data is given in Table 9.7.

The data in Table 9.7 shows 13 individuals taking pre-test and 12 individuals taking post-test. We shall ignore the 13th score since no post-test score is available for this individual and consider our sample as 12. The sign column of Table 9.7 shows that the sign of the difference between the "After" and "Before." Now, we just need to find the number of +ve and –ve signs. There are 10 positive signs and 2 negative signs. If the science and society course has no impact on the scientific temperament of participants, then the signs would be randomly equal. In this case, the population signs are equal and sample signs are similar within sampling errors. This hypothesis can be tested by using a chi-square test.

	+ve	−ve
Observed Frequency	10	2
Expected Frequency	6	6

Table 9.7. *Score on Scientific Temperament Scale Before and After Course*

Participant	After	Before	Sign
1	30	22	+
2	32	24	+
3	28	19	+
4	26	27	−
5	19	17	+
6	27	18	+
7	30	26	+
8	16	20	−
9	29	21	+
10	24	23	+
11	34	28	+
12	32	30	+
13		35	

The chi-square test statistics is as follows:

$$\chi^2 = \frac{\Sigma(f_o - f_e)^2}{f_e}$$

$$\chi^2 = \frac{(10-6)^2}{6} + \frac{(2-6)^2}{6} = 5.33$$

df=1, and the chi-square at df=1 at 0.05 level is 3.84. The obtained value is larger than 3.84 and hence we reject the model that states that frequencies are equal in population. We accept that the science and society course has an impact on increasing the scientific temperament scores of people. The Wilcoxon signed-rank test is a better alternative to sign test. Let us discuss that.

9.5.2 Wilcoxon Signed-rank Test

The logic of Wilcoxon signed-rank test is identical to Wilcoxon rank-sum test. The Wilcoxon rank-sum test is applied to the independent samples, and Wilcoxon signed-rank test is applied to the dependent samples.

Let us continue with the example of sign test.

Participant	After	Before	Difference (A−B)	Rank of (A−B)	Sign
1	30	22	8	9	9
2	32	24	8	9	9
3	28	19	9	11.5	11.5
4	26	27	−1	1.5	−1.5
5	19	17	2	3.5	3.5
6	27	18	9	11.5	11.5
7	30	26	4	5.5	5.5
8	16	20	−4	5.5	−5.5
9	29	21	8	9	9
10	24	23	1	1.5	1.5
11	34	28	6	7	7
12	32	30	2	3.5	3.5
					$R_+=71$
					$R_-=7$

The steps in Computing Wilcoxon signed-rank test are as follows:

Step 1: Obtain the data of two dependent groups in column.
Step 2: Obtain the difference between each pair of score (A–B).
Step 3: Rank the difference (A–B) disregarding the sign.
Step 4: Resupply the appropriate signs to ranks of (A–B).

The sum of the ranks with a negative sign is R_- and the sum of the ranks with a positive sign is R_+. The test statistic, T, is *whichever is smaller* between the two.

The test statistics for the present data is 7. Often textbooks provide tables to interpret the test statistics. The Wilcoxon T can be converted into Z. The sampling distribution of Wilcoxon test statistics is standard normal under the null hypothesis. The mean of the distribution is $0.25n(n+1)$ and the standard deviation is $\sqrt{\dfrac{n(n+1)(2n+1)}{24}}$

Z conversion of $T=7$ is

$$Z = \frac{T - 0.25n(n+1)}{\sqrt{\dfrac{n(n+1)(2n+1)}{24}}} = \frac{7 - 0.25 \times 12 \times (12+1)}{\sqrt{\dfrac{12(12+1)(2 \times 12+1)}{24}}} = -2.51$$

The probability of $Z=2.51$ is 0.012, which is smaller than 0.05 level. To say it simply, Z is greater than 1.96 and hence is significant at 0.05 level. The null hypothesis is rejected. The null states that the distribution of the pre-test scores and post test scores is similar. The results of the Wilcoxon signed-rank test are showing that the post-scores distribution is different than the pre-score distribution. The rank-sum shows that the post-score distribution is away from the pre-score distribution and we can conclude that the training in science and society increases the scientific temper. The last point to be noted is that the exact p-values cannot be computed with ties. The R code for the Wilcoxon signed-rank test is 9.7.

R Code 9.7. Wilcoxon Signed-rank Test
```
pre <- c(22,24,19,27,17,18,26,20,21,23,28,30)   # data before
post <- c(30,32,28,26,19, 27,30,16,29,24,34,32) # data after
wilcox.test(pre, post, paired = T)              # Wilcoxon test and output

Wilcoxon signed rank test with continuity
      correction

data: pre and post
V = 7, p-value = 0.01319
alternative hypothesis: true location shift is not equal to 0
```

The Wilcoxon signed-rank test is better than the sign test because the sign test considers only the difference between the pair of the score whereas the Wilcoxon test uses the difference as well as size of the difference (through ranking).

9.5.3 Friedman's Rank Test for *k* Correlated Samples

The Friedman's rank test for k correlated samples is non-parametric analog to one-way dependent samples ANOVA. The Friedman's test can be performed when the ANOVA for the dependent samples cannot be performed for the reason of inferiority of scale of measurement or serious violations of underlying assumptions. The test is developed by Milton Friedman, a well-known economist. The test statistics (χ_F^2) is obtained as follows:

$$\chi_F^2 = \frac{12}{nk(k+1)} \sum_{i=1}^{k} R_i^2 - 3n(k+1)$$

where χ_F^2=Friedman's statistics that follows chi-square distribution under null, n=sample size, k=number of conditions or levels of IV; $\sum_{i=1}^{k} R_i^2$=of the ranks for each condition or level and R_i is sum of the ranks for i^{th} condition. The raking of the data is row wise. Each row in the data represents one participant's scores. The scores are ranked for the participant. Similarly, scores are ranked for all the participants. The ranking is demonstrated with the data.

Example: Let us continue with behavior economics experiments. There are three most common experimental paradigms: ultimatum game, trust game, and dictator game. The ultimatum game is explained in the previous section. The dictator game takes away the freedom of the responder to decline the offer and responders have to accept any offer made. The trust game involves interesting twist—whatever amount the proposer sends to the responder is tripled and then responder can send some fraction of it back to the proposer. For example, 10 participants are subjected to all three conditions with ₹100 as the initial endowment. The data given below shows the findings of the experiment in terms of amount proposed.

Participant	Dictator	Ultimatum	Trust
A	20 (1)	47 (2)	50 (3)
B	22 (1)	50 (2)	55 (3)
C	10 (1)	48 (2)	58 (3)
D	16 (1)	45 (2)	46 (3)
E	18 (1)	52 (3)	50 (2)
F	16 (1)	52 (2)	50 (3)
G	09 (1)	60 (3)	55 (2)
H	15 (1)	57 (3)	48 (2)
I	25 (1)	54 (3)	45 (2)
J	30 (1)	52 (2)	55 (3)
Rank-sum	10	24	26

The Friedman's statistics is calculated as

$$\chi_F^2 = \frac{12}{nk(k+1)} \sum_{i=1}^{k} R_i^2 - 3n(k+1)$$

$$\chi_F^2 = \frac{12}{10 \times 3 \times 4}(10^2 + 24^2 + 26^2) - 3 \times 10 \times 4$$

$$\chi_F^2 = 0.1 \times (1352) - 120 = 15.2$$

χ_F^2 follows chi-square distribution under the null hypothesis with df=k−1. The chi-square at 0.05 level at 2 degrees of freedom is 5.99. The obtained value is 15.2 which is larger than the critical value. The obtained value is significant and null hypothesis that three groups are from the same distribution is rejected. The fractions sent by the participants differ across the three experimental game structures. One can carry out comparison of each pair by using Wilcoxon signed-rank test as well. The R Code for Friedman's test is given in R Code 9.8.

R Code 9.8. Friedman's Test for Dependent Samples
```
dg <- c(20,22,10,16,18,16,9,15,25,30)
ug <- c(47,50,48,45,52,52,60,57,54,52)
tg <- c(50,55,58,46,50,50,55,48,45,55)
data <- c(dg,ug,tg)
data1 <- matrix (data, ncol = 3, byrow = F, dimnames = list(1:10, c("DG",
"UG", "TG")))       # converting data into matrix with labels
data1                 # data matrix
```

```
friedman.test(data1)      # Friedman's test with output

  Friedman rank sum test
data: data1
Friedman chi-squared = 15, df = 2, p-value = 0.0005531
```

SUMMARY

This chapter presented a discussion on non-parametric procedures for ordinal and nominal data. There are many other options, particularly multivariate one, that are not discussed in this section. The R codes provided are useful in analyzing your own data. The bootstrapping is a growing field and in the recent future perhaps the bootstrapping would take over the non-parametric options. The popularity is also a function of the ability of the bootstrap tests to estimate parameter without the data loss which is common attribute of the non-parametric options.

EXERCISE

1. In a multiplex, out of 230 individuals, 89 choose screen 1, 60 choose screen 2, 40 choose screen 3, and remaining choose screen 4. Test the hypothesis that the screens are equally preferred.
2. Test the hypothesis that screens are preferred with 6:8:4:5 ratio.
3. Solve the problem using R.
4. In a research, 55% people chose brand A and remaining chose brand B. Test the hypothesis that proportions are identical.
5. A group of Individuals responded under five conditions. The correct answers under five conditions are 50, 45, 60, 20, 70. Test that proportion of people passing is same in population.
6. Carry out median test for a data. x=(11 10 8 13 10 13 10 9 11 12 15 8 10 12 11 10 7 9 10 10). Y=(16 12 10 14 13 13 14 7 12 13 14 12 11 14 13 13 15 12 11 10)
7. Test the hypothesis with Wilcoxon rank-sum test.
8. Assuming that 6 is dependent data, test the hypothesis that two distributions are similar.
9. Explain Kruskal–Wallis test.

10 Factor Analysis and Structural Equation Modeling

10.1 INTRODUCTION

The trickiest problem for the discipline of psychology is the unobservable nature of the object of its investigation—the mind. This creates difficulty in understanding the structural components of human mind. So much so that these difficulties lead the behavioral school of psychology to completely abolish intra-individual reality and consider observable-measureable behavior as a mind. One should note that it's not a different story for other social sciences as well when it comes to fundamental assumptions about the human mind. For example, a similar theoretical position has been taken by economics in terms of "theory of revealed preferences," primarily driven by the work of Paul Samuelson.

The discipline of psychology has two central questions: (a) What does human mind consist of? This question looks at the *structural* organization of the human mind and tries to understand various constituent aspects of mind. For example, if intelligence is assumed to be an important structure of the human mind, then we want to know the psychological attributes that constitute human intelligence. We are also interested in the interrelationship of these aspects. We may further want to know whether intelligence is one single structure or whether there are independent structures that are jointly known as intelligence. (b) How the mind works? This question is dealing with *functions* of the structures of the human mind. It also implies that structurally different attributes might work together functionally. If intelligence is a function of human mind, then we are interested in knowing how intelligence works while doing its job. We may also have an interest in understanding the various steps involved in executing this function. The first type of understanding of intelligence is reflected in theories such as Spearman's "g" factor theory and Guilford's structure of intellect model. The second type of understanding is reflected in information processing theories such as Jensen's reaction time, Nettelbeck's inspection-time, and PASS model. The first types of theories are also known as factor analytic theories of intelligence. The reason is simple. The statistical technique called factor analysis is used to derive these theoretical positions. The application of factor analysis to uncover the structure of human mind is primarily due to the pioneering work by Charles Spearman on the "g" factor theory. Since then, factor analysis has become a highly indispensable tool in the armory of psychology researchers. Understanding the structure of a given psychological attribute is one of the questions answered by factor analysis. This question has seminal importance for the discipline. Nevertheless, factor analysis is a useful instrument in psychological test development as well. This chapter as well as the next chapter shall illustrate the importance of factor analysis in test/scale construction.

Over the last 100 years, factor analysis has evolved into a diverse, effective, and application-specific tool-set. Factor analysis is not a single analysis, but there are many methods and approaches to do so. Factor analysis can be broadly classified into two major types: (a) Exploratory factor analysis (EFA) and (2) confirmatory factor analysis (CFA). The **EFA**, as the name suggests, is a data-driven process that explores the structure in the data. It doesn't necessarily start with theory and doesn't have a specified hypothesis-testing mechanism. The **CFA** is a theory-driven process that attempts to test whether the given data fit to a theoretical model. Now the CFA is considered as a part of the broad framework of structural equation modeling (SEM) (however, there are some methods that are called CFA but they are not under the framework of SEM). The SEM is an important alternative to carry out predictive analysis with variables that are not observable (latent variables). Since SEM-CFA is discussed in this chapter, it is a good idea to get us briefly introduced to full-SEMs as well. This chapter shall cover these three data-analytic methods: The EFA, CFA, and SEM.

Factor analysis is a data reduction technique. The main purpose of factor analysis is to reduce the data on all variables to small number of factors without much loss of variability in the data.

10.2 EXPLORATORY FACTOR ANALYSIS

Let's start with a correlation matrix that I have obtained on my data (Belhekar, 2008) on NEO-PI-R. The six-variable correlation matrix is chosen by considering points such as it is based on sound theoretical work (it is very clean data which is otherwise rarity). The correlation among six different variables is displayed in Table 10.1. The six variables are E1 = Warmth; E2 = Gregariousness; E6 = Positive emotion; N3 = Anxiety; N4 = Hostility; N6 = Vulnerability.

The correlation matrix generally omits the upper diagonal. I have retained it to keep appearance simple. There is one noticeable observation. The first three facets are well correlated, the last three factors are well correlated, and the first three and last three do not correlate much with each other. One way of describing the variation in this correlation matrix is to say that there are two underlying dimensions (factors): One of them is associated with extraversion measures and the second one is associated with neuroticism measures. Factor analysis is the statistical method that would identify the underlying structure. In this case it looks very easy. In reality, the data are more complex, for example, there may be correlations among the items of scale/test or intercorrelations among several measures. At times, a researcher does not start with any theory but follows the data (e.g., psych lexical personality research) wherein the patters of correlations are more complex and the underlying structure cannot be identified by just visual examination.

10.2.1 General Description

Factor analysis is a data reduction technique. It is used with cross-sectional data to identify variables in the data that form theoretically meaningful subgroups. These subgroups are expected to be independent from each other. For example, in the above data, neuroticism factor and extraversion factor are two relatively independent subsets. Variables in a subset are

Table 10.1. *Correlation Matrix of Six Personality Variables*

Variables	E1	E2	E6	N3	N4	N6
E1	1	0.493	0.523	−0.091	−0.08	−0.011
E2	**0.493**	1	0.358	−0.05	−0.048	0.051
E6	**0.523**	**0.358**	1	−0.059	−0.006	0.023
N3	−0.091	−0.05	−0.059	1	0.614	0.595
N4	−0.08	−0.048	−0.006	**0.614**	1	0.523
N6	−0.011	0.051	0.023	**0.595**	**0.523**	1

Notes: E1 = Warmth; E2 = Gregariousness; E6 = Positive Emotion; N3 = Anxiety; N4 = Hostility; N6 = Vulnerability. Values greater than absolute value .4 are shown in bold face.

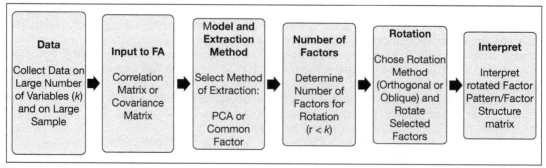

Figure 10.1. *Schematic Diagram of Steps in EFA*

related with each other and are unrelated with variables in other subsets. These subsets are called factors.

Two strands can be identified in the EFA: (a) principal component analysis (PCA) and (b) common factor analysis (FA). Some researchers call both of them factor analysis. Others do not consider PCA as a factor analysis and only consider common factor analysis as factor analysis. We shall look at the difference while discussing the issue of communality.

The following steps are taken in PCA and FA. Initially, data is obtained for large number of participants on many variables. Then the correlation matrix for the data is obtained and either using PCA or FA, the factors are extracted. Then a decision about the number of factors to be retained is made and those many factors are rotated. The results are then interpreted. Researchers often try different number of factors to understand interpretability and interpretation of factors is the most important part of EFA. If the solutions are interpretable, then the PCA and FA is a useful exercise. The schematic diagram in Figure 10.1 explains steps in EFA.

Tabachnick and Fidell (2007) describe three problems in doing factor analysis. (a) Absence of criterion variable: the analysis discussed so far (linear regression, correlation, logistic regression, *t*-test, ANOVA) have some criterion variable against which the solution is tested. The PCA and FA do not have such an external criterion. (b) Presence of mathematically identical but theoretically different solutions: a variety of methods are available for rotation providing mathematical identical solutions but each of them is slightly different in terms of interpretability and scientific utility. This may lead to different researchers choosing different rotation methods and concluding differently about the same data. (c) Factor analysis is likely to be misused by researchers in an attempt to fit some model to data when every other statistical procedure fails.

10.2.2 Factor Analysis Jargon

Let's quickly understand the meaning of the words that we shall frequently use while discussing FA.

Correlation matrix: This matrix (or covariance matrix) generally refers to the *observed correlations* (or covariances) among variables obtained on the data. The truncated factor analysis solutions always have less information than the information in a correlation matrix. After factor analysis, a well-fitting factor analysis solution should be able to give us the correlation matrix back that is closer to the observed correlation. The correlation matrix obtained from FA solution is called a *reproduced correlation* matrix. The difference between the observed and reproduced correlation matrices is called a *residual correlation* matrix. The residual matrix contains the variance that the PCA or FA did not explain.

Extraction: This is the process of transforming variance from a correlation matrix into factors or components. The PCA method provides *components* and FA provides *factors*. The

PCA extracts from the observed correlation matrix, that is, all observed variance is analyzed. The FA extracts from *shared variance* or common variance. A shared or common variance is that variance which is common to all variables. The factors are considered as underlying causes of the observable variation among the variables, and components are just accumulations of variables; thus, in one sense, variables produce components. If the correlation matrix is analyzed, then why can one method analyze common variance and the other cannot? You think for a while; the answer is on the way.

Communalities (h^2): These are estimates of shared variance for each of the variables. There are various estimates of communalities.

Rotation: This is a process of making the selected factors or components more interpretable. Rotated and unrotated matrices are mathematically identical, but with an appropriate rotation method of correct number of factors, the rotation improves interpretability. There are two types of rotation methods: orthogonal and oblique. The *orthogonal* rotation method produces factors that are independent or uncorrelated, and *oblique* rotation produces factors that are dependent or correlated.

Factor pattern matrix: This matrix is a "variables by factors" matrix. If we retain two factors for a six-variable correlation matrix, then the factor pattern matrix is a 6×2 matrix, and 12 elements of this matrix are called factor *loadings*. The number of factors is expected to be much smaller than the variables. Loading refers to the coefficient describing the unique relation between a variable and a factor. The factor pattern is evaluated for interpretation in the case of orthogonal rotation. The factor pattern and factor structure matrices are identical for orthogonal factors.

Factor structure matrix: This matrix is a "variables by factors" matrix describing the correlations of variables with factors. In the case of oblique rotations, the factor pattern and factor structure matrices are different. In the case of orthogonal rotations, they are identical.

Phi matrix: This is the inter-factor correlation matrix. In the case of orthogonal factors, the phi matrix is an identity matrix and in the case of orthogonal factors, off-diagonal elements describe inter-factor correlations.

10.2.3 Purpose of Exploratory Factor Analysis

The EFA can be carried out for various reasons. One, understanding the number of factors that can describe the existing correlation matrix is a common purpose of EFA. Two, once the rotated factors are obtained, researchers are interested in understanding the theoretical meaning of those factors. This is perhaps the most widespread purpose of doing EFA. Three, the EFA can be carried out to evaluate theory. Though, it is generally believed that the theory is evaluated by CFA, and EFA provides an exploration in the data, researchers often use EFA to evaluate theory. The EFA outputs in line with theory are generally used as evidence in favor of theory in many cases. Four, EFA factors can be saved and used as variables in analysis. When you have a large number of variables, the EFA provides a data reduction mechanism and the factors can be used as variables. Using the rotated PCs as predictors in regression analysis is becoming a common trend.

10.2.4 Specific Issues in EFA

Sample size: The general recommendation is that the sample size should be large. The sample size of 200 is perhaps the minimum requirement and a sample of size 300 and above is viewed with some respect. Though some (e.g., Sapnas & Zeller, 2002) have recommended small samples under certain conditions; however, the above recommendation of large samples is often practiced.

Normality, linearity, outliers, and multicollinearity: Univariate normality is a useful assumption; however, small deviations do not influence EFA much. Multivariate normality is a more serious requirement of the data for statistical decision in retaining factors for rotation. The absence of linearity degrades the solution. It's well known that outliers have an adverse impact on correlations and, hence, must be avoided. The multicollinearity is a serious problem when the matrix is inverted. The EFA does not require matrix inversion. However, the determinant of the correlation matrix and the eigenvalues approach zero with high multicollinearity. As a remedy, a variable with a very high squared multiple correlation (SMC) is generally removed.

Factorability of correlation matrix: A correlation matrix should be suitable for factor analysis. The factor analysis requires enough common variation in the correlation matrix. Generally, the absence of correlation above absolute value 0.3 is a problematic situation for the application of FA. Two popular measures are Bartlett's test of sphericity and the Kaiser–Meyer–Olkin (KMO) measure of sampling adequacy.

Bartlett's test is used to test the null hypothesis that the population correlation matrix is an identity matrix. The identity matrix has unities on diagonal spaces and zeros in off-diagonal spaces. Bartlett's test statistics is as follows:

$$\chi^2 = -\left(n - 1 - \frac{2k+5}{6}\right)\ln|R|$$

where χ^2 is chi-square distributed Bartlett's test statistics at df $= [k \times (k-1)]/2$, and k is the number of variables, R is the correlation matrix, $|R|$ is a determinant of the correlation matrix, and n=sample size. In the case of the above data,

$$\chi^2 = -\left(304 - 1 - \frac{2 \times 6 + 5}{6}\right)\ln|0.1986293| = 485.16$$

The df $= [6 \times (6-1)]/2 = 15$. The null hypothesis is rejected and we accept the alternative that the population correlation matrix departs significantly from the identity matrix. R code 10.1 is as follows.

R Code 10.1. Bartlett's Test of Sphericity
```
cr <- c(1, 0.493, 0.523, -0.091, -0.08, -0.011, 0.493, 1, 0.358, -0.05,
-0.048, 0.051, 0.523, 0.358, 1, -0.059, -0.006, 0.023, -0.091, -0.05,
-0.059, 1, 0.614, 0.595, -0.08, -0.048, -0.006, 0.614, 1, 0.523, -0.011,
0.051, 0.023, 0.595, 0.523, 1)    # data
R <- matrix(cr, ncol = 6)         # dada into matrix
n <- 304                          # sample size
k <- ncol(R)                      # number of variables
bt_chi <- -(n-1-(2*k+5)/6)*(log(det(R)))
df <- (k*(k-1))/2
print(bt_chi)
print(df)
print(pchisq(bt_chi, df, lower.tail=F))
library(psych)
cortest.bartlett(R, n)            # provides Bartlett's test statistics
```
Bartlett's test is particularly known for sensitivity to sample size and it increases in power with sample size. It is recommended that $(n/k) < 5$, is not a suitable sample size for EFA.

The **KMO** measure of sampling adequacy is obtained by

$$KMO = \frac{\sum\limits_{i}\sum\limits_{j\neq i}^{n} r_{ij}^2}{\sum\limits_{i}\sum\limits_{j\neq i}^{n} r_{ij}^2 + \sum\limits_{i}\sum\limits_{j\neq i}^{n} a_{ij}^2}$$

where $\sum\limits_{i}\sum\limits_{j\neq i}^{n} r_{ij}^2$ is the sum of squared correlation and $\sum\limits_{i}\sum\limits_{j\neq i}^{n} a_{ij}^2$ is the sum of squared partial correlations. The KMO would be a large value if $\sum\limits_{i}\sum\limits_{j\neq i}^{n} a_{ij}^2$ is a small value and it will be a small value if $\sum\limits_{i}\sum\limits_{j\neq i}^{n} a_{ij}^2$ is a large value. It implies that the KMO index indicates contribution of partial correlations to the ratio of correlations. Small partial correlations are functions of common variance in the correlation matrix. The KMO of 0.5 and below is considered as poor factorability. The KMO value of 0.7 and above is good and above 0.8 is excellent. For example presented in Table 10.1, the KMO is

$$KMO = \frac{\sum\limits_{i}\sum\limits_{j\neq i}^{n} r_{ij}^2}{\sum\limits_{i}\sum\limits_{j\neq i}^{n} r_{ij}^2 + \sum\limits_{i}\sum\limits_{j\neq i}^{n} a_{ij}^2} = \frac{3.351}{4.925} = 0.68$$

The KMO=0.68 is acceptable a value. It can be obtained for each variable as well with the similar logic. Variables with very poor KMO values need to be examined before inclusion. R code 10.2 describes the computation of KMO in R.

R Code 10.2. Overall and Variable-wise KMO

```
library(psych)          # Call library psych
KMO(R)                  # KMO syntax
## Output ##
Kaiser-Meyer-Olkin factor adequacy
Call: KMO(r = R)
Overall MSA = 0.68      # Overall KMO
MSA for each item =     # variable-wise KMO

E1     E2     E6     N3     N4     N6
0.62   0.69   0.66   0.67   0.72   0.72
```

10.2.5 Basic Equations

This section is organized in two parts: First explains the factor models and the second explains the matrix algebra notations for computing a factor analysis solution.

10.2.5.1 Factor Models and Communalities

The component model and the common factor model are two models of factor analysis. Different authors use different notational systems. I am following Harman (1976) with slight modification. The model for PCA or components analysis is as follows:

$$z_j = a_{j1}F_1 + a_{j2}F_2 + \cdots + a_{jk}F_k \qquad \text{for } j = 1, 2, \ldots, k$$

where z_j is the standardized form of variable j, $F_1, F_2, \ldots, F_k$ are k unrelated components such that each component, one after another, makes maximum contribution to the variance of k variables, a_{j1} is the weight for the variable j for the factor F_1, and so on. In factor analysis, only few components are retained. This approach is known for condensing maximum variance from the correlation matrix.

The *common factor model* tries to reproduce the correlation matrix described as

$$z_j = a_{j1}F_1 + a_{j2}F_2 + \cdots + a_{jm}F_m + d_jU_j \qquad \text{for } j = 1, 2, \ldots, k$$

where $m<k$, which are the common factors, U_j is unique j factors, and d_j is the weight associated with U_j. The common factors describe variations among the variables, whereas unique factors describe the remaining variance, which includes random errors of measurement. The coefficients associated with factors are known as *loadings*. With the condition that (a) common factors are uncorrelated among themselves and (b) unique factors are uncorrelated with common factors, the variance of j variables in terms of factor models can be described as

$$S_j^2 = 1 = a_{j1}^2 + a_{j2}^2 + \cdots + a_{jm}^2 + d_j^2$$

The $S_j^2 = 1$ is obvious since j is the standard normal variable. Each common factor has unique contribution to make to the variance of z_j, for example, a_{j1}^2 is a unique contribution of factor 1 to the variance of z_j. This leads to the understanding of an important concept in factor analysis called communalities (h^2). The communality (h^2) of variable z^2 is expressed as the sum-of-squares of common factor coefficients:

$$h_j^2 = a_{j1}^2 + a_{j2}^2 + \cdots + a_{jm}^2 \qquad \text{for } j = 1, 2, \ldots, k$$

The remaining part of the variance of variable z_j is uniqueness. The uniqueness can be further split into two portions: one, the portion that is specific to the variable and, two, the portion that is due to measurement error or unreliability of the variable. The variable z_j can be expressed as

$$z_j = a_{j1}F_1 + a_{j2}F_2 + \cdots + a_{jm}F_m + b_j S_j + e_j E_j \qquad \text{for } j = 1, 2, \ldots, k$$

where S_j is a specific factor and E_j is the error factor; b_j and e_j are their coefficients, respectively. With the condition that specific factors and error factors are uncorrelated, the coefficients are expressed as

$$d_j^2 = b_j^2 + e_j^2$$

Given this, the variance of z_j variable can be expressed as

$$S_j^2 = 1 = a_{j1}^2 + a_{j2}^2 + \cdots + a_{jm}^2 + b_j^2 + e_j^2$$
$$S_j^2 = 1 = h_j^2 + b_j^2 + e_j^2$$

$$\textit{variance of } z_j = 1 = \text{communality of } j + \text{Specificity of } j + \text{unrealibility of } j$$

This implies that the unit variance of z_j is partitioned into communality and unique variance. If the reliability of the variable j is conceived as

$$r_j = 1 - e_j^2$$

then the reliability can be expressed as

$$r_j = h_j^2 + b_j^2$$

A useful idea is the index of *completeness of factorization*.

$$C_j = 100 h_j^2 / \left(h_j^2 + b_j^2 \right) = 100 \times \text{communality} / (\text{reliability})$$

The C_j will not approach 100 unless $b_j^2 = 0$. The closer this number is to 100, better the factorability of the correlation matrix.

10.2.5.2 Matrix Equations for EFA

The procedure of EFA is described in terms of matrix algebra since it is a more suitable expression. Let's start with the $\mathbf{R}_{k \times k}$ correlation matrix among the variables obtained from $\mathbf{Z}_{n \times k}$ data matrix. Table 10.1 describes $\mathbf{R}_{k \times k}$. Let's have notations like n=number of observations, k=number of variables, and m=number of factors. This section describes equations about extraction and rotation.

10.2.5.3 Extraction

The correlation (or covariance) matrix can be a diagonalizable matrix. The diagonalization of the correlation matrix provides eigenvectors and eigenvalues. The eigenvalues can be defined as

$$L = V'RV$$

where $\mathbf{V}_{k \times k}$ is the $k \times k$ matrix, the columns of which are called eigenvectors. The number of eigenvectors is equal to the number of variables. The principal diagonals of L are the eigenvalues. L can be obtained by the following R code.

R Code 10.3. Eigenvalues and Eigenvectors of Correlation Matrix in R

```
eig <- eigen(R)                          # diagonalization in R
ll <- round((t(eig$vectors) %*% R %*% eig$vectors), 2)
                                         # computing eigenvalues
diag(ll)                                 # diagonal of ll matrix that
                                           is eigenvalues

eig$values                               # eigenvalues from eigen
                                           command
```

The eigen vector is as follows for the data

$$\mathbf{V}_{k \times k} = \begin{pmatrix} 0.23 & -0.57 & -0.06 & -0.01 & 0.78 & 0.12 \\ 0.17 & -0.52 & 0.72 & -0.18 & -0.37 & -0.07 \\ 0.18 & -0.54 & -0.66 & 0.09 & -0.47 & -0.14 \\ -0.57 & -0.16 & 0.02 & -0.06 & 0.18 & -0.78 \\ -0.54 & -0.18 & -0.15 & -0.66 & -0.06 & 0.47 \\ -0.51 & -0.25 & 0.13 & 0.72 & -0.07 & 0.36 \end{pmatrix}$$

The eigenvalues are as follows [R code `diag(ll)` from code 10.3].

$$L = (2.19 \quad 1.89 \quad 0.65 \quad 0.47 \quad 0.44 \quad 0.36)$$

from here the factor pattern can be obtained by

$$A = V\sqrt{L}$$

where $\mathbf{A}$ is a factor pattern matrix. The R code below explains the pattern matrix.

R Code 10.4. Factor Pattern matrix

```
pat <- eig$vectors %*% sqrt(ll) # factor pattern
pat
```

```
            [,1]        [,2]         [,3]         [,4]         [,5]         [,6]
[1,]   0.3451523 -0.7787185 -0.04906384 -0.00449217  0.51616709  0.07467316
[2,]   0.2559189 -0.7186017  0.58349191 -0.12667913 -0.24272909 -0.04258074
[3,]   0.2594754 -0.7361077 -0.53097483  0.05850587 -0.31193817 -0.08566518
[4,]  -0.8440792 -0.2249859  0.01320197 -0.03992213  0.11794080 -0.46961882
[5,]  -0.8037230 -0.2411958 -0.11913305 -0.45089457 -0.03745658  0.27928457
[6,]  -0.7613197 -0.3414094  0.10406099  0.49559014 -0.04511854  0.21617255
```

```
## reproducing R
round(pat %*% t(pat), 2) # round is used to get two digits output
```

In reality, the full solution of **A** is rarely used by researchers. Only first few factors (or columns) of **A** are selected and used for further rotation. The useful and theoretically important part is the reproduced correlation. **A** can be used to reproduce correlations:

$$R = AA'$$

When **A** is not a full solution but a truncated A is used (first few columns of **A**), then it is expressed as

$$R^* = AA'$$

where **R*** is a reproduced correlation matrix. The residual correlation matrix is the difference between the actual correlation matrix minus the reproduced correlation matrix. Thurstone referred to this "fundamental factor theorem":

$$R_{resid} = R - R*$$

Hereafter, the specific number of factors of **A** shall be selected for rotation. Either orthogonal or oblique rotation is carried out. The specific details of rotations are discussed in the section of rotation (Section 10.2.10).

10.2.6 Extraction Models

EFA requires various steps to be taken and, at each step, some decision to be made. The three important steps are extraction, decision about the number of factors to be rotated, and rotation. Let's start with extraction.

There are two models from which the researcher has to choose one. The first one is the component model and second one is the common factor model. The two methods differ because they solve the problem of communalities (h^2) differently. The off-diagonal entries of the correlation matrix contain communalities. However, the diagonal spaces of the correlation matrix contain unities. The unities are variances of the standard normal variable. As we have discussed in the earlier section, the unit variance is equal to communalities plus unique variance. Hence, if we factor analyze the correlation matrix as it is, the variance that is used is the combination of common variance and unique variance. The component model uses the unities in the diagonal spaces of the correlation matrix. As a result, the variance extracted by principle component (PC) methods is always the highest.

The common factor model provides an alternative to this problem. It attempts to insert an estimate of the communalities in the diagonal spaces of the correlation matrix. The problem in this approach is what should be used as an estimate of communalities. This problem does not have a single answer. The different estimates of communalities used in the diagonal spaces of the correlation matrix are as follows: (a) highest correlation, (b) reliability coefficients, (c) SMC, (d) iterative methods.

Highest correlation: The highest correlation of the variable with any other variable is inserted in the place of the variance of that variable.

Reliability coefficient: The reliability coefficient, computed by using any of the methods of reliability, is used as an estimate of communalities. The reliability of each of the variables is computed and the values are inserted in the diagonal of the correlation matrix. The preferred choice is Cronbach's alpha coefficient, which is a measure of internal consistency when the variable is a linear composite of the items. Given the above discussion, it's easy to infer that reliability is likely to be the overestimation of the communalities.

Squared multiple correlation: The variable is regressed on all other variables and the R^2 obtained is called SMC. The correlation and regression chapters have provided a discussion about SMC in multiple correlation. SMC of each variable is a reasonably better estimate of communalities.

Iterative method: This method of communality estimates an initial value of communalities from one of the methods (usually SMC), and diagonalizes and reproduces the correlation matrix. The difference between the trace of the initial matrix (sum of diagonal of the first matrix) and trace of the reproduced matrix (the sum of the diagonal of the reproduced matrix) is taken as a criterion. If this value is larger than some pre-decided small value (e.g., 0.001), then the diagonal of the reproduced matrix is inserted in the diagonal spaces or correlation matrix and the similar process is repeated. This is continued till the difference between the two successive estimates is very small. Then these estimates are taken as estimates of communalities and inserted in the original correlation matrix, and the EFA is carried out.

10.2.7 Methods of Extraction

There are several methods of extraction available. They are PCA, principal axis analysis, maximum likelihood method, unweighted least squares, generalized least squares (GLS), alpha factoring, image analysis, and so on.

10.2.7.1 Principal Component Analysis (PCA)

The PCA method of extraction follows the component model. The PCA is known for extracting maximum variance from the correlation matrix. The first PC, which is a weighted linear combination of variables, extracts maximum variance from the correlation matrix. The second PC is computed from the residual matrix that extracts the maximum variance of the residual matrix and it is also orthogonal to the previous PC. Similarly, the next components extracted are orthogonal to the previous components. The total number of PCs is equal to the total number of variables. This is a full solution. The full solution is seldom used. The truncated solution, with the initial few components, is retained and further rotated. The variance explained by PCs is ordered; the first PC explains maximum variance and the last one explain minimum variance. The variance explained totals to 100% (or 1). The major reason for choosing PCA is maximum variance extraction. Generally, the term "components" is used instead of factors in the case of PCA. One major limitation of the PCA is that it generates a first general factor (all variables load on first factor) and next factors are bi-dimensional (some variables positively load on the factor, whereas other load negatively). If more than one PC is to be retained, then this problem is solved by using an appropriate method of rotation.

R Code 10.5. PCA Using R
```
## The general command is as follows##
library(psych)
principal(R, nfactors = 1, residuals = FALSE,rotate="varimax",n.obs=NA,
covar=FALSE, scores=TRUE, oblique.scores=TRUE, method="regression")
# If all unrotated PC are to be computed, the use foloing code.
fit <- principal(R, nfactors = 6, residuals = FALSE,rotate="none",n.
obs=304, covar=FALSE, scores=FALSE)
fit$loadings # displays the loadings matrix.
```

The above R code is explained as follows:

```
R = correlation matrix; nfactors = number of components to be extracted;
residual = whether or not to display residuals; rotate = rotation method
("none", "varimax", "quatimax", "promax", "oblimin", "simplimax", and
"cluster" are options); n.obs = sample size (when r is entered); scores
= component scores are obtained; oblique.scores = if true then component
scores are based on structure matrix; method = method of finding component
scores.
```

10.2.7.2 Principal Axis Factoring (PAF)

The PAF method of factor extraction uses the common factor model. The PAF uses an estimate of communalities instead of the full variance of the correlation matrix. The same procedure of PCA is used by the principal-factor solution, but it is applied to a reduced correlation matrix (i.e., with estimates of communalities in the diagonal) employing the model. Obviously, the PAF would extract smaller variance than PCA. The SMC is used as starting values and communalities are estimated using an iterative process. The advantage of this method is that only common variance is analyzed and the "factors" are obtained. An important dissimilarity between PCA and PAF is that the PCs are directly expressed in terms of observed variables while PAF factors can only be attained indirectly. The PAF factors are conceived as latent variables and have a "causal" meaning associated with them. The R code for PAF is as follows:

R Code 10.6. Principal Axis Factoring
```
Library(psych)
fa(R, nfactors = 2, n.obs = 304, n.iter=100, fm="pa", rotate="varimax",
scores="regression") #principal axis
# fm = "pa" is key command. The pa stands for principal axis.
```

Note for R code 10.6: R help describes fm as follows—factoring method fm="minres" will do a minimum residual (OLS), fm="wls" will do a weighted least squares (WLS) solution, fm="gls" does a generalized weighted least squares (GLS), fm="pa" will do the principal factor solution, fm="ml" will do a maximum likelihood factor analysis, fm="minchi" will minimize the sample size weighted chi square when treating pairwise correlations with different number of subjects per pair.

10.2.7.3 Maximum Likelihood

Maximum likelihood (ML) is not the most popular method of factor extraction in spite of having an elegant underlying mathematical logic. It is the only extraction method based on statistical considerations. The method was developed by Lawley and Maxwell, and further refined by Jöreskog (1967). The idea of ML is to estimate population values of factor loading that maximize the likelihood of obtaining the sample correlation matrix from population. The chi-square statistics is used to evaluate the goodness-of-fit of a model to the data. The ML estimates in the case of the EFA are known for over-factorization. That is, the ML method is notorious for retaining more than required factors for rotation. This leads to the splitting of the loadings. Given that the ML extractions leads to over-factorization, researchers can always use the root mean square of the residuals (RMSR), *df* corrected RMSR, and BIC as additional sources of information. With fm = "ml" specification in R code 10.6, the ML extraction method can be used in R. Generally, set iteration as a large number (I use 100).

10.2.7.4 Minimum Residual Analysis (MinRes)

MinRes is a method of factor analysis that minimizes the residuals. The factor loadings are estimated such that sum-of-squares off-diagonal loadings are smaller. The effectiveness of the MinRes solution depends on the number of factors extracted. In R Code 10.6, fm = "minres" will provide the minimum residual analysis output.

10.2.7.5 Unweighted Least Squares

Unweighted Least Squares (ULS) is another method of factor extractions. It attempts to minimize the squared difference between the observed correlation matrix and the reproduced correlation matrix by considering off-diagonal elements only. The ULS can be viewed as PAF with communalities estimated at the end.

10.2.7.6 Generalized (weighted) Least Squares

The only difference between the ULS and GLS is that the GLS uses weights for variables while computing the difference between off-diagonal elements of observed and reproduced correlation matrices. For R code 10.6, use fm = "gls" to get WLS factor extraction.

10.2.7.7 Image Factoring

Image factoring is a technique that combines PCA and PAF methods. The method is based on the image of the variable. The method distributes the variance of the variable reflected by other variables into factors. The image of the variable is the obtained SMC of that variable with other variables. This method solves the problem of communalities by excluding unique variance and only keeping an estimate of communalities. Each variable is regressed on the remaining variables in order to obtain image scores. The image scores are used to obtain a covariance matrix and variances of this variance–covariance matrix are used communalities. This leads to loadings to be interpreted not as correlations but as covariance, and needs a wise interpretation.

10.2.7.8 Alpha Factoring

The alpha factoring is a method that is specifically used for "psychometric" purposes. The reliability for a single sample is conceived in terms of internal consistency and the most popular measure of internal consistency is Cronbach's alpha. The alpha factoring is carried out in such a way that the reliability of the factors is maximized. An iterative procedure to estimate communalities of the common factor model is used with the condition of maximizing the alpha coefficient. The method has an advantage when researchers set the reliability of factors as the most important criterion.

10.2.8 Number of Factors

The methods of extraction provide a full solution. The number of factors or components extracted is equal to the number of factors in the full solution. The purpose of factor analysis

Table 10.2. *Unrotated PCs, Eigen Values, and Percentage of Variance*

Variable	PC1	PC2	PC3	PC4	PC5	PC6	
E1	−0.35	0.78	−0.05	0.00	−0.52	−0.07	Sum sq = 1.00
E2	−0.26	0.72	0.58	0.13	0.24	0.04	Sum sq = 1.00
E6	−0.26	0.74	−0.53	−0.06	0.31	0.09	Sum sq = 1.00
N3	0.84	0.23	0.01	0.04	−0.12	0.47	Sum sq = 1.00
N4	0.80	0.24	−0.12	0.45	0.04	−0.28	Sum sq = 1.00
N6	0.76	0.34	0.10	−0.49	0.05	−0.22	Sum sq = 1.00
Eigenvalues	**2.19**	**1.89**	**0.65**	**0.47**	**0.44**	**0.36**	
Eigen/k	0.37	0.32	0.11	0.08	0.07	0.06	Sum = 1.00
Percentage of variance	37	32	11	8	7	6	Σ%var = 100

is to reduce the number of variables. So the full solution is seldom useful. The components or factors are extracted in such a way that they progressively contain less and less variance. The first PC/factor explains maximum variance, the second explains maximum variance from the remaining variance, and so on. As a result, except for the first few PC/factors, rest of the factors are not useful for the interpretation purpose. For example, the PCA six components for the data are shown in Table 10.2.

Table 10.2 displays a full, unrotated PCA solution. Every PC column contains loadings of each variable on the respective PC. For example, −0.35 is a loading of E1 on PC1, similarly E2's loading of PC2 is 0.72. The maximum value of loading is 1. Generally, a loading of absolute value 0.30 is considered as "important" loading. The sum-of-squares column loading provides eigenvalues. For example,

$$PC1 = (-0.35, \ -0.26, \ -0.26, \ 0.84, \ 0.80, \ 0.76)$$
$$Eigen(PC1) = \Sigma(PC1)^2 = -0.35^2 + -0.26^2 + -0.26^2 + 0.84^2 + 0.80^2 + 0.76^2 = 2.19$$

The eigenvalue of PC1 is 2.19. Similarly other eigenvalues of each of the PCs can be obtained and are reported in the table.

The percentage of variance explained by the PC can be obtained by

$$\text{Percentage of variance} = \frac{\text{Eigenvalue}}{k} \times 100$$

For example, for PC1, the percentage of variance is calculated as

$$\text{Percentage of variance (PC1)} = \frac{2.19}{6} \times 100 = 37\%$$

Similarly, the percentage of variance associated with other PCs can be obtained and is given in the last row of Table 10.2. The eigenvalues associated with PCs decrease as the next PC is obtained. Similarly the percentage of variance explained by the PC drops down progressively. The first PC explains 37% variance, the second PC explains 32% variance, the third PC explains 11% variance, and the fourth, fifth, and sixth PCs explain 8%, 7%, and 6% variance, respectively. It is clear that the first two PCs are explaining 69% variance in the correlation matrix. The remaining four PCs are explaining the remaining 31% variance. It is clear that all PCs are not needed to make sense of the correlations. First few PCs can give us a good approximation of the correlation matrix. The question that will bother most researchers (particularly in the absence of guiding theory) is "how many factors/PCs to be retained as a good approximation of correlation matrix?." Let's use this background to help us in understanding the number of factors to be rotated.

10.2.9 Methods to Decide Number of Factors

There are a number of ways to determine the number of factors/PCs to be retained. Guttmann's eigenvalue > 1 criteria, scree plot, eigenvalue larger than Monte Carlo eigenvalues, statistical test, percentage of variance, use of guiding theory, interpretability of different solutions, and so on, are among the popular approaches. Let's examine them.

1. **Guttmann's eigenvalue above 1 criterion:** The factor/PC that has an eigenvalue greater than 1 is retained. This approach assumes that eigenvalue 1 shall have a considerable variance. In psychometric research, this approach provides over-factorization. For our example, this criterion suggests retention of the first two PCs.

2. **Scree plot:** the scree plot is also called the Cattell's scree plot. The eigenvalues are plotted on the *X*-axis and component numbers are on the *Y*-axis. The scree can be plotted using the following R code (Figure 10.2).

R Code 10.7. Scree Plot
```
library (psych)
fit <- principal(R, nfactors = 6, rotate = "none")
eigen <- fit$values
pc_number <- 1:6
plot(pc_number, eigen, pch = 20, cex = 3, cex.lab = 2, cex.axis = 2, main
= "The Scree Plot", type = "b")
```

The scree plot is obviously a subjective estimate of the number of factors to be retained. However, most researchers use the scree plot to make this decision given the success of this approach. Raîche, Riopel, and Blais (2006) suggested an objective alternative to subjective scree. The details are not discussed but R code 10.8 for the same is provided in the following.

R Code 10.8. Non-graphical Solutions for the Cattell's Scree Test
```
library(nFactors)
ev <- eigen(cor(data))
ap <-parallel(subject=nrow(data),var=ncol(data), rep=100,cent=.05)
```

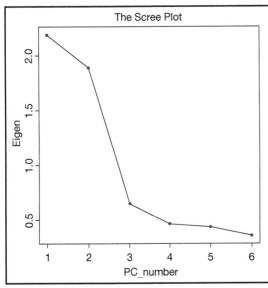

The word scree actually describes the broken rock fragments at the base of the cliffs or mountains. The scree is gradually sloping, whereas cliff is sharply sloping. The scree-plot uses a similar logic. The initial eigenvalues are large and from specific points, the eigenvalues drop down and create a scree. The PC/factors above the scree are retained. In this figure, the scree starts from the third PC. Hence, we shall retain the first two PCs. This is also described as "elbow point" because of the shape.

Figure 10.2. *The Scree Plot for R Code 10.7*

```
nS <- nScree(x=ev$values, aparallel=ap$eigen$qevpea)
plotnScree(nS)
```

3. **Parallel analysis and an eigenvalue larger than Monte Carlo eigenvalues:** The approach is proposed by Horn (1967). The approach is intuitively appealing. If the data are randomly generated, then the data will lack the structure. If we carry out PCA or common factor analysis, then the eigenvalues will be smaller than the eigenvalues for a structured (real) data. One starts with a large number of such samples (10000 or so) and for each sample k, eigenvalues are obtained. For example, for PC1 we shall have 10000 eigenvalues from random data, arranged in descending order. Now, decide some level of rejecting hypothesis, say 5%. Note the eigenvalue above which are top 5% eigenvalues for random data. If the obtained real-data eigenvalue is larger than the 5% mark eigenvalues, then we retain that PC/factor. If the obtained real-data eigenvalue is smaller than the 5% mark eigenvalue, then we stop retaining the PC/factor. The idea is simple: If the factor/PC is describing a structure, then getting large eigenvalues from random data is rare (chance less than 5%). Cota, Longman, Holden, Fekken, and Xinaris (1993) described 95th percentile eigenvalues from random data which exemplify this approach. R code 10.8 also provides parallel analysis. The R library nfactors provides parallel analysis.

4. **Percentage of variance:** A researcher pre-decides a percentage of variance that a factor analysis should explain (say, 70% for example) and keep on extracting factors till this criterion is met. This is a questionable criterion given the status of psychological theory and unreliability of measurement. This criterion is not recommended.

5. **The statistical test:** This test analyzes the residuals and tests the hypothesis to see whether residuals are large enough so that new factors are required to be computed. If residuals are large then the next factor/PC is computed. Again, residual is computed and the statistical test is carried out. The chi-square test of residuals is carried to test the fit. Unfortunately, the test statistics are sensitive to sample size and with large sample, theoretically small residuals can give significant results.

6. **Use of guiding theory:** The use of theory to decide the number of factors is a common strategy when such a theory is present. In test development, or while analyzing a large number of instruments, such a theory may not provide guidance. In the present example, the guiding theory suggests two components to be retained.

7. **Interpretability of different solution:** This is a commonly used strategy (though less reported) for making decision about the number of factors. Different numbers of factors are retained and interpretability of these solutions is verified. The most interpretable solution is finally used.

10.2.10 Factor Rotation

The number of factors retained are rotated using an orthogonal or an oblique criterion. Factor rotation is possible when the number of factors is greater than 1. The idea of rotation, reasoning for rotation, and their types are discussed.

10.2.10.1 Why Is Rotation Required?

Factor rotation is required for the following reasons:

1. The extraction methods (particularly PCA) are known to generate the first general component and the next components are bidirectional. The first PC/factor had maximum variance, the second factor explains the second best variance, and so on and so forth. The rotation is required to deal with **extraction artifact** and redistribute the variance.
2. The solution is expected to have a **simple structure**. The simple structure is indicated by one variable having the highest loading only on one factor and does not have high

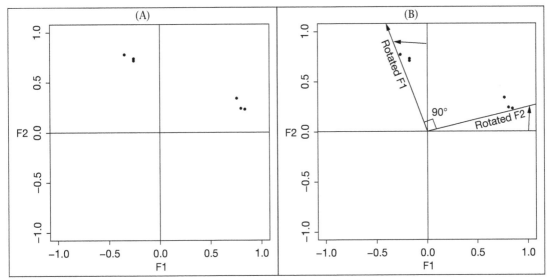

Figure 10.3 *(A) Unrotated Solution (B) Graphically Rotated Solution*

loadings (absolute value 0.30 and above) on any other factor. When one variable has high loadings on more than one factor, it is called *split loadings*. The split-loadings do not make theoretically useful meaning. The extraction methods that focus on extracting maximum variance end up disregarding a simple structure. The simple structure can be obtained by rotating the factors.

3. The factors are rotated so that they become **theoretically interpretable**. The rotation is expected to make factors theoretically more interpretable.

10.2.10.2 What Is Rotation?

Before discussing the types of rotations, let's graphically understand factor rotations. Figure 10.3(A) is an unrotated solution and Figure 10.3(B) is a rotated factor solution. The two solutions are mathematically identical. The angle of separation between the two factors for both solutions is 90°, that is, both rotated and unrotated factors are uncorrelated (orthogonal).

Figure 10.3 explains the rotation graphically. The unrotated graph has vertical axis as factor 1 and horizontal axis as factor 2. The six variables are projected into an unrotated two-dimensional factorial space. The upper left quadrant has E1, E2, and E6 and the upper right quadrant has N3, N4, and N6. For example, E1 has –0.32 and 0.78 as loadings on factor 1 and factor 2. So E1 is in the left upper quadrant. Similarly, other variables are plotted as per their scores on both factors. As we rotate the F2 axis upwards, the F1 also gets rotated to the left because we want to maintain an angle of separation of **90°** between them. In the rotated solution, all variables primarily have high scores on one factor and low scores on another factor. This is the benefit of rotation. Nowadays, no researchers follow graphical rotation. Graphical rotation was used for illustration purpose only.

10.2.11 Types of Rotation

The rotation of retained factors is of two types: orthogonal and oblique. The orthogonal rotation results in two factors that are uncorrelated with each other. The inter-factor correlation matrix (Φ) is an identity matrix:

$$\Phi = I$$

Oblique rotations results into correlated factors. In such a case, Φ needs to be computed. Generally, by definition, factors are independent higher-order abstractions that account for the relationship among the variables. The factors are grouping of variables that are correlated with each other and are not correlated with factors in other subsets. Given this, the orthogonal factor rotations are generally preferred. However, oblique rotations can be useful in obtaining a theoretically interpretable solution by introducing small dependence among the factors. The oblique rotated solutions with high inter-factor correlations are not considered desirable in the factor analysis literature. When you have many factors that show moderate relationship, a higher order factor analysis is carried out.

10.2.11.1 Orthogonal Rotation

There are many methods of orthogonal rotation in EFA. They are quartimax, varimax, trans-varimax, equamax, parsimax, and so on. Let $\mathbf{A}$ be the $k \times r$ unrotated matrix of orthogonal factors, where $r < k$ and r is the number of factors retained for rotations. The problem of orthogonal rotation is to find a transformation matrix $\mathbf{T}$ which is an orthogonal $r \times r$ matrix such that $\mathbf{B} = \mathbf{AT}$. Where the $\mathbf{TT'} = \mathbf{I}$, that is, it is an identity matrix.

The quartimax rotation is one of earliest rotations. It maximizes a quantity Q which is defined as

$$Q = \sum_{j=1}^{r} \sum_{i=1}^{k} b_{ij}^4$$

where k is the number of original variables and r is retained factors. The quartimax is considered as a special case of orthomax rotation. It maximizes the sum of squares of $\mathbf{B}$ row-wise. The quartimax rotation tends to provide a "general" rotated vector which has loading of all the variables. The quartimax method does row simplification. The varimax rotation is preferred over quartimax.

Varimax rotation is one of the popular methods of factor rotations. The method is due to Kaiser (1958). The simplification of factor in varimax rotation is achieved by maximizing the variance of the loadings within factors. The varimax is attempting column simplification. The increase in the variance of loadings makes bigger loadings in the column even larger and smaller loadings in the column even smaller. Hence, some variables will have loadings on a factor and others will not. The simple structure and interpretability are a result of this process. It also leads to the redistribution of variance and all factors have almost equal variance (unlike an unrotated solution).

The equamax rotation method is a combination of varimax and quartimax. After researchers found flaws about the behavior of equamax (Mulaik, 1972), it has become less popular.

The parsimax method is developed by Crawford (1967). As the name suggest, it tries to provide maximally parsimonious solution. Crawford tried to put together the column-simplification idea of varimax and the row-simplification idea of quartimax.

Orthogonal procrusteus rotation is another rotation that recently became popular, particularly in the context of rotations to the target matrix.[1] The initial work of Peter Schönemann (1966) provided a generalized solution of the orthogonal procrusteus problem. The factor pattern matrix $\mathbf{A}$ is rotated to a target matrix $\mathbf{B}$ by an orthogonal transformation matrix $\mathbf{T}$ such as the sum of squares of $\mathbf{E}$ is the minimum. This is a least-squares criterion. Given that the orthogonal procrusteus model is $\mathbf{AT} = \mathbf{B} + \mathbf{E}$ and a side condition is $\mathbf{TT'} = \mathbf{T'T} = \mathbf{I}$ ($\mathbf{TT'}$ is the identity matrix), the orthogonal procrusteus estimates are obtained against the least-squares criterion that $Trace(\mathbf{EE'}) = \min$.

---

[1] The method became popular due to its application to NEO-PI-R data. It was demonstrated by McCrae, Zonderman, Costa, Bond and Paunonen (1996) that procrusteus rotations are more effective than SEM-CFA. These researchers rotated NEO-PI-R factor patterns obtained on different cultures towards normative American data reported in NEO Manual. The US factor pattern was a target matrix. This research demonstrated cross-cultural generality of the FFM.

Between the orthogonal rotations, the varimax rotation is the most popular rotation among the researchers.

10.2.11.2 Oblique Rotations

Oblique rotations attempt to find a post-rotation factor solution that has correlated factors. The oblique rotations include oblimin, oblimax, promax, and so on.

The oblimax rotation criterion is proposed by Saunders (1961). The orthogonal quartimax rotation and oblique oblimax rotation uses the principle of maximum kurtosis. The Oblimin and direct oblimin are oblimin family rotations. In the direct oblimin (Jennrich and Sampson, 1966) method, the cross-products of the loadings are minimized to obtain the sample structure. It permits a wide range of inter-factor correlations. Promax is an oblique factor rotation method proposed by Hendrickson and White (1964). This method starts with a varimax rotated factor pattern and further tries to simplify it by bringing obliqueness. This is amongst one of the most popular methods of oblique rotation.

The rotations are available in R for "principal" and "fa" as rotate subcommand. You have to specify the rotation. The varimax in the case of orthogonal and promax in the case of oblique are the most popular rotations.

10.2.12 Factor Structure and Factor Pattern

The factor pattern matrix (A) is a $k \times r$ matrix. This matrix is matrix of weights associated with each factor for the variable. The inter-factor correlation matrix (Φ) is an identity matrix in the case of orthogonal factors:

$$\Phi = I$$

When the oblique rotation is used, then factors are correlated with each other. The inter-factor correlation matrix (Φ) is not an identity matrix. Then we can define a new matrix

$$C = A\Phi$$

C is a factor structure matrix. The factor structure matrix is a matrix of correlation between variables and factors when the rotation is oblique. In the case of orthogonal rotations, $\Phi = I$, and hence

$$C = AI$$

$$C = A$$

The orthogonal factors have $C = A$, implying that the factor pattern loadings are correlations of variables with the factors. The same is not the case with oblique rotations.

10.2.13 Factor Scores

One useful aspect of EFA for applied researchers dealing with a large number of variables is that once the factor rotations are performed and factors are interpreted, then the factors can be used as variables by converting them into factor scores. This is a very useful feature, particularly when we have large number of variables and some of them are analyzed by using EFA. The factor scores can be employed in the analysis as variables. They are standardized variables with mean zero and variance one for PCA. Most often, they can be used in regression as predictors. For example, suppose we have many measures of ability and we want to predict performance, then we can traditionally regress performance on all the measures of ability. However, we can do EFA with those measures of ability and obtain one or two underlying factors and save factor scores. The performance then can be regressed on those few factors. There are several ways of computing factor scores. Each of the methods provides slightly different results. The most popular method of estimating a factor score is a regression method. It provides factor scores highly correlated with the factors. The method works as follows:

First, a matrix **B** is computed which is

$$B = R^{-1}A$$

where R^{-1} is an inverse of original correlation matrix, and **A** is a factor pattern matrix. The factor score **F** is obtained for every observation by

$$F = ZB$$

where **Z** is $n \times k$ data matrix converted into a standardized score.

10.2.14 R Example of EFA

There are various packages that will be useful in doing factor analysis. The principal in psych package, fa in psych package, factanal in stats package (default package) are useful in doing factor analysis. R code 10.9 shows the PCA with varimax rotation.

R Code 10.9. The PCA with Varimax Rotation

```
library(psych) # call psych
fit <- principal(R, nfactors = 2, rotate = "varimax") # PCA with varimax
## OUTPUT##
Principal Components Analysis
Call: principal(r = R, nfactors = 2, rotate = "varimax")
Standardized loadings (pattern matrix) based upon correlation matrix
      PC1    PC2    h2    u2    com
e1  -0.05   0.85  0.73  0.27   1
e2   0.01   0.76  0.58  0.42   1
e6   0.01   0.78  0.61  0.39   1
n3   0.87  -0.08  0.76  0.24   1
n4   0.84  -0.05  0.70  0.30   1
n6   0.83   0.06  0.70  0.30   1

                        PC1    PC2
SS loadings            2.16   1.93
Proportion Var         0.36   0.32
Cumulative Var         0.36   0.68
Proportion Explained   0.53   0.47
Cumulative Proportion  0.53   1.00

Mean item complexity = 1
Test of the hypothesis that 2 components are sufficient.

The root mean square of the residuals (RMSR) is 0.1

Fit based upon off diagonal values = 0.9
```

R code 10.9 shows the command as well as output. The varimax rotated PCA is rewritten in Table 10.3 for ease of understanding.

The examination of Table 10.3 shows that the E1, E2, and E6 have loaded on PC2 and N3, N4, and N6 are loaded on PC1. The varimax rotated factor pattern shows the simple structure. The PC1 can be labeled as "neuroticism" factor and PC2 can be labeled as "extraversion" factor. The two-factor solution has explained 68% of variance.

Table 10.3. *Principal Component Analysis with Varimax Rotation*

	PC1	PC2	h^2
E1	−0.04	**0.85**	0.73
E2	0.02	**0.76**	0.58
E6	0.02	**0.78**	0.61
N3	**0.87**	−0.06	0.76
N4	**0.84**	−0.03	0.7
N6	**0.83**	0.08	0.7

Note: Values greater than absolute value.4 are shown in bold face.

This section has explained the EFA. The EFA provides various insights into psychometrics and psychological theory. However, the EFA should not be the approach of choice when the inquiry is guided by the theory. The next section explains CFA, when we have an underlying theory.

10.3 CONFIRMATORY FACTOR ANALYSIS (CFA)

10.3.1 Introduction to CFA

The CFA[2] is a special case of SEM. Classically, the SEM has two types of models: one, measurement model and, two, full-SEM model. The measurement model of the SEM is CFA. The CFA is a method of factor analysis that tests the theory. The EFA does not utilize any statistical theory to test a hypothesis that the obtained factor structure resembles the theoretically expected factor structure. At the most, the theory guides in deciding the number of factors to be rotated in the EFA. The "true" structure immerges at the end of EFA. The process of EFA is not a "scientific" process from Popperian[3] viewpoint. According to this epistemic[4] viewpoint, the science obtains knowledge by the process of "falsification" of a hypothesis. The failure to falsify a hypothesis leads to retaining the hypothesis. In the case of EFA, no such hypothesis is directly tested and subjected to the process of falsification. This casts doubt about its ability to generate knowledge and makes it an "inductive" method. The CFA, on the other hand, is a process that "tests" a theory about the structure of the variables. The CFA in that sense a "scientific" method. The purpose of EFA is primarily to describe the underlying structure, whereas the purpose of CFA is to verify a hypothesis about the underlying structure. Unlike EFA, the expected factor structure is pre-specified in the CFA. Let's continue with the example discussed in the EFA.

The example describes three measures of the extraversion domain of NEO-PI-R, namely warmth (Ex1); gregariousness (Ex2); positive emotion (Ex6), and the other three measures of the neuroticism domain of NEO-PI-R (anxiety [N3]; hostility [N4]; vulnerability [N6]). The theory of personality (Eysenckian theory, the FFM, the big-five model, and so on) states that extraversion and neuroticism are different and independent dimensions of personality. The

---

[2] This is not entirely correct. There are some methods of CFA that cannot be considered as SEM subsets. They include orthogonal and oblique procrusteus methods, multiple-groups methods, etc. However, the procrusteus are also not completely confirmatory in that sense of term. They use EFA output (either rotated or unrotated factor pattern matrix and rotates it to a target matrix). The oblique procrusteus has been criticized for generating high obliqueness to fit the data to model. I would consider procrusteous as a rotation method than CFA.

[3] Karl Popper is a well-known philosopher of science. He is remembered for his contribution to the epistemology of science.

[4] Epistemology is a branch of philosophy that deals with the question regarding what can be called knowledge. It attempts to define sources, necessary and sufficient criterion and limits of knowledge. Karl Popper and Thomas Kuhn are among the significant contributors to the epistemology of science.

variables Ex1, Ex2, and Ex6 are aspects of extraversion and variables N3, N4, and N6 are aspects of neuroticism. Theoretically, one should expect Ex1, Ex2, and Ex6 to load only on extraversion and N3, N4, and N6 only load on neuroticism. The CFA constructs a hypothesis in the beginning and carries out a process that tests such a hypothesis.

The logic of CFA is based on the assumption (which is very true in the case of psychological variables and their measures) that *measured variables* (also called observed variables, manifest variables, or indicators) are imperfect indicators of *latent variables*. Let's take an example of intelligence. Intelligence is the internal structure of mind that is not observable. Suppose an intelligence test has 30 items. An individual can pass or fails on each item. The item's scores are not intelligence themselves (and for that matter nor is the sum of scores on all the items or any standardized conversion of that total score like, z, T, and so on). Someone getting a score of IQ=120 is an indication of just a relative position. The item scores of individuals are the manifest behavior and not intelligence themselves. The central idea of latent variables is that the score on 30 items is not intelligence, but it is intelligence (a latent variable) that is causing the score on these 30 items. A **latent variable** is an unobservable, underlying construct that causes the observable and measured variables (also called manifest variables). Since the latent variables are unobservable, the measurement of the latent variables is not possible. Then what is measured is known as the imperfect indicator of the latent variables. In the case of the personality example, scores on warmth (Ex1), gregariousness (Ex2), and positive emotion (Ex6) are imperfect indicators of latent construct extraversion. Similarly, scores on anxiety (N3), hostility (N4), and vulnerability (N6) are imperfect indicators of neuroticism. This implies that the scores on observed variables are caused by latent variables. However, the observed scores are not just caused by the latent variables, but they can also be a function of random errors. So the complete model looks as follows.

The latent variables are the primary cause of manifest variables. The manifest variables can also be caused by random errors and so are considered as imperfect indicators.

$$\text{Observed Variable} = \text{Latent Variable} + \text{Random Error}$$

Often, there are more indicators or observed variables per latent variable. The researcher can test a hypothesis that the group of these indicators is caused by a pre-specified latent variable. The CFA does not allow the data to dictate, detect, and discover the latent variables. The researcher is required to specify the underlying structure and evaluate whether the observed data "fits" to a pre-specified model.

10.3.2 Steps in CFA

The researcher employing CFA needs to take the following steps:

1. **Have theory:** The CFA is a hypothesis-testing method. The CFA cannot be conducted in the absence of a theory-driven hypothesis (or at least a hunch). The hypothesis for personality example states that the manifest variables E1, E2, and E6 are caused by the latent variable extraversion, and manifest variables N3, N4, and N6 are caused by the latent variable neuroticism. The theory further specifies that the two latent variables are unrelated.

2. **Get data:** In the wake of causal theory, the researcher should get data on observable variables or indicators in the model. The sample size should be large. In addition to test the CFA hypothesis, the CFA method can be used to test various other questions (mean structures, multiple-groups, and do on), and accordingly suitable modifications are made in the data-collection process.

3. **Specify model:** The theoretical model is specified as a linear model. The model specification is discussed in details in sections to follow.

4. **Test for identification**: Identification is an important issue in CFA. A correct solution of identification problem leads to appropriate estimation of model parameters It is discussed in detail in the sections to follow.

5. **Estimate model parameters**: The model has various parameters. The parameters are estimated by one of the parameter estimation method. Most popular method of parameter estimation is ML. However, other methods might do the job better under specific circumstances.

6. **Statistical test and fit indices**: The statistical test of the "fit" between model and data is carried out. The statistical test of CFA has certain limitations. The alternatives to overcome those limitations are discussed in the appropriate section.

7. **Compare different models**: One of the alternatives is to compare different competing theoretical models and choose the best among them. The method of doing so is discussed soon.

8. **Interpret and conclude**: Once the results are obtained, the researcher has to carefully evaluate the results and decide whether the hypothesis in question is to be retained or not.

10.3.3 The Graphical Model

The model for two latent factors, extraversion and neuroticism latent variables, is shown in Figure 10.4. The model shows that the latent variable extraversion causes the Ex1, Ex2, and Ex3 indicators. These indicators are also caused by e1, e2, and e3 errors. The latent variable neuroticism causes the N3, N4, and N6 indicators. These indicators are also caused by e4, e5, and e6 errors. Please note that the causality is from the latent variables to observed variables. It's because someone has high latent trait extraversion, their score on indicators of extraversion is high. The indicators are imprecise. The imprecision of the indicators is modeled by the errors associated with each of the indicators.

The graphical presentation of the CFA model is always insightful. Some common rules of the graphical presentations are as follows (also see Table 10.4).

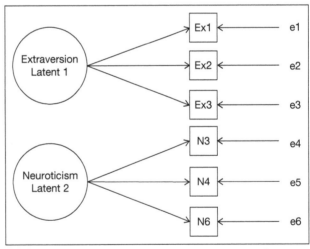

Figure 10.4. *Schematic CFA Model for Personality Data*

Table 10.4. *The Meaning of the CFA Symbols*

Sign	Description	Represents
⭕	Circle	Latent variable (unobservable, not measured)
◻	Square	Observed variable (manifest variable or indicator); directly measured
⟶	Straight arrow	Causal direction or influence path
↻	Curved double-headed arrow	Correlation/Covariance between exogenous (latent) variables or errors

The latent variables are always represented by circles. The manifest or observed variables are represented by square boxes. The straight arrows represent the direction of causality. The curved arrows represent the correlation/covariance among the variables.

10.3.4 The CFA Model

The fundamental CFA model is as follows:

$$\mathbf{X} = \mathbf{\Lambda}\boldsymbol{\xi} + \boldsymbol{\delta}$$

The $\mathbf{X}$ is an observed variable, manifest variable, or indicator. The $\boldsymbol{\xi}$ is a latent variable (pronounced as *xi* or *ksi*). $\mathbf{\Lambda}$ (lambda) is a matrix of structural coefficients associated with each of the manifest variables for the $\boldsymbol{\xi}$. The $\boldsymbol{\delta}$ is an error associated with each of the manifest variables $\mathbf{X}$ (It is also referred to as Θ_δ the theta-delta matrix).

Let's now specify this model for the personality data. $\mathbf{X}$ is an observed variable. The observed variables are warmth (Ex1), gregariousness (Ex2), positive emotion (Ex6), anxiety (N3), hostility (N4), and vulnerability (N6). So we have six $\mathbf{X}$ variables $(X_1, X_2, X_3, X_4, X_5, X_6)$. There are two latent variables ($\boldsymbol{\xi}$) in the personality model: first latent variable is extraversion (let's call it $\boldsymbol{\xi_1}$) and the second latent variable is neuroticism (let's call it $\boldsymbol{\xi_2}$). Lambda refers to the structural coefficients associated with each latent variable and its associated indicators. There are six coefficients. They are denoted by the symbol $\mathbf{\Lambda}$. The $\mathbf{\Lambda}$ is a matrix of structural coefficients which contains the six coefficients. Each coefficient is symbolized as λ with a subscript, like λ_{11} (read as lambda one, one. NOT eleven). The λ_{11} is the coefficient of the first manifest variable and the first latent variable, and similarly λ_{42} is a coefficient of the fourth manifest variable and the second latent variable, that is the coefficient associated with N3 as the manifest variable (X_4) and neuroticism ($\boldsymbol{\xi_2}$) as a latent variable. $\boldsymbol{\delta}$ are associated with each of the manifest variables. There are six $\boldsymbol{\delta}$ values $(\delta_1, \delta_2, \delta_3, \delta_4, \delta_5, \delta_6)$ each of which is associated with each manifest variable $(X_1, X_2, X_3, X_4, X_5, X_6)$. The model with all these specification is displayed in Figure 10.5.

Let's us now express this model in terms of matrices. $\mathbf{X}$ is a 6×1 column vector of six indicator variables. They are measured or directly observed through scale measurement. $\boldsymbol{\xi}$ is a 2×1 column vector of two latent variables. $\mathbf{\Lambda}$ is a 6×2 matrix of structural coefficients. $\boldsymbol{\delta}$ is a 6×1 column vector of errors associated with manifest variables. The matrix $\mathbf{\Lambda}$ specifies six lambda values λ_{11} to λ_{62}. However, the values specified are the only values that will be estimated. The values that are specified as zero are fixed values and will not be estimated:

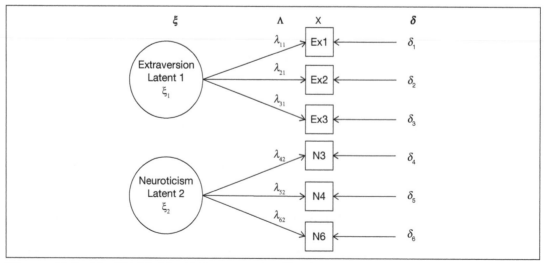

Figure 10.5. *The CFA Model with Parameter Specification*

$$
\begin{bmatrix} X_1 \\ X_2 \\ X_3 \\ X_4 \\ X_5 \\ X_6 \end{bmatrix} = \begin{bmatrix} \lambda_{11} & 0 \\ \lambda_{21} & 0 \\ \lambda_{31} & 0 \\ 0 & \lambda_{42} \\ 0 & \lambda_{52} \\ 0 & \lambda_{62} \end{bmatrix} \begin{bmatrix} \xi_1 \\ \xi_2 \end{bmatrix} + \begin{bmatrix} \delta_1 \\ \delta_2 \\ \delta_3 \\ \delta_4 \\ \delta_5 \\ \delta_6 \end{bmatrix}
$$

$$
X_{6 \times 1} = \Lambda_{6 \times 2} \ \xi_{2 \times 1} + \delta_{6 \times 1}
$$

X is a $k \times 1$ column vector of observed or manifest variables, Λ is a $k \times r$ matrix of structural coefficients, ξ is a $r \times 1$ column vector of latent variables, and δ is a $k \times 1$ column vector of random errors associated with observed variables. Here, k is the number of manifest variables/indicators; r is the number of latent variables. In the case of personality data, $k = 6$ and $r = 2$. The above matrix equation for the personality data is as follows:

$$
\begin{bmatrix} \text{Warmth} \\ \text{Gregariousness} \\ \text{Positive Emotion} \\ \text{Anxiety} \\ \text{Hostility} \\ \text{Vulnerability} \end{bmatrix} = \begin{bmatrix} \lambda_{Warmth.Ext} & 0 \\ \lambda_{Gregariousness.Ext} & 0 \\ \lambda_{Positive\ Emotion.Ext} & 0 \\ 0 & \lambda_{Anxiety.Neu} \\ 0 & \lambda_{Hostility.Neu} \\ 0 & \lambda_{Vulnerability.Neu} \end{bmatrix} = \begin{bmatrix} \xi_{Ext} \\ \xi_{Neu} \end{bmatrix} + \begin{bmatrix} \delta_{Warmth} \\ \delta_{Gregariousness} \\ \delta_{Positive\ Emotion} \\ \delta_{Anxiety} \\ \delta_{Hostility} \\ \delta_{Vulnerability} \end{bmatrix}
$$

One more matrix of our interest (which is not expressed in this model because of theoretical reasons) is PHI matrix. Φ is the variance–covariance matrix between the latent variables. When the model specifies the latent variables to be correlated, the intercorrelations between latent variables is expressed as a Φ matrix. The Φ matrix is of $r \times r$ dimensions:

$$
\Phi = E(\xi \xi')
$$

When the factors are uncorrelated, $\Phi = I$, that is, Φ is an identity matrix. Φ is expressed as

$$
\Phi = \begin{bmatrix} \sigma_{\xi_1}^2 & \sigma_{\xi_1 \xi_2} \\ \sigma_{\xi_2 \xi_1} & \sigma_{\xi_2}^2 \end{bmatrix} = \begin{bmatrix} \text{Variance latent 1} & \text{Covariance latent 1.2} \\ \text{Covariance latent 2.1} & \text{Variance latent 2} \end{bmatrix}
$$

The graphical representation uses a two-way curved arrow to express the covariation.

Now, look at errors, δ, associated with the observed variables. The errors of observed variables will have $k \times k$ variance–covariance matrix referred to as Θ_δ. The diagonal elements are variances of the errors, and non-diagonal elements will be zero, generally. Θ_δ for the personality data is as follows:

$$
\Theta_\delta = \begin{bmatrix} \sigma_{\delta_1}^2 & 0 & 0 & 0 & 0 & 0 \\ 0 & \sigma_{\delta_2}^2 & 0 & 0 & 0 & 0 \\ 0 & 0 & \sigma_{\delta_3}^2 & 0 & 0 & 0 \\ 0 & 0 & 0 & \sigma_{\delta_4}^2 & 0 & 0 \\ 0 & 0 & 0 & 0 & \sigma_{\delta_5}^2 & 0 \\ 0 & 0 & 0 & 0 & 0 & \sigma_{\delta_6}^2 \end{bmatrix} = \begin{bmatrix} \sigma_{\delta_{Ex1}}^2 & 0 & 0 & 0 & 0 & 0 \\ 0 & \sigma_{\delta_{Ex2}}^2 & 0 & 0 & 0 & 0 \\ 0 & 0 & \sigma_{\delta_{Ex3}}^2 & 0 & 0 & 0 \\ 0 & 0 & 0 & \sigma_{\delta_{N1}}^2 & 0 & 0 \\ 0 & 0 & 0 & 0 & \sigma_{\delta_{N2}}^2 & 0 \\ 0 & 0 & 0 & 0 & 0 & \sigma_{\delta_{N3}}^2 \end{bmatrix}
$$

10.3.5 Assumptions

Certain assumptions are required to estimate the structural coefficients. The assumptions are

1. $E(X)=E(\xi)=0$. The mean of the observed and latent variables is zero.
2. The relationships between the observed (X) and latent variables (ξ) are linear.
3. There are assumptions about measurement error:

   a) $E(\delta)=0$. The errors have mean zero.
   b) The errors have constant variance across observations.
   c) The errors are independent across observations.
   d) $E(\xi\delta')=E(\delta\,\xi')=0$. The errors are uncorrelated with latent variables.

10.3.6 Unrestricted and Model-implied Covariance Matrix

The CFA conceptualizes unrestricted and model-implied variance–covariance matrices. Let's start with a sample variance–covariance matrix. The variance–covariance matrix of observed variables on a sample is called a *sample* variance–covariance matrix and is symbolized as **S**. The *population* variance–covariance matrix of the observed variables is symbolized as Σ (Sigma) and is referred to as *unrestricted* variance–covariance matrix. No model restrictions are imposed on sigma (Σ). In statistics, our interest is in estimating the population parameter. For this purpose, Σ is expressed as a function of the CFA model. Σ can be expressed as

$$\Sigma = E(XX')$$

This is an unrestricted variance–covariance matrix. For the CFA model, we have defined

$$\Sigma = \Lambda\xi + \delta$$

The covariance matrix of **X** can be written as a function of θ:

$$\Sigma(\theta) = XX'$$

Since observed variables are deviations from their mean, $E(X)=0$, we have already assumed that $E(\xi\delta')=E(\delta\xi')=0$ and $E(\delta)=0$. Given this, we can substitute **X** for the CFA model and $\Sigma(\theta)$ can be re-written as

$$\Sigma(\theta) = XX'$$
$$\Sigma(\theta) = E[(\Lambda\xi + \delta)\ (\Lambda\xi + \delta)']$$
$$\Sigma(\theta) = E(\Lambda\xi\xi'\Lambda') + E(\Lambda\xi\delta') + E(\delta\xi'\Lambda') + E(\delta\delta')$$
$$\Sigma(\theta) = \Lambda E(\xi\xi')\Lambda' + E(\delta\delta')$$

Since it is shown that $\Phi = E(\xi\xi')$ and we also know that $\Theta_\delta = E(\delta\delta')$, the last line can be written as

$$\Sigma(\theta) = \Lambda\Phi\Lambda' + \Theta_\delta$$

where θ is the column vector containing p model-implied free parameters. A free parameter is a parameter to be estimated. The model implied variance–covariance matrix $\Sigma(\theta)$ can be given by

$$\Sigma(\theta) = \Lambda\Phi\Lambda' + \Theta_\delta$$

$$\Sigma(\theta) = \begin{bmatrix} \lambda_{11} & 0 \\ \lambda_{21} & 0 \\ \lambda_{31} & 0 \\ 0 & \lambda_{42} \\ 0 & \lambda_{52} \\ 0 & \lambda_{62} \end{bmatrix} \begin{bmatrix} \phi_{11} & \phi_{12} \\ \phi_{21} & \phi_{22} \end{bmatrix} \begin{bmatrix} \lambda_{11} & 0 \\ \lambda_{21} & 0 \\ \lambda_{31} & 0 \\ 0 & \lambda_{42} \\ 0 & \lambda_{52} \\ 0 & \lambda_{62} \end{bmatrix}' + \begin{bmatrix} \theta_{11} & 0 & 0 & 0 & 0 & 0 \\ 0 & \theta_{22} & 0 & 0 & 0 & 0 \\ 0 & 0 & \theta_{33} & 0 & 0 & 0 \\ 0 & 0 & 0 & \theta_{44} & 0 & 0 \\ 0 & 0 & 0 & 0 & \theta_{55} & 0 \\ 0 & 0 & 0 & 0 & 0 & \theta_{66} \end{bmatrix}$$

$$\Sigma(\theta) = \begin{bmatrix} \lambda_{11} & 0 \\ \lambda_{21} & 0 \\ \lambda_{31} & 0 \\ 0 & \lambda_{42} \\ 0 & \lambda_{52} \\ 0 & \lambda_{62} \end{bmatrix} \begin{bmatrix} \sigma_{\xi_1}^2 & \sigma_{\xi_{12}}^2 \\ \sigma_{\xi_{21}}^2 & \sigma_{\xi_2}^2 \end{bmatrix} \begin{bmatrix} \lambda_{11} & \lambda_{21} & \lambda_{31} & 0 & 0 & 0 \\ 0 & 0 & 0 & \lambda_{42} & \lambda_{52} & \lambda_{62} \end{bmatrix} + \begin{bmatrix} \sigma_{\delta_1}^2 & 0 & 0 & 0 & 0 & 0 \\ 0 & \sigma_{\delta_2}^2 & 0 & 0 & 0 & 0 \\ 0 & 0 & \sigma_{\delta_3}^2 & 0 & 0 & 0 \\ 0 & 0 & 0 & \sigma_{\delta_4}^2 & 0 & 0 \\ 0 & 0 & 0 & 0 & \sigma_{\delta_5}^2 & 0 \\ 0 & 0 & 0 & 0 & 0 & \sigma_{\delta_6}^2 \end{bmatrix}$$

$$\Sigma(\theta) = \begin{bmatrix} \lambda_{11}\sigma_{\xi_1}^2\lambda_{11} \\ \lambda_{21}\sigma_{\xi_1}^2\lambda_{11} & \lambda_{21}\sigma_{\xi_1}^2\lambda_{21} \\ \lambda_{31}\sigma_{\xi_1}^2\lambda_{11} & \lambda_{32}\sigma_{\xi_1}^2\lambda_{11} & \lambda_{31}\sigma_{\xi_1}^2\lambda_{31} \\ \lambda_{42}\sigma_{\xi_2\xi_1}^2\lambda_{11} & \lambda_{42}\sigma_{\xi_2\xi_1}^2\lambda_{21} & \lambda_{42}\sigma_{\xi_2\xi_1}^2\lambda_{31} & \lambda_{42}\sigma_{\xi_2}^2\lambda_{42} \\ \lambda_{52}\sigma_{\xi_2\xi_1}^2\lambda_{11} & \lambda_{52}\sigma_{\xi_2\xi_1}^2\lambda_{21} & \lambda_{52}\sigma_{\xi_2\xi_1}^2\lambda_{31} & \lambda_{52}\sigma_{\xi_2}^2\lambda_{42} & \lambda_{52}\sigma_{\xi_2}^2\lambda_{52} \\ \lambda_{62}\sigma_{\xi_2\xi_1}^2\lambda_{11} & \lambda_{62}\sigma_{\xi_2\xi_1}^2\lambda_{21} & \lambda_{62}\sigma_{\xi_2\xi_1}^2\lambda_{31} & \lambda_{62}\sigma_{\xi_2}^2\lambda_{41} & \lambda_{62}\sigma_{\xi_2}^2\lambda_{51} & \lambda_{62}\sigma_{\xi_2}^2\lambda_{62} \end{bmatrix} + \begin{bmatrix} \sigma_{\delta_1}^2 & 0 & 0 & 0 & 0 & 0 \\ 0 & \sigma_{\delta_2}^2 & 0 & 0 & 0 & 0 \\ 0 & 0 & \sigma_{\delta_3}^2 & 0 & 0 & 0 \\ 0 & 0 & 0 & \sigma_{\delta_4}^2 & 0 & 0 \\ 0 & 0 & 0 & 0 & \sigma_{\delta_5}^2 & 0 \\ 0 & 0 & 0 & 0 & 0 & \sigma_{\delta_6}^2 \end{bmatrix}$$

$$\Sigma(\theta) = \begin{bmatrix} \lambda_{11}^2\sigma_{\xi_1}^2 + \sigma_{\delta_1}^2 \\ \lambda_{21}\sigma_{\xi_1}^2\lambda_{11} & \lambda_{21}^2\sigma_{\xi_1}^2 + \sigma_{\delta_2}^2 \\ \lambda_{31}\sigma_{\xi_1}^2\lambda_{11} & \lambda_{32}\sigma_{\xi_1}^2\lambda_{11} & \lambda_{31}^2\sigma_{\xi_1}^2 + \sigma_{\delta_3}^2 \\ \lambda_{42}\sigma_{\xi_2\xi_1}^2\lambda_{11} & \lambda_{42}\sigma_{\xi_2\xi_1}^2\lambda_{21} & \lambda_{42}\sigma_{\xi_2\xi_1}^2\lambda_{31} & \lambda_{42}^2\sigma_{\xi_2}^2 + \sigma_{\delta_4}^2 \\ \lambda_{52}\sigma_{\xi_2\xi_1}^2\lambda_{11} & \lambda_{52}\sigma_{\xi_2\xi_1}^2\lambda_{21} & \lambda_{52}\sigma_{\xi_2\xi_1}^2\lambda_{31} & \lambda_{52}\sigma_{\xi_2}^2\lambda_{42} & \lambda_{52}^2\sigma_{\xi_2}^2 + \sigma_{\delta_5}^2 \\ \lambda_{62}\sigma_{\xi_2\xi_1}^2\lambda_{11} & \lambda_{62}\sigma_{\xi_2\xi_1}^2\lambda_{21} & \lambda_{62}\sigma_{\xi_2\xi_1}^2\lambda_{31} & \lambda_{62}\sigma_{\xi_2}^2\lambda_{41} & \lambda_{62}\sigma_{\xi_2}^2\lambda_{51} & \lambda_{62}^2\sigma_{\xi_2}^2 + \sigma_{\delta_6}^2 \end{bmatrix}$$

$$\Sigma(\theta) = \begin{bmatrix} \lambda_{11}^2\phi_{11} + \sigma_{\delta_1}^2 \\ \lambda_{21}\phi_{11}\lambda_{11} & \lambda_{21}^2\phi_{11} + \sigma_{\delta_2}^2 \\ \lambda_{31}\phi_{11}\lambda_{11} & \lambda_{32}\phi_{11}\lambda_{11} & \lambda_{31}^2\phi_{11} + \sigma_{\delta_3}^2 \\ \lambda_{42}\phi_{21}\lambda_{11} & \lambda_{42}\phi_{21}\lambda_{21} & \lambda_{42}\phi_{21}\lambda_{31} & \lambda_{42}^2\phi_{22} + \sigma_{\delta_4}^2 \\ \lambda_{52}\phi_{21}\lambda_{11} & \lambda_{52}\phi_{21}\lambda_{21} & \lambda_{52}\phi_{21}\lambda_{31} & \lambda_{52}\phi_{22}\lambda_{42} & \lambda_{52}^2\phi_{22} + \sigma_{\delta_5}^2 \\ \lambda_{62}\phi_{21}\lambda_{11} & \lambda_{62}\phi_{21}\lambda_{21} & \lambda_{62}\phi_{21}\lambda_{31} & \lambda_{62}\phi_{22}\lambda_{41} & \lambda_{62}\phi_{22}\lambda_{51} & \lambda_{62}^2\phi_{22} + \sigma_{\delta_6}^2 \end{bmatrix}$$

The hypothesized model-implied variance–covariance matrix is $\Sigma(\theta)$. If the hypothesized model is correct, then we have $\Sigma = \Sigma(\theta)$, that is, the population variance–covariance matrix is equal to the model-implied variance–covariance matrix.

10.3.7 Identification

The *identification problem* for the CFA model is whether a unique solution exists for each parameter in $\Sigma(\theta)$, that is, Λ, Φ, and Θ_δ.

The non-redundant elements of the observed variance–covariance matrix are $c = [k \times (k+1)]/2$. In the case of personality data, $c = [6 \times (6+1)]/2 = 21$. The *necessary but not sufficient condition* for identification is that the number of parameters estimated, p, are smaller than or equal to the number of non-redundant elements of the variance–covariance matrix of observed variables. That is, the condition states that if $p \le c$, then the model is identified. The p is equal to 12 if $\Phi = I$. The diagonal of Φ would be unities and off-diagonal values would be zeros. Even if we modify the model such that there exists a correlation between latent variables and assume that latent variables are standardized variables, then the number of parameters to be estimated would be 13. The only parameter added is covariance between the two latent variables (since standardized variables have variance of 1, two diagonal elements are fixed to 1 representing the variance of each latent variable in *phi*). Bollen (1989) discussed the three-indicator and two-indicator rules for identification as a *sufficient* condition. They are generally considered as useful abstractions for solving the identification problem. The two rules specify the conditions under which three and two indicators per latent variable are sufficient.

Three-indicator rule: Three indicators are sufficient for one latent variable for identification. The conditions are (a) three or more indicators are required per latent variable, (b) there is only one free parameter per row of Λ, and (c) the Θ_δ is a diagonal matrix. The three indicator rule is a sufficient condition.

Two-indicator rule: If the Θ_δ is a diagonal matrix, and each latent variable is scaled, then two indicators per latent variable are enough for identification. This is also a sufficient condition. Bollen (1989, p. 245) further modified the rule to the following conditions: (a) There is one and only one nonzero value per row of Λ, (b) there are at least two indicators per latent variable, (c) there is at least one non-zero off-diagonal element in Φ, and (d) the Θ_δ is a diagonal matrix. The difference is that some off-diagonal elements of Φ can be zero.

10.3.8 Estimation

Once the model is specified, data is available, and identification issue is taken care of, the model parameters can be estimated. **S** is a sample variance–covariance matrix and Σ is a population variance–covariance matrix. $\Sigma(\theta)$ is model-implied variance–covariance matrix. The estimation methods estimate the parameters specified in $\Sigma(\theta)$. The estimates are chosen such that $\hat{\Sigma}$ is as close as possible to **S**. There are many methods available for estimating the CFA model parameters.

The ML estimation is perhaps the most popular way of estimating parameters. The ML fitting function (F) minimized is

$$F_{\text{ML}} = \log |\Sigma(\theta)| + \text{tr}[S\Sigma^{-1}(\theta)] - \log|S| - p$$

where $|S|$ is a determinant of sample the variance–covariance matrix, p is the order of the input matrix, $|\Sigma(\theta)|$ is the determinant of the predicted variance–covariance matrix, and tr is the trace of a matrix (sum of diagonal elements). As discussed earlier, determinant is a single number that represents a generalized measure of variance. The ML minimizes the difference between Σ and **S**. Under the condition that there is a perfect model fit, the F_{ML} is zero. The $\log|S|$ and $\log|\Sigma(\theta)|$ are identical values, and $S\Sigma^{-1}(\theta)$ is an identity matrix, the trace of which is equal to p and, hence, $F_{\text{ML}} = \text{tr}[S\Sigma^{-1}(\theta)] - p = p - p = 0$. As discussed in the estimation chapter (Chapter 2), the purpose of the ML method of estimation is to find the parameter estimate such that the likelihood of obtaining the observed variance–covariance matrix is maximum. The ML estimates have asymptotic properties, that is, the estimate is closer to the property with increasing sample size. The ML estimates are asymptotically unbiased (they are biased in small samples), that is, $\lim_{x \to \infty} E(\hat{\theta}) = \theta$. The ML estimators are consistent, that is, $\text{plim}\hat{\theta} = \theta$. The ML estimators are asymptotically efficient, that is, no other estimator, among the consistent estimators, has a smaller variance than the ML estimator. The estimators are approximately normally distributed and for known standard errors, the ratio of the estimated parameter to SE follows Z-distribution. The ML estimates are generally known to be scale-invariant and scale-free. The *scale invariance* refers to the fact that F_{ML} is insensitive to the change of scale for one or more variables. For example, if the raw scores of an item are transformed to some other scale, then it is not going to influence F_{ML}. The *scale-free* property implies that the transformation from the original model and scale-changed model is possible with simple relation. A test of the overall model is provided by F_{ML} for overidentified models is an important property of F_{ML}. Most statistical packages keep ML as a default option for CFA.

The ULS has a fitting function

$$F_{ULS} = \left(\frac{1}{2}\right) \text{tr}\{[\mathbf{S} - \Sigma(\theta)]^2\}$$

F_{ULS} is minimizing the one-half of the sum of squares of elements of the residual matrix defined by $[\mathbf{S} - \Sigma(\theta)]$. The residual matrix is the difference between sample variance–covariance matrix and model predicted variance–covariance matrix. The ULS is quite similar to regression OLS discussed in Chapter 8.

The ULS provides consistent estimators of θ. However, as compared to ML, the ULS does not provide asymptotically efficient estimators. It is not scale-invariant and not scale-free as well, that is, as the impute changes from covariance to correlation, the ULS values change.

The GLS fitting function is given as

$$F_{GLS} = \left(\frac{1}{2}\right) \text{tr}\{[I - \Sigma(\theta)\mathbf{S}^{-1}]^2\}$$

The general form of the F_{GLS} is

$$F_{GLS} = \left(\frac{1}{2}\right) \text{tr}\{[\mathbf{S} - \Sigma(\theta)\mathbf{W}^{-1}]^2\}$$

The $\mathbf{W}^{-1}$ is the weight matrix for the residual matrix. Indeed, when $\mathbf{W}^{-1} = \mathbf{I}$, then the F_{ULS} becomes a special case of F_{GLS}. There are many estimates of Σ^{-1}. The most popular is $\mathbf{W}^{-1} = \mathbf{S}^{-1}$. F_{GLS} then can be expressed as

$$F_{GLS} = \left(\frac{1}{2}\right) \text{tr}\{[I - \Sigma(\theta)\mathbf{S}^{-1}]^2\}$$

F_{GLS} are scale-invariant and scale-free. However, F_{GLS} has limitation with extreme observation, and statistical tests lacks accuracy.

Among other estimators, empirical distribution theory (EDT) and asymptotically distribution free (ADF) are also frequently reported in applied research.

10.3.9 Model Evaluation

The CFA model evaluation has two strategies: one, the evaluation of the null hypothesis using test statistics, two, using fit measures to test the goodness of fit.

10.3.9.1 Evaluation of Null Hypothesis

The model parameter estimation provides parameter values—the evaluation of whether the model is fitting to the data. There are several ways of evaluating the model–data fit. The null hypothesis tested is

$$H_0 : \Sigma = \Sigma(\theta)$$
$$H_A : \Sigma \neq \Sigma(\theta)$$

The null states that $\Sigma = \Sigma(\theta)$ and if the specified model is correct, then H_0 is accepted. As a result, the residual matrix is $\Sigma - \Sigma(\theta) = 0$. Under this null hypothesis, the $n-1$ times minimum values of F_{ML} follows χ^2 distribution with df $= c-p$. The χ^2 is expressed as

$$\chi^2 = (n-1)F[S, \Sigma(\hat{\theta})]$$

If the null is correct, that is, the model-implied variance–covariance matrix and the unrestricted variance–covariance matrix do not differ in population, χ^2 at $c-p$ degrees of freedom would be insignificant (in fact, zero).

The formal χ^2 test statistics has been criticized for various weaknesses. Several assumptions are required for χ^2 statistics to be computed (e.g., multivariate normality, valid null hypothesis, and so on). In reality, it's difficult to satisfy the assumptions. The major problem of χ^2 statistics is associated with sample size. As n increases, χ^2 increases and a very minimal and unimportant difference between $\mathbf{S}$ and $\Sigma(\hat{\theta})$ is declared as significant. This is insinuating that a reasonably good model is rejected by χ^2 statistics. And on the other hand, different "weak" models can be accepted with small samples. The other problem is associated with the complexity of model. More complex models are more likely to result in insignificant χ^2 values than simpler models. More free parameters put less restriction on the model-implied variance–covariance matrix and, hence, lead to smaller values of the fitting function as well as χ^2. The last problem is that the χ^2 test cannot be possible with just identified models because the df $= c - p = 0$.

Considering these and several other limitations of the χ^2 test statistics (Kaplan, 1990), many have suggested that χ^2 value should not be viewed as a formal test statistics (e.g., Jöreskog & Sörbom, 1993). Instead, the magnitude of χ^2 at a given df is used to make decisions. The ratio of χ^2 and df is a common indicator of fit. Please recall that $E(\chi^2) = df_{\chi^2}$. Large values of this ratio indicate a bad data–model fit. In that sense, χ^2 serves as the "badness" of fit index. For example, if the $\chi^2 = 18.45$ at df $= 6$, then the ratio is $\chi^2/df = 18.45/6 = 3.075$. Whether to consider this ratio as small is the question. For example, Bollen (1989, p. 278) recommends that the ratio as high as 5 can be considered as small. Bollen further noted that this ratio is not a very acceptable solution, since $(n-1)F_{\mathrm{ML}}/df$ have the same relation with n as usual χ^2 has.

10.3.9.2 Fit Measures

The chi-square and its significance is the basic fit evaluation method. However, the null hypothesis significance testing is problematic strategy. The alternative is to evaluate goodness-of-fit by using fit measures that often make use of chi-square statistics. Several such statistics are presented in this section.

Goodness-of-fit Index (GFI) and Adjusted Goodness-of-fit Index (AGFI)

Jöreskog and Sörbom (1981) presented GFI and AGFI as model evaluation indices. The GFI and AGFI range between 0 and 1, and value closer to 1 indicates better model–data fit. Let's first understand the concept of null model. The **null model or baseline model** is the model when no model is specified for the data. Each observed variable is perfectly measured and, therefore, is equal to a latent variable (each observed has a latent variable), and the covariance matrix among the latents is assumed to be zero. This implies that all model parameters Λ, Φ, and Θ_δ are fixed and, hence, not evaluated. F_{ML} is the value of ML fit function for no model.

The GFI expresses "how much better is the model fit as compared to no model at all" (Jöreskog and Sörbom, 1993, p. 122). The GFI is

$$\mathrm{GFI} = 1 - \frac{\mathrm{tr}[(\hat{\Sigma}^{-1}S - I)^2]}{\mathrm{tr}[(\hat{\Sigma}^{-1}S)^2]} = 1 - \frac{F[S, \Sigma(\hat{\theta})]}{F[S, \Sigma(0)]}$$

$F[S,\Sigma(0)]$ is a fit function for the null model and $F[S,\Sigma(\hat{\theta})]$ is fit function for hypothesized model.

And the AGFI is

$$\text{AGFI} = 1 - \left(\frac{c}{\text{df}_h}\right)\frac{F[S,\Sigma(\hat{\theta})]}{F[S,\Sigma(0)]}$$

$$\text{AGFI} = 1 - \left(\frac{c}{\text{df}_h}\right)(1 - \text{GFI})$$

df_h is the degree of freedom for the hypothesized model and c is the number of non-redundant elements of the variance–covariance matrix. The AGFI penalizes the GFI for free parameters (i.e., for specifying more complex models) and conversely as degree of freedom approach c, the AGIF approaches GIF. For the complex models, more parameters are estimated than for the simple ones. As the number of parameters to be estimated increases, the df decreases. Consequently, c/df_h increases and AGFI decreases. This is how the AGFI is rewarding simpler models.

Normed Fit Index (NFI) and Non-normed Fit Index (NNFI)

Bentler and Bonett's (1980) suggested normed fit index (NFI) and non-normed fit index (NNFI). The understanding of independence model and saturated models is required for understanding NFI and NNFI.

The *Independence model* (M_i) is a very restrictive model. M_i hypothesize that $\Lambda = I, \Theta_\delta = 0$ and $\Phi = I$. That is, there are no latent variables (the structural coefficients are identity matrix), the observed variables are measured without error, and observed variables are independent. Most fit indices for M_i will be zero but the parsimonious fit-indices would be 1 since M_i is the most parsimonious model.

The *saturated model* (M_s) has as many free parameters as variance–covariances of observed variables and the df of the saturated model is zero. This is a trivial model because all fit measures will be perfect (1.0) but the parsimonious fit-indices would be zero since M_s is most unparsimonious model.

The *hypothesized models* by the researcher fall between these two types of models.

Generally, restrictive models (saturated models) have higher chi-square than less restrictive models. For personality data, we have a model that has not specified the correlation between latents. Let's call it Model 1 (M_1). Now let's assume Model 2 (M_2), which specifies that the latent variables are correlated. M_1 can be considered as nested within M_2. That is, if we fix $\Phi = I$ for M_2, we obtain M_1. The parameter $\sigma^2_{\xi_1\xi_2}$ in model M_2 is fixed to zero to obtain M_1. Hence, M_1 is nested

Table 10.5. *Range of Models from Independent Model to Saturated Model*

Independence Model M_i	M_j	M_1	M_2	M_k	Saturated model M_s
highest χ^2_i> Worst fit	>χ^2_j>	χ^2_1>	χ^2_2>	χ^2_k>	>χ^2_s is zero Best fit
df_i>	>df_j>	df_1>	df_2>	df_k>	>df_s

◄——►

Most restrictive model with least free parameters	Least restrictive model with most free parameters

within M_2 which is less restrictive and M_1 is more restrictive. Model M_j is said to be nested in M_k if by fixing some parameters of M_k to zero, $M_k = M_j$. Table 10.5 describes the models.

Now, we discuss the NFI and NNFI. The NFI is defined as

$$\text{NFI} = \frac{\chi_i^2 - \chi_h^2}{\chi_i^2} = 1 - \frac{F_h}{F_i}$$

χ_i^2 is independent model chi-square and χ_h^2 is hypothesized models chi-square (researcher's model, M_h). The NFI is the ratio of the difference $\chi_i^2 - \chi_h^2$ to χ_i^2. Small chi-square for model indicates a better fit. If the model is a best fit model, then $\chi_h^2 = 0$ and NFI will be 1.0. It is not possible realistically. In reality, χ_h^2 will be smaller for a better fitting model and consequently NFI will be larger (closer to 1). If the researchers model (M_h) is "bad" model, then χ_h^2 will be closer to χ_i^2 making the numerator smaller and also the NFI smaller. The problem with NFI is that it is not 1.0 for a perfect model (Bentler, 1990). Bentler and Bonett (1980), using the earlier work of Tucker and Lewis (1973), proposed a non-normed fit index (NNFI) which is also known as the Tucker–Lewis Index (TLI). The NNFI is specified as:

$$\text{NNFI} = \frac{\left(\chi_i^2/\text{df}_i\right) - \left(\chi_h^2/\text{df}_h\right)}{\chi_i^2/\text{df}_i - 1}$$

It is not normed; the values can be outside the range of 0 and 1. It enforces a penalty for degrees of freedom. More complex models are punished and more sample models are rewarded. The larger values of NNFI indicate a better model–data fit.

Comparative Fit Index (CFI)

Bentler (1990) developed CFI and FI as two indices. Let's define $l_h = [(n-1)F_h - \text{df}_h]$, and $l_i = [(n-1)F_i - \text{df}_i]$. The FI is defined as

$$\text{FI} = 1 - \frac{l_h}{l_i}$$

The FI is not restricted to the range 0 and 1. The CFI is defined as

$$\text{CFI} = 1 - \frac{l_1}{l_2}$$

where $l_1 = \max(l_h, 0)$ and $l_2 = \max(l_h, l_i, 0)$. The CFI falls within the range of 0 and 1. Bentler (1990) noted that the CFI is superior to NFI with reference to the underestimation of fit and FI is better than NNFI with reference to straying beyond the limits of 0 and 1.

Parsimonious Fit Indices

Occam's razor or Parsimony[5] is one of the central attributes of scientific theory. Proponents of parsimonious fit indices criticize the GFI and NFI. The simple way to take NFI of GFI closer to 1 is to set more and more parameters free. As a result, the model becomes more complex. There is one way to curb this tendency to penalize a model for being more complex and rewarding simpler models. The parsimony goodness of fit index (PGFI) and parsimony normed fit index (PNFI) are two parsimonious fit indices. The PGFI is specified as:

---

[5] Occam's razor or the principle of Parsimony states that among the competing explanations, the one with less assumption should be preferred.

$$PGFI = \frac{df_h}{df_n} GFI$$

where *df_h* is associated with hypothesized model (researchers model) and df_n is the number of non-redundant elements of the observed variance–covariance matrix, or df_n=c, df of the null model.

The PNFI is obtained by

$$PNFI = \frac{df_h}{df_i} NFI$$

where *df_i* is the degrees of freedom of the independence model.

Among the two, the PGFI imposes a harsher penalty for an unparsimonious model (Tanaka, 1993).

10.3.10 CFA in R

There are reasonable options available for researchers to choose from when it comes to CFA or SEM in R. The "sem" package by John Fox, the "OpenMx" developed by OpenMx core team, and the "lavaan" developed by Yves Rosseel are some of the popular options. I have used SEM and lavaan extensively. I am explaining the CFA using "lavaan" for the simple reason that it is slightly easy to use for new user. The SEM is also a very sound package. You can read the work by Fox (2006) and Fox, Nie, & Byrnes (2015).

10.3.10.1 Data

The data used for EFA is reused for CFA. The correlation matrix in Table 10.1 is reprinted here for the sake of ease.

Table 10.1. *Correlation Matrix of Six Personality Variables*

Variables	E1	E2	E6	N3	N4	N6
E1	1	0.493	0.523	–0.091	–0.08	–0.011
E2	**0.493**	1	0.358	–0.05	–0.048	0.051
E6	**0.523**	**0.358**	1	–0.059	–0.006	0.023
N3	–0.091	–0.05	–0.059	1	0.614	0.595
N4	–0.08	–0.048	–0.006	**0.614**	1	0.523
N6	–0.011	0.051	0.023	**0.595**	**0.523**	1

Note: E1=Warmth; E2=Gregariousness; E6=Positive Emotion; N3=Anxiety; N4=Hostility; N6= Vulnerability. Sample size=304.

10.3.10.2 The lavaan and CFA

Lavaan is useful for CFA, SEM, and growth models. In this section, the CFA use of lavaan is discussed. Install "lavaan" by the following code.

R Code 10.10. Preparing for CFA with lavaan
```
install.packages(lavaan, dependencies = T) # Install lavaan
library (lavaan)  # call library lavaan
example(cfa)     # run default example on Holzinger Swineford (1939) data
cr <- c(1, 0.493, 0.523, -0.091, -0.08, -0.011, 0.493, 1, 0.358, -0.05,
   -0.048, 0.051, 0.523, 0.358, 1, -0.059, -0.006, 0.023, -0.091, -0.05,
   -0.059, 1, 0.614, 0.595, -0.08, -0.048, -0.006, 0.614, 1, 0.523,
   -0.011, 0.051, 0.023, 0.595, 0.523, 1) # correlations in object cr
```

Table 10.6. *Basic Operators for lavaan*

Formula Type	Operator	Meaning	Example
Latent variable definition	=~	is manifested by; is measured by	Latent=~indicator1+ indicator2
Regression	~	is regressed on	DV~IV1+IV2
Covariance (for latents or residuals)	~~	is correlated with	Latent1~~Latent2
Intercept	~1	intercept	DV~1+IV1+IV2

```
lab <- list(c("E1", "E2", "E6", "N3", "N4", "N6"), c("E1", "E2", "E6",
  "N3", "N4", "N6")) # charachtor vector lab for variable names
R <- matrix(cr, ncol = 6, dimnames = lab) # covert cr into matrix
R              # correlation matrix with variable names
n <- 304     # sample size
```

Once lavaan is installed and the correlation matrix is written in R, the next step is to write the lavaan model for CFA.

The CFA (and even SEM for that matter) involves writing model and estimating parameters. The CFA models are written in R code 10.11. The basic operators for `lavaan` are provided in Table 10.6.

R Code 10.11. CFA Models in lavaan
```
# This code specifies three different models for the present data.
# Model1 specifies two latents with three indicators each.
# ext and neu are latents
# E1, E2, and E6 are indicators for ext
# N3, N4, and N6 are indicators for neu
# neu ~~ 0*ext specifies that latents are uncorrelated

Model1 <- 'ext =~ E1 + E2 + E6
neu =~ N3 + N4 + N6
neu ~~ 0*ext'
# Model 2 specifies correlated latents
# The only change is latents are correlated

Model2 <- 'ext =~ E1 + E2 + E6
  neu =~ N3 + N4 + N6
  neu ~~ ext'

# Model3 specifies only one latent pers
# Model hypothesizing one latent (pers) causing all indicators
Model3 <- 'pers =~ E1 + E2 + E6 + N3 + N4 + N6'
```

The `cfa()` is a dedicated CFA function of lavaan. It takes the specified model (one of three models shown in R code 10.11) and data and computes the CFA estimations. It is shown in R code 10.12 with output for Model 1.

R Code 10.12. CFA Model Estimation and Evaluation
```
# cfa() estimates model parameters
# sample.cov = R is inpute correlation matrix;
# sample.nobs = n specifies sample size
# With raw data, object in which data is stored is specified
```

```
# e.g. if raw data is stored in mydata, then cfa (Model1, mydata)

fit <- cfa (Model1, sample.cov = R, sample.nobs = n)
summary(fit, fit.measures = T) # summary of the CFA

# OUTPUT of lavaan CFA

lavaan (0.5-18) converged normally after 21 iterations

Number of observations          304
Estimator                       ML
Minimum Function Test Statistic 8.098
Degrees of freedom              9
P-value (Chi-square)            0.524

Model test baseline model:


Minimum Function Test Statistic 491.575
Degrees of freedom              15
P-value                         0.000

User model versus baseline model:

Comparative Fit Index (CFI)     1.000
Tucker-Lewis Index (TLI)        1.003


Loglikelihood and Information Criteria:

Loglikelihood user model (H0)          -2343.400
Loglikelihood unrestricted model (H1)  -2339.351
Number of free parameters                 12
Akaike (AIC)                            4710.801
Bayesian (BIC)                          4755.405
Sample-size adjusted Bayesian (BIC)     4717.347

Root Mean Square Error of Approximation:


RMSEA                           0.000
90 Percent Confidence Interval  0.000  0.060
P-value RMSEA <= 0.05           0.894

Standardized Root Mean Square Residual:

SRMR   0.035

Parameter estimates:

Information  Expected
Standard     Errors Standard

          Estimate  Std.err  Z-value  P(>|z|)
Latent variables:
ext =~
```

E1	1.000			
E2	0.685	0.098	7.007	0.000
E6	0.726	0.102	7.124	0.000

neu =~

N3	1.000			
N4	0.879	0.080	10.952	0.000
N6	0.852	0.079	10.807	0.000

Covariances:

  ext ~~

neu	0.000

Variances:

E1	0.279	0.091
E2	0.660	0.068
E6	0.618	0.068
N3	0.300	0.056
N4	0.459	0.054
N6	0.492	0.054
ext	0.718	0.118
neu	0.696	0.092

Let's understand the output for Model 1, which is the same model discussed in Section 10.3.4, and elaborated in Figure 10.5. It specified two latent variables ext and neu; ext has E1, E2, and E6 as indicators and neu has N3, N4, and N6 as indicators.

The ML estimated minimum fit function chi-square is 8.098 and df=9. The variance–covariance matrix observed has $(6 \times 7)/2 = 21$ non-redundant elements and model has 12 parameters to be estimated (six in Λ and six in Θ_δ) and, hence, df $= c - p = 21 - 12 = 9$. The chi-square of 8.098 has $p=0.524$. The chi-square is insignificant and, hence, we accept the null $\Sigma = \Sigma(\theta)$. This implies that $\Sigma - \Sigma(\theta) = 0$ under the null hypothesis. Since the model fits the data well our job actually is over. However, this is a really very well-behaved data. The chi-square is generally significant (in big way) even for good models. Hence, we continue to look at the output and examine various options. The minimum fit function chi-square for the baseline model is 491.58 at df $= c - p = 21 - 6 = 15$. In addition, $\chi/df = 8.098/9 = 0.8998$ is a very satisfactory value of this model.

Let's now look at various fit measures. In lavaan, fit measures can be obtained by R code 10.13.

R Code 10.13. Fit Measures in lavaan
```
# To get a specific fit measure like gfi
fitMeasures(fit, "gfi") # returns only GFI
gfi
0.991

# to get more fit measures together.
fitMeasures(fit, c("cfi", "rmsea", "srmr", "gfi", "agfi")) # syntax

cfi            rmsea          srmr           gfi            agfi
1.000          0.000          0.035          0.991          0.980

# To Get all fit measures
fitMeasures(fit) # all types of fit measures

# If I want certain fit measures
fitMeasures(fit, c("chisq", "df", "baseline.chisq", "baseline.df", "gfi",
"agfi", "nfi", "nnfi", "pnfi", "pgfi", "srmr", "cfi", "rmsea", "srmr"))
```

chisq	df	baseline.chisq	baseline.df	gfi
8.098	9.000	491.575	15.000	0.991
agfi	nfi	nnfi	pnfi	pgfi
0.980	0.984	1.003	0.590	0.425
srmr	cfi	rmsea	srmr	
0.035	1.000	0.000	0.035	

The GFI=0.991 and AGFI is 0.980. As we have discussed, the GFI closer to 1 indicates a better fit and the AGFI penalizes the GFI for free parameters through a downward adjustment. Both indices are very close to 1 and, hence, we conclude a reasonably good model–data fit. The NFI and NNFI are 0.984 and 1.003, respectively. This implies that the model is way better than the independent model. As we have discussed, the NNFI does not follow the limits of 0 and 1 and the NNFI obtained on the present data indicates the same. The CFI, which is a modification of NFI, is 1.00 clearly indicating the perfect data–model fit. The CFI reduces the underestimation of NFI (which is 0.984 for present example) and, hence, makes it almost 1.00. The PGFI=0.43 and PNFI=0.59 suggest lower level of parsimony. Both the indices penalize the model GFI and NFI, respectively, for dfs. The PGFI imposed penalty is highest since penalty is the ratio of df_h and df_n, where df_n is the largest possible value. Comparatively, the df_i is a smaller value and PNFI imposes less harsh a penalty. The lavaan output shows standardized root mean square residual (SRMR) value of 0.035. The SRMR below 0.08 is an acceptable fit, and below 0.05 is a good fit. The value of SRMR greater than 0.10 is indicative of a poor fit. The lavaan also provides the root mean square error of approximation (RMSEA), which falls between 0 and 1; a lower value indicates a better fit. The RMSEA below 0.06 is indicative of a reasonable model–data fit. The RMSEA of 0.00 is the lowest and indicates a very good fit. The Akaike information criterion (AIC) and Bayesian information criterion (BIC) need to be interpreted in comparison with other models; AIC and BIC cannot be interpreted in isolation. Suppose we set another model with correlated latent variables, then the model with lower AIC and BIC values is better. One can note that the covariance between ext and neu (the two latent variables) is zero since the model has set it to be zero.

10.3.10.3 Estimators in lavaan

The default estimator for lavaan is ML. The other estimators available are GLS, WLS (or at times also called ADF estimation), diagonally weighted least squares (DWLS), ULS. R code 10.14 demonstrates the specification of estimator.

R Code 10.14. Estimator in lavaan

```
# Maximum Likelihood estimator
fit <- cfa (Model, sample.cov = R, sample.nobs = n, estimator = "ML")

# generalized least squares (GLS) estimator
fit <- cfa (Model, sample.cov = R, sample.nobs = n, estimator = "GLS")

# weighted least squares (WLS) estimator
fit <- cfa (Model, sample.cov = R, sample.nobs = n, estimator = "WLS")

# diagonally weighted least squares (DWLS)
fit <- cfa (Model, sample.cov = R, sample.nobs = n, estimator = "DWLS")

# unweighted least squares (ULS)
fit <- cfa (Model, sample.cov = R, sample.nobs = n, estimator = "ULS")

## Robust estimators in lavaan

# ML with robust standard errors and a Satorra-Bentler scaled test
statistic
```

```
fit <- cfa (Model, sample.cov = R, sample.nobs = n, estimator = "MLM")

# ML with robust standard errors and a Satterthwaite mean- and variance
adjusted test statistic
fit <- cfa (Model, sample.cov = R, sample.nobs = n, estimator = "MLMVS")

# ML with robust (Huber-White) standard errors and a scaled test
statistic that is (asymptotically) equal to the Yuan-Bentler test
statistic
fit <- cfa (Model, sample.cov = R, sample.nobs = n, estimator = "MLR")

# ML with robust standard errors and a mean- and variance adjusted test
statistic
fit <- cfa (Model, sample.cov = R, sample.nobs = n, estimator = "MLMV")

# ML with standard errors based on the first-order derivatives
fit <- cfa (Model, sample.cov = R, sample.nobs = n, estimator = "MLF")

# GLS, WLS, DWLS, MLM, MLMVS, MLMV, MLR requires full data/or some
matrices specific to estimation methods. Anyways, it's desirable to have
entire data.

# lavaan provide robust estimators for DWLS and ULS estimators as well.
They are WLSM, WLSMVS, WLSMV, ULSM, ULSMVS, ULSMV.
```

The lavaan also provides parameter estimates. The two estimates with output are displayed in R Code 10.15.

R Code 10.15. Estimated Parameter Values

```
parameterEstimates(fit)    # The parameterEstimates provide values of
parameter but their standard errors and z-values as well

standardizedSolution(fit) # parameter estimates in standardized format
       lhs op  rhs    est.std  se       z         pvalue
1      ext =~  E1     0.849    0.055    15.536    0.000
2      ext =~  E2     0.581    0.052    11.136    0.000
3      ext =~  E6     0.616    0.052    11.853    0.000
4      neu =~  N3     0.836    0.035    23.846    0.000
5      neu =~  N4     0.735    0.038    19.529    0.000
6      neu =~  N6     0.712    0.038    18.540    0.000
7      ext ~~  neu    0.000    0.000    NA        NA
8      E1  ~~  E1     0.280    0.093    3.018     0.003
9      E2  ~~  E2     0.663    0.061    10.931    0.000
10     E6  ~~  E6     0.620    0.064    9.679     0.000
11     N3  ~~  N3     0.301    0.059    5.146     0.000
12     N4  ~~  N4     0.460    0.055    8.328     0.000
13     N6  ~~  N6     0.493    0.055    9.021     0.000
14     ext ~~  ext    1.000    0.000    NA        NA
15     neu ~~  neu    1.000    0.000    NA        NA

# The lavaan can also provide model implied covariance matrix

fitted(fit) # return the model-implied (fitted) covariance matrix

$cov
        E1      E2      E6      N3      N4      N6
```

```
E1   0.997
E2   0.491   0.997
E6   0.521   0.357   0.997
N3   0.000   0.000   0.000   0.997
N4   0.000   0.000   0.000   0.612   0.997
N6   0.000   0.000   0.000   0.593   0.521   0.997

$mean

E1   E2   E6   N3   N4   N6
0    0    0    0    0    0
```

Among other useful lavaan outputs are residuals. The lavaan provides unstandardized residuals and standardized residuals (for ML). It also can provide estimated parameter variance–covariance matrix for parameter estimates. Lavaan can also display the parameter specification by researchers, starting values of parameters in each model matrix, and its internal representation of model. R Code 10.15 shows this syntax without output for space constraints.

R Code 10.15. Other Syntax of lavaan
```
resid(fit, type = "standardized") # retuns standardized residuals
resid(fit)    # returns unstandardized residuals
vcov (fit)    # returns estimated covariance matrix of the parameter
estimates.
# The inspect() function has many options
inspect(fit) # returns model specification by researcher
inspect(fit, what = "start")   # returns stating values
inspect(fit, what = "list")    # returns internal representation of lavaan
```

10.3.10.4 Comparing Models

It's a common practice to compare models in the CFA literature. Researchers often specify alternative models and examine the chi-squares and other fit indices to select the best model. In case of personality data, R code 10.11 specified three different models: (a) Model 1: the first model is a model that specifies two latent constructs—ext and neu. E1, E2, and E6 are indicators for ext and N3, N4, and N6 are indicators for neu. The two latent variables are specified to be uncorrelated. The correlation between the latents is fixed to be zero. (b) Model 2: This is similar to Model 1, the only difference is that the latent variables are specified to be correlated. The correlation between the latents needs to be estimated. As a result, Model 2 has one df less than Model 1. (c) the Model 3 specifies only one underlying latent construct. All six observed variables are assumed to be manifestations of this latent construct. The theory is not supporting this model, so it is a theoretically a "bad" model. (d) A baseline model or null model: this model is not specified in R code 10.11. This model has the following specification. Specify a latent underlying each observed variable (it is observable variables which are measured without error) and specify no correlations among the latents. The model minimal fit function chi-square is a baseline or null model chi-square. The chi-square and other fit indices obtained for model 1, 2, and 3 are compared. R code 10.16 explains how to do that.

R Code 10.16. Comparing Models
```
# The models are specified in R code 10.11 are used

# parameter estimation of model 1
fit1 <- cfa (Model1, sample.cov = R, sample.nobs = n, estimator = "ML")

# parameter estimation of model 2
fit2 <- cfa (Model2, sample.cov = R, sample.nobs = n, estimator = "ML")
```

```
# parameter estimation of model 3
fit3 <- cfa (Model3, sample.cov = R, sample.nobs = n, estimator = "ML")

fm1 <- fitMeasures (fit1, c("chisq", "df", "baseline.chisq", "baseline.
df", "gfi", "agfi", "nfi", "nnfi", "pnfi", "pgfi", "srmr", "cfi", "rmsea",
"srmr", "aic", "bic"))

fm1
fm2 <- fitMeasures (fit2, c("chisq", "df", "baseline.chisq", "baseline.
df", "gfi", "agfi", "nfi", "nnfi", "pnfi", "pgfi", "srmr", "cfi", "rmsea",
"srmr", "aic", "bic"))
fm2

fm3 <- fitMeasures (fit3, c("chisq", "df", "baseline.chisq", "baseline.
df", "gfi", "agfi", "nfi", "nnfi", "pnfi", "pgfi", "srmr", "cfi", "rmsea",
"srmr", "aic", "bic"))
fm3
```

The examination of Table 10.7 clearly indicates that Model 3 is the worst model among the three models. Model 3 has no theoretical support as well. Now we need to choose from the remaining two models: Model 1 and Model 2. All the fit indices for Model 2 are slightly better than that for Model 1, except for, PNFI, PGFI, AIC, and BIC. Model 2, as compared to Model 1, has set one more parameter (correlation between latents, Φ) as a free parameter that needs to be estimated. As a result, Model 2 is more complex model with one df less. The parsimonious fit indices penalize the gain by complex models for their complexity. The PGFI and PNFI evaluate whether a model has achieved comparatively better results with increased complexity. The PGFI and PNFI inform that Model 1 is a better model than Model 2 since Model 2 with more complexity did not achieve much. The AIC and BIC are better for Model 1 and Model 2. The AIC is obtained as follows:

$$AIC = -2(\log likelihood) + 2a$$
$$AIC = -2(-2343.40) + (2 \times 12)$$
$$AIC = 4686.8 + 24 = 4710.8$$

The smaller values of AIC and BIC are indicative of a better fit. Model 1 has smaller values and, hence, Model 1 is better. In addition, Phi=−0.088 for Model 2. It implies that the two latent variables are almost uncorrelated and specifying a correlation between two latents is unnecessary. So far, the evaluation is guided by a subjective judgment. The statistical tests of whether a restrictive model (M_R) is better than unrestrictive model (M_U). The likelihood ratio test, Wald test, and Lagrangian multiplier test are useful for this purpose.

10.3.10.5 Likelihood Ratio Test (LR)

The LR test is useful in comparing two models. One is restrictive model (M_R) and other is unrestrictive model (M_U). $\hat{\theta}_R$ is the ML estimator of nested restrictive model and $\hat{\theta}_U$ is the ML estimator of model with less restrictions. The likelihood ratio is defined as

$$LR = -2[\log L(\hat{\theta}_R) - \log L(\hat{\theta}_U)]$$

which follows chi-square distribution under the null. $df_{LR} = df_R - df_U$. In usual practice, it's the difference between the two chi-squares, and it is called chi-square difference test:

$$LR = (n-1)F_R - (n-1)F_U$$

Table 10.7. *Model Comparisons for Three Models*

Models	Model Chi-sq	df	Baseline Chi-sq	Baseline df	GFI	AGFI	NFI	NNFI	PNFI	PGFI	SRMR	CFI	RMSEA	SRMR	AIC	BIC	Phi
Model 1	8.098	9	491.575	15	**0.99**	**0.98**	0.98	1.003	**0.59**	**0.43**	0.04	1	**0**	0.035	**4710.801**	**4755.405**	0
Model 2	**6.569**	8	491.575	15	**0.99**	**0.98**	**0.99**	**1.006**	0.53	0.38	0.22	0.39	0.326	0.217	5001.954	5046.558	
Model 3	299.251	9	491.575	15	0.75	0.41	0.39	-0.015	0.24	0.32							

Note: For each indices, the index in bold indicates a better data–model fit.

$$\text{LR} = \chi_R^2 - \chi_U^2$$

The LR value for the two models is obtained by

$$\text{LR} = 8.098 - 6.569 = 1.53$$

$\chi^2 = 3.84$, $p = 0.05$ and the obtained value of 1.53 is smaller than the LR value. The obtained LR is insignificant and it can be concluded that there is no difference between the two models. When two models are not different, restrictive model (simple model) is better. The LR test leads to the conclusion that Model 1 is better. The lavaan can provide the LR tests, and R code 10.17 explains this.

R Code 10.17. LR Test for CFA Model Comparisons

```
lavTestLRT(fit1, fit2)
Chi Square Difference Test
```

	Df	AIC	BIC	Chi sq	Chisq diff	Df diff	Pr(>Chisq)
fit2	8	10420	10468	6.5437			
fit1	9	10419	10464	8.0774	1.5338	1	0.2155

10.3.10.6 Wald Test (W)

The restrictive model is some constraints imposed on unrestrictive model and the restrictive model is nested within unrestrictive model. The Wald test is useful in testing the constraints placed on the unrestrictive model. Let's denote $r(\theta)$ as vector of constraints on less restrictive model. $r(\theta)$ is the function of any parameter. For example, the covariance matrix of latent variables is zero is the restriction put on the less restrictive model.

$$r(\theta) = \sigma_{\xi_{neu}\xi_{ext}}^2 = 0$$

If the restrictive model is valid, then $r(\hat{\theta}_R) = 0$ and $r(\hat{\theta}_U)$ should be within the sampling error. If the restrictive model is not valid, then $r(\hat{\theta}_U)$ should be far from $r(\hat{\theta}_R)$. The Wald test evaluates the extent to which $\hat{\theta}_U$ departs from the constraints imposed. When test consists of single constraint $\hat{\theta}_1 = 0$

$$W = \frac{\hat{\theta}_1^2}{\text{avar}(\hat{\theta}_1)}$$

where avar($\hat{\theta}_1$) is estimated asymptotic variance of $\hat{\theta}$ with df=1. R Code 10.18 explains the Wald test for testing the restriction $r(\theta) = \sigma_{\xi_{neu}\xi_{ext}}^2 = 0$.

R Code 10.18. Wald Test for CFA

```
Model1 <- "ext =~ E1 + E2 + E6
    neu =~ N3 + N4 + N6
    neu ~~ b1*ext"

fit1 <- cfa (Model1, sample.cov = R, sample.nobs = n, estimator = "ML")

lavTestWald(fit1, constraints = "b1 == 0")
$stat
[1] 1.529126
```

```
$df
[1] 1

$p.value
[1] 0.2162437
```

The test statistics is 1.529 which is insignificant. The results are similar to the LR test. Model 2 is not better than Model 1 and, hence, Model 1 which is a simpler model, is retained.

10.3.10.7 Lagrange Multiplier Test (LM Test)

Let $\log L(\theta)$ be unrestricted log likelihood function then LM statistics uses the partial derivative $\partial \log L(\theta)/\partial \theta$. The partial derivative vector is called score $S(\theta)$. The unrestricted elements of $\hat{\theta}_R$ have zero partial and if restrictions are valid then elements of $S(\theta)$ will also be zero. The validity of restriction is tested by how far $S(\hat{\theta}_R)$ is from zero. The LM test statistics evaluates the validity of restrictions:

$$LM = [S(\hat{\theta}_R)]' \, I'(\hat{\theta}_R) S(\hat{\theta}_R)$$

where $I'(\hat{\theta}_R) = \{-E[\partial \log L(\theta)/\partial \theta \partial \theta']\}^{-1}$, is evaluated at $\hat{\theta}_R$. $S(\hat{\theta}_R)$ is $S(\theta)$ evaluated at $\hat{\theta}_R$. R code 10.19 evaluates the LM test for CFA. Note that it is possible.

R Code 10.19. Lagrange Multiplier Test for CFA Models
```
Model1 <- "ext =~ E1 + E2 + E6
    neu =~ N3 + N4 + N6
    neu ~~ 0*ext
"
new = "neu~~ext"
fit <- cfa (Model1, sample.cov = R, sample.nobs = n, estimator = "ML")
lavTestScore (fit, add = new)
```

The LM test statistics also informs us that adding the new parameter is not making the model–data fit better. Hence, Model 1 is still better than Model 2.

10.3.10.8 Graphical Presentation of Model in R

The estimated model can be presented graphically in R.

R Code 10.20. CFA Plot in R
```
library(psych)
lavaan.diagram(fit)

# alternative

library(semPlot)
semPaths(fit)
```

10.3.11 Reporting CFA

The correlation matrix of six personality measures was evaluated for the factorability. The CFA was carried out to test three models: (a) Model 1: N1, N2, and N3 are indicators of neuroticism latent variable and Ex1, Ex2, and Ex3 are indicators of the extraversion latent variable. The two latents were specified to be uncorrelated. (b) Model 2: in addition to Model 1, the two latents were specified to be correlated. (c) Model 3: all six variables were specified as indicators of one latent construct. The lavaan package (Rosseel, 2012) was used to estimate the models. Various fit indices were reported in Table 10.7 for all three models. Model 1 and Model 2 are almost similar with Model 2 having slightly better values of fit measures. The examination of AIC and BIC for Model 1 (4710.80, 4755.41) and Model 2 (4711.27, 4759.59) indicated that Model 1 is slightly better. Similarly, Model 1 is better for parsimonious fit indices as well. The likelihood ratio test ($\chi^2 = 1.53$, df $= 1$, $p = 0.22$) revealed that freeing the correlation between latent parameters at the cost of df is not contributing significantly to in data–model fit. The examination of estimated correlation between the latents (phi $= -0.088$) clearly suggests that the latents are uncorrelated. Hence, a more parsimonious model, Model 1, is retained over Model 2. The CFA results support that the two independent latent variables, extraversion and neuroticism, are causing the observables as described in Model 1.

10.4 STRUCTURAL EQUATIONS MODELING (SEM)

The more general form of the CFA model is called SEM, which is closely associated with the regression models. The regression model has a dependent variable which is explained by some independent variables. We have discussed the consequences of measurement error in the regression analysis. The SEM can take care of this problem if the latent variables are assumed to be causing the IV and DV. I am avoiding a very detailed discussion of SEM. The SEM basics are introduced and the R codes are explained.

10.4.1 Data

Let's start with an example. The intelligence is causing academic achievement. The current academic achievement can be predicted by previous academic achieving as well. So we have two predictors of current academic achievement—past academic achievement, and intelligence. Let's consider all of them as latents. Now intelligence is measured by three variables (manifest variables) and previous and current academic achievement is measured by four (manifest) variables each. Let's further assume that the intelligence, previous academic achievement, and current academic achievement are all latent constructs. The latent construct intelligence (Int) is manifested by three measures of intelligence. They are verbal ability (VA), perceptual ability (PA), and working memory (WM). The latent construct previous academic achievement (Ach_pre) is manifested by four observed variables: average marks (AM_pre), seminar participation (SP_pre), teachers rating (TR_pre), and peers ratings (PR_pre). Similarly, current academic achievement is measured by four manifest variables, namely, average marks (AM_ post), seminar participation (SP_ post), teachers rating (TR_ post), and peers ratings (PR_post). The model states that the latent variable intelligence and previous academic achievement cause another latent variable current academic achievement.

The correlation matrix is given in the following table.

	VA	PA	WM	AM_pre	SP_pre	TR_pre	PR_pre	AM_po	SP_po	TR_po	PR_po
VA	1.00										
PA	0.52	1.00									
WM	0.61	0.56	1.00								
AM_pre	0.57	0.56	0.69	1.00							
SP_pre	0.50	0.46	0.65	0.85	1.00						
TR_pre	0.44	0.48	0.60	0.79	0.72	1.00					
PR_pre	0.36	0.36	0.53	0.56	0.63	0.55	1.00				
AM_po	0.59	0.60	0.71	0.89	0.76	0.69	0.52	1.00			
SP_po	0.45	0.40	0.49	0.43	0.50	0.37	0.31	0.42	1.00		
TR_po	0.38	0.30	0.41	0.27	0.22	0.31	0.24	0.20	0.28	1.00	
PR_po	0.26	0.27	0.33	0.30	0.28	0.33	0.34	0.25	0.29	0.33	1.00

By now, you have learned to get the correlation matrix in R.

10.4.2 The Model

The SEM specifies a general model and then also specifies measurement model. The SEM specifies a general latent variable model as follows:

$$\eta = B\eta + \Gamma\xi + \zeta$$

where η is a $m \times 1$ vector of endogenous variable, ξ is a $n \times 1$ vector latent exogenous variable, B is a $m \times m$ coefficients indicating influence of latent exogenous variables on each other, Γ is a $m \times n$ coefficients matrix of effects of ξ on η, and ζ is a vector containing the disturbance term. $E(\zeta)=0$, and ζ is uncorrelated with ξ.

The measurement models specified by SEM are as follows:

$$Y = \Lambda_Y\eta + \varepsilon$$
$$X = \Lambda_X\xi + \delta$$

where Y is the $p \times 1$ vector and X is the $q \times 1$ vector of observed variables, Λ_Y is $p \times m$ and Λ_X is $q \times n$ matrices relating Y with η and X with ξ. The stochastic errors ε and δ are uncorrelated with each other and have a mean zero.

The model specification for lavaan is as follows:

```
model <- '
  # measurement model
    ach_pre =~ AM_pre + SP_pre + TR_pre + PR_pre
    int =~ va + pa + wm
    ach_post =~ AM_po + SP_po + TR_po + PR_po
  # regressions
    ach_pre ~ int
    ach_post ~ int + ach_pre
  # residual correlations
    AM_pre ~~ AM_po
    SP_pre ~~ SP_po + PR_pre
    TR_pre ~~ TR_po
    PR_pre ~~ PR_po
    TR_pre ~~ PR_pre
    TR_po ~~ PR_po'
```

10.4.3 The Model Specification

The model specification implies the following:

1. There are three measurement models: (a) the latent variable intelligence is causing the indicators namely, VA, PA and WM. (b) The latent variable previous academic achievement is causing the indicators AM_pre, SP_pre, TR_pre, and PR_pre. (c) Current academic achievement is causing the indicators AM_po, SP_po, TR_po, and PR_po.
2. The latent variable intelligence is causing the latent variable previous academic achievement.
3. The latent variables intelligence and previous academic achievement are causing the latent variable current academic achievement.
4. The model is complete by the point three. The additional part is specification of residual correlations. It is obvious that average marks in previous semester and average marks in the current semester are dependent on each other and, hence, their errors also can be

conceptualized to be correlated. Similar correlation among all the errors have been specified (you would quickly recall from the chapter on regression that correlation among the errors was an issue to be sorted out, whereas in the SEM framework we have modeled them. In this sense, the SEM is closer to reality).

10.4.4 Model Estimation and R

The model estimation methods are already discussed in the CFA case. Similar methods are useful here as well. Hence, I proceed to estimation of model in R.

The R output for the SEM model is as follows:

R Code. SEM Model

```
# data into correlation matrix. Input the data interms of single row,
and following command is useful. Otherwise you can use "getCov" from
lavaan package with lower diagonal as input.
data1 <- matrix(data, nrow = 11, ncol = 11, dimnames = list(c("va", "pa",
"wm", "AM_pre", "SP_pre", "TR_pre", "PR_pre", "AM_po", "SP_po", "TR_po",
"PR_po"), c("va", "pa", "wm", "AM_pre", "SP_pre", "TR_pre", "PR_pre",
"AM_po", "SP_po", "TR_po", "PR_po")))

fit <- sem(model, sample.cov = data1, sample.nobs = 300) # estimate model
summary(fit, fit.measures = T) # summary of the model with fit measures

lavaan (0.5-20) converged normally after 64 iterations
  Number of observations             300
  Estimator                          ML
  Minimum Function Test Statistic    113.021
  Degrees of freedom                 34
  P-value (Chi-square)               0.000

Model test baseline model:
  Minimum Function Test Statistic    2251.238
  Degrees of freedom                 55
  P-value                            0.000

User model versus baseline model:
  Comparative Fit Index (CFI)        0.964
  Tucker-Lewis Index (TLI)           0.942

Loglikelihood and Information Criteria:
  Loglikelihood user model (H0)          -5177.704
  Loglikelihood unrestricted model (H1)  -5121.194
  Number of free parameters              32
  Akaike (AIC)                           10419.408
  Bayesian (BIC)                         10537.929
  Sample-size adjusted Bayesian (BIC)    10436.444

Root Mean Square Error of Approximation:
  RMSEA                              0.088
  90 Percent Confidence Interval     0.070   0.106
  P-value RMSEA <= 0.05              0.000

Standardized Root Mean Square Residual:
  SRMR                               0.052
```

Parameter Estimates:

		Expected
Information		Expected
Standard Errors		Standard

Latent Variables:

	Estimate	Std.Err	Z-value	P(>|z|)
ach_pre=~				
AM_pre	1.000			
SP_pre	0.342	0.014	25.280	0.000
TR_pre	0.287	0.013	21.578	0.000
PR_pre	0.178	0.014	12.870	0.000
int=~				
va	1.000			
pa	0.911	0.077	11.758	0.000
wm	1.359	0.095	14.288	0.000
ach_post=~				
AM_po	1.000			
SP_po	0.272	0.031	8.849	0.000
TR_po	0.237	0.029	8.176	0.000
PR_po	0.174	0.028	6.197	0.000

Regressions:

	Estimate	Std.Err	Z-value	P(>|z|)
ach_pre~				
int	3.955	0.303	13.036	0.000
ach_post~				
int	1.709	0.226	7.547	0.000
ach_ pre	0.061	0.042	1.453	0.146

Covariances:

	Estimate	Std.Err	Z-value	P(>|z|)
AM_pre~~				
AM_po	0.900	0.188	4.781	0.000
SP_pre~~				
SP_po	0.254	0.053	4.780	0.000
PR_pre	0.225	0.060	3.749	0.000
TR_pre~~				
TR_po	0.114	0.052	2.198	0.028
PR_pre~~				
PR_po	0.319	0.060	5.362	0.000
TR_pre~~				
PR_pre	0.114	0.058	1.957	0.050
TR_po~~				
PR_po	-0.112	0.053	-2.124	0.034

Variances:

	Estimate	Std.Err	Z-value	P(>|z|)
AM_pre	1.863	0.471	3.956	0.000
SP_pre	0.805	0.085	9.523	0.000
TR_pre	0.896	0.084	10.721	0.000
PR_pre	1.153	0.097	11.897	0.000
va	1.005	0.089	11.240	0.000

pa	0.963	0.084	11.409	0.000
wm	0.839	0.090	9.310	0.000
AM_po	2.260	0.214	10.560	0.000
SP_po	0.995	0.078	12.745	0.000
TR_po	0.940	0.074	12.766	0.000
PR_po	1.013	0.080	12.664	0.000
ach_pre	6.376	1.018	6.260	0.000
int	1.060	0.151	6.995	0.000
ach_post	-1.307	0.179	-7.308	0.000

The SEM model chi-square is 113.02 which is significant indicating that the model and the data do not fit. In the previous section on CFA we have already discussed the issues associated with the chi-square significance testing. More useful measures are comparing chi-square with baseline model chi-square. The CFI and TLI above 0.94 and SRMR 0.052 are indicative of a reasonable fit for the data. Most fit measures are indicating that the model–data fit is reasonable. The rest of the discussion about the model modification, and comparisons of different models is applicable almost as it is from the precious section of CFA and, hence, avoided here. You can change some of the specifications and estimate the model again. The lavaan also has similar data and model on "political democracy" data set described by Bollen (1989). You can run the data in lavaan and carry out the SEM on that data. Political democracy data is one of the very well-described data in the SEM literature.

SUMMARY

Factor analysis is a group of methods that are broadly used in analyzing the structure of the data. The number of variables is reduced by factor analysis. The variables that are correlated are grouped together and called factors. There are two types of factor analysis—EFA and CFA. The EFA is useful for understanding the structure of the data without any pre-specified theory. The EFA has principal component model (PCA) and principal axis model (PAF). The principal diagonal of the correlation matrix has unities for PCA and estimates of communalities for PAF. Communalities are common variance of the variable. The complete factor analysis solution is seldom used and truncated solution is used. Extraction refers to transforming the correlation matrix into factor matrices. The PCA method provides *components* and the FA provides *factors*. The FA extracts from *shared variance* or common variance. Determining the number of factors to be retained is decided by Cattell's scree, parallel analysis and an eigenvalue larger than Monte Carlo eigenvalues, statistical tests, and so on. There are two-factor rotation techniques—orthogonal and oblique—that result into uncorrelated and correlated factors. The CFA is useful for evaluating the factor analysis model. The CFA is useful for testing a pre-specified theory. The CFA model involves specifying theory that has latent variable, which is the cause of observed–measured traits. The models need to be just-identified; however, over-identified models can also be estimated. Under-identified models cannot be estimated. The model parameters are estimated by using a maximum likelihood estimator; in addition, GLS and ULS are also useful. The chi-square test is criticized and various measures of fit-measured are used for choosing between saturated and independent models. In addition, likelihood ratio, Wald test, and the Lagrange multiplier test are used. The R package lavaan, SEM, and openmx are useful for the same. The full SEM model is also described. The R code for evaluating the full SEM model is shown. It is recommended that one should read textbooks that are dedicated to the issue of SEM. Some of them include Bollen (1989), Mueller (1996), Loehlin (2004), and so on.

EXERCISE

1. Explain the model of EFA.
2. Describe the steps followed in EFA.
3. Discuss specific issues in EFA.
4. Describe KMO and Bartlett's tests utility.
5. For the following correlation matrix, carry out KMO and Bartlett's test.

1				
0.4	1			
0.6	0.44	1		
0.5	0.36	0.43	1	
0.7	0.54	0.48	0.6	1

6. What is the problem of communalities and how to solve it?
7. Explain the basic matrix notation of EFA.
8. Describe methods of extraction and rotation.
9. For the following 14 eigenvalues, plot the scree and decide the number of factors.

3.22	3.08	2.8	1.4	1.12	1.09	0.72	0.14	0.13	0.11	0.10	0.07	0.03

10. For the correlation matrix in exercise 5, carry out the EFA.
11. Explain the difference between EFA and CFA?
12. How to solve the problem of identification in CFA?
13. For a data of 10 observed variable with three latents, test the identification.
14. Explain the model of CFA.
15. For the correlation matrix given below, carry out CFA for the model that the first four variables are caused by latent verbal ability and the last three are caused by latent visual.

	visual speed	visual memory	spatial reasoning	mental rotation	verbal fluency	word memory	verbal flexibility
visual speed	1						
visual memory	0.45	1					
spatial reasoning	0.33	0.8	1				
mental rotation	0.56	0.3	0.3	1			
verbal fluency	0.11	−0.15	0.09	0.5	1		
word memory	0.06	−0.12	−0.2	0.45	0.67	1	
verbal flexibility	0.09	0.23	0.11	0.38	0.66	0.45	1

16. Explain fit indices of CFA.
17. Compute various fit indices for the Question 15.

11 Basic Psychometrics

11.1 INTRODUCTION

Psychological testing is the most frequently carried out activity by psychologists. It is particularly very important for the applied researchers and practitioners. Over the last 100 years of scientific practice of the discipline, the psychological testing has grown from just getting some responses from participants to well-developed statistical theories useful for the conceptualization, development, analysis, and interpretation of the data of psychological measurement. The psychometrics provides the statistical theory for psychological testing. In addition, psychometrics also works with the techniques of psychological measurement.

Let us take an example of a researcher who wants to develop a 5-item test. We understand that it is not a good idea to have a psychological test that has only five items. On an average, any good measure requires 10–20 items. The example of 5-items test is suitable to work out in a book like this. I shall not describe various aspects of test development like selecting the domain, writing items, and so on. They are very important aspects of development of psychological measures. However, the focus of this chapter is on the analysis of the data that is obtained by the researcher while developing a psychological measure.

The chapter focuses on two fundamental models of the psychometric analysis. They are: classical test theory (CTT) and item response theory (IRT). The CTT carries out the item analysis and reliability estimates. The CTT is at the basis of the most of the psychological measures that are available. The IRT is based on statistical foundation about the mental measurement. The IRT is a model that uses the latent variable idea for conceptualizing the mental measurement. The application of the IRT was not popular in the early days of IRT, however, with the availability of software (proprietary to begin with and now open-source as well) the IRT application is on the rise. The chapter shall provide R code suitable for CCT analysis and IRT analysis. The chapter is not covering various issues in psychometrics (such as item writing). It is highly recommended that you read a good textbook of psychological testing such as *Psychometric Theory* (Nunnally, 1994), *Introduction to Psychometric Theory* (Raykov & Marcoulides, 2010), *Introduction to Classical and Modern Test Theory* (Crocker & Algina, 2006), *Psychological Testing: Principles, Applications, and Issues* (Kaplan & Saccuzzo, 2012), and *Psychological Testing: A Practical Approach to Design and Evaluation* (Kline, 2005). The coverage of the chapter is the analysis under CTT and IRT.

11.2 THE CLASSICAL TEST THEORY

The CTT has been a foundation of psychological measurement for almost close to 90 years. Many well-known psychological instruments have been developed under the framework of the CTT. Let us understand the reason of the reasoning of the CTT. When individuals respond to a psychological test, they respond to an individual item. A test or scale consists of some items. After reverse scoring of reverse worded items, the scores of all the items are added (some tests/scales do weighted average). This score is called **raw score**. Most tests have some conversion of the raw score into **standard score**. The standard score conversion is converting raw score into a score that follows some known distribution. Most often (or almost always), this known distribution is the normal distribution. The conversion is into Z-score or T-score. We are not much concerned about the converted score because it is anyway just solving a problem of scaling against normative data. Let us us focus on raw score. We call the raw score $\mathbf{X}$. The CTT argues that the observed raw score (X) is made up of two components—**True score (T)** and **Random error (e)**.

$$X = T + e$$

If a person takes the test several times, then the mean of those scores is true score. It is not possible to give a test to a person several times, and hence, the nature of T is hypothetical. T is also believed to be a fixed value. For example, on intelligence test, you have some true score (say, 37, though it is never known in this fashion). If you take intelligence test, then on that specific administration you will get score of 35, or 38, or 34, or 40. If the raw score (X) is 40, then the equation for you for that administration is $40 = 37 + 3$. The error is a random, and could result due to many things like you simply guessed some answers and got them correct by chance, which is not reflecting your T but e. The other theoretical position is called domain sampling theory. There are infinite questions possible for an intelligence test. The formal psychological test has only few of them. That is, from the domain of large number of items, some items are sampled and raw score is obtained on sampled items. Score on all possible items is true score. This position now allows us to believe that the obtained test score or raw score is a random variable. Once it is a random variable, it can take certain values, and the probability distribution of the same can be worked out. The true score can be defined as an expected value of this probability distribution.

$$\mu = \sum_{k=1}^{K} X_k P_k$$

where X_k is k^{th} possible value of X, P_k is probability of X_k. The true score is sum of all the scores multiplied by their probabilities. You know that

$$\mu = \sum_{k=1}^{K} X_k P_k = E(X)$$

We can now state that

$$T_j = E(X_j) = \mu_{Xj}$$

where T_j is true score of the examinee j.
    The error can be defined as follows:

$$e_j = X_j - T_j$$

The error for the person j is the observed score of that person minus the true score of that person. e_j is also a random variable (if T_j is a constant and X_j is a variable, then e_j is also a random variable). Then we can assume a probability distribution for e, and specify an expectation and variance as well.

$$\mu_{e_j} = E(e_j) = E(X_j - T_j)$$

This can be stated that expectation of error is the sum of expectation of raw score minus expectation of the true score.

$$E(e_j) = E(X_j) - E(T_j)$$

The expectation of true scores is true score itself, since the true score is constant.

$$E(e_j) = E(X_j) - T_j$$

We have already specified that $T_j = E(X_j)$, hence

$$E(e_j) = T_j - T_j = 0$$

The expectation of the error is zero. That is errors have a mean zero.
     The assumptions of the CTT are as follows:

1. The expectation of error is zero. $E(e_j) = 0$
2. The true score and the error scores are independent. The correlation between error score and true score in the population is zero. $\rho_{Te} = 0$
3. When the scores of examinee are obtained on two separate tests, then the errors of the two tests in the population are uncorrelated. $\rho_{e1.e2} = 0$

11.2.1 Reliability, Reliability Coefficient, and CTT

Once we know what the true score, error score and raw score are, the useful information is how closely the true score (T) is associated with the total score (X). The **reliability** is conceptualized as correlation between the true score and the raw score. We have already stated that $X = T + e$
     Let us express $T - \mu_T$ as a deviation from mean T, $e - \mu_e$ is deviation of e from its mean and $X - \mu_X$ is deviation of X from its mean.

$$X - \mu_X = (T - \mu_T) + (e - \mu_e)$$

$$\rho_{XT} = \frac{\Sigma(X - \mu_X)(T - \mu_T)}{N\sigma_X\sigma_T}$$

$$\rho_{XT} = \frac{\Sigma[(T - \mu_T) + (e + \mu_e)](T - \mu_T)}{N\sigma_X\sigma_T}$$

$$\rho_{XT} = \frac{\Sigma(T - \mu_T)^2}{N\sigma_X\sigma_T} + \frac{(e + \mu_e)(T - \mu_T)}{N\sigma_X\sigma_T}$$

Since

$$\frac{(e + \mu_e)(T - \mu_T)}{N\sigma_X\sigma_T} = 0 \quad \text{and} \quad \sigma_T^2 = \frac{\Sigma(T - \mu_T)^2}{N}$$

we can re-write the above as

$$\rho_{XT} = \frac{\sigma_T^2}{\sigma_X\sigma_T}$$

To state it simply,

$$\rho_{XT} = \frac{\sigma_T}{\sigma_X}$$

That is, reliability is standard deviation of true score divided by standard deviation of total score.

11.2.2 Methods of Assessment of Reliability

There are quite a few ways of estimating the reliability. The procedures can be understood as the ones based on two test administrations and procedures that are based on single administration of the test.

11.2.3 Procedures Based on Two Test Administrations

The alternate form method and test-retest method are the two methods for the assessment of reliability that require two administrations.

11.2.3.1 Test-retest Methods

The test has a single form and two administrations of the single form are carried out with a temporal gap on the same set of participants. The Pearson's product moment correlation between the two administrations is called as test-retest reliability. The test-retest reliability is an assessment of the temporal stability of a test score and is also known as stability coefficient. The R Code 11.1 demonstrates the test-retest reliability. The t1 and t2 are two administrations with a gap of three months. The reliability is 0.93. Please note that no significance of this is required since it only tests whether the reliability is zero or not in the population. In fact the interest is in showing that it is a high value.

R Code 11.1. Test-retest Reliability
```
t1 <-c(21, 17, 20, 17, 15, 24, 23, 17, 26, 19, 19, 15, 20, 19, 20, 22,
  25, 22, 25, 25)
t2 <-c(20,18,20,18,16,22,24,16,26,19,20,15,20,20,20,23,21,21,25,25)
cor(t1,t2)

0.929817
```

11.2.3.2 Alternate Form Reliability

When a test has two equivalent forms, then the correlation between the two forms is considered as reliability. This correlation describes coefficient of equivalence. Higher value provides confidence to the researcher to use the two forms interchangeably. However, for two forms to be equivalent, it is not just reliability that is enough. The two forms are expected to have similar means, similar variances, similar standard errors of measurement, and similar relations with other constructs. This is reasonably difficult to achieve and hence generally, alternate forms are often not developed.

11.2.4 Methods for Single Administration of the Test

There are several options. Split-half method, Cronbach alpha, and Rulon's method are some of the options.

11.2.4.1 Split-half Method

The split-half method works as follows. First, the test is administered to a sample. Suppose the test has 30 items, the test is divided into two equivalent forms of 15 items each. The test is divided into equal half in different manners.

1. Group odd items into first group and even items into second.
2. Randomly assign items into two halves.
3. Rank-order items on the basis of difficulty (p) and then alternate item goes to the first half and remaining goes to the second half.

4. By matching content: when content differs in specific respects, it is necessary to match content.

The split-half method reliability is computed as

$$\rho_{XX'} = \frac{2\rho_{AB}}{1 + \rho_{AB}}$$

Look at the following data of six items for ten participants.

S No.	Items						Even Sum	Odd Sum	Total
	1	2	3	4	5	6			
1	1	1	1	0	1	1	3	2	5
2	0	1	0	0	0	0	0	1	1
3	1	1	1	1	1	1	3	3	6
4	1	0	1	1	1	0	3	1	4
5	0	0	0	0	1	0	1	0	1
6	0	1	1	1	0	0	1	2	3
7	1	1	1	1	0	1	2	3	5
8	1	1	0	1	1	1	2	3	5
9	1	1	1	0	1	1	3	2	5
10	1	1	1	1	1	1	3	3	6
						Average	2.1	2	
						SD	1.04	1	
								$\text{Cor}_{AB} = 0.48$	

$$\rho_{XX'} = \frac{2\rho_{AB}}{1 + \rho_{AB}}$$

$$\rho_{XX'} = \frac{2 \times 0.48}{1 + 0.48} = 0.65$$

The six items are responded by the ten participants. The sum of odd and even item is provided in last two columns. The correlation between the odd and even items is 0.48. However, the correlation itself is not a reliability. The correlation is based on three items each from the scale whereas the scale has six items. The reliability for six items (2–3 itmes) needs to be computed. Hence the formula of split-half makes an adjustment to adjust the reliability obtained on three items to double the items.

11.2.4.2 Cronbach Alpha: Method Based on Item Covariances

Lee Cronbach[1] in 1951 wrote one of most important papers in the field of psychometrics— "Coefficient alpha and the internal structure of tests"—in the journal *Psychometrika*.[2] The

---

[1] Lee Cronbach (1916–2001) is the most influential American psychologist for CTT applications. As a child, he was a participant in Terman's long-term study of talented children. He developed interest in psychological measurement due to the work of Thurstone on the measurement of attitudes. After his PhD (1940), he wrote two very influential papers, one is on alpha and other is on the two disciplines of scientific psychology. The second paper discussed experimental psychology and correlation psychology as the two disciplines of psychology. He was also the president of American Psychological Association. One of his most important contributions is on the dependability of behavioral measures and he also developed generalizability theory of psychological measurement. He is also instrumental in developing idea of validity of psychological tests along with Paul Meehl.

[2] *Psychometrika* is a premier journal in the field of psychometrics. The journal started in 1936 and the first issue contains articles by Hotelling on computation of principal components, and L. L. Thurstone. The journal is

paper contains synthesis of various methods for estimating reliability. The Cronbach alpha is one of the powerful ways of expressing reliability based on item covariances. The formula is

$$\hat{\alpha} = \frac{k}{k-1}\left(1 - \frac{\sum \hat{\sigma}_i^2}{\hat{\sigma}_X^2}\right)$$

where k is number of items in the test, $\hat{\sigma}_i^2$ is a variance of item i, and $\hat{\sigma}_X^2$ is a variance of the total test. An example data is shown below on 6-item test.

				Sr			
	1	2	3	4	5	6	Total
1	1	1	1	0	1	1	5
2	0	1	0	0	0	0	1
3	1	1	1	1	1	1	6
4	1	0	1	1	1	0	4
5	0	0	0	0	1	0	1
6	0	1	1	1	0	0	3
7	1	1	1	1	0	1	5
8	1	1	0	1	1	1	5
9	1	1	1	0	1	1	5
10	1	1	1	1	1	1	6
Var	0.233	0.178	0.233	0.267	0.233	0.267	3.433

The alpha can be calculated as follows:

$$\hat{\alpha} = \frac{k}{k-1}\left(1 - \frac{\sum \hat{\sigma}_i^2}{\hat{\sigma}_X^2}\right)$$

$$\hat{\alpha} = \frac{6}{6-1}\left(1 - \frac{1.27}{3.09}\right) = 0.707$$

The alpha of 0.71 is considered as a good value. The alpha is a function of number of items. Alpha increases as the number of items increases.

R Code 11.2. Cronbach Alpha
```
# Data on six items
i1<-c(1, 0, 1, 1, 0, 0, 1, 1, 1, 1)
i2<-c(1, 1, 1, 0, 0, 1, 1, 1, 1, 1)
i3<-c(1, 0, 1, 1, 0, 1, 1, 0, 1, 1)
i4<-c(0, 0, 1, 1, 0, 1, 1, 1, 0, 1)
i5<-c(1, 0, 1, 1, 1, 0, 0, 1, 1, 1)
i6<-c(1, 0, 1, 0, 0, 0, 1, 1, 1, 1)

data<- data.frame(i1,i2,i3,i4,i5,i6) # data frame
library(psych) # call package psych
alpha(data) # alpha data

## Output
Reliability analysis
Call: alpha(x = data)
```

devoted to advancement of theory and methodology of behavioral data. Many important papers in the field of factor analysis, SEM, and psychometrics are published in this journal.

```
raw_alpha  std.alpha   G6(smc)   average_r  S/N   ase   mean   sd
0.71          0.7       0.85       0.28      2.4  0.21   0.68  0.31

lower  alpha upper   95% confidence boundaries
0.29       0.71                    1.12
```

Reliability if an item is dropped:

	raw_alpha	std.alpha	G6(smc)	average_r	S/N	alpha se
i1	0.53	0.52	0.71	0.18	1.1	0.30
i2	0.72	0.72	0.80	0.34	2.6	0.23
i3	0.66	0.65	0.85	0.27	1.9	0.25
i4	0.72	0.71	0.87	0.33	2.5	0.22
i5	0.75	0.75	0.84	0.37	3.0	0.22
i6	0.55	0.54	0.69	0.19	1.2	0.29

Item statistics

	n	raw.r	std.r	r.cor	r.drop	mean	sd
i1	10	0.91	0.90	0.94	0.84	0.7	0.48
i2	10	0.46	0.48	0.46	0.25	0.8	0.42
i3	10	0.66	0.66	0.54	0.47	0.7	0.48
i4	10	0.51	0.50	0.34	0.26	0.6	0.52
i5	10	0.41	0.40	0.33	0.16	0.7	0.48
i6	10	0.86	0.87	0.91	0.75	0.6	0.52

Non missing response frequency for each item

	0	1	miss
i1	0.3	0.7	0
i2	0.2	0.8	0
i3	0.3	0.7	0
i4	0.4	0.6	0
i5	0.3	0.7	0
i6	0.4	0.6	0

The R output explains various points.

The raw alpha is based on covariances whereas the standardized alpha are based on correlations. The standardized alpha is slightly lower than the raw alpha. The G6 (smc) are Guttman's Lambda 6 reliability.[3] The average_r is average inter-item correlation. It is 0.28 for the present data. The reliability if an item is dropped is an important statistics. Look at the drop in raw alpha values. For the item 1, the drop is 0.53, which means if the item 1 is removed from the test, then the reliability of the test reduces. For the item 5, it is 0.75, which means that if the item 5 is dropped, then the reliability is increasing to 0.75. If I am using this data for item analysis, then I would retain the item 1 and remove the item 5. The r.drop is also a useful information, it contains item test-score correlation for this item against the scale without this item. In case of the dichotomous items, mean always indicates the difficulty of the item.

11.2.4.3 The Validity

Separate discussion on validity is avoided since the validity of the test involves correlation, regression, and factor analysis. These three are discussed separately in separate chapters. The

---

[3] Guttman's lambda 6 is useful reliability coefficients. The G6 (or L6) is useful when the correlations between the items are lower in relation to the SMC. It uses variance of the item accounted for SMC. They are also called as Guttman's lower-bounds.

factor analysis is useful in understanding dimensionality. Exploratory factor analysis is a common choice of psychometricians.

11.3 ITEM RESPONSE THEORY

The IRT has three important models. They are one parameter logistic model, two parameter logistic model, and three parameter logistic model. The IRT is a major shift from the traditional view of the psychometric assessment. It starts with theorizing a latent variable model. The latent variable model is discussed in the earlier chapter. The theory believes that the item responses are function of the latent traits that are much smaller in number than the items. The modern test theory or IRT is primarily a function of the seminal work by Lord and Novik[4] (1968). Recently, Hambleton and Swaminathan (1985) and Embreston and Raise (2000) have provided much comprehensive review of the IRT models for psychologists. This framework provides completely different way of understanding the measurement of psychological attributes. The IRT software are becoming more and more user-friendly and open-source which is increasing the popularity of the IRT. The IRT is not focusing on the total score. Its focus is on the assessment of the underlying latent or unobserved trait. The latent trait is not observed but is leading to the test behavior. The central assumption in IRT is that there is a connection between the trait being measured by test and a response to an item on a test.

The trait is called *latent trait*. It is denoted by the symbol theta (Θ), which refers to the ability of the person. The connection is simple: the probability of response to an item on the test is function of individual's theta level. Suppose we are measuring reasoning ability. The theta (Θ) is the individual's reasoning ability. The test of reasoning has some item on reasoning. The chance of passing the item depends on the individual's reasoning ability (Θ). As the Θ level increases, the chance of passing the item increases. If someone has high Θ, then the probability of passing an item is also high for the person. And inversely, if someone has low Θ, then the probability of passing an item is low for the person. The important part of the IRT is that it models responses of all participants for all items for various levels of theta. The IRT can estimate measurement error at any level of the theta. In CTT, the measurement errors were constant. The CTT test are useful in discriminating averagely, whereas, the IRT is useful in developing test that can have highest discrimination at particular level of theta. The IRT is useful for dichotomous responses, and polytomous responses. Various other models can be tested by IRT, for example, nominal category model, rating scale models, graded response model, partial credit models, sequential model for ordered responses, models for time limit tests, and so on. In this chapter, we shall discuss three models—one parameter logistic model, two parameter logistic model, and three parameter logistic model. All the models are useful for assessing the participants' theta level. Another advantage of the IRT is the ability to be useful for computer-adaptive testing (CAT), which is a procedure where the item is given to the responder depending on the ability.

11.3.1 Models

Let us start with models that are useful for the dichotomous data. The dichotomous data models are useful in ability testing and scaling where only dichotomous responses are invited. There are three models to be discussed. They are: one parameter logistic model, two parameter logistic model, and three parameter logistic model.

---

[4] Lord and Novik contributed a book *Statistical Theories of Mental Test Scores* that has changed the psychometrics for once and all. It was not so popular in early of the book. With the advent of high speed computing, the IRT has become popular.

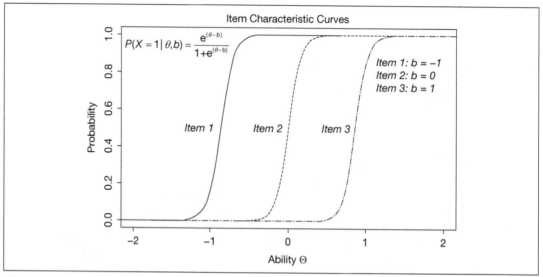

Figure 11.1. *One PL IRT Model*

11.3.1.1 One Parameter Logistic Model

One parameter logistic model is a basic model also known as Rasch model in the honor of Danish Mathematician statistician George Rasch who developed it (1960). The one parameter in the model is **difficulty**. The parameter is sometimes called threshold or location as well. The parameter difficulty is labeled as *b*, which has a mean 0 and standard deviation 1. The theta is also scaled with mean 0 and variance 1. The item with higher *b* value is more difficult and item with lower *b* value is less difficult. If there are two items, one with *b*=1 and second with *b*=−1, then the second item is an easy item than the first one. The one parameter logistic model is

$$P(X = 1 \mid \theta, b) = \frac{e^{(\theta-b)}}{1+e^{(\theta-b)}}$$

The probability that *X* takes a value of 1 given the ability of the individual and difficulty of the item is expressed. *X*=1 is success on the item. This probability is expressed in the logistic format. The probability can be expressed as

$$P(\Theta_i) = \frac{1}{\{1 + e^{-D(\theta-b_i)}\}}$$

where *D* is 1.702, *e*=2.718, *b* is item difficulty, and theta is ability of the examinee. For example, if we assume that *b*=1 (item is difficult) and theta is 0.2, then the probability of passing an item is 0.204. If we make difficulty of the item as −0.8, then the probability of passing is 0.846. This implies that the probability of passing an item with difficulty 1 is much smaller than probability of passing an item with difficulty of −0.8.

Figure 11.1 shows the 1 PL IRT model. The figure shows three-item characteristic curves. The item 1 is having *b*=−1. This is easiest of the item. The chance of passing this item is highest at ability −1 with steepest slope around the theta of −1. The item 2 is moderately difficult item with *b*=0, and item three is more difficult item with *b*=1. Both items have highest probability of passing the item at theta 0 and 1 respectively. The item 1 can be passed with low theta whereas item 3 can be passed by the person having high theta.

The R has a package ltm which is useful to carry out IRT. The Law School Admission Test data set (LSAT, Section VI) is used for the analysis of these parameters which is available in ltm. The data set has five items. Each item has a dichotomous response. It is a data of 1000 observations.

The R Code 11.3. One PL model

```
library(ltm)
fit<-rasch(LSAT)
summary(fit)
plot(fit, items = c(1, 2, 3, 4, 5))

Call:
rasch(data = LSAT)

Model Summary:

log.Lik    AIC        BIC
-2466.938  4945.875   4975.322

Coefficients:
               value     std.err   z.vals
Dffclt.Item 1  -3.6153   0.3266    -11.0680
Dffclt.Item 2  -1.3224   0.1422    -9.3009
Dffclt.Item 3  -0.3176   0.0977    -3.2518
Dffclt.Item 4  -1.7301   0.1691    -10.2290
Dffclt.Item 5  -2.7802   0.2510    -11.0743
Dscrmn          0.7551   0.0694    10.8757

Integration:
method: Gauss-Hermite
quadrature points: 21

Optimization:
Convergence: 0
max(|grad|): 2.9e-05
quasi-Newton: BFGS
```

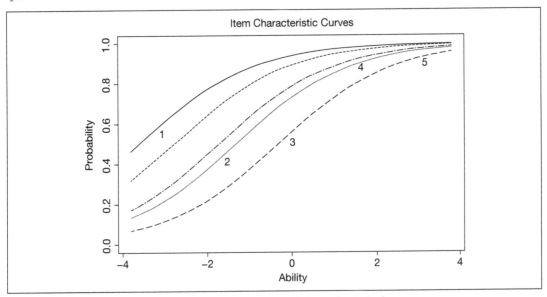

Figure 11.2. *Figure of One Parameter Logistic model from the R Code*

Figure 11.2 provides item characteristics curve. You can observe in the graph that the item 1 is the easiest of the item and item 3 being a difficult item. The log-likelihood of the model is –2466.938 and the difficulty parameter is also estimated. The estimated values of the difficulty parameter, their associated standard errors and z-values are also provided. The Item 1 has lowest difficulty value (–3.62) whereas item 3 has highest difficulty value (–0.32). However, the discrimination is constant for all the items (0.75) since this parameter is not specified. All in all, the test is at easier side.

11.3.1.2 Two Parameter Logistic Model

The two parameter logistic model has added complexity. The 1 PL model assumed equal slope for all the items, and the estimate of the discrimination parameter is indicative of the same. The two parameter logistic model has slope parameter set free which means that the item parameters are estimated such as the slope of the item is separately estimated for each item. The items can have different discrimination ability. The formal model is as follows

$$P(X = 1 \mid \theta, a, b) = \frac{e^{a(\theta - b)}}{1 + e^{a(\theta - b)}}$$

where in addition to 1 PL model, a parameter 'a' is added. The parameter a is a discrimination parameter or slope parameter.

$$P(\Theta_i) = \frac{1}{\{1 + e^{-Da_i(\theta - b)}\}}$$

The probability can be worked out. Suppose the theta is –0.2, b=0.15, and a=2, the probability is 0.23, and when the slope parameter value (a) changes to 0.5, the probability is 0.43.

Figure 11.3 shows the schematic representation of the two parameter IRT model. The Figure shows that the item 1 has a gradual slope. The probability of passing the item 1 is increasing gradually as the ability is increasing. The item 3 in contrast, has a steeper slope. The probability

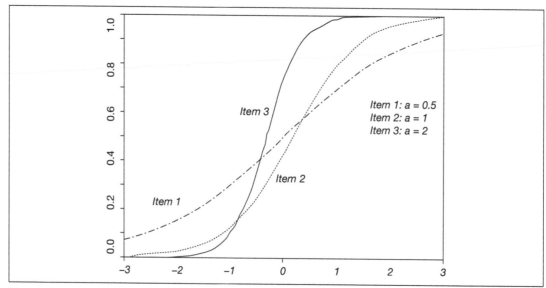

Figure 11.3. *Two Parameter Logistic Model of IRT*

of passing the item 3 is close to zero when the theta is around –1.5. From this point, the probabilities start rising sharply. The probability of passing the item 3 is reasonably high as the theta is close to 0.5. In the narrow space of theta of –1.5 to theta of 0.5, the probabilities of passing the item 3 went from zero to close to 1. The item 1 required slightly more than –3 to +3 range of theta since it was gradually sloping. In the R, for the LSAT data, the R Code 11.4 is specifying a two-parameter IRT model.

R Code 11.4. Two PL IRT for LSAT

```
fit <- ltm(LSAT ~ z1) # z1 is slope parameter set free
summary (fit)

Call:
ltm(formula = LSAT ~ z1)

Model Summary:
  log.Lik      AIC        BIC
-2466.653   4953.307   5002.384

Coefficients:
                  value    std.err    z.vals
Dffclt.Item   1  -3.3597   0.8669    -3.8754
Dffclt.Item   2  -1.3696   0.3073    -4.4565
Dffclt.Item   3  -0.2799   0.0997    -2.8083
Dffclt.Item   4  -1.8659   0.4341    -4.2982
Dffclt.Item   5  -3.1236   0.8700    -3.5904
Dscrmn.Item   1   0.8254   0.2581     3.1983
Dscrmn.Item   2   0.7229   0.1867     3.8721
Dscrmn.Item   3   0.8905   0.2326     3.8281
Dscrmn.Item   4   0.6886   0.1852     3.7186
Dscrmn.Item   5   0.6575   0.2100     3.1306

Integration:
method: Gauss-Hermite
quadrature points: 21

Optimization:
Convergence: 0
max(|grad|): 0.024
quasi-Newton: BFGS
```

The R code shows the discrimination parameter being specified for the five items. The discrimination of each of the item is estimated. All the values of discrimination are almost similar but in comparison the item 3 has higher discrimination. You can also realize that two log-likelihood are not different.

11.3.1.3 Three Parameter Logistic Model

The three parameter logistic model has increased complexity by adding one more parameter. The parameter added to the 3 PL IRT Model is parameter c, which is called guessing parameter. The parameter values indicate that the correct answers are given by guessing and not due to the ability of the persons. The model is

$$P(X = 1 \mid \theta, a, b, c) = c + (1 - c)\frac{e^{a(\theta-b)}}{1+e^{a(\theta-b)}}$$

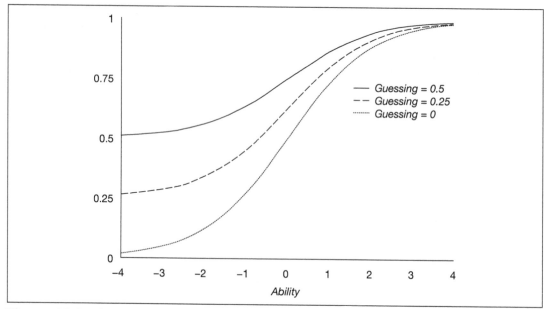

Figure 11.4. *The Three Parameter Logistic Model*

It can be stated as

$$P(\Theta_i) = c + (1-c)\frac{1}{\{1+e^{-Da_i(\theta-b)}\}} = c + \frac{1-c}{\{1+e^{-Da_i(\theta-b)}\}}$$

The model states that as the value of c increases, the probability of passing the item is higher at lowest of the theta or ability.

Figure 11.4 shows the 3PL IRT Model.

Figure 11.4 shows that the item with guessing=0 is the item on which guessing is not possible. The item with the guessing=0.5 is the item with very high amount of guessing. This item starts with probability of passing an item of 0.5 which means that one can pass this item without having any ability but just with a random guess. Modeling this parameter helps in two ways. One, it helps us detect the items that are performing badly so that these items can be removed from the test, and two, under the condition when some amount guessing cannot be stopped during the measurement, the modeling of the parameter helps in controlling the effect of this behavior on the measurement.

The three parameter model in R can be estimated as follows:

R Code 11.5. Three Parameter IRT Model
```
tpm(LSAT)
Call:
tpm(data = LSAT)

Coefficients:
        Gussng  Dffclt   Dscrmn
Item 1  0.037   -3.296   0.829
Item 2  0.078   -1.145   0.760
Item 3  0.012   -0.249   0.902
Item 4  0.035   -1.766   0.701
Item 5  0.053   -2.990   0.666

Log.Lik: -2466.66
```

The R code shows the parameter estimated model wherein third parameter of guessing is also estimated. The value of guessing parameter is higher for item 2. It is lowest for the item 3.

11.3.1.4 Samejima's Graded Response Model

The graded response model is useful for modeling the polytomous response. The 5-point Likert scales are the graded responses. The basic Samejima's graded response model is as follows

$$P_{xij}(X_{ij} = x_{ij} \mid \theta_i) = P^*_{xij}(\theta_i) - P^*_{xij+1}(\theta_i)$$

where

$$P^*_{xij}(\theta_i) = P(X_{ij} \geq x_{ij} \mid \theta_i) = \frac{e^{Da_j(\theta_j - b_{xij})}}{1 + e^{Da_j(\theta_j - b_{xij})}}$$

The Samejima models are actually in some sense binomial models. While working the probability of success on one option, rest of the responses can be considered as failures. I am not going into details of the model. The R code and graphical expression should serve the purpose.

The Samejima model in Figure 11.5 shows the plot for only one item (unlike earlier figures). The one item has five response categories. They are 1 = "strongly disagree," 2 = "disagree," 3 = "neutral," 4 = "agree", and 5 = "strongly agree." The figure is insightful. Assume that underlying trait is extraversion. Theta below 0 shows introversion and theta above 0 shows extraversion tendencies. The item is "I like to meet people." The response of 1 (strongly disagree) has a higher probability when the theta is very low. The low theta indicates introversion. This pattern implies that individuals who are very low in extroversion have very high probability to choose response 1. On the other hand, the line 5 (strongly agree) shows that as the theta is very high, the probability of choosing the "strongly agree" increases. Now look at response 2 (disagree). Individuals who are below 0 and just moderately introverted are more likely to choose 2. The figure shows that probability of choosing this response is highest at theta of

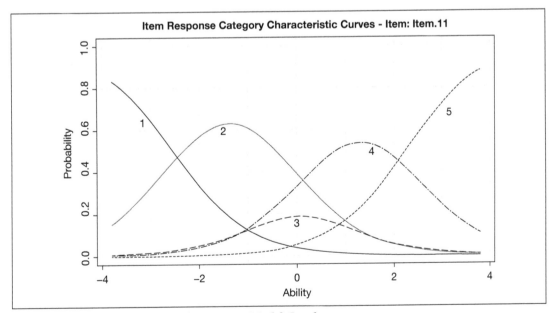

Figure 11.5. *Samejima Graded Responses Model Graph*

−1.5. You would realize that the Samejima model is very useful. The following R code can be used to estimate parameters.

R Code 11.6. Samejima Graded Response Models

```
library(ltm) #call package ltm
data<-read.csv("/Users/macbook/Desktop/scoringR.csv", header = T)
  # input data; you need to create a data matrix
attach(data)
names(data)
fit1<-grm(data, constrained = FALSE) # fitting samejima model
plot(fit1, items = c(11, 14, 15, 18, 20, 21,25, 26),lwd = 3, cex = 1.4)
abline(v = -4:4, h = seq(0, 1, 0.2), col = "lightgray", lty = "dotted")
plot(fit1, type = "IIC", items = 10, legend = TRUE, lwd = 2, cx =
  "topright") # plotting the model for items
```

11.3.2 Item Information and Test Information Function

Figure 11.6 provides item and test information function. The item information curve is another useful part of the IRT models. The information function is defined as one over sigma square. The information function can be plotted and provides a useful understanding. The R code 11.7 shows the information function.

R Code 11.7. Item and Test Information Function

```
## Item Information Curves, for the first 3 items; include a legend
plot(fit, type = "IIC", items = 1:3, legend = TRUE, lwd = 2, cx =
  "topright")
## Test Information Function
plot(fit, type = "IIC", items = 0, lwd = 2, cex.lab = 1.1, sub =
  paste("Call: ", deparse(fit$call)))
## The Standard Error of Measurement can be plotted by
vals <- plot(fit, type = "IIC", items = 0, plot = FALSE)
plot(vals[, "z"], 1/sqrt(vals[, "info"]), type = "l", lwd = 2,
xlab = "Ability", ylab = "Standard Error",
main = "Standard Error of Measurement")
```

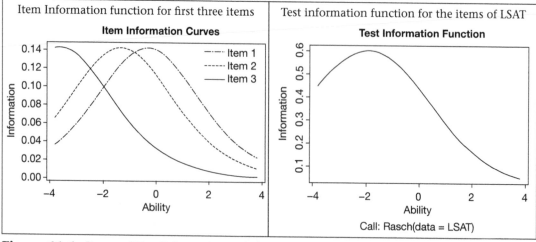

Figure 11.6. *Item and Test Information Function*

The item information curve informs us that the item 3 is maximally providing information at the theta of –4 to –3 whereas the item 1 is providing information in the theta of zero. In the test, we need items that provide us information at various theta levels. If the test has items that provide information at specific theta level, then that test is useful only to assess individual of that theta and rest of the individuals above the theta will pass or fail depending on whether they are above the theta or below the theta. The test information curve does the same for the overall test. The standard error of measurement can be plotted by the R code provided. The plot is not shown. However, the plot is almost exactly inverse of test information curve. The curve shows the standard error on *Y*-axis and theta on *X*-axis.

11.3.3 Choosing a Model

The model estimates are maximum likelihood estimates. The goodness-of-fit chi-square test can be performed and fit of the model can be evaluated. The problems associated with the chi-square test are discussed in the earlier chapter. The test evaluates whether model and data fit well. The other option is to perform likelihood ratio test. The log-likelihood for each model is available. The test is discussed in the previous chapter. One can easily do it in R. The R Code 11.8 is showing the model fit and LR test.

R Code 11.8. Goodness-of-Fit and LR Test for IRT

```
GoF.rasch(fit)

Bootstrap Goodness-of-Fit using Pearson chi-squared

Call:
rasch(data = LSAT)

Tobs: 18.34
# data-sets: 50
p-value: 0.84
fit<-rasch(LSAT)
fit1 <-ltm(LSAT ~ z1)
anova(fit, fit1)

Likelihood Ratio Table
       AIC       BIC      log.Lik    LRT    df    p.value
fit    4945.88   4975.32  -2466.94
fit1   4953.31   5002.38  -2466.65   0.57   4     0.967
```

The goodness-of-fit is resulting in insignificant chi-square. This is telling us that model fits the data well. The comparison of the two likelihood ratios for one parameter IRT model and two parameter IRT model informs us that the additional parameter specification has no gain involved. The principle of parsimony helps us to retain one parameter model over two parameter model.

11.3.4 The Applications of IRT

The IRT is useful for many purposes. The IRT is useful in scaling individuals. This is a very useful attribute of the IRT models particularly when information is available on many tests. Needless to say that IRT is a very useful tool in test construction and modifications. A new test can be developed by using the IRT theory. Existing test can be modified by using IRT model since the data are already available on them. Fascinating application of the IRT is CAT (Computer Assisted Testing), which does not provide entire test to the test taker. It only gives the items that are near test takers theta values. So initially a random item is given and then

if the individual passes that item, then item difficult than that is randomly given and if individual fails the item easier than that is randomly given. Same procedure continues and a very
narrow range ability items are reached to get a better estimate of the ability. This is possible
only under IRT framework.

SUMMARY

This chapter has provided a brief introduction about two psychometric models. The CTT is
based on assumption about error and attempts to develop a test that has a high reliability. The
IRT is mathematically elegant procedure and has multiple models and researcher can choose
appropriate model for their purpose. The item characteristic curve provides useful information. Formal statistical procedures are well developed for deciding about the suitable model,
test, and items. The chapter has also provided suitable R Codes.

EXERCISE

1. Explain CTT.
2. State assumptions of CTT.
3. Show $E(e_j) = 0$
4. Show $\rho_{XT} = \dfrac{\sigma_T}{\sigma_X}$
5. A researcher administered the same form with a gap of three weeks. The two administrations shared 81% common variance. What is the test-retest reliability?
6. t1 = (22, 15, 22, 18, 17, 28, 21, 14, 28, 22, 20, 14, 19, 20, 18, 22, 27, 21, 28, 27); t2 = (22,
   19, 23, 19, 18, 23, 23, 17, 28, 20, 22, 17, 22, 21, 20, 24, 26, 20, 29, 23)
7. Explain limitations of alternate form reliability.
8. How to create two forms for split-half reliability?
9. For the following data, compute split-half and Cronbach alpha.

S No.	Items					
	1	2	3	4	5	6
1	0	1	1	0	1	1
2	1	1	1	1	1	1
3	1	1	0	1	1	1
4	1	0	1	1	1	0
5	0	0	0	0	1	0
6	0	1	1	1	0	0
7	1	0	1	1	1	1
8	0	0	0	1	0	1
9	1	1	1	0	1	1
10	0	0	0	0	0	0

10. Explain 1 PL, 2 PL and 3 PL models of IRT.
11. Compute IRT models in R on *Mobility* data from *ltm* package.

Appendix A: Introduction to R

R is a very powerful statistical environment that provides researcher a flexibility and freedom to work in their own ways. R is open-source which can be downloaded from comprehensive R archives network website (CRAN). R can be installed on Windows, Mac, and Linux operating systems. The installation instructions are provided on R web page.

The link https://cran.r-project.org/bin/windows/base/ can provide you the most recent windows installable .exe file.

The link https://cran.r-project.org/bin/macosx/ provides the mac os pkg files.

The installation can happen from any of the CRAN mirrors available worldwide.

R opens in a console, an R editor and an R graphic window (called Quartz in Mac). Generally practice your R code in the R editor window rather than directly writing them in the console.

There are separate editors available other than the once provided by R. Tinn-R and R Studio, and the R commander are the most popular ones. The R commander provides a spreadsheet view which is not in the default setup of R.

R is used for many reasons:

1. R is free.
2. As a teacher I can give assignment to the students and they can do it on the go.
3. One can write code if one has to perform any new statistics. It is easy to write an R code.
4. R has most advanced statistical packages (such as sem, lavaan, and ltm) for most complex analysis possible.
5. The R graphics is excellent. It provides publication-quality graphs. It also provides the control to the researcher.
6. Most simulations can be carried out in R, for example, CLT. It becomes a very handy all-in-one tool for teaching statistics.
7. Most of the functions are built in. The fresh code need not be written for 95% of the functions.
8. The online help is widely available for R. Many universities have provided free R Tutorials on their websites.
9. R provides various manuals for using R on the website. Most students can benefit by referring to personality project website http://personality-project.org/r/

When you open R, you get to see the following screen.

```
R version 3.2.2 (2015-08-14) - "Fire Safety"
Copyright (C) 2015 The R Foundation for Statistical Computing
Platform: x86_64-apple-darwin13.4.0 (64-bit)

R is free software and comes with ABSOLUTELY NO WARRANTY.
You are welcome to redistribute it under certain conditions.
Type 'license()' or 'licence()' for distribution details.

Natural language support but running in an English locale

R is a collaborative project with many contributors.
Type 'contributors()' for more information and
'citation()' on how to cite R or R packages in publications.

Type 'demo()' for some demos, 'help()' for on-line help, or
'help.start()' for an HTML browser interface to help.
Type 'q()' to quit R.
```

```
[R.app GUI 1.66 (6996) x86_64-apple-darwin13.4.0]
```

```
[Workspace restored from /Users/macbook/.RData]
[History restored from /Users/macbook/.Rapp.history]
```

The window is an R Consol.

Let us look at basic operations in R.

After installing R, only a base package is installed. To install more packages, carry out following:

Start R and Type following in R and press enter. Keep computer connected to the internet. It will install various R packages that are useful to us. This may take half an hour to an hour depending on your computer and the Internet speed. After running first line, R will ask you to choose CRAN mirror you can choose any one.

```
install.packages("ctv")
library("ctv")
```

```
install.views("Psychometrics", dependencies = T) # Install packages for
psychological data analysis.
```

```
install.views("Econometrics", dependencies = T)
```

```
install.views("Distributions", dependencies = T)
```

```
install.views("ExperimentalDesign", dependencies = T)
```

```
install.views("Graphics", dependencies = T)
```

```
install.views("Multivariate", dependencies = T)
```

```
install.views("Robust", dependencies = T)
```

```
install.views("SocialSciences", dependencies = T)
```

```
install.views("gR", dependencies = T)
```

R is a case-sensitive language. FOO, Foo, and foo are three different objects!

Basic arithmetic operations in R: addition, subtraction, multiplication, and division can be performed as if it is a calculator.

```
x <- 10
y <- 5
```

```
z <- x + y
z1 <- x - y
z2 <- x/y
z3 <- x * y
```

```
# R will NOT READ things written after # sign
#square and square roots
```

```
x^2       # square of x
sqrt(9)   # square-root of 9
log(x)    # log of x
exp(1)    # exponential of 1
abs(x)    # absolute value of x
```

```
#sin(x); cos(x); tan(x); asin(x); acos(x); atan(x) are other useful
functions
```

```
# Type help(exp) to know more about exp function.
```

Most basic operator in R is as follows:

```
**        Exponentiation
<         Less than
<=        Less than or equal to
>         Greater than
>=        Greater than or equal to
==        exactly equal to
!=        not equal to
!x        not x
x | y x OR y
x & y x AND Y
Is TRUE(x)    Tests if x is True
```

Getting help in R is easy. There are many ways in which you can get help in R.

```
help.start() # general help in R
help(t.test) # help about function t.test
?t.test # samething
apropos ("t.test") # list all functions containing string t.test
example(t.test) # show an example of function t.test
```

Data input to R:

Suppose you want to input data to R, then you have two simple options. First you can input inside the editor or console.

Data is 1, 2, 3, 4, 5, 6, 7, 8, 9, 10.

```
x <- c(1,2,3,4,5,6,7,8,9,10)
# certain basic statistics can be carried out with the data.
mean(x)
[1] 5.5

sd(x)
[1] 3.02765

var(x)
[1] 9.166667

# arithmetic operations are possible on x
(x - mean(x))^2 # is a sum of squared deviations form mean.
[1] 20.25 12.25 6.25 2.25 0.25 0.25 2.25 6.25 12.25
[10] 20.25

# to get first five values of x
x[1:5]
[1] 1 2 3 4 5
```

Data type and vector in R:

```
# VECTORS
a <- c(1, 2, 2, 3, 4, 5.4, -3, 11) # numeric vector
b <- c("one", "two", "three") # character vector
c <- c(FALSE, TRUE, TRUE, FALSE, TRUE, FALSE) #logical vector
mydata <- data.frame (a, b, c) # creates data frame of three objects
mydata <- cbind (a, b, c) # binds three objects column wise
```

```
# factor as an object
gender <- c(rep("male",30), rep("female", 40))
gender <- factor(gender)
```

R can also have a matrix format data. Use the following code to get the matrix data in R:

```
y<-matrix(1:30, nrow=6,ncol=5) # y is a matrix
# another matrix 2 × 2
cells <- c(20,40,14,18)
rnames <- c("R1", "R2")
cnames <- c("C1", "C2")
mymatrix <- matrix(cells, nrow=2,ncol = 2, byrow = TRUE, dimnames= list
(rnames, cnames))
```

R can be used for generating data as well. Following are some examples for data generating mechanism in R.

```
seq(1:20)              #Generates a sequence of 1 to 20

sample(1:10)       # generate vector of 1 to 10
rep("female", 10)  # repeat "female" 10 times
rep(5, 10)            # replicate 5 10 times

rnorm(100, 10, 4) # generate random sample of size 100, man 10 and sd = 4
```

R is useful in obtaining the statistical distributions properties.

```
pnorm(1.64, lower = F)   # probability of getting value above 1.64
qnorm(.05, lower = F)    # quantile function, value above which integral
                             of pdf is .05
dnorm(1.96)              # density function at .05
rnorm (10)              # random standard normal distribution with 10
observations
```

```
# similar use of p, q, r, and d is possible with other distributions
pbinom(); qbinom().
```

The real data cannot be entered in console or editor. The users typically prefer to enter data on spreadsheet-like formats such as MS-Excel, libreOffice-calc, and so on. Once you enter data in these applications, then save it in .csv format with the headers. Generally do not use long variable names because they are difficult to manipulate. The .csv format can be called in R as follows:

```
mydata <- read.table ("path", sep=",", header=TRUE)
# for mac useres
data<- read.csv("/Users/macbook/Desktop/SEM/trial.csv", header = T)
# for windows users
data<- read.csv("C:/trail.csv", header = T)

# In case of the data in the .txt format
read.txt()

# easier way to get the data is to use following code

read.table(file.choose(),sep=",",header=TRUE) # open csv with dialogue box
```

Export of the plot
```
# Graphical output

jpeg("c:/graphs/plot.jpg")
plot(x)
dev.off()
```

The easy way to exporting a single plot is to go to file and choose "save as" option.

Writing your function: R is useful for writing your function that you can store and always use for your future purpose; you can share it with your friends and you can put it on your blog so that everyone gets to use it. I am writing a simple example for subtraction.

```
subtract = function(a,b)
{result = a-b
  return(result)}

subtract(10,6)
```

FLOW CONTROL IN R

R can be used effectively if you understand how to control the flow.
   The "if loop", for example, is written in the following way.

```
if (logical condition) {
  statements
} else {
  alternative statements
}

# else branch is optional. If else is not written and logical condition
is false, then, the loop ends.
```

The For and While Loops

```
for(i in 1:20) {
  print(i*i)
}

# similar can be done in the while loop
i=1
while(i<=20) {
  print(i*i)
  i=i+1
}
```

This appendix is just a sketchy introduction to R. Unless you explore R on your own you will not realize the potential. Two points that need to be noted. First, R learning curve is negatively accelerated, that is, initially you may find it slightly difficult to work around R but as you spend some time you would be a savvy user. Second, initially you may find the syntax difficult to remember, and may believe that it is so important to lean syntax. However, I believe in exactly inverse. It is not syntax but the logic that is important to understand. Have fun with R.

Appendix B: Basic Mathematics for Psychologists

This appendix will help you understand basic mathematical operations that are useful to psychologists.

B.1. ALGEBRA

Summation rules

Rule 1:

$$\Sigma(X+Y) = \Sigma X + \Sigma Y$$
$$\Sigma(X+Y+W+\cdots) = \Sigma X + \Sigma Y + \Sigma W + \cdots$$

Rule 2:

$$\Sigma a = na$$

Rule 3:

$$\Sigma aX = a\Sigma X$$

B.1.1. Exponents

Exponent is a number placed in a superscript position immediately after the number to indicate repeated multiplication.

$a = a^1$ if nothing is written, then 1 is the exponent. $3 = 3^1$
$a^p \times a^q = a^{p+q}$. For example, $3^2 \times 3^4 = 3^{2+4} = 3^6 = 729 = 9 \times 81$
$(a^p)^q = a^{p \times q}$. For example $(3^2)^4 = 3^{2 \times 4} = 6561$
$(a \times b)^p = a^p \times b^p$. For example, $(2 \times 3)^2 = 2^2 \times 3^2 = 4 \times 9 = 36$
$\left(\dfrac{a}{b}\right)^n = \dfrac{a^n}{b^n}$. For b is not zero. For example, $\left(\dfrac{10}{2}\right)^2 = \dfrac{10^2}{2^2} = \dfrac{100}{4} = 25$

$a^{-p} = \dfrac{1}{a^p}$. For example $2^{-3} = \dfrac{1}{3^3} = \dfrac{1}{27}$

$\dfrac{a^p}{a^q} = a^{p-q}$. For example, $\dfrac{2^4}{2^2} = 2^{4-2} = 2^2 = 4 = \dfrac{16}{4} = 4$

$$a^{1/2} = \sqrt{a}$$
$$a^{1/n} = \sqrt[n]{a}$$
$$4^{1/2} = \sqrt[2]{4} = 2$$

$$a^0 = 1 = a^{p-p} = \left(a^p\right)\left(a^{-p}\right) = \dfrac{a^p}{a^p} = 1$$

B.1.2. Basic Rules for Logarithms

$\log(a \times b) = \log a + \log b$

For example, $\log(10 \times 100) = \log 10 + \log 100 = 1 + 2 = 3 = \log 1000$

$\log(a/b) = \log a - \log b$

For example, $\log(100/10) = \log 100 - \log 10 = 2 - 1 = 1 = \log 10$

$\log(a^n) = n \log a$

For example, $\log(10^4) = 4 \log 10 = 4 \times 1 = 4 = \log 10000$

B.1.3. Permutations and Combinations

$$n! = n \times (n-1) \times (n-2) \times \cdots \times 2 \times 1$$

$$0! = 1$$

$$^n p_r = \frac{n!}{(n-r)!}$$

Where n and r are positive integers and $r \leq n$.

Example: How many ways are there to choose two members of a committee from five available candidates?

$$5p_2 = \frac{5!}{(5-2)!} = \frac{5!}{3!} = \frac{5 \times 4 \times 3 \times 2 \times 1}{3 \times 2 \times 1} = 20$$

$$^n c_r = \frac{n!}{r!(n-r)!}$$

Example: By how many ways three individuals can be selected from five individuals?

$$^5 c_3 = \frac{5!}{3!(5-3)!} = \frac{5 \times 4 \times 3 \times 2 \times 1}{3 \times 2 \times 1 \times (2 \times 1)} = \frac{120}{12} = 10$$

There are 10 ways in which 3 people can be selected from 5 individuals to form a committee. This is also known as binomial coefficient.

B.2. MATRICES

B.2.1. Matrix

A matrix is rectangular array of numbers or elements arranged in rows and columns. A matrix of order (or dimension) $M \times N$ (read as M by N) is a set of $M \times N$ elements arranged in M rows and N columns. Let the boldface capital letters denote matrices, then a matrix **A** of order $(M \times N)$ may be expressed as

$$\mathbf{A} = [a_{ij}] = \begin{bmatrix} a_{11} & a_{12} & a_{13} & \cdots & a_{1N} \\ a_{21} & a_{22} & a_{23} & \cdots & a_{2N} \\ \cdots & \cdots & \cdots & \cdots & \cdots \\ a_{M1} & a_{M2} & a_{M3} & \cdots & a_{MN} \end{bmatrix}$$

Where a_{ij} is the element appearing in the ith row and jth column of matrix **A**. $[a_{ij}]$ is an expression for the matrix **A** whose typical element is a_{ij}. The order (or dimension) of a matrix is often written as a subscript for easy reference. For example—$A_{2 \times 3}$

For example: $A_{3\times3} = \begin{bmatrix} 1 & 3 & 2 \\ 6 & 0 & 7 \\ 5 & 2 & 4 \end{bmatrix}$ $B_{2\times3} = \begin{bmatrix} 2 & 4 & 5 \\ 3 & -1 & 7 \end{bmatrix}$

Scalar: A scalar is a single (real) number. In other words, a scalar is a 1×1 matrix.

Column vector: A matrix which has M rows and only one column is called a column vector. Let the boldface lowercase letters denote vectors, and then a column vector is given as,

$$x_{3\times1} = \begin{bmatrix} 2 \\ 4 \\ 5 \\ 7 \end{bmatrix}$$

Row Vector: A matrix which has only one row and N columns is called a row vector.

$$x_{1\times3} = \begin{bmatrix} 1 & -3 & 5 \end{bmatrix}   x_{1\times4} = \begin{bmatrix} 3 & 7 & 0 & 1 \end{bmatrix}$$

B.2.2. Transposition

The transpose of a matrix A of order $M\times N$ is denoted by A' and read as A prime or A transpose. A' is a matrix of order $N\times M$ which is obtained by interchanging the rows and columns of matrix A; that is ith row of A becomes the ith column of A'. For example

$$A_{3\times2} = \begin{bmatrix} 3 & 5 \\ 0 & 1 \\ 4 & 6 \end{bmatrix}   A'_{2\times3} = \begin{bmatrix} 3 & 0 & 4 \\ 5 & 1 & 6 \end{bmatrix}$$

B.2.3. Types of Matrices

Square matrix: A matrix with the same number of rows and columns is called a square matrix.

$$A_{2\times2} = \begin{bmatrix} 1 & 2 \\ 4 & 3 \end{bmatrix}   A_{3\times3} = \begin{bmatrix} 4 & 8 & 5 \\ 1 & 0 & 2 \\ 5 & 3 & 7 \end{bmatrix}$$

Diagonal matrix: A square matrix with at least one non-zero element on the main diagonal and zeros elsewhere is called a diagonal matrix.

$$A_{2\times2} = \begin{bmatrix} 1 & 0 \\ 0 & 5 \end{bmatrix}   A_{3\times3} = \begin{bmatrix} 4 & 0 & 0 \\ 0 & -1 & 0 \\ 0 & 0 & 3 \end{bmatrix}$$

Scalar matrix: A diagonal matrix whose all diagonal elements are equal is called a scalar matrix.

$$A_{3\times3} = \begin{bmatrix} 5 & 0 & 0 \\ 0 & 5 & 0 \\ 0 & 0 & 5 \end{bmatrix}   A_{2\times2} = \begin{bmatrix} -2 & 0 \\ 0 & -2 \end{bmatrix}$$

Identity matrix: A diagonal matrix whose all the diagonal elements are 1 is called an identity or unit matrix and it is denoted by I. It is a special kind of scalar matrix.

$$I_{3\times3} = \begin{bmatrix} 1 & 0 & 0 \\ 0 & 1 & 0 \\ 0 & 0 & 1 \end{bmatrix} \quad I_{4\times4} = \begin{bmatrix} 1 & 0 & 0 & 0 \\ 0 & 1 & 0 & 0 \\ 0 & 0 & 1 & 0 \\ 0 & 0 & 0 & 1 \end{bmatrix}$$

Symmetric matrix: A square matrix whose elements above the main diagonal are mirror images of the elements below the main diagonal is called a symmetric matrix. In other words, a symmetric matrix is such that its transpose is equal to itself, that is, $\mathbf{A}=\mathbf{A}'$.

Null matrix: A matrix whose all the elements are zero is called a null matrix. It is denoted by 0.

B.2.4. Matrix Operations

B.2.4.1. Matrix Addition

Let $A=[a_{ij}]$ and $B=[b_{ij}]$

If matrix **A** and matrix **B** are of the same order then matrix addition can be given as

$$\mathbf{A}+\mathbf{B}=\mathbf{C}$$

where **C** is of the same order as **A** and **B** and is obtained as $c_{ij}=a_{ij}+b_{ij}$ for all i and j. Here, **C** is obtained by adding the corresponding elements of **A** and **B**. For example, if

$$A_{3\times3} = \begin{bmatrix} 1 & 0 & 6 \\ 3 & -2 & 2 \\ 4 & 5 & 3 \end{bmatrix} \quad B_{3\times3} = \begin{bmatrix} 1 & 3 & 4 \\ 2 & 6 & 0 \\ 8 & 1 & 7 \end{bmatrix} \quad \text{and}$$

$$\mathbf{C}=\mathbf{A}+\mathbf{B}, \text{ then}$$

$$C_{3\times3} = \begin{bmatrix} 2 & 3 & 10 \\ 5 & 4 & 2 \\ 12 & 6 & 10 \end{bmatrix}$$

B.2.4.2 Matrix Subtraction

Let $A=[a_{ij}]$ and $B=[b_{ij}]$

If matrix **A** and matrix **B** are of the same order then matrix subtraction can be given as

$$\mathbf{C}=\mathbf{A}-\mathbf{B}$$

where **C** is of the same order as **A** and **B** and is obtained as $c_{ij}=a_{ij}-b_{ij}$ for all i and j. Here **C** is obtained by subtracting the elements of **B** from the corresponding elements of **A**. For example,

$$\text{if } A_{3\times3} = \begin{bmatrix} 2 & 0 & 9 \\ 3 & -1 & 2 \\ 4 & 6 & 8 \end{bmatrix} \quad B_{3\times3} = \begin{bmatrix} 1 & 3 & 8 \\ 2 & 6 & 0 \\ 7 & 1 & 4 \end{bmatrix} \quad \text{and}$$

$$\mathbf{C}=\mathbf{A}-\mathbf{B}, \text{ then}$$

$$C_{3\times3} = \begin{bmatrix} 1 & -3 & 1 \\ 1 & -7 & 2 \\ -3 & 5 & 4 \end{bmatrix}$$

Scalar Multiplication

To multiply a matrix **A** by a scalar λ (a real number), we multiply each element of the matrix **A** by λ:

For example: if $\lambda = 2$ and $A = \begin{bmatrix} 1 & -2 \\ 3 & 4 \end{bmatrix}$ then $\lambda A = 2A = \begin{bmatrix} 2 & -4 \\ 6 & 8 \end{bmatrix}$

B.2.5. Matrix Multiplication

Let **A** be $M \times N$ and **B** be $N \times P$ then the product **AB** (in this order only) is defined to be a new matrix **C** of order $M \times P$ such that

$$c_{ij} = \sum_{k=1}^{N} a_{ik} b_{kj} \quad i = 1, 2, \ldots, M$$

$$j = 1, 2, \ldots, P$$

Here, c_{ij} the element in the ith row and the jth column of **C** is obtained by multiplying the elements of the ith row of **A** by the corresponding elements of the jth column of **B** and summing over all terms. This is called the row by column rule of multiplication.

Thus, to obtain c_{11}, the element in the first row and the first column of **C**, we multiply the elements in the first row of **A** by the corresponding elements in the first column of **B** and sum over all terms. Similarly to obtain c_{12}, we multiply the elements in the first row of **A** by the corresponding elements in the second column of **B** and sum over all terms, and so on.

Note that for multiplication to exist, the number of columns in **A** must be equal to the number of rows in **B**. In other words, matrices **A** and **B** must be conformable with respect to multiplication.

For example:

if $A_{2\times3} = \begin{bmatrix} 1 & 3 & 4 \\ 2 & 5 & 6 \end{bmatrix}$ and $B_{3\times2} = \begin{bmatrix} 2 & 7 \\ 1 & 4 \\ 3 & 1 \end{bmatrix}$ then

$$AB = C_{2\times2} = C_{2\times2} = \begin{bmatrix} (1\times2)+(3\times1)+(4\times3) & (1\times7)+(3\times4)+(4\times1) \\ (2\times2)+(5\times1)+(6\times3) & (2\times7)+(5\times4)+(6\times1) \end{bmatrix}$$

$$C_{2\times2} = \begin{bmatrix} 2+3+12 & 7+12+4 \\ 4+5+18 & 14+20+6 \end{bmatrix}$$

$$C_{2\times2} = \begin{bmatrix} 17 & 23 \\ 27 & 40 \end{bmatrix}$$

Appendix C: Statistical Tables

TABLE C.1. AREA UNDER NORMAL DISTRIBUTION

For example, to determine the area under the curve between 0 and 0.45, start at the row for 0.4, and read along until 0.45—there is the value 0.1736. Because the curve is symmetrical, the same table can be used for values going in either direction, so a negative 0.45 also has an area of 0.1736.

For Z-score of 0.45, the area between mean and Z is 0.1736. The area beyond Z is 0.50 – 0.1736 = 0.3264. The R Code to obtain them is as follows.

```
pnorm(.45, lower = F) # Results in 0.3263552
.5 - pnorm(.45, lower = F) # results in 0.1736448
```

Z	0.00	0.01	0.02	0.03	0.04	0.05	0.06	0.07	0.08	0.09
0.0	0.0000	0.0040	0.0080	0.0120	0.0160	0.0199	0.0239	0.0279	0.0319	0.0359
0.1	0.0398	0.0438	0.0478	0.0517	0.0557	0.0596	0.0636	0.0675	0.0714	0.0753
0.2	0.0793	0.0832	0.0871	0.0910	0.0948	0.0987	0.1026	0.1064	0.1103	0.1141
0.3	0.1179	0.1217	0.1255	0.1293	0.1331	0.1368	0.1406	0.1443	0.1480	0.1517
0.4	0.1554	0.1591	0.1628	0.1664	0.1700	0.1736	0.1772	0.1808	0.1844	0.1879
0.5	0.1915	0.1950	0.1985	0.2019	0.2054	0.2088	0.2123	0.2157	0.2190	0.2224
0.6	0.2257	0.2291	0.2324	0.2357	0.2389	0.2422	0.2454	0.2486	0.2517	0.2549
0.7	0.2580	0.2611	0.2642	0.2673	0.2704	0.2734	0.2764	0.2794	0.2823	0.2852
0.8	0.2881	0.2910	0.2939	0.2967	0.2995	0.3023	0.3051	0.3078	0.3106	0.3133
0.9	0.3159	0.3186	0.3212	0.3238	0.3264	0.3289	0.3315	0.3340	0.3365	0.3389
1.0	0.3413	0.3438	0.3461	0.3485	0.3508	0.3531	0.3554	0.3577	0.3599	0.3621
1.1	0.3643	0.3665	0.3686	0.3708	0.3729	0.3749	0.3770	0.3790	0.3810	0.3830
1.2	0.3849	0.3869	0.3888	0.3907	0.3925	0.3944	0.3962	0.3980	0.3997	0.4015
1.3	0.4032	0.4049	0.4066	0.4082	0.4099	0.4115	0.4131	0.4147	0.4162	0.4177
1.4	0.4192	0.4207	0.4222	0.4236	0.4251	0.4265	0.4279	0.4292	0.4306	0.4319
1.5	0.4332	0.4345	0.4357	0.4370	0.4382	0.4394	0.4406	0.4418	0.4429	0.4441
1.6	0.4452	0.4463	0.4474	0.4484	0.4495	0.4505	0.4515	0.4525	0.4535	0.4545
1.7	0.4554	0.4564	0.4573	0.4582	0.4591	0.4599	0.4608	0.4616	0.4625	0.4633
1.8	0.4641	0.4649	0.4656	0.4664	0.4671	0.4678	0.4686	0.4693	0.4699	0.4706
1.9	0.4713	0.4719	0.4726	0.4732	0.4738	0.4744	0.4750	0.4756	0.4761	0.4767
2.0	0.4772	0.4778	0.4783	0.4788	0.4793	0.4798	0.4803	0.4808	0.4812	0.4817
2.1	0.4821	0.4826	0.4830	0.4834	0.4838	0.4842	0.4846	0.4850	0.4854	0.4857
2.2	0.4861	0.4864	0.4868	0.4871	0.4875	0.4878	0.4881	0.4884	0.4887	0.4890
2.3	0.4893	0.4896	0.4898	0.4901	0.4904	0.4906	0.4909	0.4911	0.4913	0.4916
2.4	0.4918	0.4920	0.4922	0.4925	0.4927	0.4929	0.4931	0.4932	0.4934	0.4936
2.5	0.4938	0.4940	0.4941	0.4943	0.4945	0.4946	0.4948	0.4949	0.4951	0.4952
2.6	0.4953	0.4955	0.4956	0.4957	0.4959	0.4960	0.4961	0.4962	0.4963	0.4964
2.7	0.4965	0.4966	0.4967	0.4968	0.4969	0.4970	0.4971	0.4972	0.4973	0.4974
2.8	0.4974	0.4975	0.4976	0.4977	0.4977	0.4978	0.4979	0.4979	0.4980	0.4981
2.9	0.4981	0.4982	0.4982	0.4983	0.4984	0.4984	0.4985	0.4985	0.4986	0.4986
3.0	0.4987	0.4987	0.4987	0.4988	0.4988	0.4989	0.4989	0.4989	0.4990	0.4990

TABLE C.2. TABLE FOR *R* TO *Z'* TRANSFORMATION

The following R code is useful to obtain the same.

```
library(psychometric) # call library psychometric
r2z (.33) # find z for r = .33. the result is [1] 0.3428283
z' = .5 * log((1+r)/(1-r)) # formula for the same
```

r	z'	r	Z'	r	z'
0	0	0.34	0.3541	0.68	0.8291
0.01	0.01	0.35	0.3654	0.69	0.848
0.02	0.02	0.36	0.3769	0.7	0.8673
0.03	0.03	0.37	0.3884	0.71	0.8872
0.04	0.04	0.38	0.4001	0.72	0.9076
0.05	0.05	0.39	0.4118	0.73	0.9287
0.06	0.0601	0.4	0.4236	0.74	0.9505
0.07	0.0701	0.41	0.4356	0.75	0.973
0.08	0.0802	0.42	0.4477	0.76	0.9962
0.09	0.0902	0.43	0.4599	0.77	1.0203
0.1	0.1003	0.44	0.4722	0.78	1.0454
0.11	0.1104	0.45	0.4847	0.79	1.0714
0.12	0.1206	0.46	0.4973	0.8	1.0986
0.13	0.1307	0.47	0.5101	0.81	1.127
0.14	0.1409	0.48	0.523	0.82	1.1568
0.15	0.1511	0.49	0.5361	0.83	1.1881
0.16	0.1614	0.5	0.5493	0.84	1.2212
0.17	0.1717	0.51	0.5627	0.85	1.2562
0.18	0.182	0.52	0.5763	0.86	1.2933
0.19	0.1923	0.53	0.5901	0.87	1.3331
0.2	0.2027	0.54	0.6042	0.88	1.3758
0.21	0.2132	0.55	0.6184	0.89	1.4219
0.22	0.2237	0.56	0.6328	0.9	1.4722
0.23	0.2342	0.57	0.6475	0.91	1.5275
0.24	0.2448	0.58	0.6625	0.92	1.589
0.25	0.2554	0.59	0.6777	0.93	1.6584
0.26	0.2661	0.6	0.6931	0.94	1.738
0.27	0.2769	0.61	0.7089	0.95	1.8318
0.28	0.2877	0.62	0.725	0.96	1.9459
0.29	0.2986	0.63	0.7414	0.97	2.0923
0.3	0.3095	0.64	0.7582	0.98	2.2976
0.31	0.3205	0.65	0.7753	0.99	2.6467
0.32	0.3316	0.66	0.7928		
0.33	0.3428	0.67	0.8107		

TABLE C.3. VALUES OF CORRELATION COEFFICIENT UNDER NULL THAT POPULATION CORRELATION IS ZERO

Degrees of Freedom	Probability		
	0.05	0.01	0.001
1	0.997	1.000	1.000
2	0.950	0.990	0.999
3	0.878	0.959	0.991
4	0.811	0.917	0.974
5	0.755	0.875	0.951
6	0.707	0.834	0.925
7	0.666	0.798	0.898
8	0.632	0.765	0.872
9	0.602	0.735	0.847
10	0.576	0.708	0.823
11	0.553	0.684	0.801
12	0.532	0.661	0.780
13	0.514	0.641	0.760
14	0.497	0.623	0.742
15	0.482	0.606	0.725
16	0.468	0.590	0.708
17	0.456	0.575	0.693
18	0.444	0.561	0.679
19	0.433	0.549	0.665
20	0.423	0.457	0.652
25	0.381	0.487	0.597
30	0.349	0.449	0.554
35	0.325	0.418	0.519
40	0.304	0.393	0.490
45	0.288	0.372	0.465
50	0.273	0.354	0.443
60	0.250	0.325	0.408
70	0.232	0.302	0.380
80	0.217	0.283	0.357
90	0.205	0.267	0.338
100	0.195	0.254	0.321

Note: Refer to section 5.2.3.a for the R code.

It is recommended to use *t*-statistics conversion for values not the table. Generally interpolation is to be avoided.

TABLE C.4: STUDENT'S *T*-DISTRIBUTION

The following R code can provide these values:

```
qt(.05, 10, lower = F) # .05 is one tailed probability, 10 is df.
qt(.05/2, 10, lower = F) # two-tailed probability for same problem.
```

df	Two-tailed Probabilities				
	0.1	**0.05**	**0.025**	**0.01**	**0.005**
1	6.314	12.706	25.452	63.657	127.321
2	2.920	4.303	6.205	9.925	14.089
3	2.353	3.182	4.177	5.841	7.453
4	2.132	2.776	3.495	4.604	5.598
5	2.015	2.571	3.163	4.032	4.773
6	1.943	2.447	2.969	3.707	4.317
7	1.895	2.365	2.841	3.499	4.029
8	1.860	2.306	2.752	3.355	3.833
9	1.833	2.262	2.685	3.250	3.690
10	1.812	2.228	2.634	3.169	3.581
11	1.796	2.201	2.593	3.106	3.497
12	1.782	2.179	2.560	3.055	3.428
13	1.771	2.160	2.533	3.012	3.372
14	1.761	2.145	2.510	2.977	3.326
15	1.753	2.131	2.490	2.947	3.286
16	1.746	2.120	2.473	2.921	3.252
17	1.740	2.110	2.458	2.898	3.222
18	1.734	2.101	2.445	2.878	3.197
19	1.729	2.093	2.433	2.861	3.174
20	1.725	2.086	2.423	2.845	3.153
21	1.721	2.080	2.414	2.831	3.135
22	1.717	2.074	2.405	2.819	3.119
23	1.714	2.069	2.398	2.807	3.104
24	1.711	2.064	2.391	2.797	3.091
25	1.708	2.060	2.385	2.787	3.078
26	1.706	2.056	2.379	2.779	3.067
27	1.703	2.052	2.373	2.771	3.057
28	1.701	2.048	2.368	2.763	3.047
29	1.699	2.045	2.364	2.756	3.038
30	1.697	2.042	2.360	2.750	3.030
31	1.696	2.040	2.356	2.744	3.022
32	1.694	2.037	2.352	2.738	3.015
33	1.692	2.035	2.348	2.733	3.008
34	1.691	2.032	2.345	2.728	3.002
35	1.690	2.030	2.342	2.724	2.996
36	1.688	2.028	2.339	2.719	2.990
37	1.687	2.026	2.336	2.715	2.985
38	1.686	2.024	2.334	2.712	2.980
39	1.685	2.023	2.331	2.708	2.976
40	1.684	2.021	2.329	2.704	2.971
41	1.683	2.020	2.327	2.701	2.967
42	1.682	2.018	2.325	2.698	2.963
43	1.681	2.017	2.323	2.695	2.959
44	1.680	2.015	2.321	2.692	2.956
45	1.679	2.014	2.319	2.690	2.952
46	1.679	2.013	2.317	2.687	2.949

		Two-tailed Probabilities			
df	0.1	0.05	0.025	0.01	0.005
47	1.678	2.012	2.315	2.685	2.946
48	1.677	2.011	2.314	2.682	2.943
49	1.677	2.010	2.312	2.680	2.940
50	1.676	2.009	2.311	2.678	2.937
60	1.671	2.000	2.299	2.660	2.915
70	1.667	1.994	2.291	2.648	2.899
80	1.664	1.990	2.284	2.639	2.887
90	1.662	1.987	2.280	2.632	2.878
100	1.660	1.984	2.276	2.626	2.871
110	1.659	1.982	2.272	2.621	2.865
120	1.658	1.980	2.270	2.617	2.860
130	1.657	1.978	2.268	2.614	2.856
140	1.656	1.977	2.266	2.611	2.852
150	1.655	1.976	2.264	2.609	2.849
160	1.654	1.975	2.263	2.607	2.846
170	1.654	1.974	2.261	2.605	2.844
180	1.653	1.973	2.260	2.603	2.842
190	1.653	1.973	2.259	2.602	2.840
200	1.653	1.972	2.258	2.601	2.839
300	1.650	1.968	2.253	2.592	2.828
400	1.649	1.966	2.250	2.588	2.823
500	1.648	1.965	2.248	2.586	2.820
1000	1.646	1.962	2.245	2.581	2.813

TABLE C.5. THE *F*-DISTRIBUTION

The following R code is useful to obtain these values.

```
qf(.05, 2, 10, lower = F) # F value at df = 2, 10 at .05 level. Answer
is 4.102821
qf(.01, 2, 10, lower = F) # F value at df = 2, 10 at .01 level. Answer
is 7.559432
```

df denominator	Degrees of Freedom Numerator									
	1	2	3	4	5	6	7	8	9	10
1	161.45	199.50	215.71	224.58	230.16	233.99	236.77	238.88	240.54	241.88
1	4052.18	4999.50	5403.35	5624.58	5763.65	5858.99	5928.36	5981.07	6022.47	6055.85
2	18.51	19.00	19.16	19.25	19.30	19.33	19.35	19.37	19.38	19.40
2	98.50	99.00	99.17	99.25	99.30	99.33	99.36	99.37	99.39	99.40
3	10.13	9.55	9.28	9.12	9.01	8.94	8.89	8.85	8.81	8.79
3	34.12	30.82	29.46	28.71	28.24	27.91	27.67	27.49	27.35	27.23
4	7.71	6.94	6.59	6.39	6.26	6.16	6.09	6.04	6.00	5.96
4	21.20	18.00	16.69	15.98	15.52	15.21	14.98	14.80	14.66	14.55
5	6.61	5.79	5.41	5.19	5.05	4.95	4.88	4.82	4.77	4.74
5	16.26	13.27	12.06	11.39	10.97	10.67	10.46	10.29	10.16	10.05
6	5.99	5.14	4.76	4.53	4.39	4.28	4.21	4.15	4.10	4.06
6	13.75	10.92	9.78	9.15	8.75	8.47	8.26	8.10	7.98	7.87
7	5.59	4.74	4.35	4.12	3.97	3.87	3.79	3.73	3.68	3.64
7	12.25	9.55	8.45	7.85	7.46	7.19	6.99	6.84	6.72	6.62

(Table C.5. Contd.)

(*Table C.5. Contd.*)

df denominator	Degrees of Freedom Numerator									
	1	2	3	4	5	6	7	8	9	10
8	5.32	4.46	4.07	3.84	3.69	3.58	3.50	3.44	3.39	3.35
8	11.26	8.65	7.59	7.01	6.63	6.37	6.18	6.03	5.91	5.81
9	5.12	4.26	3.86	3.63	3.48	3.37	3.29	3.23	3.18	3.14
9	10.56	8.02	6.99	6.42	6.06	5.80	5.61	5.47	5.35	5.26
10	4.96	4.10	3.71	3.48	3.33	3.22	3.14	3.07	3.02	2.98
10	10.04	7.56	6.55	5.99	5.64	5.39	5.20	5.06	4.94	4.85
11	4.84	3.98	3.59	3.36	3.20	3.09	3.01	2.95	2.90	2.85
11	9.65	7.21	6.22	5.67	5.32	5.07	4.89	4.74	4.63	4.54
12	4.75	3.89	3.49	3.26	3.11	3.00	2.91	2.85	2.80	2.75
12	9.33	6.93	5.95	5.41	5.06	4.82	4.64	4.50	4.39	4.30
12	4.75	3.89	3.49	3.26	3.11	3.00	2.91	2.85	2.80	2.75
13	9.07	6.70	5.74	5.21	4.86	4.62	4.44	4.30	4.19	4.10
13	4.67	3.81	3.41	3.18	3.03	2.92	2.83	2.77	2.71	2.67
14	8.86	6.51	5.56	5.04	4.69	4.46	4.28	4.14	4.03	3.94
14	4.60	3.74	3.34	3.11	2.96	2.85	2.76	2.70	2.65	2.60
15	8.68	6.36	5.42	4.89	4.56	4.32	4.14	4.00	3.89	3.80
15	4.54	3.68	3.29	3.06	2.90	2.79	2.71	2.64	2.59	2.54
16	8.53	6.23	5.29	4.77	4.44	4.20	4.03	3.89	3.78	3.69
16	4.49	3.63	3.24	3.01	2.85	2.74	2.66	2.59	2.54	2.49
17	8.40	6.11	5.18	4.67	4.34	4.10	3.93	3.79	3.68	3.59
17	4.45	3.59	3.20	2.96	2.81	2.70	2.61	2.55	2.49	2.45
18	8.29	6.01	5.09	4.58	4.25	4.01	3.84	3.71	3.60	3.51
18	4.41	3.55	3.16	2.93	2.77	2.66	2.58	2.51	2.46	2.41
19	8.18	5.93	5.01	4.50	4.17	3.94	3.77	3.63	3.52	3.43
19	4.38	3.52	3.13	2.90	2.74	2.63	2.54	2.48	2.42	2.38
20	8.10	5.85	4.94	4.43	4.10	3.87	3.70	3.56	3.46	3.37
20	4.35	3.49	3.10	2.87	2.71	2.60	2.51	2.45	2.39	2.35
21	8.02	5.78	4.87	4.37	4.04	3.81	3.64	3.51	3.40	3.31
21	4.32	3.47	3.07	2.84	2.68	2.57	2.49	2.42	2.37	2.32
22	7.95	5.72	4.82	4.31	3.99	3.76	3.59	3.45	3.35	3.26
22	4.30	3.44	3.05	2.82	2.66	2.55	2.46	2.40	2.34	2.30
22	7.95	5.72	4.82	4.31	3.99	3.76	3.59	3.45	3.35	3.26
23	4.28	3.42	3.03	2.80	2.64	2.53	2.44	2.37	2.32	2.27
23	7.88	5.66	4.76	4.26	3.94	3.71	3.54	3.41	3.30	3.21
24	4.26	3.40	3.01	2.78	2.62	2.51	2.42	2.36	2.30	2.25
24	7.82	5.61	4.72	4.22	3.90	3.67	3.50	3.36	3.26	3.17
24	4.26	3.40	3.01	2.78	2.62	2.51	2.42	2.36	2.30	2.25
25	7.77	5.57	4.68	4.18	3.85	3.63	3.46	3.32	3.22	3.13
25	4.24	3.39	2.99	2.76	2.60	2.49	2.40	2.34	2.28	2.24
26	7.72	5.53	4.64	4.14	3.82	3.59	3.42	3.29	3.18	3.09
26	4.23	3.37	2.98	2.74	2.59	2.47	2.39	2.32	2.27	2.22
27	7.68	5.49	4.60	4.11	3.78	3.56	3.39	3.26	3.15	3.06
27	4.21	3.35	2.96	2.73	2.57	2.46	2.37	2.31	2.25	2.20
28	7.64	5.45	4.57	4.07	3.75	3.53	3.36	3.23	3.12	3.03
28	4.20	3.34	2.95	2.71	2.56	2.45	2.36	2.29	2.24	2.19
29	7.60	5.42	4.54	4.04	3.73	3.50	3.33	3.20	3.09	3.00
29	4.18	3.33	2.93	2.70	2.55	2.43	2.35	2.28	2.22	2.18
30	7.56	5.39	4.51	4.02	3.70	3.47	3.30	3.17	3.07	2.98
30	4.17	3.32	2.92	2.69	2.53	2.42	2.33	2.27	2.21	2.16
35	4.12	3.27	2.87	2.64	2.49	2.37	2.29	2.22	2.16	2.11
35	4.12	3.27	2.87	2.64	2.49	2.37	2.29	2.22	2.16	2.11
40	4.08	3.23	2.84	2.61	2.45	2.34	2.25	2.18	2.12	2.08
40	4.08	3.23	2.84	2.61	2.45	2.34	2.25	2.18	2.12	2.08
45	4.06	3.20	2.81	2.58	2.42	2.31	2.22	2.15	2.10	2.05

df denominator	Degrees of Freedom Numerator									
	1	2	3	4	5	6	7	8	9	10
45	4.06	3.20	2.81	2.58	2.42	2.31	2.22	2.15	2.10	2.05
50	4.03	3.18	2.79	2.56	2.40	2.29	2.20	2.13	2.07	2.03
50	4.03	3.18	2.79	2.56	2.40	2.29	2.20	2.13	2.07	2.03
60	4.00	3.15	2.76	2.53	2.37	2.25	2.17	2.10	2.04	1.99
60	4.00	3.15	2.76	2.53	2.37	2.25	2.17	2.10	2.04	1.99
70	3.98	3.13	2.74	2.50	2.35	2.23	2.14	2.07	2.02	1.97
70	3.98	3.13	2.74	2.50	2.35	2.23	2.14	2.07	2.02	1.97
80	3.96	3.11	2.72	2.49	2.33	2.21	2.13	2.06	2.00	1.95
80	3.96	3.11	2.72	2.49	2.33	2.21	2.13	2.06	2.00	1.95
90	3.95	3.10	2.71	2.47	2.32	2.20	2.11	2.04	1.99	1.94
90	3.95	3.10	2.71	2.47	2.32	2.20	2.11	2.04	1.99	1.94
100	3.94	3.09	2.70	2.46	2.31	2.19	2.10	2.03	1.97	1.93
100	3.94	3.09	2.70	2.46	2.31	2.19	2.10	2.03	1.97	1.93

Note: The values for df denominator are repeated. The first value is 0.05 level and second is 0.01 level. For example, df1=2 and df2=6, then 5.14 is a 0.05 level value and 10.92 is a 0.01 level value.

TABLE C.6. THE STUDENTIZED RANGE STATISTICS

The following R code is useful to obtain these values.

```
qtukey(.05, 3, 10, lower =F) # .05 is level of significance, nmeans = 3,
  and df = 10. Answer is 3.876777
qtukey(.01, 3, 10, lower =F) # .01 is level of significance, nmeans = 3,
  and df = 10. Answer is 5.270162
```

df for Error Term	k=Number of Treatments								
	2	3	4	5	6	7	8	9	10
5	3.64 5.70	4.60 6.98	5.22 7.80	5.67 8.42	6.03 8.91	6.33 9.32	6.58 9.67	6.80 9.97	6.99 10.24
6	3.46 5.24	4.34 6.33	4.90 7.03	5.30 7.56	5.63 7.97	5.90 8.32	6.12 8.61	6.32 8.87	6.49 9.10
7	3.34 4.95	4.16 5.92	4.68 6.54	5.06 7.01	5.36 7.37	5.61 7.68	5.82 7.94	6.00 8.17	6.16 8.37
8	3.26 4.75	4.04 5.64	4.53 6.20	4.89 6.62	5.17 6.96	5.40 7.24	5.60 7.47	5.77 7.68	5.92 7.86
9	3.20 4.60	3.95 5.43	4.41 5.96	4.76 6.35	5.02 6.66	5.24 6.91	5.43 7.13	5.59 7.33	5.74 7.49
10	3.15 4.48	3.88 5.27	4.33 5.77	4.65 6.14	4.91 6.43	5.12 6.67	5.30 6.87	5.46 7.05	5.60 7.21
11	3.11 4.39	3.82 5.15	4.26 5.62	4.57 5.97	4.82 6.25	5.03 6.48	5.20 6.67	5.35 6.84	5.49 6.99
12	3.08 4.32	3.77 5.05	4.20 5.50	4.51 5.84	4.75 6.10	4.95 6.32	5.12 6.51	5.27 6.67	5.39 6.81
13	3.06 4.26	3.73 4.96	4.15 5.40	4.45 5.73	4.69 5.98	4.88 6.19	5.05 6.37	5.19 6.53	5.32 6.67
14	3.03 4.21	3.70 4.89	4.11 5.32	4.41 5.63	4.64 5.88	4.83 6.08	4.99 6.26	5.13 6.41	5.25 6.54
15	3.01 4.17	3.67 4.84	4.08 5.25	4.37 5.56	4.59 5.80	4.78 5.99	4.94 6.16	5.08 6.31	5.20 6.44
16	3.00 4.13	3.65 4.79	4.05 5.19	4.33 5.49	4.56 5.72	4.74 5.92	4.90 6.08	5.03 6.22	5.15 6.35
17	2.98 4.10	3.63 4.74	4.02 5.14	4.30 5.43	4.52 5.66	4.70 5.85	4.86 6.01	4.99 6.15	5.11 6.27
18	2.97 4.07	3.61 4.70	4.00 5.09	4.28 5.38	4.49 5.60	4.67 5.79	4.82 5.94	4.96 6.08	5.07 6.20
19	2.96 4.05	3.59 4.67	3.98 5.05	4.25 5.33	4.47 5.55	4.65 5.73	4.79 5.89	4.92 6.02	5.04 6.14
20	2.95 4.02	3.58 4.64	3.96 5.02	4.23 5.29	4.45 5.51	4.62 5.69	4.77 5.84	4.90 5.97	5.01 6.09
24	2.92 3.96	3.53 4.55	3.90 4.91	4.17 5.17	4.37 5.37	4.54 5.54	4.68 5.69	4.81 5.81	4.92 5.92
30	2.89 3.89	3.49 4.45	3.85 4.80	4.10 5.05	4.30 5.24	4.46 5.40	4.60 5.54	4.72 5.65	4.82 5.76
40	2.86 3.82	3.44 4.37	3.79 4.70	4.04 4.93	4.23 5.11	4.39 5.26	4.52 5.39	4.63 5.50	4.73 5.60
60	2.83 3.76	3.40 4.28	3.74 4.59	3.98 4.82	4.16 4.99	4.31 5.13	4.44 5.25	4.55 5.36	4.65 5.45
120	2.80 3.70	3.36 4.20	3.68 4.50	3.92 4.71	4.10 4.87	4.24 5.01	4.36 5.12	4.47 5.21	4.56 5.30
infinity	2.77 3.64	3.31 4.12	3.63 4.40	3.86 4.60	4.03 4.76	4.17 4.88	4.29 4.99	4.39 5.08	4.47 5.16

Note: The first value in each cell is 0.05 level value and second value is 0.01 level value.

TABLE C.7. KENDALL'S TAU VALUES AT THREE LEVELS OF SIGNIFICANCE

n	p-values		
	0.1	**0.05**	**0.01**
4	1		
5	0.8	1	
6	0.733	0.867	1
7	0.619	0.714	0.905
8	0.571	0.643	0.786
9	0.5	0.556	0.722
10	0.467	0.551	0.644
11	0.418	0.491	0.6
12	0.394	0.455	0.576
13	0.359	0.436	0.564
14	0.363	0.407	0.516
15	0.333	0.39	0.505
20	0.274	0.326	0.421
25	0.24	0.287	0.367
30	0.218	0.255	0.333

Note: Please refer to 5.6.3.c for R code for obtaining significance.

It is recommended to use the distribution conversion rather than the table.

TABLE C.8. CRITICAL VALUES OF THE KOLMOGOROV–SMIRNOV TEST STATISTICS

Sample Size (N)	p-Values		
	0.10	**0.05**	**0.01**
1	0.950	0.975	0.995
2	0.776	0.842	0.929
3	0.642	0.708	0.828
4	0.564	0.624	0.733
5	0.510	0.565	0.669
6	0.470	0.521	0.618
7	0.438	0.486	0.577
8	0.411	0.457	0.543
9	0.388	0.432	0.514
10	0.368	0.410	0.490
11	0.352	0.391	0.468
12	0.338	0.375	0.450
13	0.325	0.361	0.433
14	0.314	0.349	0.418
15	0.304	0.338	0.404
16	0.295	0.328	0.392
17	0.286	0.318	00.381
18	0.278	0.309	0.371
19	0.272	0.301	0.363
20	0.264	0.294	0.356
25	0.240	0.270	0.320
30	0.220	0.240	0.290
35	0.210	0.230	0.270

TABLE C.9. CHI-SQUARE DISTRIBUTION

The following R code is useful for the same.

```
qchisq(.05, 3, lower =F) # chi-square value at .05 level for df = 3 is
    computed.
```

df	0.995	0.990	0.975	0.950	0.900	0.100	0.050	0.025	0.010	0.005
1	0.00004	0.0002	0.00	0.00	0.02	2.71	3.84	5.02	6.64	7.88
2	0.01	0.02	0.05	0.10	0.21	4.61	5.99	7.38	9.21	10.60
3	0.07	0.12	0.22	0.35	0.58	6.25	7.82	9.35	11.35	12.84
4	0.21	0.30	0.48	0.71	1.06	7.78	9.49	11.14	13.28	14.86
5	0.41	0.55	0.83	1.15	1.61	9.24	11.07	12.83	15.09	16.75
6	0.68	0.87	1.24	1.64	2.20	10.65	12.59	14.45	16.81	18.55
7	0.99	1.24	1.69	2.17	2.83	12.02	14.07	16.01	18.48	20.28
8	1.34	1.65	2.18	2.73	3.49	13.36	15.51	17.54	20.09	21.96
9	1.74	2.09	2.70	3.33	4.17	14.68	16.92	19.02	21.67	23.59
10	2.16	2.56	3.25	3.94	4.87	15.99	18.31	20.48	23.21	25.19
11	2.60	3.05	3.82	4.58	5.58	17.28	19.68	21.92	24.73	26.76
12	3.07	3.57	4.40	5.23	6.30	18.55	21.03	23.34	26.22	28.30
13	3.57	4.11	5.01	5.89	7.04	19.81	22.36	24.74	27.69	29.82
14	4.08	4.66	5.63	6.57	7.79	21.06	23.69	26.12	29.14	31.32
15	4.60	5.23	6.26	7.26	8.55	22.31	25.00	27.49	30.58	32.80
16	5.14	5.81	6.91	7.96	9.31	23.54	26.30	28.85	32.00	34.27
17	5.70	6.41	7.56	8.67	10.09	24.77	27.59	30.19	33.41	35.72
18	6.27	7.02	8.23	9.39	10.87	25.99	28.87	31.53	34.81	37.16
19	6.84	7.63	8.91	10.12	11.65	27.20	30.14	32.85	36.19	38.58
20	7.43	8.26	9.59	10.85	12.44	28.41	31.41	34.17	37.57	40.00
21	8.03	8.90	10.28	11.59	13.24	29.62	32.67	35.48	38.93	41.40
22	8.64	9.54	10.98	12.34	14.04	30.81	33.92	36.78	40.29	42.80
23	9.26	10.20	11.69	13.09	14.85	32.01	35.17	38.08	41.64	44.18
24	9.89	10.86	12.40	13.85	15.66	33.20	36.42	39.36	42.98	45.56
25	10.52	11.52	13.12	14.61	16.47	34.38	37.65	40.65	44.31	46.93
26	11.16	12.20	13.84	15.38	17.29	35.56	38.89	41.92	45.64	48.29
27	11.81	12.88	14.57	16.15	18.11	36.74	40.11	43.20	46.96	49.65
28	12.46	13.57	15.31	16.93	18.94	37.92	41.34	44.46	48.28	50.99
29	13.12	14.26	16.05	17.71	19.77	39.09	42.56	45.72	49.59	52.34
30	13.79	14.95	16.79	18.49	20.60	40.26	43.77	46.98	50.89	53.67
40	20.71	22.16	24.43	26.51	29.05	51.81	55.76	59.34	63.69	66.77
50	27.99	29.71	32.36	34.76	37.69	63.17	67.51	71.42	76.15	79.49
60	35.53	37.49	40.48	43.19	46.46	74.40	79.08	83.30	88.38	91.95
70	43.28	45.44	48.76	51.74	55.33	85.53	90.53	95.02	100.43	104.22
80	51.17	53.54	57.15	60.39	64.28	96.58	101.88	106.63	112.33	116.32
90	59.20	61.75	65.65	69.13	73.29	107.57	113.15	118.14	124.12	128.30
100	67.33	70.07	74.22	77.93	82.36	118.50	124.34	129.56	135.81	140.17

References

Agresti, A. (1990). *Categorical data analysis*. Hoboken, NJ: Wiley.

———. (2007). *An introduction to categorical data analysis*. Hoboken, NJ: Wiley.

———. (2010). *Analysis of ordinal categorical data* (2nd ed.). Hoboken, NJ: Wiley.

Anderson, T. W. (1962). On the distribution of the two-sample cramer-von mises criterion. *The Annals of Mathematical Statistics, 33*, 1148–1159.

Anderson, T. W., & Darling, D. A. (1952). Asymptotic theory of certain "goodness of fit" criteria based on stochastic processes. *Annals of Mathematical Statistics, 23*, 193–212.

———. (1954). A test of goodness of fit. *Journal of the American Statistical Association, 49*, 765–769.

Anscombe, F. J., & Glynn, W. J. (1983). Distribution of the kurtosis statistic b 2 for normal samples. *Biometrika, 70*(1), 227–234. doi:10.1093/biomet/70.1.227

Balling, J. D., & Falk, J. H. (1982). Development of visual preference for natural environments. *Environment and Behavior, 14*, 5–28.

Banaji, M. R., & Greenwald, A. G. (1995). Implicit gender stereotyping in judgments of fame. *Journal of Personality and Social Psychology, 68*(2), 181–198. doi:10.1037/0022-3514.68.2.181

Baron, R. M., & Kenny, D. A. (1986). The moderator-mediator variable distinction in social psychological research—conceptual, strategic, and statistical considerations. *Journal of Personality and Social Psychology, 51*, 1173–1182.

Bartlett, M. S. (1935). The effect of non-normality on the t-distribution. *Proceedings of the Cambridge Philosophical Society, 31*, 223–231.

Behrens, W. U. (1929). Ein Beitrag zur Fehlerberechnung bei wenigen Beobachtungen [A contribution to error estimation with few observations]. *Landwirtschaftliche Jahrbücher* (Berlin: Wiegandt and Hempel) 68, 807–837.

Belhekar, V. M. (2008). Personality correlates of creativity: *A Study Using Eysenckian Model and the Five-Factor Model*. Unpublished doctoral thesis). University of Pune, India.

Belhekar, V. M., & Sabnis, S. V. (2011). The five-factor model and borderline personality. *Indian Journal of Clinical Psychology, 38*, 6–16.

Benjamini, Y., & Hochberg, Y. (1995). Controlling the false discovery rate: A practical and powerful approach to multiple testing. *Journal of the Royal Statistical Society, Series B, 57*, 289–300.

———. (2000). On the adaptive control of the false discovery rate in multiple testing with independent statistics. Journal of Educational and Behavioral Statistics, 25(1), 60–83. doi:10.3102/10769986025001060

Boland, P. J. (1984). A biographical glimpse of William Sealy Gosset. *The American Statistician, 38*(3), 179. doi:10.2307/2683648

Bonferroni, C. E. (1935). *Il calcolo delle assicurazioni su gruppi di teste, Studi in Onore del Professore Salvatore Ortu Carboni* [The calculation of insurance on the heads of groups, Studies in Honor of Professor Salvatore Ortu Carboni] Rome, 13–60.

Bonferroni, C.E. (1936). *Teoria statistica delle classi e calcolo delle probabilità, Pubblicazioni del R Istituto Superiore di Scienze Economiche e Commerciali di Firenze* [Statistical theory of classes and probability. Publications of R Institute of Economic and Commercial Sciences of Florence, 8, 3–62.

Boole, G. (1854). *An investigation of the laws of thought on which are founded the mathematical theories of logic and probabilities*. Macmillan.

Borkenau, P., & Ostendorf, F. (1992). Social desirability scales as moderator and suppressor variables. European Journal of Personality, 6, 199–214. doi:10.1002/per.2410060303

Bentler, P. M. (1990). Comparative fit indexes in structural models. Psychological Bulletin, 107(2), 238–246.

Bentler, P. M., & Bonett, D. G. (1980). Significance tests and goodness of fit in the analysis of covariance structures. Psychological Bulletin, 88, 588–606.

Bollen, K. A. (1989). *Structural equations with latent variables*. New York: John Wiley & Sons.

Borroni, S., Somma, A., Andershed, H., Maffei, C., & Fossati, A. (2014). Psychopathy dimensions, big five traits, and dispositional aggression in adolescence: Issues of gender consistency. *Personality and Individual Differences, 66*, 199–203. doi:10.1016/j.paid.2014.03.019

Bortkiewicz, L. von (1898). *Das Gesetz der kleinen Zahlen* [The law of small numbers]. Leipzig.

Bower, G. H. (1981). Mood and memory. *American Psychologist, 36*, 129–148. doi:10.1037/0003-066x.36.2.129

Box, G. E. P. (1949). A general distribution theory for a class of likelihood criteria. *Biometrika, 36*, 317–346.

———. (1953). Non-normality and tests on variances. *Biometrika, 40*, 318–335.

———. (1954). Some theorems on quadratic forms applied in the study of analysis of variance problems, II. Effects of inequality of variance and of correlation between errors in the two-way classification. *Ann. Math. Statist., 25*, 484–498. doi:10.1214/aoms/1177728786

Brown, M. B., & Forsythe, A. B. (1974). The ANOVA and multiple comparisons for data with heterogeneous variances. *Biometrics, 30*, 719–724.

Chambers, J. M., Cleveland, W. S., Kleiner, B., & Tukey, P. A. (1983). *Graphical methods for data analysis*. Monterey, CA: Wadsworth Publishing Company.

Champely, S. (2015). *PWR: Basic functions for power analysis* (R package version 1.1–3). Retrieved from http:// CRAN.R-project.org/package=pwr (accessed on May 19, 2016).

Cochran, W. G. (1954). Some methods of strengthening the common chi-square test. *Biometrics, 10*, 417–451.

Cochran, W. G., & Cox, G. M. (1957). *Experimental designs* (2nd ed.). New York: Wiley.

Cohen, J. (1960). A coefficient of agreement for nominal scales. *Educational and Psychological Measurement, 20*, 37–46.

———. (1977). *Statistical power analysis for the behavioral sciences*. New York: Academic Press.

———. (1988). *Statistical power analysis for the behavioral sciences* (2nd ed.). Hillsdale, NJ: Lawrence Erlbaum.

Conover, W. J. (1980). *Practical nonparametric statistics* (2nd ed.). New York: John Wiley and Sons.

———. (1999). *Practical nonparametric statistics* (3rd ed.). New York: John Wiley and Sons.

Cosmides, L. (1989). The logic of social exchange: Has natural selection shaped how humans reason? Studies with the Wason selection task. *Cognition, 31*, 187–276.

Cota, A. A., Longman, R. S., Holden, R. R., Fekken, G. S., & Xinaris, S. (1993). Interpolating 95th percentile eigenvalues from random data: An empirical example. *Educational and Psychological Measurement, 53*, 585–596.

Cramér, H. (1946). *Mathematical methods of statistics*. Princeton, NJ: Princeton University Press.

Crawford, C. (1967, April 1). *A general method of rotation for factor analysis*. Paper read at the Spring Meeting of the Psychometric Society, Madison, WI.

Crawford, J. R., & Howell, D. C. (1998). Comparing an individual's test score against norms derived from small samples. *The Clinical Neuropsychologist, 12*, 482–486.

Crocker, L. & Algina, J. (2006). *Introduction to classical and modern test theory*. Ohio: Cengage Learning.

Cronbach, L. J. (1951). Coefficient alpha and the internal structure of tests. *Psychometrika, 16*, 297–334. doi:10.1007/bf02310555

Cumming, G. (2012). *Understanding the new statistics: Effect sizes, confidence intervals, and meta-analysis*. New York: Routledge.

D'Agostino, R. B. (1970). Linear estimation of the normal distribution standard deviation. *The American Statistician, 24*, 14–15.

———. (1970a). Transformation to normality of the null distribution of gi. *Biometrika, 57*, 679–681.

———. (1970b). Simple compact portable test of normality: Geary's test revisited. *Psychological Bulletin, 74*, 138–140.

———. (1971). An omnibus test of normality for moderate and large size samples. *Biometrika, 58*, 341–348.

———. (1986). Graphical analysis. In R. B. D'Agostino & M. A. Stephens (Eds.), *Goodness-of-fit techniques* (pp. 7–62). New York: Marcel Dekker, Inc.

D'Agostino, R. B., & Lee, A. F. S. (1977). Robustness of location estimators under changes of population kurtosis. *Journal of the American Statistical Association, 72*, 393–396.

D'Agostino, R. B., & Pearson, E. S. (1973). Tests for departure from normality. Empirical results for the distributions of b_2 and $\sqrt{b_1}$. *Biometrika, 60*, 613–622.

D'Agostino, R. B., Belanger, A., & D'Agostino, Jr., R. B. (1990). A suggestion for using powerful and informative tests of normality. *The American Statistician, 44*, 316–321.

Dallal, G. E., & Wilkinson, L. (1986). An analytic approximation to the distribution of Lilliefors's test statistic for normality. *The American Statistician, 40*, 294–296.

Darlington, R. B. (1990). *Regression and linear models*. New York, NY: McGraw-Hill.

Darlington, R. B., & Carlson, P. M. (1987). *Behavioral statistics: Logic and methods*. New York: The Free Press.

Davis, J. A. (1967). A partial coefficient for Goodman and Kruskal's gamma. *Journal of the American Statistical Association, 62*, 189–193.

Dunn, O. J. (1961). Multiple comparisons among means. *Journal of the American Statistical Association, 56*, 52–64.

———. (1964). *Multiple comparisons* using rank sums. Technometrics, 6, 241–252.

Dunn, O. J., & Clark, V. (1969). Correlation coefficients measured on the same individuals. *Journal of the American Statistical Association, 64*(325), 366–377. doi:10.1080/01621459.1969.10500981

Dunnett, C. W. (1955). A multiple comparison procedure for comparing several treatments with a control. *Journal of the American Statistical Association, 50*, 1096–1121.

———. (1964). New tables for multiple comparisons with a control. *Biometrics, 20*, 482–491.

———. (1980). Pairwise multiple comparisons in the homogeneous variance, unequal sample size case. *Journal of the American Statistical Association, 75*, 789–795.

Dutton, D. (2009). *Art instinct: Beauty, pleasure, and human evolution*. NY: Bloomsbury Press.

Eals, M., & Silverman, I. (1994). The hunter-gatherer theory of spatial sex-differences: Proximal factors mediating the female advantage in recall of object arrays. *Ethology and Sociobiology, 15*, 95–105.

Edwards, A. L. (1984). An introduction to linear regression and correlation (2nd ed.). New York: W. H. Freeman and Company.

Efron, B., & Tibshirani R. J. (1993). An Introduction to the Bootstrap. New York: Chapman & Hall/CRC.

Egan W. J., & Morgan, S. L. (1998). Outlier detection in multivariate analytical chemical data, *Anal. Chem. 70*, 2372–2379.

Einot, I., & Gabriel, K. R. (1975). A study of the powers of several methods of multiple comparisons. *Journal of the American Statistical Association, 70*, 574–583.

Embreston, S. E., & Raise, S. P. (2000). *Item response theory for psychologists*. Mahwah, NJ: Lawrence Erlbaum.

Eysenck, H. J. (1995). *Genius: The natural history of creativity*. Cambridge: Cambridge University Press.

Fisher, R. A. (1915). Frequency distribution of the values of the correlation coefficient in samples from indefinitely large population. *Biometrika, 10*, 507–521.

———. (1921). On the "probable error" of a coefficient of correlation deduced from a small sample. *Metron, 1*, 3–32.

———. (1930). Inverse probability. *Proceedings of the Cambridge Philosophical Society, 26*, 528–535.

———. (1930). The moments of the distribution for normal samples of measures of departure from normality. *Proceedings of the Royal Society of London A, 130*, 16–28.

———. (1935). The fiducial argument in statistical inference. *Annals of Eugenics, 8*, 391–398.

———. (1956). *Statistical methods and scientific inference*. Edinburgh: Oliver & Boyd.

Fisher, R. A., & Yates, F. (1957). *Statistical tables for biological, agricultural and medical research* (4th ed.). Edinburgh: Oliver and Boyd.

Fligner, M. A., & Killeen, T. J. (1976). Distribution-free two-sample tests for scale. *Journal of the American Statistical Association, 71*(353), 210. doi:10.2307/2285771

Forgas, J. P. (2002). Feeling and doing: Affective influences on interpersonal behavior. *Psychological Inquiry, 13*(1), 1–28. doi:10.1207/s15327965pli1301_01

———. (2002). Toward understanding the role of affect in social thinking and behavior. *Psychological Inquiry, 13*(1), 90–102. doi:10.1207/s15327965pli1301_03

Fox, J. (1991). *Regression diagnostics*. Newbury Park, CA: SAGE Publications.

———. Structural equation modeling with the SEM package in R. *Structural Equation Modeling, 13*(3), 465–486 .

Fox, J., Nie, Z. & Byrnes, J. (2015). SEM: Structural Equation Models. R package version 3.1–6. http://CRAN.R-project.org/package=sem

Freidlin, B., & Gastwirth, J. L. (2000). Should the median test be retired from general use? *The American Statistician, 54*, 161.

Furnham, A., & Chamorro-Premuzic, T. (2004). Personality, intelligence and art. *Personality and Individual differences, 36*, 705–715.

Gabriel, K. R. (1978). A simple method of multiple comparisons of means. *Journal of the American Statistical Association, 73*(364), 724–729.

Geary, R. C. (1935). The ratio of the mean deviation to the standard deviation as a test of normality. *Biometrika, 27*, 310–332.

———. (1947). Testing for normality. *Biometrika, 34*, 209–242.

Geyer, C. J. (2003, September 30). *Maximum likelihood in R*. Retrieved, from http://www.stat.umn.edu/geyer/5931/mle/mle.pdf (accessed on May 19, 2016).

Gigerenzer, G. (2004). Mindless statistics. *The Journal of Socio-Economics, 33*(5), 587–606. doi:10.1016/j.socec.2004.09.033

Gigerenzer, G., Swijtink, Z., Porter, T., Daston, L., Beatty, J., & Krüger, L. (1989). *The Empire of Chance. How Probability Changed Science and Every Day Life*. Cambridge: Cambridge University Press.

Glejser, H. (1969). A new test for heteroskedasticity. *Journal of the American Statistical Association, 64*, 315 –323.

Gnanadesikan, R. (1977). *Methods for statistical data analysis of multivariate observations*. New York: Wiley.

Goldfeld, S. M., & Quandt, R. E. (1965). Some Tests for Homoscedasticity. *Journal of the American Statistical Association, 60*, 539–547.

Good, P. I. (1999). *Resampling methods: A practical guide to data analysis*. Boston: Birkhäuser.

Goodman, L. A., & Kruskal, W. H. (1954). Measures of association for cross-classification. *Journal of the American Statistical Association, 49*, 732–764.

——— (1972). Measures of association for cross classifications, IV: Simplification of asymptotic variances. *Journal of the American Statistical Association, 67*(338), 415–421. doi:10.1080/01621459.1972.10482401

Goodman, W. K., Price, L. H., Rasmussen, S. A., Mazure, C., Fleischmann, R. L., Hill, C. L., Heninger, G. R., & Charney, D. S. (1989). The Yale–Brown obsessive compulsive scale (Y-BOCS): Part I. Development, use, and reliability. *Arch Gen Psychiatry, 46*, 1006–1011.

Green, S. B. (1991). How many subjects does it take to do a regression analysis? *Multivariate Behavioral Research, 26*, 449–510.

Greenhouse, S. W., & Geisser, S. (1959). On methods in the analysis of profile data. *Psychometrika, 24*, 95–112.

Greenwald, A. G., & Banaji, M. R. (1995). Implicit social cognition: Attitudes, self-esteem, and stereotypes. Psychological Review, *102*(1), 4–27. doi:10.1037/0033-295x.102.1.4

Grissom, R. J., & Kim, J. J. (2005). *Effect sizes for Research: A broad practical approach*. Mahwah, NJ: Lawrence Erlbaum, Marie Dasborough.

Hadi, A. S., & Simonoff, J. S. (1993). Procedures for the identification of multiple outliers in linear models. *Journal of the American Statistical Association, 88*(424), 1264. doi:10.2307/2291266.

Hall, R. E., Lilien, D.M., Sycoyoshi, G., Engle, R. Johnson, J., and Ellsworth, S. (1995). *Eviews user guide*. Irvine, CA: Quantitative Micro Software.

Hambleton, R. K., & Swaminathan, H. (1985). *Item response theory: Principles and applications*. Boston: Kluwer.

Harman, H. H. (1976). *Modern factor analysis* (3rd ed.). Chicago: University of Chicago Press.

Harvey, A. C., & Phillips, G. D. A. (1974). A comparison of the power of some tests for heteroscedasticity in the general linear model. *Journal of Econometrics, 2*, 307–316.

Hayes, A. F. (2013). *Introduction to mediation, moderation, and conditional process analysis*. NY: The Guilford Press.

Hayes, A. F., & Cai, L. (2007). Further evaluating the conditional decision rule for comparing two independent means. *British Journal of Mathematical and Statistical Psychology, 60*(2), 217–244. doi:10.1348/000711005x62576

Hays, W. L. (1981). *Statistics* (3rd ed.). New York: Holt, Rinehart & Winston.

Hayter, A. J. (1986). The maximum familywise error rate of Fisher's least significant difference test. *Journal of the American Statistical Association, 81*, 1001–1004.

Healy, M. J. R. (1968). Multivariate normal plotting. *Applied Statistics 17*, 157–161.

Hedges, L. V. (1981). Distribution theory for Glass's estimator of effect size and related estimators. *Journal of Educational Statistics, 6*, 107–128.

Hedges, L. V., and Olkin, I. (1985). *Statistical methods for meta-analysis*. San Diego, CA: Academic Press.

Hendrickson, A. E., & White, P. O. (1964). PROMAX: A quick method for rotation to oblique simple structure. *British Journal of Statistical Psychology, 17*, 65–70.

Henze, N., & Zirkler, B. (1990). A class of invariant consistent tests for multivariate normality. *Communications in Statistics—Theory and Methods, 19*, 3595–3617.

Hochberg, Y. (1974). Some conservative generalizations of the t-method in simultaneous inference. *Journal of Multivariate Analysis, 4*, 224–234.

Hofstede, G. (2001). *Culture's consequences: Comparing values, behaviors, institutions, and organizations across nations* (2nd ed.). Thousand Oaks, CA: SAGE Publications.

———. (2003). *Culture's Consequences: Comparing Values, Behaviors, Institutions and Organizations across Nations* (2nd ed.) Thousand Oaks, CA: SAGE Publications.

Holm, S. (1979). A simple sequentially rejective multiple test procedure. *Scandinavian Journal of Statistics, 6*, 65–70.

Holmes, T. H., & Rahe, R. H. (1967). The social readjustment rating scale. *Journal of Psychosomatic Research, 11*(2), 213–218.

Horn, J. L. (1967). On subjectivity in factor analysis. *Educational and Psychological Measurement, 27*, 811–820.

Hotelling, H. (1940). The selection of variates for use in prediction with some comments on the general problem of nuisance parameters. *Annals of Mathematical Statistics, 11*, 271–283.

Howell, D. C. (2008). *Statistical methods for psychology*. Belmont, CA: Wadsworth.

Hsu, C. T., & Lawley, D. N. (1939). The derivation of the fifth and sixth moments of b2 on samples from a normal population. *Biometrika, 31*, 238–248.

Huber, P. J. (1964). Robust estimation of a location parameter. *The Annals of Mathematical Statistics, 35*, 73–101.

Huberty, C. J., & Olejnik, S. (2006). Applied MANOVA and discriminant analysis. *Wiley Series in Probability and Statistics*. doi:10.1002/047178947x

Huberty, C. J., & Petoskey, M. D. (2000). Multivariate analysis of variance and covariance. In H. Tinsley and S. Brown (Eds.), *Handbook of applied multivariate statistics and mathematical modeling* (pp. 183–208). New York: Academic Press.

Huynh, H., & Feldt, L. S. (1976). Estimation of the box correction for degrees of freedom from sample data in the randomized block and split plot designs. *Journal of Educational Statistics, 1*, 69–82.

Illari, P., & Russo, F. (2014). *Causality: Philosophical theory meets scientific practice*. Oxford: Oxford University Press.

Isen, A. M. (1984). Toward understanding the role of affect in cognition. In R. S. Wyer, Jr & T. K. Srull (Eds.), *Handbook of Social Cognition* (Vol. 3, pp. 179–236). Hillsdale, NJ: Erlbaum.

Jarque, C. M. & Bera, A. K. (1980). Efficient tests for normality, homoscedasticity and serial independence of regression residuals. *Economics Letters, 6*, 255–259. doi:10.1016/0165-1765(80)90024-5.

——. (1987). A test for normality of observations and regression residuals. *International Statistical Review, 55*(2), 163–172.

Jennrich, R. I., & Sampson, P. F. (1966). Rotation for simple loadings. *Psychometrika, 31*, 313–323.

Jöreskog, K. G. (1967). Some contributions to maximum likelihood factor analysis. *Psychometrika, 32*(4), 443–482. doi:10.1007/bf02289658

Joreskog, K. G., & Sorbom, D. (1981). *Analysis of linear structural relationships by maximum likelihood and least squares methods* (Research Report 81–8). Uppsala: University of Uppsala.

——. (1993). *LISREL 8 user's reference guide*. Chicago: Scientific Software International.

Judd, C. M., & McClelland, G. H. (1989). *Data analysis: A model comparison approach*. San Diego, CA: Harcourt Brace Jovanovich.

Jung, S., (2013). Exploratory factor analysis with small sample sizes: A comparison of three approaches. *Behavioural Processes, 97*, 90–95. dx.doi.org/10.1016/j.beproc.2012.11.016

Kaiser, H. F. (1958). The varimax criterion for analytic rotation in factor analysis. *Psychometrika, 23*, 187–200.

Kaplan, D. (1990). Evaluating and modifying covariance structure models: A review and recommendation. *Multivariate Behavioral Research, 25*(2), 137–155.

Kaplan, R. M., & Saccuzzo, D. P. (2012) *Psychological testing: Principles, applications, and issues* (8th ed.). Belmont, CA: Wadsworth Publishing Company Inc.

Kelley, K., & Maxwell, S. E. (2003). Sample size for multiple regression: Obtaining regression coefficients that are accurate, not simply significant. *Psychological Methods, 8*, 305–321.

Kendall, M. G. (1938). A new measure of rank correlation. *Biometrika, 30*(1–2), 81–93. doi:10.1093/biomet/30.1-2.81

——. (1948). *Rank correlation methods*. London: Griffin.

——. (1952). *The advanced theory of statistics* (Vol. 1). London: Charles Griffin and Co. Ltd.

Kendall, M. G., & Babington–Smith, B. (1939). The problem of *m* rankings. *Annals of Mathematical Statistics, 10*, 275–287.

Kenny, D. (1979). *Correlation and causality*. New York: John Wiley & Sons Inc.

Keppel, G.(1991). Design and analysis: A researcher's handbook. Englewood Cliffs, NJ: Prentice-Hall.

Keuls, M. (1952). The use of studentized range in connection with an analysis of variance. *Euphytica, 1*, 112–122.

Kim, S. H. & Cohen, A. S. (1998). On the Behrens–Fisher problem: A review. *Journal of Educational and Behavioral Statistics, 23*, 356–377.

Kirk, R. E. (1995). Experimental design: Procedures for the behavioral sciences (3rd ed.). Pacific Grove, CA: Brooks/Cole Publishing Company.

Kline, T. J. B. (2005). *Psychological testing: a practical approach to design and evaluation*. Thousand Oaks, CA: SAGE Publications.

Kolmogorov, A. (1933). Sulla determinazione empirica di una legge di distribuzione [On the empirical determination of a distribution law]. *Inst. Ital. Attuari, Giorn., 4*, 1–11.

Kowalski, C. J. (1970). The performance of some rough tests for bivariate normality before and after coordinate transformations to normality. *Technometrics, 12*, 517–544.

Kuiper, N. H. (1960). Tests concerning random points on a circle. *Proceedings, Akademie van Wetenschappen A, 63*, 38–47.

Kvålseth, T. O. (1985). Cautionary note about R². *The American Statistician, 39*, 279–285.

Larzelere, R. E., & Mulaik, S. A. (1977). Single-sample tests for many correlations. *Psychological Bulletin, 84*, 557–569.

Lehmann, E. L. (1993). The Fisher, Neyman–Pearson theories of testing hypotheses: One theory or two? *Journal of the American Statistical Association, 88*(424), 1242–1249. doi:10.1080/01621459.1993.10476404

Levene, H. (1960). Robust tests for the equality of variance. In I. Olkin (Ed.), *Contributions to probability and statistics*. Palo Alto, CA: Stanford University Press.

Lilliefors, H. W. (1967). On the Kolmogorov–Smirnov test for normality with mean and variance unknown. *Journal of the American Statistical Association, 62*, 399–402.

Lin, C. C., & Mudholkar, G. S. (1980). A simple test for normality against asymmetric alternatives. *Biometrika, 67*, 455–461.

Locke, C., & Spurrier, J. D. (1977). The use of U-statistics for testing normality against alternatives with both tails heavy or both tails light. *Biometrika, 64*, 638–640.

Loehlin, J. E. (1992). Latent variable models: An introduction to factor, path, and structural analysis (2nd ed.). Hillsdale, NJ: Lawrence Erlbaum.

Loehlin, J. C. (2004). *Latent variable models: An introduction to factor, path, and structural equation analysis* (4th ed.). Mahwah, NJ: Erlbaum.

Lord, F. M., & Novick, M. R. (1968). *Statistical theories of mental test scores*. Reading, Massachusetts: Addison-Wesley.

Mantel, N., & Haenszel, W. (1959). Statistical aspects of the analysis of data from retrospective studies of disease. *Journal of the American Statistical Association, 22*, 719–748.

Marascuilo, L. A., & McSweeney, M. (1977). *Nonparametric and distribution-free methods for the social sciences.* Monterey, CA: Brooks/Cole Publishing Company.

Mardia, K. V. (1970). Measures of multivariate skewness and kurtosis with applications. *Biometrika, 57*, 519–530.

———. (1971). The effect of nonnormality on some multivariate tests and robustness to nonnormality in the linear model. *Biometrika, 58* (1), 105–121.

Maxwell, S. E., & Delaney, H. D. (1990). Designing experiments and analyzing data. Belmont, CA: Wadsworth Publishing Company.

McCrae, R. R. (1987). Creativity, divergent thinking and openness to experience. *Journal of Personality and Social Psychology, 52*, 1258–1265.

McCrae, R. R., & Costa Jr, P. T. (1983). Social desirability scales: More substance than style. *Journal of Consulting and Clinical Psychology, 51*, 882–888.

McCrae, R. R., Zonderman, A. B., Costa, P. T. Jr., Bond, M. H., & Paunonen, S. V. (1996). Evaluating replicability of factors in the Revised NEO Personality Inventory: Confirmatory factor analysis versus procrustes rotation. *Journal of Personality and Social Psychology, 70*, 552–566.

Menard, S. (2000). Coefficients of determination for multiple logistic regression analysis. *The American Statistician, 54*, 17–24.

———. (2001). *Applied logistic regression analysis* (2nd ed.). Thousand Oaks. CA: SAGE Publications.

Mittlbock, M., & Schemper, M. (1996). Explained variation in logistic regression. *Statistics in Medicine, 15*, 1987–1997.

Mood, A. M. (1954). On the asymptotic efficiency of certain nonparametric two-sample tests. *The Annals of Mathematical Statistics, 25*(3), 514–522. doi:10.1214/aoms/1177728719

Mueller, R. O. (1996). *Basic principles of structural equations modeling. An introduction to LISREL and EQS.* The Neherlands: Springer.

Mulaik, S. A. (1972). *The foundations of factor analysis.* New York: McGraw-Hill Book Company.

Mumford, S., & Anjum, R. L. (2011). *Getting causes form powers.* Oxford: Oxford University press.

Nagelkerke, N. J. D. (1991). A note on a general definition of the coefficient of determination. *Biometrika, 78*, 691–692.

National Crime Records Bureau. (2011). *Accidental and suicidal deaths in India.* New Delhi: Ministry of Home Affairs, Government of India.

Newman, D. (1939). The distribution of the range in samples from a normal population, expressed in terms of an independent estimate of standard deviation. *Biometrika, 31*, 20–30.

Nosek, B. A., Greenwald, A. G., & Banaji, M. R. (2007). The implicit association test at age 7: A methodological and conceptual review. In J. A. Bargh (Ed.), *Social psychology and the unconscious: The automaticity of higher mental processes* (pp. 265–292). New York: Psychology Press.

Nunnally, J., & Bernstein, I. (1994). *Psychometric theory.* New York: McGraw-Hill.

Oja, H. (1981). Two location and scale free goodness of fit tests. *Biometrika, 68*, 637–640.

Orians, G. H., & Heerwagen, J. H. (1992). Evolved responses to landscapes. In J. H. Barkow, L. Cosmides & J. Tooby (Eds.), *The adapted mind* (pp 555–579). Oxford: Oxford University Press.

Ott, R. L, Larson, R., Rexroat, C., & Mendenhall, W. (1992). *Statistics: A tool for the social sciences* (5th ed.). Boston: PWS–Kent Publishing Company.

Pagano, M., & Gauvreau, K. (1993). *Principles of biostatistics.* Belmont, CA: Duxbury Press.

Park, R. E. (1966). Estimation with heteroscedastic error terms. *Econometrica, 34*, 888.

Pearl, J. (2009). *Causality: Models, reasoning and inference.* Cambridge: Cambridge University press.

Pearson, E. S. (1930). A further development of tests for normality. *Biometrika, 22*, 239–249.

———. (1931). Analysis of variance in case of non-normal variation. *Biometrika, 23*, 114–133.

———. (1935). A comparison of and Mr. Geary's criteria. *Biometrika, 27*, 333–352.

Pearson, E. S., & Please, N. W. (1975). Relation between the shape of population distribution and the robustness of four simple test statistics. *Biometrika, 62*, 223–241.

Piedmont, R. L., McCrae, R. R., Riemann, R., & Angleitner, A. (2000). On the invalidity of validity scales: Evidence from self-reports and observer ratings in volunteer samples. *Journal of Personality and Social Psychology, 78*, 582–593.

Rachman, S. (1997). A cognitive theory of obsessions. *Behaviour Research and Therapy, 35*, 793–802. doi:10.1016/s0005-7967(97)00040-5

———. (1998). A cognitive theory of obsessions: Elaborations. *Behaviour Research and Therapy, 36*(4), 385–401. doi:10.1016/s0005-7967(97)10041-9

Raîche, G., Riopel, M., & Blais, J. G. (2006). *Non graphical solutions for the Cattell's scree test.* Paper to be presented at the International Meeting of the Psychometric Society, HEC, Montréal, June 16, 2016.

Rasch, G. (1960). *Probabilistic models for some intelligence and attainment tests.* (Copenhagen: Danish Institute for Educational Research). 1980 expanded edition with foreword and afterword by B. D. Wright (Chicago: The University of Chicago Press).

Raykov, T., & Marcoulides, G. A. (2010). *Introduction to psychometric theory.* New York: Routledge.

Razali, N. M., & Wah, Y. B. (2011). Power comparisons of Shapiro–Wilk, Kolmogorov–Smirnov, Lilliefors and Anderson–Darling Tests. *Journal of Statistical Modeling and Analytics, 2,* 21–33.

Rao, C. R. (1948). Large sample tests of statistical hypotheses concerning several parameters with application to problems of estimation. *Proceedings of the Cambridge Philosophical Society, 44,* 50–57.

Rosseel, Y. (2012). Lavaan: An R package for structural equation modeling. *Journal of Statistical Software, 48*(2), 1–36. Retrieved, from http://www.jstatsoft.org/v48/i02/ (accessed on May 19, 2016).

Royston, J. P. (1982). An extension of Shapiro and Wilk's W test for normality to large samples. *Applied Statistics, 31,* 115–124.

———. (1983). Some techniques for assessing multivariate normality based on the Shapiro–Wilk W. *Applied Statistics, 32,* 121–133.

Runco, M. A., & Pezdek, K. (1984). The effect of television and radio on children's creativity. *Human Communication Research, 11,* 109–120.

Ryan, T. A. (1960). Significance tests for multiple comparisons of proportions, variances, and other statistics. *Psychological Bulletin, 57,* 318–328.

Sapnas, K. G., & Zeller, R. A. (2002). Minimizing sample size when using exploratory factor analysis for measurement. *Journal of Nursing Measurement, 10,* 135–154.

Satterthwaite, F. E. (1946). An approximate distribution of estimates of variance components. *Biometrics Bulletin, 2,* 110–114.

Saunders, D. R. (1956). Moderated variable in prediction. *Educational and Psychological Measurements, 16,* 209–222.

———. (1961). The rationale for an "oblimax" method of transformation in factor analysis. *Psychometrika, 26,* 317–324.

Scheffé, H. (1943). Statistical inference in the non-parametric case. *The Annals of Mathematical Statistics, 14*(4), 305–332. doi:10.1214/aoms/1177731355

Scheffé, H. A. (1953). A method for judging all possible contrasts in the analysis of variance. *Biometrika, 40,* 87–104.

———. (1959). *The analysis of variance.* New York: John Wiley and Sons.

Schönemann, P. H. (1966). A generalized solution of the orthogonal Procrustes problem. *Psychometrika, 31,* 1–10.

Shapiro, S. S. (1980). *How to test normality and other distributional assumptions.* Milwaukee, WI: American Society for Quality Control.

Shapiro, S. S., & Wilk, M. B. (1965). An analysis of variance test for normality (complete samples). *Biometrika, 52,* 591–611.

Sheskin, D. J. (2007). *Handbook of parametric and nonparametric statistical procedures.* Boca Raton: Chapman & Hall/CRC. Taylor & Francis Group.

Šidák, Z. (1967). Rectangular confidence regions for the means of multivariate normal distributions. *Journal of the American Statistical Association, 62,* 623–633.

Siegel, S., & Castellan Jr, N. J. (1988). *Nonparametric statistics for the behavioral sciences* (2nd ed.). New York: McGraw–Hill Book Company.

Smirnov, N. (1939). Sur les écarts de la courbe de distribution empirique [On the differences in the empirical distribution curve]. *Rec. Math. [Mat. Sbornik] N.S., 6*(48), 1, 3–26.

Somers, R. H. (1962). A new asymmetric measure of association for ordinal variables. *American Sociological Review, 27,* 799–811.

Spearman, C. (1904). The proof and measurement of association between two things. *American Journal of Psychology, 15,* 72–101.

Steiger, J. H. (1980). Tests for comparing elements of a correlation matrix. *Psychological Bulletin, 87,* 245–251.

———. (2004). Beyond the F test: Effect size confidence intervals and tests of close fit in the analysis of variance and contrast analysis. *Psychological Methods, 9,* 164–182.

Stephens, M. A. (1967). Tests for the dispersion and the modal vector of a distribution on a sphere. *Biometrika, 54,* 211–223.

———. (1974). EOF statistics for goodness of fit and some comparisons. *Journal of the American Statistical Association, 69,* 730–737.

———. (1986). Tests based on EDF statistics. In D'Agostino and Stephens (Eds.), *Goodness of fit techniques* (pp. 97–194). New York: Marcel Dekker.

Stoline, M. R., & Ury, H. K. (1979). Tables of the studentized maximum modulus distribution and an application to multiple comparisons among means. *Technometrics, 21*(1), 87. doi:10.2307/1268584

Student [Gossett, W. S.] (1908). The probable error of a mean. *Biometrika, 6,* 1–25. doi:10.1093/biomet/6.1.1.

Subrahmaniam, K., Subrahmaniam, K., & Messeri, J. Y. (1975). On the robustness of some tests of significance in sampling from a compound normal distribution. *Journal of the American Statistical Association, 70,* 435–438.

Sukhatme, P. V. (1938). On Fisher and Behrens' test of significance for the difference in means of two normal samples. *Sankhya, 4,* 39–48.

Sukhatme, P. V., Thawani, V. D., Pendharkar, V. G., & Natu, N. P. (1951). Revised tables for the d-test of significance. *Journal of the Indian Society of Agricultural Statistics, 3,* 9–23.

Tabachnick, B. G., & Fidell, L. S. (2007). *Using multivariate statistics* (5th ed.). Boston: Allyn and Bacon.

Tamhane, A. C. (1979). A comparison of procedures for multiple comparisons of means with unequal variances. *Journal of the American Statistical Association, 74*(366a), 471–480. doi:10.1080/01621459.1979.10482541

Tanaka, J. S. (1993). Multifaceted conceptions of fit in structural equation models. In K. A. Bollen & J. S. Long (Eds.), *Testing structural equation models* (pp. 10–39). Newbury Park, CA: SAGE Publications.

Theil, H. (1971). *Principles of econometrics.* NY: Wiley.

Thode, H. C. (2002). *Testing for normality.* New York: Marcel Dekker Inc.

Torrance, E. P. (1974). *Torrance test of creative thinking: Norms and technical manual.* Lexington, MA: Personal Press/Ginn and Co.

Tucker, L. R., & Lewis, C. (1973). A reliability coefficient for maximum likelihood factor analysis. *Psychometrika, 38*(1), 1–10.

Tukey, J. W. (1960). A survey of sampling from contaminated distributions. In I. Olkin, S. G. Ghurye, W. Hoeffding, W. G. Madow & H. B. Mann (Eds.), *Contributions to probability and statistics* (pp. 448–485). Stanford, CA: Stanford University Press.

———. (1977). *Exploratory data analysis.* Reading, MA: Addison-Wesley.

Voyer, D., Postma, A., Brake, B., & Imperato-McGinley, J. (2007). Gender differences in object location memory: A meta-analysis. *Psychonomic Bulletin & Review, 14*(1), 23–38. doi:10.3758/bf03194024

Wallis, W. A. (1939). The correlation ratio for ranked data. *Journal of the American Statistical Association, 34,* 533–538.

Watson, G. S. (1961). Goodness of fit tests on a circle. *Biometrika, 48,* 109–114.

Welch, B. L. (1938). The significance of the difference between two means when the population variances are unequal. *Biometrika, 29,* 350–362.

———. (1951). On the comparison of several mean values: An alternative approach. *Biometrika, 38,* 330–336.

Welsch, R. E. (1977). Stepwise multiple comparison procedures. *Journal of the American Statistical Association, 72,* 566–575.

White, H. (1980). A heteroskedasticity-consistent covariance matrix and a direct test for heteroskedasticity. *Econometrica, 48,* 817–838.

White, J. M. (2010, April 21). *Doing maximum likelihood estimation by hand in R.* Retrieved from http://www.johnmyleswhite.com/notebook/2010/04/21/doing-maximum-likelihood-estimation-by-hand-in-r/ (accessed on June 8, 2016).

Wilcox, R. R. (1987). New designs in analysis of variance. *Annual Review of Psychology,* 38, 29–60.

Wilcox, R. R. (2003). *Applying contemporary statistical techniques.* Laguna Hills, CA: Elsevier.

Wilcox, R. R. (2016). *Understanding and applying basic statistical methods using R.* Hoboken, NJ: Wiley.

Wilcox, R. (2005). *Applying contemporary statistical techniques.* CA: Elsevier Science.

———. (2012a). *Introduction to robust estimation and hypothesis testing* (3rd ed.). San Diego, CA: Academic Press.

———. (2012b). *Modern statistics for the social and behavioral sciences: A practical introduction.* Boca Raton, FL: CRC Press.

Wilks, S. S. (1932). Certain generalizations of the analysis of variance. *Biometrika, 39,* 471–494.

Williams, E. J. (1959). The comparison of regression variables. *Journal of the Royal Statistical Society (Series B), 21,* 396–399.

Yule, G. U. (1938). Notes of Karl Pearson's lectures on theory of statistics. *Biometrika, 30,* 198–203.

Yule, G. U. (1911). *An introduction to the theory of statistics.* London: Charles Griffin.

Zandt, T. V. (2002). Analysis of response time distributions. In H. Pashler & J. Wixted (eds). *Stevens' handbook of experimental psychology: Volume 4: Methodology in experimental psychology* (pp. 461–516). New York: John Wiley & Sons, Inc. doi:10.1002/0471214426.pas0412

Zeller, R. A. (2006). *Statistical tools in applied research.* Retrieved July 10, 2008, from http://www.personal.kent.edu/~rzeller/Ch.%2010.pdf

Zivot, E. (2012, July 26). *Maximum likelihood estimation.* Retrieved, from http://faculty.washington.edu/ezivot/econ424/maximumLikelihoodPowerpoint.pdf (accessed on May 20, 2016).

Index

akaike information criterion (AIC), 184
alpha factoring, 325
basic mathematics for psychologists
algebra, 6A
basic rules for logarithms, 6A–7A
classical test theory (CTT), 362–363
exponents, 6A
matrix, 7A–8A
methods for single administration of test, 365–369
methods of assessment of reliability, 365
operations in matrices, 9A–10A
permutations and combinations, 7A
procedures based on two test administrations, 365
transposition, 8A
types of matrices, 8A–9A
analysis of variance (ANOVA), 244
foundations of, 245–246, 248
error sum of squares, 247
MSE and MSW, 247
treatment sum of squares, 247
logic of, 245
axiom, 4–5

Bernoulli trial, 11–13
conditional expectation, 34–35
conditional probability, 29
bootstrapping for t-test
independent samples, 242–243
one-sample method, 241–242

categorical/nominal data, 142
chi-square
contingency coefficient (C), 144–145
Cramér's V, 145
phi coefficient (f), 143–144
test for independence, 143–144
CMH statistic, 148–149
Kappa (k)-agreement between ratters, 149–150
likelihood ratio test (LR test), 147–148

measures of association
odds ratio (OR), 146–147
Yule's Q, 145–146
correlation
association and, 111
basic aspects
direction, 109
linearity, 110–111
strength, 110
causality and, 112
meaning and interpretation, 108
testing hypothesis for, 112
types, 111–112
correlation coefficient
testing difference
Fisher's Z-transformed value, 132
more than two independent correlations, 133–134
null hypothesis, 132
two independent correlations, 132–133
two non-independent correlations, 134–135
Z-value, 133
cultural dimension theory by Hofstede, 38n1
beta distribution, 29
chi-square distribution, 26–27
continuous random variables, 20–21
exponential distribution, 23
F-distribution, 27–28
gamma distribution, 29
normal distribution, 24–25
probability density function, 22
standard normal distribution, 25–26
student's t-distribution, 28
types, 22–23
uniform random variable, 23
Weibull distribution, 29

dependent samples
Friedman's rank test for k correlated samples, 311–313
sign test, 309–310
Wilcoxon signed-rank test, 310–311
dependent samples t-test, 230
confidence interval (CI), 233

effect-size calculation, 233
principles and computation, 231–232
reporting results, 233–234
effect-size and power
treatment effect, 253
Cohen's f, 255
eta-squared (^{2}), 254
omega-squared (w^2), 254–255
epistemology, 333n4
description, 315–316
equation, 319–322
exploratory factor analysis (EFA), 314
factor analysis jargon, 316–317
factor rotation, 328–329
factor scores, 331–332
factor structure and pattern, 331
issues, 317–319
methods of extraction, 323–325
methods to decide number of factors, 327–329
models, 322–323
number of factors, 325–326
purpose, 317
R example, 332–333
estimation process for mean estimation, 39–40
expectation of X and Y, 31–32
jointly distributed random variable, 30–31
estimators, 39
small-sample properties
efficient, 50
linearity and BLUE, 51
minimum variance, 50
MSE, 51
unbiased, 49–50
event, 3

factor analysis, 314

Gauss–Markov theorem, 159–161
Geary's test, 87–88
generalized (weighted) least squares, 325
Goodman and Kruskal's gamma (g), 111, 139–141
Goodness-of-fit Index (GFI), 342–343
graphical representation of data
Box–Whisker Plot, 71–72

ggplot2 and lattice, data
  visualization with R, 76
histograms, 72–73
Kernel density plots, 73–74
pie charts, 75–76
steam-and-leaf graph, 70–71
Guilford's structure of intellect
  model, 314
Guttman's lambda, 6, 368

heteroscedasticity
  Breusch-Pagan-Godfrey test,
    188–189
  data, 190
  Glejser test, 187
  Goldfeld-Quandt (GQ) test, 188
  graphical methods, 187
  Park test, 187–188
  White general test for, 189
t-test, 207
  estimating sample size, 235
    dependent samples *t*-test,
      240
    one-sample *t*-test, 236
    one-sample *t*-test, determin-
      ing, 237–240
  mean, sampling distribution,
    209–211
  principles, 207–209
  variance, sampling distribution,
    211–213

image factoring, 325
  item response theory (IRT)
    applications, 377–378
    choosing model, 377
    item information and test
      information function,
      376–377
independent samples
  Kruskal-Wallis H test, 308–309
  median test, 304–305
  Wilcoxon rank-sum test,
    306–308
independent samples *t*-test
  assumptions, 220–222
    confidence interval (CI), 223
    distribution of difference
      between means, 218–220
  effect-size, 223
    magnitude of treatment, 224
  heterogeneous variances
    Behrens–Fisher problem,
      226–228
    homogeneity of variances,
      229–230
    robustness of *i*-statistic, 230

Welch–Satterthwaite solu-
  tion, 228–229
non-zero value, calculations,
  225–226
reporting results, 224–225
interval estimation, 48–49

Jensen's reaction time, 314
Kendal's tau (t_{xy}), 111
  coefficient
    computational alternative
      for, 137–138
    logic and computation of,
      136–137
    significance testing of, 138
  ranking data, 135–136
    correlation for, 136

Lagrange multiplier test (LM Test),
  355
large sample properties, 51
  asymptotic unbiasedness, 52
  consistency, 52
  efficient estimator with asymp-
    totic variance, 52
  normal distribution, 53
  sufficiency, 53
logistic regression, 196
  classification, 203–204
  fundamentals of, 197–199
  odds ratio, 203
  significance testing of the
    coefficients, 199
    information criteria, 202–203
    log-likelihood statistics,
      200–201
    R and R^2, 201–202
    Wald statistics, 201
  writing the results, 204

measures of central tendency
  mean, 64–66
  median (Mdn), 64, 66
  mode, 65–66
measures of variability
  average deviation, 67
  interquartile range (IQR), 67
  median absolute deviations
    (MAD), 67
  range, 66
  standard deviation (SD), 68–70
  variance, 67–68
methods of estimation
  Bayes' rule, 58
  Bayesian inference, 58
  bootstrap or resampling, 58
  method of least squares, 53–54

method of maximum likeli-
  hood (ML), 54–56
  Lagrangian multiplier test,
    56–57
  likelihood ratio (LR), 56–57
  Wald, 56–57
method of moments (MOM),
  53
multiple comparison procedures
  basic ideas in
    error rates, 257
    post-hoc and planned
      comparisons, 257
    significance of *F*, 257–258
  planned comparisons, 258
    Bonferroni–Dunn (BD) test,
      261–263
    Holms test, 263
    Larzelere test, 263
    Mulaik test, 263
    multiple *t*-test, 261
    orthogonal comparisons,
      259–260
    with contrasts, 259
  post-hoc tests
    Benjamini–Hochberg test,
      269–270
    Dunnett T3, 269
    Dunnett's procedure, 264
    Games–Howell procedure,
      266–267
    Hochberg GT2, 268–269
    LSD, 263–264
    MCP comparison and selec-
      tion, 270–272
    Newman–Keuls procedure,
      267–268
    Ryan–Einot–Gabriel–Welsch
      Q (REGWQ) procedure, 268
    Scheffé test, 267
    studentized range statistics
      (*q*), 265
    Tamhane T2, 269
    Tukey's HSD/WSD test,
      265–266
    Tukey–Kramer procedure, 266
    Waller–Duncan (WD) test, 270
multiple regression, 175
  additional model selection
    criterion, 183
    AIC and SIC, 184
    Mallows's C_p criterion, 184
  hypothesis testing
    predictor variable, testing
      significance of, 181–182
    testing significance of model,
      179–181

importance of IVS, 185
issues in
  detecting multicollinearity, 186–187
  heteroscedasticity, 187–190
  independent error, 190
  model specification errors, 190–193
  multivariate outliers, 185
  sample size, 185
  singularity and multicol-linearity, 185–187
mediated and moderated variable regression
  moderated variable regression, 196
  simple mediation model, 193–196
purpose of, 176
types of, 182–183
multivariate analysis of variances (MANOVA), 102, 287
assumptions
  covariance matrices, homo-geneity of variance, 289
  homogeneity of regressions, 289
  linearity assumption, 289
  mutlicollinearity and singu-larity, 289
  MVN and outliers, 288
  reliability of covariates, 289
  sample size, 289
example with R, 294–296
null and alternative hypothesis for, 290
results, 296
small sample worked out example
  SSCP, 291–293
statistical test, 290
testing homogeneity of variances
  Box's M test, 293–294
  log-likelihood ratio test, 293
multivariate normal distribution (MVN), 288
assessing multivariate normali-ty, statistical tests
  Henze–Zirkler's MVN test, 104–106
  MANOVA, 102
  Mardia's MVN test, 103
  Royston's MVN test, 103

NEO Personality Inventory 3 (NEO-PI-3), 1n1

null hypothesis
  Fisher and Neyman–Pearson on, 42–43
  testing and sampling distri-bution, 43–44
probability
  axiomatic approach, 4–5
  simple propositions, 6–7
  standard error of statistics, 40
  basic idea, 39
  statistical inference, 38
Nettelbeck's inspection-time, 314
non-normal data, problems and solutions
  bootstrapping, 99
    merits and demerits, 100
  data transformation, 99
  non-parametric statistics, 99
non-normed fit index (NNFI), 343–345
non-parametric methods
  chi-square test
    assumptions of, 300–301
    for goodness-of-fit, 298–299
normal distribution
  historical aspects, 78–79
  IQ, 83–84
  percentile, 83–84
  properties of, 80
  standard normal and score, 81
  T-score, 83–84
  testing for normality
    history, 79–80
  Z scores, 81–83
normed fit index (NFI), 343–345
null hypothesis, 88, 341–342
  critical value, 46
  directional and non-directional hypothesis, 46
  Fisher and Neyman–Pearson, 42–43
  level of significance, 46
  rejection and acceptance, region of, 45
  testing and sampling distribu-tion, 43–44
  types of errors, 45–46
  use of P, 44
null model or baseline model, 342

one-way ANOVA (ANOVA)
  assumption of sphericity, 277
  computation of repeated measures, 274
  calculations, 275–276

independent samples
  ANOVA computations, 249–252
  homogeneity of variances, 248–249
  independence, 249
  normality, 248
  null and alternative hypothesis, 249
  ramifications, 252–253
post-hoc test
  with Tukey's HSD, 276–277
repeated measures
  basic ideas, 272–273
  counterbalancing, 272
  crossover designs, 272
  Latin square designs, 272
  randomization of orders, 273
  structural model for, 273
outliers, 288

partial correlation (rp), 127–128
  multiple correlation coefficient, 131–132
  Pearson's correlation, 130
  regression residuals, 130
  semipartial correlation (r_{sp}), 130–131
  use of, 129–130
PASS model, 314
Pearson's correlation coefficient, 111, 112
  assumptions, 121
  computation of, 115
    adjusted correlation coeffi-cient, 116–117
  factors influencing
    bivariate outliers, presence of, 122
    combining heterogeneous subgroups, 121–122
    linearity, absence of, 122–123
    sampling restricted range, 121
  hypothesis testing, 116–117
    confidence interval (CI), 119–120
    population correlation, 118–119
    sample size, power calcula-tion, 120–121
  logic of, 112–113
    correlation coefficient, 114–115
proportions test
  independent proportions, 303–304

McNemar's chi-squared test,
301–303
psychometrics, defined, 362
Psychometrika, 366*n*2

random error (e), 363

Rao–Blackwell–Kolmogorov
theorem, 61
raw score, 362–363
R, introduction
data input, 381A–382A
export of plot, 382A–383A
flow control, 383A
uses, 379A–381A
writing function, 383A
reliability and reliability coefficient, 364
assumption, 338
confirmatory factor analysis
(CFA), 314
estimation, 340–341
graphical model, 335–336
identification, 339–340
in R, 345–355
introduction, 333–334
model, 336–337
model evaluation, 341–351
reporting, 355–356
steps, 334–335
Ryan–Einot–Gabriel–Welsch Q
(REGWQ), 268

Samejima's graded response model, 375–376
sampling distribution, 39–42
mean estimation
estimation process for, 40
of statistics mean, 40
R code, result of, 41
theoretical, 42
sampling distribution of statistics,
40–41
Schwarz information criterion
(SIC), 184
sequential multiple regression, 182
simple linear regression
accuracy of prediction, 162, 164
coefficient of determination,
163
assumptions underlying,
170–174
basics of, 156
computation of OLS,
157–158
Gauss–Markov theorem,
159–161
interpretation of, 161–162

OLS, estimation method, 157
standardized regression
coefficients, 162
confidence limits, 170
hypothesis testing in, 164–165
confidence interval (CI), 167
significance of, 166–167
two independent values,
167–168
model, 154–155
R with output, 168–170
scatterplot and regression,
155–156
writing up, 175
single-sample *t*-test, 213
mean test, 214
one-sample mean with, 214
alternate use, 217–218
confidence interval (CI),
216–217
one-tailed and two-tailed
tests, 215–216
Spearman's "g" factor theory,
314
Spearman's rho (r_s), 111
ranking data, 135–136
correlation for, 136
special correlations
biserial (r_b), 126
Pearson's correlations
phi coefficient, 123–126
phi correlation (*f*), 125–126
point-biserial correlation
(r_{pb}), 123–126
t-test and effect-size, 124–125
tetrachoric correlation (r_{tet}), 127
standard score, 363
statistical tables
area under normal distribution, 11A
chi-square distribution, 19A
F-distribution, 15A–17A
Kendall's Tau values, 18A
Kolmogorov–Smirnov test
statistics, 18A
R to Z transformation, 12A
student's T-distribution,
14A–15A
studentized range statistics,
17A
statistical inference
central limit theorem (CLT), 59
Cramer–Rao inequality, 59–60
law of large numbers, 59
Rao–Blackwell–Kolmogorov
theorem, 61
statistical or stepwise regression,
183

statistical theories of mental test
scores, 369*n*1
data, 356–357
estimation and R, 358–360
model, 357
structural equation modeling
(SEM), 315
statistics, 39

test-retest reliability, 365
testing normality, 84
D'Agostino's D, 95
goodness-of-fit test, 88
Anderson–Darling test (AD
test), 91–92
Cramér and von Mises,
92–93
D'Agostino–Pearson test
(D'Agostino K² test),
94–95
Jarque–Bera test (JB test),
93–94
Kolmogorov–Smirnov test
(K-S test), 89–90
Kuiper's V test, 91
Lilliefors test, 90–91
Shapiro–Wilk test, 94
graphical methods, 95
plotting probability, 96–98
plotting raw data, 96
likelihood ratio (LR) tests, 95
Lin and Mudholkar's test, 95
Oja's test, 95
statistical tests for univariate
normality
Geary's test, 87–88
Kurtosis test, 86–87
population and sample
moments, 85
skewness test, 86–87
two-way completely independent
ANOVA
factorial analysis of variance
basic ideas, 278
completely repeated mea-
sures, 286
computational formula,
281–285
data and calculation,
281–285
interaction effect, 279–280
main effect, 278–279
mixed-factorial, 285–286
partitioning sum of squares,
280–281
structural model, 280–281

union and intersection, 3*n*3

random variable
    expected value, 9–10
    probability distributions, 7–9
unrestricted and model-implied
    covariance matrix,
    338–339
unweighted least squares (ULS),
    325

variance, 10–11
    discrete random variable
        Bernoulli random variable
          and distribution, 11–13
        binomial random variable
          and distribution, 13–15
        Poisson random variable and
          distribution, 16–19

Wald test (W), 354–355
wholly significant difference
    (WSD). *See* honestly
    significant difference
    (HSD)

zero correlation, 109